C000162060

THE ASHGATE RESEARCH COMPANION TO MONSTERS AND THE MONSTROUS

This volume awakens the monster as an academic topic. Combining John Block Friedman's historical-literary approach with Jeffrey J. Cohen's theoretical concerns, Asa Simon Mittman and Peter Dendle have marshaled chapters that comprise a seminal work for everyone interested in the monstrous. Wide-ranging chapters work through various historical and geographic views of monstrosity, from the African Mami Wata to Pokémon. Theoretical chapters consider contemporary views of what a monster is and why we care about them as we do. Taken together, the essays in The Ashgate Research Companion to Monsters and the Monstrous *reveal that monsters appear in every culture and haunt each of us in different ways, or as Mittman says, the monstrous "calls into question our (their, anyone's) epistemological worldview, highlights its fragmentary and inadequate nature, and thereby asks us … to acknowledge the failures of our systems of categorization."*

David Sprunger, Concordia College, Minnesota, USA

An impressively broad and thoughtful collection of the ways in which many cultures, ancient and modern, have used monsters to think about what it means to be human. Lavishly illustrated and ambitious in scope, this book enlarges the reader's imagination.

Lorraine Daston, Director of the Max Planck Institute
for the History of Science, Germany

ASHGATE
RESEARCH
COMPANION

The *Ashgate Research Companions* are designed to offer scholars and graduate students a comprehensive and authoritative state-of-the-art review of current research in a particular area. The companions' editors bring together a team of respected and experienced experts to write chapters on the key issues in their speciality, providing a comprehensive reference to the field.

The Ashgate Research Companion to Monsters and the Monstrous

Edited by

ASA SIMON MITTMAN
California State University, Chico, USA

WITH

PETER J. DENDLE
Pennsylvania State University, Mont Alto, USA

Routledge
Taylor & Francis Group

LONDON AND NEW YORK

First published 2013 by Ashgate Publishing

Published 2016 by Routledge
2 Park Square, Milton Park, Abingdon, Oxon OX14 4RN
711 Third Avenue, New York, NY 10017, USA

Routledge is an imprint of the Taylor & Francis Group, an informa business

Copyright © 2013 Asa Simon Mittman and Peter J. Dendle

Asa Simon Mittman and Peter J. Dendle have asserted their right under the Copyright, Designs and Patents Act, 1988, to be identified as the editors of this work.

All rights reserved. No part of this book may be reprinted or reproduced or utilised in any form or by any electronic, mechanical, or other means, now known or hereafter invented, including photocopying and recording, or in any information storage or retrieval system, without permission in writing from the publishers.

Notice:
Product or corporate names may be trademarks or registered trademarks, and are used only for identification and explanation without intent to infringe.

British Library Cataloguing in Publication Data
The Ashgate research companion to monsters and the
   monstrous.
   1. Monsters. 2. Monsters--History. 3. Animals--
   Abnormalities. 4. Abnormalities, Human. 5. Monsters in art.
   6. Monsters in literature.
   I. Monsters and the monstrous II. Mittman, Asa Simon, 1976-
   III. Dendle, Peter, 1968-
   398.4'5-dc22

Library of Congress Cataloging-in-Publication Data
Mittman, Asa Simon, 1976-
   The Ashgate research companion to monsters and the monstrous / by Asa Simon
Mittman with Peter J. Dendle.
      p. cm.
   Includes bibliographical references and index.
   ISBN 978-1-4094-0754-6 (hardback)
   1. Monsters. I. Dendle, Peter, 1968- II. Title.

   GR825.M57 2011
   001.944--dc23

                                                                              2011025755

ISBN 9781472418012 (pbk)
ISBN 9781409407546 (hbk)

MIX
Paper from
responsible sources
FSC   FSC® C013985
www.fsc.org

Printed in the United Kingdom
by Henry Ling Limited

Contents

PART I: HISTORY OF MONSTROSITY

PART II: CRITICAL APPROACHES TO MONSTROSITY

For Grendel
Welcome into the hall

List of Figures

List of Contributors

Persephone Braham received her BA in political science from Columbia University and her PhD in Spanish from the University of Pennsylvania. She is the author of *Crimes Against the State, Crimes Against Persons: Detective Fiction in Cuba and Mexico* (2004) and numerous articles on monsters in Latin American literature and film. She is the Director of the Latin American and Iberian Studies program at the University of Delaware, where she teaches Latin American literatures and cultures.

Jeffrey Jerome Cohen is Professor of English and Director of the Medieval and Early Modern Studies Institute at the George Washington University. His books include *Hybridity, Identity and Monstrosity in Medieval Britain*; *Medieval Identity Machines*; and *Of Giants: Sex, Monsters, and the Middle Ages*. He is the editor of the collections *Cultural Diversity in Medieval Britain*; *The Postcolonial Middle Ages*; and *Monster Theory: Reading Culture*.

Surekha Davies is a Leverhulme Early Career Fellow in the Department of History, Classics, and Archaeology at Birkbeck, University of London. Her research interests include cultural encounters, travel writing, history of knowledge, exploration, cartography, monstrous bodies, and global medicine circa 1400–1800. She currently examines representations of African, Asian, and American peoples across textual and visual genres. She has published in *Imago Mundi*, *Terrae Incognitae* and *Renaissance Studies*, and has articles forthcoming in *The Historical Journal* and *History and Anthropology*. She has completed a monograph, provisionally titled *America's Inhabitants on Maps and the Construction of Ethnographic Knowledge, 1500–1650*. She is co-editing special issues of *History and Anthropology* and the *Journal of Early Modern History*.

Peter J. Dendle is an Associate Professor of English at Pennsylvania State University, Mont Alto, where his research focuses on constructs of the demonic past and present. His publications include two monographs (*Satan Unbound: The Devil in Old English Narrative Literature*, 2001, and *The Zombie Movie Encyclopedia*, 2001), two more to appear shortly (*Demon Possession in Anglo-Saxon England* and a zombie movie follow-up book), and numerous articles on medieval and modern literature, folklore, and ritual.

Henry John Drewal received his BA from Hamilton College. After graduation, he joined the Peace Corps, and during his two years in Nigeria apprenticed himself to a Yoruba sculptor. That experience was transformative. He studied at Columbia University in African Studies with an interdisciplinary specialization in African art history and culture, receiving two Masters degrees and a PhD. Since 1991, he has been the Evjue-Bascom Professor of Art History and Afro-American Studies at the University of Wisconsin-Madison and Adjunct Curator of African Art at the Chazen Museum of Art, UW-Madison. He has published several books and edited volumes and many articles on African/African Diaspora arts, and curated several major exhibitions, among them *Yoruba: Nine Centuries of African Art and Thought*; *Beads, Body, and Soul: Art and Light in the Yoruba Universe*; *Mami Wata: Arts for Water Spirits in Africa and Its Diasporas*; and most recently *Dynasty and Divinity: Ife Art in Ancient Nigeria*, which opened in Spain.

D. Felton is Associate Professor of Classics at the University of Massachusetts Amherst. In addition to her book *Haunted Greece and Rome: Ghost Stories from Classical Antiquity*, she has published on various aspects of folklore in classical literature. Her current project is a book on serial killers in the ancient world.

Michael Dylan Foster is Assistant Professor in the Department of Folklore and Ethnomusicology and the Department of East Asian Languages and Cultures at Indiana University. He has written extensively on the monstrous and supernatural in Japanese culture and is the author of *Pandemonium and Parade: Japanese Monsters and the Culture of Yōkai* (2009), which was awarded the 2009 Chicago Folklore Prize for the year's best book-length work of folklore scholarship.

John Block Friedman is Professor Emeritus of English and Medieval Studies from the University of Illinois at Urbana Champaign. He is the author of many books and articles on medieval topics, including *The Monstrous Races in Medieval Art and Thought* (Harvard University Press, 1981, repr. Syracuse University Press, 2000) and, most recently, *Brueghel's Heavy Dancers: Transgressive Clothing, Class and Culture in the Late Middle Ages* (Syracuse University Press, 2010). He is presently completing the commentary volume for a facsimile edition of the *Secrets of Natural History* (BN fr. 22971) for the Spanish publisher Siloé. He lives in Columbus, Ohio.

Francesca Leoni is the Yousef Jameel Curator of Islamic art at the Ashmolean Museum of Art and Archaelogy, University of Oxford, after holding posts at Rice University (2008–2010) and the Museum of Fine Arts Houston (2008–2011). Her interests include the Islamic arts of the book in the pre-modern and early modern times; cross-cultural exchanges between the Islamic world, the Western world and Asia; and the history and circulation of technologies. Among her recent publications are contributions to the exhibition catalogue *Light of the Sufis: The Mystical Arts of Islam* (2010); "Diplomacy and Gift Giving at the Court of Fath 'Ali Shah," in *Gifts of the Sultan: The Arts of Giving at the Islamic Courts*, ed. Linda Komaroff (2011); and the article "Picturing Evil: Images of Divs and the Reception of the *Shahnama*," in *Shahnama Studies II*, ed. Charles Melville and Gabrielle Van den Berg (2011).

Michelle Osterfeld Li received her PhD in East Asian Studies from Princeton University in 2000, focusing on pre-modern Japanese literature, history, and religion. She also has an MA in modern Japanese literature from Ochanomizu Women's University in Tokyo. Currently an affiliate fellow at the Ho Center for Buddhist Studies at Stanford, she has taught classes in modern Japanese language and literature at San José State University and classes in pre-modern Japanese literature at Stanford and, most recently, the University of Iowa. She authored *Ambiguous Bodies: Reading the Grotesque in Japanese Setsuwa Tales* (2009).

Matthew Looper is Professor in the Department of Art and Art History at California State University, Chico. He received his PhD in Art History from the University of Texas at Austin in 1995. His research interests include classic Maya art and writing, Maya textiles, and Maya dance traditions, in all periods. His most recent book is *To Be Like Gods: Dance in Ancient Maya Civilization* (2009).

Patricia MacCormack is Reader in English, Communication, Film and Media at Anglia Ruskin University, Cambridge. She has published extensively on continental philosophy, particularly Deleuze, Guattari, Serres, Irigaray, and Blanchot. Her work has appeared in *Women: A Cultural Review; New Formations; Theory Culture and Society; Queering the Nonhuman;* and *Body and Society,* among others. She is the author of *Cinesexuality* (2008) and the co-editor of *The Schizoanalysis of Cinema* (2008).

Sarah Alison Miller is an Assistant Professor of Classics at Duquesne University. Her book, *Medieval Monstrosity and the Female Body* (2010), analyzes monstrous representations of female corporeality in late-medieval poetic, gynecological, and mystical texts.

Partha Mitter is a renowned scholar, a recipient of numerous fellowships and awards who has lectured and taught throughout the world, including the Getty Research Institute in Los Angeles, Columbia, Princeton, Oxford and Cambridge universities, as well as the Institute for Advanced Study in Princeton. He is currently Emeritus Professor in Art History at the University of Sussex and a member of Wolfson College, Oxford University.

Asa Simon Mittman is an Associate Professor of Art History at California State University, Chico. He is the author of *Maps and Monsters in Medieval England* (2006), co-author of *Inconceivable Beasts: The Wonders of the East in the Beowulf Manuscript* (with Susan Kim, forthcoming), as well as author of several articles on the subject of monstrosity and marginality in the Middle Ages. He is the president of MEARCSTAPA (Monsters: the Experimental Association for the Research of Cryptozoology through Scholarly Theory And Practical Application). He is currently working on *Digital Mappaemundi,* co-designed with Martin Foys and Shannon Bradshaw.

Karin Myhre received her PhD in East Asian Languages from the University of California, Berkeley and has been awarded grants for work at Peking University as well as the National Central Library in Taipei. Her research centers on Chinese vernacular materials, especially drama from the Song through Ming periods (circa 10th–16th centuries). Particular interests include humor, violence, and the representation of ghosts.

Dana Oswald is Associate Professor of English at the University of Wisconsin-Parkside. She received her PhD from the Ohio State University in 2005, where she studied Old and Middle English language and literature under Nicholas Howe. Her abiding fascination with monsters and the monstrous is reflected in her book, *Monsters, Gender and Sexuality in Medieval English Literature* (2010), and in essays published in *Exemplaria* and *Different Visions*. She is currently pursuing projects focused on two kinds of transgressive medieval bodies: those of transgendered monsters and those of mothers.

Abigail Lee Six is Professor of Spanish at Royal Holloway, University of London. She has been researching in the field of Gothic Studies for the past three years and has published two monographs on aspects of the Gothic in Spanish literature from the nineteenth century to the present day.

Karl Steel is Assistant Professor of English at Brooklyn College, City University of New York. He is the author of, among other things, *How to Make a Human: Animals and Violence in the Middle Ages* (2011), and the editor, with Peggy McCracken, of "The Animal Turn," a special issue of the journal *Postmedieval*. Since 2006, he has blogged at <www.inthemedievalmiddle.com> with Jeffrey Jerome Cohen, Eileen A. Joy, and Mary Kate Hurley.

Debra Higgs Strickland is Director of the Glasgow Centre for Medieval and Renaissance Studies and teaches History of Art at the University of Glasgow. She is an editorial board member of *Different Visions: A Journal of New Perspectives on Medieval Art* and an associate editor of *The Grove Encyclopedia of Medieval Art* (forthcoming). Her major publications include *Medieval Bestiaries: Text, Image, Ideology* (1995); *The Mark of the Beast* (1999); and *Saracens, Demons, and Jews: Making Monsters in Medieval Art* (2003). She is completing a new book on *The Epiphany of Hieronymus Bosch: Imagining Antichrist and Others from the Middle Ages to the Reformation*.

Hannah Thompson is a Senior Lecturer in French at Royal Holloway, University of London. She has published widely on Emile Zola and the questions of the body in nineteenth-century French literature. She is currently completing a book on bodily taboos of pornography, gender confusion, disability, incest, illness and pain in nineteenth-century French prose fiction.

Chet Van Duzer, currently an Invited Research Scholar at the John Carter Brown Library and a Kislak Fellow at the Library of Congress, has published extensively on medieval and Renaissance cartography. He recently published a monographic study of Johann Schöner's globe of 1515, and his book *Sea Monsters on Medieval and Renaissance Maps* will be out soon from the British Library.

Jeffrey Andrew Weinstock is Professor of American Literature and graduate program coordinator at Central Michigan University. He is the author of *Scare Tactics: Supernatural Literature by American Women; The Rocky Horror Picture Show, Charles Brockden Brown, and Vampires: Undead Cinema*, and is the editor of the Ashgate *Encyclopedia of Literary and Cinematic Monsters*. He has also edited four volumes of the fiction of horror author H.P. Lovecraft for Barnes & Noble.

Acknowledgments

We wish to thank Dymphna Evans for her insight and acumen, for helping shepherd this project through the process so smoothly, and for listening to Asa's excited ranting about monsters over a cup of coffee in a London café. We also thank Ashgate Publishing for their support for this topic, their generosity in illustrating this collection, and their patience as we worked to get the last recalcitrant fangs and scales in place.

We would also like to thank our contributors. It has been a pleasure to work with this exceptional group of scholars, many of whom relied on and assisted one another. This process has been, in our estimation, a model of collaborative scholarship. Each editor would also like to thank his fellow editor, as their respective strengths and specialties complemented each other superbly, and made it a pleasure to work in tandem. As Georges Braque said of his productive relationship with Pablo Picasso, we are all "roped together like mountain climbers."

Many members of the scholarly community have helped us throughout the planning, writing, and editing of this volume. In particular, though, we thank Derek Newman-Stille, with whom we sustained a conversation throughout the process, and whose work influenced our thinking about monsters and inspired a section of the foreword. Our thanks to Marcus Hensel for compiling the extensive index, without which a book cannot really be considered a "research companion." We also wish to thank those contributors who took the time to read and comment on the collection as a whole—their knowledge and expertise have helped strengthen the collection significantly.

Dr Michael Doncheski, Director of Academic Affairs of the Mont Alto campus of Penn State, and Dr Sandra E. Gleason, Associate Dean for Faculty and Research in the Office of the Vice President for Commonwealth Campuses, are to be thanked for their commitment to scholarship and their support for faculty. Shirley Ketrow-Crawford is an invaluable resource, for making things happen seamlessly and effectively. It is also a pleasure to thank Alica White, Peggy Angelovich, and Tom Reinsfelder, for expert and reliable library support. Dr Francis Achampong was also very supportive of this project.

The Department of Art and Art History at California State University, Chico, had the courage to hire (and tenure) "the monster guy," and their support and friendship are deeply appreciated. Thanks to Professor Matthew Looper and Professor Elise Archias, and Chair of the Department Professor Teresa Cotner. Dean Joel Zimbelman has been consistently supportive. Erin Herzog in the Ira

Latour Visual Resources Center was patiently helpful on a number of occasions, and the staff of the Interlibrary Loan office, Flora Nunn and Jo Ann Bradley, make research possible, up in the North State. Susan Kim should be thanked for her longstanding collaboration (and friendship) that has greatly influenced Asa's thinking on monsters and the monstrous in so many ways.

Michele Mittman continues to show generous understanding of Asa's various afflictions, monster studies among them. And yes, Lela, your dad really did help make another book on monsters.

Finally, of course, we wish to thank the raucous, boisterous, terrifying mass of creatures herein contained: dragons and demons, headless men, heartless killers, soulless ogres, vampires, hunchbacks, giants, mermaids, shape-shifters, dog-heads, ghosts, starry deer crocodiles, *taotie, oni,* and centaurs, border-walkers and margin-steppers, monsters, *mearcstapas* all.

The treacherous imagination is everybody's maker—we are all the invention of each other, everybody a conjuration conjuring up everyone else. We are all each other's authors.

—Philip Roth, *The Counterlife* (1986)

Foreword

John Block Friedman

Since I first began to study monstrosity about 37 years ago, there has been a remarkable surge of interest in the topic. My original focus was a narrow one: Western European literary and artistic responses to the "otherness" of portentous individual human and animal births, and to the alleged presence of races of monstrous men and women, largely human in appearance, in remote parts of the world. By "otherness" I mean that the way writers and artists treating such beings encapsulated inchoate fears of losing human status. Narrow because folkloric monsters, stories of monstrous beings in non-European myth, and Asian and Islamic artistic representations of these beings did not seem relevant to my concern for "alterity" in the late classical period and in the European Middle Ages. Moreover, I had clearly defined limits of time and space: antiquity to New World exploration, and Europe, and European perceptions of the Middle East and Africa. I would never have thought of mingling monsters, those on the medieval Hereford and Ebstorf maps for example (see Figures 17.1, 18.1 and 18.2), with monsters to be found in Second World War comic books or contemporary forms of popular culture such as vampire novels and films. And the Far East and South and Central America played no part in my interest in monsters.

In these past three decades, the proliferation of books and articles, both scholarly and popular (including websites in many languages), and the degree to which the subject of monsters broadly understood has occupied the attentions of cultural and psycho-analytical critics has led to a number of general overviews and specific treatments of monsters from classical myth, such as Malcolm South's *Mythical and Fabulous Creatures: A Source Book and Research Guide* (1987) with essays ranging over griffins to centaurs, vampires to werewolves and giants. No book, to my knowledge, however, has the cultural, geographic, and temporal range of the present volume. Indeed, that there should even be a need for a "Companion" to monster studies which could appeal both to specialists and the cultivated general reader is a sign of just how far what one contributor calls the interest in "the posthuman" has gone and how complex has become what had hitherto—spatially and temporally—been a fairly narrow topic.

In my own early research on monsters, I was chiefly concerned with those that were largely malign, representing the darker side of nature and culture. Even the places where they were found were dangerous to or uninhabitable by ordinary

Figure 0.1   The Heap, Hillman Comics, 1940

Source: © 2011 Todd McFarlane Productions, Inc.

mortals. But it is now clear that in many cultures, the Mayan and Aztec, the very early Buddhist, and the most contemporary Japanese, monsters can be comic, even playful, and can have positive cosmological significance. And they are ubiquitous. Guy de Bazoches, echoing a remark by Saint Jerome, observed that "only France has no monsters"[1] and he was perhaps more correct than he could imagine. For as this Companion shows, monsters are all around us, in our dreams, our children's reading, in accounts of postcolonial capitalism and exploitation and in films detailing the power relations of men and women, in our perceptions of disabled people in the streets; sometimes, even, they are us.

As any good book should do, this one produces every few pages an "aha" reaction, where childhood experiences that have passed for years as insignificant suddenly take on numinous meanings, becoming significant in retrospect. Several of our contributors speak of the shifting boundaries between monstrosity and humanity and how the monster can represent aspirations, even heroic ones. For me, this brings to mind a comic book series, The Heap, which in 1943 I spent a great deal of time reading and to this day I recall clearly in imagination, but whose significance only now do I fully understand (Figure 0.1). In one incarnation or another, The Heap continued on in comic books for several decades.

The comic had a sort of archetypal mantra to the effect that the protagonist "fell, died, lived, and rose again." The plane of an actual First World War flying ace Baron Eric von Emmelman was shot down over a Polish swamp. The pilot did not die, but retained for decades a shred of life, amalgamating with the marsh water, vegetation and soil to become a gigantic hairy heap like a walking bale of peat moss. At the onset of the Second World War, the Heap rose from his swamp and roamed about rather like Lancelot in his madness, eventually turning on his fellow Germans, now Nazis, and doing occasional good deeds for the Allied cause. The story had everything: the monster was of good family, brave and valiant, skilled as a pilot, and politically right thinking, even if exiled to the margins for his ugliness and uncertain humanity. The Heap also had a youthful human sidekick, Ricky, whom I envied immensely at the time. Though I only recognized it recently in reading some of these essays, the Heap partook of most of the features of high monster culture, belonging in spirit with Dindymus, king of the cave dwelling Bragmanni, and sharing the remote or uncivilized habitat of many of the monsters in Western European narratives.

Five of these chapters, those of Steel, Van Duzer, Strickland, Felton and Davies, bring the reader up to date on the Western European traditions of Plinean monstrous races of men originating in classical antiquity, as well as on the fortunes of the largely Roman tradition of monstrous individual births and their significance for the city or the nation. In the early modern period these monsters by birth had a new life in sectarian religious controversy. Felton, Steel and Davies's chapters chart the development of monsters from the ancient Greeks through the age of the Desert Fathers and beyond into the Middle Ages and early modern period. It is primarily

---

1   W. Wattenbach (ed.), *Die Apologie des Guido von Bazoches* (Berlin: Sitzungsberichte der Königlich Preussischen Akademie der Wissenschaften zu Berlin, 1893), p. 34.

out of this tradition that the present volume—and the modern academic study of monsters which it reflects and defines—has grown, though it casts a far wider net in its geotemporal scope. While the Greeks obviously derived much of their monster lore from very ancient and extensive Near Eastern legends, in their literature and art they developed what would be the particular character of the Western European monster tradition and its Latin inheritance. From cosmological encounters and wars between monsters and gods and later between monsters and men, as in the stories of Odysseus's wanderings among the Sirens and adventures with creatures like Polyphemus, developed an archetype of reason and beauty in eternal conflict with the irrational and the chaotic. The earliest cosmologies associate monsters with chaos and unreason, out of which form itself emerged and on occasion, as with Medusa and Scylla, this chaos is tied to the primal female nature.

Eventually the Greek monsters move from heaven to earth and heroes battle these irrational and uncivilized giants and hybrid creatures. Probably the *Odyssey* and the *Aeneid* are the best-known examples here, and it is indeed from Virgil that a host of hybrid monsters came into the early medieval imaginary. Greek travelers, for example, Herodotus, Ctesias, Scylax, and Megasthenes, located whole races or tribes of men monstrous in appearance or customs or social order and dietary practice in India, which became a new focus—along with Ethiopia to a lesser extent—of terrestrial rather than heavenly or chthonic monsters. Such beings, in their very remoteness from the Hellenic "center," conveniently removed the irrational and uncivilized from that center.

Roman encyclopedists Pliny and Solinus widened the world of the monstrous to catalogue individual races as recognized forms of humanity. Authors frequently located them in deserts, by rivers, in mountains—primarily in India—and listed their customs, appearance, and social organization in what might be called early ethnography. The medieval inheritance of Pliny and Solinus was a fascination with the East, reflected in illustrated narratives like the adventures of Alexander the Great, romances, wonders collections like the Anglo-Saxon examples now in the British Library, and encyclopediae, not to mention works of travel, usually fictional, like *Mandeville's Travels*. For example, in an early fifteenth-century illustrated French collection made to please the armchair traveler called *Secrets of Natural History*, 56 countries, regions and islands are described in elaborate detail as to flora and fauna, manners and the like. India is by far the longest entry, running to 19 pages, most of it about the customs and appearances of its various people and animals, real and imaginary, primarily based on antique sources.[2]

The ancient Romans were just as intrigued by monsters as the ancient Greeks, and in addition to races of such beings, were also fascinated by what has come to be known as teratology, the study of deformed births believed to be omens of impending events affecting the nation. Two-headed babies, hunchbacks, dwarves, giants and the like were, as Plutarch indicated, subjects for popular interpretation and wonder; and they were often exposed in marketplaces for a fee, as in modern

---

2   I am preparing a facsimile edition of the latest manuscript of this work, Paris, Bibliothèque Nationale MS Fr. 22971, and will quote here from my transcription by folio number.

side-shows. So widespread was the Roman interest in monsters that it was even parodied as a national trait by Lucian, and indeed it is with this aspect of monster lore that we begin to find monsters as essentially a new epistemological subject, one having a separate and independent literary, scientific and geographical existence in works like the *Etymologiae* of Isidore of Seville and the *De Naturis Rerum* of Rhabanus Maurus.

This new subject forms a more fully developed and independent area of human knowledge and investigation from the 1240s onward, with the appearance of *De Monstruosis Hominibus Orientis*, making up the third book of the medieval encyclopedia *De Naturis Rerum* of the thirteenth-century Flemish Dominican Thomas of Cantimpré. The presence of this book considering the history, origins, significance, and place in an ordered universe of monsters as a subject of investigation was very unusual. The contents of Book III were borrowed from Pliny, Solinus, Saint Augustine, Isidore of Seville, Jacques de Vitry, and others, but the idea of separating such beings from the standard books on the human body, the soul, and the elements which typically form the early portions of such encyclopediae was new. A brief preface opens Book III, and the first question raised therein is whether or not monstrous men descended from Adam, an issue explored by Augustine. And the first concrete illustration of the question of whether they were human or not is brought up by the mention of the centaur-like being which Saint Antony meets in the desert in Jerome's *Life of Saint Paul*, as discussed by Steel.

About 50 years after the *De Naturis Rerum* was first circulated, a verse spin-off of Book III, now moralized and illustrated with 49 magnificent miniatures, appeared as a separate work, called *De Monstruosis Hominibus*. As a sign of the increasing popularity of works on monsters and the East for the bourgeoisie and literate aristocracy, this poem, written in Old French, adds new details to Thomas, and even augments it with new races such as hybrid men whose lower half is canine, and through rhetorical flourishes makes the races even uglier and more monstrous than they had been in Thomas and in his source Pliny. The author, obviously a cleric, also stresses that these beings are not random but part of a divine plan, for "God has made nothing in vain." The titillative aspect of the monstrous races is also brought out, for by comparison to these beings, "God has made us handsome beyond all other creatures, according to his image," and the poet appears to laud the good fortune of his audience: "in foreign nations they are not a bit/Like they are here. You know/truly that the Oriental is quite otherwise than we are."[3]

The Old French poet also elaborates the story of Saint Antony's meeting with the onocentaur, mentioned in the preface to Thomas's book on monstrous men of the East, and gives the creature and its location, not the meeting, a special moral significance:

---

3   See Alfons Hilka (ed.), "Eine altfranzösische moralisierende Bearbeitung des Liber de Monstruosis Hominibus Orientis von Thomas von Cantimpré, De Naturis Rerum," in *Abhandundgen der Gesellschaft der Wissenschaften zu Göttingen: Philologisch-Historische Klasse 7* (Berlin: Weidmannsche Buchhandlung, 1933), pp. 1–73. See ll. 13, 32–4, 1–11.

> *True it is what others witness and say, that in the East are men horrible, vile, villainous and bad, who do not dwell in towns but in deserts and mountains. They have very strange faces and are men above the waist but animals in many strange ways below. Cruel, bad, stinking, and fierce, they come from adultery.*[4]

A particular causation is therefore offered for the monster who is or was a man suffering from species corruption brought about as a punishment for sin. In many ways, the story of Antony's meeting with the onocentaur—widely circulated in the Middle Ages, as Steel shows—was a paradigm for the "Christianization" of monsters, their incorporation into a cohesive religious worldview in which they are explained in several ways.

It was in the period of the encyclopediae, as well, that speculation on the exact status of monstrous beings, especially those from Equatorial Africa, in the Great Chain of Being became common and the analytic tools of scholastic philosophy was brought to bear upon them. Though there had been brief disquisitions earlier, such as those of Honorius of Autun and Ratramnus of Corvey (who wondered about the cynocephalus), it was Peter of Auvergne (1304) who devoted a whole *quodlibet* to the matter of whether or not Pygmies were actually men, even though they had language and other evidence of reason, common elements in medieval definitions of humanity.

Racial ideas—the notion of whole groups superior or inferior to others by reason of skin color and other features—seem to have been an inevitable concomitant of such cataloging of monsters. The term *gens/gentes*, or "people" in Latin, comes, by the period of about 1000, to mean race as well as merely the abstract "people." Catalogs in travel works and the great encyclopediae such as the *Specula* of Vincent of Beauvais could now include "gentes" such as Muslims, Jews, Mongols, "Seres" or Chinese, and animist "Ethiopians," as well as Amazons, dog-heads and backward-footed men, who by reason of coloration, religious practices or lack of them, physical "deformity," aberrant dietary and sexual practices, lack of or incomprehensible languages, cannibalism, or even social practices like those of the matriarchal Amazons, come to play an important role in "group" thinking about monsters, as Strickland notes in her chapter on race and monstrosity. The projection of fears and fantasies by Western Europeans on to cultural "others" led inevitably to this concept of "race" and to what today might be called "racism." It is in this emerging area of racism associated with monstrosity and moral disorder that we can also situate medieval anti-Semitism, for Jews were often caricatured as so grotesque in appearance as to be monstrous. Finally, the idea of three originary tribes descending from the Noachic division of the world, with the black peoples of "Africa" the cursed children of Ham, produced a convenient framework for racial stereotypes and the exclusion of cultural others from the body politic based first on color and later on appearance, religion, and social practices, as well.

---

4   Ibid., ll. 32–43.

A passage from the *Secrets of Natural History* mentioned above contrasts the "perfection" and superiority of Europe and Europeans with the unattractiveness and weakness of Africa and its inhabitants by reasons of climate and geographical location. Europe is:

> the third part of the habitable world and is situated towards the north, quite opposite to Africa, which is located towards the middle and is subject to the miserably burning heat of the sun ... The inhabitants of this region ... are handsomer, stronger, and bolder than those in the hot country of Africa. And the reason for this is the sun's great heat, that continuously shining on the Africans dries the humours and natural virtues of their bodies and prevents them from growing. In consequence, they are short, thin, dry, and black as coal and have kinky hair. And because of the continual heat in which they live, their pores are always open, letting the vital spirits escape from their bodies. And quite otherwise are the Europeans and the northerners who live far from the sun. For by the continual cold in which they live, their pores remain closed, restraining their vital spirits, by which they engender good men, virtuous with regard to their humoural complexions. And thus the Europeans are more temperate and moderate in their deeds.... for through the retention of vital spirits they are all the stronger, bolder and have greater courage.[5]

Though Ptolemy's *Tetrabiblios* had already argued that moral deformity and physical ugliness were the result of climatic conditions, it was really in the Middle Ages that we begin to see the singling out of Africans as monstrous on the basis of climatic determinism. Added here was the notion of inner moral turpitude from the practice of non-Christian religion, most particularly Islam. The line in the

---

5 "Europpe est la tierce partie de la terre habitable et est situee par devers Septentrion, toute a lopposite de Affricque, qui est situee devers le midy. Et est subgecte a la miserable ardeur et challeur du souleil. Erodoctus dit que les hommes et les femmes de la region dEurope sont plus beaulx et plus fors et plus grans et plus hardiz que ilz ne sont en chault pais dAffricque. Et la cause si est du souleil qui continuellement est sur les Africquans et vertuz du corps et pour ce ilz ne pevent croistre ni ameliorer et sont petiz, maigres, et secs et noirs comme charbon, et ont les chevreux crespez. Et pour la continuelle challeur en quoy ilz sont, ilz ont les pores touzjours ouvres, et ainsi se tinportent les esperilz naturelz et yssent hors de leurs corps. Et pour ce sont ilz failliz en couraige, paoureur, et sans hardiesse. Et autrement est des Euoppeans et Aquillonnaires qui sont loing du souleil, car pour la froidure foraine ilz ont les pores reffrains au dedans du corps, par quoi se engendrent humeurs bonnes et naturelles a humaine complexion. Et aussi sont les gens de celle region plus attemprez et moderez en leur fait. Et auxi sont a la foiz plus hardiz et courageux, car pour labsconsion de la bonne challeur et humeur qui est dedans leurs esperilz ilz sont plus fors et plus hardiz et ont plus grant courage." (Paris, Bibliotèque Nationale, MS Fr. 22971, folios 23v–24.)

Song of Roland that "The pagan cause is wrong, the Christian right"[6] suggests the perception of whole peoples made monstrous through choice of religion.

Through the earlier Middle Ages, this view applied largely to dark-skinned and Eastern peoples, but as Davies shows, by the Reformation we begin to see that monstrosity could lie in *interpretation*, characterizing people who in most respects looked like and lived near us but who, through defects of birth or religious choice, could be interpreted as monstrous through error. The older Roman view that such births were bad omens of a general nature gave way to the idea that they signified God's punishment for individual moral failings of religious or even political error, or they could result from the mother's sinful thoughts at the instant of conception. Thus to be spiritually or politically wrong was to be monstrous.

The Renaissance brought with it not only the well-known veneration of all things "classical" but also a renewed interest in collecting and interpreting *terata* or unnatural births and the beginnings of the *cabinet* mentality with its fashionable acquisition of wonders and freaks, where we seek out and revel in things that fill us with a sort of pleasure mixed with horror and repugnance. Ambroise Paré's vernacular *Des monstres et prodiges* of 1573 is an example of this sort of treatise; it indicated a new subjectivity in monster study, for to the author monstrosity was a matter of appearance rather than fact, as in the case of children who *seem* to be born against nature. Caspar Peucer, for example, argued that one should examine one's own feelings immediately upon the sight of a monster as a guide to characterizing it.[7]

Increasingly in the early modern period, monsters are home-grown rather than primarily found in India and Africa, though there was a corollary interest in exporting to the New World imagined races more usually indigenous to those exotic parts, such as the Anthropophagi and dog-heads which Columbus spoke of, discussed here by Davies and Braham. Chet Van Duzer's chapter focuses on precisely this moment when monstrosity moves gradually from the edges of the earth, as in its treatments in Greek and Roman authors like Megasthenes and Pliny, and its representation on early medieval world maps like the Hereford and Ebstorf maps, to a more domestic placement. By the late fifteenth and early sixteenth centuries "monsters can be among us" relative to the location of the author or the map maker, and they are increasingly transported from the edges to the center. Some of this is due to the pomp and vanity of monarchs. The desire of European rulers to import from their habitats exotic creatures ranging from elephants to aboriginal peoples altered popular focus on monsters. The Romans had brought hippopotami and crocodiles for the amusement of the emperor and the populace and later European emperors had continued this practice, as Francis Klingender's monumental *Animals in Art and Thought* well illustrates.[8] As Van Duzer notes: "The

---

6   See Howard S. Robertson (trans.), *The Song of Roland* (London: Dent, 1972), LXXIX, l. 1015, p. 30.

7   See Surekha Davies's article in this collection.

8   Francis Donald Klingender, *Animals in Art and Thought to the End of the Middle Ages* (Cambridge, MA: MIT Press, 1971).

ability to display the exotic wonders from distant realms symbolized the emperor's power over most of the known world."

As exploration diminished the possible existence of monstrous beings in Africa and the East, they were transferred to the "new world" in accounts of matriarchal Amazons, Patagonian giants, and even Pygmies in Canada. Interestingly, though these literary reports continued well into the eighteenth century, the representation of monsters gradually declined on world maps and globes as practical navigation and exploration expanded.

While the interest in monsters waxed and waned or served largely political and theological ends in Europe, monsters were vital cultural forces elsewhere in the world: China, Japan, the Islamic sphere, and even in the ancient Americas and the Caribbean, in contexts as wide-ranging as postcolonial fiction and cosmological creation myths, Buddhist narratives and popular Japanese folklore, as the chapters by Leoni, Myhre, Foster, Li, Looper and Braham show with a wealth of detail.

Though we often think of Islamic art and decoration as non-representational, at least of human and divine figures, there are many hybrid creatures in such art which seem cognates of Western European monster representation, just as elements in the Qur'an have counterparts in Hebrew scripture. As with the Greeks, Islamic monsters seem largely hostile to humans. A version of Satan called Iblis and a type of demon called the White Div are very like satanic and demonic representations in Romanesque art, for example, with features such as gigantic stature, claws, horns, and grotesque heads. Iblis is an inferior or earth demon that rebels against God, much as did Satan in Milton's *Paradise Lost*, and is made a monster in punishment. The Div seems to exist outside any human or animal group. Both represent the evil coming from disharmony and the more id-like aspects of human nature.

Chinese monsters, as ancient as those of the Greeks or more, lurked at the boundaries between familiar and unfamiliar forms of existence, as demonstrated by Myhre. They appear, for example, as early as the seventeenth century BCE in bronze masks representing entities called *taotie*. Features of these monsters still appear in Chinese art, such as round or protruding eyes, horns, and gaping mouths, often seen on Foo dogs. Appealing to the armchair traveler of the sort I mentioned in conjunction with Western works like *Mandeville's Travels* was the third-century BCE *Classic of Mountains and Seas*, which treated with illustrations non-Chinese geography, and monsters to be found outside the realm, as well as a variety of topics like omens relating to wonders. In Chinese art of later periods, monsters had human figures but bulging expressive eyes, snouts for noses, fangs, horns, and striking coloration often intended to represent non-Chinese, showing the familiar fear of the "other" on home ground.

In contrast to Chinese monsters generally, which are inimical to humanity, their Japanese counterparts, as Li and Foster show, have a much more ambiguous significance. The *oni* are Japanese monsters or spirit creatures who are found in collections of tales from the ninth to the fourteenth centuries and their representations appear down into the seventeenth century on roof tiles as well. They are also depicted on Buddhist scrolls symbolizing forces of nature such as thunder. Unlike some of the evil monsters we have so far seen, *oni* are more mischievous and might be seen as corresponding to Western fairies or elves, though they can have the fanged, clawed, horned aspect of Chinese monsters, and be brightly colored. So too, like Western spirits, they make music or play instruments.

Modern Japanese culture remains alive with monsters, as the Pokémon game would suggest. Two features distinguish contemporary Japanese monsters from those elsewhere: their playful nature and their role in intellectual culture. As we saw in the case of the Western medieval polymaths Thomas of Cantimpré and Vincent of Beauvais, Japanese scholar-folklorists categorize them and arrange them in encyclopediae and compendia, which are important in Japanese historical scholarship. The *yōkai* were shape-shifting monsters; the term is very elastic and can range in meaning from goblin to demon. They are sometimes gigantic, on occasion malign or benign, but always ambiguous. As with Roman tutelary spirits like Cloacus, the god of sewers, there were anthropomorphic *yōkai* living by rivers and other bodies of water who were the spirits of the outhouse, who would reach up and extract organs from the unfortunate persons using the seats.

Yōkai are endemic in Japanese life, appearing in Kabuki dance, on decorative scrolls and woodcuts, even on playing cards. During the rise of Japanese nationalism, *yōkai* were important in the developing concept of Japan's dynamic military and industrial growth as something to resist against, for some of the tales were debunked as rustic and out of keeping with modern industrial life. But there was a contrary movement in which, like the American idealization in 1950s films of the period of Western expansion in the 1870s, the *yōkai* from the same period onward appealed to a sense of nostalgia in older persons. In recent years there have been books, films, stories, comics, video games and websites about these monsters, so that perhaps among all the cultures studied in this Companion, the Japanese monster has the most current and active life.

New World monsters, though less well known and less frequently studied, have had a long life on the North and South American continent as well, both before and after colonization. As Looper shows, crocodile hybrids were basic to Aztec religious cosmology, combining deer, crocodile, iguana, and snake forms; they personified the forces of the earth and of the sky in public art. Such monstrous forms were often used in the iconography of rulers to show their control over cosmic and terrestrial forces.

In this terrestrial world, categories of gender that bend or do not adhere to the male–female binary have long been considered monstrous. Here, behavior and choice or physical features not immediately visible to beholders fulfill the conditions of monstrosity. The virgin, the hyper-masculine man, and the hermaphrodite can all be imagined as monstrous, for there are liminal and shifting categories between those of normative gender, as Oswald points out in her chapter. Those who fall outside this "masculine/feminine binary" have traditionally been viewed as monstrosities. *Mandeville's Travels*, for example, treats virgins as having serpents in their wombs, who poison the men who enter them in a variant of the *vagina dentata* motif discussed by Miller in her chapter on monstrous sexuality. The Amazons are also discussed from the perspective of monstrous virgins; they are monstrous through their legendary matriarchal social organization, self-mutilation to be able to pull the bow further to the chest, killing of men after they breed with them, and willingly adopted celibacy. This group of militant quasi-virgins lent its name to a New World river and to matriarchal and cannibal tribes associated with it. The myth of the Amazons participates in masculine fear of loss of power to women and of the *vagina dentata*. At the other end of the spectrum lie hyper-masculine male monsters, including cannibal rapist giants like Dinnabuc in the Arthurian legends, blood-drinking vampires, and flesh-eating werewolves, hirsute beast-men exhibiting aggressive eating and sexuality.

Monsters become more mythic and archetypal in Caribbean culture, as analyzed by Braham, especially in postcolonial fiction, where the idea of the unknown was inextricably tied to monsters who both attracted and repelled. As we have seen, Western European monsters were transported to this region through European exploration, as evidenced by the Amazon River, cannibals, and Patagonian giants. In the modern period these archetypes serve largely as symbols for slavery and postcolonial exploitation of indigenous peoples and their landscape. Perhaps the most important early figure in Caribbean monster lore was Amerigo Vespucci, who spoke heatedly of tattooed savages and libidinous cannibal women who ate one of his shipmates before his eyes. Nakedness, anthropophagi, and especially enlarged female genitalia became an early construct in the myths of the New World.

In Caribbean literature, monsters and monstrous archetypes are associated with the rise of "regional" fiction. For instance, in certain Brazilian novels the female cannibal of Vespucci's narrative returns now as a castrating cannibalistic figure. One such novelist, José Eustasio Rivera, author of *La vorágine*, is a bit like Conrad in *Heart of Darkness* in criticizing the destructive capitalism of rubber plantation culture. The heroes' conflicts are with cannibalistic and emasculating women and landscapes, flora and fauna, as well as specific women who destroy the heroes through their greed and sensuality.

Many of these themes involving monsters dangerous to male control and masculinity itself in Latin American literature also appear in contemporary North American fiction and cultural studies. Miller's chapter on monstrous sexuality, with its focus on the *vagina dentata*, treats an archetype inherent in Vespucci's early narrative about New World matriarchal cannibal and libidinous women. Such alluring monsters mingle desire with potential pain; Miller traces back this concept as early as Scylla, one of the monsters encountered by Odysseus and treated by Ovid in the *Metamorphoses*. Allegories of the story make it a conflict between the beastly female and the rational male principles in the human being, for Scylla was a hybrid, a form of Siren with a female human body above and toothed dog mouths below.

Scylla and the fear she engenders in men lies behind the film *Teeth* (2007) about a girl with teeth in her vagina who punishes men who rape her so that they bleed to death, subverting the helpless victim of male sexuality motif common to many Hollywood films. As Miller points out: "The *vagina dentata* becomes, then, a monster that cannot be conquered by male bravery, strength, or wit. Its teeth— whether they materialize punishment or recapitulate sexual violation—become a feature of female sexual and reproductive identity." Thus monstrous sexuality in such women sends "mixed messages," luring yet destroying and "represent[ing] the barred entrance to humanity's primordial home."[9]

While many of the monsters treated in the Companion come from antiquity or the Middle Ages, when concern for the precise nature and stability of human status was high, there are, as I have remarked earlier, monsters of different types with us today in novels, films, comics, and even perceived among the disabled people we see daily on the street. Weinstock's study of postmodern monsters reveals that we actually make our own monsters according to the changes in our conception of what is human. Our changing anxieties and desires can alter our views of the "natural" and thus that which is *contra naturam*. Lee-Six and Thompson chart the origins of these trends in the romantic period, covering seminal works like Shelley's *Frankenstein* and Stevenson's *The Strange Case of Dr Jekyll and Mr Hyde*. Monstrosity, from the nineteenth century to the present, has been largely "decouple[d from] physical abnormality, from intelligence, character, or morals."[10] Increasingly, modern monsters are seen as the products of social forces and can be victims, sympathetic, and even heroic and noble.

David Lynch's film *Elephant Man* (1980), set in Victorian London, shows such a victim. The hero's monstrosity was caused by a birth over which he has no control. Exploited commercially as a freak, the Elephant Man is taken up by a benevolent surgeon, Dr Treves, and eventually, when at ease with his benefactor, reveals his intelligence and innate decency. The Elephant Man is so horrible in appearance that he must wear a bag or hood over his face at all times. Two forces then work on him: his exploiter, aptly named Bytes, who keeps carrying him off for profit as a freak, and keeps then forcing him into monstrosity, and the kindness and medical care of his benefactor, leading him spiritually if not physically out of it. So the Elephant Man is mocked as a monster, profits his "owner" as such and horrifies the uninstructed observer, but a contrary current ennobles him as a victim of nature and nurture.

Since the 1970s and especially in more recent days, the Elephant Man paradigm has been reversed in films such as *Psycho* (1960), *The Manchurian Candidate* (1962), *The Day of the Jackal* (1973), *Silence of the Lambs* (1991), and *American Psycho* (2000). These show us psychopaths and terrorists who are physically invisible to us, but monstrous within. Characters such as Norman Bates and Hannibal Lecter are quite or relatively normal in appearance, even initially appealing at first glance, and yet monstrous morally.

And in some cases, as with John Gardener's novel *Grendel* and Anne Rice's vampire novels, where we have relatively sympathetic first-person monster narrators, we can admire if not necessarily aspire to their condition. Rice's vampires are creatures of enviable grace and elegance, whatever else they may be. Now, morality rather than physical appearance indicates true monstrosity. In the post-war and conformist 1950s, monstrosity became an "escape from hegemonic social forces of normalization," and this continued for several decades.

---

9   See Sarah Alison Miller's essay in this collection.
10   See Abigail Lee Six and Hannah Thompson's essay in this collection.

Even more recently, films and fiction explore the idea that giant corporations or impersonal viral contagions are monsters that greedily invade all aspects of human life. AIDS, Ebola, mysterious germs about to annihilate the world, are all forms of monstrosity and appeal to the paranoia about infection, for germs are actually a miniaturized "other" to be feared. Natural forces too can be monstrous: global warming, tidal waves and such caused by human misuse of the earth take us full circle to the Roman and later medieval idea that monstrosity and its attendant ills are God's punishment for sinful men.

While almost all the cultural constructs involving monstrosity which I have mentioned have been largely literary and artistic, engagement with disability studies raises some new and different questions, by taking a more sociological approach to monstrosity than those usually found in such discussions.[11] Disability studies is a discipline with strong ties to the social history of monstrosity. Just as so many cultures exiled their anxieties onto distant monsters, so the able person seeing the disabled thinks "how fortunate I am that I am what I am and not like that." In an apotropaic fashion, then, the disabled person bears away this collective bad fortune.

Not only from a sociological but also from a literary and artistic perspective, this pairing of disability and monstrosity has many important ramifications. As early as Saint Augustine, the "crippled" person was associated with some sort of moral deformity, and Gerald of Wales spoke of "cripples" in that region who were connected with werewolves and other hybrids. Monsters often seem to be disabled, covered with sores, or, as with the hunchback Igor in the old Frankenstein films,[12] limping and distorted.

Disabled people make us nervous; we don't know where to put our eyes. They remind us of our mortality and the fragility of our good fortune. And yet we are fascinated by them; indeed, children who are unfiltered in responses will stare until corrected. Just as with the monster, there is something frightening about "them."[13] In short, they seem an intrusion in our orderly and healthy society and can even seem contagious, as is literalized in figures like the vampire, who transmits its monstrosity into the victim's blood stream through a bite.

---

11 I am endebted here to the work of Derek Newman-Stille, who presented on "Monstrosity and Disability in the Middle Ages" in a session organized by Mittman at the International Medieval Congress in Leeds in 2009, and who is currently working on this subject.

12 Technically, the hunchbacked assistant in James Whale's *Frankenstein* (1931), played by Dwight Frye, was named "Fritz." Bela Lugosi's character "Ygor" in *Son of Frankenstein* (1939) and *The Ghost of Frankenstein* (1942) was not a hunchback. However, in popular conception and a vast number of subsequent versions, these seem to merge into the hunchbacked assistant "Igor."

13 See Rosemarie Garland-Thomson, "Integrating Disability, Transforming Feminist Theory," in Bonnie Smith and Beth Hutchison (eds), *Gendering Disability* (New Brunswick: Rutgers University Press, 2004), pp. 73–103; Rod Michalko, *The Difference that Disability Makes* (Philadelphia: Temple University Press, 2002); and Tanya Titchkosky, *Disability, Self, and Society* (Toronto: University of Toronto Press, 2003). My thanks to Derek Newman-Stille for these references.

Such ideas of illness perceived as monstrous are quite old, and in a medieval encyclopedia of 1408, John de Foxton's *Liber Cosmographiae*, for example, we find the idea that intercourse with a menstruating woman will produce destruction and even monstrosity. So dangerous is this blood to living things that "so powerful is its affect as physicians say, that if it is poured on the roots of a tree or on seeds, they will not grow, and if a dog tastes it he will at once go mad and die."[14] Thus female genitalia, even in the dry medical commentary of the encyclopedist, has the power to destroy the landscape. But there is more. A cause of the prohibition against sexual contact with a menstruating woman is that "the child conceived then will have leprosy, be a hunchback, and monstrous."[15]

Let me illustrate this point about monstrous contagion of the "disabled" and the idea that monstrosity is somehow catching with the recent fictionalized account of the life of our most eminent photographer of the bizarre, freakish, and unreal. This film is Steven Shainberg's *Fur: An Imaginary Portrait of Diane Arbus* (2006), where the lead is played by Nicole Kidman. The film conjoins three genres, that of the modern biopic of the artist coming to find herself aesthetically, with the much earlier *Freaks* of Tod Browning (1932) (with numerous genre scenes of what we would today called the disabled—circus "midgets," bearded ladies and the like), and a fairy-tale love-of-a-sympathetic-monster story modeled on Cocteau's *Beauty and the Beast* (1946), one of the finest fantasy films ever produced. Some of Shainberg's film follows the life of the photographer and some is pure invention, though heavily indebted to Cocteau and Browning. In brief, Arbus, a well-to-do New Yorker and daughter of a furrier family, is married to a commercial photographer. Serving as his sexually and creatively unawakened assistant, she does not yet take any photographs herself.

Early on, she is showed as fetishizing hairiness in men. She notices a curious masked man—in a reprise of the *Elephant Man* film mentioned earlier, who has moved into her apartment building and with whom she becomes obsessed. Eventually, entering his apartment, she discovers he is completely covered in fur, like La Bête in Cocteau's film, and bears a strongly leonine resemblance to that character. Moreover, his name is Lionel (surely a nod to Stephan Bibrowsky, whose hypertrichosis led him to perform as the famous "Lionel the Lion-Faced Man"), played by Robert Downey Jr. The furred man explains his medical condition to Arbus (though he does not reveal that he is dying of an associated lung condition) and remarks "don't be afraid, it is not catching." Arbus, now in love with Lionel, begins to use her camera, and is introduced to a world of his freakish friends—dwarves, transvestites and the like, in a variety of genre scenes of their lives, parties, and romances—whom she will later recall photographically. Symbolically, she shaves Lionel's monstrous fur before they make love, to return him to human normalcy.

Thus, Lionel is clearly a monster and his masked, furred condition, part werewolf in his sexually aggressive relation to Arbus (at the beginning of their

---

14 See John B. Friedman (ed.), *John de Foxton's Liber Cosmographiae (1408)* (Leiden: J.J. Brill, 1988) C. 88, p. 257.

15 Ibid., C. 88, p. 256.

encounters he recognizes in her something she cannot yet know about herself), part Elephant Man, requiring that he go about New York in a full head mask or bag, indicates his otherness. Arbus's husband Alan (a somewhat conventional commercial photographer) is repelled by Lionel's appearance, though to get his wife back, Alan grows a very full beard, assuming ("catching") the condition of monstrous disability to no avail.

Another form of less fantastic disability is perceived as monstrous, though not contagious, in a recent novel. Jeffrey Eugenides's novel *Middlesex* treats the question of fluid gender categories with a hermaphroditic hero/heroine/hero. Calliope/Cal's very name harks back to the classical antecedents of this condition. Indeed, the author' reference to Tiresias, the blind hermaphroditic prophet of Thebes, occurs very early in the novel. The hermaphroditic child was a portent like those examined in other parts of the Companion and not a good one, since Eugenides observes that "confronted with such a child, the Spartans had left the infant on a rocky hillside to die."[16]

The narrator Calliope, through adolescence, claims "my genitals have been the most significant thing that ever happened to me."[17] Monstrosity in this case is naturally created through an odd chromosomal count (and inbreeding), as with some of the science fiction-like explanations of monstrosity in the films mentioned earlier. Eventually, at 14, her concerned parents take Calliope from Michigan to New York to a clinic for "Sexual Disorders and Gender Identity." During the period when she is undergoing various tests at the clinic, she also pays a visit to the New York Public Library, as she has made little sense of the complex medical diagnoses and observations that the doctors at the clinic offered her parents about her. As she goes to the large Webster's dictionary in the Reading Room, she finds under "hermaphrodite" a definition and then "'See synonyms at MONSTER.' ... There it was, *monster*, in black and white, in a battered dictionary in a great city library ... Monster. That was what she was ... For a second Callie saw herself that way. As a lumbering, shaggy creature pausing at the edge of woods."[18] Calliope is profoundly disabled, then; her state of being neither boy nor girl but with the organs of both makes her unable to enter into "normal" life; she fears being perceived as "other." The "lumbering shaggy creature pausing at the edge of woods" sounds very like the comic book character the Heap, with which I opened this discussion. And, like Lionel Sweeney in *Fur*, who makes Diane Arbus shave him before making love, Calliope, looking in the mirror at her girl's face, plucks a couple of boy's mustache hairs from her lip.

Calliope allows us to see into the "other" in a way that was rarely done in antique and medieval accounts of monsters. She is entirely modern, yet her Greek heritage, her rather mythic genealogy—her grandparents were brother and sister—and her name all allow us to see her against the vast canvas on which so many different cultures have painted their differing conceptions, as outlined in this Companion.

---

16 Jeffrey Eugenides, *Middlesex* (New York: Picador, 2003), p. 410.
17 Ibid., p. 401.
18 Ibid., p. 431.

Introduction
The Impact of Monsters and Monster Studies

Asa Simon Mittman

Monsters do a great deal of cultural work, but they do not do it *nicely*.[1] They not only challenge and question; they trouble, they worry, they haunt. They break and tear and rend cultures, all the while constructing them and propping them up. They swallow up our cultural mores and expectations, and then, becoming what they eat, they reflect back to us our own faces, made disgusting or, perhaps, revealed to always have been so. It is not only the Doppelgänger of Shelley or Poe that is our evil twin. All monsters—from headless (but human?) blemmyes to bestial dragons to the amorphous, disembodied forces of the virus—all "monsters" are our constructions, even those that can clearly be traced to "real," scientifically known beings (conjoined twins and hermaphrodites,[2] for example, as seen through pre-modern lenses); through the processes by which we construct or reconstruct them, we categorize, name, and define them, and thereby grant them anthropocentric meaning that makes them "ours."

But why should we study them? Why should we read, write, and teach about monsters and the monstrous? Why should we use them as theoretical constructs to apply to other subjects? I will try here to offer some initial answers, as well as frame the necessarily heterogeneous contents of this volume. At the very outset, though, I wish to note my amazement that, in the space of a few years, the study of monsters has moved from the absolute periphery—perhaps its logical starting point—to a much more central position in academics.

I will begin with an anecdote: during a job interview a few years ago, I was asked: "Where do you see yourself in 20 years?" I replied: "I'd like to be the head of the world's first academic center for Monster Studies." After this session of the interview, a member of the department called me into his office. He told me that he

---

1   My thanks to Marcus Hensel for his helpful comments on a draft of this essay.
2   These figures are discussed in Michel Foucault, *Abnormal: Lectures at the Collège de France, 1974–75*, trans. Graham Burchell (New York: Picador, 2003), pp. 66–75.

had been teaching in the program for 50 years, and that he had some advice for me. In what I think he intended as a gruffly avuncular manner, he leaned on his desk and said: "Listen, Asa, you've got to drop all this monster stuff and start doing *real* scholarship."

I really did not know what to make of this at the time, but have thought about it quite a lot since. "Drop all this *monster stuff.*" "*Real* scholarship." What is "real scholarship?" What constitutes a worthwhile subject of study? What was I *supposed* to be working on? For a medieval art historian, perhaps images of Jesus or cathedral architecture or illustrations of saint's lives would be seen as "real." But not *monsters*, and certainly not the made-up field of "Monster Studies" or, as Jeffery Jerome Cohen (whose ground-breaking work appears like a leitmotif throughout these essays) first phrased it, "Monster Theory," a phrase that serves as the title of his collection of essays from 1996 that in some ways can be seen as having inaugurated the field.[3]

Still, and with all due deference to Cohen (who makes no such claim) and his insightful work, the study of monsters can hardly be said to have begun in 1996. The essays in this collection—exemplary rather than encyclopedic[4]—examine a wide range of significant texts, images, and other forms of important cultural representations, some scholarly and others not, from literary and artistic to scientific and geographical, from theoretical to theological to mythological, and ranging from the most ancient of history to the present day, and from Africa to Europe to Asia to the Americas. *The Epic of Gilgamesh*, replete with monstrosity as a central theme, is the world's earliest extant epic, written in Sumerian around 2000 BCE.[5] Debbie Felton examines the vast range of monstrosity in the classical world, from Gilgamesh forward. Karin Myhre opens her study of China with monsters contemporaneous to those in the ancient West, focusing on *taotie* masks that "function as a central decorative motif" in Shang Dynasty (ca. 1600–1000 BCE) art, and carries her discussion up to the twentieth century. Matthew Looper finds monstrous figures in the art of the Maya of the Classic (ca. 250–900 CE)

---

3   Jeffrey Jerome Cohen (ed.), *Monster Theory: Reading Culture* (Minneapolis: University of Minnesota Press, 1996). The study of monsters has gone by a number of terms, including not only the new "Monster Studies" and "Monster Theory." An older term is "teratology," from the Greek τέρας (monster, prodigy), primarily used in the Enlightenment to refer to the medical study of "unnatural births." *The Oxford English Dictionary* attests to its usage as early as 1678 to refer to "a discourse of prodigies and wonders." A century and a half later, in 1842, the term is first attested to refer to its more common usage, "the study of monstrosities or abnormal formations in animals or plants." (teratology, n., 2nd edn, 1989; online version November 2010, <http://oed.com:80/Entry/199333>, accessed March 12, 2011. Earlier version first published in *New English Dictionary*, 1911.) The term has, though, recently returned to its original broader valence, appearing in several essays here to refer to the study of monsters more generally.

4   Other volumes are in progress of more encyclopedic nature, such as the forthcoming *Encyclopedia of Literary and Cinematic Monsters* ed. Jeffrey Andrew Weinstock (Farnham: Ashgate, 2013).

5   Maureen Gallery Kovacs, *The Epic of Gilgamesh* (Stanford: Stanford University Press, 1989), p. xxiii.

and Post-classic (ca. 450–1500 CE) periods, more or less equating to the period covered by Karl Steel in his work on the European Middle Ages, and with much chronological overlap with Francesca Leoni's essay on the monstrous in the Islamic visual tradition from the tenth through the sixteenth centuries. Surekha Davies examines the early modern period, and Abigail Lee Six and Hannah Thompson cover the fertile nineteenth century. Michelle Li focuses on Japanese monsters in the eighth through the sixteenth centuries, and Michael Dylan Foster then carries them through to the present, where they are juxtaposed with Jeffrey Weinstock's work on present-day monstrosity in the West. Persephone Braham tackles the monstrous Caribbean, beginning in 1492, also concluding in the present. Henry Drewal examines the monstrous in modern Africa. And this list only covers the first part of this collection, containing a series of geo-historical essays.

What are we to make, then, of the assertion that the study of monsters is not "real scholarship," in light of this tremendous breadth of global cultural interest? In the European tradition, for example, some of the most influential scholars of the early Christian and medieval periods sweated over the definition and etymology of *monstra* [monster], and the problem of the presence of monsters within God's supposedly perfect creation. Influential passages by Augustine and Isidore are cited in many works that cover the subject, and by Chet Van Duzer, Karl Steel, and Debbie Felton, here.

We can, though, tread further back, to the Roman period, when, in the first century of the common era, Pliny the Elder could be said to have been a scholarly practitioner of Monster Studies, writing at length about the wonders at the edges of the known world, as well as others closer to home;[6] and we might travel back to his source for these, Herodotus, the putative "Father of History" himself; and to two influential sources, Megasthenses (ca. 350–290 BCE), Greek ambassador to India, and Ctesias of Cnidus, a Greek writer of the fifth-century BCE, who probably journeyed to the 'East,' where he claims to have seen wondrous peoples and animals. Both wrote now fragmentary texts called *Indica*.[7]

Of course, as a modern academic field of study and theoretical discipline, Monster Studies is relatively new on the horizon, the most recent in a long series of thematic fields from Women's Studies to Gender Studies to Transgender Studies, from Africana Studies to Peace Studies to Jewish Studies. But Jeffrey Cohen's *Monster Theory* is 15 years old, and a great wealth of scholarly literature on the monstrous is available. The challenge of this volume, and this introduction, then, is not a paucity of scholarship—as it might have been 20 years ago—but an overabundance thereof.

---

6   See, especially, Book VII of Pliny, *Natural History*, ed. and trans. H. Rackham, 10 volumes (Cambridge: Harvard University Press, 1940 and 1958).

7   See Van Duzer's essay in this collection, as well as William Latham Bevan and H.W. Phillott, *Mediæval Geography: An Essay in Illustration of the Hereford Mappa Mundi* (London: E. Stanford, 1873; reprint, Amsterdam: Meridian, 1969), p. 159, and John Block Friedman, *The Monstrous Races in Medieval Art and Thought* (Cambridge, MA and London: Harvard University Press, 1981), p. 5, among others. See Friedman, *Monstrous Races*, p. 212, n. 2, for detailed references.

Still, there is one apparent difference between Monster Studies and these other thematic disciplines: monsters, of course, do not exist. To assert that they do is to enter into the realm of cryptozoology, as carefully articulated by Peter Dendle, co-editor of this collection. I am often asked if medieval people believed that the monsters—the one-legged men, elves, dragons and so on—were real. My colleagues working on monsters in other subject areas meet the equivalent questions. The short (if slightly misleading) answer is generally yes, they did.[8] This binary of real and unreal, though, is as problematic when applied to monsters as it is when applied to scholarship. In both cases, there are two troubling implications: first, they suggest that fictitious or constructed subjects are not worthy of study (though who questions the study of Shakespeare's Puck, or of Beowulf himself?) Second, they imply that the "real" and "unreal" exist in a binary arrangement, while careful consideration of the monstrous reveals a great deal of what Cohen has termed (in another context) "difficult middles."[9]

The reality of monsters (or the belief therein) has been discussed in several studies. Cohen, arguing for the "simultaneous repulsion and attraction at the core of the monster's composition," directly answers the question:

> *Perhaps it is time to ask the question that always arises when the monster is discussed seriously ... Do monsters really exist?*
>
> *Surely they must, for if they do not, how could we?*[10]

---

8   For a full discussion of this in regard to the European Middle Ages, see Asa Simon Mittman and Susan Kim, *Inconceivable Beasts: The 'Wonders of the East' in the Beowulf Manuscript* (Tempe, AZ: ACMRS, forthcoming), chapter 6: "Framing 'the Real': Spatial Relations on the Page and in the World."

9   Jeffrey Jerome Cohen, *Hybridity, Identity and Monstrosity in Medieval Britain: On Difficult Middles* (New York: Palgrave Macmillan, 2006).

10   Cohen, "Monster Culture (Seven Theses)," in Jeffrey Jerome Cohen (ed.), *Monster Theory: Reading Culture* (Minneapolis: University of Minnesota Press, 1996), p. 20. This article, foundational to the field, was the subject of a roundtable which I organized at the 44th International Congress on Medieval Studies in 2009, "Monster Culture: Seven Theses (A Roundtable)," featuring Larissa Tracy, Mary Kate Hurley, Karma de Gruy, Stuart Kane, Jeff Massey, Derek Newman-Stille, and Jeffrey Jerome Cohen. Each thesis was examined and discussed, and the influence of the work as a whole considered. The standing-room only attendance spoke to the interest in the subject and the positive tone and tenor of the discussion confirmed the inclusive nature of the article and the field. The roundtable was sponsored by MEARCSTAPA (Monsters: the Experimental Association for the Research of Cryptozoology through Scholarly Theory And Practical Application), an academic association that takes its acronymic title from the Old English for border-walker, one of the terms applied to Grendel and his mother in the Anglo-Saxon epic *Beowulf* (R.D. Fulk, Robert Bjork, and John Niles (eds), *Klaeber's Beowulf*, 4th edn [Toronto: University of Toronto Press, 2008], line 1348). Note: all quotations from *Beowulf* are from this edition, and all translations are my own.

I would like to briefly tackle the question again, from two angles: the localized beliefs of individual societies and the utility of a notion of belief in current academic studies. Part of the trouble (if that is what it is) that inspires the question over and over again may be located in the term "monster," which bears a varying host of culture-specific associations. In seeking authors for the collection, we found scholars working in some periods to be very receptive to the term, whereas others were either hesitant about or resistant to applying the label to phenomena in their areas of subject. It is my hope, though, that this volume will work to expand productively the scope of the monstrous, a subject that is, by its nature, heterogeneous or even heterodox.

Though there is considerable study of the etymology of "monster" in the volume, and its period-specific meanings at prior points in history, there is little discussion, directly, of its *present scholarly* valence, of its meaning in the volume's title. Modernity would, I think, generally define a literal "monster" (in contrast with the more metaphorical use of the term to refer to particularly depraved people, such as the serial killers discussed by Weinstock) as that which is horrible, but *does not actually exist*: silly sea monsters, in contrast to terrifying but real creatures like the oarfish or frilled shark.[11] The *Oxford English Dictionary* tells us, for example:

> *Originally: a* mythical *creature which is part animal and part human, or combines elements of two or more animal forms, and is frequently of great size and ferocious appearance. Later, more generally: any* imaginary *creature that is large, ugly, and frightening. The centaur, sphinx, and minotaur are examples of "monsters" encountered by various mythical heroes; the griffin, wyvern, etc., are later heraldic forms.*[12]

This suggests that the difference between animal and monster is not the degree of terror it induces, how horrible it is, how hodgepodge in appearance or apparent construction, but its reality or lack thereof.

As a point of contrast, the Middle Ages might well have defined a monster as "a creature" with such qualities, leaving out the qualifiers that it be "mythical" or "imaginary." We are thus faced with two approaches to the question of the "reality" of the monsters in other periods, neither one of which we wish to accept here—either that medievals, or whomever the group in question might be, like us, wisely and rationally viewed sea serpents and *oni* and centaurs and *yōkai* and the

---

11   Photographs can tellingly be found at both *National Geographic* ("Rare 'Prehistoric' Shark Photographed Alive," October 28, 2010, <http://news.nationalgeographic.com/news/2007/01/photogalleries/frilled-shark/index.html>, accessed March 12, 2011) and *Deep Sea Monsters* ("Frilled Shark," no date, <http://www.deepseamonsters.com/component/content/article/59-frilled-shark.html>, accessed March 12, 2011).

12   "monster, n. and adv. and adj." 3rd edn, August 2010; online version November 2010, <http://oed.com:80/Entry/121738>, accessed March 12, 2011. An entry for this word was first included in the *New English Dictionary*, 1908. Emphasis added.

like as metaphors, and never *really* believed all that nonsense, or that they were "superstitious" and "benighted" products of a dark age, unable to arrive at rational conclusions in the same manner as modern people. However, as David Stannard argues in respect to the Puritan period:

> We do well to remember that the [pre-modern] world ... was a rational world, in many ways more rational than our own. It is true that this was a world of witches and demons, and of a just and terrible God who made his presence known in the slightest acts of nature. But this was the given reality about which most of the decisions and actions of the age, throughout the entire Western world, revolved.[13]

Belief in monsters was common throughout the pre-modern world, and continues, as Dendle, Foster, and Weinstock demonstrate, today. Their importance, their significance, extends well beyond the base question of their reality, though. Whether we believe or disbelieve the existence of a phenomenon is not what grants it social and cultural force. The question is not therefore "Did people believe in monsters?"—they did, and still do—but rather, "What is a monster?"

I wish to argue here that a monster is not really known through observation; how could it be? How could the viewer distinguish between "normally" terrifying phenomena and abnormally terrifying monstrosity? Rather, I submit, the monster is known through its *effect*, its impact.[14] Therefore, from this perspective, all the monsters are real. The monsters in all of the traditions discussed here had palpable, tangible effects on the cultures that spawned them, as well as on neighboring and later cultures. Beliefs die very slowly, and while it is a common trope that we live with the ghosts of the past, so too, we live with the monsters of the past. We still live with the horned Jew and the giant Saracen, with Japanese water monsters,

---

13   David E. Stannard, *The Puritan Way of Death* (Oxford: Oxford University Press, 1977), p. 69.

14   Several of our contributors have argued related points, explicitly and implicitly, most especially Patricia MacCormack: "Defined through this word 'marvel,' teratology describes a study of relation more than of an object;" Cohen: "It is true that some of us have never glimpsed a monster. Yet none of us have beheld time, or oxygen, or the wind. We vividly perceive their effects, and from this evidence we postulate agency and cause. The effects of the monster are undeniable;" and Jeffrey Weinstock: "The recurring concern underlying contemporary monster narratives is that, through a sort of retroactive causality, we now can only determine the monster's presence through its effects." See also Noël Carroll, *The Philosophy of Horror or Paradoxes of the Heart* (New York: Routledge, 1990), especially page 14: "Like suspense novels or mystery novels, novels are denominated horrific in respect of their intended capacity to raise a certain affect. Indeed, the genres of suspense, mystery, and horror derive their very names from the affects they are intended to promote—a sense of suspense, a sense of mystery, and a sense of horror. The cross-art, cross-media genre of horror takes its title from the emotion it characteristically or rather ideally promotes; this emotion constitutes the identifying mark of horror."

with Frankenstein's monster and (over and over again) the vampire. We live with the *vagina dentata*, the cyborg, the hostile alien living beyond our reach (though we live within its). As we cannibalize the Others of others, as we tear them apart and stitch them back together, we continually redefine the parameters of the monstrous.

Finding and Defining the "Monstrous"

How might we locate the monstrous, how might we, like the casual art observer, "know it when we see it?" I would argue that the monstrous does not lie solely in its embodiment (though this is very important) nor its location (though this is, again, vital), nor in the process(es) through which it enacts its being, but also (indeed, perhaps primarily) in its *impact*. Yes, the paradigmatic Grendel is larger than a man ("næfne he wæs mara Þonne ænig man oðer"[15] [except he was greater than any other man]); yes, he has a claw or talon of some sort ("hæÞenes handsporu"[16] [heathen's claw]); and yes, he lives at the periphery of civilization, far from the mead hall ("hælærna mæst; scop him Heort naman"[17] [greatest of halls; he assigned it the name "Heorot"]), in a churning, dragon-filled mere ("Nis Þæt heoru stow!"[18] [That is not a pleasant place!]); but this is costume and set-design, whereas the heart of the monstrosity lies in the missing head of Æschere:

> Ne frin Þu æfter sælum! Sorh is geniwod Denigea leodum./Dead is Æschere.[19]
> [Ask you not after joy! Sorrow is renewed among the people of the Danes.
> Dead is Æschere.]

No study could hope to pin down the monstrous in terms of physicality, though this is its most obvious marker. That which is "monstrous" in one culture (dark skin according to some medieval Christian texts, light skin according to some medieval Muslim texts, and so on) does not translate to others' Others. Certainly, hybridity is common, as are giantism and dwarfism, and other forms of excess or lack (too many arms, too few, though these can just as well be markers of divinity), as well as certain activities, like anthropophagia, but the common ought not be substituted for the constitutive. I could not hope to describe the physical, behavioral or geographic parameters of the monstrous, here or anywhere. By definition, the monster is outside of such definitions; it defies the human desire to subjugate through categorization. This is the source, in many ways, of their power. Instead, then, I would look to the impact(s) of the monstrous. This might

---

15   *Beowulf*, line 1353. All translations are mine.
16   *Beowulf*, line 986.
17   *Beowulf*, line 78.
18   *Beowulf*, line 1372.
19   *Beowulf*, lines 1322–3.

be manifest in the horror of excessive violence, but is rooted in the vertigo of redefining one's understanding of the world.[20] As Noël Carroll writes: "monsters are not only physically threatening; they are cognitively threatening. They are threats to common knowledge."[21] Massimo Leone writes relatedly about the process of religious conversion, arguing that such moments of destabilization draw our attention to the "stability" we thought we had, producing a vertigo that:

> *reveals that what is called equilibrium is nothing but a zero degree of the presence of the body in a given space. Nevertheless, it is only through a pathological condition, an alteration of normality, that this point of departure of perception can itself be perceived.*[22]

Above all, the monstrous is that which creates this sense of vertigo, that which calls into question our (their, anyone's) epistemological worldview, highlights its fragmentary and inadequate nature, and thereby asks us (often with fangs at our throats, with its fire upon our skin, even as we and our stand-ins and body doubles descend the gullet) to acknowledge the failures of our systems of categorization.

The above deals with how cultures define monstrosity from within. As some of our authors remind us, though, monsters are defined from without, as well. Again, there are real impacts, as when external perspectives declared Indian[23] or Maya[24] or African[25] deities to be monstrous. Similar processes are enacted within individual cultures to marginalize segments of their own populace: sexual, gender,[26] ethnic and religious[27] minorities, or the disabled. Monster theory can be, for marginalized groups and cultures, empowering, much as the closely related project of postcolonial theory has been, as a means of understanding and describing the tools used to abject, to reject and exclude people from the warmth of the mead hall.

---

20   Timothy K. Beal, *Religion and its Monsters* (New York: Routledge, 2002), p. 7, refers to a "vertigo-like" experience resulting from interaction with the mysterious be it religious, monstrous or both.

21   Carroll, *The Philosophy of Horror*, p. 34.

22   Massimo Leone, *Religious Conversion and Identity: The Semiotic Analysis of Texts* (New York: Routledge, 2004), pp. x–xi. See also Massimo Leone, "Literature, Travel, and Vertigo," in Jane Conroy (ed.), *Cross-Cultural Travel: Papers from the Royal Irish Academy Symposium on Literature and Travel, National University of Ireland, Galway, November 2002* (New York: Peter Lang, 2003), pp. 513–22.

23   See Mitter's essay in this collection.

24   See Looper's essay in this collection.

25   See Drewal's essay in this collection.

26   See Oswald's essay in this collection.

27   See Strickland's essay in this collection.

Inclusion and Exclusion

In a volume on monsters and the monstrous, inclusion and exclusion are vital, reoccurring themes. Location inside, at the heart of a culture, is predicated on the banishment of others. Peter Dendle and I were sharply aware of this issue, as we considered how to construct and frame this collection, since any act of framing is, in a sense, an establishment of boundaries, an act of violence. As John Gillies writes of Heidegger, "the act of enframing ruptures as much as it encloses."[28] With the acknowledgement that total inclusivity would not be possible, we nonetheless aimed, in defining our subject, to cast as broad a net as we could, striving to find scholars working on monsters and monstrous subjects throughout global history. Sometimes, there was an embarrassment of riches (as with the European Middle Ages and the nineteenth century), sometimes a small number of scholars working boldly, without a large network of monster-focused colleagues (Middle Eastern Studies, China), and in a few cases, we were simply unable to find scholars working on the subject (South-East Asia, Australia). This may well be our failings and language limitations; perhaps there is good work out there, in local and regional languages, that does not appear in our databases, that is not turned up by our searches. And perhaps in some areas, the term "monster" is simply not very meaningful, or even is a rejected term of colonial imperialism (India, as discussed elegantly by Partha Mitter here[29] and elsewhere).

Frequently, we negotiated with our authors as we came to understand the role of the monstrous in their geo-historical periods of study. In some cases, the monster is all body, in others, disembodied spirit. In some cases, the "monsters" are quite real in the conventional sense, even if amplified, and in others, clearly fictional or mythical. In some cases, they very closely mirror their creators, while in others they are non-anthropomorphous. Again, the defining features cannot be considered essential, as it were, as the sources are too varied, too wonderfully divergent to be summarized or contained by such characteristics. We have therefore encouraged contributors to find their own definitions, rather than to ascribe to our preconceptions. It is through my reading of these excellent essays that the present thesis regarding monstrous impact was derived, rather than from a pre-existing mandate.

The volume is divided into two halves, "Part I: History of Monstrosity" and "Part II: Critical Approaches to Monstrosity." Part I seeks to contextualize monsters, seeing how they function within individual cultures. Part II strives to find theories by which we might understand them, and also to use the monsters themselves as theoretical constructs by which we might gain greater understanding of the cultures by which they are produced. Part II should also serve to extend the coverage beyond the geo-historical periods we were able to cover in Part I, as

---

28   John Gillies, "Posed Spaces: Framing in the Age of the World Picture," in Paul Duro (ed.), *The Rhetoric of the Frame: Essays on the Boundaries of the Artwork* (Cambridge: Cambridge University Press, 1996), p. 25.

29   See Mitter's essay in this collection.

these broad themes can be found in monsters, wherever and whenever they arise. There is, of course, a great deal of productive overlap between these sections, and among essays within them. Ordering such material presents challenges. Cohen, in his preface to *Monster Theory*, notes:

> *The most obvious organization for a book of this kind would perhaps be a chronological ordering of the contents, but such a valorization of time as the primary determinant of meaning goes against what much of this collection asserts. The monster as a category that is not bound by classificatory structurations, least of all one as messy and inadequate as time. To order the contents of the volume diachronically would implicitly argue for a progress narrative that ... does not—cannot—exist.*[30]

As our collection ranges across the globe (East Asia, South Asia, Europe, the Caribbean, Mesoamerica, the Middle East, North America, Africa) as well as across time (ancient civilizations to the contemporary world), and with some essays treating very particular historical moments, while others cover many centuries, and all of them with start- and stop-points that cannot be linked up one after another or neatly placed in parallel, a simple chronological arrangement— desirable or inappropriate—simply would not be possible. We might have presented loose groupings (the ancient world, the Middle Ages), but to do so would be to superimpose Western chronological divisions—arbitrary enough in the context for which they were designed—upon the rest of the world in a way that does not arise organically from each culture's internal history and progression.

We have therefore arranged the geo-historical essays alphabetically by author name, which will impose on them an order no more arbitrary, and hopefully less embedded in traditional narratives, than other systems we might have chosen. We have designed the collection to be read as a whole, as each essay bears implications for the others, and we invite our readers to seek out associations that are individual, idiosyncratic, and speculative. To order them by period or group them by geography would be to discourage readers to look beyond their own research areas. As editor of the collection, reading the full range of essays has been a pleasure and, at times, a thrill.

Though it has remained largely peripheral in the broader context of most humanities, the monstrous has not been wholly ignored. In the past two decades, some scholars have begun the critical work of understanding the monstrous in a number of disciplines and for a number of periods, especially the Middle Ages. Medieval monstrosity has received great attention in the past two decades, including Cohen's several publications,[31] but also Bettina Bildhauer and Robert

---

30   Jeffrey Jerome Cohen, "Preface: In a Time of Monsters," in Jeffrey Jerome Cohen (ed.), *Monster Theory: Reading Culture* (Minneapolis: University of Minnesota Press, 1996), p. ix.

31   Among numerous articles and other related books, see: Cohen, *Hybridity, Identity and Monstrosity in Medieval Britain; Hybrids, Monsters, Borderlands: The Bodies of Gerald of Wales* (New York: St Martin's Press, 2000); and *Of Giants: Sex, Monsters, and the Middle*

Mills's collection on *The Monstrous Middle Ages* (2003)[32] and Andy Orchard's *Pride and Prodigies: Studies in the Monsters of the Beowulf-Manuscript* (1995).[33] It also serves as the focus of a few earlier, highly influential texts that have proven seminal, such as John Block Friedman's *The Monstrous Races in Medieval Art and Thought* (1981),[34] Rudolf Wittkower's "Marvels of the East: A Study in the History of Monsters" (1942),[35] and even J.R.R. Tolkien's "Beowulf: The Monsters and the Critics" (1936).[36] Arguably, the Middle Ages represented an especially fertile period for the forging of cultural constructions in recognizably modern formulations. But this important approach has much to tell us, potentially, about many other periods and cultures, and it is my hope that the scope, the insights, and the promise of the current collection can help spur fresh research and stimulate further discussion on this challenging yet crucial topic. My hope is that these essays cohere enough for the volume as a whole to maintain some measure of integrity, rather than for it to become a straightforward and harmonious whole. As Cohen writes, "hybridity is a fusion *and* a disjunction, a conjoining of differences that cannot simply harmonize."[37] Such should be the nature of a collection on monsters and the monstrous.

Conclusion

I would like to close with another anecdote, this one darker than the one with which I began. Last year, toward the end of my extended unit on monsters in my medieval survey, we covered depictions of Jews. We read the relevant chapter of Debra Strickland's compelling *Demons, Saracens and Jews*,[38] and were discussing the images of the twelfth-century Winchester Psalter. This is a work that appears in the major global art historical survey textbooks, which showcase the striking Hellmouth scene, rather than the shockingly anti-Semitic images of the Passion. Here, the Jews are literal monsters, with sharp fangs and distorted, grimacing faces, savages with great, hooked noses carrying not only rough clubs but even weapons

Ages (Minneapolis: University of Minnesota Press, 1999).

32 Bettina Bildhauer and Robert Mills (eds), *The Monstrous Middle Ages* (Cardiff: University of Wales Press, 2003).

33 Andy Orchard, *Pride and Prodigies: Studies in the Monsters of the Beowulf-Manuscript* (Cambridge: D.S. Brewer, 1995).

34 Friedman, *Monstrous Races*.

35 Rudolf Wittkower, "Marvels of the East: A Study in the History of Monsters," *Journal of the Warburg and Courtauld Institutes* 5 (1942).

36 J.R.R. Tolkien, "Beowulf: The Monsters and the Critics," *Proceedings of the British Academy* (1936), reprinted in John Ronald Reuel and Christopher Tolkien (eds), *The Monsters and the Critics, and Other Essays* (Boston: Houghton Mifflin, 1984).

37 Cohen, *Hybridity, Identity and Monstrosity in Medieval Britain*, p. 2.

38 Debra Higgs Strickland, *Saracens, Demons, and Jews: Making Monsters in Medieval Art* (Princeton: Princeton University Press, 2003).

made of giant bones (see Figure 17.7). Having set the Psalter in the context of the *Wonders of the East* and related monster texts, I believed that I had set the stage for a thoughtful discussion of the careful manner in which illuminators, especially in the twelfth and thirteenth centuries, subtly altered the narrative of the Passion by substituting grotesquely caricatured Jews in the place of the Romans throughout the story. Through the use of images, since the scriptural text could not be altered, Pontius Pilate becomes a Jew, and Roman soldiers become Jews; according to the Gospel of John, Jesus was arrested by a group consisting of both Roman soldiers and Jewish temple police, but all figures here are caricatured Jews.[39] Moreover, through the frequent use of contemporary clothing, the figures become contemporary Jews, rather than those of over a thousand years earlier. This fostered the narrative that the Jews were, *and remained*, the killers of Christ, a very important pillar in anti-Jewish rhetoric and action throughout the Middle Ages and well beyond, leading to the claims of Blood Libel, host desecration, and other entirely fictional acts of defamation that suggested that, in the medieval present, Jews carried ceaselessly on, killing Christ through ritual re-enactments of the crucifixion.[40]

One of my students raised her hand after this discussion, with a look of confusion and anger on her face. She said that she did not understand what I was "trying to get at," what my point was, since, she said, with a quaver of emotion in her voice, with the Winchester Psalter's image of the Arrest of Christ on the screen (see Figure 17.7), that I was making too much out of nothing, since this *is* what Jews look like, more or less. And anyway, she continued, the Jews *are* Christ-killers. She then screamed out the text of John 19:15, saying "the Jews shouted, 'Kill him! Kill him! Crucify him!'" She was quoting, interestingly, from the "God's Word Translation,"[41] the most violent English translation I have been able to find, since most read "take him" or "away with him," where this one version reads "kill him." The comparative accuracy of translation from the Greek is irrelevant, here, since she was not inspired by reading the original, but rather a modern English version. David Burke, former Director of Translations

---

39   John 18:3. The medieval designers of this image and others like it would have been working from the Latin Vulgate, which reads "Iudas ergo cum accepisset cohortem et a pontificibus et Pharisaeis ministros venit illuc cum lanternis et facibus et armis" [Therefore Judas having accepted a division of soldiers along with police and servants of the chief priests and Pharisees came there with lanterns and torches and arms] (*Biblia Sacra: Iuxta Vulgatam Versionem*, ed. Bonifatius Fisher, Robert Weber and Roger Gryson [Stuttgart: Deutsche Bibelgesellschaft, 1994], p. 1690). As clarified by a note in the *New Oxford Annotated Bible*, ed. Bruce M. Metzger and Roland E. Murphy, new revised standard version (Oxford: Oxford University Press, 1994), p. 153, "Both Roman *soldiers* and the Jewish temple *police* made the arrest." Emphasis in original.

40   It bears mention that only in 2011 did the current pope, Benedict XVI, declare, as one headline put it, "Jesus' death cannot be blamed on Jewish people" (John Thavis, Catholic News Service, March 2, 2011, p. xxxi, <http://www.catholicnews.com/data/stories/cns/1100846.htm>, accessed March 12, 2011).

41   God's Word to the Nations Bible Mission Society, *God's Word* (Grand Rapids: World Publisher, 1995).

for the American Bible Society, has critiqued this translation, noting that "'poorly informed' readers are likely to interpret the polemic against 'the Jews' in the New Testament as if 'Jews of all time are somehow implicated.'"[42] In this way, the modern translation and the medieval image are in concert with one another, and the resulting impression, conveyed by my student, was that the Jewish monster was real. The impact of these imagined monsters has been all too real, from the Middle Ages onward.

I was struck temporarily speechless, but as I soundlessly worked my jaw in an effort to formulate a reply, I saw in the eyes of all the other students a shocked recognition that, in essence, answers the question posed at the outset, here: all of this *matters*. All of this is *relevant*. I was trying to show how medieval images were designed to allow *medievals* to confuse one group of Jews from the first century with *all* Jews in their own day, and here, in twenty-first-century America, my students saw this same notion quite alive. Their horror at the spectacle served to demonstrate that images of monsters from another time and place are not just curios, dead relics of a lost age. And that it was images of Jews that brought this out ought not be given too much weight. We could have had the same sort of outburst based on images of Muslims, or of "Africans" or "Indians." Indeed, it is the latter two groups that are most often depicted as deeply monstrous, since *all* of the Wonders of the East, covered at length by Felton, Davies, and Van Duzer— the lying, homophagic Donestre, giant-eared Panotii, ass-bodied Onocentaur, and on—are all peoples who are supposed to dwell in India and Africa.

I close with an account of this very disturbing classroom episode, not because contemporary racism, often rooted in millennium-old bigotry, is the only or even the most important relevance for our study of monsters. Rather, it should serve to demonstrate the vast spread of the aftershocks that follow the arrival of the monstrous, the power and durability of its impact and import. In their distorted aping of their creators and their world, monsters show us how a culture delimits its own boundaries, how it sees itself; what it respects and desires is revealed in these portraits of scorn and disgust. This classroom moment of hate and fear, uncomfortable as it was for my students and me, should also remind us that when we study the monsters of the past, we study our own demons as well.

How might we begin to move beyond the demonization of one another? MacCormack turns the lens back on the reader, writing: "in the most reduced sense then, through concepts of adaptability and evolution itself, all organisms are unlike—*we are all, and must be monsters* because nothing is ever like another thing, nor like itself from one moment to the next."[43] Perhaps, in answer to the question above, we might begin with an examination of the monstrous, which time and

---

42   Michael Marlowe, "Against the Theory of 'Dynamic Equivalence'" (revised, August 2009) <http://www.bible-researcher.com/dynamic-equivalence.html#nota41>, with interior quotes from David G. Burke, "Translating *Hoi Ioudaioi* in the New Testament," *TIC Talk* 24 (1993).

43   MacCormack's chapter in this collection, p. 204, emphasis added.

again highlights the porous nature of the boundary that ought separate "us" from "them."

Whatever one can say about monsters past and present, one thing is certain: this field is a renewable and self-sustaining one, and the subject of our study will be available for a long time to come. The monster has shown its enduring importance within a wide range of cultural landscapes, from the Ancient Near East to the contemporary Digital Age, and though it is hunted over and over again, shows no danger of being hunted to extinction. The protean nature of the monstrous is among its key traits, and no doubt our contemporary societies—whether we know it or not—hold the nascent, embryonic kernels of monsters for future generations.

PART I
History of Monstrosity

The Monstrous Caribbean

Persephone Braham

Man is the animal that must recognize himself as human to be human.
Giorgio Agamben[1]

How did it happen that whole regions of Latin America—Amazonia, Patagonia, the Caribbean—are named for the monstrous races of women warriors, big-footed giants, and consumers of human flesh? Across time and across cultures, monsters appear in origin myths and prophecies of decline and fall, populating human imaginings of resurrection and renovation, fecundity and transformation, decline and death. But it is most particularly in Latin America, whose discovery coincided with the birth of modernity, that Amazons, cannibals, sirens and other monsters have become enduring symbols of national and regional character. Embodying exoticism, hybridity, and excess, monsters sustained the ongoing conceptualization of the unknown that was a prerequisite to conquest and colonization; after independence, monsters became metaphors for a series of problems ranging from indigenous and African slavery to dictatorship and postcolonial identity. The Caribbean Caliban, the anthropophagous Amazonian landscape, Haiti's living dead, and the sirens of the seas loom in Latin America's identity literature as incarnations of imminence, desire, and dread. This study seeks to expose symbolic rationales of Latin America's discourse of self-discovery, beginning with the portentous encounters of 1492, in the Sea of Cannibals.

From the earliest European travels in the East, tales of strange creatures and marvelous peoples accompanied accounts of scientific and military exploration. The great Greek conqueror, Alexander, reportedly alerted Aristotle to the natural wonders and monstrous races of the East.[2] Pliny the Elder's *Natural History* (first-century CE) includes Amazons, androgeni (hermaphrodites), anthropophagi (man-eaters), hairy men and women, Cynocephali (dog-headed men), and many

---

1   Giorgio Agamben, *The Open: Man and Animal* (Stanford: Stanford University Press, 2004), p. 26 (his italics).
2   John Block Friedman, *The Monstrous Races in Medieval Art and Thought* (Cambridge, MA and London: Harvard University Press, 1981), p. 7.

other fantastic humanoid creatures.[3] In addition to travel, scientific, and military accounts, monsters figure as portents of God's intention in didactic texts such as the third- and fourth-century *Physiologus* and Augustine of Hippo's *City of God*.[4]

The Iberian Bishop Isidore of Seville (d. 636 CE) integrated the scientific and didactic interpretations of monsters in his hugely influential *Etymologies*, which contains an encyclopedic accounting of all the world's phenomena from language and laws to imaginary animals. Along with sheep, horses, lions, and beavers, Isidore treated griffins, dragons, basilisks, mandrakes, phoenixes, and unicorns.[5] Affirming the existence of monstrous races such as "the Gigantes, Cynocephali, Cyclopes, and the rest,"[6] he located these primarily in the East, according to convention the symbolic locus of Paradise:

> Paradise is located in the east. Its name, translated from Greek into Latin, means "garden." In Hebrew in turn it is called Eden, which in our language means "delights." The combination of both names gives us the expression "garden of delights," for every kind of fruit-tree and non-fruit bearing tree is found in this place, including the tree of life. It does not grow cold or hot here, but the air is always temperate.[7]

As Chet Van Duzer notes elsewhere in this collection, in the medieval imaginary, monsters frequently populated unexplored parts of the world such as Scythia, Ethiopia, Japan, and Sicily.[8] Olympian creatures and other marvelous beasts served as a foil for Christianity, standing in for various virtues and vices in exemplary texts such as the bestiaries. In the Iberian literature of the time, travel narratives often delivered allegories of the Christian journey through vice and temptation; for example, in the fourteenth-century *Libro de Buen Amor* (*The Book of Good Love*), travelers must brave the savage, lusty *serranas* (mountain women), who combine elements of the Scythian Amazon legend with the European wild man tradition. Similarly, chivalric romances (*novelas de caballería*) like the *Libro de Alexandre*, in which the great soldier visited with the queen of the Amazons, combined marvelous elements from the *Iliad* and Isidore's

---

3   Pliny, *Natural History*, trans. H. Rackham (The Loeb Classical Library, 1958). Karl Steel's essay in this collection explores medieval perspectives on the cynocephali and other humanoid monsters.

4   Augustine of Hippo, *City of God*, vol. V, Books 16–18.35 (The Loeb Classical Library, 1966), Book 16, Chapter 8.

5   Compendia such as the medieval bestiaries included both existing and imagined animals. Cf. Pamela Gravestock, "Did Imaginary Animals Exist?" in Debra Hassig (ed.), *The Mark of the Beast: The Medieval Bestiary in Art, Life, and Literature* (New York: Garland, 1999), pp. 119–35.

6   *The Etymologies of Isidore of Seville*, ed. and trans. Stephen A. Barney et al. (New York: Cambridge University Press, 2006), XI.iii.12.

7   Ibid., XIV.iii.2.

8   Chet Van Duzer, "*Hic sunt dracones*: The Geography and Cartography of Monsters," in this collection. Van Duzer rightly notes the tendency to describe monsters as a function of their distance from the (mostly European) locus of the subject.

Etymologies, reinforcing the proximity of monsters to the enterprise of conquest and the longed-for recovery of the Earthly Paradise.

Discovery and Conquest

Christopher Columbus is without a doubt the single greatest influence in the creation of monsters of the Latin American imaginary. An avid reader, Columbus was well acquainted with the variety of monstrous beings he might expect to encounter in his travels, as well as their value as portents of virtue, vice, wealth, or divine intention. It is well known that he studied Marco Polo's thirteenth-century accounts of his travels to the East; the apocryphal fourteenth-century text *The Travels of Sir John Mandeville* (which supported Columbus's theory that the Earth was circumnavigable); Pierre d'Ailly's fifteenth-century *Imago Mundi*; and Pliny's *Natural History*.

When he arrived in the Caribbean Sea, Columbus was convinced that he had arrived in the mythical East. He was astonished by the beauty, heat, and lushness of the landscape, and interpreted these as signifiers of possible wealth and, as Isidore had written, divine providence. On January 8, near the "Rio del Oro" on present-day Haiti, he reported encountering three *serenas* (sirens), and described them matter-of-factly as "not so beautiful as they are painted, though to some extent they have the form of a human face."[9] He had seen similar creatures off what was called the Grain Coast of Guinea, where a coveted spice was harvested; his comparison of the two suggested that they were harbingers of gold. His descriptions of the tropical flora matched Isidore's garden of delight, and by the fourth voyage he had located the primordial seven-foot serpents.[10] Commemorative images of the Discovery were populated with sirens, tritons, and other fantastic creatures (Figure 1.1).

Columbus tried, for the most part, to emphasize the natives' natural receptivity to Christian customs and their freedom from the defects attributed to the monstrous races.[11] However, both his Letter to Luis de Santángel of April 1493 and the diary

---

9 Julius E. Olson and Edward Gaylord Bourne (eds), *The Northmen, Columbus, and Cabot, 985–1503: The Voyages of the Northmen* (New York: Charles Scribner's Sons, 1906), p. 218.

10 There are numerous commentaries on Columbus's attempts to reconcile what he was finding with what he expected; the lack of immediate wealth such as gold made it important to emphasize other, more symbolic readings of the territory. Cf. in particular Beatriz Pastor Bodmer, *The Armature of Conquest: Spanish Accounts of the Discovery of America, 1492–1589*, trans. Lydia Longstreth Hunt (Stanford: Stanford University Press, 1992), pp. 28–9.

11 Stephen Greenblatt argues that Columbus tried to differentiate between the monstrous and the marvelous and in fact demonstrated skepticism regarding monsters: "the former are vivid, physical violations of universal norms, the latter are physical impressions that arouse wonder." *Marvelous Possessions* (Chicago: University of Chicago Press, 1991), p. 75.

Columbus primus inuentor Indiæ Occidentalis. VI.

C OLVMBVS *trans Gades in Portugalliam, & omnem illam Oceani oram nauigans, fæpenumero animaduertit, & diligenter obferuauit, ventos quofdam ftatis anni temporibus ab occafu flare, qui multos dies conftanti tractu fpirarent: quos quum non aliunde, quam ex tranfmarina ora pro-ficifcipoffe iudicaret, tamdiu circa eam rem cogitando animum verfauit, vt eius certitudinem quærere aliquando conftitueret. Quapropter & Reipub. Genuenfi, & Principibus aliquot fuam operam obtulit, vt illam oram indagaret: fed ab omnibus neglectus, tandem fumptibus Ferdinandi & Ifabellæ Re-gum Hifpaniæ, nauigationem inftituit.*

B 3   Colum-

Figure 1.1   Christopher Columbus arrives in the Caribbean surrounded by sirens and tritons. Jan van der Straet, 1592, published by Theodor de Bry in *Americae pars quarta* (Frankfurt, 1594). Courtesy of the John Carter Brown Library at Brown University.

of the first voyage (later retold by Bartolomé de Las Casas)[12] include second-hand reports of anthropophagy, purportedly received from indigenous interlocutors. After evincing a good deal of skepticism regarding these reports, Columbus announced rather startlingly at the very end of the Letter that, although he had neither seen human monsters *nor received news of any*, the women of Matinino, the island closest to Spain, lived without men and "practice[d] no female usages," but used arms and copper armor, of which they were exceedingly fond. These women consorted, he continued, with the man-eating inhabitants of Caribo, the second island; moreover, the inhabitants of Cuba were all bald and possessed "incalculable gold."[13] From Las Casas's edition of the Diary, as well, we have the following episodes:

> *Fourth of November: [Columbus] also understood that, far away, there were men with one eye, and others with dogs' noses who were cannibals, and that when they captured an enemy, they beheaded him and drank his blood, and cut off his private parts.*[14]

> *Twenty-Sixth of November: It appears that these Indians do not settle on the sea-coast, owing to being near the land of Caniba. When the natives who were on board saw a course shaped for that land, they feared to speak, thinking they were going to be eaten; nor could they rid themselves of their fear. They declared that the Canibas had only one eye and dog's faces. The Admiral thought they lied, and was inclined to believe that it was people from the dominions of the Gran Can who took them into captivity.*[15]

However apocryphal or contradictory, Columbus's reports of cannibals and warrior women were widely circulated and became integral to tales of the *Mar de caníbales* or Cannibal Sea, and subsequently *Tierra Firme*, as the mainland became known. The New World loomed in the European imagination as a prodigy and an opportunity, as attested by numerous accounts of marvels in the chronicles of

---

12 See Margarita Zamora's meticulous commentary on the editing and diffusion of Columbus's accounts of the first voyage in *Reading Columbus* (Berkeley: University of California Press, 1993). Zamora analyzes the roles played by various interests including the Spanish Crown, Columbus's son Ferdinand, and Fray Bartolomé de Las Casas in the editing and diffusion of the accounts. She believes that this text, uncovered in 1989 by Antonio Rumeu de Armas, was the draft of the more polished Letter to Santángel dated February of that year: the predated February letter was edited (censored) for circulation by the Catholic monarchs (pp. 9ff).
13 Olson and Bourne, *The Northmen, Columbus, and Cabot*, p. 270. These two islands recall Marco Polo's description of the islands of Masculia and Femenina. All four references to the Matinino women in the text are worded this way, just as the three references to "Caribs, who eat men" are similarly worded.
14 Ibid., p. 138.
15 Ibid., p. 157.

conquest and exploration that circulated in the sixteenth century.[16] As Europeans began to discover Pliny's shortcomings, they were able to substitute new, equally astounding or monstrous phenomena for his blemmyes and sciopodes. Scholars have described this discursive production—the rhetoric of wonder evoked by the New World—as the "discourse of the marvelous," the "discourse of miracles," and the "discourse of abundance."[17] Well-known maps by Sebastian Münster (1540) and others represented *Tierra Firme* (present-day Brazil, Venezuela, and Colombia) as the land of the cannibal, and the New World was allegorized as a cannibal warrior woman. As less welcoming indigenous populations were encountered, the inference of cannibalism became a convenient justification for conquest, enslavement, and other abuses. Amazons, sirens, and cannibals represented the wealth of the Indies, and resistance to the Spanish right to it.[18]

From Cannibals to Amazons

> *Probably no male human being is spared the terrifying shock of threatened castration at the sight of female genitals.*
>
> Sigmund Freud, 1927

Anyone who questions the ascendency of the cannibal in the Latin American imaginary need only consult Carlos Jáuregui's monumental *Canibalia* (2008), an encyclopedic analysis of cannibalism as a cultural trope. As he points out, the cannibal does "not respect the boundaries that stabilize difference:"[19] it

---

16   The meeting of symbolic and empirical interpretations of the New World has been thoroughly examined (especially around the 1992 quincentennial of the Encounter) in numerous works, including Vladimir Acosta, *El continente prodigioso* (Caracas: Universidad Central de Venezuela, 1992); Anthony Pagden, *European Encounters with the New World from Renaissance to Romanticism* (New Haven: Yale University Press, 1993); Greenblatt, *Marvelous Possessions*; Jorge Magasich-Airola and Jean-Marc de Beer, *America Magica: When Renaissance Europe Thought It Had Conquered Paradise* (London: Anthem Press, 2006); and many others.

17   Greenblatt, *Marvelous Possessions*; Rolena Adorno (various); Julio Ortega, "The Discourse of Abundance," *American Literary History* 4/2 (1992), pp. 369–85.

18   This interpretation is widely held. See Sara Castro-Klaren, "What Does Cannibalism Speak? Jean de Léry and the Tupinamba Lesson," in Pamela Bacarisse (ed.), *Carnal Knowledge: Essays on the Flesh, Sex, and Sexuality in Hispanic Letters and Film* (Pittsburgh: Tres Ríos, 1993), pp. 23–41; Michael Palencia-Roth, "Cannibalism and the New Man of Latin America in the 15th- and 16th-Century European Imagination," *Comparative Civilizations Review* 12 (1985), pp. 1–27; and Peter Hulme, "Columbus and the Cannibals," in Bill Ashcroft, Gareth Griffiths and Helen Tiffin (eds), *The Post-Colonial Studies Reader* (London: Routledge, 1995), pp. 365–9.

19   "no respeta las marcas que estabilizan la diferencia." Carlos Jáuregui, *Canibalia: Canibalismo, calibanismo, antropofagia cultural y consumo en América Latina* (Madrid/ Frankfurt: Iberoamericana/Vervuert, 2008), p. 13.

problematizes binaries such as *interior/exterior* and *self/other* that we depend on to define our humanity. From Columbus's *de facto* coinage of the word *caníbal* to critiques of capitalism, the cannibal has mediated Latin American intercourse with others and itself. Latin America has always been inscribed from an ethnographic point of view, whether by sixteenth-century *cronistas*, nineteenth-century naturalists, or twentieth-century anthropologists and sociologists.[20] Cannibals and Amazons are metaphors for identifiable discursive currents such as barbarism, but also alert us to the difficulties of maintaining the boundaries between self and other that attend the objective investigation of one's own culture.

From the moment that cannibalism was first mentioned in connection with the New World, it was construed as a threat to masculinity. Entirely free from Columbus's fussy ambivalence, the lucky and enterprising Amerigo Vespucci introduced a fascinated Europe to a brave new world populated by "strange and monstrous" pierced and tattooed natives, "innumerable serpents, and other horrible creatures and deformed beasts" of the vast forests, and the bestial, libidinous women.[21] Vespucci stated that "human flesh is an ordinary article of food" for the indigenous, and described seeing a shipmate clubbed and eaten before his very eyes by a group of women with whom he was attempting to communicate.[22] Perhaps recalling his own readings about the Amazons, he commented in detail on the native women's strength and marksmanship. He returned repeatedly to the themes of anthropophagy and female sexual perversity, and described with horror the women's licentious custom of using snake venom to enlarge their men's penises, often resulting in castration:

---

20   As Roberto González Echevarría argues, the tools of ethnography and anthropology enabled twentieth-century intellectuals to "generate a discourse capable of containing and expressing those myths": in other words, to author Latin America itself. *Myth and Archive: A Theory of Latin American Narrative* (Durham, NC: Duke University Press, 1998), p. 143. Such endeavors require certain symbolic and rhetorical maneuvers to sustain. Carlos Alonso explains that "through its preoccupation with autochthony the subject necessarily enters into a relationship of mediation with respect to its own culture, a circumstance that opens the way to counterfeit, exoticism or ideological expediency ..." *The Spanish American Regional Novel: Modernity and Autochthony* (New York: Cambridge University Press, 1990), p. 3.

21   Clements R. Markham (trans., notes, and intro.), *The Letters of Amerigo Vespucci and Other Documents Illustrative of His Career* (London: Printed for the Haylukt Society, 1894), p. 46. Letter on his Third Voyage from Amerigo Vespucci to Lorenzo Pietro Francesco di Medici, March (or April) 1503. Some scholars doubt the authenticity of the *Mundus Novus* letter to Pier Francesco de' Medici and the "Four Voyages" letter to Piero Soderini, and most agree that the first voyage of 1497 was a fiction. However, the letter to Lorenzo di Medici, known as the *Mundus Novus* and narrating the third voyage of 1501 (published in Florence in 1503), and the letter to Piero Soderini summarizing the four voyages (published in Florence in 1505 or 1506), were both published in Vespucci's lifetime and are generally regarded as authoritative.

22   Markham, *The Letters of Amerigo Vespucci*, p. 37. Upon seeing that the women were reluctant to speak with his party, Vespucci retired and sent an "agile and valiant youth" to initiate communications. He was promptly knocked on the head.

> Another custom among them is sufficiently shameful, and beyond all human credibility. Their women, being very libidinous, make the penis of their husbands swell to such a size as to appear deformed; and this is accomplished by a certain artifice, being the bite of some poisonous animal, and by reason of this many lose their virile organ and remain [sic] eunuchs.[23]

Like many early chroniclers, Vespucci had difficulty interpreting the nakedness of the indigenes, alternating between salacious speculation and utter mystification. The account of his first voyage describes with relish the mysterious and contradictory female sex:

> Although they go naked, yet they are fleshly women, and, of their sexual organ, that portion which he who has never seen it may imagine, is not visible, for they conceal with their thighs everything except that part for which nature did not provide, which is, speaking modestly, the pectignone [pubis] ... [T]hey showed an excessive desire for our company.[24]

Vespucci would have been familiar with Isidore of Seville's *Etymologies*, which commented both on the "shame" of the pudenda and the innate dishonesty of the siren, whose genitals are inaccessible to the eye.[25] His remarks also resonate several centuries later in Sigmund Freud's commentary on the structural origins of female perversity: "in the woman [sexual life] is veiled in impenetrable darkness, partly in consequence of cultural stunting and partly on account of the conventional reticence and dishonesty of women."[26]

The association between women's sexual and gastronomic appetites and men's misadventures was systematically inscribed in early textual and graphic representations of Amazonia, allegorizing "America" as a cannibal woman (Figure 1.2). Hans Staden's story of his captivity among the Tupinamba of Brazil from 1552 to 1555 brought together cannibalism, female sexuality and emasculation. The Jesuit Father José de Anchieta described how the Tupi women defiled their male victims' bodies before devouring them:

---

23 Ibid., p. 46.

24 "Letter to Pier Soderini," in Germán Arciniegas, *Amerigo and the New World*, trans. Harriet de Onís (New York: Alfred A. Knopf, 1955), p. vii.

25 "The parts of the body called genitals (*genitalia*) receive their name, as the word itself shows, from the begetting (*gignere*, ppl. *genitus*) of offspring, because with them one procreates and begets. They are also known as 'organs of modesty' (*pudenda*) on account of a feeling of shame (cf. *pudor*, 'shame'), or else from 'pubic hair' (*pubis*), by which they are also hidden with a covering. However, they are also called the 'indecent parts' (*inhonestus*), because they do not have the same kind of comeliness as limbs that are placed in open view." *The Etymologies of Isidore of Seville*, XI.i.102.

26 Sigmund Freud, *Three Contributions to the Theory of Sex*, 2nd edn, trans. A.A. Brill (Mineola, NY: Dover, 2001), p. 30.

Figure 1.2   "America." Philippe Galle, circa 1581. New York Historical Society.

128   A M E R I C Æ

remſubigunt,Mingau vocatam, quam illæ adhibitis liberis abſorbent. Laĉtes
comedunt, tum carnes circa caput derodunt. Cerebrum, lingua, & quicquid

eſui eſt in capite, pueris cedit. Finitis hiſce ritibus, ſinguli domum repetunt, aſ-
ſumpta pottione ſua. Auĉtor cædis aliud adhuc nomen ſibi imponit. Regulus
tugurii brachiorum muſculos ſupernos ſcalpit dente cuiuſdam animantis oc-
ciſori:vbi vulnus conſolidatum eſt,relinquitur veſtigium,quod honori magno
ducitur. Quo die cædes perpetrata eſt, auĉtor eius ſe quieti dare neceſſe habet,
& in leĉto ſuo retiformi decumbere totum eum diem: præbetur illi arcus non
ita magnus,cum ſagitta,quibus tempus fallit,& ſcopum ex cera adornatum petit. Quod fit,ne brachia ex terrore cædis obtuſa, ſeu exterrita fiant tremula in
ſagittando. Hiſce omnibus ego ſpeĉtator, & teſtis oculatus interfui.
    Numeros non vltra quinarium norunt: ſi res numerandæ quinarium ex-
cedant,indicāt eas digitis pedum & manuum pro numero demôſtratis. Quod
                             ſi nu-

Figure 1.3   A cannibal feast among the Tupinamba Indians of Brazil, published
by Theodor de Bry, *Americae tertia pars memorabilē provinciæ Brasiliæ
historiam* (Frankfurt, 1592). Anne S.K. Brown Military Collection, John
Hay Library.

They killed another one of their enemies, whom they soon tore into pieces with great rejoicing, especially the women, who went around singing and dancing; some [of the women] pierced the cut off members [of the body] with sharp sticks, others smeared their hands with [the victim's] fat and went about smearing [the fat on] the faces and mouths of others, and it was such that they gathered [the victim's] blood in their hands and licked it, an abominable spectacle, such that they had a great slaughter on which to gorge themselves.[27]

The Frenchman Jean de Léry lived among the Tupi Indians of Brazil for some months during 1557–58, and made extensive observations of their anthropophagic customs. A Protestant, Léry drew parallels between Tupi ritual and what he saw as Catholic excesses. However, he also differentiated between the "holy" anthropophagy of the Christian Eucharist and the ceremonial or pleasure-based anthropophagy of the Tupi. He observed that the designated victims were often given many wives before they were sacrificed and eaten, reinforcing the (by now routine) conflation of sexual and gastronomic pleasure, sacrament, and orgy. Theodor de Bry's enormously popular images of cannibal "cookouts," (see Figure 1.3) published in the late sixteenth and early seventeenth centuries, illustrated these stories for all Europe.[28]

The German natural philosopher Alexander von Humboldt, who undertook the exploration of the Spanish-held territories between 1799 and 1804, greatly influenced Latin American thought.[29] Humboldt attributed reports of monsters in Amazonia to Indian legends that the missionaries exploited for entertainment value. In light of this skepticism, his reaction to the Amazon legend seems oddly credulous:

---

27 Quoted in Marvin Harris, *Good to Eat: Riddles of Food and Culture* (New York: Simon and Schuster, 1985), pp. 208–9.

28 The 13 volumes of de Bry's *Great Voyages* (1590–1634) were illustrated editions of voyage narratives, often edited and supplemented without respect for the original author's text or the true reality of the Americas. Volume 3 was based on accounts by Hans Staden and Jean de Léry. An astute businessman as well as an artist, de Bry worked from Staden's own illustrations, liberally mixing in elements of different narratives, regions, cultures, and traditions in his portrayal of the Indians. Hence, a representation of the Tupinamba cannibals in Brazil combines elements from Léry's descriptions such as "tonsured" hair, with archetypal features of the Wild Man—hairy bodies, long hair and beards, and so on—, biblical figures such as Adam and Eve and Leviathan, and figures from classical mythology and Pliny's taxonomy, Thévet's *Cosmography*, and other sources. Among these generally idealized images are, as Bernadette Bucher notes, a number of hag-like female figures with sagging breasts, associated in medieval tradition with "maleficent women, vampires, witches, demons, the incarnation of Envy and Lust, and the depiction of Death." Bernadette Bucher, *Icon and Conquest: A Structural Analysis of the Illustrations of de Bry's Great Voyages*, trans. Basia Miller Gulati (Chicago: University of Chicago Press, 1981), p. 38.

29 Cf. Mary Louise Pratt, *Imperial Eyes: Travel Writing and Transculturation*, 2nd edn (New York/London: Routledge, 2008).

> *A taste for the marvelous and a wish to describe the New World with some of the tones of antiquity no doubt contribute to the reputation of the Amazons. But this is not enough to reject a tradition shared by so many isolated tribes. I would conclude that women, tired of the state of slavery in which men have held them, united together and kept their independence as warriors. They received visits once a year from men, and probably killed off their male babies. This society of women may have been quite powerful in one part of Guiana.*[30]

Humboldt's response to stories of cannibalism among the Guiana was equally non-empirical. In a long description of indigenous cannibalistic practices (which he never witnessed first-hand), he suggested that, based on language differences, they did not recognize the "universal" concept of humanity but only that of family. He was much more incredulous about reports of earth-eating Indians, and took pains to measure the phenomenon by scientific observation.[31]

Humboldt's influence is obvious in the writings of Argentine intellectual Domingo Faustino Sarmiento, who, writing against the savage dictatorship of Juan Manuel de Rosas (1826–52), used monstrous imagery to define the terms of civilization and barbarism. Sarmiento's *Facundo* is widely considered fundamental to the development of Argentinean and Latin American identity, and may be the single most influential text of that region's nineteenth and twentieth centuries. Sarmiento described Argentina gynomorphically, as the man-eating Theban Sphinx: "half cowardly woman, half bloodthirsty tiger;" the seductive but sterile pampas awaiting the enlightened "penetration" and "fertilization" of a Tocqueville-like father figure. In short, Argentina was *una vorágine*—a sucking vortex or Charybdis enticing the unwary (although enlightened) European to his demise.[32] Sarmiento's discourse of civilization and barbarism, and the association of the feminine with the barbaric side of society, resonated well beyond Argentina throughout the nineteenth and twentieth centuries, shaping the thinking of positivists, determinists, and regionalists, as will be seen in the representative works described below.

After a century of looking to Europe and the United States for cultural models, Latin Americans turned in the 1920s and 1930s toward the autochthonous and the regional in their search for cultural definition. Regionalism was a literary and philosophical movement that sought to characterize the particulars of a given region through the particularities of its language, traditions, flora, fauna, and topography; the Latin American character was seen as deeply inflected by

---

30 Alexander von Humboldt, *Personal Narrative of a Journey into the Equinoctial Regions of the New Continent*, trans. Jason Wilson (New York: Penguin, 1995), pp. 240–1.

31 Ibid., p. 245.

32 Domingo Faustino Sarmiento, *Facundo: Civilization and Barbarism*, trans. Kathleen Ross (Berkeley, CA: University of California Press, 2003), p. 32. Oedipus defeated the Theban Sphinx (daughter of Echidna, part woman and part snake, along with the Chimaera, the Hydra and other monsters) by answering her riddle, whereupon she threw herself off the Acropolis in despair.

its environment. Roberto González Echevarría argues convincingly that this turn led to a re-encounter with, and re-evaluation of, indigenous and regional cultures through ethnography: "the crisis of the West ... removed natural science as the mediating discourse in Latin American narrative, and made way for a new one, that of anthropology."[33]

Unlike the French in Africa or the British in the Middle East, the Latin American student of his own culture could not comfortably define his activity as an empire-building encounter with dark-skinned primitives. Nor could he, like the German folklorists, catalog the folkways of a homogeneous pre-modern culture as the building blocks of national splendor. If Latin Americans characterized the non-modern as aberrant or monstrous, in many instances they also questioned the viability of the modern in a Latin American setting. In this way, as Carlos Alonso suggests, the discourse of regional or national autochthony became a rationale for the failures and contradictions of modernity in Latin America. By focusing on the telluric or non-modern aspects of regional tradition, literary production foregrounded "the fundamental *eccentricity* of Latin America vis-à-vis modernity."[34]

The Brazilian *antropofagia* movement of the 1920s was a notable expression of this confluence of irrationalist thought, anthropological discourse, and the quest for autochthony with respect to European and US modernity. As Prado Bellei defines it, *antropofagia* is "the ambivalent strategy of incorporation by means of which the strength of the cultural other is used for the creation of a separate cultural identity."[35] Oswald de Andrade's notorious 1928 "Anthropophagist Manifesto" emphasized recovering "primitive wisdom" to both defend against and profit from modern technological society, suggesting that a stronger, more authentic Brazilian culture would result from the cannibalistic incorporation of selected aspects of modern technical culture by the primitive.[36] *Antropofagia* was a short-lived but very intense movement that generated several important

---

33   González Echevarría, *Myth and Archive*, p. 150. Julie Skurski describes the outcome of these tensions as the "irrationalist" movement, and also suggests that its utility to the *novela de la tierra* (specifically in Gallegos's case) was precisely in its valorization of the "spiritual and instinctual dimensions of life," as opposed to the foregoing positivist movements' emphasis on the material, the rational and the empirical. "The Ambiguities of Authenticity in Latin America: Dona Bárbara and the Construction of National Identity," *Poetics Today* 15/4 (1994), p. 606.

34   Alonso, *The Spanish American Regional Novel*, p. 24, my emphasis. For Alonso, the rise of the regionalist novel in the first 30 years of the twentieth century reflects the influence of Nietzsche and Bergson in Latin America, as well as the imminent hegemony of the United States. Anthropology unavoidably defines (exoticizes, marginalizes) the objects of its analysis, and is much more implicated in social policies enacted upon its objects than used to be recognized.

35   Sérgio Luiz Prado Bellei, "Brazilian Anthropophagy Revisited," in Francis Barker, Peter Hulme, and Margaret Iversen (eds), *Cannibalism and the Colonial World* (New York: Cambridge University Press, 1998), p. 99.

36   Osvaldo de Andrade, "The Anthropophagist Manifesto" [1928], trans. Alfred Mac Adam in *Latin American Literature and Arts* 51 (1995), pp. 65–8.

works in poetry, narrative, and the visual arts. Brazilian artists and intellectuals would revisit *antropofagia* in the 1970s as a way of critiquing the modernizing programs undertaken by the dictatorship: a representative work is Nelson Pereira dos Santos's 1971 film *Como era gostoso o meu frances* (*How Tasty Was My Little Frenchman*).

The great Latin American regionalist novels of the 1920s again engage the dilemmas of establishing a positive Latin American identity within Western binary paradigms: modern/primitive, metropolitan/colonial, universal/autochthonous, civilized/barbarous. These novels depict the struggle for Latin America's future as an epic battle between modern man and a feminized, atavistic landscape, whose avatars—grasping, sensual women, bloodthirsty animals, and exotic topographical features—echoed its castrating and/or anthropophagic capacities. The two most influential and widely disseminated regionalist novels, *La vorágine* (Colombia, 1924) and *Doña Bárbara* (Venezuela, 1929), were clearly influenced by the tradition of natural science that began with Humboldt and culminated in positivism, as well as the mythological preoccupations of post-war anthropological thought, with its intense scrutiny of local beliefs, customs, and artifacts.

La vorágine (*The Vortex*), by José Eustasio Rivera, is commonly regarded as the foundational work in the *novela de la tierra*, or telluric genre. Rivera was a connoisseur of the major foreign explorations of the Orinoco and Rio Negro, and worked as a surveyor and ardent defender of Colombian territory against Venezuelan and Peruvian incursions. His novel denounces the abuses of the rubber companies working in the jungle, which he saw as devouring the humanity of the workers. The novel's histrionic protagonist, Arturo Cova, goes into the Amazonian jungle in pursuit of a woman and is, presumably, devoured. Cova's hypermasculine self-image is continually undermined by his appalling failure in the performances of masculinity (his clumsiness at a round-up allows his horse to be gored, and his leadership of a jungle search party is strikingly inept). Threats to Cova's life and virility are equally embodied in corrupt, sensual women and the fleshly, life-draining land. His descriptions of the jungle are transparently gynomorphic and evocative of castration, mind-altering drugs and aphrodisiacs, and flesh-eating diseases like syphilis and leprosy.[37] The jungle is a hungry mouth awaiting its prey: "a man-consuming hell, a gaping mouth swallowing men whom hunger and disappointment place in its jaws."[38] Termites and other devouring insects mimic sexually transmitted diseases, felling (manly) trees and men:

---

37   Both diseases were of great concern in Colombia in the 1920s as they were considered obstacles to national progress. Cf. Diana Obregón, "Building National Medicine: Leprosy and Power in Colombia, 1870–1910," *Social History of Medicine* 15/1 (2002), pp. 89–108. The Colombian ethnographer and medical man Luis Cuervo Márquez assured his readers in 1915 that leprosy was imported from Europe in *Geografía médica y patológica de Colombia: Contribución al estudio de las enfermedades intertropicales* (Bogotá: Librería Colombiana, 1915), p. 168.

38   José Eustasio Rivera, *The Vortex*, trans. Earle K. James (New York: Putnam, 1935), p. 242.

The comején grub gnaws at the trees like quick-spreading syphilis, boring unseen from within, rotting tissue and pulverizing bark ... Here the aphrodisiac parasite that covers the ground with dead insects; the disgusting blooms that throb with sensual palpitations, their sticky smell intoxicating as a drug; the malignant liana, the hairs of which blind animals, the pringamosa that irritates the skin ... crunching jaws are heard, devouring with the fear of being devoured.[39]

The anthropophagic jungle, with its devouring ants and miasmic, paralyzing, leech-filled swamps, breathing "the sopor of death, the enervating process of procreation,"[40] is mirrored in the fleshy oriental succubus Madona Zoraida Ayram, who inhabits its depths. The novel is strewn with mutilated male bodies: Millán the *domador* or horse-tamer who is gored by a bull; the disarmed Indian Pipa; the trees "castrated" by the *caucheros*; various peons sucked into swamps or eaten by voracious ants; Luciano, the guide's long-dead son and the victim of the Madona's mercenary sexuality. Arturo succumbs as well to the Madona Zoraida, remarking bitterly: "This insatiable she-wolf has burned up my virility with her breath. She wastes me like a candle that burns upside-down."[41] The novel's final scene, where Arturo kills his rival and recovers his lover Alicia, culminates in the rival's corpse being consumed by the voracious Caribe fish, prefiguring Arturo's own final deglutition by the jungle.

Doña Bárbara is a thesis novel in which, as in Sarmiento's *Facundo*, Bolívar's *Carta de Jamaica*, and earlier allegorical representations of America, civilization and barbarism are embodied respectively as man (the city lawyer Santos Luzardo, whose name denotes his enlightenment) and woman (the cattlewoman of the plain, Doña Bárbara, or the Barbarous Lady). The well-known critic Donald Shaw once called it Latin America's best-known novel;[42] its author went on to become president of Venezuela. The symbolic character Doña Bárbara is a *mestiza* whose birth originated in a rape. The novel opens with her own rape; this conquest of her body—and implicitly her mother's Indian body—mirrors that of the land, generating her vengeful hunger for the territory and cattle of Santos Luzardo's ranch Altamira, and for castrating any man who would oppose her. Doña Bárbara's sexual voracity (mirroring her lust for power) is demonstrated by the wasted figure of the "*ex-hombre*," her estranged husband Lorenzo Barquero, who was emasculated and broken through an excess of enforced sexual activity with Doña Bárbara.[43] Doña Bárbara is estranged from her own maternity (a possible avenue of redemption), through the neglect of her daughter Marisela.

---

39 Ibid., pp. 230–1.
40 Ibid.
41 Ibid., p. 290.
42 Donald Shaw, "Gallegos' Revision of Doña Bárbara 1929–30," *Hispanic Review* 42/3 (1974), pp. 265–78. It should be noted that his remarks were made well after the publication of Gabriel García Márquez's *100 Years of Solitude*.
43 Rómulo Gallegos, *Doña Bárbara* [1929] (Mexico: Porrúa, 1981), p. 16.

Doña Bárbara is referred to as Amazon, Sphinx and "devourer of men." She is associated with *el Tuerto*, an ancient man-and-steer-eating alligator whom she supposedly controls, and the feminized *tremedal* or quicksand bog, *la Chusmita*, where she beholds a *culebra de agua* or water serpent strangling a yearling. Like Doña Bárbara, the *llano* or plain is a chaotic "devoradora de hombres" —its extension unbounded and its rivers filled with the small, ravenous Caribe fish—and like Doña Bárbara it is gradually conquered and tamed by Santos Luzardo. This reclamation consists of the systematic frustration of her sexual wiles, and destruction of her spurious claims on masculine territory, as Santos breaks horses, faces down her agents, castrates renegade bulls, and runs off the sinister big-game hunter Mister Danger, all to a persistent chorus of Altamira's men cheering his virility. Once the untamable Doña Bárbara has returned to her origins, the blooming, newly domesticated Marisela takes her place, presumably to help Santos populate the *llano*. The cannibal's defeat is the harbinger of progress.

Ricardo Güiraldes's *Don Segundo Sombra* (1926), the middle novel of the classic Regionalist triumvirate, is an elegiac set-piece that celebrates the most manly of archetypes, the Argentine *gaucho* or cowboy. There are few feminine characters in the story and none who explicitly menace the male characters. However, in one anomalous episode, the protagonist Fabio Cáceres and his horses are almost sucked into a crab-infested swamp, or *cangrejal*. Afterwards, he cannot stop thinking about being devoured by crabs as the earth swallows him up:

> I could not get the crab bed out of mind. The pampa must suffer because of it! And God help the bones of whoever fell in! Next day they'd be picked clean. To feel the ground giving way underfoot, to feel oneself sinking down, inch by inch. And mud pressing the ribs! To die drowned on land! And then the crabs tearing and picking the flesh—belly, entrails, bones, making all of them a mass of blood and filth! The thousands of shells acrawl within one, turning the torture of death into a vertigo of voraciousness![44]

The telluric dimensions of the female characters in *Doña Bárbara* and *La vorágine* are so conspicuous that enumerating them here paradoxically seems to underplay their actual power. The *Don Segundo* case is at once more subtle and more shocking: a single image of the earth slowly ingurgitating a helpless man, hundreds of crabs voraciously devouring his bowels, his "parts" transformed into a "mass of blood and filth." In all three novels, then, elements of the feminized terrain—animal, vegetable, and mineral— conspire to emasculate and consume the unwary adventurer.

The fact that the drama of this encounter is couched so unequivocally in terms of a threatened or compromised masculinity is also reflective of the *novela de la tierra*'s

---

44   Ricardo Güiraldes, *Don Segundo Sombra*, trans. Harriet de Onís (New York: New American Library, 1966), pp. 109–10. Onís renders rather delicately the original "Y saber que el bicherío le va a arrancar de a pellizcos la carne ... *Sentirlos llegar al hueso, al vientre, a las partes, convertidas, en una albóndiga de sangre e inmundicias*, con millares de cáscaras dentro, removiendo el dolor en un vértigo de voracidad ..." Güiraldes, *Don Segundo Sombra* (Madrid: Alianza, 1982), p. 126.

anthropological subtext. As many scholars have noted, the three novels can be read on a continuum, from the anguished and chaotic *La vorágine* to the stately *Don Segundo*, to the optimistic, even triumphal *Doña Bárbara*. The fate of the protagonists reflects their ability to impose themselves on the landscape and its avatars through a series of encounters, delineated equally by each protagonist's relative objectivity and his normative masculinity. Hence, in *Don Segundo*, Fabio Cáceres learns to be a man in terms which allow him to bridge the divide between past and future, while in *La vorágine*, a disoriented, debilitated Arturo Cova is entirely swallowed up by the maw of the jungle, sending out a final flare in the figure of his infant son. Arturo's intense, hallucinogenic solipsism never leads to self-knowledge. He never recognizes the dangers of the external landscape as a reflection of his failures, nor the perfidy of the women as a reaction to his own corruption. In psychoanalytic terms, the novel enacts the universal mythic archetype of the devouring Great Mother: "beheading and dismemberment … express the dread that masculine consciousness has of being swallowed up by the unconscious feminine."[45]

The recurrence of certain binary themes in the Latin American literary and critical tradition—aesthetics versus ethics, universal versus local, civilization versus barbarism—along with the more conciliatory but equally oppressive elaborations on *mestizaje* or racial mixture, are the inevitable result of an ongoing, inherently ethnographic effort to locate and describe autochthonous or national culture(s), but also to locate and describe the self. As natural science and amateur ethnography before it, anthropology (and indeed any study of social man that calls itself science) brings together the imperatives of objectivity with the problematics of what we now recognize as the modern subject. But as anthropologists have discovered, anthropology itself is a product of its own culture and history: a story built on other stories and informed by acknowledged archetypes. The authority of the cannibal woman in the Latin American identity discourse of the 1920s is, perhaps, a reflection of the changing nature of ethnographic sensibility from one firmly rooted in positivist objectivity to one that recognizes the incongruity of such a stance.

Sirens

Sirena: supuesto animal marino, leemos en un diccionario brutal.
Jorge Luis Borges[46]

The sirens of classical and medieval tradition dwelt alongside Scylla, the hyperdentate sea-hydra; Charybdis, the crushing sea-vortex (or *vorágine*) who devoured passing ships, and her ally, the primordial sea-serpent Leviathan of the *Revelation*.

---

45 Richard J. Callan, "The Archetype of Psychic Renewal in 'La Vorágine,'" in Carmello Virgillo and Naomi Lindstrom (eds), *Woman as Myth and Metaphor in Latin American Literature* (Columbia, MO: University of Missouri Press, 1985), p. 19.

46 Jorge Luis Borges, *Libro de los seres imaginarios* (Buenos Aires: Kier, 1967), p. 57.

Isidore of Seville identified sirens as "harlots,"[47] and some bestiaries presented them as avatars of the devil. Elsewhere in this collection, Dana Oswald examines the siren in the context of gendered monstrosity. As Oswald remarks, the monstrosity of the siren lies in its gender and also its hybridity.

A study of the distribution of siren images through the Middle Ages places about 30 percent of these images in Spain, specifically Castille, Navarre, and Catalonia.[48] In medieval Spanish lyric, the siren was a metaphor for flattery and the treachery of the senses (Juan de Mena's *Coplas*) or the transience of good fortune (the Marquis of Santillana's sonnets). The beautiful Melosina, tragically transformed each Saturday into a serpent below the waist, figured in a popular 1489 Spanish translation of the French *Mélusine* by Jean d'Arras.[49] Melosina has many sons, all of whom have bizarre disfigurations (a missing or extra eye, a protruding fang, asymmetrical ears or eyes). In Spanish Golden Age literature, Calderón de la Barca's zarzuela *El golfo de las Sirenas* retells Odysseus's encounters with Scylla, Charybdis, and the sirens. Francisco Quevedo's unnamed siren represents the treacherous senses; the man who stops his ears and covers his eyes is safely insulated from her danger.[50] Sirens were rumored to eat men who did not satisfy them sexually, and Spanish fishermen and sailors had to swear an oath against coupling with them. Sirens were, paradoxically, present at the birth of modern science: Carlos I and Felipe II of Spain reportedly saw sirens dissected in Andreas Vesalius's operating theater. Carolus Linnaeus, the founder of modern taxonomy, included sirens in the same class as man and apes.[51]

A denizen of both the Caribbean and Mediterranean seas, the siren embodied the lure of exploration and conquest. Caressing and tempestuous, teeming with commerce, the two seas were the thresholds between Europe and the great wealth of unknown continents. For the great Caribbean scholar Germán Arciniegas, the intrepid Amerigo Vespucci and his beautiful cousin Simonetta, the model for Botticelli's amphibious Venus (the siren of the Renaissance), personify these mirrored seas.[52] Inhabiting the liminal space between the Old and New Worlds, the hybrid siren offered a metaphor for Latin American intellectuals seeking political and cultural independence from Europe. At the same time, the racial, cultural, and national hybridity attributed to the *criollos* of the Americas was regarded as voluptuous, degenerate, and impure.[53]

---

47   *The Etymologies of Isidore of Seville*, XI.iii.31.

48   Jacqueline Leclercq-Marx, *La Sirène dans la pensée et dans l'art de l'Antiquité et du Moyen Âge: du mythe païen au symbole chrétien* (Brussels: Académie Royale de Belgique, 1997).

49   In her investigation of the Melosina texts, Ivy Corfis suggests that the wide diffusion of the translation under the Catholic Kings was meant to reinforce the image of the female head of state and mother of empire. See "Beauty, Deformity, and the Fantastic in the Historia de la linda Melosina," *Hispanic Review* 55/2 (1987), pp. 181–93; and "Empire and Romance: Historia de la linda Melosina," *Neophilologus* 82/4 (1998), pp. 559–75.

50   Paul Julian Smith, "Quevedo and the Sirens: Classical Allusion and Renaissance Topic in a Moral Sonnet," *Journal of Hispanic Philology* 9/1 (1984), p. 36.

51   Agamben, *The Open*, p. 24.

52   Germán Arciniegas, *Biografía del Caribe* (Buenos Aires: Sudamericana, 1963), p. 20.

53   The terms creole and criolization have divergent meanings in the Anglophone,

At the birth of modern Latin America, the Liberator Simón Bolívar described Spain as an unnatural stepmother, and the newly independent Americans as her abject offspring: neither European nor indigenous, never properly enslaved nor truly free.[54] The prolific Alejandro Tapia y Rivera (1826–82), considered the father of Puerto Rican literature, was also one of the great Puerto Rican patriots of the nineteenth century, a time when the island's late colonial status was a constant source of debate and anxiety among its intellectuals (and, indeed, remains so today). *La Antigua Sirena* (1862) took up the theme of the hybrid or liminal status of Puerto Rico. The novel is framed allegorically as the tale of Venice's greatness destroyed by the political intrigues of a dissolute oligarchy. Tapia represents Venice (implicitly Puerto Rico, as the mainland colonies before her) as a wasted Amazon deprived of her glory by incompetent masters. All the characters represent aspects of Venetian society: the sybaritic oligarchy; the manly hero destroyed by jealous politicians; the virtuous citizen persecuted by malicious rivals; the tragic artist; and the ignorant, trusting people. The eponymous Sirena is a beautiful young woman who seduces and destroys all those around her. She is a monster of political intrigue who undermines the most idealistic and patriotic young men: a "double lie" whose external beauty belies her moral corruption and whose all-consuming devotion to power runs contrary to the feminine ideal of self-abnegation: "Sirena was, then, a double lie: a lie as a beauty, a lie as an abnegation, the second and principal beauty of woman."[55] The Siren, indeed, represents the political intrigue in the Spanish court and its deleterious effects on the noble, fatally misused American Amazon.

In the aftermath of the Cuban–Spanish–American War of 1898, the United States was exerting new hegemonic powers through both military action and a policy of pan-Americanism. Latin Americans responded with pan-Latin Americanist movements such as *mundonovismo* and *hispanoamericanismo* that advocated cultural autonomy for Latin America. José Enrique Rodó's essay *Ariel* (1900) represented the US as a voracious, soulless Caliban intent on despoiling the noble, spiritual Latin American Ariel.[56] Latin American *modernismo* (1880–1910), probably the single most important aesthetic movement to come from Latin America, rejected the materialism of the US and growing middle classes at home, creating a highly erudite, interiorized literature that was dense with symbolism and sensation.

Francophone and Hispanophone Americas. For Spanish Americans, *criollo* identified ethnic Spaniards and Africans born in the Americas. The term eventually came to identify the rural landowning classes who prided themselves on their Spanish heritage but identified strongly as American.

54 Simón Bolívar, *Letter from Jamaica* (1815), trans. Lewis Bertrand, in *Selected Writings of Bolivar* (New York: Colonial Press, 1951). Bolívar lamented Spanish incompetence with respect to its colonies in comparison to the great enslavers of history.

55 "Sirena era, pues, una doble mentira, mentira como hermosa, mentira como abnegación, la segunda y principal belleza de mujer." Alejandro Tapia y Rivera, *La Antigua Sirena* (Mexico: Orión, 1959), p. 118.

56 His inversion of the Shakespearean paradigm was later reversed in the Cuban Roberto Fernández Retamar's 1971 essay *Calibán*, which asserted the hungry virility of Latin America against the flabby decadence of the US.

Modernista poets evoked the siren as muse, but also as Caliban's collaborator in soulless commerce. Rubén Darío's untitled poem IX from *Cantos de Vida y esperanza* (1905) deploys the siren (*la pérfida sirena*) and the cannibal as metaphors for the philistines (*el bestial elemento*) who churn in a sea of petty striving at the feet of the eternal towers of poetry. Latin American *modernista* and decadentist novels teem with remote, idealized women (the domestic ideal) and manipulative, domineering sirens who suck out their lovers' souls.[57] For Latin American positivists—the students of Freud, Lombroso, Taine, Nordau, Krafft-Ebing, and Sarmiento who used psychobiological models to address social ills—mermaids represented the seductive but atavistic internal "other," which could, perhaps, be domesticated through modern, taxonomically driven practices such as eugenics, sociology, and education.

The Venezuelan Manuel Díaz Rodríguez's 1902 novel *Sangre patricia* (*Patrician Blood*) locates the siren, symbol of the Caribbean and America, at the center of this encounter with modernity. Like Sarmiento and Bolívar before him, and Gallegos and Rivera afterwards, Díaz Rodríguez's literary production was only a part of a wider civic and intellectual project that included political activism, journalism, diplomacy, and other endeavors. His *modernista* novel is a meditation on the debates of his day, on the ethics of intellectual activity amid the modernizing project, and the place of Latin America in the world.

Neither fish nor fowl, in *Sangre patricia* the hybrid siren becomes a metaphor for the protagonist's dilemma and that of the era: whether salvation lies in the pursuit of the sublime (the Arielist view), or the material (bourgeois modernity supported by political activism). The novel's protagonist Tulio Arcos is the last of a family whose history recapitulates Venezuela's: descending from an Andalusian conquistador to statesmen under the Republic, their lineage has degenerated under the dictatorships of the later nineteenth century. Fleeing Venezuela after a failed revolution, Tulio awaits his bride Belén[58] in Paris, but she dies during the crossing and her body is buried at sea. Tulio undertakes the archetypal Mediterranean odyssey of forgetting, but he gradually becomes submerged in the nostalgic apprehension of Belén and estranged from the material world. Finally he decides to return to Venezuela and his political calling, but during the return voyage, he succumbs to the song of a siren and throws himself into the tropical sea.

As a siren, Belén escapes the empirical and taxonomic paradigms that underlay the positivist discourse of the period. Hybrid images of Belén as white lily/woman and white coral/labyrinth cross domains from animal to vegetable to mineral and open a door between sexual sensation and death. Tulio's hallucinatory dream-state increasingly impinges on his waking perceptions, and even those of the people around him, who begin to perceive Belén in fleeting sensory fragments: as a song, a fragrance, or an apparition. Although the narrator is careful to state that her miraculous beauty is not an "*espejismo*" or projection of male desire, but rather "a

---

57 For example, José Martí's jealous *Lucia Jerez* (1885) and Emilio Bobadilla's parasitical Alicia in *A fuego lento* (1903).

58 Spanish for Bethlehem, the contested city.

nearly perfect reality," her image is always indirect, a series of *animae* projected by the male passengers: one sees her in a quasi-domestic attitude, another as Venus rising from the foamy waves (echoed by references to Botticelli throughout the text).[59] Belén's supremely flexible persona enthralls without ever becoming accessible as a concrete reality.[60]

The seas, and indeed water in general (rivers, rivulets, streams, vapors), saturate the pages of *Sangre patricia*. The narrative's circular structure links three oceans—the Caribbean, point of origin for Belén's journey; the Atlantic, where she dies near the Azores; and the Homeric Mediterranean, where Tulio ceremonially "buries" Belén and imagines himself as the amphibious sea-god Glaucus, the mythical lover of Scylla. Díaz Rodríguez represents these seas as a tropical, feminized continuum rather than as discrete entities. In its feminine mode, the sea is also hungry: when Belén's body is buried at sea among the sea grapes, the sea—atypically feminized as *la mar*—"close[s] its blue and insatiable mouth on that fruit of beauty."[61] As the synesthetic Belén, variously and fragmentally perceived as image, sound, scent, and taste, erases the boundaries between reality and fantasy, the three seas intermix in the continuum, and the spiritual and the material planes of Tulio's existence gradually merge.

Uvas del trópico was the novel's original title, reflecting Tulio's lineage, the sea grape trees of Caribbean beaches and, perhaps, inspired by Darío's "cool grapes" of carnal temptation in *Lo fatal* (1905). *Uvas del trópico* also describes the theme of *arraigo* (cultural attachment or rootedness) and *desarraigo* (rootlessness) that so preoccupies Tulio and his friends. In leaving the *patria* for Europe, they risk being overtaken by nostalgia, a well-known pathology characterized by a fatal sense of longing and uprootedness. The double meaning of *uvas del trópico* (rooted Caribbean beach trees and floating, non-rooted tunicates) refers to Tulio's dilemma, as well as to Belén as the cause of his nostalgia. The title *Sangre patricia*, on the other hand, plays on the positivist theme of lineage and degeneration on a national scale.

The usual analysis of *Sangre patricia* suggests a total rejection of the real—political activism and economic materialism—in favor of the *bello ideal*, analogous to that in Rodó's *Ariel*. Several conversations among Tulio and his friends recapitulate this debate. However, Tulio's voluptuous correspondence with Belén's image has concrete carnal repercussions, as he appears physically debauched to his friends. The siren's erotic lure transforms Tulio's impulse towards the sublime into devastating desire, or as Bram Dijkstra puts it, "spells death to [his] transcendent soul."[62] The meeting of the sublime and the mundane is more optimistically represented in

---

59   Manuel Díaz Rodríguez, *Sangre patricia* [1902] (Caracas: Ayacucho, 1992), p. 57.
60   See Henry Drewal's essay in this collection for a discussion of the origins and diffusion of the African serpent-woman/mermaid figure known as Mami Wata. Renowned for her mutability, Mami Wata has avatars in most of the cultures of the greater Caribbean.
61   "cerró su boca insaciable y azul sobre aquel fruto de belleza," Díaz Rodríguez, *Sangre patricia*, p. 36.
62   Bram Dijkstra, *Idols of Perversity: Fantasies of Feminine Evil in Fin-de-siècle Culture* (New York and Oxford: Oxford University Press, 1986), p. 266.

the aptly named Martí,[63] who reconciles pragmatic living with sublime art, and science with the supernatural, telling Tulio of the siren who washed up on the Breton coast, and of recent scientific proof of Leviathan's existence. Far from being fatally deracinated, Martí's Caribbean origins allow him to operate in a continuum across spiritual, supernatural, and empirical boundaries.

As Mary Douglas suggests in her discussion of Leviticus, monsters can be both abject and sacred, and defilement is a prerequisite for order.[64] Giorgio Agamben and David Williams speak of the monster as both a symptom of our lost unity with God and a promise of imminent redemption.[65] Díaz Rodríguez likewise uses the siren to exemplify the ramifications of this middle way. He explains in his essay "Sobre el modernismo" that modernist expression is, like water, the medium in which the apparent dichotomy between the mystical and the natural (and other implied, analogous dichotomies—Mediterranean/Caribbean, Ariel/Caliban, local/universal) can be harmoniously resolved: "Two predominant and constant tendencies that, always in harmony, course along related, parallel channels, when they don't become entwined and comingled, transforming from two separate and distinct ways to one alone."[66] Díaz Rodríguez's hybrid, synesthetic mermaid simultaneously incarnates the lure of this reconciliation and the dangers that await the seeker of the middle way.

Zombies, *soucouyants* and *loups-garoux*: The Caribbean Gothic

Zombies were not present at the very first encounter between Europe and the Americas; indeed, zombies as we know them are not even a Caribbean construct anymore, and have cultural uses vastly different from those that surround their African origins and Caribbean evolution.[67] However, even this exportation of

---

63   Presumably named for the great Cuban patriot and modernist poet José Martí, who personified the lettered soldier.

64   Mary Douglas, *Purity and Danger: An Analysis of Concepts of Pollution and Taboo* (New York: Praeger, 1966), p. 42.

65   Agamben, *The Open*. David Williams, *Deformed Discourse: The Function of the Monster in Mediaeval Thought and Literature* (Montreal: McGill-Queen's University Press, 1996).

66   "Dos tendencias predominantes y constantes que, siempre en armonía, discurren por cauces fraternales y paralelos, cuando no se entrelazan y confunden, hasta quedar los dos, en un principio separadas y distintas, convertidas en una sola." Manuel Díaz Rodríguez, "Sobre el modernismo," in *Narrativa y ensayo* (Caracas: Biblioteca Ayacucho, 1982), p. 351.

67   The recent proliferation of popular culture zombies in film, literature, television, and games—mostly in the US and UK—echoes that of the vampire. Few to none of these numerous twenty-first-century zombies have anything at all to do with Africa or Haiti; instead, they stand in for new anxieties around consumerism, contagion, and cultural degeneration.

zombies can be understood as part of the wider economic exploitation of Latin America from the moment of the Encounter, and in particular the function of the Caribbean as the nexus of this relationship.

Columbus introduced sugar cane to the Caribbean on his second voyage, setting the stage for the establishment of the cane plantation system, the annihilation of the Arawak natives, the introduction of the Atlantic slave trade, and the resulting structures of poverty, dictatorship, dependence, and racial and sexual alienation that afflict the Caribbean today. The first African slaves came to Hispaniola (today Haiti and the Dominican Republic) in 1502, and slavery was the central economic and existential fact of the Caribbean for four centuries after the Discovery.[68] The slave economy of the Caribbean, indeed, was the seat of "the anthropophagic logic of modernity:"[69] the transcontinental flow of goods, people, capital, and culture that we now call globalization. Zombies became a potent symbol for the colonial and postcolonial relationship—based on the abjection and exploitation of human bodies and the extraction of resources—between Europe, the United States, Africa, and the Caribbean. The sociologist Mimi Sheller makes a compelling argument in *Consuming the Caribbean* that the monsters attributed to the Caribbean simply reflect the anthropophagic patterns inherent to the capitalist enterprise, which consumed the bodies of between one and three million Arawaks on the island of Hispaniola and between four and eight million Central and West Africans through "capture, forced transport, 'seasoning,' work regimes, physical punishment, mutilation, disease, sexual exploitation, and the appropriation of children from their parents,"[70] and now consumes their island descendants metaphorically through military bases, tourist spectacles, and sex tourism. All this consumption, she writes, is "connected by the international exercise of gendered sexual power."[71] The modern-day zombie symbolizes, then, the collective erasure that occurs in the Caribbean at the nexus of colonialism, patriarchy, and capitalism, and the desire and fear of the powerful who enter into the territory of the oppressed.

As slavery depends on the theft or capture of the body, zombiism is predicated on the theft or capture of the soul. Zombiism is related (though not at all central) to the major Afro-Latin American religions such as Haitian *Vodou*, Afro-Caribbean *santería*, Brazilian *candomblé* and *macumba*, which all incorporate some form of

---

68   Ironically, it was the well-intentioned Bartolomé de Las Casas who, having witnessed the torture and death of the enslaved Indians first hand as an *encomendero* or plantation owner, pleaded with the Spanish Crown to import Africans as they were more able to withstand the rigors of plantation work.
69   May Joseph, *Nomadic Identities: The Performance of Citizenship* (Minneapolis: University of Minnesota Press, 1999), p. 136.
70   Of the approximately ten million slaves imported to the New World, about 40 percent went to the Caribbean and 45 percent to Brazil and other Central and South American colonies. As Sheller points out, mortality was far higher in the tropics and under the conditions of sugar production than it was in North America; in addition, as many Africans were killed in the enslavement process as were imported as slaves. Mimi Sheller, *Consuming the Caribbean* (London: Routledge, 2006), pp. 150–1.
71   Ibid., p. 163.

ritual possession entered through music and dance as a conduit for spirits or *loas* to communicate with the devoted. During a trance, the possessed person, usually a priest or other adept, is regarded as exempt from responsibility for any actions, and is not expected to remember anything that transpires. Zombies likewise lack subjectivity, memory, and free will. Zombies can be bodies without a spirit or (less generally known) spirits without a body. They are people whose souls have been stolen by a *bokor*, or Vodou priest, who then has complete power over them and uses them as slaves. Tales of zombies arise when a neighboring farmer is successful with his crops (the implication being that he secretly employs zombies as slave labor), or when people are unexpectedly lucky or unlucky. Zombies have been studied almost exclusively in connection with Haiti, but they have cousins and analogs throughout the Caribbean, including the Jamaican *jumbie*, the *djombi* of Surinam, the Cuban *fúmbi*, and the blood-sucking *soucouyant* of the Anglophone Caribbean.

Far from being defined by zombiism, the Vodou religion is in many cases one of resistance and rebirth, which, through potions, trances, and lycanthropic transformations, offers many avenues for its practitioners to communicate with the divine and escape the toils of poverty and tyranny. As the Cuban author Alejo Carpentier wrote in his famous prologue to the 1949 novel of Haiti's history, *El reino de este mundo* (*The Kingdom of this World*), Vodou has been part of this struggle since the great slave revolts of Mackandal and Boukman, which opened the way to independence:

> I found myself in daily contact with something that could be defined as the marvelous real. I was in a land where thousands of men, anxious for freedom, believed in Mackandal's lycanthropic powers to the extent that their collective faith produced a miracle on the day of his execution. I had already heard the prodigious story of Boukman, the Jamaican initiate. I had been in the Citadel of La Ferrière, a work without architectural precedent, its only forerunner Piranesi's "Imaginary Prisons." I breathed in the atmosphere created by Henri Christophe, a monarch of incredible zeal, much more surprising than all of the cruel kings invented by the Surrealists, who were very much affected by imaginary tyrannies without ever having suffered a one. I found the marvelous at every turn.[72]

For Carpentier, the apprehension of the real marvelous is "the privileged revelation of reality" particular to the Caribbean and the Latin American: it does not recognize the binaries embedded in modern Western thought. Therefore, the power embedded in the Vodou faith allows Haitians to realize the marvelous in reality, in both cruelty and grandeur, far beyond the feeble fantasies of civilized Europeans.

---

72   Alejo Carpentier, Prologue to *The Kingdom of this World*, trans. in Lois Parkinson Zamora and Wendy B. Faris (eds), *Magical Realism: Theory, History, Community* (Durham, NC: Duke University Press, 1995), pp. 75–89, at 86–7.

Westerners have willfully confused Vodou, a powerful and complex religion, with the abjection of zombiism and sensationalized rituals. Implicated in the slave rebellion that led to the creation of the first black republic in the Western hemisphere (and the first Latin American independence from colonial powers), Vodou was carefully suppressed during the long US occupation of Haiti (1915–34): contemporary racists found in Vodou rituals all the evidence they needed that they were indeed locked in a battle to save the Caribbean from dark and infernal forces. Ironically, the US occupation also re-enslaved the Haitians, reinstating the plantation system, forcing Haitians to build roads, and brutalizing thousands of peasants.[73] Under the US occupation, outsiders' interest in zombies grew. The notorious Haitian dictator Papa Doc Duvalier (1957–71), who was himself a Vodou priest and medical doctor, officially sponsored the practice of Vodou. This was partly an expression of the new ascendance of the black majority, with its folk traditions, over the traditional mulatto elites, and partly a convenient tool for terrorizing his enemies. The Duvalierist secret police, the *Tontons macoutes*, were widely perceived as powerful zombies, immune to pain and devoid of empathy. For outsiders, the quasi-mind control that Duvalier exercised on the population through the *macoutes* (which in other contexts might be described using forensic terms like domestic intelligence, surveillance, or national security) evoked the zombie phenomenon and confirmed both the supposedly pathological despotism of tin-pot Caribbean dictators and the childlike passivity of the natives.[74] Because of zombies, the critic Joan Dayan writes, "perhaps no other Caribbean island has inspired such extreme invention, such impressive paraphrase" as Haiti.[75]

Besides zombies, a number of monstrous and evil spirits are present in the Haitian tradition, including *lougawou* or vampires (the French *loups-garoux*, or werewolves, acquire vampirical attributes in the Caribbean context), *djables* (she-devils), *soucriants* (old women who shed their skin at night and suck human blood), and *bizango* (who eat children). However, it is Americans, not Caribbeans, who are primarily responsible for the spread of the zombie figure and the convergence of zombiism and Vodou generally with cannibalism, vampirism, and the gothic. Introduced in accounts like William Seabrook's *The Magic Island* (1929), and Hollywood movies like *White Zombie* (1932), *I Walked with a Zombie* (1943), *Ouanga* (1935), and others, the zombie soon became implicated in vampire/cannibal rituals, child sacrifice, depraved sexual excesses, and other tales of inhuman savagery supposedly witnessed by outsiders in Haiti. This conflation can be seen in Richard Leoderer's *Voodoo Fires in Haiti* (1932), where the author describes his introduction to "Congo Bean Stew:"

---

73   Cf. Joan Dayan, *Haiti, History, and the Gods* (Berkeley: University of California Press, 1998), p. 37; Jennifer Fay, "Dead Subjectivity: *White Zombie*, Black Bagdad," *The New Centennial Review* 8/1 (2008), pp. 81–101; Mary A. Renda, *Taking Haiti: Military Occupation and the Culture of US Imperialism, 1915–1940* (Chapel Hill: University of North Carolina Press, 2001).

74   Sheller, *Consuming the Caribbean*, p. 139.

75   Dayan, *Haiti, History, and the Gods*, p. 32.

> *A great Voodoo festival had been announced and these two made arrangements for a child-sacrifice. The victim finally decided upon was Jeanne's little twelve-year-old niece, Claircine, who was carried off into the jungle and kept a prisoner in the temple until the time arrived. It is unnecessary to go into details about what actually happened. On the great night there was a large assembly of worshippers. The priests cut the child's throat and drank the blood according to ritual, and with the flesh they cooked a Congo Bean Stew; for, according to Haitian connoisseurs, human meat tastes best when boiled with Congo beans. The negroes were delighted with the dish, and the night finished up with the customary wild dances and licentious sexual performances.*[76]

US Marine John Houston Craige's *Black Bagdad* (1932) and *Cannibal Cousins* (1934) and many others told similar stories.[77] Folklorist Zora Neale Hurston and ethnobiologist Wade Davis give sympathetic, if positivist, accounts of zombies, while Haitian academics have scrambled to disprove their existence through scientific treatises and anti-superstition campaigns.[78]

As a symbol of the "black magic" associated with what John Cussans calls the Voodoo Construct,[79] zombies are a convenient metaphor for the way in which the self-oriented Westerner defines and acts upon the non-Western Other. The zombie embodies everything that makes the Caribbean mysterious, fearful, and alluring to the imperial imagination, and all that justifies Western domination of the region by

---

76   The original was published in German in 1932, and the English translation in 1935. Third edition, ed. Lois Wilcken (Gretna, LA: Pelican, 2005), p. 18.

77   John Houston Craige, *Cannibal Cousins* (New York: Minton, Balch & Co, 1934); Steven Gregory, "Voodoo, Ethnography, and the American Occupation of Haiti: William B. Seabrook's *The Magic Island*," in Christine Ward Gailey (ed.), *Dialectical Anthropology: Essays in Honor of Stanley Diamond, I: Civilization in Crisis: Anthropological Perspectives; II: The Politics of Creativity: A Critique of Civilization* (Gainesville: University Press of Florida, 1992), II: pp. 169–207. As J. Michael Dash points out, this kind of writing continues to this day in reflections on the US role in Haiti: "The (Un)kindness of Strangers: Writing Haiti in the 21st Century," *Caribbean Studies* 36/2 (2008), pp. 171–8.

78   Cf. Zora Neale Hurston, *Tell My Horse: Voodoo and Life in Haiti and Jamaica* (Philadelphia: Lippincott, 1938); Wade Davis, *The Serpent and the Rainbow: A Harvard Scientist's Astonishing Journey into the Secret Societies of Haitian Voodoo, Zombis, and Magic* (New York: Touchstone, 1985), and *Passage of Darkness: The Ethnobiology of the Haitian Zombie* (Chapel Hill, NC: University of North Carolina Press, 1988).

79   Cussans defines voodoo (as opposed to Vodou) as: "a set of ubiquitous and enduring, popular cultural motifs evoked by the word for people outside of societies where Vodou is a lived religion. This set of motifs I will call the Voodoo Construct. It is made up of four predominant interwoven motifs which recur whenever someone who has no special knowledge is asked to describe what voodoo is. For the current purposes the Voodoo Construct is made up of (i) the voodoo doll, (ii) the zombie, (iii) the voodoo witch-doctor and (iv) voodoo possession." John Cussans, "Voodoo Terror: (Mis) Representations of Vodu and Western Cultural Anxieties," presented for "Feels Like Voodoo Spirit—Haitian Art, Culture, Religion," *The October Gallery* (London, 2000), <http://codeless88.wordpress.com/voodoo-terror>.

various means since the Encounter. The zombie quickly became an instrumental figure in the Caribbean tourist's vocabulary of desire (and, indeed, soon escaped the Caribbean altogether). Lizabeth Paravisini-Gebert gives a detailed account of the erotic codification of this "spectral Haiti" originating in a 1909 case of the zombification of Marie M., a young upper-class (hence light-skinned) girl. It was Seabrook's retelling of this case that popularized the gothic zombie narrative that would be immortalized and elaborated in Hollywood films. The elements of this story include "the coveting of a beautiful, light-skinned or white upper-class girl by an older, dark-skinned man who is of lower class and is adept at sorcery; the intimation of necromantic sexuality with a girl who has lost her volition; ... the girl's eventual escape from the bokor in her soiled wedding clothes ...; her ultimate madness and confinement in a convent or mental asylum."[80] Erotic desire for lighter-skinned women is an analog of the dark bokor's social ambition. This is the basic thread that runs through the early zombie movies, and, indeed, ultimately inflects some Caribbean literature as well, for example, Jacques-Stephen Alexis's "Chronique d'un faux-amour" (1960) and René Depestre's *Hadriane dans tous mes rêves* (1988), which privilege the erotic/racial element over the heavy and heroic content of Haiti's history.

One of the foundational white zombie movies, *I Walked with a Zombie* (1943), which is based on Charlotte Brontë's famous gothic novel *Jane Eyre*, cemented the seemingly inevitable insertion of the zombie into the gothic genre. With its allegorical view of racial and gender relations, the gothic reenacts the guilt and paranoia of the colonial subject under the conditions of patriarchy, colonialism, and capitalism that engendered the eroticized Voodoo Construct. The gothic heroine, typically a virgin without family or social status, is generally trapped in a mysterious and hostile environment, sexually menaced by unknown or sinister forces. In *Jane Eyre*, the fair, virginal, articulate heroine gradually uncovers the mystery of Rochester's homicidal Jamaican wife, Bertha Antoinetta Mason. Bertha represents the savage Caribbean Caliban: dark and violent, lustful and inchoate, she howls like an animal and attempts to destroy the Prospero-like Rochester. Jane's triumph is essentially in outlasting Bertha to become Rochester's rightful wife, concluding her long journey of self-inscription into the legal and social codes of the day. *I Walked with a Zombie* is generally regarded as the most nuanced of the early zombie films, which perhaps lends the zombie gothic a certain appeal for women writers who wish to explore the complexities of the monstrous feminine.

Several Caribbean women writers have used the zombie gothic to critique the gender and racial issues attendant on their postcolonial Caribbean status. A classic of postcolonial Caribbean literature, the Dominican writer Jean Rhys's *Wide Sargasso Sea* recreates the antecedents of Bertha's madness in the relationship between the

---

80   Lizabeth Paravisini-Gebert, "Women Possessed: Eroticism and Exoticism in the Representation of Woman as Zombie," in Margarite Fernandez Olmos and Lizabeth Paravisini-Gebert (eds), *Sacred Possessions: Vodou, Santeria, Obeah, and the Caribbean* (New Brunswick, NJ: Rutgers University Press, 1997), pp. 37–58, at 40.

colonized Antoinette and the colonizer Rochester.[81] Daughter of a former slave-owner and a beautiful but distant mother, Antoinette is a social orphan who is rejected by the British white and Jamaican black populations equally. There is a strong zombie subtext to Rhys's novel.[82] Both Antoinette and her mother, Annette, are denigrated as zombies. Rochester, suspecting Antoinette of poisoning him, reads avidly of zombies, and effectively destroys Antoinette's will, renaming her Bertha before taking her away to exile in England and imprisoning her in the attic of his house. By telling the story from Antoinette's perspective, Rhys inverts the white zombie formula and displaces the burden of monstrosity onto Rochester.

The critically acclaimed Ana Lydia Vega is a Puerto Rican writer whose passions—history and story-telling—come together in her hybrid pseudo-gothic story/novel *Pasión de historia y otras historias de pasión*. A professor of French literature and Caribbean studies, she has received two prestigious literary prizes, the Premio Casa de las Américas (1981) and the Premio Juan Rulfo (1982). She represents a generation of Puerto Rican writers whose meditations on the problematic status of the island are expressed through linguistic and generic play and parody. Following Rhys's model, Vega sets out to recover the stories of Caribbean women who have been disappeared. Her protagonist Carola, a writer who is being stalked by her married ex-lover, tries to reconstruct the story of Malén (Magdalen), the victim of an "honor" killing who is being reviled in the tabloid press. Carola escapes to France to visit her friend, the voluptuous Vilma, in her "exotic paradise," the south of France, thinking that the trip will transform her from a "sad creature of the Tropics," the object of the masculine colonial gaze, to a postcolonial anthropologist of Empire.[83] There, Carola discovers that the repressive patriarchal norms of her tropical island are magnified in the sadistic, jealous husband of Vilma, abetted by his mother, described as the "Mrs Danvers" (Daphne du Maurier's archetypal gothic villainess) of the house. As she watches helplessly, her friend the "Taíno princess" (an allusion to the erotically charged Caribbean Mulatta figure) slowly becomes another Bertha Mason—"unchaste … gross, impure, depraved"—before her eyes.[84] Paralyzed by her ambivalence, a debilitating head cold, and writer's block, Carola becomes increasingly zombified: mute, powerless to help her friend and, what is worse, unable to continue her investigation into the Malén case. On her return to the island, her letters to Vilma are returned: Vilma has been swallowed up in Bluebeard's castle. Carola's tale ends abruptly, with an editor's note informing the reader that the author was killed by an unknown stalker, bringing the story full circle. The erasure of women, then, is embedded in all phases and facets of the colonial construct.

Vega explores the white zombie gothic more explicitly in her novella *El baúl de Miss Florence* (*Miss Florence's Trunk* from *Falsas crónicas del Sur*, 1991), which depicts the experience of a Victorian English governess in a Puerto Rican sugar hacienda.

---

81   Jean Rhys, *Wide Sargasso Sea* [1966], intro. Francis Wyndham (New York: Norton, 1982).
82   Cf. Thomas Loe, "Patterns of the Zombie in Jean Rhys's Wide Sargasso Sea," *Journal of Postcolonial Writing* 31/1 (1991), pp. 34–42.
83   Ana Lydia Vega, *Pasión de historia* (San Juan, PR: Ediciones de la Flor, 1991), p. 13.
84   Charlotte Brontë, *Jane Eyre* [1847] (New York: Relford, Clarke, & Co., 1885), p. 262.

An outspoken and sensible woman, Miss Florence finds herself increasingly unable to protest the injustice she sees, or to effect any meaningful change in the cruel environment around her. Vega explains how the logic of slavery negates the agency of all parties in the colonial system:

> I wanted to show how an independent woman who had her own career as a tutor, who came from England where feminism was developing at the time (although it was the Victorian era) could, within the institutions of slavery, fall into a state of psychological bondage. What we see then, is this process within Miss Florence to liberate herself.[85]

The protagonist's ability to break free lies in her comprehension of the parallels between her position, that of women generally, and that of the slaves on the hacienda, as well as the implication of the colonial system in their common repression. For Vega, the skeleton in Puerto Rico's gothic closet is African identity, which was historically downplayed in favor of the indigenous in the Puerto Rican imaginary:

> ... On the other hand, you learned absolutely nothing about our African heritage because it was "taboo." It was completely concealed. So, I thought that in order to achieve our own personal liberation, it was mandatory to begin the process here, in a search for the hidden history, a search for our roots, and to underscore these roots as well.[86]

Mayra Montero is a prolific and very popular Cuban-born writer and activist who has lived in Puerto Rico since the mid-1960s. Montero also uses the zombie trope as a way of understanding the colonial legacy. Her novel *Tú, la oscuridad (In the Palm of Darkness)*[87] describes the years following President Jean Bertrand Aristide's first exile in 1991, when approximately 5,000 Haitians were assassinated and many thousands more raped, tortured, and terrorized by ex-*macoutes* and paramilitaries serving the Raoul Cédras regime. For Montero, the zombie symbolizes the Westerner's incomprehension of the Caribbean, and, at the same time, the deadly retaliation of the Caribbean subaltern against the "anthropophagic logic of modernity."

The novel's North American narrator, herpetologist Victor Grigg, contracts Thierry Adrien, a Haitian tracker, to help him search for the last remaining specimen of a rare blood frog. As Thierry and Victor hunt the frog from the Mont des Enfants Perdus to the Casetaches, they are themselves hunted by the shadowy

---

85   Elizabeth Hernández and Consuelo López Springfield, "Women and Writing in Puerto Rico: An Interview with Ana Lydia Vega," *Callaloo: A Journal of African American and African Arts and Letters* 17/3 (Summer 1994), pp. 816–25, at 821.

86   Ibid., p. 824.

87   Mayra Montero, *Tú, la oscuridad* (Barcelona: Tusquets, 1995). Two additional novels by Montero deal with Haiti: *La trenza de la hermosa luna* (1987); and *Del rojo de su sombra* (1992). Additionally, her short story "Corinne, muchacha amable" has a zombie theme.

soldiers of the drug lord Cito Francisque. The competing narratives of Thierry (folk/magical) and Victor (rational/scientific) are intercut with cryptic news items reporting the sudden decline or disappearance of frog species in various corners of the world. These items typically end on a note of utter futility, as the abrupt, increasingly numerous disappearances remain stubbornly unexplained. The scientific attitude towards the impenetrable tragedy of the frogs reflects the consternation and impotence of the international community faced with the spectacle of Haiti's destruction, ultimately a result of the many formulas for exploitation, rationalization, and modernization imposed on it by the same powers, from Spain in the sixteenth century and France in the eighteenth century to the United States in the twentieth century.

There have been many attempts to explain zombiism scientifically,[88] all of which have failed to some degree because they impose a Western binary framework on the zombie question. Montero's work treats this framework as irrelevant. The story of the zombies in *Tú, la oscuridad* begins in Thierry's childhood, when his father and his colleagues were *pwazon-rats*, contracted by the zombies' owners to trap and kill errant zombies. Once zombies reach the mountains they (like runaway slaves) are beyond redemption, because they recover their memory of being and become filled with murderous vengeance. Thierry's father died at the hands of the evil zombie-woman Romaine La Prophetesse, who caught him with his pants down (literally) and took his skin. For Thierry, however, the zombies of the past were an indication of happiness and abundance: a source of danger that also represented a livelihood and a certain social order. In the 1990s, however, the zombies have been supplanted by distinctly non-magical, non-erotic mutilated corpses and burning dogs. As Thierry interprets this "language" to Victor, Victor willfully dismisses his readings as driven by magical thinking or personal ambition. Victor's scientific refusal to conceive of reality in terms of a continuum, rather than a conflict between the rational (modern) and the magical (non-modern), prevents him from acknowledging their interconnectedness. Zombie-like, he gradually loses his bearings and his ability to communicate with the rational outer world. For his part, Thierry pities Victor's positivist "excuses" for the frogs' disappearance (acid rain, herbicides), knowing that their flight is part of the great extinction predicted by the god Damballah.[89]

---

88 See Hans-W. Ackermann and Jeannine Gauthier, "The Ways and Nature of the Zombi," *The Journal of American Folklore* 104/414 (1991), pp. 466–94, for a critique of Western efforts to explain the zombie. The Haitian diplomat and scholar Jean Price-Mars defended Vodou and decried the sensationalism of external analyses of zombiism. See also Erika Bourguignon, "The Persistence of Folk Belief: Some Notes on Cannibalism and Zombis in Haiti," in *Journal of American Folklore* 72/283 (1959), pp. 36–46; C.H. Dewisme, *Les zombis; ou, Le secret des morts-vivants* (Paris: Bernard Grasset, 1957), p. 138. Mars (1945, 1947) and Alfred Métraux (*Le Vaudou Haitien*, Paris: Gallimard, 1968) rationalized zombiism as a variety of mental illnesses.

89 Montero, *Tú, la oscuridad*, p. 132.

For Thierry, to name, to classify, to capture and preserve, is necessarily to kill, under the "perverse light" of modernity.[90] Ultimately, he points out, the frogs could stand in for any other animal: like the frogs, Thierry's family and children (many of whom were born with mutations) have died or disappeared one by one. Victor's family, too, is sterile and, though he does not know it, dying—as are his herpetologist colleagues. The frogs' apocalyptic predicament thus illustrates the potentially worldwide ramifications of Haiti's dying ecosystem. For Montero, Haiti is not a mysterious, savage Other, but a symptom of the darker ramifications of the rational West and a warning of a future in which zombies, frogs, and humans (Caribbean and non-Caribbean alike) are doomed to extinction.

Conclusion

Alejo Carpentier's epiphany exemplifies a twentieth-century Latin American intellectual perspective that drew an unbroken line from Columbus to magical realism:

> *The presence and vitality of this marvelous real was not the unique privilege of Haiti but the heritage of all of America, where we have not yet begun to establish an inventory of our cosmogonies. The marvelous real is found at every stage in the lives of men who inscribed dates in the history of the continent and who left the names that we still carry: from those who searched for the fountain of eternal youth and the golden city of Manoa to certain early rebels or modern heroes of mythological fame from our wars of independence ...*[91]

The third of Jeffrey Jerome Cohen's Seven Theses on Monstrosity states that monsters signal epistemological crisis by undermining or transgressing binary classifications and resisting integration into accepted orders of thought; the sixth, that the fear of monsters is mediated by desire. These two "theses" sum up in relatively few words what a great many scholars have expressed over the years about monsters and their meaning within human culture. The monsters of Haiti, the Caribbean, and Latin America are not materially different from the monsters found in other cultures. However, the narratives that emerged at the junction of three cultures under the conditions of early modern globalization established monsters as a preeminent mode of discourse between Latin America and the colonial powers that interacted with it, and ultimately inflected the tropes used by Latin Americans themselves in efforts to explain, diagnose, or correct their eccentricity.

---

90 For further interpretation of the roles of darkness and light in the novel, see Carmen Rivera Villegas, "Nuevas rutas hacia Haití en la cartografía de Mayra Montero," *Revista Hispánica Moderna* 54/1 (2001), pp. 154–65.

91 Carpentier, Prologue, p. 88.

The Unlucky, the Bad and the Ugly: Categories of Monstrosity from the Renaissance to the Enlightenment[1]

Surekha Davies

In his diary entry for August 24, 1661, Samuel Pepys described how he came face-to-face with a monster:

> We are called to Sir W. Battens to see the strange creature that Captain Holmes hath brought with him from Guiny; it is a great baboone, but so much like a man in most things, that (though they say there is a species of them) yet I cannot believe but that it is a monster got of a man and she-baboone. I do believe that it already understands much English, and I am of the mind it might be tought to speak or make signs.[2]

Pepys's difficulty lay in two uncertain boundaries of his age and, perhaps, all ages, between human and beast, and between nature and monstrosity. As far as Pepys was concerned, this so-called baboon was so like a human that it was more plausible that it was a singular monster of unnatural causes than a regular animal resembling all its kin. One of several conceptual frameworks on which monsters existed in the early modern period was a continuum between human and animal.

Pepys thus points us towards one of the three interpretative traditions of Renaissance teratology, each based in turn on textual prototypes from classical

---

1   For comments on this chapter, I thank Andrew Curran, Glyn Davies, Jennifer Spinks, and the anonymous reader. I am grateful for the support of the Leverhulme Trust.
2   Samuel Pepys, *The Diary of Samuel Pepys: A New and Complete Transcription*, ed. Robert Latham and William Matthews, 11 volumes (London etc., 1970–83 [2000 printing]), II, 160, no. 24. Robert Holmes had returned from West Africa the previous month. He may have brought back a chimpanzee or a gorilla.

antiquity.[3] One of these traditions can be traced to Aristotle's *Generation of Animals* (ca. 350 BCE).[4] It considered monsters as occasional errors in nature, brought about as a result of the working of nature on the brute, occasionally unresisting substance of matter. Anything that did not resemble its parents, particularly its father, was a monster in Aristotle's view. Thus even women, who lacked the perfection of men, were a kind of monster. These monsters did not, for Aristotle, illustrate or portend anything, apart from showing that female generative secretions had triumphed over male seed and caused a departure from a normal male child—a monstrous birth.[5] A second tradition existed within a discourse of omens and prodigies founded by Cicero's *On Divination* (44 BCE).[6] Cicero perceived monstrous births as signs of impending calamity. Subsequent classical and Christian authors continued this approach.[7] The medieval chronicle tradition interpreted a range of prodigies, from comets to floods to conjoined twins, as general signs of impending political upheaval or war.[8] The third tradition was of monsters as wonders of nature. Largely based on Pliny the Elder's *Natural History* (ca. 77–79 CE), authors in this tradition added the possibility of entire races of monsters dwelling in the far corners of the earth. The monstrosity of distant peoples was characterized by physical or behavioral abnormalities—such as having one leg rather than two, or living on an exclusive diet of smells—and defined by two central features. First, these deviations were found across a population, rather than being restricted to a few unnatural individuals. Second, it occurred at the edges of the known world[9]—somewhere distant from the observer's point of view.[10] As Pliny put it, "India and parts of Ethiopia especially

---

3   See, for example, Zakiya Hanafi, *The Monster in the Machine: Magic, Medicine, and the Marvelous in the Time of the Scientific Revolution* (Durham, NC: Duke University Press, 2000), p. 7; Lorraine Daston and Katherine Park, "Unnatural Conceptions: The Study of Monsters in Sixteenth- and Seventeenth-Century France and England," *Past and Present* 92 (1981), pp. 20–54, at 22–3; Jean Céard, *La Nature et les prodiges: l'Insolite au XVIe siècle*, 2e édition revue et augmentée (Geneva: Droz, 1996), pp. 3–20.
4   Aristotle, *Generation of Animals*, trans. A.L. Peck (London and Cambridge, MA: Harvard University Press, 1963).
5   Ibid., II.iii and IV.iii–iv. See also Hanafi, *Monster in the Machine*, p. 8; Marie-Hélène Huet, *Monstrous Imagination* (Cambridge, MA etc.: Harvard University Press, 1993), pp. 3–4.
6   Cicero, *De senectute; De amicitia; De divinatione*, trans. William Armistead Falconer (London and Cambridge, MA: Heinemann and Harvard University Press, 1971).
7   Hanafi, *Monster in the Machine*, p. 8; Céard, *Nature et les prodiges*, p. 3.
8   For positive interpretations of prodigious births in pre-Reformation Germany, see Jennifer Spinks, *Monstrous Births and Visual Culture in Sixteenth-Century Germany* (London: Pickering & Chatto, 2009), chapters 1 and 2.
9   John Block Friedman, *The Monstrous Races in Medieval Art and Thought* (Syracuse, NY: Syracuse University Press, 2000), pp. 1, 37–8.
10   See Francesc Relaño, *The Shaping of Africa: Cosmographic Discourse and Cartographic Science in Late Medieval and Early Modern Europe* (Aldershot: Ashgate, 2002), pp. 28–41 (overview), 84–6 (Africa); Asa Simon Mittman, *Maps and Monsters in Medieval England* (New York, NY and London: Routledge, 2006), pp. 12–15. For monsters and "symbolic extremes" in the East, see Mary W. Helms, *Ulysses' Sail: An Ethnographic Odyssey of*

teem with marvels."[11] These elements distinguished extra-European monstrosity from domestic forms. In the fifth century CE, these beings were incorporated into a Christian framework in St Augustine of Hippo's *City of God*.[12] St Augustine suggested that "either the written accounts of certain races are completely unfounded or, if such races do exist, they are not human; or, if they are human, they are descended from Adam."[13] For medieval Christian thinkers, all humans were by definition Adam's descendants. The uncomfortable implication was that if monstrous peoples were rational, thinking, and therefore human beings, they shared their ancestry with the rest of humanity. Isidore of Seville, the medieval bishop, historian, and encyclopedist, paraphrased and rearranged material from St Augustine and other sources in his *Etymologies*. Isidore neatly encapsulated the difference between monstrous races and monstrous individuals thus: "Just as, in individual nations, there are instances of monstrous people, so in the whole of humankind there are certain monstrous races, like the giants, the Cynocephali [dog-headed people], the Cyclopes, and others."[14]

Much has been learned by looking in depth at specific types of monster in isolation from one another. To some extent, the paths taken by modern scholars reflect the separate traditions through which monsters had long been discussed: those of prodigy, natural history, and monstrous peoples. However, European conceptions of monstrosity were wider than any one of these. In many cases in our period, the appropriate framework was uncertain or contested, as is illustrated by Pepys's encounter with a baboon. The nature of the monster/human divide in the ethnology of distant others was much debated between the Renaissance and the Enlightenment, circa 1400–1800. During the Renaissance, while the classical typology of prodigious, natural, and distant monsters (and their medieval variants) continued to inform expectations, the three categories overlapped and intersected in practice. Although a particular text might appear to deal with one type of monster, its author would have been aware of the other types and, in some cases, drew on these traditions, or referred explicitly to their monsters.

Power, Knowledge and Geographical Distance (Princeton, NJ: Princeton University Press, 1988), pp. 213–17.

11 Pliny the Elder, *Natural History*, ed. and trans. H. Rackham, 10 volumes (Cambridge, MA: Harvard University Press, 1969), VII:ii.21: "Praecipue India Aethiopiumque tractus miraculis scatent."

12 St Augustine, *The City of God Against the Pagans*, trans. Eva Matthews Sanford and William McAllen Green, 7 volumes (London and Cambridge, MA: Heinemann and Harvard University Press, 1965), V, book XVI.viii–ix.

13 Ibid., XVI.viii (for text and translation): "Aut illa quae talia de quibusdam gentibus scripta sunt, omnino nulla sunt; aut si sunt, homines non sunt; aut ex Adam sunt, si homines sunt." Earlier in this section, Augustine asserts that any human being, that is, a "rational mortal creature" ("animal rationale mortale"), was descended from Adam, no matter how strange they might be in appearance, custom, or nature.

14 Isidore of Seville, *The Etymologies of Isidore of Seville*, ed. and trans. Stephen A. Barney et al. (New York: Cambridge University Press, 2006), XI.iii.12; also quoted in Céard, *Nature et les prodiges*, p. 43.

While the natural or immediate causes of monsters continued to divide them into three categories, monsters across these categories were increasingly considered together in interpretations of their ultimate causes and deeper significances. In order to better understand the interdependency of the three textual traditions of monsters as omens, errors, or wonders, I shall focus here on those monsters that appeared in more than one tradition or whose secondary causes were contested.

Perhaps the biggest problem for those who tried to make sense of the monsters they saw or read about was deciding what they meant. For monsters of all causes *looked* the same: unnatural. There was no consensus on whether beings like (say) headless infants were one of nature's errors, a sign of their mother's sin, portents of communal doom or—if they dwelled far from Europe—members of a monstrous people. God used the same instruments of nature for all his actions and messages. Thus the interpretation of monsters was a contested enterprise. The story of monsters and the monstrous between the Renaissance and the Enlightenment is, in essence, a story of competing interpretations pushed by different groups for the same phenomena.

This essay begins by tracing in turn the trajectories of the theories of prodigious, natural, and distant monsters circa 1400–1800. It will outline the discourses within which these theories were discussed, highlighting instances of ambiguity and overlap in monster types and broader discourses. It concludes by suggesting a series of themes that were common in discussions of all categories of monster in this period, and the possible impact of the blurring of boundaries between monsters in this period for the subsequent paths of discourses about monsters.

Monsters as Signs of Divine Displeasure

Since classical antiquity, monsters had been seen as religious signs, and were closely associated with miracles in early Christian literature.[15] One of the three interpretations offered of monsters in the early modern period was that they were signs of divine displeasure. From the late medieval period, there was an increasing interest in divination via monstrous births.[16] During the Renaissance they were taken as signs that a community was practicing the traditional biblical sins, such as greed, vanity, and adultery, and foretold subsequent punishment through natural catastrophes such as floods or plagues.[17] The late fifteenth century and the earliest years of the Reformation marked a shift in the interpretations of monsters, from portents of general misfortune to signs of particular crimes and impending divine retribution for a new range of failings indicating wrongful political and religious

15   Céard, *Nature et les prodiges*, pp. 21–9.
16   Ottavia Niccoli, *Prophecy and People in Renaissance Italy*, trans. Lydia G. Cochrane (Princeton, NJ: Princeton University Press, 1990), p. 32.
17   Lorraine Daston and Katherine Park, *Wonders and the Order of Nature, 1150–1750* (New York, NY: Zone Books, 1998), pp. 182–3.

Figure 2.1   P. Melanchthon and M. Luther, *Deuttung der zwo grewlichen figuren Bapstesels zu Freyburg en Meyssen funden, mit anzaygung des jungstentags* (Wittenberg, 1523), sigs [A.i.*v*.–A.ii.*r*.], Papal Ass and Monk Calf, Classmark F152.d.1.30 (reproduced by kind permission of the Syndics of Cambridge University Library).

allegiances. Stories of monstrous human, animal, and (often) hybrid births began to serve propagandistic purposes. Both Protestants and Catholics would produce prints, pamphlets, and broadsheets that interpreted monstrous births as evidence of the wrongness of their opponents.[18] Thus monstrous births became signs of divine disapprobation that revealed through their particularities the sin that had been committed.

In 1523, an influential pamphlet penned by Martin Luther and Philipp Melanchthon interpreted monsters as divine criticism of a specific group: monastic institutions and their papal overlords.[19] The pamphlet combined two monsters: the creatures they called the Papal Ass and the Monk Calf (Figure 2.1). The Papal Ass

18   For anti-Lutheran prophecy, see also Spinks, *Monstrous Births and Visual Culture*, chapter 5; R. Po-Chia Hsia, "A Time for Monsters," in Laura Lunger Knoppers and Joan B. Landes (eds), *Monstrous Bodies/Political Monstrosities in Early Modern Europe* (Ithaca, NY and London: Cornell University Press, 2004), pp. 67–92; Niccoli, *Prophecy and People*, pp. 126–36.

19   Julie Crawford, *Marvelous Protestantism: Monstrous Births in Post-Reformation England* (Baltimore, MD and London: The Johns Hopkins University Press, 2005), p. 27.

had appeared in Rome on the banks of the Tiber in 1495. It sported the head of an ass, a woman's breast and belly, an elephant's foot instead of a right hand, a hoof and claw in the place of feet, and a dragon's head on its posterior.[20] The Monk Calf had appeared near Freiberg in Saxony in 1522. It was devoid of fur, had a flap of skin around its neck (read as a monk's cowl), and a mark on the top of its head in the manner of a tonsure.[21] Luther and Melanchthon analyzed the elements of these creatures' monstrous bodies as symbols of the pope and his faulty regime. This kind of pamphlet often contained apocalyptic overtones.[22]

Monsters could also signal the errors of a single individual. They could, for example, be the result of a mother's secret desires and active imagination. Monstrous births might be judged to be the result of sex between women and animals, or even the devil.[23] A child resembling anyone other than its lawful father was sometimes interpreted as evidence that the mother had been thinking of someone else at the moment of conception.[24] The monstrous birth thereby publicly signalled divine retribution for impure thoughts or deeds. It also served as a mechanism for identifying crimes that were difficult to detect, notably adultery; as one scholar has noted: "monsters themselves are texts ... [that] render the private beliefs and behaviours of early modern men and women spectacularly visible."[25]

Of course, as the French physician Nicolas Venette asserted, an adulterous woman might conceal her crime by thinking about her husband: thus "resemblance is not proof of filiation."[26] The juridical implications of this were far-reaching. Marie-Hélène Huet's wide-ranging study of perceptions of the monstrous maternal imagination, drawing on medical works, philosophy, literature, and other subjects, illustrates how these discourses cross-fertilized freely between the Renaissance and the Enlightenment. Huet argues that the importance played by resemblance in theories of generation imposed a superficial order on the unverifiability of paternity, which was "unmasked" by monstrosity.[27] In other words, since a monster's attributes did not allow it to be tied definitively to specific natural causes or significances, the converse was also true: the resemblance of a baby to its mother's husband was no proof that it was not monstrous, a subversion of natural order. The proper interpretation of such observations was deemed to require the judicious consideration of context—was the

---

20   For the circulation of news of this monster and the political uses to which it was put, see Niccoli, *Prophecy and People*, pp. 35–60.

21   For English examples of flaps of skin being compared to Catholic vestments, see Alexandra Walsham, *Providence in Early Modern England* (Oxford: Oxford University Press, 1999), pp. 195–6.

22   For analysis of the pamphlet, see Spinks, *Monstrous Births and Visual Culture*, pp. 59–72. For apocalyptic dimensions, see Daston and Park, *Wonders*, p. 187.

23   Huet, *Monstrous Imagination*, pp. 5–6.

24   Ibid., chapter 4.

25   Crawford, *Marvelous Protestantism*, pp. 3, 22–4, 62–78. See also Walsham, *Providence*, pp. 201–2.

26   Quoted in Huet, *Monstrous Imagination*, p. 80.

27   Ibid., p. 34.

mother a "known" adulterer, for example? Perhaps the greatest danger of monsters was the shadows they cast over normality, which, in turn, became unverifiable.

The relations between a monstrous body, such as a ruffed calf or a two-headed baby, and its meaning were multiple and protean. In the early seventeenth century, the Puritan parish rector William Leigh offered two different interpretations of the same monstrous "double child." In one, he read the monster (born dead) as a judgment of an individual's moral wrongdoing. In the other, he claimed that it was a warning that signaled God's imminent, more general punishment of English religious wrongdoers, both heretical Catholics and those avowed Protestants whose thoughts and deeds were too close to "Romish" practices.[28] The problem was that observation alone was not enough to determine whether or not a monster was a sign of individual or collective sin and thus also of divine displeasure and impending punishment. The implications of a monster were dependent on the interpretation of the viewer, rather than on any visible characteristics of the monster.

Ideas of providence shaped the worldviews of individuals across all social strata in early modern England.[29] They informed the interpretation of monstrous births as divine fingers pointing at sinful individuals and social groups— "larum-bels" sent by God as "lesons & scholynges for us all."[30] During the English Civil War and the Restoration, metaphors of the state as a body, and as particular forms of government as akin to monstrous bodies, were widespread in intellectual thought, popular culture, and political theory.[31] Religious fanaticism, political polemics, gender politics, portents, and divine retribution were welded together in popular explanations of headless births in 1640s England. A 1646 pamphlet, detailing a headless baby born to a certain "Mrs Houghton, a Popish Gentlewoman," recounted on its title-page that it had "the face of it upon the breast, and without a head (after the mother had wished rather to bear a Childe without a head than a Roundhead) and had curst the Parliament."[32] Births such as these were held up as proof of God's displeasure at individuals and the political and religious views they espoused.

In the 1640s and 1650s, during the civil wars and the Interregnum, English pamphlets depicting monstrous births proliferated. The headless monster was a common motif during a period in which beheading—the punishment for a traitor—was frequent. Royalist pamphlets drew on the concern that, with the

---

28 For discussion, see Crawford, *Marvelous Protestantism*, chapter 3.
29 Walsham, *Providence*, pp. 2–3.
30 *Strange News out of Kent* (London, 1609); cited in Walsham, *Providence*, p. 195.
31 See, for example, William E. Burns, *An Age of Wonders: Prodigies, Politics and Providence in England, 1657–1727* (Manchester: Manchester University Press, 2002); Laura Lunger Knoppers, "'The Antichrist, the Babilon, the great dragon': Oliver Cromwell, Andrew Marvell, and the Apocalyptic Monstrous," in Knoppers and Landes (eds), *Monstrous Bodies/Political Monstrosities*, pp. 93–123.
32 *A Declaration, of a Strange and Wonderfull Monster: Born in Kirkham Parish in Lancashire* (London, 1646), discussed, with further examples, in David Cressy, "Lamentable, Strange, and Wonderful: Headless Monsters in the English Revolution," in Knoppers and Landes (eds), *Monstrous Bodies/Political Monstrosities*, pp. 40–63.

beheading of Charles I, England was itself headless. In some cases, depictions of headless women showed them giving birth to headless offspring. These women emblematized several perceived threats: women who did not obey their husbands; the unnatural power of Parliament; and divine retribution for one's sins.[33] Thus instances of monstrous deformation of the head were particularly resonant in this period, with beings that were headless, bore the wrong number of eyes and ears, or exhibited other unnaturally shaped heads being interpreted as signs that England was politically monstrous.[34] In the case of fashion and cosmetics, where the head and body were consciously deformed, the deployment of the body metaphor for the state was particularly ingenious.

Following the Glorious Revolution of 1688, commentators on prodigies interpreted them against deism and atheism. Rather than necessarily being a divine portent of future menace, the prodigy was often evidence of God's existence, and of punishment of a particular sin committed by an individual.[35] While to some, the loss of the monarchy rendered the body politic monstrous, to others, the presence of a female monarch was a monstrous aberration. Women on and behind the throne, including Elizabeth I, Mary Tudor, and Catherine de Medici, provoked the ire of many.[36] John Knox's *The First Blast of the Trumpet against the Monstrous Regiment of Women* (1558), published anonymously, railed against the horror of female leaders, and in particular Queen Mary: "a woman promoted to sit in the seate of God (that is, to teache, to judge, or to reigne above man), is a monstre in nature."[37]

Between the Reformation and the late seventeenth century there was a marked increase in the variety of explanations given for prodigious monsters. Monstrous births were often tied to particular political or religious agendas. Nevertheless, there remained much uncertainty over whether such monsters might signal the reprehensibility of an entire social group (and, if so, which group?), or merely the reprehensible thoughts and behavior of their own mothers. In this way, prodigious monsters overlapped with monsters as errors within nature, as we shall see.

Monstrous Births and the Order of Nature

The maternal imagination did not merely give rise to monsters through divine punishment. Monsters could also appear as a natural consequence of more benign

---

33 Crawford, *Marvelous Protestantism*, chapter 4.
34 William E. Burns, "The King's Two Monstrous Bodies: John Bulwer and the English Revolution," in Peter G. Platt (ed), *Wonders, Marvels, and Monsters in Early Modern Culture* (Newark, DE and London: University of Delaware Press and Associated University Presses, 1999), pp. 187–202, at 189–91.
35 Burns, *Age of Wonders*, pp. 126–7.
36 See Sharon Jansen, *The Monstrous Regiment of Women: Female Rulers in Early Modern Europe* (Basingstoke: Palgrave Macmillan, 2002), p. 1, n. 2 for relevant literature.
37 [John Knox], *The First Blast of the Trumpet against the Monstrous Regiment of Women* (Geneva, 1558), f. 17r.

desires or blameless experiences. A mother's thoughts and imagination were believed to influence the shape of her unborn child not only during conception but also through pregnancy. This view had its roots in ancient thought, particularly that of Aristotle, and continued to inform explanations about unnatural births into the early nineteenth century.[38] In 1697, the Sussex vicar William Turner described a girl with "the figure of a fish" on her leg, and a boy with "a mulberry growing upon his forehead," and explained that both aberrations were caused by maternal cravings during pregnancy.[39]

The very sight of something unnatural, alarming, striking, or desirable during pregnancy, including misshapen animals and statues, could enter a mother's imagination and thereby affect the form of the foetus.[40] The French philosopher Nicolas Malebranche was a fervent believer in the power of the maternal imagination over the shape of a foetus. In *De la recherche de la vérité* (1674) or *The Search for Truth*, he stressed the fragility of the foetus, and its ability to receive, and be shaped by, impressions formed in the mother's mind. In a memorable passage, he notes how a mother who saw a criminal executed on the wheel gave birth to a child who manifested the same injuries: "At the sight of this execution, so capable of frightening a woman, the violent flow of the mother's animal spirits passed very forcefully from her brain to all the parts of her body corresponding to those of the criminal, and the same thing happened in the child."[41]

By the late sixteenth century, a range of specialized medical writing about monsters existed, both as sections of broader works about nature or human generation, and as monographic treatments of monsters.[42] Germany in the 1550s saw the emergence of wonder books that combined monstrous births with other natural wonders. *Des Monstres et prodiges*, a treatise by Ambroise Paré, chief surgeon to the kings of France, was published in Paris in 1573. It covers some 40 marvels and monstrous individuals.[43] For Paré, monsters were a motley bunch: some were animals, others were human, and some were a mixture of the two, like the hermaphrodite, winged, horned, human-faced, one(-griffin)[44]-legged wonder

---

38 Huet, *Monstrous Imagination*, pp. 3–7, 13–16.

39 William Turner, *A Compleat History of the Most Remarkable Providences* (London, 1697), Part II, 1.

40 Huet, *Monstrous Imagination*, pp. 16–24.

41 Ibid., pp. 47–8.

42 Daston and Park, *Wonders*, p. 192; see n. 47 for examples.

43 Ambroise Paré, *Des Monstres et prodiges* (Paris, 1573). For a modern edition, see idem, *Des Monstres et prodiges*, ed. Jean Céard (Geneva: Droz, 1971). Note that this is a revised edition of the work as it appeared in Paré's *Les Oeuvres d'Ambroise Paré* (Paris, 1585). The text is discussed in Céard, *Nature et les prodiges*, chapter XII; C.J.S. Thompson, *The Mystery and Lore of Monsters: With Accounts of Some Giants, Dwarfs and Prodigies* (London: Williams & Norgate, 1930), chapter V.

44 The mythical griffin commonly had the wings and forelegs of an eagle and the body and hindquarters of a lion. Thus a bird-like leg of a griffin—what Paré terms "pied de griffon" on the Ravenna monster—was indistinguishable from that of an eagle. It is unclear why Paré decided that this hybrid monster with a feathery lower body must, on balance, have

of Ravenna, that even sported a third eye in the middle of its leg. Paré's work included land and marine animals and birds, thus turning monstrous humans into a phenomenon that was part of a broader natural history and pathology (Figure 2.2).[45] Such works drew on the prodigy tradition for some of their source materials.[46] Paré outlined the causes of monsters, which ranged from the divine (God's glory or wrath), to the natural (wrong quantity of semen), to the mechanical ("the mother's indecent sitting position") to the diabolical.[47] What distinguished Paré from writers of prodigy literature was the proportion of monsters that were considered to portend something. For Paré, most monsters merely demonstrated nature's curious mechanisms, and were neither portents, signs, nor errors. Monsters evoked curiosity and wonder rather than fear or horror.

Distinguishing a prodigy from a misbirth was a complex and subjective process. Paré wrote that monstrous misbirths merely appeared to be against the course of nature. Nonetheless, others believed that while the secondary cause of a monster might be natural, this did not preclude the possibility that it had ultimately been sent from God as a sign, since he used nature as an instrument. Thus, the secondary cause of a monstrous birth might be the mother's impure thoughts, while the primary cause was God's wrath at her sin. Monsters like the one born in Ravenna, so bizarre that no natural process could be posited, were clearly caused solely by God.[48] The Protestant scholar Caspar Peucer suggested that in order to tell a prodigy from a misbirth, one should pay attention to one's emotions at the moment of seeing it: monsters that show something "have always terrified human minds, overcome by presages of sad and calamitous events, and affected them with wonder and fear." Monsters that were not interpreted as portents evoked other emotions, such as wonder.[49]

The close link between emotion and cognition in the case of monsters was part of a broader response to unexplainable phenomena between the medieval period and the eighteenth century. It lies at the center of an important critical approach to responses to monsters, in the seminal *Wonders and the Order of Nature* by Lorraine Daston and Katherine Park. Focusing on monsters within Europe, the authors

---

the leg of the (already hybrid) griffin rather than that of an eagle. By 1579, in the revised and extended second edition of his *Les Oeuvres d'Ambroise Paré*, he had changed his mind, describing the creature as having "vn seul pied semblable à celuy d'vn oyseau de proye" (a single foot resembling that of a bird of prey; *Les Oeuvres*, IX.^{C}XXIIII). The monster's description and illustration varied, as did the number and type of its legs; the earliest known testimony ascribes to it a hairy leg with a devil's hoof and a human leg with an eye in the middle: see Niccoli, *Prophecy and the People*, pp. 35–46.

45   Céard, *Nature et les prodiges*, p. 304.
46   Ibid., p. 295.
47   Paré lists 13 causes in chapter I. For the list translated, see Marie-Hélène Huet, "Monstrous Medicine," in Knoppers and Landes (eds), *Monstrous Bodies/Political Monstrosities*, pp. 127–47, at 129.
48   Daston and Park, *Wonders*, pp. 192–3.
49   Caspar Peucer, *Commentarius de praecipuis generibus divinationum* (Wittemberg, 1560), ff. 442v–3v; translation from Daston and Park, *Wonders*, p. 193.

Figure 2.2   Ambroise Paré, *Oeuvres d'Ambroise Paré* (Paris, 1628), monster of
            Ravenna (in his *Des Monstres et prodiges*, first published in Paris in
            1573), Classmark K.7.30 (reproduced by kind permission of the
            Syndics of Cambridge University Library).

suggested that ideas about monsters emerged from "three separate complexes
of interpretations and associated emotions—horror, pleasure, and repugnance—
which overlapped and co-existed during much of the early modern period." The
particular interpretation made by an individual scholar was culturally contingent,
often informed by local political or religious upheaval.[50]

---

50   Daston and Park, *Wonders*, pp. 180, 187–90. For monsters as wonders that evoked
        pleasure, see p. 73.

Daston and Park assert that ideas about monstrous births underwent several key changes in the sixteenth and seventeenth centuries. At the turn of the sixteenth century, monsters were increasingly found within Europe, rather than being confined to distant regions. The belief that monsters were signs from God was shared by popular and educated culture. Not only did a plurality of interpretations co-exist in the medieval period—supernatural, divine, portentous and natural—but these continued in many ways in the early modern period.[51] The seventeenth century witnessed the gradual withdrawal of learned culture from prodigious ideas about monsters. This did not come about for epistemological reasons, but rather was encouraged by some for political ones. Monsters began to elicit indifference or repugnance rather than curiosity or pleasure.[52] In 1605, Sir Francis Bacon of the Royal Society in London had argued that monsters were part of the order of nature, and that they could be used to improve the causal explanations that characterized natural philosophy.[53] Despite Bacon's vision, argue Daston and Park, monsters and other "strange facts" received limited attention by the Society.[54]

Some aspects of this view have been challenged in recent years. It is now clear that monsters played an important part in seventeenth- and eighteenth-century learned culture, particularly natural philosophy. Recent scholarship has indicated the continuing interest of the Royal Society in curiosities and monstrous births. Palmira Fontes da Costa has shown that members of the Royal Society continued to discuss instances of monstrous births in their meetings, to which some beings were even brought along as specimens, well into the 1750s. The subjects and specimens included children born without brains (1697, 1711), various dwarfs and "gigantic" children (1744, 1746, 1750, 1751), a child born with the figure of a robin on its neck after its mother had been frightened by the sight of a dead robin (1751), a monstrous calf (1697, 1706), a monstrous pig (1700), and a monstrous sheep (1752). The Society had its own cabinet of curiosities, the Repository, until 1779.[55]

In eighteenth-century Paris, the Académie Royale de Sciences debated for decades over whether monstrous births were the work of God (through preformed seed) or the result of physical shocks suffered by the foetus after conception. If monsters were the latter, they were effectively accidental—a conclusion that implied that there were limits to God's power. What was more, such explanations of monsters even allowed for the possibility of new species emerging by chance. This

---

51   Daston and Park, *Wonders*, pp. 173–80. This approach constituted a revision of their earlier groundbreaking article "Unnatural Conceptions." There, they had suggested that there was a progressive shift, between the medieval period and the Enlightenment, of explanations of monstrous births as supernatural portents and punishments, to objects of wonder, to natural phenomena to be subjected to scientific inquiry.

52   Daston and Park, *Wonders*, pp. 201–5.

53   Sir Francis Bacon, *The Two Bookes of the Proficiencie and Advancement of Learning* (London, 1605).

54   Daston and Park, *Wonders*, chapter 5.

55   Palmira Fontes da Costa, *The Singular and the Making of Knowledge at the Royal Society of London in the Eighteenth Century* (Newcastle Upon Tyne: Cambridge Scholars Publishing, 2009), pp. 46–65 and Appendix A.

conflict over the origin of monsters pitched providentialist physicians, naturalists, and philosophers, such as the king's physician Joseph Du Verney, against those who favored "accidentalist" theories, such as Louis Lemery.[56] For Enlightenment *philosophes* like Voltaire, defining the notion of monster was highly problematic. Denis Diderot went so far as to deny the monster's separate existence, thereby subsuming monstrosity within humanity.[57]

Nevertheless, evidence of the continuing interest of some scholars in monsters as signs is provided by *A Discourse Concerning Prodigies* (1663) by John Spencer, a Cambridge antiquarian. This hefty tome was clearly aimed at the wealthier sections of the reading market, which must therefore still have entertained the possibility of prodigies and signs. The work is a methodical critique of every possible reason given for prodigies, and attempts to prove at every turn that they are not divine signs.[58] The sophistry and detail of Spencer's diatribe against prodigies, speckled with numerous Latin and Greek quotations (the latter in Greek script), suggests that it was the educated members of society that he was trying to convince. Spencer urged them to assess prodigies critically, "to let no vulgar notions commence our perswasions, before they have past the scrutiny of our reason, and appear to merit our assent."[59] For Spencer, the dangers of beliefs in prodigies were clear. He outlined them in his preface: "the common reverence of prodigies doth greatly trespass upon" religion.[60] In addition, it jeopardized political power, for "how mean a value and regard shall the issues of the severest debates, and the commands of authority, find, if every pitifull prodigy-monger have credit enough with the people to blast them, by telling them that heaven frowns upon them and that God writes his displeasure against them, in black and visible characters, when some sad accident befalls the complyers with them?" Spencer asserted that his "book may be profitable to serve the just interest of state," outlining three key reasons: "it tends to secure the honour of acts of state and the results of publick counsel," "it ministers to the quiet and tranquillity of the State," and "as it tends to make men more manageable to the commands of authority, which easy men may quickly be frighted from by such images of straw, as the relations of monsters and strange sights are."[61] Spencer then laid out natural, non-prodigious explanations for every conceivable type of prodigy. For those who still remain unconvinced, he asserted that: "If God do write *Fata hominum* in these mystick characters, there is none on earth found able to read the writing, and (with any certainty) to make known the

---

56   Andrew Curran and Patrick Graille, "The Faces of Eighteenth-Century Monstrosity," introduction to Andrew Curran, Robert P. Maccubbin, and David F. Morrill (eds), *Faces of Monstrosity in Eighteenth-Century Thought, Eighteenth-Century Life* 21, n.s., 2 (1997), pp. 1–15, at 4–6.

57   Ibid., pp. 9–10.

58   John Spencer, *A Discourse Concerning Prodigies: Wherein the Vanity of Presages by them is Reprehended, and their True and Proper Ends are Indicated* (Cambridge, 1663). For Spencer's strategies, see Burns, *Age of Wonders*, pp. 58–68.

59   For example, Spencer, *Discourse Concerning Prodigies*, p. 4.

60   Ibid., sig. A.3.r.

61   Ibid., sig. A.4.r.–B.1.r.

interpretation thereof."[62] By stressing the difficulty in reading God's signs, Spencer hoped to discourage his readers from doing so—or worse, from falling prey to those sign-readers who sought to overturn the rightful church and state.

It is also important to note that there was no consensus in learned circles for the best way of dealing with the political and religious dangers of beliefs about prodigies. The clergy was an important group that continued to write about monsters as portents, into the eighteenth century. Simon Ford, the rector at Old Swinford, compiled ancient and local, contemporary examples of monstrous births in his *Discourse Concerning Gods Judgements* (1678).[63] Ford stressed the value of such births as signs of individual sin, rather than as rhetorical devices for arguing against rival political or religious factions. The Sussex vicar William Turner claimed that his *Compleat History of the Most Remarkable Providences* (1697) would be "useful to ministers in furnishing topicks of reproof and exhortation, and to private Christians for their closets and families."[64] It includes a substantial section devoted to divine judgement on various transgressions, from cursing to sabbath-breaking. As with Spencer's volume against prodigies as signs, the book is a large tome, hardly a cheap pamphlet for the masses.

We may never be able to ascertain the extent to which members of the clergy believed that monsters were portents, or merely wished their flock to improve their ways through fear of portents. Nevertheless, their approach for increasing the authority of the church included the strategic encouragement of belief in prodigies. As such, the clergy's publication, into the eighteenth century, of both pamphlets and large treatises demonstrating the meanings of prodigious births must be understood as an important approach to monsters in this period, which was at odds with that of certain other sectors of learned culture (emblematized by Spencer's view), which considered any belief in the portentous nature of prodigies to be dangerous. By the eighteenth century, beliefs in prodigies as signs seem to have been primarily linked to sins of individuals rather than of political and religious groups. If that is the case, it would suggest that there was a return, in some ways, to pre-Reformation perceptions of monstrous births as natural, wondrous, or indicators of individual sin, rather than as devices of political polemic.

Understanding the relationship of monstrous births to the order of nature was highly problematic in this period. In terms of interpreting their significance, there was an uneasy continuum between births that heralded general misfortune or divine punishment, births that were in themselves punishments for an individual (their mother), and births that were caused by natural accidents during pregnancy. Learned culture was divided over the proper way to explain monstrous births. While, on the one hand, these births might hold the keys to a better understanding of nature and generation, and could even be used to make political arguments, the malleability of observations to different political and religious agendas made them

---

62   Ibid., p. 4.
63   Simon Ford, *A Discourse Concerning Gods Judgements* (London, 1678).
64   Turner, *Compleat History.*

highly unpredictable tools for social control. As John Spencer put it, they opened the doors for "every pitifull prodigy-monger" to deceive people.

Monstrous Peoples at the Ends of the Earth

Until the sixteenth century, individual monstrous births and exotic monstrous peoples belonged to different traditions and were largely understood through distinct explanations. During the Renaissance and the early modern period, monstrous births and monstrous races began to converge in several discourses, particularly in the context of natural history, as we have seen. Nevertheless, ideas about monstrous races that had been prevalent in classical antiquity and the medieval period continued to inform European thought between the Renaissance and the Enlightenment. During the first two centuries of printed books, beings such as apple-smellers, troglodytes, anthropophagi, and sciapods, who had sniffed, huddled, chomped, or hopped their way across medieval manuscripts of the *Marvels of the East* and Pliny the Elder's *Historia naturalis*, continued to pass through the hands and minds of European writers, readers, and viewers. Of the classical sources, Pliny was the most widely cited authority on monstrous races in the early modern period. Also popular in the sixteenth century were encyclopedic texts such as St Augustine's *City of God* and Isidore's *Etymologies*.[65] The books of Marco Polo and John Mandeville were printed widely into the seventeenth century. Mandeville's fictional narrative, for instance, was one of the earliest of all works to be printed, and the most popular incunable by a medieval prose writer.[66] Outlining his alleged pilgrimage to the Holy Land, it had appeared in at least 72 printed editions by the end of the sixteenth century.[67] While the majority of the vellum-inches in Marco Polo's and Mandeville's accounts were devoted to folk who were not monstrous, Mandeville in particular was frequently cited as an author who described monsters dwelling in the furthest parts of the world, as we shall see.[68]

Traditional ideas about monstrous peoples also circulated via contemporary geographies and maps. These selected and reformulated information from travel accounts, encyclopedias, biblical works, and other sources.[69] One example is a

---

65 Isidore, *Etymologies*, XI.iii.12–30.
66 Mary B. Campbell, *The Witness and the Other World: Exotic Eastern Travel Writing 400–1600* (Ithaca, NY and London: Cornell University Press, 1988), p. 122.
67 Rosemary Tzanaki, *Mandeville's Medieval Audiences: A Study on the Reception of the Book of Sir John Mandeville (1371–1550)* (Aldershot: Ashgate, 2003), p. 1, n. 1; this study focuses on manuscripts.
68 See also, in this collection, Braham, "The Monstrous Caribbean," p. 18.
69 For mapmakers' contributions to the shaping of ethnographic knowledge, including ideas about monstrous races, see in particular Surekha Davies, "Representations of Amerindians on European Maps and the Construction of Ethnographic Knowledge, 1506–1624," PhD dissertation, University of London, 2009. This research is the basis of a forthcoming monograph provisionally entitled *America's Inhabitants on Maps and the*

globe produced in 1492 (before Columbus's return from his first landfall in the Caribbean) by Martin Behaim, a Nuremberg mapmaker and merchant. It refers to Marco Polo and Mandeville in the light of both ancient writings and contemporary travels. Behaim makes precise references to Marco Polo's *Description*, giving book and chapter references.[70] A legend in the south-eastern Indian Ocean states that "in the last book of Marco Polo in the sixteenth chapter it is written that the people of this island, Angama, have heads, eyes and teeth like dogs, and are thoroughly misshapen, and savage, for they prefer human flesh to other flesh."[71]

What was new about monstrous races during the long sixteenth century was the nature of their march across the globe. The mid-fifteenth century had heralded the age of oceanic expansion: European navigators began to sail south along the coast of West Africa and around it to India, and west across the Atlantic to what became known as the Americas. As the theoretical span of the world laid out by scholars started to be traversed by men in ships, the possibility of meeting monsters theoretically became increasingly likely. Contemporary travel literature became an important new source for monsters. A key question in the minds of these travelers and their readers was the relationship between the monsters they expected to see and the beings newly being observed in the field. Their expectations were informed by broad ethno-geographical ideas. One related to the roundness of the world:[72] if you sailed west for long enough, you would eventually reach the east. Thus Columbus and other travelers to America considered the peoples they encountered in the light of their expectations about the Far East—which included the possibility of monstrous races.[73]

The anthropophage was the first monstrous being to be identified in America. Of the inhabitants of the Antilles islands, Columbus wrote to Luis de Santángel, *Escribano de Ración* (keeper of the royal privy purse) that:

> In these islands I have so far found no monstrous people [ombres monstrudos], as many expected … except on one island … which is inhabited by people who are held in all the islands to be very ferocious and who eat human flesh.[74]

Construction of Ethnographic Knowledge, 1500–1650.

70 This precision allows us to identify the redaction that Behaim used; see my "The Wondrous East in the Renaissance Geographical Imagination: Marco Polo, Fra Mauro and Giovanni Batista Ramusio," *History and Anthropology* 23/2 (2012, forthcoming), near n. 56.

71 For transcription and translation, see E.G. Ravenstein, *Martin Behaim: His Life and His Globe* (London: G. Philip & Son, 1908), p. 88.

72 Contrary to popular belief, medieval scholars were well aware that the earth was spherical. See Louise M. Bishop, "The Myth of the Flat Earth," in Stephen J. Harris and Bryon Lee Grigsby (eds), *Misconceptions about the Middle Ages* (London and New York, NY: Routledge, 2008), pp. 97–101.

73 Columbus also sailed south: for the broader implications of this, see the important study, Nicolás Wey-Gómez, *The Tropics of Empire: Why Columbus Sailed South to the Indies* (Cambridge, MA and London: MIT Press, 2008).

74 Christopher Columbus, *Letters from America: Columbus's First Accounts of the 1492 Voyage*, ed. and trans. B.W. Ife (London: King's College London, School of Humanities,

Not only were monstrous people what "many expected," but Columbus himself reflected on the islanders within this tradition. He uses the widest definition of *monstrudos*, encompassing behavioral aberrations. In his unpublished journal known as the *Diario*, he also raises the possibility of physical monsters. On November 4, 1492, in conversation with the inhabitants of Cuba known today as the Taíno, Columbus "understood that, far from there, there were one-eyed people and others with dogs' muzzles who ate human beings; and that upon seizing a person, they cut his throat and drank his blood and cut off his genitals."[75]

Several traditional monsters appear here: the one-eyed cyclops of classical mythology, the dog-headed cynocephalus, and the anthropophage. Columbus reports their existence on the basis of indigenous testimony, but one cannot help wondering how much of the Indians' speech he could have understood after a few weeks in the region.[76] His interpreter spoke Hebrew, Aramaic, and some Arabic, languages Columbus expected to hear when he reached Asia.[77] Even the interpreter was absent here, having been sent on a reconnaissance mission on November 2. These monsters seem to be as much about what Columbus expected to find as anything the Taíno might have said.[78] An important feature here is that it is not a first-hand observation, but rather an attempt to substantiate a point on the authority of *ear*witnessing something: hearing it from someone who had witnessed it firsthand—an eyewitness.[79] Similar moments appear in relation to monstrous peoples in a number of early modern travel narratives.[80]

Early modern audiences were divided over the credibility of monstrous peoples in distant regions. After all, it was widely known that travelers, along with the old, were able to fabricate safely, since few could collaborate their testimony. Maximilianus Transylvanus, secretary to Charles V of Spain, had been present at the Spanish court at Valladolid when the members of the Magellan circumnavigatory expedition (1519–22) were interviewed.[81] Maximilianus's letter to his father, the

---

75 Christopher Columbus, *A Synoptic Edition of the Log of Columbus's First Voyage*, ed. Francesca Lardicci (Turnhout: Brepols, 1999), DB48.8 (includes English translation to which I have made minor changes): "Entendió ... que lexos de allí avía hombres de un ojo, y otros con hoçicos de perros que comían los hombres, y que en tomando uno lo degollavan y le bevían la sangre, y le cortavan su natura."

76 For Columbus's (mis)understanding of situations, see, for example, Peter Mason, *Deconstructing America: Representations of the Other* (London; Routledge, 1990), p. 101.

77 Peter Hulme, *Colonial Encounters: Europe and the Native Caribbean, 1492–1797* (London: Methuen, 1986), p. 20.

78 This point is also made in David Abulafia, *The Discovery of Mankind: Atlantic Encounters in the Age of Columbus* (New Haven, CT and London: Yale University Press, 2008), p. 153.

79 For the concept of earwitnessing in the early modern period, see, for example, Andrea Frisch, *The Invention of the Eyewitness: Witnessing and Testimony in Early Modern France* (Chapel Hill, NC: University of North Carolina Press, 2004), pp. 22–3.

80 See, for example, Davies, "Representations of Amerindians," chapter 7.

81 Antonio Pigafetta, *Magellan's Voyage: A Narrative Account of the First Circumnavigation*, ed. and trans. R.A. Skelton (New York: Dover Publications, 1994), p. 5.

Cardinal-Archbishop of Salzburg, dated October 22, 1522,[82] wrote approvingly of the explorers' testimony: "they appeared in their narrative, not merely to have abstained from fabulous statements, but also to contradict and refute those made by ancient authors."[83] Moreover, he added, "who ever believed that the Monosceli, the Sciapodes, the Scyrites, the Spithamaei, the Pygmies or other of this kind were rather monsters than men?"[84] Maximilianus does not rule out the possibility that such beings exist, but considers that the traditional Plinian races—if they existed—were most likely both human and non-monstrous.

Therein lay the greatest problem in understanding monstrous races: how could you be sure that they were truly monstrous races of the Plinian sort, rather than 1) one-off monstrous births; 2) slightly unusual people; or 3) merely fabulous fabrications. In 1596, the English mathematician Thomas Blundeville produced a tirade against accounts of monstrous races:

> they are meere lies that are woont to be told of the pigmeans, in that they should bee but a foote and a halfe high, and like wise that which hath bene spoken of people, that should haue their heads, their noses, their mouthes, and their eies in their breastes, or of those that are headed lyke a dog, or of those that haue but one eie, and that in their forehead, or of those that haue but one foote and that so great, as that it covereth and shadoweth all their bodie, or of those that haue greate eares hanging downe to the ground. All these are meere lyes, invented by vain men to bring fooles into admiration, for monsters are as well borne in Europe, as in other partes of the world.[85]

Blundeville's list of unlikely beings echoes the list of monstrous peoples in Pliny's *Historia naturalis*. Perhaps most interesting is the reason given for not believing in them: "for monsters are as well borne in Europe, as in other partes of the world." For Blundeville, European monsters were singular individuals; there was no reason for aberrations in distant lands to be any different, either in frequency or characteristics. The explanations for domestic monsters were sufficient to explain any distant ones; any observations that did not fit must have been "invented." Blundeville's and Maximilanus's reservations point to a key ontological ambiguity: the uneasy boundary between monsters in Europe and monsters abroad. Not even the criterion of inherited, widespread prevalence

---

82 Maximilianus Transylvanus, *De Moluccis Insulis* (Rome, 1523).

83 Ibid., sig. B.i.*v*.: "non modo nihil fabulosi afferre, sed fabulosa omnia alia a veteribus authoribus prodita, refellere et reprobare, narratione sua viderentur." Translations, with minor amendments, are from Antonio Pigafetta and Maximilianus Transylvanus, *First Voyage Around the World by Antonio Pigafetta and "De Moluccis Insulis" by Maximilianus Transylvanus*, ed. and trans. Carlos Quirino (Manila: Filipiniana Book Guild, 1969), p. 111.

84 Maximilianus Transylvanus, *De Moluccis Insulis*, sig. B.i.*v*–B.ii.*r*; idem, *First Voyage*, ed. Quirino, p. 111. For further discussions of Maximilianus's and Blundeville's views on distant monsters, see Davies, "Representations of Amerindians," chapters 6 and 7.

85 Thomas Blundeville, *Exercises* (London, 1594), p. 262.

Agere

Figure 2.3   Ulisse Aldrovandi, *Monstrorum historia* (Bologna, 1642), p. 18, one
of the Gonzales sisters, Classmark M.13.43 (reproduced by kind
permission of the Syndics of Cambridge University Library).

of a monstrous characteristic was sufficient to fully separate European and
distant monsters in practice. Just as monstrous portents and natural misbirths
could not be distinguished by observation alone, so were the characteristics of
monstrous races also elements found among monstrous individuals in Europe.
For Blundeville, this dissolved the alleged monsters of the Plinian tradition until
they no longer constituted a category of their own.

The family of Petrus Gonzales was a case in point. Inheritors of a genetic condition now termed *hypertrichosis universalis*, their bodies and much of their faces were covered in hair (Figure 2.3).[86] Petrus was born on the Canary Islands—arguably a distant land, but one that had come under Spanish rule in the late fifteenth century.[87] Their hairiness meant that they were also explicable via traditional beliefs about wild folk who were deemed to be hairy and to live in forests and mountains in Europe. Notions of wild people appeared in Christian and folkloric traditions. While St Augustine and most medieval writers considered them to be descended from Adam and Eve, and therefore human, they were generally viewed as non-human and dangerous in medieval and fifteenth-century popular culture.[88]

During the sixteenth century, the wild man was often portrayed positively. He became a family protector on coats-of-arms. Perhaps the most extreme example of this was the idea of the wild man as the ancestor of civilized Germans. Tacitus's *Germania*, written in the first century CE, had described the Germans as wild people who lacked many of the civilized practices of the Romans. The text was unknown during the medieval period, but was re-discovered in 1420, and began to circulate in print in the 1470s. During the early sixteenth century, German humanists began to associate wild people with a heroic stage in the evolution of contemporary Germans.[89] By implication, wildness had become a state between the monstrous and the human.

Just as monstrous births in Europe could be given multiple meanings in different social contexts and discourses, monstrous races could be rationalized in a variety of ways. Indeed, monstrous races and non-European peoples existed on an ethnological continuum: the more different a people's customs and physical appearance, the more likely it was that terms such as monstrous, wild, savage, and barbarous would be applied to them. The term "monstrous" might be used for social practices, such as body-piercing, tattooing, or the eating of human flesh. Those who inflicted monstrosity upon themselves constituted a category distinct from both monstrous individuals and monstrous races. At this point, monstrosity began to blur into savagery and barbarism. The Tartars of north-east Asia were said to have physical and behavioral deformities. In 1636, Donald Lupton drew from this the inference that: "The Tartarians are [the] most deformed of all men."[90] Such approaches to alterity were nothing new; the ancient Greeks had, of course, used the term *barbaroi* to denote people who did not speak Greek, but who, from the Greek perspective, merely babbled incomprehensibly in a monstrous simulation

---

86 For an accessible microhistorical study of sixteenth-century Europe and its ways of making sense of "others," told through responses to the hairy family, see Merry Wiesner-Hanks, *The Marvelous Hairy Girls: The Gonzales Sisters and Their Worlds* (New Haven, CT and London: Yale University Press, 2009).

87 For European contact with indigenous Canary Islanders, see Abulafia, *Discovery of Mankind*, chapter 4.

88 Wiesner-Hanks, *Marvelous Hairy Girls*, pp. 32–4.

89 For this argument, see Stephanie Leitch, "The Wild Man, Charlemagne and the German Body," *Art History* 31/3 (2008), pp. 283–302.

90 See Mark Thornton Burnett, *Constructing "Monsters" in Shakespearean Drama and Early Modern Culture* (Basingstoke: Palgrave Macmillan, 2002), p. 43.

of "true" language.[91] In the medieval period, Islam had offered an antithesis to many inhabitants of Latin Europe; Saracens were sometimes identified with dog-headed beings.[92] Such anxieties were at least partly based on the difficulty of establishing the relationships between religions, peoples, and their histories and thus of delineating where the self ended and the other began.

The ascription of monstrosity (broadly defined to include aberrant practices) to inhabitants of distant regions had implications for European colonial and imperial objectives. In the 1580s, the first English observers of the Algonquian tribes of present-day Virginia and North Carolina had stressed their fine physical form. Their simple but ordered ways of life were seen as evidence that they lived in an earlier state of civility, as had Britain's own Pictish ancestors, and could be "raised to civility."[93] Such views chimed well with the promotional purpose of early colonial literature, which was aimed at encouraging English settlers. During the early seventeenth century, after the massacre of English colonists at Jamestown, Virginia, in 1622, English writing about the Algonquians changed radically, now arguing that these peoples were barely human. Edward Waterhouse, a first-hand witness and Virginia official, used arguments grounded on their "savage" practices to suggest that these "rude, barbarous, and naked people" should be hunted down with horses and bloodhounds, "and mastiues to teare them, which take this naked, tanned, deformed sauages, for no other then wild beasts."[94] Waterhouse and other commentators read the Algonquians' customs and manners as barbarous in the light of their resistance to English colonists and to the true religion. The negative interpretations of Algonquian life in turn led to negative portrayals of their physical appearance. European perceptions of non-European monstrosity were thus inextricably linked to broader approaches to interpreting human diversity on the basis of customs, appearance, and religion.[95]

For some commentators, one need not be born a monster; one could choose to become one. Put another way, religious, moral, or political transgressions were monstrous, figuratively speaking.[96] In the years following the appearance of the

---

91   This lack of intelligible speech was linked to limitations in reasoning power and social practices. See Anthony Pagden, *The Fall of Natural Man: The American Indian and the Origins of Comparative Ethnology* (Cambridge: Cambridge University Press, 1986), pp. 16–18.

92   See Debra Higgs Strickland, *Demons, Saracens, and Jews: Making Monsters in Medieval Art* (Princeton, NJ and London: Princeton University Press, 2003), p. 160; and, in this collection, idem, "Monstrosity and Race in the Late Middle Ages," p. 374.

93   See especially Thomas Harriot, *A Briefe and True Report of the New Found Land of Virginia* (Frankfurt am Main, 1590), which contained fine engravings derived from watercolors produced by a first-hand observer, the artist John White. The *Report* was first published in 1588 as an unillustrated pamphlet.

94   Edward Waterhouse, *A Declaration of the State of the Colony in Virginia [1622]* (Amsterdam and New York: Da Capo Press, 1970), p. 24.

95   See Joan-Pau Rubiés, "New Worlds and Renaissance Ethnology," *History and Anthropology* 6 (1993), pp. 157–97.

96   Andrew Curran, "Afterword," in Knoppers and Landes (eds), *Monstrous Bodies/Political*

Lutheran Monk Calf engraving, similar monsters began to appear in a variety of textual genres as "fashion monsters." These metaphorical creatures served to critique the morals of those who wore particular items of clothing, such as slashed hose and smart ruffs. For those Protestants who would come to be termed Puritans, not only were the vestments of "popish" heresy problematic, but so too were secular sartorial excesses, which could be signs of lecherousness or vanity — moral/behavioral rather than physical monstrosity.[97] In both cases, the monstrosity hinged on the power of clothing to transform its wearer.[98] Those who chose to preen themselves into "fashion monsters" were seen to be no better than non-Europeans. Such views were held, for example, by Samuel Purchas, an Anglican clergyman and editor of travel accounts. He devoted a chapter of his *Historie of Man* (1619) to "The vanitie of the whole bodie together in divers vices; and of fashions in generall."[99] In a swingeing critique of "moderne fashions," Purchas noted that a vain person "strives to cut, race, pinke, print, iagge and fashion himselfe out of humane feature, to put off a man, and put on a monster, in a humour of gallantrie." Such fashions were hardly better than the nose- and lip-rings of the Amerindians, who "esteeme themselues gallants, thus accoultred." In this way, both the "ethnicke" and the Christian "stripped himselfe of his best clothing" — the naked body that God had bestowed upon him, which "clothed him with beautie admired of angels."[100] Monstrosity, then, could be a(n im)moral choice, rather than a physical characteristic present since birth. Directives against this brand of monster often brought together distant savages and European gallants. The French Protestant Jean de Léry had asserted that the embarrassment of rich clothing preferred in Europe was no less immoral than the widespread nudity he encountered among the inhabitants of Brazil.[101]

The practices of distant nations could be used to critique practices closer to home. In his *Anthropometamorphosis* (1650), the London physician John Bulwer discussed physical alteration — inborn or self-inflicted. For Bulwer, the English interest in cosmetic fashion, particularly "cosmetical conceits from barbarous nations," threatened to corrupt English nature.[102] Bulwer paid particular attention

Monstrosities, pp. 227–45, at 243; and James A. Steintrager, "Perfectly Inhuman: Moral Monstrosity in Eighteenth-Century Discourse," in Curran, Maccubbin, and Morrill (eds), *Faces of Monstrosity*, pp. 114–32, at 116. For notions of ethical monstrosity in Enlightenment France, see also Andrew Curran, *Sublime Disorder: Physical Monstrosity in Diderot's Universe* (Oxford: Voltaire Foundation, 2001).

97 Crawford, *Marvelous Protestantism*, pp. 31–55.

98 For the cultural import of clothing in this period, see, for example, Peter Stallybrass and Ann Rosalind Jones, *Renaissance Clothing and the Materials of Memory* (Cambridge: Cambridge University Press, 2000).

99 Samuel Purchas, *Microcosmus or The Historie of Man* (London, 1619), chapter XXV.

100 Ibid., pp. 225–6.

101 Jean de Léry, *Histoire d'un voyage fait en la terre du Brésil, 1557 [1580]*, ed. Frank Lestringant (Montpellier: Max Chaleil, 1992), chapter VIII.

102 John Bulwer, *Anthropometamorphosis: Man Transform'd; or, the Artificial Changeling* (London, 1650).

to deformations of the head, such as the painting of spots and shapes on the face, in order to make claims about the dangers of "deforming" the body politic, particularly its head.[103] Indeed, those who deformed themselves were, in Bulwer's eyes, guilty of treason against the law of nature.[104]

The majority of the material in *Anthropometamorphosis* was ethnographic, insofar as it comprised descriptions of distant peoples, culled from a variety of sources that can often be traced to some sort of eyewitness. As Mary Campbell has noted, for Bulwer, the foreign and the monstrous overlapped almost completely.[105] One might add that they also overlapped with the seditious and the immoral. In this way, ethnology and teratology were part of a continuum for describing both selves and others. The anxiety caused by monsters and their possible meanings lay in the implications of positioning individuals, groups, and selves along that continuum.

The superficial characteristics of distant monstrous peoples with physical deformities—headless men, giants, and the like—were, at one level, indistinguishable from those of monstrous individuals. In addition, readers of travelers' accounts also had to contend with the possibility that their sources contained fabrications that they could not easily verify independently.

The slipperiness of the category of monstrous people extended to those with behavioral deformities. Behavioral monstrosity lay between and blended Europeans with others, metaphorical aberrations and physical ones. Monstrous, barbarous, and civil behaviors existed on a continuum; reconfiguring one had the potential to disrupt the others. When mid-seventeenth century Englishmen turned against the Virginia Algonquians, they characterized their minds and bodies as savage and deformed. Less than 50 years previously, these very minds and bodies had been seen as pleasing, partly civilized—and similar to those of the ancient Britons.

Monsters Amalgamated

The catalog of monsters compiled by Ulisse Aldrovandi, a sixteenth-century naturalist and encyclopedist, was published in 1642.[106] Despite its focus on individual monsters, mostly coming from first-hand observation or eyewitness accounts, it begins with an array of monstrous beings from distant lands, such as the "four-eyed Ethiopian" (*Aethiops quatuor oculis*) (Figure 2.4).[107] Aldrovandi

---

103 Burns, "King's Two Monstrous Bodies"; Crawford, *Marvelous Protestantism*, chapter 4.

104 For further discussion of Bulwer's state/body metaphors, see Burns, "King's Two Monstrous Bodies," pp. 192–9, especially 195.

105 For an analysis of Bulwer's text, see Mary Baine Campbell, *Wonder and Science: Imagining Worlds in Early Modern Europe* (Ithaca, NY: Cornell University Press, 1999), pp. 233–50, especially 238–9.

106 Ulisse Aldrovandi, *Monstrorum historia* (Bologna, 1642). Aldrovandi died in 1605; for his collection, see Paula Findlen, *Possessing Nature: Museums, Collecting, and Scientific Culture in Early Modern Italy* (Berkeley: University of California Press, 1994), chapter 1.

107 Aldrovandi, *Monstrorum historia*, p. 9.

Figure 2.4   Ulisse Aldrovandi, *Monstrorum historia* (Bologna, 1642), p. 11, four-
eyed Ethiopian, Classmark M.13.43 (reproduced by kind permission
of the Syndics of Cambridge University Library).

drew on a variety of classical, medieval, and contemporary sources, from Pliny to
Antonio Pigafetta, a supernumerary on the Magellan circumnavigatory voyage. He
also included the hairy family of Petrus Gonzales and human–animal hybrids such
as a fish resembling a monk. He covered monsters as anatomical misbirths and as
prodigies, and monstrous animals.[108] The *Monstrorum historia* is one of a number of
sources that indicates that, between Paré's *Des Monstres et prodiges* of 1573 and the

---

108   Ibid., pp. 16–18, 28, 34–8.

mid-eighteenth century, the category of monster expanded enormously, while its subdivisions became less pronounced.

Such admixtures of phenomena mirrored a wider interest in the unnatural or unusual as a source of wonder and pleasure. From at least the sixteenth century, in cabinets of curiosity, monstrous births jostled with corals, creatures of the deep, and even artifacts and costumes of distant peoples. Members of a wide range of social groups would have heard of or seen such beings at fairs and shows. The wealthy could pay for these performers to entertain them and their select friends in the privacy of their own homes. The audiences for such entertainment included members of the general public with limited education, scholars, naturalists, and the aristocracy. Members of the Royal Society, including John Evelyn, Samuel Pepys, and Robert Hooke, attended exhibitions of monsters.[109] The monsters displayed at fairs, like those to be found in cabinets of curiosity, ranged from malformed humans to non-European others (notably Native American Indians) to exotic or deformed animals and aquatic creatures. Such spaces constructed monsters and marvels through what one scholar has called "practices of enfreakment."[110]

One such fair was Bartholomew Fair in West Smithfield, London, which was first chartered in 1133 and ran, amazingly, until 1855. This three-day summer fair attracted all manner of marvelous, curious, and grotesque exhibits and entertainments. A 1641 pamphlet noted its popularity among "people of all sorts, high and low, rich and poore, from cities, townes, and countrys, of all sects ... and of all conditions, good and bad, vertuous and vitious, knaves and fooles, cuckolds and cuckholdmakers ..."[111] In 1802, William Wordsworth wrote of Bartholomew Fair's:

> albinos, painted Indians, dwarfs, the Horse of knowledge, and the learned pig
> The stone-eater, the man that swallows fire, giants, ventriloquists, the
> Invisible Girl ...
> All freaks of nature, all Promethean thoughts
> Of man; his dulness, madness, and their feats
> All jumbled up together to make up
> this Parliament of monsters.[112]

This jumble of monstrous births, unusual folks, animals, talented individuals, and non-Europeans that constituted a palette of "freaks of nature" in Wordsworth's

---

109 Paul Semonin, "Monsters in the Marketplace: The Exhibition of Human Oddities in Early Modern England," in Rosemarie Garland Thomson (ed.), *Freakery: Cultural Spectacles of the Extraordinary Body* (New York, NY and London: New York University Press, 1996), pp. 69–81, at 70; Richard D. Altick, *The Shows of London* (Cambridge, MA and London: Harvard University Press, 1978), pp. 36–7.

110 Rosemarie Garland Thomson, "Introduction," in *Freakery: Cultural Spectacles of the Extraordinary Body*, ed. idem (New York, NY and London: New York University Press, 1996), pp. 1–19, at 14.

111 Ibid., p. 3. See also Semonin, "Monsters in the Marketplace," pp. 76–7.

112 Quoted in Altick, *Shows of London*, p. 36: William Wordsworth, *The Prelude*, 1805 version VII.662–94.

eyes underlines the blurriness of the boundaries between the traditional typology of monsters. From the mid-sixteenth century, such fairs exhibited inhabitants of America, Africa, and even Asia with increasing frequency.[113]

This essay began with Samuel Pepys's discussion of a baboon/monster. But Pepys was not the only person in his household who had an interest in the monstrous. Pepys's manservant, James Paris du Plessis, created his own illustrated manuscript compendium of monsters, and sold it to Sir Hans Sloane around 1733. The first few monsters illustrate the variety across the volume: a child with two heads born at Pithiviers in France; a Tartar with a horse's head; and "a man with a monstrous goiter ... being a terrour to all big bellyed women that saw him."[114] "A spotted negro prince was sold in London and show'd publickly at the age of 10 years in 1690." James Paris saw him then, and again in 1725. The prince was taught to speak English quite well, his monstrosity presumably limited to the fact that his "jet black" body was "intermixt with a clear and beautifull white, spotted all over."[115] By contrast, a black wild man from the East Indies, "covered all over the body and arms and hands with very thick long black hair, could never larn to speak, read nor rite." He, too, "was sold to a company of rope dancers."[116]

Paris's extensive interest in collecting stories about monsters might have been prompted by a childhood encounter in Pithiviers. A "gentlemans wife" who saw a two-headed monster in an almanack gave birth, in Paris's mother's house, to a dead two-headed child. This was buried with great secrecy in Paris's own bit of the garden, where he accidentally dug it up.[117] As if that were not enough, Paris also relates a tale about his own mother-in-law, who gave birth to "a child in the form of a lobster" after seeing a lobster in Leadenhall Market.[118]

Conclusion

Between the Renaissance and the Enlightenment, monsters could be categorized according to either secondary causes or deeper significances. These two methods cut across one another: they might bring together innocent victims of circumstance, like pregnant mothers frightened by lobsters, and individuals who had deliberately challenged the social order, as in the case of adulterers. One consequence was that it was difficult to determine even a monster's secondary cause—could one be sure that a mother had committed adultery with the person whom her child resembled, rather than having merely been surprised by him during pregnancy? The warrants connecting observed monsters to both secondary causes and meanings were

---

113 See Altick, *Shows of London*, pp. 45–8, for examples.
114 London, British Library, Department of Manuscripts, MS Add. 5246, ff. 6r–8v.
115 Ibid., ff. 11r–14v.
116 Ibid., ff. 53v.
117 Ibid., f. 5r.
118 Ibid., ff. 13r. –18r.

subjective and contested, the consequence of observation, analysis, comparison with precedent, *realpolitik*, and emotional responses. From the Reformation onwards, as the meanings ascribed to prodigious births became increasingly specific, particular interpretations of monsters—notably the Papal Ass and the Monk Calf—were used to critique religious and political opponents.

Monster-sceptics doubted both the existence of certain types of monster— notably monstrous races—and the significance of their monstrosity. Whether a monster was deemed to be an omen, an error, or a natural wonder of distant lands, observable evidence of monster-genesis was hard to come by. In many cases, there were few eyewitnesses. It is perhaps for this reason that, with the emergence of natural history as a discipline in the Renaissance, and the increasing importance of observational evidence in the late seventeenth century, learned circles focused on individual cases of monsters that they could see with their own eyes.

The mid-sixteenth and seventeenth centuries witnessed the increasing assimilation of discussions of monstrosity within a number of independent textual genres and intellectual disciplines. These included travel writing, moralistic and exemplary tales, anatomy, embryology, and comparative ethnology. By the mid-eighteenth century, numerous types of monster appeared in a variety of spaces in Western culture and intellectual thought, where different explanations of their meanings and causes were posited. Cabinets of curiosity, popular fairs, and James Paris's collection of monsters all drew together misbirths, distant peoples, and animals. They indicate how the category of "monster" expanded to perhaps its greatest extent in the decades around 1800. The late medieval division of monsters into natural, prodigious, and distant types was modified by the close interaction of monsters with discussions about the rest of nature, and about human society and (un)civility. Monstrosity could also be either actual or metaphorical, forming a continuum that stretched from one-legged wonders to "fashion monsters." The monstrous hairiness of Petrus Gonzales's family linked it to the wild ancestors of Europe, who were in turn linked to inhabitants of distant lands by their ways of life. In effect, a new liminal category, comprising those beings that could not be definitively identified as either monstrous or normal, became an accepted part of Western thought.

Beauteous Beast: The Water Deity Mami Wata in Africa

Henry John Drewal

Mammy-wota ... You can always tell them, because they are beautiful with a beauty that is too perfect and too cold.

Chinua Achebe (1972, p. 43)

If you see Mami Wata oh, never you run away ...

Sir Victor Uwaifo (1967)

Every child swims in its mother's womb before taking a first breath of air. In this sense and in others "water is life." In Africa and the African Atlantic world, people recognize the essential and sacred nature of water by honoring and celebrating a host of water spirits.[1] The identities of these divinities, however, are as slippery and amorphous as water itself. Only the frames of history, art, and culture can contain them, giving them shape, contour, substance, and specificity. Yet even these frames are subject to change, and when they undergo a metamorphosis, so do the attributes, personalities, identities, and actions of these fascinating and ambiguous spirits.

This chapter is about a renowned African water divinity called Mami Wata (pidgin English for "Mother Water" or "Mistress Water"), and more broadly, a vast "school" of countless female and male African aquatic spirits known generically as *mami watas* and *papi watas*. Is she a "mother," "mistress," or "monster"? Like the fluidity of water itself, Mami Wata may be all these things, depending on the frames of history, culture, and the perspectives of communities

---

1   This is a revised and condensed version of my chapter in Henry John Drewal, *Mami Wata: Arts for Water Spirits in Africa and Its Diasporas* (Los Angeles: Fowler Museum-UCLA, 2008). See also, Drewal (ed.), *Sacred Waters: Arts for Mami Wata and Other Divinities in Africa and the Diaspora* (Bloomington: Indiana University Press, 2008), for a collection of 46 essays and a DVD on arts for Mami Wata and other water spirits from across the African continent and in the African Atlantic world. Our thanks to Rebecca Feldstein for her help with these notes.

Figure 3.1 Dona Fish, Ovimbundu people, circa 1950–1960, wood, pigment, metal, sacrificial material, 75 cm, Fowler Museum.

and individuals. Monstrosity, as described through this collection, can be as much applied from without as inhering within beings. Mami Wata is celebrated by many, but demonized as monstrous by Christian Pentecostalism and fundamentalist Islam, These two invasive faiths bring with them notions of a clear-cut divide between good and evil, and ideas about original sin and notions of redemption—concepts absent from indigenous African religions. In much African religious theology, belief, and practice, good and bad are always present in all things. As the Yoruba say, *tibi/tire ni* ("everything has both good and bad together"). Intentions and actions determine which aspects dominate. Both are always in dynamic play and tension. Western/European concepts and terms such as "witch," or "magic," or "fetish," when applied to certain persons, actions, or things in Africa, distort and misrepresent how they are understood by Africans—as both/either positive or negative depending on the specific cultural and historical circumstances. Even though Pentecostals and Muslims have adopted a position of authority in claiming an ability to neutralize with a "superior" faith such "evil" forces as Satan and Mami Wata, we need to explore the deeper philosophical foundations of such concepts to arrive at more nuanced understandings.

Mami Wata, often portrayed with the head and torso of a woman and the tail of a fish, is at once beautiful, jealous, generous, healing, empowering, seductive, and potentially deadly (Figure 3.1). A water spirit now widely known across Africa, Mami Wata's origins are sometimes said to lie "overseas"—beyond Africa's shores—yet she manifests the attributes of many ancient and indigenous African water deities and has been thoroughly incorporated into local beliefs and practices. Her powerful and pervasive presence results from a number of factors. Of special note, she can bring good fortune in the form of money, and as a "capitalist" par excellence, her power increased between the fifteenth and the twentieth centuries, the era of growing trans-oceanic, international trade between Africa and the rest of the world.

Mami Wata's very name is in pidgin English, a language developed to lubricate trade. The countless numbers of Africans who were torn from their homeland and forcibly carried across the Atlantic between the sixteenth and nineteenth centuries as part of this "trade" brought with them their beliefs and practices honoring Mami Wata and other ancestral deities. They re-established, revisualized, and revitalized these spirits and deities, who often assumed new guises: Lasirèn, Watra Mama, Maman de l'Eau, or Mae d'Agua. Subsequently, these "new" faiths flourished. Worshippers of Mami Wata have typically selected local as well as global images, arts, ideas, and actions; interpreted them according to indigenous precepts; invested them with new meanings; and then re-presented them in novel and dynamic ways to serve their own specific aesthetic, devotional, social, economic, and political aspirations.

Mami's powers, however, are believed to extend far beyond economic gain. Although for some she bestows good fortune and status through monetary wealth, for others, she aids in concerns related to procreation—infertility, impotence, or infant mortality. Some are drawn to her as an irresistible, seductive presence who offers the pleasures and powers that accompany devotion to a spiritual force. Yet she also represents danger, for a liaison with Mami Wata often requires a substantial sacrifice, such as the life of a family member or celibacy in the realm of mortals. Despite this, she is capable of helping women and men negotiate their sexual desires and preferences. Mami also provides a spiritual and professional avenue for women to become powerful priestesses and healers of both psycho-spiritual and physical ailments, and to assert female agency in generally male-dominated societies. Rapid socioeconomic changes and the pressures of trying to survive in burgeoning African urban centers have increased the need for the curative powers of Mami Wata priestesses and priests.

Half-fish and half-human, Mami Wata straddles earth and water, culture and nature. She may also take the form of a snake charmer (Figure 3.2), sometimes in combination with her mermaid attributes and sometimes separate from them.

Figure 3.2 Mami Wata shrine figure, Annang Ibibio peoples, Nigeria, 1950s–1960s, wood, pigment, metal, sacrificial materials, 87.6 cm, Michael J. Carlos Museum, Emory University, 1994.3.9. Photograph by Bruce White.

In addition to her primary manifestation, the existence of *mami watas* and *papi watas* must also be acknowledged, a vast and uncountable "school" of indigenous African water spirits with local names and distinctive personalities. These are honored in complex systems of beliefs and practices that may or may not be shared with the water spirit Mami Wata.

An Efik sculpture portraying Mami Wata as a human-fish-goat-priestess handling a bird and a snake demonstrates her hybridity and powers of transformation.[2] She can also easily assume aspects of a Hindu god or goddess without sacrificing her identity.[3] She is a complex multivocal, multifocal symbol with so many resonances that she feeds the imagination, generating, rather than limiting, meanings and significances: nurturing mother; "sexy mama"; provider of riches; healer of physical and spiritual ills; embodiment of dangers and desires, risks and challenges, dreams and aspirations, fears and forebodings. People are attracted to the seemingly limitless possibilities which she represents, and at the same time, they are frightened by her destructive potential. She inspires a vast array of emotions, attitudes, and actions among those who worship her, those who fear her, those who study her, and those who create works of art about her. What the Yoruba peoples say about their culture is also applicable to the histories and significances of Mami Wata: she is like a "river that never rests."

Mami Wata is part of the magical world of mermaids and other fantastic creatures who exhibit terrifying yet seductive powers. This essay explores arts, beliefs, and practices surrounding Mami Wata, and the themes of globalization, capitalism, and the power of traveling images and ideas to shape the lives of people and communities. Further, it explores how human imagination and cross-cultural exchange serve as catalysts in the artistic representation of these marvelous water divinities. It traces various streams of the far-flung, diverse, and complex artistic and devotional traditions for Mami Wata.

Tracing the visual cultures and histories of Mami Wata and other African water divinities is surely a daunting task, and in view of the mutability of water itself, it seems appropriate to approach this inquiry employing what Jan Vansina has termed "a streaming model" of history.[4] Such an approach considers the dynamics of multiple sources: diffusions and dispersals; independent inventions; confluence, divergence, and re-convergence; rapid movement; stagnation; currents, ebbs and flows, whirlpools, and eddies. Water metaphors seem to make sense when we speak of the fluidity and complexities of visual cultures and art histories over time and space. The following offers a broad overview of possible

---

2   See Drewal, *Mami Wata*, p. 26, figure 3: Mami Wata masquerade headdress, Efik peoples, south-eastern Nigeria, 1950s, wood, pigment, animal skin, cloth, raffia, 91.4 cm, private collection.

3   See Drewal, *Mami Wata*, p. 27, figure 4: Agbagli Kossi (b. circa 1945; Lome, Togo; active 1960–1990s),standing figure of Mami Wata, 1970s (?), wood, pigment, 91.4 cm, Ignacio and Caroline Villarreal/Ignacio A. Villarreal Collection.

4   Jan Vansina, *Art History in Africa* (New York: Longman, 1998), pp. 185–95.

visual histories of African water divinities, suggesting sources and currents for Mami Wata.

Sacred Waters: Ancient and Indigenous Arts for African Water Deities

From early evidence of image making on the continent and throughout the millennia, diverse African cultures have stressed the value and power of water not only as a source of sustenance, but also as a focus of spiritual and artistic expression. Many depictions of such spiritual entities assumed the form of hybrid creatures, part-human, part-aquatic. In other words, the cosmological and artistic frameworks were already present in many local contexts to make the introduction of newer water divinities, such as Mami Wata, a natural progression.

The earliest images of African water deities may be paintings on rock dating to more than 28,000 years before the present. They depict various underwater spirit beings that continue to populate the folklore of hunter-gatherers in southern Africa.[5] In some of these paintings, human–animal hybrids known as therianthropes (not unlike the half-human, half-fish mermaids and mermen who appear much later in time) float among various aquatic creatures including fish, snakes, and the mythic "rain bull" of the San peoples. These depictions may be intended to represent the trance journeys of a shaman or healer attempting to find water or bring rain to the parched Kalahari Desert.[6]

A primordial female water spirit sometimes known as Tingoi/Njaloi epitomizes ideal yet unattainable beauty, power, and goodness. She presides over female initiation rites among various peoples in Sierra Leone and Liberia, including Mende, Temne, Bullom, Vai, Gola, Dei, Krim, Kissi, and Bassa.[7] Tingoi/Njaloi

---

5   See Drewal, *Mami Wata*, p. 29, figure 5: rock painting from the Kalahari Desert shows transformed humans floating easily among fish, snakes, and the mythic "rain bull" of San peoples. Photograph by Dr Fred Block.

6   But also see Anne Solomon, who critiques Lewis-Williams and offers another perspective on the issue of "meaning" in San rock art: Anne Solomon, "The Myth of Ritual Origins? Ethnography, Mythology, and Interpretation of San Rock Art," *South African Archaeological Bulletin* 52 (1997), pp. 3–13; Anne Solomon, "Landscape, Form, and Process: Some Implications for San Rock Art Research," *Natal Museum Journal of the Humanities* 9 (1997), pp. 57–73; Anne Solomon, "Ethnography and Method in Southern African Rock Art Research," in C. Chippindale and P.S.C. Taçon (eds), *The Archaeology of Rock Art* (Cambridge: Cambridge University Press, 1998); Anne Solomon, "Meanings, Models, and Minds: A Reply to Lewis-Williams," *South African Archaeological Bulletin* (June 1999), pp. 51–60; and J.D. Lewis-Williams, *Believing and Seeing: Symbolic Meaning in Southern San Rock Paintings* (London: Academic Press, 1981).

7   Frederick Lamp, "Cosmos, Cosmetics, and the Spirit of Bondo," *African Arts* 18 (1985), pp. 28–43, 98–99; Ruth B. Phillips, *Representing Woman: Sande Masquerades of the Mende*

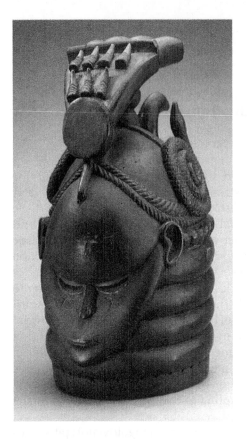

Figure 3.3 Sowei/Nowo headdress, Sherbro-Bullom peoples, Sierra Leone, late nineteenth century, wood, pigment, 41.9 cm, Fowler Museum X65.4778. Gift of the Wellcome Trust.

is often likened to a mermaid, and Muslim Mende peoples speak of her as a female *jina*, or spirit, with the lower body of a fish.[8] It seems likely that this view represents a pre-Islamic tradition of female water spirits who permeate beliefs and merge with Muslim practices in this region, as opposed to male spirits who are generally associated with the forest.[9] Sowei/Nowo initiation headdresses from this region offer deep and complex allusions to Tingoi/Njaloi, as well as to social practices and cosmic forces. They are worn by women elders during the initiations of young girls. A zigzag motif found on the forehead of some of these headdresses may be a glyph for water, and young Sande/ Bondo girls are said to "go under the

---

of Sierra Leone (Los Angeles: UCLA Fowler Museum of Cultural History, 1995), p. 37; and Sylvia A. Boone, *Radiance from the Water: Ideals of Feminine Beauty in Mende Art* (New Haven: Yale University Press, 1986).

8   Phillips, *Representing Woman*, pp. 53–4.

9   Mermaid images may also have entered Africa via Islamic culture. If present traditions of a *jinn* spirit in the form of a mermaid (*nguva*) along the Swahili coast of eastern Africa are old, then African, Arab, and South Asian sailors traversing the Indian Ocean since the seventh or eighth centuries could have brought her (see Eileen Moyer, "Death of the Mermaid and Political Intrigue in the Indian Ocean," in Drewal (ed.), *Sacred Waters*, pp. 451–65. *Jinn* are generally troublesome, but sometimes helpful. Mermaid *jinn* ideas may also have come with the spread of Islam into sub-Saharan Africa beginning in the tenth or eleventh centuries, as part of widespread beliefs and practices associated with healing trance cults such as Bori in Nigeria and Niger and Zar in Sudan. Tigani Eltahir (personal communication, March 30, 2000), who has done extensive research on Zar in Sudan, told me about one category of *jinn* that manifests as "ladies, Egyptian maids, and mermaids." Their color is pink. Another reference to water *jinn* and Mami Wata comes from Timbuktu, Mali. The Hawka, a Muslim brotherhood, honors Harakoy, mother of spirits, vault of the sky, and mistress of water. Harakoy is represented by the 1955 Indian edition of the snake charmer print of Mami Wata (see Viviana Pacques, *L'arbre cosmique* (Paris: Institut d'Ethnologie, Travaux et Mémoires 70, 1964), figure 585).

water" during the first part of their initiation.[10] Among the Temne, as Frederick Lamp notes, "water is the gestating fluid of rebirth, called, in the esoteric language of initiation, *yankoila*, 'Mother Water.'"[11]

A rare and elegant late nineteenth-century Sowei/Nowo headdress from the Sherbro-Bullom peoples of Sierra Leone features the idealized attributes and beauty of a young woman (Figure 3.3). The ringed neck suggests ripples of water, as if the spirit has just emerged from the depths.[12] It may also resemble the chrysalis of a moth or butterfly as a sign of beauty and female transformation.[13] The snakes that appear coiled on either side of the head are among the most frequent motifs depicted on Sowei/Nowo headdresses. Generally considered to be water creatures, snakes reveal a constellation of ideas about ancient African water spirits and, later, Mami Wata. They are the guardians of the medicines of Sande/Bondo, and shrine sculptures often depict a female-headed coiled snake or a female head and neck encircled by a snake.[14] Wall paintings of Tingoi/Njaloi sometimes show her as a serpent-fish with a human head adorned by elegantly arranged and luxuriant hair.[15]

This elaborate coiffure resonates with later descriptions and representations of Mami Wata. Among the Sherbro, rich, full hair is a sign of beauty and health, and women interweave black cotton with their own hair to achieve volume.[16] For the Mende, the thickness and length of hair are emblematic of the productive organic growth and fertility essential to femininity.[17] The flat circular form over the broad forehead in the illustrated headdress may be a mirror or older form of amulet. Mirrors often refer to the surface of water and are attributes of mermaids, as well as of the graduates of Sande/Bondo who, during their "coming out" ceremony, sit in state and gaze meditatively into them.[18]

These are but two of countless comparable examples of arts for water spirits on the African continent. Despite enormous diversity in styles and imagery, such works frequently fuse human and aquatic elements emblematic of the spiritual transformations that are fundamental to many African religions. They visualize a widespread aspect of African religious rituals: altered states of consciousness or trance. These are fundamental and essential. Possession is proof of the embodiment

---

10 Boone, *Radiance from the Water*, pp. 50, 170.
11 Lamp, "Cosmos, Cosmetics, and the Spirit of Bondo," p. 42.
12 Ibid., p. 36.
13 Ibid., p. 32.
14 Phillips, *Representing Woman*, p. 146, figure 7.6.
15 Ibid., p. 54, figure 3.6.
16 Carol P. MacCormack, "Proto-Social to Adult: A Sherbro Transformation," in C.P. MacCormack and M. Strathern (eds), *Nature, Culture, and Gender* (Cambridge: Cambridge University Press, 1980), p. 106.
17 For a discussion of Mami's hair among the Igbo, see Sabine Jell-Bahlsen, "Dada-Dreadlock-Hair: The Hidden Messages of Mammy Water in Southeastern Nigeria," in Drewal (ed.), *Sacred Waters*, pp. 245–57. See also Boone, *Radiance from the Water*, pp. 96–7, 138.
18 Phillips, *Representing Woman*, p. 84, figure 4.12.

of spiritual forces for the benefit of humans. Hybrid or composite animal–human images visualize the transformation that occurs during trance. Feared and revered, desired yet unattainable, these ancient indigenous divinities resonated deeply and prepared the way for the arrival and incorporation of another divine part-human, part-fish creature—the mermaid from overseas.

The Mermaid: Arrival of a European Water Spirit Image in Africa

Mermaids, and to a lesser extent mermen, have populated the human imagination for millennia. Some of the earliest have their origins in the fertile river valleys of Mesopotamia (for example, the merman spirit of River Urat, circa 900 BCE, in the Museum of Ethnology, Berlin-Dahlem), Africa's Nile Valley, and later the Mediterranean world of the Phoenicians, Minoans, Greeks, and Romans. For the Greeks and Romans, mermaids—like the part-bird, part-human sirens—symbolized danger. In medieval Christian Europe, the mermaid entered bestiaries and other arts in the twelfth and thirteenth centuries where she usually appeared in a strongly moralizing context as a symbol of vanity, immorality, seduction, and danger.[19]

By the fifteenth century, when Europeans began to explore beyond Mediterranean waters, they carried with them images of mythic creatures—dragons, griffins, unicorns, centaurs, and especially the mermaid (see Figures 18.1 and 18.2).[20] These images assumed different forms within the visual/material culture of sailors, merchants, and explorers and might appear as book illustrations, prints, playing cards, flags and other heraldic devices, trademarks (like the mermaids and mermen on Dutch clay pipes traded in many parts of Africa since the seventeenth century), watermarks, and perhaps tattoos. Songs, dances, games, and the playing of musical instruments may also have made direct reference to sirens or mermaids. European belief in the existence of such creatures is confirmed by the fact that in January, 1493 Christopher Columbus recorded the sighting of three mermaids off the coast of Haiti, then known as Hispaniola. He wrote that they "came quite high out of the water" but were "not so beautiful as painted, though to some extent they have the form of a human face."[21]

---

19 See Debra Hassig (ed.), *The Mark of the Beast* (New York: Garland, 1999). Also Debra Strickland's chapter in this collection.

20 See Drewal, *Mami Wata*, p. 35, figure 12: saltcellar, Sapi peoples, Sherbro Island, late fifteenth century, ivory, 16 cm, the National Museum of Denmark, Copenhagen. Photograph © The National Museum of Denmark, Ethnographic Collection.

21 Christopher Columbus, *The Journal of Christopher Columbus* [1493], trans. Clements R. Markham (Boston: Adamant Media Corporation, 2001), p. 154 (reprint of the 1893 edition by the Hakluyt Society, London). Also see Braham in this collection for further discussion of this passage.

And what did Africans think and do when they first saw Europeans and their depictions of water spirits or mermaids? According to the accounts of some of the earliest European travelers and to some African oral histories, many Africans associated Europeans with the sea and water spirits, an impression that would have been reinforced by the sight of their large sailing vessels coming into view from below the horizon. One of the earliest European accounts of African ideas about Europeans was written by Alvise da Cadamosto, who voyaged to the western coast of Africa near Cape Verde in the years 1455 and 1456:

> It is asserted that when for the first time they saw sails, that is, ships, on the sea (which neither they nor their forefathers had ever seen before), they believed that they were great sea-birds with white wings, which were flying, and had come from some strange place ... some of them ... thought that the ships were fishes ... Others again said that they were phantoms that went by night ... Thus, as they did not understand the art of navigation, they all thought that the ships were phantoms.[22]

These curious-looking visitors, their possessions, and especially their icons, must have made a profound impression on Africans of the time. João De Barros's fifteenth-century accounts described "Abbyssinians [Africans]" who "bowed down and adored the figurehead of the Portuguese flagship—a wooden statuette of the Angel Gabriel."[23] Written descriptions from the centuries that followed these early African–European encounters tell a similar tale. Thomas Astley, for example, includes an account that occurred during the voyage of the Frenchman Andre Brue to the islands of Bissao and Bissagos in 1700. When a visiting African was questioned as to why he had elaborately sacrificed a rooster aboard the ship carrying Brue, he indicated "that the People of his Country looked on the Whites as the Gods of the Sea; that the mast was a Divinity that made the Ship walk, and the Pump was a Miracle, since it could make Water rise-up, whose natural Property is to descend."[24]

Others have documented similar responses in the nineteenth and twentieth centuries. D. Amaury Talbot cited an origin myth for Kalabari Ijo masked dances in honor of water spirits that links them with Europeans.[25] G.I. Jones noted the Igbo belief that Europeans originated from the water.[26] And the Kongo had their own views about Europeans as water spirits, for they were "white" and came

---

22 Gerald R. Crone, *The Voyages of Cadamosto and Other Documents on Western Africa in the Second Half of the Fifteenth Century* (London: Hakluyt Society, 1937), pp. 20–1.

23 K.G. Jayne, *Vasco da Gama and His Successors* [1910] (New York: Barnes and Noble,1970), p. 47.

24 Thomas Astley, *A New General Collection of Voyages and Travels* [1745], vol. 2 (New York: Barnes and Noble, 1968), pp. 104–5.

25 D. Amaury Talbot, *Woman's Mysteries of a Primitive People: The Ibibio of Southern Nigeria* [] (London: Cassell, 1915; Frank Cass, 1968), p. 309.

26 G.I. Jones, "Mbari Houses," *Nigerian Field* 6 (1937), p. 79.

from the sea, the passage between this world and the next, and they brought "rich gifts unknown in 'this' world."[27] Despite the difficulties encountered in verifying and interpreting early European accounts, which are drenched in prejudice and ignorance about Africa and Africans, the number and persistence of such reports from different parts of Africa and different eras may offer certain insights for assessing the early reception of Europeans and their visual culture.[28]

The ambiguities of these first encounters, when Europeans and Africans shared many views about water spirits and monstrous others, seem to have initially provoked a mixture of curiosity, attraction, revulsion, and wonder. Fears of the unknown balanced a desire to learn and benefit from a new commercial opportunity in a situation that had not yet devolved into the asymmetrical power relationships of aggressors/captors and victims of the nascent slave trade. Wealth and power loomed as potential rewards brought by these strange, white water-beings from overseas who sailed in floating vessel-shrines covered in images of their aquatic protectors—mermaids, mermen, and other fantastic hybrid creatures.

Africanizing the Mermaid: A Sapi Version

At about the same time that Christopher Columbus was seeing mermaids in the Atlantic, an African sculptor, a member of the Sapi peoples living on Sherbro Island off the coast of Sierra Leone, was carving the image of one on an ivory saltcellar, commissioned by a visiting Portuguese explorer or merchant. As his model, the artist used an image supplied to him by his Portuguese client.[29] Though the mermaid was copied from a European model, the Sapi sculptor immediately "Africanized" her for she is flanked by two crocodiles, ancient African symbols for water spirits and a central image associated with water spirits among the descendants of the Sapi, the Bullom, and the Temne.[30] As their familiarity with European mermaid

27   Anne Hilton, *The Kingdom of Kongo* (Oxford: Clarendon, 1985), p. 50.
28   For a detailed and insightful discussion of African (Sapi, Benin, Kongo), perceptions and representations of Europeans in the era of first contact, see Suzanne Preston Blier, "Imaging Otherness in Ivory: African Portrayals of the Portuguese ca. 1492," *Art Bulletin* 75 (1993), pp. 375–96.
29   See note 20 above. A second Sapi ivory saltcellar from Newcastle-on-Tyne on loan to the British Museum depicts "semi-nude female figs with fish tails." In Douglas Fraser, "The Fish-Legged Figure in Benin and Yoruba Art," in Douglas Fraser and Herbert M. Cole (eds), *African Art and Leadership* (Madison: University of Wisconsin Press, 1972), pp. 275–6.
30   Crocodiles are prominent in stories of Sowo women among the Temne, Bullom, and Baga: "A Bundu woman plays tricks with crocodiles. A strong and fearsome swimmer, she dives amidst the reptiles and stirs them from sleep, calling to them as she flirts the water into their eyes, making them follow her as she swims rapidly away." (See Lamp, "Cosmos, Cosmetics, and the Spirit of Bondo," p. 34, citing nineteenth- and early twentieth-century sources, Butt-Thompson and Blyden). The first Europeans to

lore increased, Africans interpreted, adapted, and transformed the image of a European mermaid (and, later, other images) into a representation of an African deity—Mami Wata—and developed elaborate systems of belief and sacred visual and performance arts in the process.

Although the wellspring of the visual culture and history of Mami Wata will always remain conjectural,[31] I would suggest that much textual and visual evidence indicates that the concept of Mami Wata, if not her name,[32] originated long before the massive dispersal of Africans to the Americas (from the sixteenth to nineteenth centuries) and the colonial era (1900–1957). The antiquity and prevalence of indigenous African beliefs in water deities, widely imaged as hybrid human–aquatic creatures,[33] served as a basis to understand and translate European mermaid myths and images into African ones from the first momentous Euro-African contacts in the fifteenth century.

---

arrive in Africa were the Portuguese, who in 1462 made contact with the Sapi people on Sherbro Island off the coast of present-day Sierra Leone. Establishing trading, they commissioned the sophisticated stone and ivory Sapi sculptors to create saltcellars, pyxes (Christian liturgical vessels), spoons, fork and knife handles, and oliphants (hunting horns) based on European models, probably consisting of prints, drawings, or book illustrations (Ezio Bassani and William B. Fagg, *Africa and the Renaissance: Art in Ivory* [New York: The Center for African Art and Prestel, 1988], p. 111).

31 One Mami Wata priestess believes her ancient origins are in Mesopotamia and Egypt as written in Mamaissii Vivian Hunter-Hindrew (Mama Zogbé, Hounon-Amengansie), *Mami Wata: Africa's Ancient God/dess Unveiled*, 2 volumes (Augusta, GA: Mami Wata Healing Society, 2004); in Barbara Paxon, "Mammy Water: New World Origins?" *Baessler-Archiv* 31 (1983), pp. 407–46, she suggested an origin among Africans in the New World and a return to Africa. Several scholars theorize that Mami Wata is a colonial-era invention (Jeremy Coote and Jill Salmons, "Mermaids and Mami Wata on Brassware from Old Calabar," in Drewal (ed.), *Sacred Waters*.

32 Historical evidence of a pidgin Dutch name for Mami Wata in the African Atlantic world comes from Surinam in the eighteenth century (1775) with discussions of Watra Mama dances feared by whites, something that may have been introduced by Papa/Popo Africans (Ewe-Mina, coast of Republic of Benin) who came in large numbers between circa 1675 and 1775. See Alex van Stipriaan, "The Ever-Changing Face of Watramama in Suriname: A Water Goddess in Creolization since the Seventeenth Century," in Drewal (ed.), *Sacred Waters*, pp. 525–47.

33 One African aquatic creature, the manatee—a mammal that suckles its young—may have also fostered ideas about mermaids and wealth from the sea. See Jean M. Borgatti, "Tale of the Achikobo: It Is the Tail That Is Mine," in Drewal (ed.), *Sacred Waters*, pp. 105–13, for a discussion of *achikobo* among the Okpella, although the name (*achi*=horse, *kobo*=coin money/penny) suggests the colonial era. Bohumil Holas, *Mission dans l'est libérien* (Dakar: IFAN, 1952), pp. 426–7, notes another widely dispersed tradition that seems to bridge ancient indigenous aquatic spirits possibly derived from manatee lore with Mami Wata. He discusses and illustrates wall paintings depicting "Mami Ouata" (a variant of Liberian pidgin English). She is shown with her hair parted in the middle, a fish body and tail, two human legs, and high-heeled shoes on her feet. Holas says that Mami Ouata is widely dispersed all along the coast among the Putu and Tchien peoples (Liberia), as well as the Dida, Ebrie, Avikam, and Godie peoples in Côte d'Ivoire.

Given their ideas about Europeans, Africans could have quite easily come to regard European icons, such as the figureheads on ships and other marine sculptures, as representations of water spirits.[34] Several works have been documented in African water spirit shrines in widely dispersed locales across the continent that support this supposition. Among the Bidjogo on the West African coast, a Baroque-style (1550–1750) figurehead dominated a shrine on Formosa Island.[35] A figurehead from a ship wrecked off the coast of southern Africa in the 1870s was allegedly acquired by Africans and incorporated into a shrine in honor of local sea divinities.[36] Another, a Janus marine sculpture, formerly in the Daniel Brooks Gallery, New York, was allegedly collected in south-eastern Nigeria before 1975. Most likely it came from a trading vessel plying the West African coast. Red pigmentation around the eyes, often used on people and on sculptures in eastern Nigeria, suggests that it may have been used in a ritual context.[37]

Mami Wata and the Image of the Snake Charmer

Half-human, half-serpent images for water spirits, widespread throughout Africa—like the half-human, half-fish creatures discussed above—set the stage for the arrival and incorporation of a very particular European image of an "Oriental other" that resonated deeply within African water spirit arts: the snake charmer. The West has had a long and enduring fascination with the "exotic."[38] By the second

---

34   Saints' statues carried aboard ships found their way into African shrines by the seventeenth century (Timothy Garrard, "Figurine Cults of the Southern Akan," in Christopher Roy (ed.), *Iowa Studies in African Art* [Iowa City: The School of Art and Art History, University of Iowa, 1984], pp. 167–90.

35   Hugo Adolf Bernatzik, *Im Reich der Bidyogo: Geheimnisvolle Inseln in Westafrika* (Leipzig: Koehler and Voigtländer, 1944), plate 177.

36   P. Pinckney, *American Figureheads and Their Carvers* (New York: W.W. Norton, 1940), pp. 27, 130.

37   G.I. Jones, *The Art of Eastern Nigeria* (Cambridge: Cambridge University Press, 1984), p. 33.

38   By the end of the eighteenth century and with the development of romanticism, exoticism became a theme of growing importance in the arts and in culture. Romanticism, with its focus centered on "any time but now, and any place but here" (cf. William Fleming, *Arts and Ideas* (New York: Holt, Rinehart and Winston, 1980), p. 376), sought its inspiration in the past, in nature, and in the exotic. The exotic included almost everywhere beyond a narrowly defined Western Europe. Orientalism meant not only the distant lands of Asia, but the Mediterranean (North Africa and the Near East) and Eastern Europe (Russia) as well. This was also a time when trade goods from around the world were entering European markets and missionaries set out to spread the Christian doctrine. The arts reflected this new fascination and tapped the growing popular interest in the "other." Jean-Georges Noverre choreographed *Les fêtes Chinoises* (1749) in Paris. As early as 1759, Arthur Murphy presented a play called *The Orphan of China*, Gluck wrote the opera *Pilgrims to Mecca* (1764), and Mozart's music was set in a

half of the nineteenth century, this interest had spread beyond the European upper and middle classes to a much wider audience. During the Victorian era, with its rigid social norms, people turned to the exotic to provide a "temporary *frisson*, a circumscribed experience of the bizarre."[39] Institutions such as botanical and zoological gardens, ethnographic museums, and especially circuses provided vehicles for such escape.

While illustrated accounts of adventures abroad proliferated in books, magazines, and newspapers, the exotic became tangible as a growing number of African, Asian, and Indian sailors appeared in the port of Hamburg and other European maritime centers.[40] Carl G.C. Hagenbeck worked as a fish merchant in St Pauli, a port area and popular "entertainment" center for sailors and others. In 1848, a fisherman who worked the Arctic waters brought some sea lions to Hagenbeck, which he in turn exhibited as a zoological "attraction." The immediate success of this venture led to a rapidly enlarged menagerie of exotic animals from Greenland, Africa, and Asia.[41]

Sensing the public's enormous appetite for the bizarre, Hagenbeck decided to expand his imports to include another curiosity—exotic people. The first of these arrived in 1875, a family of Laplanders, who had accompanied a shipment of reindeer. This was the modest beginning of a new concept in popular entertainment known as the Volkerschauen, or "People Shows."[42] In order to advertise his new attractions, Hagenbeck turned to Adolph Friedlander, a leading printer who quickly began to produce a large corpus of inexpensive color posters for Hagenbeck. Hagenbeck's most extravagant spectacle was doubtless his "International Circus and Ceylonese Caravan," 70 artists, craftspeople, jugglers, magicians, and musicians, together with many wild animals. The caravan was witnessed by over a million people within a six-week period.[43]

Hagenbeck hired a famous hunter named Breitwieser to travel to south-east Asia and the Pacific to collect rare snakes, insects, and butterflies. In addition to these,

---

Turkish harem in 1785 (Fleming, *Arts and Ideas*, pp. 379–80). Kew Gardens in London had rococo pavilions, Greek temples, Gothic chapels, a Muslim mosque, a Moorish palace, and a house of Confucius (Fleming, *Arts and Ideas*, p. 380). At Brighton between 1815 and 1821, John Nash built an "Arabian Nights extravaganza" for the Prince Regent in a style called "Indian Gothic," a cluster of minarets, cupolas, pinnacles, and pagodas with an interior filled with oriental lacquerware, Chinese Chippendale, and painted dragons (Fleming, *Arts and Ideas*, p. 381). See also essays by Mitter, Davies, and Van Duzer in this collection.

39 James Clifford, "On Ethnographic Surrealism," *Comparative Studies in Society and History* 23 (1981), p. 542.

40 Urs Bitterli, *Die "Wilden" und die "Zivilisierten"* [1976] (Munich: Beck. Benninghof-Luhl, 1984); and H.C. Debrunner, *Presence and Prestige: Africans in Europe* (Basel: Basler Afrika Bibliographien, 1979).

41 Guenter H.W. Niemeyer, *Hagenbeck* (Hamburg: H. Christians, 1972), p. 247.

42 Sibylle Benninghof-Luhl, "Die Ausstellung der Kolonialsierten: Volkershauen von 1874–1932," in *Andenken an den Kolonialismus* (Tubingen: Attempto, 1984).

43 Niemeyer, *Hagenbeck*, p. 251.

Breitwieser brought back a wife who, under the stage name "Maladamatjaute," began to perform as a snake charmer in Hagenbeck's production.[44] A chromolithograph poster made for Hagenbeck by Friedlander's company in the 1880s featured her.[45] A Hamburg studio photograph, taken in about 1887, shows Maladamatjaute attired for her performance.[46] The style and cut of her bodice, the stripes made of buttons, the coins about her waist, the armlets, the position of the snake around her neck and a second one nearby, the non-functional bifurcated flute held in her hand, and her facial features and coiffure, all duplicate those seen in a snake charmer chromolithograph from the Friedlander lithographic company, the original of which has not yet been found. What we do have, however, is a reprint (Figure 3.4)[47] made in 1955 in Mumbai (Bombay), India, by the Shree Ram Calendar Company from an original sent to them by two (Indian?) merchants in Kumase, Ghana. In a letter to me dated June 17, 1977, the manager of the Calendar Company stated that the print had been copied "without changing a line even from the original."

There can be little doubt, therefore, that Maladamatjaute was the model for the image. Her light brown skin placed her beyond Europe, while the boldness

---

44 It seems that Breitwieser did much of his "hunting" in south-east Asia and the Pacific, and it seems likely that Maladamatjaute came from that part of the world, possibly from Samoa or Borneo. Soon after she arrived in Hamburg with Breitwieser, in about 1880, she began to perform as a snake charmer in one of Hagenbeck's shows (Wilhelm Zimmermann, personal communication, 1984). Within a short time she had become an international attraction, performing in the United States in about 1885. A P.T. Barnum circus newspaper/courier shows her in a small fenced area surrounded by many snakes and holding aloft two large snakes above her head, while another wraps around her body. Her full head of hair flares outward, parted in the middle, and her name has changed to "Nala Damajanti—the Empress of the Reptile World—the Greatest and Most Astounding snake charmer of Hindoostan—the bravest of the brave—Python sorceress of mighty power." She wears a tight bodice, armlets, necklace, and hoop earrings. This was published in Philadelphia in 1885 in a newspaper-like format as an advertisement for the circus. Maladamatjaute also inspired others to become snake charmers, according to an article in *The World* (March/April 1888, courtesy of the John and Mable Ringling Museum of Art). As her fame grew, she continued to perform internationally in Europe and the United States under slightly different stage names. What remains constant, however, are the representations of her thick, full head of black wavy hair parted in the middle, and elements of her "Hindoo/Oriental" dress—jewelry, necklace, tight bodice, and hoop earrings.

45 Ruth Malhotra, *Manege Frei! Artisten-und Circusplakate von Adolf Friedlander* (Dortmund: Harenberg Kommunikation, 1979), p. 99.

46 See Drewal, *Mami Wata*, p. 50, figure 30: studio photograph of Maladamatjaute attired for her performance, Hamburg, Germany, circa 1887.

47 My thanks to Ruth Malhotra for much information on the Friedlander posters and permission to illustrate one of the posters. She noted that some of the early examples in the 1880s were numbered—perhaps the "#4" at the bottom of the 1955 Bombay edition was copied from the original. The style of the work is very similar to that of Christian Bettels, the chief lithographer and one of the few artists working for Friedlander who signed his work (Ruth Malhotra, personal communication, 1980).

Figure 3.4   Adolph Friedlander Company (possibly Christian Bettels), *Der Schlangenbandiger* (*The Snake Charmer*), originally commissioned 1880s, reprinted 1955, chromolithograph (reprinted from the original by the Shree Ram Calendar Company, Bombay, India), 35.6 cm. Henry John Drewal and Sarah K. Khan Collection.

of her gaze and the strangeness of her occupation epitomized for Europeans her "otherness" and the mystery and wonder of the "Orient." As Maladamatjaute's fame as a snake charmer spread, her image began to appear in circus flyers and show posters for the Folies Bergère in Paris (see, for example, Musée des Arts Décoratifs, Paris, no. 480), as well as in the United States. Soon after, and probably unknown to Maladamatjaute, her image spread to Africa—but for very different reasons and imbued with very new meanings.

The Snake Charmer as Mami Wata in Africa

Not long after its publication in Europe, the snake charmer chromolithograph reached West Africa, probably carried by African sailors who had seen it in Hamburg. European merchants stationed in Africa, whether Germans or others, may have also brought Maladamatjaute's seductive image to decorate their work or domestic spaces.[48]

For African viewers, the snake charmer's light brown skin and long black wavy hair suggested that she came from beyond Africa, and the print had a dramatic and almost immediate impact. By 1901, about 15 years after its appearance in Hamburg, the snake charmer image had already been interpreted as an African water spirit, translated into a three-dimensional carved image, and incorporated into a Niger River Delta water spirit headdress that was photographed by J.A. Green in the Delta town of Bonny (Figure 3.5).[49] The headdress clearly shows the inspiration of the Hamburg print. Note especially the long, black hair parted in the middle, the garment's neckline, the earrings, the position of the figure's arms and the snakes, and

---

48 A nineteenth-century photograph of the Kauffman Traders shop in Caracas, Venezuela, circa 1894, shows two men surrounded by walls covered in framed paintings, photographs, and prints of a variety of subjects, but mostly women in sedate "pinups" (Museum für Hamburgische Geschichte Bildarchiv). The same could have occurred in Africa. Two major Hamburg companies (Woermann and Brigg) were doing business in Liberia, Dahomey (present-day Benin), and Lagos by the mid-nineteenth century. See also Martha G. Anderson and Philip M. Peek (eds), *Ways of the Rivers: Arts and Environment of the Niger Delta* (Los Angeles: UCLA Fowler Museum of Cultural History, 2002), p. 62, figures A3 and A4, for nineteenth-century views of a trader's quarters in New Calabar and a warehouse in the Niger Delta—with many pictures, prints, and photographs on the walls.

49 I found this image buried in a folder of random photographs in the archive, along with others by Green, a Bonny photographer who documented many aspects of life in the Delta, including the presence of Europeans. Many of his photographs are in the Unilever PLC archives. Martha G. Anderson, Lisa Aronson, Christraud M. Geary, and E.J. Alagoa are presently conducting research on J.A. Green with the support of a Getty Collaborative Research Grant. The project includes archival research in the United States and Great Britain, as well as fieldwork in Nigeria. They plan to organize an exhibition of the late photographer's work.

Figure 3.5   Photograph of a water spirit headdress, J.A. Green, Niger River Delta
town of Bonny, by 1901. Photograph courtesy of the Nigerian National
Museum, neg. no. 106.94.17.

the low-relief rendering of the inset with a kneeling flute player surrounded by four
snakes. The image of Maladamatjaute, the "Hindoo" snake charmer of European
and American renown, had begun a new life as the primary icon for Mami Wata, an
African water divinity with overseas connections, joining and sometimes replacing
her manifestation as a mermaid.

The style and iconography of the print help to explain its rapid, widespread
acceptance. Its naturalism contributed to its being understood by Africans as a
"photograph" of a foreign spirit. As one Igbo priestess told me, "someone must
have gone under the water to snap it."[50] As a product of Western technology, this
"photograph" was an instance of the medium reinforcing the message. The snake,
an important and widespread African symbol of sacred water and the rainbow
(especially along the Ghana/Togo/Benin/Nigeria coast), was a most appropriate
subject to be shown surrounding, protecting, and being controlled by Mami Wata.
The position of one snake arching over the head of Mami Wata reinforced its link

50   M. Opara (Owerri-Igbo priestess, Lagos), personal communication (October 4, 1975).

with the rainbow, as is seen in several Mami Wata shrine murals along the West African coast.

Other elements in the print linked it with myths concerning images of mermaids. The snake charmer shared the complexion, facial features, long, flowing hair, and breathtaking appearance of mermaids. Without exception African respondents have stressed the extraordinary beauty and power of her bold, intense gaze and composure. One Yoruba man, recalling the first time he saw the Mami Wata chromolithograph during his youth in Lagos, around 1921, admitted that he nearly "peed in his pants" when he beheld the striking beauty with her long flowing hair and her snakes.

As Africans usually depict complete figures in their arts, the rendering of Mami Wata as a half-figure in the chromolithograph was taken to be significant by African viewers. In discussing this aspect of the print, devotees pointed out that the unseen lower portion of the snake charmer indicated that Mami Wata was "hiding her secret," that is, her fish tail. The ambiguous rendering of the cloth below the waist, which is reminiscent of scales, probably reinforced this idea. The overall blue-green background and the absence of contextual images such as buildings or a landscape (except for the rocks in the inset with the flute player) contribute to the impression of an underwater scene. These features seem to have inspired the shrine environments of some Mami Wata devotees.[51]

In the nearly 112 years since the arrival of the snake charmer print in Africa (and especially after 12,000 copies were printed in Bombay, India, in 1955 and sent to traders in Kumase, Ghana),[52] the image has traveled widely, first in West and subsequently in Central Africa. In the 1960s, the snake charmer print was also reproduced in London (and other locales as well), with stronger color contrasts and a darker-complexioned Mami. Artists in many different places, inspired by the image, have created an imaginative array of forms celebrating Mami Wata. Various copies of copies continue to circulate widely in sub-Saharan Africa where, as of 2005, the influence of the print can be discerned in at least 50 cultures in 20 countries, from Senegal to Cameroon and beyond.

Mami Wata and Hindu Gods and Goddesses

Between the fifteenth and nineteenth centuries, the vast majority of visitors from overseas that Africans encountered were European or American. By the early

---

51 Drewal, *Mami Wata*, chapters 3 and 5.
52 In 1955, the print was sent from Kumase, Ghana, to Bombay, India, to be copied by the Shree Ram Calendar Company. When the 12,000 copies made reached the Indian traders who had ordered them in Kumase in about 1956, they were distributed and sold widely. This very successful business venture aroused the curiosity of African picture merchants, as well as devotees (of Mami Wata and other divinities) concerning these Indian entrepreneurs and their vast array of cheap, colorful images of gods and goddesses.

twentieth century, however, as Europeans established a colonial presence in Africa, other peoples from European-influenced areas, such as Lebanon and the British colony of India, began to arrive. They came as traders and, like the Europeans before them, were associated by Africans with wealth from overseas. In the 1930s and 1940s (possibly inspired in part by Mahatma Gandhi's successful campaign for India's independence), Indian material culture in the form of images in books, pamphlets, films, and popular devotional chromolithographs,[53] as well as the votive practices of Indian traders in Africa, came to have a profound impact on Mami Wata worshippers, their icons, and ritual actions.[54]

Another new episode in the development of the visual culture of Mami Wata began in the 1940s–1950s. The popularity of the snake charmer lithograph and the presence of Indian merchants (and films) in West Africa led to a growing fascination with Indian prints of Hindu gods and goddesses. In various places, especially along the Ghana–Nigeria coast, people began to interpret these deities as representations of a host of *mami* and *papi wata* spirits associated with specific bodies and levels of water. Using these prints as guides for making icons in wood, clay, and other media, performing rituals, and preparing altars known as "Mami Wata tables," devotees expanded the pantheon of water spirits, fostering an ever-growing complexity in Mami Wata worship, which includes elements of Christianity, Hinduism, Buddhism, Western astrology, European spiritualist and occult beliefs and practices, and so forth.[55] The openness of such belief systems offers "eternal potential."[56] As Dana Rush notes, the Hindu chromolithographs that have flooded *vodunland* (that is, Ghana, Togo, and Benin) possess both external and internal mobility. They are easily reproduced and transported, and they

---

53   James H. Bae, *In a World of Gods and Goddesses: The Mystic Art of Indra Sharma* (Novato, CA: Mandala Publishing, 2003).

54   Indra Sharma was one of the major artists of Indian calendar art depicting Hindu gods and goddesses. He began to paint in 1942 and launched his professional career in 1951–52. From 1946 to 1960 he lived in the poor Borivili district of Bombay before moving to Peddar Road. In the early years he struggled to make a living with portraits of wealthy Gujarati businessmen and cinema posters (paid on the basis of one rupee per foot). Then the S.S. Brijwasi and Sons Company hired him to paint calendar pictures of Hindu gods and goddesses (probably in the 1950s). He also worked for Daburs company in Bombay and Graphite Private Ltd in Calcutta, and continued to produce calendar art from 1975 to 1995, completing about 35 to 40 paintings a year (Bae, *In a World of Gods and Goddesses*, pp. 23–4). It is the millions of cheaply produced copies of his paintings and those of other artists before him (see Dana Rush, "The 'Convulsive Beauty' of Mami Wata," MA thesis, University of Iowa, 1992, p. 63) that have crossed oceans to enter the minds and hearts, and shape the devotions, of Mami Wata's followers.

55   Henry John Drewal, "Interpretation, Invention, and Re-Presentation in the Worship of Mami Wata," *Journal of Folklore Research* 25 (1988), pp. 101–39; Drewal, "Mermaids, Mirrors, and Snake Charmers: Igbo Mami Wata Shrines," *African Arts* 21 (1988), pp. 38–45, 96; Drewal, "Performing the Other: Mami Wata Worship in West Africa," *The Drama Review* T118 (1988), pp. 160–85; Drewal (ed.), *Sacred Waters*.

56   Rush, "The 'Convulsive Beauty' of Mami Wata"; Dana Rush, "Eternal Potential: Chromolithographs in Vodunland," *African Arts* 32 (1999), p. 61.

are "inwardly mobile" since their "inherent forms and meanings do not remain stationary."[57] They continually move, change, shift, and multiply.

Take, for example, the chromolithographic image of the triple-headed, multi-armed Hindu deity Dattatreya.[58] For Ewe Mami Wata worshippers, it represents Densu, a *papi wata* spirit associated with a river in Ghana. He is called the "triple gift giver" and is a source of enormous wealth, as explained by the artist of the mural in the shrine of renowned Mami Wata priestess Affi Yeye in Benin. In the shrine of Igbo healer and Mami Wata priest Dido in Nigeria, the spirit has a different name but still serves to give valuables with its many hands.

As a Yoruba Mami Wata devotee who sells popular Hindu prints in Togo has explained:

> [F]ormerly, during the colonial period, we had the pictures [Hindu images], but we didn't know their meaning. People just liked them to put in their rooms. But then Africans started to study them too—about what is the meaning of these pictures that they are putting lights, candles, and incense there every time. I think they are using the power to collect our money away, or how? So we started to befriend the Indians to know their secret about the pictures. From there the Africans also tried to join some of their societies in India and all over the world to know much about the pictures. Reading some of their books, I could understand what they mean.[59]

His account illustrates how meanings are constructed, as well as how Mami Wata ritual practices evolve and spread so dramatically. The print seller uses books on Buddhism, Hinduism, and occultism as references for his synthesis of foreign and indigenous divinities and the paraphernalia necessary for their worship. When African clients express an interest in the deities illustrated in particular prints, the print seller provides the English, Hindu, and African names of the gods and goddesses and explains their powers, attributes, and the materials required for their worship. Each spirit, he explains, has its own incense or perfume because Mami Wata likes pleasant scents, and the fragrances "drive away evil spirits." He adds that Mami Wata abhors filth and loves beautiful things. Therefore, her shrine must be spotless, well arranged, and covered in white cloth or clean sand. The remaining requirements include flowers, "sweet" foods (such as candy, bananas, oranges, and eggs), candles, either a bound notebook or sheets of paper, money,

---

57   Ibid., p. 62.

58   See Drewal, *Mami Wata*, figure 41: print of the Hindu deity Dattatreya, before 1975, chromolithograph, 20.3 x 15.2 cm, private collection.

59   [Ogunbiyi, personal communication, 1975]. The importance of books and writing in Mami Wata beliefs and practices seems to have been inspired by writing associated with overseas strangers and the presence of books in some Hindu chromolithographs, especially those for Lakshmi (see Drewal, "Mermaids, Mirrors, and Snake Charmers," p. 45, figure 13; and Drewal, "Interpretation, Invention, and Re-Presentation in the Worship of Mami Wata,' pp. 122–3, figures 11, 12).

perfume, and talcum powder, as well as sweet music to soothe Mami Wata's heart.[60] All these ritual elements resonate with the devotions of Hindu merchants, studied by African devotees of Mami Wata for the purpose of obtaining the same good fortune as those successful merchants from overseas.

Mami Wata Maligned as a Monster[61]

Since the late 1970s, however, Mami Wata's engagement with modernity, morality, Christianity, and Islam has led to dramatic transformations in the ways she is depicted and understood. For some, her dangerous and seductive attributes align her with the forces of Satan. Mami Wata has thus become a primary target of a widespread and growing religious movement led by evangelical (Pentecostal) Christians and fundamentalist Muslims who seek to denigrate and demonize indigenous African faiths.[62] For these groups, Mami Wata has come to personify immorality, sin, and damnation. She is considered one of the most powerful presences of Satan, one whose work is to seduce women and men away from the "path of righteousness."[63] In their eyes, she epitomizes the monster—a terrifying and evil entity who engages in shocking, immoral behavior.

Two newspaper articles from Zaire demonstrate the view of Mami Wata as "evil seductress."[64] The first tells the story of five market women who are believed to be *mami watas*. When people buy foodstuffs from these women and prepare them, they have no taste and their quantity rapidly diminishes. The women are described

---

60   Henry John Drewal, with Charles Gore and Michelle Kisliuk, "Siren Serenades: Music for Mami Wata and Other Water Spirits in Africa," in Linda Phyllis Austern and Inna Naroditskaya (eds), *Music of the Sirens* (Bloomington: Indiana University Press, 2006), pp. 294–316.

61   This section title alludes to Partha Mitter's groundbreaking study, *Much Maligned Monsters: A History of European Reaction to Indian Art* (Oxford: Clarendon Press, 1977). See also Mitter's essay in this collection.

62   See Charles Gore, "Mami Wata: An Urban Presence or the Making of a Tradition in Benin City, Nigeria," in Drewal (ed.), *Sacred Waters*; and Joseph Nevadomsky, "Mami Wata, Inc," in Drewal (ed.), *Sacred Waters*, pp. 351–9, for more contemporary disputes and negotiations between Mami Wata followers and Pentecostal Christians in Benin City, Nigeria.

63   See several essays on this topic in Drewal (ed.), *Sacred Waters*, including Meyer, Gore, Elleh, Hackett, Kisliuk, and Moyer; see also Michelle Gilbert, "Shocking Images: Ghanaian Painted Posters," in *Ghana Yesterday and Today* (Paris: Musée Dapper, 2003), pp. 353–79, and n. 17, who cites a similar situation in Cameroon, the Democratic Republic of the Congo, and Sierra Leone in the works of Peter Geschiere, *The Modernity of Witchcraft: Politics and the Occult in Postcolonial Africa* (Charlottesville, VA: University of Virginia Press, 1997); and Rosalind Shaw, *Memories of the Slave Trade: Ritual and the Historical Imagination in Sierra Leone* (Chicago: University of Chicago Press, 2002).

64   My thanks to Zoe Strother for sending me these newspaper articles.

Figure 3.6   Kwame Akoto, aka Almighty God (Kumase, Ghana, b. 1950), *Do Not Go to Maame Water*, 2001(?), board, oil paint, 61 x 81.3 cm, Fowler Museum, x2007.2.1. Gift of Doran H. Ross.

as "brown" in color with "a beauty like the Virgin Mary." All day they remain seated on containers that are reputed to hold "fetishes." Their lower bodies are covered with cloths in order to hide their fish tails. The women are said to live with *bisimbi*, male spirits who dwell under the water. The leader of these market women is claimed to be ruled by Satan.[65] The second story praises the musician Mayaula-Mayoni for composing a song entitled "Mamie-Wata" that criticizes prostitution by women (*mami watas*) who "excel in the commerce of charm" and use their "bodies instead of their intelligence" to make money for their boyfriends/pimps.[66]

The artist Kwame Akoto, who took the name "Almighty God" after his conversion to Pentecostalism, exemplified the movement to demonize Mami Wata. Akoto, who operates one of the most prolific painting workshops in Kumase, Ghana, founded his business in the 1970s and approximately 15 master painters working in Ghana today have apprenticed under him at one time or another. Over the years Akoto complained about being bothered by Mami Wata (and seductive women in general), the forest spirit Tata Buta, and Saint Anthony.[67] In 1991, Akoto underwent a religious conversion when he met his future wife, Faustina, who persuaded him to enter the Living Faith Centre Pentecostal Church. At that time he began to create moralizing pictures based upon his new faith and expressing his

---

65   Anonymous article, *Forum des As*, April 22–23, 1995, no page number.
66   Anonymous article, *Le Compatriote*, no. 231, July 15, 1995, no page number.
67   See Drewal, *Mami Wata*, p. 49, figure 66, Kwame Akoto, aka Almighty God (Kumase, Ghana, b. 1950), *Self Portrait with the Artist's Tormentors*, 1997, wood, paint, 92 cm, Fowler Museum X97.10.5; museum purchase.

Figure 3.7   Daniel Laryea, aka Sowwy (b. 1966, Accra, Ghana), *Splash*, circa 1995, paint on canvas, Ernie Wolfe Gallery, Los Angeles.

opposition to smoking, drinking, and prostitution.[68] His painting entitled *Do Not Go to Maame Water* (Figure 3.6) is an autobiographical work depicting his religious torment. It shows the seductive mermaid crossed out.

Ghana has also become the site of a burgeoning local film and video industry that often reflects the dramatic rise of Pentecostal Christianity and its obsession with witchcraft and Satanic forces. In this context Mami Wata is recast as a "Christian demon in league with the Devil."[69] The advertisements for such films are often large-scale, hand-painted posters executed by the vast army of sign painters (including Kwame Akoto) throughout the country. Such graphic artists used to create larger murals for Mami Wata shrines and for other indigenous faiths, but as the devotions to Mami Wata and other ancestral deities have come under attack, these commissions have greatly diminished. Now they create movie posters, such as one inspired by the Hollywood film *Splash* (Figure 3.7). The somewhat muscular and aggressive appearance of the mermaid may have been calculated to evoke fear of Mami Wata, who is described by Pentecostals as a "fallen angel" driven out of heaven with Satan.[70] Birgit Meyer, a scholar who has done extensive work on contemporary Ghanaian religions and Mami, argues that "Mami Water is an image that condenses the eroticism of forbidden, yet compelling pleasures and speaks to urbanites' ambivalent views about modern life ... [This image shows] how in Christian imagination, Mami Water appears to be virtually uncontrollable."[71] Painted as a dangerous, destructive, and immoral force, Mami Wata has become the focus of attacks on the dangers of terrible "marine spirits" who must be avoided and conquered at all costs.

Conclusion

The outline of the visual histories and cultures of Mami Wata and of the multitude of *mami* and *papi watas* that has been sketched above reveals the fluidity and dynamic creativity of arts, beliefs, and practices celebrating water spirits in Africa. These encompass local images celebrating ancient and indigenous water spirits, global examples that capture the transcultural nature of Mami Wata, and contemporary ideological and theological controversies concerning good and evil. This historical overview is complemented in several detailed case studies in the catalog that accompanied a traveling exhibition on Mami Wata and related divinities, and more extensively in an edited volume.[72] The analyses of scholars and devotees in these

---

68 Doran H. Ross, "Artists Advertising Themselves: Contemporary Studio Facades in Ghana," *African Arts* 37 (2004), p. 74.

69 Birgit Meyer, "Mami Water as a Christian Demon: The Eroticism of Forbidden Pleasures in Southern Ghana," in Drewal (ed.), *Sacred Waters*, pp. 383–98, at 387.

70 Ibid., p. 385.

71 Ibid., p. 385.

72 Drewal, *Mami Wata*; and Drewal (ed.), *Sacred Waters*.

two volumes demonstrate how, why, and where specific persons and communities have created images and ideas of Mami Wata in their own individual and collective ways for their own purposes. Both macro and micro perspectives help us comprehend the extraordinary diversity and complexity of the circumstances that shape the artistic, religious, and cultural practices of those who deal with Mami Wata, whether as nurturing protector or evil seducer, as mother or monster.

Rejecting and Embracing
the Monstrous in Ancient Greece
and Rome

D. Felton

Introduction

The Greeks adapted many of their monsters from the Near East, but it was in ancient Greek culture that monsters reached an apogee of sorts, with both pictorial and literary depictions of monsters flourishing to a degree not seen before.[1] For the Greeks, monsters embodied a variety of fears: the potential of chaos to overcome order, of irrationality to prevail over reason; the potential victory of nature against the encroaching civilizations of mankind; the little-understood nature of the female in contrast to the male. The Greek myths repeatedly present monsters being conquered by gods and men; the forces of order, reason, civilization, and patriarchy inevitably prevail in Greek thought.

That is to say, to a large extent monsters are culturally determined. Each culture has its own preoccupations and fears, its own definitions of "normal," its own manner of looking at reality.[2] As Catherine Atherton observes, monsters "get defined in relation to communities and to their standards of what is good, acceptable, normal, or natural … . In different times, places, and cultures, or from different viewpoints within a single culture, different answers will emerge."[3] Monsters often arise from the desire to domesticate and thus disempower what a

---

1   See David D. Gilmore, *Monsters: Evil Beings, Mythical Beasts, and All Manner of Imaginary Terrors* (Philadelphia: University of Pennsylvania Press, 2003), p. 37; also Jan Bremmer, "Monsters en fabeldieren in de Griekse cultuur," *Vereniging van Vrienden Allard Pierson Museum Amsterdam: Mededelingenblad* 68 (1997), pp. 2–5, at 2. The author is inexpressibly grateful to Asa Mittman and Peter Dendle for all of their thoughtful comments, careful editing, and endless patience in the development of this chapter.

2   Bremmer, "Monsters en fabeldieren in de Griekse cultuur," p. 2.

3   Catherine Atherton (ed.), *Monsters and Monstrosity in Greek and Roman Culture*, vol. 6, *Nottingham Classical Literature Series* (Bari: Levanti Editori, 1998), p. x.

culture finds threatening.[4] So, what the Greeks and Romans considered monstrous gives us insight into what those cultures feared. Among other things, monsters were the opposite of the ordered, rational society idealized by the Greeks.

But what, more specifically, defines the "monstrous" in ancient Greece and Rome? The Greek term *teras* referred both to a portent and, in the concrete sense, a physical monstrosity. The English word itself comes from the Latin *monstrum*, which to the Romans signified very generally a supernatural event thought to be a portent from the gods, a warning of some sort (from the root *monere*, "to warn").[5] But, as with the Greek term, the Latin word also commonly denoted a physically unnatural being of any sort, whether humans (or animals) exhibiting morphological abnormalities, or mythological monsters.[6] What constitutes "unnatural" or "abnormal," then, is often something that is not clearly human or animal but rather in-between, a disturbing hybrid mixture, what Jeffrey Jerome Cohen refers to as "ontological liminality";[7] a creature of amazing size; a creature unlike anything anyone has ever seen before; a creature that evokes revulsion. As Atherton puts it, monsters are often "prime bearers of 'taxonomic perversity'" in relation to the cultures that create them.[8]

Thus, although the Greeks told of a very wide variety of monstrous beings, the creatures tended to have certain traits in common. Greek mythological monsters were indeed usually immense. They were nearly always morphological oddities, such as loathsome multi-headed or multi-limbed hybrids, often reptilian. They usually had extraordinary physical powers, which were at least partially a result of their anatomical superfluity.[9] Some monsters were not even identifiably animal; they were closer to mere abstractions of frightening concepts, as we shall see in Hesiod. Many were also imbued with malice; one does not tend to find giant, hybrid, incredibly strong monsters in Greek myth that are also benevolent.[10] The Greek monsters, like those of many other cultures, tend to be inherently destructive, exhibiting tremendous hostility toward humans.

There were certainly other types of being that the Greeks and Romans considered monstrous. The Romans sometimes referred to ghosts as *monstra*, for example, and various supernatural creatures abounded in the ancient imagination, such as werewolves who fed not only on livestock but on human flesh, and the Greek *empousae* and *lamiae*, vampire-like female beings who attacked new mothers

---

4   Jeffrey Jerome Cohen (ed.), *Monster Theory: Reading Culture* (Minneapolis: University of Minnesota Press, 1996), p. viii.

5   See Steel's essay in this volume for more on the etymology of *monstrum*.

6   Robert Garland, *The Eye of the Beholder: Deformity and Disability in the Graeco-Roman World* (Ithaca: Cornell University Press, 1995), p. 4.

7   Cohen, *Monster Theory*, p. 6.

8   Atherton, *Monsters and Monstrosity in Greek and Roman Culture*, p. xiv. For a modern example of this relativism, consider "The Eye of the Beholder" episode of *The Twilight Zone* (Season 2, Episode 42, 1960).

9   See, for example, the discussion in Adrienne Mayor, *The First Fossil Hunters: Paleontology in Greek and Roman Times* (Princeton: Princeton University Press, 2000), pp. 196–7.

10   Unlike, for example, the dragons of Chinese mythology.

and their children or who seduced and devoured young men. Roman literature tells of witches who robbed graves, performed gruesome necromantic ceremonies, and murdered children. These various beings, it was believed by some, could be encountered in real life by ordinary men. And men themselves were capable of monstrous, savage, lawless behavior that made them little different from the terrifying hybrid creatures of myth fought by heroes of the distant past. In such cases, the concept of monstrosity is based not on a physical deformity but on abhorrent moral values.[11]

Non-human monsters almost invariably dwelled outside of civilized, urban areas. Mountains, rocks, caves, cliffs, and other natural places untamed by culture were home to most of the monsters of Greek myth. The Sphinx, for example, lived on Mt Phikion outside of Thebes; the Cyclops Polyphemus lived in a cave; the Sirens sang from rocky cliffs. Similarly, bodies of water including lakes, marshes, and the often hostile sea, toward which the Greeks had an ambivalent attitude, held many monsters.[12] As Jan Bremmer observes, this is not surprising since wilderness is where "unordered" things such as monsters rightly belong.[13]

Because the Greeks regularly identified women with the wildness of nature—defined by the Greeks as whatever existed beyond the boundaries of an ordered civilization—it is not surprising to find that a very large proportion of monsters in Greek mythology are female. Sue Blundell explains that women's capacity for child-bearing aligned them with natural forces beyond male control.[14] That women could also sometimes produce children with physical abnormalities only added to the perception of women as potentially terrifying and destructive. Creatures such as Medusa, Scylla and Charybdis, the Harpies, and the Furies, among many others, all spoke to men's fear of women's destructive potential. The myths then, to a certain extent, fulfill a male fantasy of conquering and controlling the female. But ultimately our interpretation of monsters in Greece and Rome may remain more general as we examine the evidence. David Gilmore suggests: "For most Western observers the monster is a metaphor for all that must be repudiated by the human spirit. It embodies the existential threat to social life, the chaos, atavism, and negativism that symbolize destructiveness and all other obstacles to

---

11 For a discussion of people behaving monstrously, see Weinstock's essay in this volume.

12 Mountains in particular, far from the bounds of ordered cities, were often the places where atrocious things happened: Actaeon, killed by his own hunting dogs for seeing the goddess Artemis bathing; Pentheus, torn to shreds by maenads for his impiety toward the god Dionysus.

13 Bremmer, "Monsters en fabeldieren in de Griekse cultuur," p. 3. Van Duzer's essay in this volume discusses climate as a main geographical principle that traditionally determined regions inhabited by monsters, particularly in the Middle Ages and early Renaissance. Although some ancient authors, such as Hippocrates and Diodorus Siculus, mention climate as a factor in monstrosity (as Van Duzer notes), climate does not seem as significant as topography in accounting for the location or type of the majority of mythical monsters in Greek and Roman literature.

14 Sue Blundell, *Women in Ancient Greece* (Cambridge, MA: Harvard University Press, 1995), pp. 17–19.

order and progress."[15] This was particularly true for the ancient Greeks. For the Romans, too, monsters represented the barbaric and uncivilized, but the Romans also demonstrated a fascination with the monstrous that the Greeks did not. The Romans consequently sought out the monstrous in a manner quite unlike the Greeks, as we shall see.

Monstrous Origins

Some of the earliest monsters in Greek literature appear in the Greek creation myth, the most detailed version of which survives in Hesiod's eighth-century BCE *Theogony* ("origin of the gods"). This 1022-line poem describes the physical origins and organization of the cosmos. At first there is nothing but Chaos, an empty void;[16] then Gaia, the Earth, comes into being, and Tartarus, a dim, underworld-like region. The fourth original entity is Eros, an abstraction representing the reproductive impulse, necessary for continued creation in the cosmos.

These early entities begin a tortuous, chaotic, and essentially experimental process of reproduction resulting in various monstrous creatures. Chaos produces several generations of abstractions that Hesiod considered monstrous in the sense that they brought misery to mankind: for example, from Chaos came Night, which bore Doom, Ruin, Death, and Deception, among many others.[17] Gaia, reflecting the fertility attributed to the Earth by early societies, produces many offspring via parthenogenesis including Ouranos, the Sky; thus, as in many early cosmologies, the two primary beings are Earth and Sky. Mating with Ouranos, Gaia births the twelve Titans. Hesiod does not describe these beings physically in any detail but seems to conceive of them as semi-anthropomorphic and even describes one of them as "lovely."[18] Hesiod envisions the other offspring of Gaia and Ouranos as deformed: three Cyclopes, terribly strong giants with one huge, round eye in the middle of their foreheads; and three Hecatoncheires or "Hundred-Handers," each

---

15   Gilmore, *Monsters*, p. 12. He also offers a Freudian interpretation and comments that monsters are impressive and fearful because they break the rules—they observe no limits, respect no boundaries, and attack and kill without compunction. Monsters may be projections of a more general wish fulfillment—the wish to be able to do as we please. He suggests that monsters and their behavior represent the Freudian *id*. This theory finds a literal representation in the 1956 film *Forbidden Planet*. Although Freudian psychoanalytic theory has fallen somewhat out of favor, his many ideas about the unconscious and dream symbolism can still be helpful in the realm of myth, as Gilmore demonstrates (pp. 14–18).

16   The Greek word *chaos* indicates a vast empty space or infinite dark void, and should not be confused with the English word "chaos" meaning "disorder" or "confusion," though the English derives directly from the Greek.

17   *Theogony* 211–14.

18   The Titaness Tethys, *Theogony* 136. The word *erateine*, deriving from *eros*, means "lovely" or "charming," and Hesiod also applies it to Thalia, one of the three Graces, in line 909.

with 100 hands and 50 heads. Hesiod describes the latter as not only "immense" but as too terrible to be approached or even spoken of.[19]

In short, the early Greek cosmos filled quickly with a wide variety of monstrous creatures during the process of creation. This tumultuous, experimental early universe became the setting for a cosmic struggle toward order that would come about in the third generation after Gaia with Zeus and his divine siblings. The concept of successive generations of gods battling both their elders and monstrous creatures for power over the cosmos was familiar to the Greeks from Near Eastern myths, including the Babylonian creation story found in the epic *Enuma Elish* and the Hurrian-Hittite poems *Kingship in Heaven* and *Song of Ullikummi*.[20] In these stories a warrior-god from the younger generation gains cosmic supremacy by defeating older generations of gods, some of whom were depicted as terrifying monsters, and others of whom enlisted fearful monstrosities representative of the old universe to fight on their behalf.

Gods and Monsters

Many Near Eastern religions and social systems rested on an allegorical origin myth of a man battling a monster. In every case, a young warrior-god who represents harmony and order as well as nationhood goes forth to battle a "chaos-monster" that threatens the world order. In the aftermath of such apocalyptic confrontations, civilizations emerge, prosper, and flourish, and humanity takes its rightful place as master of the Earth. The monster myths proclaim our ownership over the world and justify the present order.[21] So, for example, the Babylonian warrior Marduk conquers the monstrous Tiamat, the embodiment of primeval chaos who also happens to be his mother; and the Sumerian god Ninurta defeats a multi-headed dragon-like creature. The succession myth of Hesiod's *Theogony* provides no exception to the pattern.

After the universe came into tumultuous existence, the cosmos still lacked order. The earliest beings were savage and cruel, poor rulers. When Gaia bore his children, Ouranos, afraid of being overthrown, forced them all back into her womb. She conspired with the youngest of them, Cronos, who castrated Ouranos, disempowering him and symbolically separating Earth and Sky.[22] Cronos freed the other Titans but was no better than his father: when his

---

19 *Theogony* 151, 153.
20 M.L. West (ed. and comm.), *Hesiod: Theogony* (Oxford: Clarendon Press, 1966), p. 19, explains: "This Succession Myth has parallels in oriental mythology which are so striking that a connexion is incontestable. They occur principally in Hittite and Akkadian texts." For details, see his extended discussion, pp. 20–31.
21 Gilmore, *Monsters*, pp. 28–9.
22 This mirrors the Hurrian-Hittite sources, in which the usurping god Kumarbi bites off and swallows the elder god Anu's genitals and becomes pregnant.

sister/wife Rhea bore children, Cronos, equally afraid of being overthrown, swallowed them himself. His unnatural and gruesome attempt to prevent a son from replacing him as universal sovereign emphasizes the monstrous nature of Zeus's predecessors, the Titans.[23] For the Greeks, Zeus's overthrowing of Cronos represented the triumph of civilization over savagery. This came about as Cronos's youngest child, Zeus, escaped the fate of his siblings when Rhea substituted a stone for the baby. Gathering his (regurgitated) siblings and aided by the Cyclopes and Hundred-Handers, Zeus succeeded in overthrowing the older generation in a conflict known as the Titanomachy. This new, third generation was more civilized, and Zeus began to bring order to the cosmos. His main obstacle, brought forth by Gaia as a "final attempt to circumvent undisputed male rule of the universe"[24] and as a test of whether Zeus was fit to rule the cosmos, was the monster Typhoeus, who represented the old female, chthonic order. The most fearsome creature in the *Theogony*, Typhoeus appears as an embodiment of violent nature out of control:

> From its shoulders
> sprouted a hundred heads of snaky, dreadful dragons
> flickering sooty tongues; and under its brows, from its eyes
> flames flashed, and fire burned from all its glaring heads.[25]

Add to this the unearthly shrieking which Hesiod describes a few lines later[26] and Typhoeus presents "a frightening alternative to Zeus's benevolent despotism."[27] In an explosive epic battle, Zeus defeats Typhoeus, who hurls all the forces of nature at him: earthquakes, fire, hurricanes, tidal waves. The conflagration that ravages Earth during Zeus's war with Typhoeus represents a patriarchal assault on the early female-dominated cosmos. As Sarah Pomeroy observes: "Hesiod details the divine progression from female-dominated generations, characterized by natural, earthy, emotional qualities, to the superior and rational monarchy of Olympian Zeus."[28]

---

23   See, for example, Francisco José de Goya y Lucientes's "Saturn devouring one of his children," which depicts Cronos's horrifying cannibalism.

24   Stephen L. Harris and Gloria Platzner, *Classical Mythology: Images and Insights*, 6th edn (New York: McGraw-Hill, 2012), p. 85.

25   *Theogony* 824–8. This and all other translations are my own, unless otherwise noted.

26   *Theogony* 830–35.

27   Harris and Platzner, *Classical Mythology*, p. 85.

28   Sarah B. Pomeroy, *Goddesses, Whores, Wives, and Slaves: Women in Classical Antiquity* (New York: Schocken Books, 1975), p. 2. This is not to say that such a progression in myth corresponds to an actual historic change in Greek society and religion, such as a shift from worshipping female divinities to worshipping male deities. Pomeroy is careful to point out that the existence of a mother goddess in prehistory is still highly theoretical and unproven, though it remains a popular theory (pp. 13–14). The progression in myth is metaphorical, representative of the relative importance that reason claimed over irrationality in Greek thought. A certain level of misogyny, evident in the Greek

Figure 4.1   Armed with his lightning bolt, Zeus battles the winged, serpent-
legged Typhoeus. Greek (Chalcidian) black-figure hydria (water-jug),
circa 540 BCE.

The chthonic imagery present in Hesiod's description of the earlier cosmic
generations becomes quite important when studying the monsters of Greek
myth. Typhoeus is only the first of many creatures to have serpent-like attributes
and a connection to the primordial mythological period before the ouranian gods
gained power. The depiction of Typhoeus itself goes back to the Near Eastern
creation myths in which Tiamat, for example, is a snake-like monster. Serpents
represent many different concepts in ancient mythologies, but prominent among
them is the serpent as early goddess figure or consort of Earth goddess.[29] Many
Greek monsters are either born of Earth herself or of Typhoeus and serve as
metaphors for the struggle of man over nature. Hesiod and other Greeks thus
conceived of Zeus as a bringer of culture, as echoed in Greek art. In Figure 4.1,
for example, Zeus with his lightning bolt, representing Sky, confronts Typhoeus,
whose snaky legs indicate his origin from Earth.[30] Zeus's status as a culture hero
is also borne out by his strongly anthropomorphic appearance and his ability
to control nature (particularly by subordination of the female), as well as his
progeny—such civilizing forces as the Muses and the Graces, for example.

archaic period, likely also influenced the creation story.
29   See, for example, Anne Baring and Jules Cashford, *The Myth of the Goddess: Evolution of
an Image* (London: Arkana Penguin Books, 1991), pp. 64–6 and 499–500.
30   In Greek iconography, the wings on Typhoeus and other creatures, both chthonic and
ouranic, indicate not that these beings are associated with the sky but only that they
belong to the non-human realm.

Figure 4.2 Athena fighting the giant Alkyoneus, who gained strength whenever he touched his mother, Earth. Eastern frieze, Great Altar of Pergamon, first half of the second century BCE.

Other works than Hesiod's *Theogony*, such as the *Bibliotheca* attributed to Apollodorus,[31] add another battle before Zeus and the Olympian gods can truly bring order to the cosmos. This tradition holds that Gaia bore monstrous offspring called the Gigantes, or Giants. These creatures were not only huge and brutish but had legs ending in the tails of snakes. The Giants challenged the Olympians for supremacy, resulting in the conflict known as the Gigantomachy. In keeping with their savagery, the Giants fought by hurling huge boulders and uprooted trees, whereas the Olympians used the various crafted weapons representative of a more advanced culture, such as arrows and swords. The tradition of the Gigantomachy tells that it was *after* the Giants were defeated that Zeus fought Typhoeus, but the ancient sources at least agree that after vanquishing these various creatures a triumphant Zeus took his place as rightful ruler of the cosmos.

The Gigantomachy was perhaps even more popular in Greek art than in Greek literature, appearing on monumental works of sculpture for centuries. In archaic Greece, the Gigantomachy served as a metaphor for reason and order triumphing over chaos, as, for example, in the pediment of the Temple of Artemis at Corfu (circa 580s BCE). In classical Greece, after the Persian Wars (490–479 BCE), the Gigantomachy symbolized the victory of the Greeks (Olympians) over the barbarian Persians (Giants), as on the east metopes on the Parthenon. The battle of the gods and Giants thus became a visual expression of the victory of the Athenians over their enemies. The most well-known surviving representation of the Gigantomachy in art is that on the Great Altar of Pergamon (circa 180–160 BCE).[32] Figure 4.2 shows a scene from the eastern frieze of the altar, wherein the Olympian goddess Athena, grasping the Giant Alkyoneus by the hair, separates him from his mother, Gaia, who is attempting to rise from her earthly domain to aid in the battle. The winged goddess of victory, Nike, approaches at the upper right, signifying the Olympians' impending victory over the Giants. For the Pergamenians, as for the Athenians, the Gigantomachy symbolized their victory over their enemies. And, as Max Kunze observes: "Such representations also clearly conceal a rulership ideology which saw the myth as a negative confrontation between divine order and barbarianism to be interpreted not only to their own advantage but also to be used for their own propagandistic ends. Their victory was the victory of order over chaos."[33]

---

31 Apollodorus (second century BCE) wrote a *Bibliotheca* ("Library") of Greek mythology, but the extant work by that name attributed to him actually dates to the first or second century CE.

32 Pergamon was an ancient Greek city in what is now modern Turkey.

33 Max Kunze, *The Pergamon Altar: Its Rediscovery, History, and Reconstruction* (Mainz: Verlag Philipp von Zabern, 1995), p. 24. In antiquity there were other interpretations as well; for example, the Roman poet Claudian (early fifth century CE) wrote an epic *Gigantomachia* in which the battle was metaphorical for catastrophic geological change. Similarly, as noted in Harris and Platzner, *Classical Mythology* (p. 85), the massive conflicts which Hesiod describes in the battle between Zeus and Typhoeus have been interpreted as possibly being "a faint memory of some distant geological catastrophe, such as the devastating prehistoric eruptions" of Thera (Santorini).

The representation of Alkyoneus and the other Giants in this monumental sculpture is worth a brief mention. Susan Woodford, noting that the subject of the Gigantomachy was popular in both art and literature for a very long time, observes that: "it is not always easy to decide which of the two took the lead in the transformation of the ways in which the giants came to be represented."[34] In fact, the earliest artistic representations focused on the actual fighting and the Giants were regularly depicted simply as warriors with conventional armor and conventional weapons. This is the case despite the literary versions of the myth in which the Giants were not just warriors who attacked the gods but barbaric enemies challenging the Olympian order.[35] The Giants' barbarism was increasingly stressed in the course of the fifth century BCE, and after the middle of the century this barbaric aspect of the giants became increasingly prominent.[36] In the fourth century BCE, probably influenced by the images of other Olympian enemies such as Typhoeus, artists began to depict the Giants not merely as barbaric but as partly animal.[37] By the Hellenistic period, Giants whose torsos ended in snaky limbs had become common, as we see on the Pergamon Altar.

The pattern of warrior-god fighting "chaos monster" was repeated by other Greek gods, most notably by Zeus's son Apollo. To establish his importance as a god, Apollo came to Delphi to found his own sacred sanctuary, only to find the place terrorized by a monstrous serpent. Some accounts say that the serpent was female, while others say it was male; some say it was nameless, others that it was called Python; some say it was born of Gaia, others that Hera (sister/wife of Zeus) produced the creature. But sources agree that the serpent was a remnant of the older days when Gaia's matriarchy held sway.[38] The *Homeric Hymn to Apollo* tells how Apollo slew the serpent, and it is not exactly an epic battle: Apollo fells the serpent with one arrow. Despite the apparent ease with which Apollo kills the serpent, however, the significance of this episode should not be underestimated. As if reflecting the "historical transition from chthonic powers to sky gods" apparent in Hesiod's *Theogony*, the story of Apollo's victory over the serpent of Delphi also involves "an epochal battle between female and male principles of

---

34   Susan Woodford, *Images of Myths in Classical Antiquity* (Cambridge: Cambridge University Press, 2003), p. 122.

35   Ibid., p. 123.

36   Ibid., pp. 123–4: Woodford points out that this development was probably influenced by the spectacular work of art that was Phidias's sculpture of Athena, placed in the Parthenon sometime after 447 BCE. The shield held by the goddess was decorated with a scene of Athenians fighting Amazons in relief on the exterior and with a depiction of the gods fighting Giants painted on the interior. Only hints of what this painting looked like survive, but apparently the Giants were mostly animal-skin-clad, savage creatures who used primitive weapons such as rocks and tree trunks.

37   Ibid., p. 125.

38   Variation is typical in Greek myth because of its origins in oral tradition, and it is thus not uncommon to find literary variants in opposition to each other—such as versions of this Apollo myth disagreeing as to the sex of the serpent.

divinity," given the respective origins of Apollo and of the serpent.[39] Moreover, Apollo voluntarily undergoes punishment and purification to atone for having killed the guardian serpent of Gaia's shrine, indicating that the new male order must at least acknowledge the past power of feminine divinity.

Heroes and Monsters

The pattern set by Zeus and Typhoeus in the creation of the Greek mythological cosmos carried down not only into stories of other Greek gods but into later mythological generations of men in which heroes inevitably had to fight monsters in a re-enactment of the battle for order in the cosmos—the younger, male generation trying to overcome the elder female order; civilization and rationality trying to overcome savagery and emotion.[40] This, too, was patterned on Near Eastern mythology such as the story of Gilgamesh and his companion Enkidu fighting the gigantic primitive monster Humbaba.[41] But added to the stories of heroes—starting with that of Gilgamesh—was the concept of immortality: facing these monsters, and in particular traveling to the land of the dead and facing monsters there, represented coming to accept one's own mortality. Heroes such as Gilgamesh came to realize that the only way for a mortal to become immortal is to do great service to society and to leave behind a noble reputation.[42]

In killing the serpent at Delphi, Apollo abolished the old savage, chthonic order and brought reason and culture in its place. Similarly, the hero Cadmus had to kill a dragon before founding a new city in Boeotia in central Greece. He first needed to sacrifice to the goddess Athena and sent several men to bring water from a

---

39   Harris and Platzner, *Classical Mythology*, p. 232.

40   In the literature of ancient Greece and Rome the serpents and other dragon-like creatures fought by gods and heroes did not specifically represent Evil as they did in Christian literature. In such stories as St George fighting the dragon or St Patrick driving the snakes out of Ireland, for example, the serpents symbolize a variety of evils, such as sin and paganism (respectively). The Christian concept of the snake as evil hearkens back to the characterization of the serpent in the Garden of Eden.

41   Note, too, that in conquering Humbaba, the heroes cut down many trees in the Cedar Forest with their metal weapons: nature versus culture (*Gilgamesh*, Tablet V).

42   The epic of *Gilgamesh* opens and closes with the exhortation to the audience to look at the walls of Uruk, a lasting physical monument and testimony to the accomplishments of Gilgamesh. Similarly, the Greeks and Romans recognized that immortality could be achieved only by leaving memorable works for future generations. Literature was a main accomplishment to this end. The fifth-century BCE historian Herodotus opened his work by explaining that his reason for writing is to prevent the wars between the Greeks and Persians from being forgotten; the first-century BCE Roman poet Catullus remarked of his work, *"plus uno maneat perenne saeclo,"* "may it last for more than one age" (Poem 1.10). See also Horace, *Ode* 3.30: *"non omnis moriar,"* "I will not die entirely," a sentiment expressed in relation to his poetry as a monument that would survive him.

nearby spring for the ritual, but they did not return. Upon investigation, Cadmus found that a huge serpent, a guardian of the spring (which was sacred to Ares), had devoured his men. He killed the snake and, after atoning for shedding the guardian's blood, was able to found the city of Cadmeia, which became Thebes. The killing of a dragon to found a settlement represents, for the Greeks, the advance of culture over nature.[43]

Essentially, in Greek mythology, once Zeus calmed the cosmos, order had to be established in the world of men as well. The older generations of gods may have been deposed, but their monstrous progeny lived on: Typhoeus, for example, had fathered the Chimaera, the Hydra, Cerberus, the Sphinx, the Nemean lion, and Scylla, among many others. The stability represented by the reign of Zeus was mythologically concurrent with the age of men, and it was up to men to civilize the world in the same way in which Zeus had tamed the cosmos. So among men, heroes arose who would bring social order by ridding the earth of the monstrous creatures from elder times, making the countryside and the roads—the latter particularly emblematic of civilization—safe for their fellow man. Thus the monsters in Greek myth, such as anthropophagus giants, tended to represent uncivilized, lawless forces, as did untamed elements of nature often represented by the monstrous female. These elements were to be conquered and replaced by the culture-bringing male.

The earliest generation of heroes included Perseus, Bellerophon, and Heracles (Hercules to the Romans). Perseus is best known as the slayer of Medusa, one of three snaky-haired Gorgon sisters. Perseus traveled to the Gorgons' lair in the far west to cut off her head, viewing her reflection in a shield to avoid looking at her petrifying gaze directly. This early myth reflects the theme of the younger, patriarchal society replacing an older, pre-agricultural, Gaia-dependent world, as the Gorgons had come into existence in the earliest days of the cosmos, their snaky hair reflecting their chthonic origins.[44] Perseus also encounters one of the first major sea monsters in Greek mythology. After slaying Medusa, Perseus passes Ethiopia where he sees the princess Andromeda chained to a rock, about to be sacrificed to appease a monster. Early literary sources do not describe the monster in detail, but its name, Cetus, also means "whale."[45] Perseus slays the

---

43 The fact that images of monsters are scarce in Paleolithic and Neolithic art, and that such images became widespread with the emergence of early cities and states in the Near East about five millennia ago, lends support to this primary theme underlying stories of heroes fighting monsters.

44 The Gorgons were either children or grandchildren of Gaia, depending on the variant. Also, Hellenistic versions of the myth say that Medusa was a lovely young woman turned into a hideous Gorgon for angering Athena and was thus not one of the original Gorgons.

45 Cetus and other sea monsters of Greek myth represent not only the chthonic connection (given their serpent-like bodies) but also the dangers of the sea and sea travel. Because Perseus, Andromeda, Cassiopeia, and even Cetus were, according to myth, turned into constellations at their deaths, a detailed version of their story appears in one of the lesser-known Roman epic poems, Marcus Manilius's *Astronomica* (first century CE). Manilius includes a lengthy digression to explain the origin of the constellation

creature with his sword.[46] Thus, wielding the emblem of a "civilized" (that is, metalworking) culture, Perseus proves himself a worthy defender of society.

From Medusa's severed neck the winged horse Pegasus was born, a hybrid creature that was, somewhat ironically, instrumental in killing another hybrid creature—the Chimaera. One of Typhoeus's many offspring, the fire-breathing she-monster had three heads: those of a lion, a goat, and a snake.[47] The creature was ravaging the countryside around Lycia (in Anatolia), until the hero Bellerophon, after taming Pegasus, flew on the stallion to Lycia and killed the Chimaera with arrows. Again a hero saves society from a monstrous female hybrid remnant of the early female-dominated generations of the cosmos. Pegasus himself, though a hybrid, was evidently considered by the Greeks to be a wondrous winged horse rather than a horrifying deformity, as so many of the other hybrid creatures of myth were.[48] Like the Olympian descendants of Gaia who rebelled against their chthonic ancestors, Pegasus, also a descendant of Gaia, helped conquer another representative of the old order—but only after being himself domesticated and manipulated by a male hero for this purpose.

The deeds of Perseus and Bellerophon seem minor, however, in comparison with those of Heracles, best known for his twelve Labors. Heracles was not only physically stronger than any other hero of Greek myth; he experienced more hardships, more tortures, and faced more monstrous creatures than any of the others, partially because the goddess Hera bore an unusually strong grudge against him. Even in Heracles's infancy Hera tried to kill him but, already exhibiting prodigious strength, Heracles strangled the snake she placed in his crib. This childhood incident was only a miniature predictor of the monstrous battles to come. Assigned the twelve Labors to atone for killing his wife and children— which he did in a fit of madness brought on by Hera—Heracles faced increasingly incredible obstacles; his tasks became more fantastical as they moved farther and farther from mainland Greece.

Heracles's first six Labors were confined to the Peloponnese, the landmass that comprises southern Greece. Here his job was to clear the countryside of the various monstrous creatures that were killing herds and inhabitants alike. Most of these creatures were basically exaggerated versions of known animals; Heracles's Labors would get more fantastical when he left the Peloponnese, presenting the familiar trope that creatures become more monstrous as we move further from the heart of "civilization." His first task was to save the region of Nemea from a monstrous lion, a cave-dwelling offspring of Typhoeus sent purposely by Hera. This huge creature's hide was impervious to weapons, so Heracles had to strangle it with his

---

Andromeda (5.538–618). For a detailed literary analysis, see Paul Murgatroyd, *Mythical Monsters in Classical Literature* (London: Duckworth, 2007), pp. 154–61.

46   Not, as the 1981 and 2010 films *Clash of the Titans* would have you believe, by exposing it to Medusa's head.

47   Or, in some variants, the front parts of a lion, the middle of a goat, and the tail of a snake.

48   According to Hesiod, Pegasus was even a favorite of the Muses.

bare hands. After saving Nemea, Heracles proceeded to the neighboring region of Lerna to confront the swamp-dwelling, multi-headed snake known as the Hydra, a daughter of Typhoeus.[49] Hera had sent this creature, too, as a threat to Heracles. In addition to destroying the countryside, the Hydra represented an actual danger associated with stagnant pools in that it breathed noxious fumes, fouling the air. Heracles tried cutting off its heads, but to his dismay every severed head grew back until he hit upon the strategy of cauterizing each neck stump. Gilmore comments: "The Hydra's monstrosity consisted not only in its multi-cephalic nature but also in ... its ability to grow back its nine heads when lopped off by humans."[50] But its monstrosity consisted also in its association with the chthonic.

Heracles's other Peloponnesian Labors also brought him up against unusually dangerous animals.[51] Then Heracles's Labors became increasingly bizarre the farther he traveled from mainland Greece, going first to Crete, then Thrace, then Scythia in the east before heading to the far west.[52] There, in the Garden of the Hesperides, he had to kill Ladon, another gigantic, multi-headed serpent, guardian of the Golden Apples. Heracles's last Labor was the most fantastical of all: he had to fetch Cerberus, the watchdog of Hades. Another monstrous offspring of Typhoeus, Cerberus had 50 heads, according to Hesiod,[53] but only three according to most other ancient sources.[54] Some writers and a number of vase paintings also gave the monstrous hound a snake's tail and snaky heads jutting from his back, cementing his association with the chthonic world—as if being guardian of Hades were not enough to do so. In Figure 4.3, for example, Heracles presents the monstrous dog to the cowardly Eurystheus, who has taken refuge in a large storage jar.[55] Heracles, depicted with his traditional attributes, the club and lion skin,[56] holds Cerberus rather loosely on a leash while the dog, jaws agape, leaps forward. Note the snakes emanating from Cerberus's heads and limbs.

Having successfully completed all his Labors, Heracles had made the Greek countryside and the world safer for mankind. Lurking under his story, as with those of other heroes, we find the same basic pair of themes: first, of the younger, male generation overthrowing representatives of the older, female generation, as

---

49   The exact number of heads attributed to the Lernaean Hydra varies widely—from five or six up to 100.

50   Gilmore, *Monsters*, p. 40.

51   These Labors were the Erymanthian Boar; the Ceryneitian Hind; the Horses of the Augean Stables (or, more specifically, their dung); and the Stymphalian Birds.

52   These Labors were the Cretan Bull; the Mares of Diomedes; the Belt of the Amazon Queen Hippolyta; and the Cattle of Geryon, near Gibraltar.

53   *Theogony* 312.

54   See Woodford, *Images of Myths in Classical Antiquity*, pp. 174–5, for discussion of the number of Cerberus's heads as represented in Greek art.

55   Eurystheus, a king of Myceneae and cousin of Heracles, was in charge of assigning the twelve Labors. After Heracles killed his own wife and children in a Hera-induced fit of madness, the Delphic oracle required the hero to serve Eurystheus for twelve years.

56   Heracles wears the skin of the Nemean lion, reflecting his own dual nature as a creature of society but also as a creature of superhuman strength and brutality.

Figure 4.3   Heracles has captured Cerberus. Caeretan black-figure hydria
              attributed to the Eagle Painter, circa 525 BCE. Note the snakes
              emanating from Cerberus's heads.

many of the threats which Heracles faces are female or chthonic in their nature; and
second, the notion that the farther one goes from Greece, the more barbaric, alien,
and monstrous the creatures that inhabit those far lands.

In between his Labors, Heracles participated in the hero Jason's quest for
the Golden Fleece, a voyage that demonstrated once again that the farther from
Greece the heroes traveled, the stranger their adventures.[57] The same was true of
Theseus, who fought highway robbers on the road to Athens but the Minotaur on
the island of Crete. The Theseus myth cycle arose relatively late compared to other
Greek hero myths, having developed in the late sixth century BCE as a political

---

57   The Argonauts were headed to Colchis on the far shore of the Black Sea and encountered
      first giants and then the Harpies before coming up against fire-breathing bulls and
      a giant serpent guarding the Fleece. The Harpies ("Snatchers") were hybrid female
      monsters from the pre-Olympian generations described variously as birds with the
      faces of women or women with the wings and talons of birds of prey. See discussion
      below on Vergil's *Aeneid*.

reflection of the Athenians' desire to have their own local hero in contrast to the pan-Hellenic hero Heracles.[58] The myth of incestuous Theban hero Oedipus, unlike that of Theseus, developed early—before the eighth century BCE.[59] The presence of the Sphinx in the story, however, is generally agreed to be a later development. Vase paintings showing Oedipus with the Sphinx are mainly fifth century BCE and later, as is much of the literature narrating Oedipus's encounter with the creature.[60] The Sphinx ("Strangler"), mythologically yet another of the monstrous, hybrid offspring of Typhoeus, had the face of a woman, the body of a lion, and the wings of a bird of prey.[61] Sent down to a mountain near Thebes to punish the city for the pedophiliac crime of its former king Laius, the Sphinx ravaged the countryside around Thebes and killed any passers-by who could not answer her famous riddle. This made Thebes a rather unpopular destination. Oedipus saved the city by solving the riddle of the Sphinx, resulting in her suicide. Oedipus, in some ways the ideal rational and clever Greek hero, bested a monster that, like many others, represented the less rational, more enigmatic, more emotional female.

Perhaps the most detailed literary episodes of heroes encountering monsters occur in Greek and Roman epic poetry, particularly Homer's *Odyssey* and Vergil's *Aeneid*. Odysseus's journey homeward from Troy starts off relatively realistically, with a raid on a coastal town inhabited by the Cicones, a tribe of men allied with King Priam.[62] Similarly, his encounter with the Lotus-Eaters is quite strange and disturbing, but not entirely outside the realm of the possible. From there, however, the progress of the hero's journey belongs to the realms of the fantastic.[63] Odysseus and his ships arrive at the island of the Cyclopes, whom he describes as a race with no laws, no organized society of any kind; worse, "they show no concern for each other."[64] The gigantic,

---

58   The myth may also reflect a shift in the center of power in the Mediterranean from the Minoan society on Crete to the Mycenean and Athenian societies on the mainland (Harris and Platzner, *Classical Mythology*, p. 299). Theseus as a mythological character does appear in earlier Greek literature but is not specifically associated with Athens until the late sixth century BCE. On the possible origins of Theseus, see Henry J. Walker, *Theseus and Athens* (Oxford: Oxford University Press, 1995), pp. 9–15.

59   See, for example, *Odyssey* 11.271–80. That is, the myth of Oedipus's having killed his father and married his mother was known before the eighth century BCE, as these lines make clear.

60   The Sphinx began to appear in Greek art in the orientalizing period of the late eighth and seventh centuries BCE, when Near Eastern hybrid creatures gained popularity in the Greek imagination. Early Greek depictions of the Sphinx show her apparently raping or killing young men; the Sphinx also appears as a decoration on grave steles in Greece. See Emily Vermeule, *Aspects of Death in Early Greek Art and Poetry* (Berkeley, Los Angeles, London: University of California Press, 1979), pp. 171–3.

61   There are few detailed literary descriptions of the Theban Sphinx in ancient literature. One appears in the *Oedipus* of the Roman playwright Seneca (first century CE), lines 95–100.

62   The Cicones lived on the south-western coast of Thrace.

63   R.J. Clare, "Representing Monstrosity: Polyphemus in the *Odyssey*," in Atherton (ed.), *Monsters and Monstrosity*, pp. 1–17, at 1.

64   *Odyssey* 9.115.

one-eyed Cyclopes live in caves on mountaintops, and Odysseus stresses their lack
of the technology usually associated with advanced civilizations: not only do they
not build ships, but they are pre-agricultural.[65] When the Cyclops Polyphemus finds
Odysseus in his cave, his actions prove even more monstrous than his appearance:
seizing two of Odysseus's men, he smashes their brains out on the ground, and
then devours them, "feasting on their entrails and flesh and marrow-filled bones, /
leaving nothing."[66] The Cyclopes' lack of advanced technology is also apparent when
Odysseus and his remaining crew sail away: Polyphemus tears away the top of a
huge mountain and hurls it at the ships, barely missing.

The next monstrous race which Odysseus and his men encounter is the
Laestrygones. This tribe appears to be more advanced than the Cyclopes because
they have a citadel, city, and society, ruled by a king. But they, too, are gigantic,
"as tall as a mountain-top,"[67] and when Odysseus's men are summoned to the
king's presence, he immediately eats one of them. The Laestrygones, hurling huge
boulders from the cliffs, destroy all but one of Odysseus's ships. Like the Giants
fighting the Olympians—a similarity Odysseus points out[68]—and like Polyphemus,
the Laestrygones do not have the technology to produce advanced weapons.[69] And
the presence of a social hierarchy does not guarantee what the Greek considered
civilized behavior: the farther away one goes from Greece, the more barbaric and
monstrous the races. After their unfortunate encounters with the Cyclopes and the
Laestrygones, Odysseus's crew use these episodes as warnings to Odysseus not to
be too curious to explore, as when he wants to investigate Circe's island.

With Circe, Odysseus's adventures become increasingly fantastic. The
enchantress turns Odysseus's men into swine—though it should be noted that *she*
considers *men* to be savages and gives them a form to fit her opinion.[70] After making

---

65 Charles Segal, "Divine Justice in the *Odyssey*: Poseidon, Cyclops, and Helios," *The
American Journal of Philology* 113/4 (1992), pp. 489–518, at 495, explains that the Cyclopes
make their appearance in "an unstable conjunction of opposites. They occupy both a
Golden Age paradise where 'trusting to the gods' they receive the earth's fruits without
toil, and a subhuman condition of dwelling in mountain caves with only a rudimentary
social organization and isolated nuclear families (9.106–15). Odysseus' arrival brings
out the negative side of their primitive society, for just this 'lack of concern for one
another' prevents them from coming to Polyphemus' aid (cf. 9.399–412) … Polyphemus,
in other words, crystallizes the savage side of the Cyclopes' precivilized world." See
also Cohen, *Monster Theory*, p. 14.

66 *Odyssey* 9.292–3. Note that, although this is anthropophagy, it is not necessarily
cannibalism since the Cyclops is not eating his own kind. The same is true of the
Laestrygones, below.

67 *Odyssey* 10.113.

68 *Odyssey* 10.120–22.

69 But they have spears of some sort: "piercing the men like fish, they carried them away
for a joyless feast" (10.124)—joyless from Odysseus's point of view, that is. The phrase
seems to refer either to fishing spears or to roasting spits.

70 Modern audiences might consider Circe a type of monster, or at least consider her
behavior monstrous. The Greeks considered her dangerous because she was a witch,

Figure 4.4   Scylla. Etruscan cinerary urn, circa second century BCE.

peace with Odysseus, however, she turns his crew back into men and helps direct them home, advising them on how to visit Hades to speak with the seer Teiresias and warning them against the dangers that they will later encounter: the Sirens and Scylla and Charybdis. Homer does not physically describe the Sirens and the text gives us no reason to think of them as bird-like. But post-Homeric tradition gives them a genealogy and claws so that even now they are thought of as monstrous, dangerous, hybrid, cliff-dwelling female creatures that lure men to their deaths with beguiling song.[71] In addition to reflecting the male/female conflict that we

---

but also referred to her as a goddess or as a nymph. Odysseus refers to her as "an amazing deity with a human voice" (*Odyssey* 11.8). As Odysseus bests her with some help from the god Hermes, the encounter between Circe and Odysseus does relate to the overall pattern of Olympian-generation male overcoming chthonic-connected female. Circe also lives isolated on an island, fitting the topography of monsters.

71   Bremmer, "Monsters en fabeldieren in de Griekse cultuur," p. 4, suggests the association of Sirens with birds may have come from Egypt, and from Egyptian and Greek depictions of the soul as a small winged creature, but it is also possible that they became associated in Greek thought with the Harpies (on which, see below). For a detailed literary analysis of the Sirens, see Murgatroyd, *Mythical Monsters*, pp.

have seen before, the Sirens also, perhaps more mundanely, represent the dangers of sea travel and this episode points out how sailors must not allow themselves to be distracted.[72]

Circe emphasizes the Sirens' voices rather than their appearance, but in warning Odysseus about Scylla, she describes the creature in great physical detail. Scylla is a "baneful monster" dwelling in a cave very high in a cliff. Her voice sounds like puppies yelping. Worse:

> She has twelve feet, all splayed out,
> and six serpentine necks, on each a terrifying head
> crowded with three thick rows of teeth
> teeming with black death.
> From her waist she lies hidden in her hollowed cavern,
> but stretching out her heads from the dreadful dwelling
> she fishes there, glancing greedily around the rocks.[73]

In this earliest literary description of Scylla, the monster has six snaky heads emanating from her upper torso. In later depictions in both literature and art, the snaky heads emerge from her waist.[74] In Figure 4.4, for example, a relief sculpture on an Etruscan cinerary urn depicts Scylla with vast snaky limbs comprising her entire lower body, reaching out and grasping passing sailors.[75] The "yelping" alludes to the tradition of Scylla's heads being those of dogs, as also depicted in later art and literature.[76] Despite Scylla's obvious connections to the chthonic—her cave, her snaky necks—Odysseus does *not* vanquish her, but instead loses six of his men, having followed Circe's advice to pass closer to Scylla than to Charybdis, described as an immense whirlpool sucking in the sea and spewing it forth again. An encounter with Charybdis would have destroyed his entire ship. In this

---

44–56, which examines the Sirens not only in classical literature but also in medieval, Renaissance, and later authors.

72 In ancient Greece, particularly in the archaic period (eighth to early fifth centuries BCE), serious concern about and aversion to the hardships and dangers of seafaring was a normal Greek attitude. See M.L. West, *Hesiod: Works and Days* (Oxford: Clarendon Press, 1978), pp. 313–14.

73 *Odyssey* 12.89–95.

74 In Vergil's *Aeneid*, for example, Scylla has a human face and a maiden's breasts, but her lower body is that of a sea monster, with a "womb of wolves" (3.426–8).

75 Scylla, along with other scenes from the *Odyssey*, was a popular motif on cinerary urns throughout the Hellenistic period in Etruria. Mythologically, Scylla and Charybdis were thought to inhabit the Straits of Messina by Sicily, south of Etruria. See Richard De Puma, "The Tomb of Fastia Velsi from Chiusi," *Etruscan Studies* 11/1 (2008), pp. 135–49.

76 A noteworthy artistic example is the Scylla sculpture group (first century CE) from Sperlonga, Italy, which depicts Scylla with the face of a woman but with dogs' heads on snaky necks emanating from her waist. Several unlucky sailors are caught in the dogs' jaws. The sculpture group is very crowded, however, and the details not easily distinguished in images of the type reproduced in this chapter.

instance, the dangers posed by the sea—or by female sexuality—overwhelm the theme of male dominance.[77]

The other hero who encounters monsters on his way from Troy is Aeneas, as he flees his destroyed city for Italy. In the Strophades islands in the Ionian Sea, he and his men encounter the Harpies, than which there is "no monster more dire."[78] Aeneas describes the Harpies' "maidenly faces" but adds that they have:

> ... a most disgusting discharge from their bellies,
> clawed hands, and faces always pale with hunger.[79]

The Harpies are also filthy and emit a horrible odor. The description of discharge dripping from their bellies suggests menstruation,[80] and the monsterization of this essential female function is an even more blatant expression of fear of the feminine than Vergil's descriptions of Scylla and Charybdis,[81] whom Aeneas and his crew go on to avoid, just barely, after driving away the Harpies.

Vergil's epic describes many other monsters, most notably the two vast serpents that strangle Laocoön and his sons, and the various nightmarish creatures which Aeneas sees in Hades. In short, Greek and Roman hero myths contain a great profusion of monstrous beings, most of which demonstrate the same prevalent general themes: the male must overcome the female and various representatives of her chthonic origins; and the male must control nature and replace disorder with order, chaos with culture.

Monstrous Races and Unnatural Animals

Greek myths tell of various monstrous races such as the Cyclopes and Laestrygones, the giant, man-eating tribes mentioned above. Other monstrous races of classical mythology are mostly animal–human hybrids such as the Tritons, half-human sea beasts; the satyrs and silenoi, lustful horse-men associated with the god

---

77   For an extended discussion of Scylla as a prototype for the *vagina dentata*, see Miller's essay in this volume. Charybdis, too, is a frightening depiction of female sexuality: a giant, devouring black hole.

78   *Aeneid* 3.214.

79   *Aeneid* 3.216–18.

80   The more usual interpretation is that *foedissima ventris/proluvies* (3.216–17), "a most foul discharge from the belly," refers to excrement, because of the Harpies' constant hunger (see Nicholas Horsfall, *Vergil, Aeneid 3: A Commentary* [Leiden: Brill, 2006], pp. 187–8). But *venter* was an extremely common Latin word for "womb" as well as "belly" in the late Republic and early Imperial period, and *proluvies* often meant "flood," and did not exclusively refer to discharge from the bowels.

81   See also Miller's essay in this volume, which discusses the association of female fertility with monstrosity.

Dionysus;[82] and the centaurs, half-human, half-horse hybrids. But in addition to mythological stories, we have various ethnographical accounts written by Greeks who traveled to faraway places and saw wondrous sights or heard amazing rumors and recorded them. Stephen Asma explains: "As explorers, soldiers, and traders penetrated strange lands, they absorbed local legends and encountered unfamiliar creatures, bringing all this back to urban Greece and Rome."[83] As in the mythological accounts of hero journeys, these "real" accounts of ethnographers and historians describe races that are stranger, more barbaric, less human, and less humanoid the farther away from Greece one travels. Most ancient Greeks and Romans considered all human ethnic groups other than their own to be barbarians, that is, less civilized. And, as Asma puts it, "the literature of the ancients reveals a continuum of degrees, whereby races of men decline further and further away from their ethnocentric starting place."[84] For example, foreign races on the fringes of the Greek world, such as the Thracians and Scythians to the north and east or the Egyptians to the south, have different customs and different physical features from the Greeks but are not monstrous; farther away races that the Greeks saw rarely (or not at all) are much more strange, deformed, and overall physiologically unlikely if not impossible, such as the races farther south in Libya and farther east in India.[85] It seems that the Greeks sublimated many instinctive fears in the monsters of their myths, but they also rationalized those fears in another, non-mythological form with their increasingly exaggerated descriptions of monstrous races and animals, most of which they imagined to live very far away.[86]

The historian and ethnographer Herodotus (second half of the fifth century BCE) provides in his *Histories* some of the earliest descriptions of fantastic races, recording nearly everything he was told, though he remains highly skeptical. For example, regarding tales of a one-eyed race of men in northern Scythia known as Arimaspians, he remarks: "I don't believe one-eyed men exist."[87] Similarly, he remarks, "I don't believe" in a race of goat-footed men or reports of a race of men

---

82 Satyrs were conceived of as half-horse, half-man but differing from centaurs in having essentially human form with only a horse's tail and pointed ears. Occasionally satyrs were depicted with goats' legs.

83 Stephen T. Asma, *On Monsters: An Unnatural History of Our Worst Fears* (Oxford: Oxford University Press, 2009), p. 27.

84 Ibid., p. 36.

85 Herodotus often matches his increasingly uncertain information with increasing distance from the Greco-centric world: see Tim Rood, "Herodotus and Foreign Lands," in Carolyn Dewald and John Marincola (eds), *The Cambridge Companion to Herodotus* (Cambridge: Cambridge University Press, 2006), pp. 290–305.

86 Rudolf Wittkower, "Marvels of the East: A Study in the History of Monsters," *Journal of the Warburg and Courtauld Institutes* 5 (1942), pp. 159–97, at 159.

87 Herodotus 3.116.2. See also discussion of these races in David Asheri, Alan Lloyd, and Aldo Corcella, *A Commentary on Herodotus Books I–IV* (Oxford: Oxford University Press, 2007), p. 504.

who sleep for six months out of the year.[88] And in recording the existence in eastern Africa of races of dog-headed men and headless men with eyes in their breasts, he cautions the reader: "at least, that's what the Libyans *say*."[89] Hearing a Scythian belief that a tribe called the Neuri are werewolves, Herodotus comments: "they do not convince *me*" that such things are true.[90]

Herodotus's *Histories* also contains descriptions of fabulous animals. He seems less skeptical when describing the gold-digging ants of India, "smaller than dogs but larger than foxes";[91] Arabian flying snakes;[92] and gold-guarding griffins.[93] The gold-digging ants are, in fact, "one of the most famous Herodotean *mirabilia*."[94] The story of these ants continued to be enlarged and modified by subsequent authors and enjoyed great success in antiquity until the late Roman period. Herodotus has followed here a motif centered on the theme of a treasure guarded by fabulous animals and the dangers which its theft might involve, and in keeping with tradition the Greeks "set such legends in the furthest regions of the known world."[95] Similar motifs also existed in other literatures of the ancient world: the Indian epic *Mahabharata*, for example, mentions the *pipillika* ("gold of the ants") in relation to northern India.[96] In fact, Herodotus also remarks that both the animals and birds of India are much larger than anywhere else.[97] India, as one of the farthest-known countries from Greece, was the source of much fascination in the West. The first separate Greek treatise on India appeared in the late fifth/ early fourth century BCE, written by Ctesias of Cnidos, a Greek doctor at the court of the Persian king Artaxerxes II. Ctesias wrote his *Indika* mainly to record Persian beliefs about India,[98] and the work survives only in fragments included in later authors, many of whom doubt his credibility but record the fascinating tales anyway. Even these few fragments contain far too many descriptions of

---

88   Herodotus 4.25.1.
89   Ibid. 4.191.4. The emphasis here and below is in the original Greek.
90   Ibid. 4.105.2. See also Asheri et al., *Commentary*, pp. 656, 713–14, for discussion of the Neuri.
91   Herodotus 3.102.
92   Ibid. 3.107–8.
93   Ibid. 3.116. Throughout his *Histories*, Herodotus alternates between being highly logical and astonishingly credulous. For discussion, see James Romm, *Herodotus* (New Haven and London: Yale University Press, 1998), pp. 132–47. Herodotus also mentions these griffins at 4.13 and 4.27. On griffins in the ancient Greek and Roman world, see Asma, *On Monsters*, pp. 27–30; and Mayor, *The First Fossil Hunters*, pp. 15–52. For more on Herodotus's descriptions of animal and human monsters, see Van Duzer's essay in this volume.
94   Asheri et al., *Commentary*, p. 498.
95   Ibid., pp. 498–9. He notes that the motif of the gold-guarding ants was picked up in the Middle Ages, for example, in the epistle of "Prester John" to Frederik II.
96   Ibid., p. 499. Given the date of composition of the *Mahabharata* (late fifth century BCE), it is possible, though unlikely, that Herodotus's story influenced the Indian version.
97   Herodotus 3.106.
98   As Van Duzer also points out, Ctesias did not himself travel to India.

monstrous races and animals to list here, but they certainly agree with Herodotus in insisting that the animals and birds of India are unusually large. Ctesias records, among other immense creatures, roosters of enormous size, dogs so huge that they fight with lions, sheep and goats larger than asses, and a worm at least seven cubits long (circa twelve feet).[99] But it is the monstrous hybrid animals and bizarre races of men that received the most attention. Besides mentioning the gold-guarding griffins familiar from Herodotus, Ctesias gives us the first extant description of the manticore (*martichora*, "man-eater"), "which has a human face, is the size of a lion, and is red like cinnabar":[100]

> *It has three rows of teeth, human ears, and light blue eyes like a man's. It has a tail like a land scorpion on which there is a stinger more than a cubit long. It also has stingers on either side of the tail as well as on the end like a scorpion ..."*[101]

But the most extensive surviving fragments of Ctesias are devoted to the race of dog-headed men, mentioned briefly by Herodotus but given the full treatment in the *Indika*. Known as the Cynocephaloi ("Dog-headed"), this race has "larger teeth than dogs and claws that are similar but larger and more rounded," and tails that are "just above the rear end, like that of a dog" in addition to their dog heads.[102] They live in caves in the mountains, communicate by howling and making gestures, and live by hunting.[103] Ctesias also describes people who lack necks and have eyes on their shoulders, and the Monocoli ("One-legged"), a race who "have one leg but show amazing agility by jumping. These same men are also called the Sciapodes because when it is hot, they lie on the ground on their back and shade themselves with their feet."[104] These races all live on the fringes of "civilized" society and, in

---

99 See Andrew Nichols, *The Complete Fragments of Ctesias of Cnidus: Translation and Commentary with an Introduction*, unpublished PhD dissertation, University of Florida, 2008, pp. 111–25.

100 Nichols, *Complete Fragments*, pp. 111 and 116–17.

101 Ibid., p. 111.

102 Ibid., p. 113. Also see Steel's essay in this volume for extended discussion of medieval accounts and images of Cynocephaloi.

103 See Nichols, *Complete Fragments*, pp. 113–14 and 121–2; also James S. Romm, *The Edges of the Earth in Ancient Thought: Geography, Exploration, and Fiction* (Princeton: Princeton University Press, 1992), pp. 77–81.

104 The Sciapodes ("Shade-footed" or "Shady-feet") were also described by an earlier writer, Scylax of Caryanda (fifth century BCE), who, according to later sources, recorded that "the Sciapodes have very broad feet and at midday they drop to the ground, stretch their feet out above them, and give themselves shade." Scylax also wrote of "countless other strange marvels" similarly recorded by Ctesias (Nichols, *Complete Fragments*, pp. 116 and 125; see also Wittkower, "Marvels of the East," p. 160). It is possible—perhaps even likely—that many of these accounts arose through misinterpretation of Indian stories. Various Indian epics, for example, contain a legend about the Ages of Man, wherein the lengths of the Ages decrease along with righteousness, and men grow

addition to being geographically distant, live in topographically wild areas such as caves, lacking the basics of culture.

The Greek fascination with India, particularly with its bizarre races and fauna, grew even more intense in the fourth century BCE following the expeditions of Alexander the Great, whose invasion of India in 326 BCE changed and added to the Western conception of the country. Information passed down by those who accompanied Alexander on his campaigns made its way into the works of various writers, including the *Indika* of Megasthenes (circa 350–290 BCE), an Ionian Greek who went on several embassies to the court of the Indian king Chandragupta.[105] Though marred by his credulous acceptance of folktale, Megasthenes's *Indika* provided the fullest account of India yet and, along with the *Alexander Romance* by Pseudo-Callisthenes (circa third century BCE), became the source for many centuries for Western knowledge of India. Megasthenes repeated much of what Herodotus and Ctesias had already said, but "added considerably to the list" of oddities, writing of serpents with wings like bats; men without mouths, who lived on the smell of roasted meat and the perfumes of fruit and flowers; and people with no nostrils, among others.[106] Similarly, the *Alexander Romance* "attaches to Alexander a number of encounters with fabulous humans and creatures in distant regions," which, in addition to the Cynocephaloi and men with no heads, included a crab the size of a man's torso with pincers six feet long, and three-eyed lions.[107] Wittkower notes that the belief in a dog-headed race was known in all parts of Asia, and that one-eyed races appear in the *Mahabharata* and other Indian epics, where they were apparently also considered barbaric.[108] Nevertheless, it was the classical conception of India as a land of fabulous races and marvels that kept its hold on the European imagination all the way into the fifteenth and sixteenth centuries, until far more accurate reports by travelers "made it impossible to maintain the old views about India."[109]

---

smaller in stature and their lifespan contracts until they beget children at age ten and are white-haired at 16 (West, *Hesiod: Works and Days*, pp. 174–6). Ctesias tells of an Indian tribe having eight digits on each hand and foot, and whose children are born with white hair; travelers may have heard the metaphorical story of the Ages of Man and taken it as an account of a real race.

105　As with the writings of Ctesias, Megasthenes's work survives only in fragments preserved in later authors. For Chandragupta, the Greeks had several different names: Sandrokyptos, Sandrokottos, and Androcottus. In his chapter in this volume, Van Duzer uses "Sandrocottus."

106　See Wittkower, "Marvels of the East," p. 162; also Asma, *On Monsters*, pp. 19–22 on Alexander's encounters with monstrous animals. Regarding the names for various races, I have been following the sources, giving proper names where they do. Herodotus, for example, uses "cynocephaloi" to describe the race but does not use it as a name, as opposed to his use of "Neuri" and "Scythian." For Ctesias, I have followed Nichols's text.

107　Murgatroyd, *Mythical Monsters*, p. 19.

108　Wittkower, "Marvels of the East," p. 163.

109　Ibid., p. 194.

Romans and Monsters

The Romans of the late Republic and early Empire adapted the Greek prototypes of monsters without changing much, just as the Romans adapted the Greek pantheon. Despite their lack of innovation, however, the Romans certainly appear to have been just as entranced by monsters as the Greeks were—if not more so.[110] Thus, rather than keeping the monstrous at arms' length as the Greeks preferred, the Romans embraced the monstrous and allowed the grotesque and bizarre to "spill over into every aspect of Roman life."[111] The Romans were, in short, interested in what they considered freaks of nature, which included not only monstrous animals but also what in their view were deformed and thus monstrous humans, such as dwarfs and hunchbacks.[112] The Romans' predilection for the unusual may have been in part an expression of their expansionist mentality, influenced by the changing boundaries of the Empire.

The Roman naturalist Pliny the Elder (first century CE), whom Asma terms "one of the most important characters in the history of monsterology,"[113] describes so many monstrous creatures and races in his *Natural History* that they cannot all be listed here, though we should note that his work was so influential that it became one of the main sources for medieval monster lore.[114] Aside from monsters mentioned by earlier authors such as the manticore, griffin, and werewolves, Pliny gives us one of the earliest written descriptions of the basilisk, noting that anyone who looks the creature directly in the eyes immediately dies. He continues:

> It is not more than twelve inches long ... All other serpents flee at its hiss, and it does not move forward by means of much coiling as other serpents do, but proceeds upright with its middle held high. It destroys plants not only with its touch but with its breath; it burns up grass and breaks rocks.[115]

Other bizarre creatures on Pliny's list include the amphisbaena, an African two-headed snake; the catoblepas, a monstrous animal the size of a bull, with a horse's mane, and which, like the basilisk, had a gaze fatal to anyone who met it; and a tree-climbing octopus that was at home on land as well as in the sea.[116] In cataloging such creatures, Pliny was not only reflecting the "encyclopedic mentality" that

---

110   Carlin A. Barton, *The Sorrows of the Ancient Romans: The Gladiator and the Monster* (Princeton: Princeton University Press, 1993), p. 85.
111   Ibid., p. 85.
112   Ibid., p. 86.
113   Asma, *On Monsters*, p. 33.
114   Wittkower, "Marvels of the East," p. 166. Also, as Van Duzer notes, Pliny's descriptions of monstrous races were themselves heavily influenced by Ctesias (for example, his description of the manticore, *Natural History* 8.30.75).
115   *Natural History* 8.33.78.
116   On this last, see Camilla Asplund Ingemark, "The Octopus in the Sewers: An Ancient Legend Analogue," *Journal of Folklore Research* 45/2 (2008), pp. 145–70.

was becoming popular during his time, but also aiming for that audience of Romans interested in the unusual and strange. Increasing curiosity in the world around them, a result of Roman military and economic expansion, "served only to stimulate rather than modify such interest: the more extraordinary the actual discoveries, the greater the hope of still more wondrous things to come."[117] Pliny himself commented: "Nature always persuades me, when I observe her, that nothing about her is impossible to believe."[118]

We also have a good example of the Roman interest in hybrids and other oddities of nature in the *Mirabilia* of the Greek author Phlegon of Tralles (second century CE).[119] Phlegon's work includes an entire section on monstrous births, such as a child that had four heads, a child born with a head growing out of its left shoulder, and a child born with the head of the Egyptian god Anubis (the head of a jackal).[120] Children with such manifest congenital abnormalities were often believed to be portents sent by angry gods, which did not bode well for the children: "In Rome a certain woman brought forth a two-headed baby, which on the advice of the sacrificing priests was cast into the River Tiber."[121] At the same time, Plutarch, writing in the first and second centuries CE, describes—

---

117 Mary Beagon (trans. and comm.), *The Elder Pliny on the Human Animal: Natural History Book 7* (Oxford: Clarendon Press, 2005), p. 17.

118 *Natural History* 11.2.6.

119 Phlegon of Tralles's *Mirabilia* is probably the most famous classical example of paradoxography, a genre of literature dealing with abnormal occurrences and inexplicable phenomena in nature.

120 William Hansen (trans. and comm.), *Phlegon of Tralles' Book of Marvels* (Exeter: University of Exeter Press, 1996), p. 46. Hansen, p. 151, notes that "Persons, mostly infants, possessing a greater or smaller than usual inventory of external body parts appear very frequently in the list of prodigies compiled by Julius Obsequens" (*Liber Prodigiorum*). Garland, *The Eye of the Beholder*, pp. 155–6, discusses Aristotle's theory, set forth in his *Generation of Animals*, that a fusion of sperm causes such deformities. Regarding the child with the head of Anubis, Hansen comments (p. 153): "Rather than simply saying that the child had the head of a dog, Phlegon compares it to Anubis either because the overall image of the child's human body and canine head was most familiar as that of the mixed-form god Anubis, or because the child's head resembled that of Anubis specifically in being jackal-like. Moreover, he may have wished to avoid the word 'dog-headed', which was somewhat imprecise," since it might be taken as a reference to the Cynocephaloi.

121 Hansen, *Phlegon of Tralles' Book of Marvels*, p. 47. Of course, it was not unusual for children born with physical disabilities or abnormalities to be exposed in the wilderness or allowed to die in some other manner, as such children would have been both a financial burden and an embarrassment to their parents (Hansen, p. 150). Hansen (p. 128) adds that "the usual term for strikingly abnormal offspring in Greek is *teras*, from which derives the modern term 'teratology', the study of congenital malformations." The Greek *teras* differed from the term *ektrapéloi*, which meant "deviants" (literally, "turning from the path") and referred to humans whose deformities were not obvious at birth but who developed abnormally as they grew. As Pliny the Elder notes, there was no Latin equivalent term for the Greek *ektrapéloi* (*Natural History* 7.16.76).

and, it should be added, deplores—a "monstrosities market"[122] frequented by the Romans, who would browse for such oddities as persons without calves, with unusually short arms, with three eyes, with ostrich heads, and in general for creatures of mixed form.[123] It is unclear from Plutarch's description "whether the Monstrosities Market was an actual market-place for the buying and selling of human curiosities or a place for viewing them for a fee,"[124] much like the "freak shows" popular in circuses and carnivals in the US in the nineteenth and early twentieth centuries.[125] Ancient authors also reported the occasional capture and public display of fabulous beings such as hippocentaurs[126] and Tritons; doubtless some of these exhibits were instances of erroneous identification or deliberate fraud along the lines of P.T. Barnum's "Fiji Mermaid."[127] There were semi-permanent collections of such wonders in various temples that basically served as museums: in the Temple of Athena in Tegea, for example, "you could see such mythological wonders as the skin and tusks of the Calydonian Boar."[128] Other items on display around the ancient world included gigantic bones; the skeleton of the sea monster that threatened Andromeda; and the hair of Medusa (which had evidently lost its petrifying effect).[129] In fact, aside from their gladiatorial games, a favorite Roman pastime was the collection of monster artifacts, many of which were commercial hoaxes, but no matter; they were still status symbols.[130] Many Roman patricians were vastly wealthy and able to afford such rarities and curiosities. The Roman emperors in particular were avid collectors, not only of material curiosities such as giant bones but also of living human oddities. Garland suggests that this is partially because a monster, like an emperor, is "something of a social anomaly," and "their exclusion from the world of the able-bodied made the deformed ideal companions and confidants of emperors," a fad that may have originated with the Egyptian pharaohs.[131] The Romans' interest in monstrosities may also have been related to their imperialistic tendencies, to "the emperor's ever-lengthening quest in a shrinking world for something new and

---

122 "the *teraton* agora" (Plutarch, *De Curiositate* 10, also *Moralia* 520c).
123 Plutarch, *De Curiositate* 10 and *Moralia* 520c; see also Hansen, *Phlegon of Tralles' Book of Marvels*, p. 150; Barton, *The Sorrows of the Ancient Romans*, p. 86; and Garland, *The Eye of the Beholder*, p. 47.
124 Hansen, *Phlegon of Tralles' Book of Marvels*, p. 150.
125 P.T. Barnum, for example, provided many human curiosities to his audiences starting in the 1940s. See also Tod Browning's 1932 film "Freaks," which starred men and women with real deformities, and Robert Bogdan, *Freak Show: Presenting Human Oddities for Amusement and Profit* (Chicago: University of Chicago Press, 1990).
126 Like "centaur," a creature with the upper body of a human and the torso and legs of a horse, but distinguished from the centaurs of myth, which were a specific hybrid race from Thessaly. See Hansen, *Phlegon of Tralles' Book of Marvels*, p. 170.
127 Ibid., pp. 171–6; Garland, *The Eye of the Beholder*, p. 55.
128 Hansen, *Phlegon of Tralles' Book of Marvels*, p. 175.
129 Ibid., pp. 175–6; Garland, *The Eye of the Beholder*, pp. 54–5.
130 Gilmore, *Monsters*, p. 45; see also Mayor, *The First Fossil Hunters*, pp. 230–3.
131 Garland, *The Eye of the Beholder*, p. 49.

exotic to relieve his aching boredom."[132] At the same time, we might consider why we ourselves find such exhibits fascinating: people still flock to the dinosaur halls in museums and to the many Ripley's "Believe It Or Not" exhibitions around the country; Diane Arbus's photos of human "deviants" remain controversial but highly popular; and the number of visitors to the Mutter Museum (of human pathology) in Philadelphia increases with each passing year.[133]

Conclusion

Representations of monsters in the ancient world in both art and literature became so common that various ancient authors mocked their countrymen's obsessions with them.[134] We have already seen Herodotus's skepticism and Plutarch's disgust at people's gullibility and fascination with monsters. The Greek geographer Strabo (first century CE) and the Roman grammarian Aulus Gellius (second century CE) were also highly critical of such beliefs. The second-century CE author Lucian, in his *True History*, parodies the tales of monstrous creatures and races found in Homer, Herodotus, Ctesias, and other authors by creating even more exaggerated creatures and races such as three-headed vultures as large as horses; birds with grass for feathers and lettuce-leaves for wings; and a race of eel-eyed, lobster-faced people, to name only a few.[135] These creatures succeed as parodies in being hybrids even more bizarre than those found in previous authors: animals are mixed with vegetable matter, for example. Lucian also places his vastly exaggerated fabulous races at an even farther distance than any other ancient author: these races live on the *Moon*.[136] Lucian, in announcing up front that the *True History* is a parody of Homer, Ctesias, and others,[137] invites his readers to spot the allusions, exaggerations, and allegories.[138]

---

132 Ibid., p. 50.
133 The Ripley's museum exhibits contain alleged examples and real documentation of human "freaks," and the Mutter Museum includes such exhibits as a plaster cast of co-joined twins Chang and Eng; skeletons of a giant and a midget; and a collection of (fatal) baby deformities.
134 Gilmore, *Monsters*, p. 37, giving Horace and Vitruvius as examples, in addition to Lucian.
135 Interestingly, Lucian's *True History* is also one of the only works of fiction from antiquity that includes giant *insects* and arachnids rather than reptilian or animal monsters. Lucian describes spiders as large as islands, ants 200 feet long, gigantic mosquitoes, and fleas the size of twelve elephants. Although the gold-digging ants were popular from Herodotus on (see above), no other work from antiquity contains a proliferation of gigantic insects and arachnids on Lucian's scale.
136 An equally large number of strange races and fabulous creatures live on the Sun. On the monstrous in Lucian, see also Van Duzer's essay.
137 Lucian, *True History* 1.2–4.
138 For a detailed analysis of Lucian's *True History* as parody and philosophy, see Aristoula

Despite the occasional skepticism and satire, stories of monstrous creatures retained their popularity throughout classical antiquity. For the Greeks and Romans, the cultural realization of monsters often expressed their anxiety over essential antagonisms, with the themes underlying the stories remaining quite consistent: the struggle of order against chaos; of the known against the unknown, the familiar against the unfamiliar and remote; of the rational against the irrational and inexplicable; of the masculine against the feminine; of culture against nature, as the heroes— representatives of civilization—confronted monsters embodying uncontrollable aspects of the natural world. In short, monsters represented the untamed forces of nature that presented a dangerous threat to orderly human society.[139] But these monsters were, and still are, necessary. By constantly challenging man's attempt to impose order on his environment, monsters ensure "that the civilized order is kept flexible and permeable to changing influences of a creative power that has not yet ceased to flow."[140] Monsters remind us that our environment is *not* always controllable. The earth keeps changing, and we must continue to adjust; we must continue to be creative and heroic in our efforts to bring order to the chaos constantly threatening us, and thus to accept the monstrous even while trying to keep it at bay. The Greeks and Romans, in their literature and society, realized that even as we reject monsters, we embrace them; even as we fear them, we enjoy them and the challenges they represent. We cannot live without them.

Georgiadou and David H.J. Larmour, *Lucian's Science Fiction Novel* True Histories: *Interpretation and Commentary* (Leiden: Brill, 1998). They suggest possible origins for Lucian's monstrous creatures. On the three-headed vultures, for example, they comment, "having three heads is appropriate for creatures whose function is to guard something," such as triple-headed Hecate (goddess of the crossroads) and Cerberus (p. 96).

139 Other interpretations are not inconsistent with these themes: Gilmore, for example, suggests that, given the often ancestral nature of many monsters—with an earlier epoch of the cosmos inhabited by huge, monstrous, powerful creatures—"one can also view the tales of heroes and monsters as a kind of metaphor for the parent–child relationship, in which the monsters are fantasized images of one's own parents, who seem immense to their own children, and all-powerful and dominating and therefore threatening" (*Monsters*, p. 46). This would certainly be in keeping with the often-Oedipal patterns present in early succession myths, with younger generations of gods overthrowing their elders. See, for example, Richard Caldwell, *The Origin of the Gods: A Psychoanalytic Study of Greek Theogonic Myth* (New York and Oxford: Oxford University Press, 1989).

140 John and Caitlin Matthews, *The Element Encyclopedia of Magical Creatures* (London: Harper Element, 2005), pp. xviii–xix.

Early Modern Past to Postmodern Future: Changing Discourses of Japanese Monsters

Michael Dylan Foster

Japanese monsters have already taken over the world. In the guise of card games, animated television features, manga, and video games, Pokémon—literally "pocket monsters"—have infiltrated popular culture and leisure time in almost every corner of the globe.[1] Pokémon is an interactive form of entertainment that can be played through a number of platforms, from handheld electronic "gameboy" consoles to trading cards. Currently, there are over 400 individual monsters in the Pokémon universe, each with a distinct name, habitat, and set of characteristics. Success in the game is predicated on mastery of details about these creatures, and there are numerous handbooks and catalogs to map, list, illustrate, and describe them.[2]

Despite its newness and commercial context, the contemporary Pokémon phenomenon provides a good starting point for a chapter on historical and vernacular Japanese monsters. Indeed, a number of Pokémon characters are explicitly derived from earlier monsters of Japanese folklore. More importantly, however, the Pokémon universe—with its multimedia presentation, its profusion of characters, and its requirement of expert knowledge—neatly reflects several overarching characteristics of the Japanese monster world more generally. To a greater or lesser degree, these characteristics have been part of Japanese monster discourse for almost 400 years.

---

1   Since their introduction in Japan in 1996, over 200 million units of Pokémon video games have sold worldwide—and there seems to be no end in sight. See "Pokemon Black Version and Pokemon White Version Coming to North America in Spring 2011," *Business Wire*, May 28, 2010, ABI/INFORM Dateline, ProQuest, Web, June 23, 2010.

2   See Tawara Seiji (ed.), *Poketto monsutaa zukan* (Tokyo: Ascii, 1997); also Nakazawa Shin'ichi, *Poketto no naka no yasei* (Tokyo: Iwanami shoten, 1997); Joseph Tobin (ed.), *Pikachu's Global Adventure: The Rise and Fall of Pokémon* (Durham: Duke University Press, 2004); Anne Allison, *Millennial Monsters: Japanese Toys and the Global Imagination* (Berkeley: University of California Press, 2006).

First, just like Pokémon, Japanese monsterdom is characterized by *abundance* and *variation*. Not only are the sheer numbers in the pantheon overwhelming, but there is also a dazzling variety of phenomena. These monsters have both indigenous and foreign origins and are constructed from a dynamic mixture of past and present folk ideas, individual creativity, visual imagery, narrative innovation, and commercial inspiration. Secondly, the predominant strategy for coming to terms with this variety and abundance has been through taxonomic processes of collection, classification, and ordering—what I refer to as *encyclopedic* discourse. And finally, even as they are sometimes believed, feared, or scientifically debunked, Japanese monsters have often been infused with a lively sense of playfulness, treated in a *ludic* fashion that neatly complements more serious encyclopedic discourses.

With these overarching principles as a backdrop—abundance/variation, encyclopedic discourse, and ludic sensibilities—this chapter introduces the broad concept of the monster in Japan and the diverse cultural meanings that it has assumed from the early modern period to the present. Alternately frightening and fun, horrible and humorous, repulsive and cute, Japanese monsters are remarkably mutable and resilient. Not only have they withstood the rationalizing forces of Japan's modernity, but today they are more popular than ever, proliferating in new ways within an increasingly global marketplace. But in Japan, as elsewhere, monsters cannot be understood without also considering the disciplines and the people who have examined them.[3] Along with the role of monsters themselves, then, I introduce the academic study of monsters in Japan—intellectual and popular undertakings that inevitably reflect particular historical moments. I also briefly present some specific monsters to illustrate not only the heterogeneity of Japanese monsters themselves, but also their diverse origins and their constantly changing function within the cultural imaginary.

Time, Words, Concepts

In Japan, as elsewhere, inexplicable phenomena and mysterious creatures have existed since the earliest records. Both divine and demonic, such phenomena as ogre-like *oni*, cunningly vicious *kitsune* (foxes), or animated household objects collectively called *tsukumogami*, have long haunted religious and secular discourses. This chapter will focus only on the last four centuries: from the early modern era, known as the Edo period (circa 1600–1868), to the present. Within this long historical span, we observe distinct changes in the understanding of monsters. The Edo period provides an especially good starting point because it has often been characterized as a time when monsters became notably more visible in the Japanese popular imagination—appearing frequently in written and illustrated texts,

---

3   For a detailed cultural history of Japanese monsters during these periods, see Michael Dylan Foster, *Pandemonium and Parade: Japanese Monsters and the Culture of Yōkai* (Berkeley: University of California Press, 2009).

dramatic performances, and even in board games. This vivacity can be attributed to relative political stability, increased urbanization, high literacy rates, innovations in printing technology, and the concomitant rise of a vibrant artistic and literary culture. Within this milieu, monsters migrated from rural environments and from folk and Buddhist religious contexts to find new spawning grounds in the world of popular culture.

I should explain here the language of Japanese monstrosity. In the Japanese case, the English word "monster" can be misleading and I use it here only out of convenience. Historically, a range of different terms have been invoked to indicate the strange and mysterious in Japan. During the Edo period, perhaps the most common was *bakemono*, which can be translated literally as "changing thing." Embedded in *bakemono*, and the related *obake*, is an emphasis on transformation, and indeed many—though certainly not all—Japanese monsters are characterized by their shape-shifting abilities.[4] Both *bakemono* and *obake* are still used today in some academic and literary discourses, and also in vernacular conversation (*obake* has a somewhat childish ring to it). Currently, however, the word of choice seems to be *yōkai*, a term made up of two Chinese characters, both of which denote strangeness, mystery, or suspicion. Although the word itself has semantic roots in China and can be found in Japan as early as the mid-Edo period, it was not until the Meiji period (1868–1912) that it started to be invoked as a technical term for things beyond the realm of explanation. Today *yōkai* appears frequently in both academic and popular writing; it has become an umbrella signifier that can be variously translated as monster, spirit, goblin, ghost, demon, phantom, specter, fantastic being, lower-order deity, or any unexplainable experience or numinous occurrence.[5]

This inclusiveness is significant: in distinction to many conceptions of monstrousness in the West, the category of *yōkai* is vexingly diffuse. At one end of the spectrum we find phenomenal occurrences, strange events such as poltergeists or mysterious lights. At the other end are somatic *yōkai*, material things and anomalous animal bodies, such as shape-shifting foxes or the *kappa* water goblin discussed below. At least in general *yōkai* discourse, then, there is a continuum between the spiritual and the material. That is, the concept of *yōkai* represents a hybrid of weird corporeality with something numinous or mysterious, a linking of the tangible and intangible, of object and phenomenon.

Along with *yōkai*, another word often translated as monster is *kaijū*, which might be rendered literally "mysterious beast." The difference between *kaijū* and *yōkai* is a murky one at best, but today *kaijū* are usually associated with gigantic creatures such as Godzilla, Mothra, and Gamera that feature in the genre of *kaijū*

---

4   For Edo-period meanings of *bakemono*, see Adam Kabat, "Bakemono zukushi no kibyōshi no kōsatsu: Bakemono no gainen o megutte," in Komatsu Kazuhiko (ed.), *Yōkai* (Tokyo: Kawade shobō shinsha, 2000), pp. 141–64.

5   Komatsu Kazuhiko, "Yōkai: Kaisetsu," in Komatsu (ed.) *Yōkai*, pp. 435–6. See also Kyōgoku Natsuhiko, "Yōkai to iu kotoba ni tsuite (sono 2)," *Kai* 12 (December 2001), pp. 296–307.

eiga or "monster movies."[6] In the pages that follow, I focus primarily on *yōkai* as conceptions that have come to be associated in the popular imagination with folk culture, in distinction to the *kaijū's* more explicit commercial origins (and grander corporeality). However, one point of this chapter is in fact to underscore the impossibility of making such sweeping characterizations or disentwining the multiple threads of cultural production.

Finally, it is also worth noting the blurriness between the demonic and the deific, between monster and god. Japanese indigenous belief is full of *kami*, Shintō deities often locally associated with natural features such as mountains, rocks, trees, and rivers. Similarly, Japanese Buddhist systems also feature numerous figures, both frightening and benevolent, of monstrous proportions and supernatural proclivities. There is a certain amount of ambiguity between *kami*, these sacred manifestations of belief, and conceptions of *yōkai*. In fact, the founding scholar of Japanese folkloristics, Yanagita Kunio, once posited that *yōkai* should be thought of as *kami* that have "degraded" over time.[7] But the continuum is not just diachronic: a water spirit, for example, may be worshipped as a *kami* by families for whom the river provides ample irrigation, and despised as a *yōkai* by families downriver who experience drought. Perhaps, as folklorist and anthropologist Komatsu Kazuhiko suggests, *yōkai* are "unworshipped" *kami* and *kami* are "worshipped" *yōkai*.[8] Similarly, although they may cause mischief, mayhem, and even commit murder, *yōkai* are not necessarily defined by bad behavior. The example of the *yōkai/kami* water spirit is instructive: in the zero-sum game of human survival, an act that benefits one person may very well hurt another. If any generalization can be made, it is that Japanese monsters are ambiguous—like monsters around the world, they mock definitive categorization.

Changing *Yōkai* Discourses

Japanese fantastic creatures have long been found in folkways and local belief systems, featured in legends and folktales, and even celebrated in festivals and rituals. With increasing urbanization during the Edo period, they came to be prevalent in all sorts of popular cultural products, including woodblock prints (*ukiyo-e*), kabuki theatre, *rakugo* storytelling, and lighthearted illustrated texts called *kibyōshi*.[9] And during

---

6   For more on these distinctions, see Saitō Jun, "Yōkai to kaijū," in Tsunemitsu Tōru (ed.), *Yōkai-henge* (Tokyo: Chikuma shobō, 1999), pp. 66–101.

7   *Yanagita Kunio, Teihon Yanagita Kunio shū 5* (Tokyo: Chikuma Shobō, 1969), p. 125. All translations from Japanese texts are my own.

8   Komatsu Kazuhiko, *Yōkaigaku shinkō: Yōkai kara miru Nihonjin no kokoro* (Tokyo: Shōgakkan, 1994), pp. 33–40, 162–73.

9   For the important relationship of *yōkai* with the *kibyōshi* genre, which flourished between 1775 and 1806, see Adam Kabat, *Edo bakemono zōshi* (Tokyo: Shōgakkan, 1999); *Ōedo bakemono saiken* (Tokyo: Shōgakkan, 2000).

Japan's modern period and into the present, they have remained a constant presence in literature, manga, film, and now video games. In one sense we can think of Japanese monsters as being, in the terminology of contemporary media discourse, *multi-platform*—that is, the question of "origins" and "authenticity" is quickly subsumed by the fact that they are at home in a wide range of environments and media. In outlining the history and nature of something as multi-faceted as *yōkai*, then, it is impossible to separate the creatures themselves from the historical and discursive contexts in which they appear, as well as from the individuals who have contemplated, played with, and written about them. One way to explore their changing role within the Japanese cultural imaginary, therefore, is to focus on how they have been studied.

Early Modern Monsters

Indeed, since at least the Edo period, scholars have made concerted efforts to grapple with these mysterious creatures. In Japan this early modern period was characterized by the prominence of a strain of neo-Confucian thought that promoted the "investigation of things" (*kakubutsu chichi*) in order to understand the structure of nature and the proper order of society. This drive for understanding inspired the importation of numerous natural history texts and pharmacopeias from China, and also fostered the development of indigenous natural history studies accessible to people in different social strata. Included in these books were some of the monsters we have come to call *yōkai*. One particularly impressive work was a 105-volume encyclopedia called the *Wakan-Sansaizue* (circa 1715), which not only incorporated knowledge (and images) from numerous Chinese sources, but also presented indigenous learning.

Figure 5.1   Mōryō from *Wakan-Sansaizue.*

A number of the creatures that would come to be known as *yōkai* are seamlessly folded into the various sections of this massive compendium. In the section on "fish types," for example, there is a succinct entry for a *ningyo*, or mermaid, which includes a matter-of-fact description of its appearance, reference to Chinese and Japanese texts, and a casual mention that *ningyo* bones can be made into a poison with "wonderful effect."[10] There is also an entire chapter devoted to different types of dragons, and elsewhere we find real animals, such as elephants and tapirs, that do not exist in Japan; within the context of this inclusive catalog, it is easy to imagine their conflation with creatures of a more fantastic bent. Another section contains a panoply of odd beings—one-legged mountain spirits (*sansei*), the monkey-like *enkō*, mountain witches (*yamauba*)—all more or less anthropomorphic. Again, most descriptions refer back to Chinese texts, and include a straightforward presentation of physical characteristics, habits, and habitats. A creature called a *mōryō*, for example, is described as being the size of a "three-year-old child, black and red in color, with red eyes, long ears and beautiful hair." The entry goes on to note, casually, that, according to a particular Chinese text, *mōryō* "like to eat the livers from dead bodies." The author also adds his own suggestion, based on his reading of a classic Japanese text (*Nihonshoki*), that the *mōryō* may be a "mountain deity."[11] The image included with the encyclopedia entry emphasizes the creature's childlike appearance rather than its gruesome diet (Figure 5.1).

The *Wakan-Sansaizue* was a serious encyclopedic effort born of an intellectual milieu that valued taxonomy—naming, listing, categorizing, ordering—what I call encyclopedic discourse.[12] But even as this period in Japanese history was distinguished by such earnest scholarly undertakings, it was also infused with a lively and creative spirit of play. This ludic mode of expression can be found, for example, in a popular form of entertainment called *hyaku-monogatari*, literally "100 stories," in which people gathered together to exchange spooky tales.[13] A 1718 text summarizes the procedure: "First light one hundred lamps (wicks) with blue paper around them, and hide all weapons. Now, for each frightening tale, extinguish one lamp (wick) … when all one hundred flames have been extinguished, a monster [*bakemono*] will most definitely appear."[14] In other words, after each story, a light

---

10   Terajima Ryōan, *Wakan-Sansaizue* 7 (Tokyo: Heibonsha, 1994), pp. 183–4.

11   Terajima, *Wakan-Sansaizue* 6, pp. 156–7.

12   The *Wakan-Sansaizue* entailed amalgamation and compilation akin to—but several decades earlier than—Diderot's famous *Encyclopédie* of 1751–72.

13   More accurately, such a gathering was called a *hyaku-monogatari kaidan kai*.

14   From *Wakan kaidan hyōrin*, quoted in Tachikawa Kiyoshi (ed.), *Hyaku-monogatari kaidan shūsei* (Tokyo: Kokusho kankōkai, 1995), p. 354. Most *hyakumonogatari* collections include fewer than 100 tales; the number may simply indicate a large amount. Nakazawa Shin'ichi suggests that 100 also "clearly possesses a qualitative meaning," underscoring the profusion of different *yōkai* and a sense of wonder at their variety. Their classification and ordering, he argues, was a "pleasure" discovered by the people of the Edo period and represents a sensibility that distinguishes them from previous generations. "Yōkai-ga to hakubutsugaku," in Komatsu (ed.), *Yōkai*, p. 79.

would be extinguished until the gathering was thrown into blackness—and a real monster would show itself.

Because this otherworldly contact had no explicitly serious objectives beyond the thrills and chills of contact itself, it was likely that many participants approached the experience with tongue firmly set in cheek. Informing this playfulness was a desire for the monstrous, a tempting of fate and bravery, and a will to experience the unexplainable. The origins of the monsters themselves were as varied as the participants: there were stories with Chinese literary origins, folk narratives from the Japanese countryside, personal experience narratives, and tales created expressly for the game.[15] The popularity of these oral sessions soon led to their collection and publication in books, where they were shared widely throughout the country.

Hyaku-monogatari, then, is a way of playing with monsters that may have had its beginnings as an oral pastime but soon tapped into urban, literary, and commercial sensibilities. Out of this environment emerged one of the key figures in the early modern understanding of monsters: Toriyama Sekien (1712–88), an artist and cataloger whose work continues to inform understandings of *yōkai* today. Between 1776 and 1784, Sekien produced four sets of illustrated bestiaries, in codex form, that collectively document over 200 different *yōkai*.[16] These texts neatly embody the coalescence of encyclopedic and ludic articulation. Each page features an illustration of a particular *yōkai*, often complete with description. At the same time, however, the accompanying text and illustration often contain lively word and image play. Sekien may have been cataloging *yōkai*, but he and his readers were having fun in the process. In fact, while clearly knowledgeable about traditional beliefs, Sekien was apparently not averse to inventing his own monsters. One analysis posits that of over 200 distinct creatures, most are derived from Japanese folklore, art, or literature, 14 come directly from Chinese sources, and 85 may have been fabricated.[17]

Sekien's catalogs did not necessarily become working lists from which artists and writers borrowed characters, but his hybrid of encyclopedic and ludic modes served to extract monsters from their narrative and local contexts so that they could become free agents, mutable metaphors for all sorts of purposes. And during the last 100 years of the Edo period, *yōkai* haunted the literature, art, and popular culture of Edo, Osaka, and Kyoto. They appeared in wood block prints, kabuki, popular literature, illustrated texts, and numerous parodies and satires. They also found a place in popular games and entertainments—board games, *yōkai* shooting galleries,

15   Komatsu Kazuhiko, *Shutendōji no kubi* (Tokyo: Serika shobō, 1997), p. 251.
16   *Gazu hyakkiyagyō*, 1776; *Konjaku gazu zoku hyakki*, 1779; *Konjaku hyakki shūi*, 1781; *Hyakki tsurezure bukuro*, 1784. All four texts are reproduced in Inada Atsunobu and Tanaka Naohi (eds), *Toriyama Sekien gazu hyakki yagyō* (Tokyo: Kokusho kankōkai, 1999). Throughout this essay, I follow Japanese scholarly protocol and refer to Toriyama Sekien simply as Sekien; I refer to all other Japanese individuals mentioned here by their family names.
17   Tada Katsumi, *Hyakki kaidoku* (Tokyo: Kōdansha, 1999), p. 20.

spectacle shows, even a "*bakemono* candle" that would project the eerie flickering silhouette of a monster.[18] One game known as *yōkai karuta* especially epitomizes the blending of encyclopedic and ludic sensibilities. Developed during the last third of the Edo period, *yōkai karuta* was an association card game in which each card featured a particular monster; a player's skill was determined by familiarity with associated characteristics and legends.[19] The similarities between this game and contemporary Pokémon play are remarkable.

Scientific Modernity

Toriyama Sekien never explicitly questioned the ontological veracity of *yōkai*. This is not to say that *yōkai* were universally immune to critical analysis during the Edo period—indeed, mysterious phenomena were subject to explanation from a variety of Confucian and Buddhist perspectives. But it was not until the Meiji period (1868–1912) and Japan's vigorous push for "civilization and enlightenment" (*bunmei kaika*), that the importation of Western scientific principles inspired scholars and ideologues to actively debunk *yōkai*. In particular, Buddhist philosopher Inoue Enryō (1858–1919) created the discipline of *yōkaigaku* (*yōkai*-ology or "monsterology") with a specific objective: to rationally explain away supernatural beliefs so that Japan could become a modern nation-state.[20] To this end, Inoue collected volumes of data on *yōkai*-related beliefs from around Japan and developed analytical categories to systematically filter out "superstitions" and "false mystery" from what he defined as "true mystery" (in a religious sense).

Inoue was an early student and teacher of psychology and an enthusiastic scholar of philosophical traditions from around the world; in 1887 he founded his own university in order to teach a heady mixture of Western and Eastern learning. He was also a passionate anti-*yōkai* campaigner who traveled throughout Japan (and China) lecturing on monsters and attempting to debunk local beliefs. To be sure, his didacticism may have been informed by nationalistic objectives and a pejorative attitude toward the folk, but he was also an enthusiastic storyteller who seemed to

18   Kagawa Masanobu, "Yōkai to goraku," *Kai* 11(August 2001), pp. 306–7. See also Kagawa, *Edo no yōkai kakumei* (Tokyo: Kawade shobō shinsha, 2006), pp. 181–239; Iwata Noriko, "Bakemono to asobu: Nankenkeredomo bakemono sugoroku," *Tōkyō-to Edo-Tōkyō hakubutsukan hōkoku* 5 (February 2000), pp. 39–52. Takeuchi notes that in art: "The depiction of supernatural themes reached an apogee during the nineteenth century, an age when artists vied with each other to satisfy the public's quickened appetite for images of the bizarre and the macabre." Melinda Takeuchi, "Kuniyoshi's Minamoto Raikō and the Earth Spider: Demons and Protest in Late Tokugawa Japan," *Ars Orientalis* 17 (1987), p. 5.

19   Tada Katsumi, *Edo yōkai karuta* (Tokyo: Kokusho kankōkai, 1998); Kagawa, *Edo no yōkai kakumei*, pp. 189–92; Foster, *Pandemonium and Parade*, p. 73.

20   Figal coins the word "monsterology" in his discussion of Inoue's *yōkaigaku* and its place within modernity. Gerald Figal, *Civilization and Monsters: Spirits of Modernity in Modern Japan* (Durham: Duke University Press, 1999).

enjoy sharing monster tales. His lectures and writing were widely accessible, often published in newspapers, and extremely entertaining. Although his professed purpose was to disenchant monsters with scientific reason, certainly one effect of his efforts was to popularize and transmit narratives from one region to another; Inoue's work was significant not only as a reflection of emerging scientific and psychological paradigms, but also because it tapped into a broad public fascination with the weird and mysterious. Most importantly, perhaps, it established a valuable archive of monster beliefs collected just at this critical moment in which Western rationalism was coloring traditional interpretive paradigms.

Early Twentieth-Century Development of Folkloristics

While Inoue's objective was to explain away the possibility of monsters, in the early twentieth century another scholar emerged with a more humanist, cultural approach to the same problem. Yanagita Kunio (1875–1962), one of modern Japan's most influential thinkers, is generally credited with establishing the discipline of folkloristics (*minzokugaku*). Early in his career, Yanagita began exploring the role of monsters in Japanese culture; unlike Inoue, he did not debunk *yōkai* as superstitions, but rather set out to collect and preserve them as relics of disappearing belief systems. In addition to numerous short essays, one result of this process was "Yōkai meii" (*Yōkai* glossary, 1938–39), a short text describing *yōkai* from information culled from a variety of local gazetteers and folklore collections.[21]

The glossary, of course, fits neatly into the encyclopedic mode of discourse which we have seen before. But significantly, for Yanagita the collecting of monsters can also be seen as acknowledgment of their value as cultural commodities evocative of an idealized past rapidly being displaced by Western industrial modernity. Yanagita's objectives may have been critically distinct from Inoue's, yet they also similarly positioned monsters as central to Japan's identity as a modern nation-state. Classifying *yōkai* as a way to demarcate an "authentic" Japan also had the effect of converting them into historical remainders shorn of living mystery and existing only as museum pieces in the folkloric archives of the modern nation.

Post-War Monster Redux

Although many other voices participated in the discourse of *yōkai* from the Edo period to the present, Sekien's catalogs, Inoue's *yōkaigaku*, and Yanagita's folkloristics are emblematic of historically shifting interpretive paradigms with regard to monstrous phenomena. In the second half of the twentieth century, during the rapid economic expansion and industrial growth that characterized Japanese society after the Second World War, monsters took on yet another meaningful role

---

21 Originally published in the journal *Minkan denshō*, "Yōkai meii" is reprinted in *Teihon Yanagita Kunio shū* 4 (Tokyo: Chikuma Shobō, 1970), pp. 424–38.

within the cultural imaginary. Just as Yanagita had painted them as relics from a disappearing Japan, now they became infused with a deep sense of nostalgia as desired icons from a more "innocent" and "authentic" pre-war Japan.

The individual most responsible for making monsters relevant during this period was manga/anime artist Mizuki Shigeru (b. 1922). Starting in the 1960s, Mizuki enthusiastically revitalized the image of *yōkai* in the popular imagination, breathing life into their weird forms so that they would once again playfully enchant children and adults alike, but at the same time retain their nostalgic association with an earlier Japan. Mizuki's anime and manga are familiar to anybody who grew up watching television or reading manga in Japan since the late 1960s, and today he continues to make an impact on a whole new generation.

Mizuki's most famous manga and anime series, *Gegege no Kitarō* (Spooky Kitarō), focuses on the adventures of a charming boy monster and his gang of *yōkai* friends. Though Kitarō himself was created by Mizuki, many of the *yōkai* that appear in the series are drawn from existing folklore and previous documentation. In fact, along with his popular narratives, Mizuki is well known for his extensive scholarly research and has published numerous illustrated catalogs that recall Edo-period bestiaries. Indeed, in many ways the *yōkai* phenomenon comes full circle with Mizuki: like Toriyama Sekien two centuries earlier, he exploits the popular media of his time while neatly combining the ludic and encyclopedic modes. And like Sekien as well, he celebrates the abundance and diversity of monsters. Just as Sekien's eighteenth-century images exerted a powerful influence on the concept of *yōkai* for years to come, so too Mizuki's work has shaped the meaning of *yōkai* within the popular imagination of late twentieth-century and early twenty-first-century Japan. Moreover, Mizuki himself has become a cultural hero, and every year thousands of tourists travel to the small village of Sakaiminato, where he grew up. Among the many monster-related tourist attractions is a shopping street lined with over 120 bronze *yōkai* figurines.[22]

Illustrative Examples of Monsters

Keeping in mind the abundance and variety of monsters within the Japanese cultural imagination, in the pages that follow I select five specific monsters— some well known, some obscure—that illustrate the historical processes outlined in the preceding sections. While the Japanese panoply contains many charismatic and notable creatures—from bird-like *tengu* mountain goblins to trickster *tanuki* (raccoon dogs)—the ones introduced below provide particular insight into the origins, uses, contexts, and transmission of monstrous knowledge and images. They also demonstrate the influence of individual texts and authors on broader cultural understandings and articulations.

---

22   See Michael Dylan Foster, "Haunted Travelogue: Hometowns, Ghost Towns, and Memories of War," *Mechademia* 4 (2009), pp. 164–81.

Kappa

The *kappa* is one of the most wide-ranging and oldest *yōkai*: a *kappa*-like creature even appears in the early mytho-historical *Nihonshoki* (720). Like most folkloric monsters, the *kappa* varies significantly with historical and geographical context. Having said that, they are almost always portrayed as small anthropomorphic creatures that live in the water, usually a river or pond. They can be deadly, with a penchant for pulling horses into the water, drowning small children, and reaching up through a victim's anus to extract the liver or other internal organ. Or they can simply be mischievous: during the Edo period, they were occasionally found lurking in outhouses, where they would reach up to stroke the buttocks of unsuspecting occupants. The *kappa* often has a carapace on its back like a turtle, and a concave saucer filled with water on its head; if the water spills, the *kappa* loses its notorious supernatural strength. Hence, one well-known method for defeating a *kappa* is to make it bow.

Kappa are found throughout Japan, though often under variant names—such as *kawatarō* or *suiko*—and feature in numerous local legends and folktales.[23] Not surprisingly, there is an extensive entry on the *kappa* in the *Wakan-Sansaizue* (where it is called *kawatarō*):

> *About the size of a ten-year-old child, the kawatarō stands and walks naked and speaks in a human voice. Its hair is short and sparse. The top of its head is concave, and can hold a scoop of water. Kawatarō usually live in the water but in the light of the late afternoon, many emerge into the area near the river and steal melons, eggplants and things from the fields. By nature the kawatarō likes sumō; when it sees a person, it will invite him [to wrestle] ... If there is water on its head, the kawatarō has several times the strength of a warrior ... The kawatarō has a tendency to pull cattle and horses into the water and suck blood out of their rumps. People crossing rivers must be very careful ...*[24]

It is worth noting here that unlike most of the other entries in the *Wakan-Sansaizue*, the kappa description does not reference any Chinese precedents; indeed, while water sprites are certainly a transcultural monstrous form, the *kappa*'s particular combination of characteristics seems to be indigenous to Japan.

Toriyama Sekien includes a *kappa* in his first *yōkai* catalog; Yanagita discusses the *kappa* in various different works; and Mizuki even has a manga series, *Kappa no Sanpei* (Sanpei the Kappa), featuring a *kappa* protagonist. In contemporary Japan, the *kappa* has become much more playful, especially within popular and commercial culture, where it serves as a mascot character for everything from *sake* manufacturers to banks. Sushi shops in Japan (and elsewhere) sell *kappa* rolls

---

23   For a discussion of the many names and characteristics associated with the *kappa*, see Ishikawa Juni'ichirō, *Shinpan kappa no sekai* (Tokyo: Jiji tsūshinsha, 1985); Nakamura Teiri, *Kappa no Nihonshi* (Tokyo: Nihon editāsukūru shuppanbu, 1996).

24   Terajima, *Wakan-Sansaizue* 6, p. 159.

Figure 5.2   Playful image of a *kappa* used on a sign urging people to "work together to make a livable environment" (Shizuoka Prefecture). Photograph by the author.

(*kappa maki*), a rice and cucumber combination named for the *kappa*'s supposed love of cucumbers. And near rivers throughout Japan, signs exhort people to keep the water clean so *kappa* will return; these days, apparently, it is the humans who frighten *kappa* (Figure 5.2).

Tenjōname

Whereas the *kappa* has a long and storied presence in local folklore, other *yōkai* have much more dubious origins. In Mizuki's catalogs, for example, there is an ugly monster called a *tenjōname*, or literally "ceiling licker": a tall, bony creature with frilly hair and an extraordinarily long tongue. Mizuki's illustration shows it seemingly suspended in mid-air, licking a wooden ceiling. "When there is nobody around in an old house, temple, or shrine," Mizuki writes, this monster "comes out and licks with its long tongue ... if they found stains on the ceiling, people in the old days thought it was the work of the *tenjōname*."[25] As an explanation for the otherwise unexplainable, the *tenjōname* fulfills a common function of

---

25   Mizuki Shigeru, *Zoku yōkai jiten* (Tokyo: Tokyo-dō Shuppan, 1984), pp. 152–3.

Figure 5.3   Close-up of bronze figurine of Mizuki's *tenjōname* in Sakaiminato. Photograph by the author.

the monstrous. Significantly, however, Mizuki—writing for a modern urban–suburban readership—endows the creature with a nostalgic rural hue. As a child growing up in a small village before the war, he goes on to explain: "there was an old woman in the neighborhood who was particularly knowledgeable about *yōkai*. On occasion, she used to stay at our place, and she looked at the stains on the ceiling of our house and said, 'Look! The *tenjōname* comes out at night and makes those stains'" (Figure 5.3).[26]

With this brief narrative, then, Mizuki positions the *tenjōname* firmly in rural tradition. But it turns out that Mizuki's illustration is remarkably similar to one by Sekien who, intriguingly, provides a completely different explanation—nothing at all about stains on the ceiling, but rather a sophisticated and playful allusion to a fourteenth-century literary text. In fact, some scholars think that the *tenjōname* was simply fabricated by Sekien.[27] Was Sekien's invention then introduced into oral tradition and village folklore to become, centuries later, an explanation for stains on the ceiling? Whether or not we believe Mizuki's account, it demonstrates the dynamic and non-linear relationship between the oral and the literate (and the

---

26   Ibid., p. 152.
27   Komatsu, *Yōkaigaku shinkō*, p. 63; Murakami Kenji, *Yōkai jiten* (Tokyo: Mainichi shinbunsha, 2000), p. 235.

visual), as well as the constant lively interplay of tradition and individual creativity in the making of monsters.

Ninmenju

In one of his many encyclopedic compendia of *yōkai*, Mizuki describes a tree in Aomori Prefecture that, according to legend, would bleed when cut. He suggests that this strange plant might be a version of the *ninmenju* or *jinmenju*, a monstrous tree with human heads instead of flowers.[28] The *ninmenju* was pictured two centuries earlier by Sekien, who explains that it is found "in the mountains and valleys. Its flowers are like human heads. They do not speak, but merely laugh constantly. If they laugh too much, it is said, they will fall off."[29] The tree in Sekien's illustration skirts the left-hand side and top border of the page, with a spiky leafed branch bearing bald heads. Sekien apparently borrowed his tree from one similarly portrayed in the *Wakan-Sansaizue*, but intriguingly the *Wakan-Sansaizue* illustration features not only the tree, but also a man standing to the right of it. More intriguing still is that this entry is not in the section of the encyclopedia dedicated to plants; rather it is located in the section on "peoples from foreign lands."[30] In fact, what is featured here is not the tree itself, but the land with which it is associated, a place called "Daishi." The *Wakan-Sansaizue* passage refers to an earlier Chinese text, the *Sancaituhui* (circa 1609), where the land is called "Da-shi," possibly a transliteration of "tazi," a Persian word meaning "Arab." Continuing this journey back in time and down the Silk Road, we find different versions of the great Persian epic poem, *Shahnama* (Book of Kings) by Firdawsi (d. 1020), containing illustrations of a man conversing with a human-headed tree. The man, it turns out, is Sikandar, or Alexander the Great, and the illustrations portray his legendary encounter with a talking tree, sometimes called the Wakwak Tree, which prophesized his death.[31]

I trace (very superficially) this complex lineage simply to underscore the dynamic movement of imagery and ideas across space, time, and cultures. Here a picture of Alexander the Great becomes associated with "foreign lands" and enters Japan (through China) during the Edo period (a time, ironically, known for its relative isolation). Eventually man and place are elided and we are left only with a mysterious tree located somewhere in "the mountains and valleys" — a plant

---

28   Mizuki Shigeru, *Zusetsu Nihon yōkai taizen* (Tokyo: Kōdansha, 1994), p. 249.
29   Inada and Tanaka, *Toriyama Sekien*, p. 191.
30   Terajima, *Wakan-Sansaizue* 3, p. 319.
31   See, for example, "Iskandar at the Talking Tree," an illustration by an unknown artist from the fourteenth century, which shows a man on a white horse seemingly in conversation with a tree with human heads: <http://www.asia.si.edu/collections/zoomObject.cfm?ObjectId=10115>, accessed July 5, 2010. On legends of the Wakwak Tree, see David Williams, *Deformed Discourse: The Function of the Monster in Mediaeval Thought and Literature* (Montreal: McGill-Queen's University Press, 1996), p. 210.

monster to join the expanding pantheon of Japanese *yōkai*. The tree, in turn, not only becomes part of the national cultural imaginary, but is specifically associated with a local legend in one corner of Japan. The process illustrates the discursive transmission and transformation of legend and imagery over time, space, and cultural context, and demonstrates one of many ways in which a "Japanese" monster can come into being. A seemingly indigenous *yōkai*, it turns out, may have begun as an Islamic illustration of Alexander the Great!

Gojira

Commercial and political factors also contribute to the creation and promulgation of Japanese monsters. Perhaps the most internationally famous of all Japanese monsters is, of course, Godzilla—or *Gojira* in the Japanese original. As mentioned earlier, *Gojira* is generally labeled *kaijū* or fantastic beast. The original 1954 film (in contrast to the Hollywood re-edit of 1956) explicitly critiques American Cold War policy and Japan's burgeoning post-war democracy. *Gojira*, a deep-sea monster awakened from its slumbers by American weapons testing, works as a powerful metaphor of culture versus nature and for the terrors unleashed by the nuclear age and the unforeseeable forces—political, environmental, technological—that would influence everyday lives in the decades after the war.

Gojira, both movie and monster, also influenced the commercial world of popular culture, spawning an entire genre of monster films. While later creations did not possess the same gravitas as *Gojira*, many of their stories followed a similar narrative pattern: an ancient slumbering beast is brought to life and violence through inadvertent human intervention, be it technological carelessness (*Gamera*; 1965) or commercial ambition (*Gappa*; 1967). In most cases, the *kaijū* in question comes from somewhere offshore, either a distant Japanese island or foreign lands/waters. In this context, Japan's own native folk monsters, the *yōkai*, seem quaint and anachronistic.[32]

Kuchi-sake-onna

Indeed, given post-war Japan's vibrant media culture, rife with monster movies, manga, and anime, it is tempting to believe that the folklore-inspired *yōkai* of the past are no longer viable. In 1979, however, a new phenomenon emerged that

---

32 In a mash-up of *kaijū* movies with more traditional *yōkai*, a recent (2010) film called *Death Kappa* features a gargantuan *kappa* rampaging through the cityscape. For more on *Godzilla* and other monster movies, see William Tsutsui, *Godzilla on My Mind: Fifty Years of the King of Monsters* (New York: Palgrave Macmillan, 2004); William M. Tsutsui and Michiko Ito (eds), *In Godzilla's Footsteps: Japanese Pop Culture Icons on the Global Stage* (New York: Palgrave Macmillan, 2006); Takahashi Toshio, *Gojira no nazo: Kaijū shinwa to Nihonjin* (Tokyo: Kōdansha, 1998).

demonstrated that monsters were still alive and well, despite the industrialization and urbanization that were reshaping the landscape. Or rather, it was these very factors that contributed to the birth of a new legendary monster, the *kuchi-sake-onna*, literally "Slit-Mouthed Woman," who would haunt the urban and suburban streets. A seemingly attractive young woman, *kuchi-sake-onna* always wore a white surgical mask, not in itself unusual in Japan for somebody suffering from a cold; in her case, however, it covered up a mouth hideously slit from ear to ear. As one person recalls from childhood:

> This woman with a white mask and long hair would come from behind and tap you on the shoulder. When you turned to look, she would ask, "Am I pretty?" [Watashi kirei?] If you said, "Yes, you're pretty," she would say "Even like this?" [Kore demo?] and remove the mask and threaten you. Or if you said, "You're not pretty," she would come chasing after you. When I parted with my friends on the way home from school, and it was getting dark, I would be frightened when I thought about it.[33]

For six months, this contemporary legend traveled at explosive speeds throughout Japan, assuming local characteristics wherever it was told, making children frightened to walk home from school alone and, in several locations, even inspiring extra police patrols.[34]

Kuchi-sake-onna draws on a long line of frightening female monsters and ghosts in Japan—from the *yuki-onna* ("Snow Woman") to *ubume* (literally, "Birthing Woman")—but also clearly reflects very contemporary concerns, such as the alienation of concrete apartment complexes, environmental illnesses, educational pressures on children, and anxiety over changing societal roles for women.[35] Moreover, *kuchi-sake-onna*'s rapid diffusion throughout Japan has been attributed to the popular media: her story was broadcast on television and late-night radio, and discussed in weekly magazines and ubiquitous tabloid-like "sports newspapers." Although the initial excitement and fear surrounding her died down after about six months, when the dust settled, she had become a staple of the Japanese bestiary, almost always invoked in discussions of "modern" *yōkai*. She has also resurfaced in Korea, and more recently become a film star, protagonist in a series of Japanese horror movies (*Kuchi-Sake-Onna* [*Carved: The Slit-Mouthed Woman*], 2007; *Kuchi-Sake-Onna 2* [*The Scissors Massacre*], 2008).

---

33   Quoted in Saitō Shūhei, "Uwasa no fōkuroa: Kuchi-sake-onna no denshō oboegaki," *Kenkyū kiyō* 7 (March 30, 1992), p. 90.

34   Asakura Kyōji, "Ano 'Kuchi-sake-onna' no sumika o Gifu sanchū ni mita!" in Ishii Shinji (ed.), *Uwasa no hon* (Tokyo: JICC Shuppan kyoku, 1989), p. 140.

35   Michael Dylan Foster, "The Question of the Slit-Mouthed Woman: Contemporary Legend, the Beauty Industry, and Women's Weekly Magazines in Japan," *Signs: Journal of Women in Culture and Society* 32/3 (Spring 2007), pp. 699–726.

Figure 5.4   Bronze figurine of Mizuki's *kuchi-sake-onna* in Sakaiminato. The cute, almost comical, image is typical of Mizuki's manga style; while retaining features of the monster of legend, the creature is domesticated enough for popular consumption. Photograph by the author.

Japanese Monsters/Global Monsters

Although the examples cited here represent just a tiny selection of hundreds within the informal pantheon, I hope that they suggest the wealth and heterogeneity of Japanese monster culture, and the difficulty of generalizing about such an expansive and bewildering teratology. I began this chapter with a reference to the Pokémon phenomenon because it encapsulates, in a very contemporary guise, so many of the traditional features of the monster world in Japan: the abundance and variety of creatures and an engagement with both the encyclopedic and ludic modes. Pokémon also clearly reflects a transnational, transcultural nature that has long been a part of the history of Japanese monsters, as evident from the complex lineage of the *ninmenju*, but is currently turbocharged by the internet and other technology.

149

Since the 1980s Japan has experienced a so-called "*yōkai* boom" within popular culture; in recent years this monster mania has spread beyond the borders of Japan and the Japanese language. Indeed, Pokémon is only the tip of the iceberg of an expanding global subculture obsessed with Japanese monsters. Internationally circulated media products, such as the anime of Miyazaki Hayao (Studio Ghibli) and blockbuster films such as Takashi Miike's *The Great Yōkai War*, not only arouse an interest in *yōkai* and *kaijū* as exotic foreign monsters, but also inspire creative participation on commercial and folk levels right at home (however defined). Japanese monsters are part of a burgeoning, media-driven, global cultural imaginary of the weird. There are websites dedicated to (encyclopedically) listing and describing *yōkai*. They appear (ludically) in video games (for example, a *tanuki* in the Mario series) and internet role-playing games. There are manga, such as Nina Matsumoto's *Yōkaiden* series and Stan Sakai's *Usagi Yojimbo: Yokai*, written in English for an English-language readership. There are public art shows dedicated to illustrating "original" *yōkai*, and even a cursory glance at DeviantART.com reveals thousands of *yōkai* images posted by budding artists all around the world.

Although Japanese monsters in folklore and popular culture are so often tied to place—specific pools of water, old farmhouses, suburban streets—now it seems that they are also able to travel. This does not mean that they are necessarily detached from the places they once haunted, but their narratives can be told and reinvented in other cultures and other languages, their images consumed, appreciated, and redrawn in new contexts. Just as *yōkai* in post-war Japan became nostalgic icons of an imagined purer and more innocent time, so too perhaps, to people in countries far from Japan, the *yōkai* of global popular culture reflect a desire for an imagined Japan, an "otherworld" where monsters—and the mysterious excitement they embody—is still possible. It remains to be seen whether the monsters of Japan will take up permanent residence in new settings, but whatever happens, it is clear that they are already exerting an influence on conceptions of the monstrous and mysterious in cultures around the world. Perhaps we can no longer call them "Japanese."

On the Monstrous in the Islamic Visual Tradition[1]

Francesca Leoni

Monsters and monstrosity are mostly uncharted subjects in the context of the Islamic cultural sphere. This is fairly surprising given the wealth of creatures populating the related material, and specifically artistic, production that could be considered "monstrous." From fabulous beasts such as harpies and sphinxes insinuated in the decorative friezes of metal and ceramic vessels, to the dragons and demonic creatures inhabiting pages of manuscripts and albums, grotesque beings appear to have repeatedly nourished the creativity of Muslim artists, and have yet rarely been examined beyond their decorative role.[2]

---

1   This chapter is dedicated to the memory of Professor Oleg Grabar (1929–2011), an extraordinary mentor and enlightened scholar, whose enthusiasm for this topic was of great inspiration and support.

2   The few existing studies mostly address the origin and iconographic development of specific groups of images. Such is the case of the giants and demons attributed to Muhammad Siyah Qalam, which appear in a series of *muraqqa*'s (albums) examined in the course of a colloquium held in London in 1980. The proceedings, gathered in the volume *Between China and Iran: Paintings from Four Istanbul Albums* (London: University of London, 1985) edited by Ernst J. Grube and Eleanor Sims, are introduced by an article by Ernst Grube in which he asks whether some of these creatures could be called "monsters" rather than demons ("The Problem of the Istanbul Paintings," pp. 1–30, especially 17–30). However, the author does not further elaborate on the distinction between the two concepts. A much more recent volume dedicated to the same images explores the symbolic and psychological value of Muhammad Siyah Qalam's creatures (Mine Haydaroğlu (ed.), *Ben Mehmed Siyah Kalem, Insanlar ve Cinler Ustasi* [Istanbul: T.C. Kültür ve Turizm Bakanligi, 2004]). The term "monster" is also applied to some of the *'aja'ib al-makhluqat* (wonders of creation) featured in an exhibition dedicated to concepts of marvels and marvellous in Islamic lands (*L'étrange et le merveilleux en terres d'Islam. Paris: Musée du Louvre, 2001: 23 avril–23 juillet 2001* [Paris: Réunion des Musées Nationaux, 2001]), although in this genre the word is used mostly as a synonym of wondrous or odd creatures.

It is important to note that the traditional notion—or better, notions—of monstrosity, essentially developed in the context of Western scholarship, may not prove useful to explain the existence and significance of comparable phenomena in the diverse cultural contexts that produced them.[3] What appear as "monsters" to the eyes of modern observers, in other words, may not have been received or perceived as such at home and/or in the past. At the same time, recent theoretical developments in the field of teratology have distilled a series of premises that contribute to delineate a more culture-neutral analytical category for the phenomenon of the monster, so much as is possible.[4] These "postulates"—which include the idea of monsters as cultural constructs, their shifting and, therefore, indefinable nature, and their role as "dialectical Other"[5]—contribute, in part, to generate a "universal" canon for the monster, and can, therefore, assist scholars, particularly specialists of non-Western traditions, in approaching phenomena of monstrous nature available at different latitudes.[6]

With these conceptual tools in mind, this chapter offers an initial discussion on the subject of monstrosity in the Islamic context by focusing on two meaningful and little explored examples—Iblis, the Islamic Satan, and the *div-i safid*,[7] or white demon—in the context of their respective literary genres, history, and epics. The purpose is not only to analyze what makes these creatures monsters, but also to consider the specific function or functions satisfied by their being or becoming monstrous.

Iblis, the Cursed One

A passage of the *Tarikh al-rusul wa'l-muluk* (*Annals of the Prophets and Kings*), one of the most influential Islamic historical works, composed in the tenth century by Muhammad b. Jarir al-Tabari (d. 923), narrates the creation of Adam, the first man

---

3 The problematic nature of discursive categories generated in the West but used to investigate non-Western phenomena is equally addressed by Matthew Looper, "The Maya 'Cosmic Monster' as a Political and Religious Symbol," and Karin Myhre, "Monsters Lift the Veil: Chinese Animal Hybrids and Processes of Transformation," also in this collection.

4 See, in particular, Jeffrey J. Cohen, "Monster Culture (Seven Theses)," in Jeffrey J. Cohen (ed.), *Monster Theory: Reading Cultures* (Minneapolis, MN: University of Minnesota Press, 1996), pp. 3–25.

5 Ibid., p. 7.

6 Several articles in this collection confirm this. See, in particular, Michael Dylan Foster, "Early Modern Past to Postmodern Future: Changing Discourses of Japanese Monsters."

7 The Persian word *div* is conveniently translated as "demon," although the term does not possess the strictly religious connotation that it has in the West. "Monster" and "fiend" are also used as synonyms for the term (*Encyclopaedia Iranica*, s.v. "div" [Mahmud Omidsalar], http://www.iranica.com/articles/div; last accessed on November 13, 2010). Traditionally, *div*s are ill-natured spirits constantly engaged in troubling mankind.

and first prophet according to Islam.[8] The text reports how God took some soil from the earth and moistened it, making it into "sticky clay," which He then left fermenting and drying for 40 days. With this matter God fashioned the new being, and infused His spirit in him. Once alive, He ordered all angels to bow, and pay homage to the creature. The angels obeyed, and all prostrated except for one, Iblis.

Iblis, as the Qur'an notes, was "from the *jinns*," a group of inferior spirits that ruled the earth before the arrival of mankind.[9] Their disobedient and ill-inclined nature had spread chaos and violence in the world, which God decided to fight by sending an army of angels. Some texts relate that Iblis was a baby-*jinn* who was spared by the angels in the course of this battle, and brought back to heaven to be raised among them.[10] According to other traditions, Iblis was already the guardian of Paradise at the time of the dispute, and headed the army that banished his fellow *jinns* from the world.[11] As beautiful and blessed as the angels, he nonetheless possessed the rebellious temperament of his kind, which eventually brought him to refuse God's order to bow to Adam.[12] As a result of this, Iblis lost his "angelic" status. Offended by his pride, "God 'bedeviled' him (*ablasahu*)," records Tabari, "that is, He eliminated any hope for him to attain some good and made him a stoned Satan as punishment for his disobedience."[13] Iblis was not born a devil (*shaytan*), but became such after his rebellious act.[14] Because of this, he was banished from Paradise, and condemned to a perpetual existence of misery.

Iblis's rebellion is captured by a rare image included in a fifteenth-century historical miscellanea attributed to the Timurid chronicler Hafiz-i Abru,[15] and

---

8 Muhammad b. Jarir al-Tabari, *The History of al-Tabari. Volume One: General Introduction and From the Creation to the Flood*, trans. Franz Rosenthal (New York: State University of New York Press, 1989), pp. 257–66.

9 Qur'an, 18:50.

10 Various versions of this story appear in Zakariyya b. Muhammad al-Qazvini, *Kitab 'aja'ib al-makhluqat wa ghara'ib al-mawjudat* [1414] (Frankfurt: Jumhuriyya Almaniya al-Ittihadiyya, 1994), p. 368.

11 Tabari, *The History of al-Tabari*, p. 253, n. 528.

12 Iblis's reaction to God's order was also prompted by the inferior nature of the first man. The former was created from fire, a matter nobler than clay, the substance used to fashion Adam (ibid., p. 265). The issue is discussed in Giovanna Calasso, "L'intervento di Iblis nella creazione dell'uomo. L'ambivalente figura del 'nemico' nelle tradizioni islamiche," *Rivista degli Studi Orientali* 45/1–2 (1971), pp. 71–90.

13 Tabari, *The History of al-Tabari*, p. 265. Rosenthal notes how the meaning of the Arabic verb *ablasa* (from the same root as the Iblis, b-l-s), "to make someone despair," may have been produced based on the meaning of the name Iblis, which implies that the loss of all hope of salvation resulted from his disobedient act (ibid., p. 265, n. 617).

14 The Arabic term *shaytan* (pl. *shayatin*), generally translated as "devil," or "satan," is connected by Muslim lexicographers to the verb *shatana* which signifies "to detain somebody in order to divert him from his intention and destination" (*Encyclopaedia of Islam, New Edition*, s.v. "shaytan" [Toufiq Fahd and Andrew Rippin], pp. 406–9, at 406).

15 Hafiz-i Abru (d. 1430), the most prominent historian of the first half of the fifteenth century, was not only responsible for the compilation of large historical works such as the *Majma' al-tawarikh* (*Gathering of Histories*) and miscellanea such as the one

comprising part of the Persian translation of Tabari's *Tarikh al-rusul wa'l-muluk* by Abu 'Ali Bal'ami (Figure 6.1).[16] The painting presents a group of angels near a large water basin bowing down in front of Adam, the princely figure standing on a high throne. Behind them is a tree leaning towards the first man, with a move that almost imitates the bending curve of the angelic creatures below. Right next to it stands a horrid being, Iblis, pointing in the direction of Adam with his left hand, while his right hand grasps his long, white beard in a gesture that communicates perplexity.

Three inscriptions in Persian accompany the figures; from right to left, they read "Adam, the vehement" (*adam-i 'arim*), "the powerful angels" (*mala'ikat-i 'arim*), and "the cursed devil" (*shaytan-i la'in*). Due to the obvious appearance of the characters, the viewer is left to wonder what the purpose of this verbal specification is.[17] Significantly, the phrases not only identify the protagonists but also remark on their condition: Adam and the angels are the "strong" beings, who are such because they share God's approval; Iblis, instead, is the damned creature, who has fallen from grace and lost divine favor.

The distinction between blessed and damned is indeed made clear by the way in which the protagonists are represented. Adam is depicted as a prince, with fair complexion and Asian facial features, a classic convention of human representation in the Islamic tradition.[18] His slender body is elegantly dressed with two long-

---

considered here, but also for the copy and refurbishment of older historical works such as the *Jami' al-tawarikh* (*Compendium of Chronicles*), completed by the Ilkhanid vizier Rashid al-Din at the beginning of the fourteenth century. Such a strong preoccupation with history can be explained in light of the interest of the Timurids (1370–1507) to link their political activity to their Mongol ancestors, the Ilkhanids (1258–1336), from which their funder Timur descended. Situating the dynasty's achievements within the context of Mongol history and the history of Islam effectively legitimized their claim to power. The use of historiography as an ideological tool is discussed in John Woods, "The Rise of Timurid Historiography," *Journal of Near Eastern Studies* 46/2 (1987), pp. 81–108. The artistic facets of the Timurid historiographic production are addressed by Thomas W. Lentz and Glenn D. Lowry, *Timur and the Princely Vision: Persian Art and Culture in the Fifteenth Century* (Los Angeles: Los Angeles County Museum of Art; Washington, DC: Arthur M. Sackler Gallery, Smithsonian Institution, 1989), especially pp. 98–104.

16   The image is discussed in Eleanor Sims, *Peerless Images: Persian Painting and its Sources* (New Haven and London: Yale University Press, 2002), p. 264, cat. no. 180, but the text is mistakenly identified as Tabari's *Annals*. The correct information about this manuscript, conserved in the Topkapı Saray Library with shelf number B. 282, is given in Elton L. Daniel, "Manuscripts and Editions of Bal'ami's 'Tarjamah-i Tarikh-i Tabari,'" *Journal of the Royal Asiatic Society of Great Britain and Ireland* 2 (1990), pp. 282–321, at 288, n. 23.

17   I have not been able to examine the manuscript personally, and to ascertain whether the inscriptions are contemporary with the painting and, thus, part of the iconographic program, or were added at a later time, therefore expressing the opinion of a later user of the manuscript.

18   Although occurring already in the artistic production of the Seljuk dynasty (1040–1194), Asian facial features came to define a canon of beauty that was rapidly adopted in the Persianate world after the Mongol invasions, completed by the mid-thirteenth century.

Figure 6.1   Angels bowing in front of Adam. Hafiz-i Abru, *Kulliyat*, Herat, AH 818/1415 CE Topkapı Saray Library, Istanbul, B. 282, folio 16r. Reproduced by permission of the Topkapı Palace Museum, Istanbul.

sleeved robes, the blue one decorated with a sumptuous gold cloud collar, and his long hair is gathered under a precious jeweled crown, gently curling on his shoulders.[19] The angels share Adam's facial features, fancy coiffure, and princely attire to the point that nothing, except for the wings, distinguishes them from the latter. The same cannot be said for Iblis, who is instead depicted as a monstrous creature. A hybrid, dark-skinned being, the rebellious angel has a human-like

---

An overview of specific figural types in the related pictorial tradition is given in Sims, *Peerless Images*, pp. 209–66. On the status held by Asian, specifically Chinese, art and aesthetics in the Islamic world, see David J. Roxburgh, *The Persian Album, 1400–1600: From Dispersal to Collection* (New Haven and London: Yale University Press, 2005), especially pp. 295–301.

19   Colors carry strong associations in the Islamic world. Blue and red are generally associated with royalty, while green is traditionally the color of prophecy. The fact that Adam's robes are blue and red may indicate the intention to present the prophets as earthly leaders and, thus, approximate them to the secular rulers whose lives are also recorded in Tabari's work.

body, claws, tail, and a hideous, disproportioned head with horns, big ears, large flaming eyes, and a long white beard with mustaches. Differently from the angels, his disharmonious body remains unclothed, except for a short skirt split in the middle covering him from his waist to his knees. Yet, similar to them, he has wings, an attribute that probably refers to the fact that he belonged to their select circle prior to his fall, their burned edges being a further sign of his decayed status.

In this painting, physical beauty and monstrosity become the signs of a spiritual status that is in accordance with, or divergent from, God's will, offering an iconographic solution that best interprets the distinction asserted in the narrative. Indeed, the first lines of text that follow the illustration remark on the change of Iblis's condition from an angelic one (hal-i firishta) to that of the devil (hal-i iblis). Likewise, elsewhere in the text, the author stresses God's intentional "deformation" of the rebellious creature in order to humiliate him.[20] The devil's ugliness and monstrosity—which are even more surprising given that he is known to have been created beautiful[21]—are, thus, the stains of his insubordinate attitude, and the tangible marks of the Creator's resentment. The radiance and prince-like appearance of the creatures who respected the command, instead, characterize a visual formula that expresses their moral rightfulness and affinity with God.

The layout of the image also emphasizes the contrast of opposites by means of precise compositional choices. Located in the upper half of the page, the illustration's frame exceeds the width of the text block, confining Iblis to the section that extends into the margin. This fact, which could be determined by the need to accommodate a larger composition than initially planned, intelligently exploits the border to underscore the devil's new marginalized status. Iblis is included in the scene, but remains distant and critical of the event occurring in the main field by means of his sideways position. By the same token, Adam's figure forces the spatial limits of the depiction along the vertical axis, by having his crowned head breaking through the upper frame, and invading the page's top border. This vertical stretch seems to indicate another deliberate choice by the painter, meant to emphasize the superior status of the human being over the rest of the creatures, giving visual expression to the several Qur'anic references that consider Adam endowed with a higher knowledge than anyone else.[22] Finally, the hand gestures of Adam and Iblis are suggestive of opposite morals. While the devil uses them to communicate his reservation about God's most recent creative act, Adam's movements admonish Iblis's behavior. His left hand points at the devil—calling for his attention as much as for that of the viewer—while the right one is directed towards the angels as to suggest what he should do, that is, to obey God's order and bow.

---

20 Tabari, *The History of al-Tabari*, p. 249.
21 Ibid.
22 Qur'an 2:23–28; 7:10–17; and 20:115.

With the call to prostrate to the first man, God requested an act of obedience that complies with the message of total submission at the core of Islam.[23] By pointing at the exemplary behavior of the angels, and their maintained bliss, but also noting the divergent attitude of the devil and his consequent (and visible) damnation, the figure of Adam reminds the readers and viewers of the necessity of surrendering to God's will, thereby fulfilling his role of prophet. Hence, while illustrating a famous episode in the history of mankind, the painting invites the viewer to reflect on true devotion and to ponder on the consequences of apostasy.

A look at the religious climate of the first half of the fifteenth century justifies the possibility of a propagandistic intent behind the visual production sponsored by members of the Timurid dynasty, under whose tenure the present manuscript was executed. To contrast the growing Shi'i sympathies of the population and eradicate heterodox movements that proved especially attractive among the military fringes of the empire, the energies of Shah Rukh (1409–47)—the ruler in charge and primary supporter of the royal *kitabkhana* (library and pictorial workshop)—were primarily spent in the revivification of Sunni orthodoxy.[24] Started with the transfer in 1409 of the empire's capital from Samarqand to Herat, known as the "dome of Islam" (*qubbat al-Islam*) for its Sunni allegiance, the process continued with the substitution of the Turko-Mongol laws with the *shari'a* (Islamic law), and the construction of a large *madrasa* (Qur'anic school) in Herat for the study of Islamic jurisprudence (*fiqh*), Qur'anic exegesis (*tafsir*), and prophetic traditions (*hadith*).[25] Shah Rukh was directly responsible for appointing the teachers of this important institution, and one of them in particular, Jalal al-Din Qayini, was not only a militant proselytizer,[26] but also the author of a book of advice, the *Nasa'ih-i Shah-Rukhi* (*Counsels for Shah Rukh*), conceived to assist the ruler in the exercise of political leadership in the light of orthodox prescriptions. A detailed analysis of this text is beyond the scope of this article, but its stress on justice and proper governance, its observations on the

---

23 The word *islam* itself means "submission to God."

24 Sunnism and Shi'ism represent the two main branches of Islam. Sunnism (from *sunna*, or way of the prophet Muhammad) recognizes the "four rightly-guided caliphs" and the following dynasties as the rightful leaders of the Islamic community following the death of the Prophet in 632. Vice versa, Shi'ism (from *shi'a* or "party" of 'Ali) only acknowledges the descendants of 'Ali, cousin and son-in-law of Muhammad, as the proper successors and spiritual guides. The split between Sunnis and Shi'is in the Islamic community occurred at the very beginning of Islamic history, and led to a number of sects and subdivisions within each branch.

25 Maria E. Subtelny and Anas B. Khalidov, "The Curriculum of Islamic Higher Learning in Timurid Iran in the Light of the Sunni Revival under Shah Rukh," *Journal of the American Oriental Society* 115/2 (1995), pp. 210–36.

26 Qayini was dispatched to various regions of the empire to "revive the *shari'a*," as noted by Maria E. Subtelny, "The Sunni Revival under Shah Rukh and its Promoters: A Study of the Connection between Ideology and Higher Learning in Timurid Iran," in *Proceedings of the 27th Meeting of Haneda Memorial Hall Symposium on Central Asia and Iran, August 30, 1993* (Kyoto: Institute of Inner Asian Studies, Kyoto University, 1994), pp. 14–23, at 17. I would like to thank Dr Christiane Gruber for sharing this article with me.

Figure 6.2   Angels bowing in front of Adam. *Qisas al-anbiya'*, Turkey, AH
983/1575-6 CE Topkapı Saray Library, Istanbul, H. 1227, folio 11r.
Reproduced by permission of the Topkapı Palace Museum, Istanbul.

dangers of tyranny, and, most of all, its discussion of the punishments of apostates and infidels, confirm the primacy of ethics in the exercise of power and the urge to address heresy at a normative level.[27]

While the *Nasa'ih-i Shah-Rukhi* was not illustrated, another text produced by Shah Rukh's workshop, the *Mi'rajnama* (*Book of Ascension*), chose to elaborate on the consequences of amoral behaviors.[28] The text, dedicated to the night journey of the prophet Muhammad in the afterworld (*mi'raj*), includes a complete pictorial cycle of the torments awaiting various categories of sinners in hell as witnessed by the Prophet. The hanging bodies of religious hypocrites scorched by fire, and the tortures reserved for those who cast sedition, are persuasive examples of the admonitory instruction pursued in this and other texts, offering a further demonstration of the variety of resources employed by Shah Rukh to further his moral reformation.[29] Similar to works of history and literature, the *Mi'rajnama* relied on a mixture of textual and pictorial resources in order to fulfill its educational goals, "promoting an orthodox exposition that could help people embrace a lifestyle pleasing to God."[30] Yet, thanks to their ability to communicate to wider (and not necessarily literate) audiences, images ultimately augmented the didactic impact of the narratives and secured their correct reception, a fact that explains why the arts of the book and book painting developed so prominently in the Timurid period.[31]

The creation of Adam is narrated and illustrated in other literary genres produced in the Islamic sphere, first and foremost the *Qisas al-anbiya'* (*Stories of the Prophets*).[32] Several texts were produced with this title in the early centuries of Islam, although the Arabic version of al-Kisa'i, datable to the eighth century, the eleventh-century work of al-Tha'labi, and the contemporary Persian edition by al-Naysaburi became the most popular.[33] In the course of the sixteenth century, this

---

27 Ibid., p. 20.

28 Bibliothèque Nationale de France, Paris, Suppl. Turc 190. The manuscript's artistic and cultural value is thoroughly discussed by Christiane J. Gruber, *The Timurid "Book of Ascension" (Mi'rajnama): A Study of Text and Image in a Pan-Asian Context* (Valencia: Ediciones Patrimonio, 2009), especially pp. 267–99.

29 Both are illustrated in folio 57.

30 Gruber, *The Timurid "Book of Ascension,"* p. 288.

31 A good overview of book production under the Timurids is contained in Lentz and Lowry, *Timur and the Princely Vision*, chapters 2 and 3.

32 Episodes and images of prophets, including Adam, also appear in copies of the *Falnama* (*Book of Omens*), and of the *Majalis al-'ushshaq* (*Seances of the Lovers*), both of which became particularly popular in the course of the sixteenth century, when most of the extant illustrated copies were executed. The genres are discussed respectively in Massumeh Farhad with Serpil Bağcı, *Falnama: The Book of Omens* (Washington, DC: Arthur Sackler Gallery, Smithsonian Institution, 2009), and Lâle Uluç, *Turkman Governors, Shiraz Artisans, and Ottoman Collectors: Sixteenth-century Shiraz Manuscripts* (Istanbul: İş Bankası Kültür Yayınları, 2006), especially chapter 4.

33 The identity of this author and the whole development of the genre are discussed in Rachel Milstein, Karin Rührdanz, and Barbara Schmitz, *Stories of the Prophets: Illustrated Manuscripts of the Qisas al-Anbiya'* (Costa Mesa, CA: Mazda Publishers, 1999), pp. 7–15.

textual tradition was also consistently illustrated in the Ottoman world, possibly as a means to inspire piety and renew spirituality in a moment of intense religious and ideological discussions.[34] The related group of illustrated manuscripts, examined at length by Rachel Milstein, Karin Rührdanz, and Barbara Schmitz, offers a series of alternative pictorial interpretations of Adam's creation when compared to the one examined above.[35]

Figure 6.2, which accompanies a copy of the *Qisas al-anbiya'* dated 983 AH/1575–76 CE, currently in the Topkapı Saray Library, Istanbul, exemplifies one of the most common representations of the subject, based on a layout that is reminiscent of scenes of royal enthronement in outdoor settings. The interesting aspect for my discussion is that Iblis is omitted from this and similar images belonging to this cycle. The painting shows a crowned and haloed Adam kneeling on a throne located at the center of a blooming garden, the Garden of Eden, surrounded by angels bowing at his feet, and offering trays filled with light, a symbol of prophecy. Similar to Figure 6.1, both Adam and the angels are radiant, white-skinned creatures, dressed in brocaded robes and elaborate headgears, including crowns, leaves, and pearl strings. The angels are disposed in a circle around the new creature, an arrangement that enhances the celebratory tone of the image meant to commemorate Adam's receipt of the prophetic gift, which is literally being poured on him by the heavenly messengers.

As convincingly argued by Rachel Milstein, this iconographic scheme responds to the ideological program of the text, which intended to present the prophets as shadows of God on earth, and models of moral rectitude for religious as much as secular leaders. The emphasis on "the notion of a personal test" for the prophets who, as noted by Milstein, "emerge triumphant from the religious inquisition, from a spiritual death, and … are reborn to bring the message to their followers," contributed to establish distinctive iconographic solutions that privileged individual trials, and exemplary reactions to these.[36] Similar to texts of history, hagiographic works such as the *Qisas al-anbiya'* were in fact highly regarded for their didactic value, and often consulted by monarchs whose conduct could find a source of inspiration in these saints' exemplary lives.[37] In this specific context, Satan's sinister and dissonant presence would have appeared superfluous, because

I thank Dr. Milstein for sharing some of her images from the *Qisas* manuscripts analyzed in her work.

34   While Sunnism remained predominant in the Ottoman and Mughal Empires, the sixteenth century witnessed the definitive adoption of Shi'ism in Iran under the Safavid dynasty (1501–1736).

35   Milstein et al., *Stories of the Prophets*, especially pp. 41–64.

36   Ibid., p. 37.

37   Ibid., p. 34. In the course of their history, the Ottoman historiographic production absorbed the lives of the prophets, creating a continuous historical narration from pre-Islamic times down to the sixteenth century that further legitimized the dynasty. Adam, as well as Solomon, appear to have held special positions, providing ideal archetypes of prophet-kings that the Ottomans embraced. This issue is also elaborated upon by Milstein in ibid., pp. 34–7.

Figure 6.3   Expulsion of Adam and Eve from Paradise. *Qisas al-anbiya'*, Turkey, AH 987/1579-80 CE Topkapı Saray Library, Istanbul, R. 1536, folio 16v. Reproduced by permission of the Topkapı Palace Museum, Istanbul.

161

his act of rebellion to Adam's creation did not have direct consequences for the first prophet, nor did it affect the specific subject addressed by the text. The absence of Iblis from this and other *Qisas* paintings can, thus, be justified in the light of the genre's priority, that of highlighting the individual experience of the various prophets, and the spiritual challenges that their special condition posed them.[38]

An interesting facet of Adam's experience is yet worth noticing, as it conceptually and visually elaborates upon an aspect—nakedness—that, as we have seen, is what reveals Iblis's monstrous transformation as a result of his corruption. Following his own disobedience of God's command and expulsion from Paradise, Adam's figure is deprived of his precious royal apparel, and left in ashamed nudity (Figure 6.3). The passage from Kisa'i's version of the *Qisas al-anbiya'* relative to this event contains interesting details regarding the presence of clothing and jewelry as indicators of moral uprightness, and is, therefore, worth quoting in full:

> ... *no sooner had Adam tasted, one of the ears of grain that was on the crown fell off his head, his rings squirmed off from his hand and everything that had been on both him and Eve fell off—their clothes, jewelry, and ornaments. Each article, as it flew from them, cried out: "O Adam! O Eve! Long may your sorrow and may your affliction be great! Peace be with you until the Day of Resurrection, for we made a covenant with God that we should clothe only obedient, humble servants." ... Then, none of their clothing remained on them, and they hurriedly began to cover themselves with leaves ... (but) the leaves of the trees also fell from them so that they were not able to cover themselves with anything. When Adam came near a tree, it would shout at him saying: "Go away from me, O disobedient one!" The dove which had shed light on Adam's crown drew near and said: "O Adam, where is your crown, your jewels, your finery? O Adam, after beauty and magnificence, you have come to be cursed!" And everything shouted rebuke after him from all sides, and the angels also; and he looked at them with longing and regret.*[39]

The loss of the positive moral condition previously expressed in the elaborate attire of Adam and Eve is instantly mirrored in the sudden exposure of their bodies. That their naked bodies were felt to disclose the mutated disposition of their souls is aptly synthesized by Eve's hair which refuses to cover her by saying: "O you *whose evil is so obvious,* how can you cover yourself, having thus disobeyed your Lord?"[40]

---

38   Ibid. Milstein also notes that in a few occasions, Iblis appears in a corner of the composition, depicted as a dark-skinned man with a strange object around his neck (ibid., p. 107).

39   Wheeler M. Thackston, *The Tales of the Prophets of al-Kisa'i* (Boston: Twayne Publishers, 1978), pp. 41–2, emphasis added.

40   Ibid., emphasis added. It is also interesting to note the metamorphosis of the she-serpent responsible for the fall of Adam and Eve. At the beginning of the story, in fact, the serpent "was shaped like a camel, and, like a camel, she could stand erect. She had a multicolored tail, red, yellow, green, white, black, a mane of pearl, hair of topaz, eyes like the planets Venus and Jupiter, and an aroma like musk blended with ambergris"

Differently from Iblis, Adam and Eve's sin did not transform them into monsters, possibly for the different role they were meant to hold in the history of mankind. And yet, similar to Satan, their nudity implies a fault, a fact that strengthens the link between nakedness and moral deficiency, making it a readable sign of disgrace in the pictorial context.[41]

As a history narrated through the experiences of spiritual and political leaders, Tabari's *Tarikh al-rusul wa'l-muluk* evidently possessed a different rationale and purpose from the *Qisas al-anbiya'*. First of all, Tabari's text testifies to the progressive Islamization of historiographic practice, with events enounced in chronological order beginning with God's creation, and a tendency to incorporate a range of historical (and non-historical) strands derived from the diverse cultural traditions that had been incorporated into the Islamic empire. The work's strong didactic quality, which is clearly put forth at the beginning by the author, is likewise determinant in establishing the educational intent of the text, prone to stress the importance of specific virtues within an Islamic framework. By narrating the history of some of God's creatures, and by referring to instances of obedience and devoted leadership as much as to examples of insubordination, the *Tarikh al-rusul wa'l-muluk* aimed to offer significant advice on political leadership, and the exercise of just and upright authority. Interestingly, Bal'ami's translation of Tabari's text, which is the work in which Figure 6.1 appears, is more strongly based on the Qur'an, and reveals a marked interest for pre-Islamic prophets, implying a more pronounced religious and ethical inflection than its Arabic model.[42]

Considered in this light, the account of Iblis reported in the text acquires a special value. Iblis is not only the first creature who received a leading role by becoming the keeper of Paradise, and who could therefore offer a significant model of behavior due to the authoritative task received; he is also the first one who failed to maintain it because of his ingratitude, and his inability to respect God's superior authority, revealing the dangers of excessive pride in the exercise of power. For this reason, his negative experience provides a meaningful lesson and gives the reader an opportunity to reflect on what defines laudable conduct and upright leadership. The painting accompanying the story is an essential component of this educational pursuit, because of its compelling use of aesthetic difference to underscore the virtuous or corrupt nature of the characters involved in the tale. While Iblis's

---

(ibid., p. 38). However, after being corrupted by Iblis, and having seduced the first man, the angels came to Heaven to expel her and "dragged her on her belly until her legs were deformed. She became elongated, malformed and deprived of the power of speech, mute and fork-tongued" (ibid., p. 46). Also in the case of this animal, the decadence from a charming and well-shaped creature to a deformed one associates with the external form the loss of an inner, originally virtuous, disposition.

41 Criminals are traditionally shown with limited clothing as a sign of the social estrangement caused by their wrongful acts. A few examples are illustrated in Uluç, *Turkman Governors*, p. 145, figure 95, and p. 159, figure 106.

42 Bal'ami's reshaping of Tabari's *Tarikh al-rusul wa'l-muluk* is extensively discussed in A.C.S. Peacock, *Medieval Islamic Historiography and Political Legitimacy: Bal'ami's Tarikhnama* (London and New York: Routledge, 2007), especially pp. 76–105.

monstrosity occurs as a result of the transformation of originally pleasant forms, and carries the effects of an experience that occurred in a specific moment in time, it ultimately conveys an ominous message, presaging the marks of eternal perdition that would perpetually brand the damned in the afterlife.

The White Demon (*div-i safid*)

With the *div-i safid*, or white demon, we move to a different literary genre—the epic—and its most representative text—the *Shahnama* or "Book of Kings." This poem, written at the beginning of the eleventh century by Abu'l-Qasim Firdawsi, narrates the history of the kings of Iran from the beginning of time up to the Arab conquest in the mid-seventh century.[43] Therefore, although compiled in Islamic times, the text celebrates the principles and values of the monarchic institution as experienced in the course of the region's pre-Islamic history.

Amidst the deeds and adventures of princes and heroes, battles against monstrous foes are given a considerable space. Yet, the fight of Rustam against the white *div* is not only the most famous of such extraordinary exploits, but also a highly meaningful event, for reasons that will be elucidated below. Rustam is the legendary ally of the kings of Iran, and a constant source of support to the crown. When the ruler in charge, Kay Kavus, falls prisoner to the *divs* after attempting to reconquer the region of Mazandaran from their tyranny, the hero is summoned to court and asked to rescue him. In order to reach the ruler, the paladin has to face a number of trials, the last of which requires killing the white *div*, the demon-king of Mazandaran. This is not only because the latter is the jailer of Kay Kavus, but also because it is through the monster's liver that the shah's eyesight can be restored, and legitimate rulership reinstated. After crossing seven valleys and killing hundreds of *divs*, Rustam reaches the lair of their chief and prepares to face him. Lost in the cave's darkness, the hero's initial encounter with the monster is thus described by Firdawsi:

> *There, sword in hand, he paused;*
> *No room was there for fight or flight.*
> *He rubbed his eyelids, bathed his eyes, and searched*
> *the cave till in the gloom he saw a Mountain*
> *that blotted all within, with sable face*
> *and hair like lion's mane—a world to see!*[44]

---

43   The text merges legends, myths, and historical material. The most recent and comprehensive edition of the text, in eight volumes, is by Djalal Khaleghi-Motlagh, *The Shahnameh* (New York: Bibliotheca Persica, 1988–2008).

44   For the English translation, see Arthur G. Warner and Edmund Warner, trans., *The Shahnama of Firdousi Done into English*, 9 volumes (London: K. Paul, Trench, Trübner & Co., 1905–25), II: 59–60, § 12, vv. 21–6; for the Persian verses, see Khaleghi-Motlagh, *The Shahnameh* II: 42, vv. 566–9.

Figure 6.4   Rustam kills the *div-i safid* (white demon). *Shahnama* of Muhammad
Juki, Herat, circa 1440. Royal Asiatic Society, London, Ms. 239, folio 44v.
Reproduced by permission of the Royal Asiatic Society of Great Britain
and Ireland.

Awoken by Rustam's roar, the white *div* throws himself at him, and the two wrestle until the hero severs the monster's leg. He then raises the creature's weakened body, hurls it to the ground, and, once firmly above him, stabs the *div*'s belly to extract the liver that later will be used to heal the shah.

Figure 6.4, an illustration to the *Shahnama* produced for the Timurid prince Muhammad Juki around 1440, captures the moment in which Rustam, after stabbing the *div*, extracts the liver.[45] The event takes place inside a dark cave aptly located in an isolated, mountainous spot, and witnessed by nobody else other than Rustam's local guide Ulad (tied to a tree to prevent his escape), and the hero's steed, Rakhsh. Set against a black ground, the core of the image presents the lifeless monster lying on his back with his left leg severed, while the hero is firmly on him pulling out the organ from his body.

A number of aspects are worthy of notice, beginning with the difference in size of the combatants. In order to convey the "mountain-like" size of the monster, the body of the white *div* is rather large, and exhibits clawed feet and a misshaped, disproportioned horned head. Rustam is, in contrast, depicted as a much smaller character, a choice that contradicts his proverbial "elephantine" stature, but that further emphasizes his foe's abnormal size. Their opposite expressiveness is also significant. The monster's face is contracted in a pained grimace, in visible contrast with the hero's composed expression, which he keeps regardless of the emotional and physical tension produced by the fight. Finally, equally suggestive is the way in which their bodies are presented. The *div*'s nakedness indicates his uncivilized and unaffiliated condition. Rustam, instead, carries the signs of his aristocratic lineage—his military outfit made of a long robe, high boots, and defensive armor and helmet—in addition to the mark of his "superhuman" status—a tiger skin that, according to the legend, granted him talismanic powers.[46]

This specific episode of the *Shahnama* generated an impressive number of pictorial adaptations,[47] not only in the context of illustrated manuscripts, but also on a variety of other media, including tilework.[48] Its popularity raises the question as to why in a poem that celebrates the kingdoms of illuminated past rulers, the tale that most captivated people's imagination was the myth of a legendary hero

---

45   This is a unique instance, as the most frequent way in which the battle is depicted sees Rustam plunging his dagger in the monster's belly.

46   The tiger skin and/or leopard's headgear are recurrent attributes of Rustam. A discussion of their origin and meaning is provided in Abolala Soudavar, *Art of the Persian Courts: Selections from the Art and History Trust* (New York: Rizzoli, 1992), p. 186, n. 12.

47   Rustam's killing of the white *div* is the most frequently illustrated story of the *Shahnama*. The online database of illustrated *Shahnama* manuscripts produced between the fourteenth and the nineteenth centuries, co-ordinated by Cambridge University (Shahnama Project Website), currently lists a total of 260 illustrations of the story out of the some 500 manuscripts and fragments currently uploaded: http://shahnama.caret. cam.ac.uk/shahnama/faces/user/index; last accessed August 15, 2010.

48   Large friezes of *cuerda seca* tiles depicting Rustam stabbing the white demon decorate the walls adjacent to the throne room in the Gulistan Palace in Tehran, and the entranceway of the citadel of Shiraz.

and a monster. The answer possibly lies in the "cathartic" quality of the tale, which stages a clash of extremes that best interprets the epic's leitmotif, the perennial battle of good and evil.

Because of the transient quality of earthly existence, stressed by Firdawsi at various junctures throughout the poem, men's primary goal is to seek happiness by pursuing truth, order, and justice, and by rejecting cruelty, avarice, and evil. It is in the story of Rustam and the white *div* that these opposite sets of principles are best expressed and, through their accompanying pictorial adaptations, most powerfully asserted.[49] On the one hand is the fierce paladin of Iran depicted as a confident and valorous warrior. Manly in appearance—he is regularly represented with a beard, a traditional symbol of virility and maturity in the Persianate pictorial tradition— and sheltered by human and superhuman protection, he expresses the confidence and vigor associated with the ruling class. His physical harmony, composure, and audacity are the visual manifestations of his value, loyalty, and heroism. On the other hand is the *div*, the prince of all demonic beings, portrayed in all his exuberance and decadence. He is the incarnation of chaos and disharmony, which are reflected on his hybrid body, an unpredictable blend of human, animal, and grotesque features whose unnatural combination communicates his perverse nature.

This range of contrasting physical and emotional features exposed the moral implications of the story by triggering a number of mental associations and considerations about the characters' virtuous or bad nature that enabled a full understanding of the ethical message embedded in the tale. Indeed, the specific pictorial formulation of the wicked character—whose appearance, it is worthwhile noticing, is never fully described in the poem, thus leaving the artists free to shape it—ended up valorizing the one who incarnated the positive values, putting the final accent on the valorous figure(s). Monstrosity is hence not an end in itself, but an instrument to reflect on the normal and acceptable ideal, itself subject to constant correction and progressive redefinition.[50]

The white *div* is yet the perfect scapegoat, as he is persecuted and condemned for the shah's defects and excesses.[51] Kay Kavus's decision to invade Mazandaran is in fact one of his many caprices, and one severely discouraged by his courtiers and counselors. The land of Mazandaran had traditionally remained a land of sorcery and demonic creatures, and none of the previous rulers had ever dared to invade it. Yet a demon disguised as a minstrel arrives at court one day and, praising

---

49   Rustam is an example of loyalty, and the defender of authority in more than one way. Kay Kavus's ineptitude and changeable nature is balanced by the hero's faithful and courageous conduct, to the point that the reader tends to identify himself more with the latter, and take his example more than that of the ruler, contrary to what happens in the rest of the poem.

50   The role of abnormality in the definition of the proper standard is widely discussed in relation to the Western tradition by David Williams, *Deformed Discourse: The Function of the Monster in Medieval Thought and Literature* (Montreal and Kingston: McGill-Queen's University Press, 1996), especially pp. 107–227.

51   The notion of monsters as scapegoats was previously remarked upon by Jeffrey Cohen, "Monster Culture," pp. 17–18.

Figure 6.5   Tahmuras defeats the *divs*. *Shahnama* of Shah Tahmasp, Tabriz, circa
1525. The Metropolitan Museum of Art, New York, 1970.301.3 (photo
credit: The Metropolitan Museum of Art/Art Resource NY).

the beauty of the region, manages to convince the shah to reconquer it.[52] In this sense, although inspired by someone else, the shah's choice gets attention precisely to underscore his weak nature, and the consequences of his presumptuousness and foolishness, which led to the loss of the throne and his imprisonment. The fight against the white *div* can, thus, be interpreted as a battle against the irrational side of mankind, which needs to be domesticated and brought under control. This is ultimately why the monster is at once the cause of Kay Kavus's fall and the remedy for his redemption. Eliminating him is a way to purge the soul from all excesses and regain the right balance. Configured as the Other, the *div* stands as the personification of human limits—the temptations, arrogance, and selfishness that are perceived as extraneous and that can lead one astray, but that, nonetheless, still belong to human nature.[53] The battle is, thus, not only a way to restore the right order (in this case by relocating the shah on his throne), but also an act of self-preservation and purification.

The idea of the *div* as the embodiment of lower human drives and irrationality finds an interesting pictorial elaboration in relation to another episode of the *Shahnama*, the fight of the early ruler Tahmuras—nicknamed *div-band*, "binder of divs"—against the demons in the legendary section of the poem (Figure 6.5). One of the most vivid adaptations of the subject is found in a painting that was once part of the so-called *Shahnama-yi Shahi* or Shah Tahmasp's *Shahnama*, an exceptional royal copy of the Persian epic produced in Tabriz between the 1520s and 1540s for the second Safavid ruler Shah Tahmasp (r. 1524–76).[54] In a flourishing meadow tinged with vibrant hues, humans and demons face each other in a primordial battle for power and for the triumph of human civilization. One of the first mythical kings of Iran, Tahmuras, is leading the fight against the evil horde troubling the world. Depicted as a handsome knight with full royal insignia, Tahmuras occupies the very center of the painting, and from his saddle he is immortalized while crushing his heavy mace on a seemingly scared black *div*. A number of other terrified *divs* gravitate around the fighters, while a group of submissive monsters, relegated to the lower left corner of the page, grind their teeth in sign of protest against the soldiers carrying away a tamed fellow.

In addition to a growing emphasis on unregulated emotions, the *divs* occurring in this manuscript are the first to exhibit a distinct sexuality.[55] The captured pink *div* in the lower register of the painting, in particular, is characterized by male genitalia, a detail that must have inspired various reactions in the manuscript's viewers,

---

52   Khaleghi-Motlagh, *The Shahnameh* II: 10, vv. 45–117.

53   The idea of the demon as negative surrogate of men is also discussed by Talat Parman in her article "The Demon as a Human Double," in Haydaroğlu, *Ben Mehmed Siyah Kalem*, pp. 129–34.

54   A thorough study of the manuscript before its dispersal is Martin B. Dickson and Stuart C. Welch, *The Houghton Shahnama* (Cambridge, MA: Harvard University Press, 1981).

55   The only precedent is found, once again, in the demonic characters of Siyah Qalam; see Mazhar S. Ipširoglu, *Siyah Qalem* (Graz: Akademische Druck- u. Verlagsanstalt, 1976), plates 50–51.

especially when we consider how unusual the exposure of the body, let alone of its intimate parts, was in the Islamic context. Indeed, the lassoed demon is the one whose monstrous nature and instincts are offered to the viewer in their entirety. The fact that the painter decided to sexualize this specific *div* among all those that occur in the painting (and leave him entirely naked) suggests the intention to distinguish him, encouraging the viewer to regulate the lowest drives and lustful passions, of which the *div*'s ithyphallic and polluted body is an emblematic incarnation.[56]

Scholars have repeatedly commented on the ethical dimension of works of literature such as the *Shahnama*, observing how the examples of good justice and virtuosity of old kings were not only things to remember, but also valuable lessons for successive generations of rulers.[57] Mahmud of Ghazna (r. 997–1030), the poem's dedicatee, is reported to have reproached the Buyid Majd al-Dawla after the capture of Rayy for his unethical behavior, apparently unworthy of the kings of the past, thereby establishing the idea of the *Shahnama* as a repository of moral paradigms from its inception.[58]

Undoubtedly, in the course of its history the literary success of the *Shahnama* was also due to its strong didactic quality. A unique instance of the "mirror for princes" genre, the poem is attested to have been regularly included in the curricula for the education of princes, providing instances of moral excellence and value through the exemplary lives of some of its protagonists.[59] Speaking of the scholarly curriculum of princes, the twelfth-century historian Nizami 'Aruzi puts a stress on those works that provide models of behavior and offer ethical advice, inviting the rulers and their secretaries to absorb their lessons in order to stimulate their mind, refine their wit, and enkindle their soul.[60] The *Shahnama* of Firdawsi is listed

---

56 A close look at the image reveals several scars on the epidermis of this and other demons, a further indicator of their impurity. The lassoing of a hypersexualized *div* is repeated in another instance in the same manuscript. The painting illustrating the capture of Bahman Castle by Kay Khusraw, now in the David Collection, Copenhagen (inv. no. 31/1998), equally features a scene of fierce battle between humans and demons, culminating in the capture of a naked *div*. The image is reproduced in Kjeld von Folsach, *For a Privileged Few: Islamic Miniature Painting from the David Collection* (Humlebæk: Louisiana Museum of Modern Art and The David Collection, 2007), pp. 88–9, no. 34.

57 Charles-Henri de Fouchécour, *Moralia: Les notions morales dans la litterature persane du 3/9 au 7/13 siècle* (Paris: Editions Recherche sur les civilisations, 1986), pp. 107 and ff.

58 "'Have you not read the *Shahnama*, which is the history of the Persians, and the *History of Tabari*, which is the history of the Muslims?' said Mahmud. 'Yes,' replied Majd al-Dawla. 'Your conduct is not that of one who has.'" The anecdote is found in Ibn al-Athir, *Al-Kamil fi'l-Tarikh* [1386], ed. C. Tornberg (Beirut: Dar Sadir, 1966), IX: 371–2, quoted and translated in Peacock, *Medieval Islamic Historiography*, p. 13.

59 The issue is discussed in Julie Scott Meisami's article "The *Shahname* as a Mirror for Princes: A Study in Reception," in Christophe Balaÿ, Claire Kappler, and Ziva Vesel (eds), *Pand-o Sokhan: Mélanges Offerts à Charles-Henri de Fouchécour* (Tehran: Institut Français de Recherche en Iran, 1995), pp. 265–73.

60 'Aruzi's passage from his work *Chahar Maqala* (Four Discourses), composed in 1155, is quoted in David J. Roxburgh, "Baysunghur's Library: Questions Related to its

among such recommended readings, and judging from the numerous royal copies commissioned throughout the centuries by princes and rulers, the book's celebrity was assured by its contents, whose perpetuation remained worth pursuing.[61] Therefore, the numerous images of heroes defeating monstrous *divs* would have provided stark exemplars not only for proper action, but also for the very nature of the "good prince," who is invariably powerful and beautiful, as well as victorious, all aspects that, while threatened and contradicted by their hideous foes, eventually remained the principles that continued to inspire the many generations of rulers that reigned in the area.

Conclusions

Iblis and the white *div* represent two different monstrous experiences that nonetheless serve similar purposes. Iblis personifies the monstrous degeneration of an originally noble being due to his sinful behavior. His is a story of transformation in which the initial condition, the angelic one, is never entirely erased, but maintained and exhibited in corrupted form as a constant reminder of the fault that caused it, and, consequently, of the dangers that may derive from assuming the same behavior. The white *div*, instead, is a fictitious enemy produced from the dislocation of the despicable and inadmissible aspects of human nature, and, as such, represents an ideal source of expiation and redemption. Differently from Iblis, who becomes a monster, the *div* is presented as one from the beginning, although gradual shifts in his portrayal from one time period to the next reveal his volatile nature and changing roles. Either resulting from a metamorphosis or from a hybrid combination,[62] both monsters reveal the profound ethical concerns informing the textual traditions in which they appear.

This is not surprising if we bear in mind the edifying goals of Tabari's *Tarikh al-rusul wa'l-muluk* and Firdawsi's *Shahnama*. On the one hand, the historical framework of Tabari offers examples of spiritual and political leadership that serve to reflect

---

Chronology and Production," *Journal of Social Affairs* 18 (Winter 2001), pp. 11–41, at 29.

61   Among the best-known examples of royal commissions are: the so-called Great Mongol *Shahnama*, datable to the 1330s, and executed under the patronage of the last Ilkhanid ruler, Abu Sa'id (r. 1316–35); the versions produced under the Timurid princes Ibrahim Sultan (1394–1435), Baysunghur Mirza (1397–1434), and Muhammad Juki (1402–44) in the years comprised between 1430 and 1440; and the already mentioned *Shahnama-yi Shahi*. While the copies of the Timurid rulers are still intact and are respectively conserved in the Bodleian Library, Oxford (Ouseley Add. 176), the Gulistan Palace Library (MS. 61), and the Royal Asiatic Society in London (MS. 239), the other two major commissions were dispersed in the course of the twentieth century and now lie scattered in numerous public and private collections around the globe.

62   The idea of hybridity and metamorphosis as "sites of ... competing and changing understandings" is explored in Caroline Walker Bynum, *Metamorphosis and Identity* (New York: Zone Books, 2001), p. 21, and passim.

on what qualities define proper and acceptable conduct and leadership. Deviations from it, as demonstrated by Iblis's experience, are, thus, especially relevant as they expose the immediate and irrevocable consequences of inappropriate behaviors. On the other hand, the entertaining tales of Firdawsi's epic build their instructive capacity on the juxtaposition of characters with opposite qualities. The most evocative episodes stage the clash of human and demonic beings, which can be easily read as symbols of the rational and instinctual spheres characterizing human nature. The victory of intellect and good sense over passions and irrationality is necessary not only to fulfill specific narrative goals, but also to teach the readers what defines virtuous conduct, which remains unattainable without the proper control of man's lowest drives. Significantly, in both texts instruction is the product of the synergy of textual and pictorial resources which complement each other in order to elaborate a set of suitable behavioral models that are ultimately informed by an Islamic ethos.

The effort to present a commendable, and therefore embraceable, ethical code of conduct lies at the core of the two textual traditions considered in this chapter. The *Shahnama* had inherited and perpetuated the didactic mode of Sasanian manuals of statecraft known as *a'innama* (Book of Principles) and *pandnama* (Book of Counsels), and had, thus, easily served the educational needs of young, and less young, princes. This appears to have been particularly so in the Timurid period, as confirmed by the three royal copies of the *Shahnama* produced for three of Shah Rukh's sons.[63] Bal'ami's translation of Tabari's history, on the other hand, satisfied a specific historical interest (and propagandistic inclination) of the Timurid dynasty, who sought in current and previous history a way to validate their political activity and align it with that of illustrious predecessors.[64] In works of history, as much as in hagiography, eschatology, and a number of belletristic texts, the pedagogical intent is, thus, the common thread, especially considering the audience of these texts, primarily, though not exclusively, belonged to the royal circle. These diverse narratives, coupled to subtly orchestrated pictorial cycles, not only assured the transmission of specific textual materials, but also ultimately promoted ideals that contributed to the transmission and inculcation of acceptable social mores and codes of conduct.

63   See note 60.
64   See note 14.

Human of the Heart: Pitiful *Oni* in Medieval Japan

Michelle Osterfeld Li

Introduction

No spirit-creature figures as prominently in Japan as the *oni*, responding to the fears and aspirations of diverse people across centuries, sometimes challenging the social systems and political orders while elsewhere sustaining them. *Oni* have always been part spiritual and part material, associated with an invisible realm and a sense of mystery, and elusive by nature. They are often thought of as Buddhist creatures, but their relationship with Buddhism is complex.

Oni tend to be humanized through Buddhist concepts, especially karma or the sense of them having interrelated pasts, presents, and futures shaped by actions, as well as the need for sympathy from others. For example, two tales discussed below—"How Nichizō Shōnin Encounters an *Oni* on Mt Yoshino" in *Uji shūi monogatari* (*A Collection of Tales from Uji*, circa 1190–1242), and "How Gyokusenbō of Mt Hiei Becomes an *Oni*" in *Sangoku denki* (*Legends of the Three Lands*, between 1407 and 1446)—involve *oni* who are pitiful and can be helped. The shift toward *oni* who evoke sympathy occurs mainly in the medieval period (circa 1185–1600), when their potential for spiritual growth is considered. Even as they remain dangerous monsters, the reasons why they became *oni* and their potential for change start to matter.

The renowned noh performer, playwright, and aesthetician Zeami Motokiyo (1363–1443) developed a type of *oni* who have "the form of *oni* yet a human heart," favoring this rendering over a more forceful but less refined type.[1] Furthermore,

---

[1] Konishi Jin'ichi (ed.), "Shūgyoku tokka," in *Zeami shū*, Nihon no shisō 8 (Tokyo: Chikuma shobō, 1970), pp. 324–5. See also J. Thomas J. Rimer and Yamazaki Masakazu (trans.), *On the Art of the Nō Drama: The Major Treatises of Zeami* (Princeton, NJ: Princeton University Press, 1984), p. 144; and Michelle Osterfeld Li, *Ambiguous Bodies: Reading the Grotesque in Japanese Setsuwa Tales* (Stanford: Stanford University Press, 2009), pp. 124–5. For Japanese texts, Japanese names will be written according to Japanese convention, with family names first.

in "Oni' no kanashimi" ("The Sorrow of *Oni*"), scholar Ikegami Jun'ichi focuses on the loneliness, sorrow, and shame of medieval *oni*, asserting that they are in essence people of that time. While *oni* are still other, "sad and lonely as they gaze at the human world with longing,"[2] their emotions and experiences remain close to that of humans in part because they were formally people who by some misfortune crossed over to the *oni* side of existence. Ikegami's examples include the most famous *oni* of the Muromachi period (1392–1573), Shuten dōji, literally "saké-imbibing boy," who kidnaps and consumes people, especially beautiful young women (as will be discussed below). His earliest example is a woman in the collection *Kankyo no tomo* (*A Companion in Solitude*, 1222), whose remarkable tale influenced stories in *The Tale of the Heike* (mid-thirteenth century) and the noh play *Kanawa* (*The Iron Crown*, circa fifteenth century) of the demonic Hashihime (Lady at the Bridge).[3] A woman extremely resentful at the neglect of her lover disguises herself as an *oni*, even forming five horns by plastering bunches of hair with syrup. After murdering the man, she discovers that she has truly transformed into an *oni* and cannot revert to her former self. She goes into hiding. About 30 years have passed when the villagers, having lost some foals and calves to her appetite, discover that an *oni* inhabits a dilapidated temple.[4] They form a crowd and, after some reservation about burning a temple, set it on fire. The creature emerges and begs them to let her speak. Through her voice, the tale offers a glimpse of how she suffers as an *oni*, experiencing hunger, internal burning, and regret for wasting a life. Before throwing herself into the flames, she requests that a Buddhist offering be made on her behalf.[5]

---

2   Ikegami Jun'ichi, "'Oni' no kanashimi: chūsei no 'ningen' rikai," *Kokugo tsūshin, tokushū: chūsei o ikiru hitobito*, no. 266 (June 1984), pp. 12–18. The story in *The Heike* is the source for the play, so an indirect connection exists. See Terry Kawashima, *Writing Margins: The Textual Construction of Gender in Heian and Kamakura Japan* (Cambridge, MA: Harvard University Asia Center, 2001), p. 12. On a monster who experiences exclusion from the human realm similar to that of *oni*, see the discussion of Grendel in Cohen's postscript to this volume.

3   Ikegami, p. 265. On Hashihime, see Kawashima, pp. 217–87, and Noriko T. Reider, *Japanese Demon Lore: Oni from Ancient Times to the Present* (Logan: Utah State University Press, 2010), pp. 53–60.

4   The line concerning horses and cows seems somewhat open to interpretation. In *Writing Margins*, p. 324, Kawashima translates the relevant line as "the demon would snatch up young children who herd horses and cows and eat them." Similarly, Rajyashree Pandey writes that the *oni* would "catch the young lads tending horses and cows, and eat them," in "Women, Sexuality, and Enlightenment: *Kankyo no Tomo*," *Monumenta Nipponica* 50/3 (Autumn, 1995), pp. 325–56. See also Koizumi Hiroshi et al. (eds), *Kankyo no tomo*, in *Hōbutsu shū, Kankyo no tomo, Hirasan kojin reitaku*, Shin Nihon koten bungaku taikei 40 (Tokyo: Iwanami shoten, 1993), p. 423. The two translations mentioned in the following note indicate that the *oni* snatches and eats the young of horses and cows, which seems to make more sense since no distraught parents are depicted, despite the grammar and diction of the Japanese seemingly leaning toward the other interpretation.

5   Koizumi et al., *Kankyo no tomo*, pp. 422–4. The two most recent translations of this tale are: Michael Emmerich (trans.), "How a Deeply Resentful Woman Became a Living

The tale reveals an understanding of the *oni* as ultimately lonely and pitiful, and with human pain despite her transformation. Toward the end, the narrator comments that there is something touching and sad (a certain deep pathos expressed with the term *aware*) about the creature. Yet, the ambivalence toward *oni* seems to remain: the narrator claims not to have been told whether or not the Buddhist offering was made, an act that would have potentially freed the *oni* from her demonic state by insuring a higher rebirth. In this way, the tale suggests a compassionate response to an evil creature, but falls short of illustrating it.

We can better our understanding of the monstrous in ancient through medieval Japan by considering how *oni* are somewhat humanized and how Buddhism plays a role in that process. *Oni* change functionally depending on when in history they appear: through the twelfth century they act mostly in response to the behaviors of others, but they later begin to reveal their own vulnerability and evoke the sympathy of humans. While one type of *oni* (perhaps the oldest) is comprised of invisible and presumably formless malevolent spirits, I address those who are embodied at some point in the narrative (in part or fully).[6]

Oni were shaped not only by Buddhism, but also by mythical or seemingly non-Buddhist concepts of *oni* or figures suggesting them, some of which have traditionally been seen as indigenous. Connections of *oni* to the human exist from the beginning of extant Japanese literature. One such link can be seen in the figures sometimes considered the first *oni*: female creatures who pursue the creation deity Izanagi when he travels to the underworld, Yomi, to visit his deceased wife, Izanami. According to the myth, included in the histories *Kojiki* (712) and *Nihon shoki* (720), Izanami angrily dispatches *shikome* to pursue Izanagi because he shamed her by glimpsing her corpse, decaying and maggot-infested, after she beseeched him not to look.[7] While the word "shikome" is not written with the Chinese character for *oni*, "shiko" is one early reading of that character.[8] In the *Nihon shoki* version, the Chinese character combination for *shikome* means "ugly woman."[9] A link of the mythical creature to the human is apparent not only in the use of the character for "woman," but also in the somewhat realistic depiction of the corpse in decay, albeit animated.

Demon," in Haruo Shirane (ed.), *Traditional Japanese Literature: An Anthology, Beginnings to 1600* (New York: Columbia University Press, 2007), pp. 692–3; and Burton Watson (trans.), *The Demon at Agi Bridge and Other Japanese Tales*, Translations from the Asian Classics (New York: Columbia University Press, 2010), pp. 121–3.

6   I will not explore here depictions of foreigners/human enemies as *oni*.

7   For the myths in English, see Donald L. Philippi (trans.), *Kojiki* (Tokyo: University Press, 1968), pp. 61–3, and W.G. Aston (trans.), *Nihongi: Chronicles of Japan from the Earliest Times to AD 697* (Rutland, VT: Charles E. Tuttle, 1972), pp. 24–5. Samplings of these translations in adapted form are in Shirane (ed.), *Traditional Japanese Literature*, pp. 23–49.

8   Other early renderings include "mono" and "kami," according to Ōwa Iwao, *Oni to tennō* (Tokyo: Hakusuisha, 1992), pp. 28–9.

9   Kojima Noriyuki et al. (eds), *Nihon Shoki*, Nihon koten bungaku zenshū 2 (Tokyo: Shōgakkan, 1994), 1:44–5.

Whether or not these mythical beings can be considered *oni* is debatable, but certain non-Buddhist creatures, possibly dating back to before Buddhism entered Japan and related to fears of death and the unknown, as well as of the female body from a male perspective, were likely to have merged with Buddhist demons. Yomi is not associated with punishment, as are Buddhist hells, but, connected with the dead, *shikome* convey a sense similar to that of *oni*, of horrible, threatening creatures reminding us of our vulnerability and mortality.

Designating *Oni*

The question of what to consider *oni* is relevant to all historic periods. Scholars sometimes use "*oni*" as an umbrella term, referring to an assortment of fantastic creatures or even deviant human beings such as pirates or bandits.[10] I use the term mainly to indicate spirit-creatures called *oni* within their respective narratives — that is, when "*oni*" is written with the Chinese character 鬼 or in one of the two Japanese syllabic scripts (*katakana* or *hiragana*). In Chinese contexts, the character 鬼, read "gui," can refer to gods (pre-Han Dynasty), ancestral spirits, demons, and other monsters, but primarily indicates "lingering spirits of the dead."[11] The lines between ghosts and demonic figures are often blurred in Japan as well; *oni* are frequently threatening spirits of the deceased, inherently connected to the human. Such *oni* overlap with another concept: that of restless and angry spirits of the deceased, *onryō* (*vengeful spirit*) or *goryō* (*venerated spirit*, usually that of a political figure, so-called because it has been divinized to appease it) that cause natural disasters, disease, and death. In contrast to *oni*, *onryō* in early literature usually remain unembodied.

Additionally, *gaki* (餓鬼), designated by a combination of Chinese characters including 鬼, can occasionally be considered to be forms of *oni* or at least closely related to them. As apparent in two tales discussed below, understandings of *oni* and of *gaki* can merge. *Preta* in Sanskrit, *gaki* are, in Buddhism, former people reborn in the second lowest of the six realms of existence (hell, preta, animal, asura, human, deva)[12] because of excessive desire or jealousy, but they can also wander in this world searching for food. They can never be satiated, as apparent in depictions of them with thin necks, in the illustrated scroll *Gaki zōshi* (circa late twelfth century) and

---

10   See, for example, Baba Akiko, *Oni no kenkyū* (Tokyo: Sanichi shobō, 1971; reprint, Chikuma shobō, 1988).

11   Judith Zeitlin, *The Phantom Heroine: Ghosts and Gender in Seventeenth Century China* (Honolulu: University of Hawai'i Press, 2007), pp. 4–5.

12   On the six realms (*rokudō*), see William LaFleur, *The Karma of Words: Buddhism and the Literary Arts of Medieval Japan* (Berkeley: University of California Press, 1983), pp. 26–59. He defines *asura* (*ashura*) as "titans whose killings in the past have given them a warlike and ever warring nature" (p. 28). Deva are born into one of the Buddhist Heavens, where attaining enlightenment can be difficult because of the comfort and pleasures there.

Figure 7.1 "Hell of Measures (section 2)," from *Scroll of Hells* (*Jigoku zōshi*), twelfth century, one scroll (photograph provided by Nara National Museum, the Collection from Nara National Museum).

elsewhere, with which they can swallow little while their huge bellies ache to be filled.[13] They experience extreme hunger and thirst. Usually translated as "hungry ghosts" in English, the "ghost" or *ki* of *gaki* is the character 鬼, which by itself is *oni*. The translation of *ki* as ghost is imprecise if we think of ghosts as resembling their former selves enough to be recognized by people; along with *oni*, a complete transformation/transmigration takes place when someone becomes a *gaki*.

Physically, *oni* start to become formalized around the late twelfth century, particularly in art. The male and female creatures of the illustrated scroll *Jigoku zōshi* (*Scroll of Hells*) are the most famous depictions of *oni* from this period. Scrolls showing the damned were thought to have had a wide audience even in medieval Japan.[14] In Figures 7.1 and 7.2 the *oni*-wardens of hell (*gokusotsu*) are shown punishing sinners. The *oni* in the first, who forces sinners to ceaselessly

---

13 Komatsu Shigemi (ed.), *Gaki zōshi*, in *Gaki zōshi, Jigoku zōshi, Yamai zōshi, Kusō shi emaki*, Nihon no emaki 7 (Tokyo: Chūō kōron sha, 1987), pp. 1–37.

14 Haruko Wakabayashi, "Hell Illustrated: A Visual Image of *Ikai* that Came From *Ikoku*," in Susanne Formanek and William R. LaFleur (eds), *Practicing the Afterlife: Perspectives from Japan* (Vienna: Verlag der Österreichischen Akademie der Wissenschaften, 2004), pp. 287–8.

Figure 7.2   "Hell of the Iron Mortar (section 3)," from *Scroll of Hells*, see details
for Figure 7.1 (photograph provided by Nara National Museum, the
Collection from Nara National Museum).

weigh burning hot coals because, in human life, they caused others suffering
through their method of weighing merchandise (that is, they cheated people),
has the features of a very old woman—sagging breasts, white hair, and wrinkled
skin—in addition to the monstrous third eye, sharp teeth and nails, and overall
wild appearance. A similar figure in the second scene seems gleeful, with a broad
smile and a gleam in at least two of her three eyes as she carries a container of
human blood and bones. The representations of her three male colleagues, the
executioner, pushing the damned into a huge mortar to crush them, and his
helpers, similarly combine human facial and bodily features with others that are
strange, exaggerated, and horrific.[15]

According to historian Haruko Wakabayashi, images of *gokusotsu* solidified
by the thirteenth century.[16] While figures appearing in paintings from then on
are not the same as those in *Jigoku zōshi* (for example, they often have horns
and tighter, more muscular bodies), they share many similar features with the
earlier representations. Even *oni* not associated with Buddhist hells developed
along the following lines: as large humanoids with fangs and other sharp teeth
and horns, sometimes a strange number of round eyes (often three, with one
centered on the forehead) and/or fingers or toes with sharp nails or claws, wild
hair or sometimes a hairy body, and lacquer-colored skin (red, black, blue, or
green). Most have many but not all of these features. Male *oni* usually wear
a loincloth, typically either red material or tiger-skin. There are ox and horse-
headed *gokusotsu* as well, but they had little impact on depictions of creatures

---

15   For both the text and pictures, see Komatsu Shigemi, *Jigoku zōshi*, in *Gaki zōshi, Jigoku
zōshi, Yamai zōshi, Kusō shi emaki*, Nihon no emaki 7 (Tokyo: Chūō kōron sha, 1987),
pp. 54–7. See also Fernando G. Gutierrez, "Emakimono Depicting the Pains of the
Damned," *Monumenta Nipponica* 22/3–4 (1967), pp. 278–89.
16   Wakabayashi, "Hell Illustrated," p. 296.

appearing outside hells and in tales. A horse-headed demon chanting about the evanescence of life does disrupt an aristocrat and a courtesan in *Uji shūi*, but an appearance in this world is extremely rare.[17]

Oni and *Setsuwa*

In the Heian (794–1185) and Kamakura (1185–1333) periods, most *oni* appear in *setsuwa*, short tales gathered in collections predominately between the ninth and mid-fourteenth centuries.[18] Juxtaposing the ordinary and the extraordinary in a way that mixes historical fact, including historical figures and events, with fictive elements, *setsuwa* illustrate basic Buddhist principles or sometimes other Asian religious and philosophical teachings (and frequently have Indian or Chinese origins), and transmit cultural and historical knowledge. The tales incorporate elements of the folk and portray people from various social classes, but are generally associated with aristocrats and literate Buddhist monks and priests. There are many secular *setsuwa*; however, most are either overtly Buddhist, emphasizing a particular belief or practice—with certain tales and collections presumably used in preaching—or less tightly tied to Buddhist thought.

The previously mentioned *Uji shūi*, *Sangoku denki*, and *Kankyo no tomo* are three of numerous *setsuwa* tale collections. *Setsuwa* present a variety of *oni*, ranging from eerie invisible presences to embodied beings. While tales rarely describe *oni* in any complete sense, when stories do mention the creatures in non-human form, one or more of the features listed above are included. The wardens of hell depicted in paintings are not the only visual representations to influence *oni* in *setsuwa* and other literature (various gods and demons in Buddhist sculpture also do), but they likely had the greatest impact.

While "oni" is best used for creatures designated as such in texts, there is an exception: *rasetsu* or *rasetsunyo* (*nyo* indicates "female") are a subcategory of *oni* that typically impersonate women. In a tale from *Dainihonkoku hokekyōkenki* (*Miraculous Tales of the Lotus Sutra*, 1040–44), a government official leaves home for his office on horseback before dawn and, bewitched by an invisible *oni*, loses his way. At sundown, he seeks to stay the night at a small house in a desolate field. A refined, beautifully dressed woman, the type a man of his status might not even come across

---

17 Tale 24 in Book 12, Miki Sumito et al., *Uji shūi monogatari. Kohon setsuwa shū*, Shin Nihon koten bungaku taikei 42 (Tokyo: Iwanami shoten, 1990), p. 319. D.E. Mills, *A Collection of Tales from Uji: A Study and Translation of Uji Shūi Monogatari* (Cambridge: Cambridge University Press, 1970), p. 377. Royall Tyler (trans.), *Japanese Tales* (New York: Pantheon, 1987), p. 241. Below, when tales are numbered in the same way in multiple Japanese editions of a *setsuwa* collection, as is usually the case, I will simply give the text title and tale number, providing that I have already given information about one edition and am not citing a direct quote.

18 On the genre of *setsuwa*, see Li, *Ambiguous Bodies*, pp. 15–30.

in the capital, greets him. The official flees, realizing that such a person would hardly appear in the middle of nowhere and therefore must be a *rasetsu*. Chasing him, the woman turns into a ten-foot tall, flesh-hungry creature with two red eyes that resemble large mirrors either in how they reflect light or in size and four fangs, flaming from its eyes, ears, and mouth.[19] The narrator calls this creature both *rasetsu oni* and simply *rasetsu*. Although unstated, the *oni* who initially bewitched him may be the same creature. In the *Konjaku monogatari shū* (*Tales of Times Now Past*, circa 1120), *rasetsu* appears in the tale title while the narrative uses only *oni*. The *rasetsu* devours the horse while the man is saved by a speaking Chinese character, 妙 (*Myō*), the first of the *Lotus Sutra*, from a copy once buried inside a stupa long since destroyed by the elements.[20] A common motif, the demonic creature impersonating a beautiful woman, serves as a warning against women and female sexuality, seen as threats to religious practice and spiritual progress. While the man here is not a monk, the creature and the personified 妙 (*Myō*) are juxtaposed to demonstrate the efficacy of Buddhist scripture to protect against forces that lead people—even ordinary men setting out to do mundane tasks—astray and toward harm.

The term *rasetsu* comes from the Sanskrit *rākṣasa*. Dating to the Vedic period in India (circa 1500 BCE to 500 BCE), it likely initially referred to certain destructive humans opposed to Vedic cults, later imagined as supernatural humanoids who often "sport monstrous deformities"[21] such as multiple heads or eyes. The key characteristics of both *rākṣasa* and *oni/rasetsu*, that they are flesh-eating and shape shifting, are found in Hindu mythology, but, by the time *rākṣasas* traveled through China to Japan, Buddhism had long appropriated them. *Avadāna* and *jātaka* tales (which explain events of the present life of illustrious Buddhists in terms of previous karma, with *jātaka* addressing past lives of the Buddha) stress the destructive

---

19 The parts of *oni* are sometimes compared to familiar objects, perhaps to convey a sense of a connection to the material world. However, the phrase *naoshi ōkinaru kagami no gotoshi* (exactly like/as large mirrors) lacks clarity. If the eyes are large precisely as the mirrors are large, we still do not know what sized mirrors the storyteller had in mind, although one pictures the round, hand-held bronze mirrors of the time. It is also possible that the eyes are thought to be like mirrors in that they reflect light.

20 Abbreviated as *Dainihonkoku hokekyōkenki* (abbr. *Hokkegenki*), Book 3: tale 110 in Inoue Mitsusada and Ōsone Shōsuke (eds), *Ōjōden, Hokkegenki*, Nihon shisō taikei 7 (Tokyo: Iwanami shoten, 1974), pp. 191–4; Yoshiko K. Dykstra (trans.), *Miraculous Tales of the Lotus Sutra: The Dainihonkoku Hokekyōkenki of Priest Chingen* (Honolulu: University of Hawai'i Press, 1984), pp. 128–9. Also in Book 12: tale 28, Mabuchi Kazuo, Kunisaki Fumimaro, and Inagaki Taiichi (eds), *Konjaku Monogatarishū*, Shinpen Nihon koten bungaku zenshū 35 (Tokyo: Shōgakkan, 1999). Marian Ury (trans.), *Tales of Times Now Past: Sixty-two Stories from a Medieval Japanese Collection* (Berkeley: University of California Press, 1979; Ann Arbor: Center for Japanese Studies, University of Michigan, 1993), pp. 87–9. Tyler, *Japanese Tales*, pp. 209–11. Discussed in Li, *Ambiguous Bodies*, p. 149, and Charlotte Eubanks, *Miracles of Book and Body: Buddhist Textual Culture and Medieval Japan* (Berkeley: University of California Press, 2011), p. 165.

21 N.N. Bhattacharyya, *Indian Demonology: The Inverted Pantheon* (New Delhi: Manohar, 2000), p. 41.

nature of such spirit-creatures to justify their conquests or conversion, and affirm the spiritual power of Buddhism. In the Dhāraṇī chapter of the *Lotus Sutra*, ten *rākṣasīs* (female *rasetsu*) become protectors of reciters of that sutra. Other flesh-eating demons introduced with Buddhism in both their demonic and converted forms, *yakṣas* (*yasha*) also merged with *oni*, but are less common than *rasetsu* in *setsuwa* and often function in similar ways.

In ancient India, *yakṣas* began as nature spirits and were "semi-divine beings with supernatural power that brings good or bad to people."[22] Significantly, since the categories of *yakṣas and rākṣasas* were blurred (even in India), pre-Hindu and pre-Buddhist *yakṣīs* appear in sculpture "in the form of dryad or aquatic nymph," and suggest "benign female sexuality and rampant fertility."[23] In literature, both Hinduism and Buddhism came to respond to such beings with demonization, apparently because they were associated with female sexuality and male desire, which distract men from religious practice and hence prevent men from achieving enlightenment, conflating them with *rākṣasīs* and other demons.[24] While Indian sculptural images of *yakṣīs* affirm female sexuality, literary representations present it as threatening, linking the beauty that attracts men to the demonic. *Setsuwa* inherited this negative sense of *yakṣīs/rākṣasīs*. While Buddhism appropriated both types of creatures as guardians, that sense of them is rare in *setsuwa*.

An Indian Buddhist sense of *yakṣīs/rākṣasīs* that influenced Japanese representations of female *oni* appears in "How Sōkara and Five Hundred Merchants Go Together to the Land of the Rākṣasīs," in the Tenjiku (India) section of *Konjaku* and in *Uji Shūi*. The tale, which has earlier *jātaka* versions, relates how a ship of men is blown to an island of *yakṣīs* and *rākṣasīs* who impersonate beautiful women but eat men. The men enjoy pleasurable erotic lives but are endangered. Almost all are ultimately saved by the bodhisattva Kannon (Avalokiteśvara). Sōkara receives imperial sanction to conquer the land, but only after his *rasetseu*-wife follows the men back to Tenjiku to complain about being abandoned, becomes involved with the king, and eats all but his head.[25] In *setsuwa* set in Japan, *rasetsu* (often *rasetsunyō* for females) are most often demonic creatures who transform into women to victimize men. By casting female sexuality as monstrous, Buddhism attempted to discourage men, particularly monks, from forming attachments believed to interfere with the pursuit of enlightenment and to threaten the insularity and stability of the monastic community.

---

22 Ibid., p. 59.

23 Gail Hinich Sutherland, *The Disguises of the Demon: The Development of the Yakṣa in Hinduism and Buddhism*, SUNY Series in Hindu Studies (Albany: State University of New York Press, 1991), p. 137. See also pp. 7–24 in the chapter "The Yakṣa and the Waters."

24 Ibid., p. 51, and Chapter 5, "Yakṣīs," pp. 137–47.

25 *Konjaku* Book 5: tale 1, and *Uji shūi* Book 6: tale 9; Mills, *Tales from Uji*, pp. 266–9. See also Li, *Ambiguous Bodies*, p. 148. On the Indian tale and the place of the island in Japanese literature and art, see D. Max Moerman, "Demonology and Eroticism: Islands of Women in the Japanese Buddhist Imagination," *Japanese Journal of Religious Studies* 36/2 (2009), pp. 351–80.

Oni as Minimally Described

While representations of *oni* impersonating attractive, sexually available men are few, they, too, exist. A bride consumed on her wedding night believes she is with a loving groom and a woman eaten on the palace grounds trusts a suitor pulling her gently into the shadows of trees.[26] Terrifyingly, *oni* can appear as anyone, including lovers and relatives. What victims last see before an attack is often a human being rather than a monster. They may never face the *oni* in monstrous form at all: in a tale about hunters threatened by their demon-turned-mother, the brothers learn the identity of the *oni* only because they recognize the hand which one hunter severs from a hidden creature after the other feels it pulling at his topknot and calls for help.[27]

Even when *oni* are said to appear in frightening form, descriptions of them are sparse and enough details to create a substantial mental picture are rare. When two *oni* greet an abbot shortly after his death, they are merely said to be large.[28] *Oni* are minimally portrayed in *setsuwa*, even in descriptions of the nocturnal procession of 100 demons, mentioned in at least nine tales. When, in *Uji shūi*, an itinerant monk encounters the procession in a deserted temple, entering with torches come "three one-eyed creatures and all sorts of others. They are eerie creatures, not at all human. Sporting horns and with heads that cannot be described, they are utterly terrifying."[29] That is, there were features of *oni* considered unimaginable and word-defying, rendering the creatures all the more frightening. Or a tale may imply that an *oni* appears and not describe it. An ill minister dreams that fearsome *oni* shake and torture him until a handsome boy comes and chases them away with a whip, but the tale does not say what about their looks is scary.[30] Finally, part of an *oni* may be substituted for the whole: at the abandoned Kawara mansion, only a hand (and probably an arm) of an unidentifiable thing reaches out and grabs a woman. Her body is later found sucked dry, hanging from a laundry rod.[31]

At the other end of the spectrum are *oni* in monstrous form, but even then the details are not numerous. The description of the creature blocking access to Agi Bridge in one *Konjaku* tale is among the most detailed. A young man boasts to

26   Tale 2:33 in *Nihon ryōiki*, including the edition by Osamu Izumoji (ed.), *Nihon ryōiki*, Shin Nihon bungaku taikei 30 (Tokyo: Iwanami, 1996), and *Konjaku* 20:37. See also Kyoko Motomochi Nakamura (trans.), *Miraculous Stories from the Japanese Buddhist Tradition: The Nihon ryōiki of the Monk Kyōkai* (Cambridge, MA: Harvard University Press, 1973; reprint, Richmond, Surrey: Curzon Press, 1997), pp. 205–6. The tale of a woman eaten on palace grounds are *Konjaku* Book 27: tale 8 and Nagazumi Yasuaki and Shimada Isao (eds), *Kokon chomonjū*, 17:589, vol. 2, Nihon koten bungaku taikei 84 (Tokyo: Iwanami shoten, 1966), pp. 271–2. See also, Li, *Ambiguous Bodies*, pp. 141–5.
27   *Konjaku* 27:22; Ury, *Tales of Times Now Past*, pp. 163–5, and Tyler, *Japanese Tales*, pp. 316–17. Li, *Ambiguous Bodies*, pp. 179–86.
28   *Uji shūi* tale 3:13; Mills, *Tales from Uji*, pp. 204–5.
29   *Uji shūi* tale 1:17; Mills, *Tales from Uji*, pp. 154–5.
30   *Konjaku* 14:35.
31   *Konjaku* 27:17; Li, *Ambiguous Bodies*, pp. 128–9.

his friends that he can cross the haunted bridge; they, in turn, urge him to prove it. Arriving at the bridge on horseback, he encounters a beautiful woman who appears to have been abandoned. Not fooled, he refuses to stop. She chases him, transforming into an *oni* with a nine-foot green verditer body, a vermillion face with the broad round shape of a flat sitting cushion (*enza*), one amber eye, and hair as tangled as Japanese mugwort. The three fingers on each hand have knife-like nails five inches long.[32] In another tale, an ascetic plagued by desire for Empress Somedono transforms into an *oni*. He is called to the palace to exorcize the empress of evil spirits, but after curing her, catches a glimpse of her through a gap in a curtain and feels burning passion. He violates her, is caught and thrown into prison, whereupon he "vows in tears, 'I will die immediately, become an *oni*, and as long as the empress is in this world, be intimate with her whenever I desire.'"[33] The creature he becomes towers about eight feet tall and has skin as black as lacquer, eyes resembling metal bowls, sword-like teeth, as well as upper and lower fangs. He wears nothing but a red loincloth with a mallet stuck in the waistband.[34] The *oni* charms the empress, who remains unaware of his monstrous form. The amount of detail in both these examples is substantial for *setsuwa*, which are often more bone than flesh. The significance of these last two tales will be discussed further in the next section.

Oni as Response or Resistance

In addition to the illustrated scrolls mentioned above, certain Buddhist statues would also have influenced how audiences of *setsuwa* imagined *oni*, not only in terms of their looks but also functions. The nature of the relationship between conqueror or queller and *oni* is especially important. Often the very encounter affirms the privileged status of the person confronting the creature. *Jaki*, written as "evil oni" and considered a form of *yasha*, are pinned beneath the feet of the *Shitennō* (four kings of the heavens) who, clad in armor and carrying weapons, serve as temple guardians and protectors of the four directions, as in Figure 7.3. The trampled *jaki* convey the sense that unruly and threatening forces, whether internal or external, must and can be subjugated, but their position is precarious. If the *Shitennō* shift the wrong way, the *jaki* may wriggle free; the *jaki* cannot go anywhere, but then neither can the *Shitennō*.

In relatively older Buddhist tales, *oni* exist as responses to the behavior of people—to their shifting. *Oni* tend to enforce the laws of karma, so that the demonic

---

32   *Konjaku* 27:13; Tyler, *Japanese Tales*; Li, *Ambiguous Bodies*, pp. 166–75 (trans. with discussion); and Watson, *The Demon at Agi Bridge*, pp. 74–8. On this *oni* in connection to the figure of Hashihime, see Kawashima, *Writing Margins*, pp. 255–71.

33   Mabuchi Kazuo, et al., *Konjaku Monogatarishū*, Nihon koten bungaku zenshū 35 (Tokyo: Shōgakkan, 1999), 3:48.

34   *Konjaku* tale 20:7; Tyler, *Japanese Tales*, pp. 178–80; and Li, *Ambiguous Bodies*, pp. 90–103.

Figure 7.3   Statue of *Zōchōten* (Sanskrit: Virūḍhaka), a directional guardian (south), standing on a *jaki*, circa 747, Kaidan-in, the temple Tōdaiji, Nara; photograph provided by Nara National Museum with permission from Tōdaiji.

encounter is ultimately about the person or people encountering the *oni*. At the same time or alternatively, *oni* may serve to express the discontent of people who failed to benefit from a particular dominant ideology or practice. These people were often aristocrats with weak or no ties to the leading house, the northern branch Fujiwara, or Buddhist practitioners unaffiliated with institutions.

In the previously cited tale of the consumed bride, of which one version is in *Nihon ryōki* (*Miraculous Stories of Japan*, circa 823) and the other in *Konjaku*, the parents lose their daughter when they allow her to marry a rich suitor, actually an *oni*, only because of the treasures he brings. They hear the young woman crying out from the couple's bedroom on their wedding night, "Oh, it hurts. Oh, it hurts,"[35] and mistakenly attribute her distress to a painful first sexual experience. The next morning, the mother finds the bloody head and a finger of her daughter, and the treasures have become animal bones. The *Nihon ryōki* version of this tale suggests that the woman and her parents suffer because of resentment from another life, whereas the *Konjaku* emphasizes immediate retribution for their behavior: the *oni* appears in response to their greed. Additionally in *Konjaku*, the *oni* functions to undermine the politically motivated or otherwise opportunistic marriage practices of the most prosperous aristocrats, especially the northern branch Fujiwara, displaying the collective displeasure of other aristocrats who did not benefit from the key alliances. Such people would have had to suppress their disappointment and resentment all the more because the practice was common and outwardly accepted. The fate of the *oni* is not an issue in this tale because the *oni* is an instrument rather than an individual.[36]

Similarly, the tale of Empress Somedono and her *oni* lover is at one level a political statement against the Fujiwara and the lineage of Somedono. The audience is not given a sense of the ascetic-turned-*oni* deserving pity or sympathy. Copulating with the empress in front of the emperor, the minister (also father of the empress), and others in the court, he becomes a raw embodiment of lust, beastly, both comic and grotesque. Numerous stories related to this tale but created slightly later in time are about a particular Buddhist priest, Shinzei, also called Kakimoto no ki (800–860) but, in this early version, the man goes unnamed and his fate is never considered. Along with the tales about the consumed bride, this story directs attention to what the *oni* does to or for other people.[37]

As for the tale about the *oni* at Agi Bridge, the protagonist displays foolish pride and misdirected energy when he boasts that he can cross. The man initially escapes from the *oni* but, shortly after, the *oni* appears disguised as his brother and kills him. His wife inadvertently plays a role in his death when she tries to prevent her husband from killing the being she believes is her brother-in-law. In biting off

---

35   Mabuchi Kazuo, et al., *Konjaku Monogatarishū*, vol. 3, p. 132.

36   For a discussion of both versions, *Nihon ryōiki* 2:33 and *Konjaku* 20:37, see Li, *Ambiguous Bodies*, pp. 127–35. It includes translations of the *Konjaku* tale and the preface of the *Nihon ryōiki* tale. A full translation of the *Nihon ryōiki* tale is in Nakamura, *Miraculous Stories*, pp. 205–6.

37   *Konjaku* tale 20:7. For a detailed analysis, see Li, *Ambiguous Bodies*, pp. 90–103.

the man's head, the *oni* serves to implement a consequence for the man's lack of judgment and unfounded bravado, as well as, reflecting a bias of the time, for the overconfidence of the woman in her own judgment.[38]

The Connection of *Oni* to Human Emotions

Personified and humanoid forms of *oni* took precedence in Heian and medieval Japan in numbers as well as interest level, measured by how certain representations and motifs, or entire stories, are repeated in various texts. Along with the physical similarities came emotional connections. The trend to emphasize the link of the emotions of *oni* to human feeling reaches a peak in the Muromachi period, as suggested by the previously mentioned emphasis of Zeami on *oni* with human hearts. Moreover, in "The Sorrow of *Oni*," Ikegami discusses first Shuten dōji as he appears not only in the story relating his defeat, *Shuten dōji* (the Shibukawa edition, circa 1716–29), whose earliest extant version is *Ōeyama ekotoba* (*The Illustrated Tale of Mount Ōe*, early fourteenth century), but also in a presumably slightly later account of the early life of Shuten dōji before his move to Mount Ōe, *Ibukiyama Shuten dōji* (*Shuten dōji of Mount Ibuki*).[39] While the story of conquest relates how Shuten dōji is tricked into entertaining enemies, encouraged to drink a wine that debilitates *oni*, and, once intoxicated, decapitated, the fictive biography establishes many details of his personal history. In the second, Shuten dōji is a child of a human mother and a violent or raging mountain *kami* (deity), Ibuki Daimyōjin. He begins life with an unruly nature that ultimately leads him away from his part human half and toward the raging *kami* side.[40] He is fond of saké, even as a young child. His maternal grandfather sends him to a monastery, Enryakuji on Mount Hiei, to be trained as an acolyte, but the effort to tame him fails. One day, he dances an "*oni*-dance" during a celebration and is later unable to remove the *oni*-mask donned. He flees in fear and, after living for a while with his mother in a cave on Mount Ibuki because his grandfather and father refuse to help him, finally relocates to Mount

---

38   *Konjaku* tale 27:13. See Li, *Ambiguous Bodies*, pp. 166–75.
39   There are two types of *Ibukiyama Shuten dōji*. One is very similar to the story of conquest in *Ōeyama Shuten dōji*; on the differences, see Reider, *Japanese Demon Lore*, pp. 32–3. The second type has a different focus, as discussed above.
40   There is a fine line between violent god and *oni*; ultimately, the difference is often a matter of who is worshipped. Irene H. Lin has written on how the symbol of the demonic child is employed to reveal the powers behind the creation of a system of "ruling elites and influential families (*kenmon*)" in "The Ideology of Imagination: The Tale of Shuten Dōji as a *Kenmon* Discourse," in Bernard Faure and François Lachaud (eds), *Buddhist Priests, Kings, and Marginals: Studies on Medieval Japanese Buddhism*, Cahiers d'Extrême Asie 13 (2002–2003), pp. 379–410. According to her, the storing of the decapitated head of Shuten dōji in the Treasure House of Uji as a relic, which occurs at the end of the conquest tale, constitutes an act of "managing his turbulent power, and bringing it back to the center to regenerate order" (p. 410), while also reinstating Shuten dōji as a *kami* (god).

Ōe. The story of his conquest gives a different account of why and how he must flee, wander, and find a new home, but, in both stories, he necessarily settles on a way of non-human being and in a place appropriate to it.[41]

Ikegami sees the tragedy of Shuten dōji in his loss of a human life. Driven from the world, he finds himself in a lonely, hell-like existence mainly because of his inherent *oni* nature. Yet, when about to be conquered, he is naïve and trusting. He wants to like the visiting mountain priests who are really warriors set on killing him, but the people he seems to think are friends deceive and betray him.[42] More than one scholar has written on Shuten dōji in terms of the marginalized other whose position is critical to defining central authority.[43] Yet, what most pushes him away from society is internal—who or what he is and was preventing him from being human despite his ties to humanity.

The personification or humanization of *oni* does not begin in the Muromachi period. It stems largely from the idea, dating from the ninth century or earlier, of people reborn as *oni*. Even the oldest *setsuwa* collection, *Nihon ryōiki*, demonstrates a sense of *oni* as a restless spirit of a dead person. An *oni* who murders acolytes in the belfry of Gangō Temple turns out to be the spirit of a deceased wicked slave. He is conquered by a boy, who grows up to be a famous Buddhist.[44] While the *oni* is included in the tale mainly to demonstrate the remarkable abilities of the child, it remains significant that no one cares about him. Here and in most *setsuwa* about *oni*, no attempt at understanding is made, and so there is also no sense of pity. This attitude is precisely what changes.

Oni that Evoke Sympathy

The *setsuwa* discussed in this section depict *oni* about whom audiences are more apt to care. In two tales linking the monstrous to spirits of the recently deceased, the spirit transformed out of the human realm still remembers something about who he was and what he did. He cannot progress to a better place without assistance and is humanized by both memory and that need.

In "How Nichizō Shōnin Encounters an *Oni* in the Yoshino Mountains," an *oni* seeks spiritual assistance from Nichizō Shōnin (904–85?, also called Dōken),

---

41   The text which Ikegami uses for the early life of the *oni* is "Ibukiyama Shuten dōji," in Yokoyama Shigeru and Matsumoto Ryūshin (eds), *Muromachi jidai monogatari taisei*, vol. 2 (Tokyo: Kadokawa shoten, 1973), pp. 358–65. See also Lin, "The Tale of Shuten Dōji," pp. 405–6, and Ikegami, "'Oni' no kanashimi," p. 13. Recent translations of the conquest story are Noriko Reider, "Shuten Dōji: Drunken Demon," in *Asian Folklore Studies* 64 (2005), pp. 207–31, and R. Keller Kimbrough, "The Demon Shuten Dōji," in Shirane (ed.), *Traditional Japanese Literature*, pp. 1123–38.

42   Ikegami, "'Oni' no kanashimi," p. 13.

43   The concept of marginalization is integrated in the discussion in Lin, "The Tale of Shuten Dōji," and Reider, "Shuten Dōji," in *Japanese Demon Lore*, pp. 42–8.

44   *Nihon ryōiki* Book 1: tale 3; Nakamura, *Miraculous Stories*, pp. 107–8.

a Buddhist mountain ascetic known for his spiritual and mystic prowess. As in many tales, the encounter of a person and an *oni* underscores the eminence of the former. Nichizō is best known for traveling to other realms of the Buddhist cosmos after a temporary death. This account contributed to the deification as the thunder god of scholar, poet, and statesman Sugawara no Michizane (845–903), who died during an unjust exile. His angry spirit was blamed for the deaths of certain political rivals, including four killed when lightning struck the palace and Emperor Daigo (885–930, r. 897–930) slightly afterwards, as well as his son, a crown prince, prior to those tragedies.[45] Stories of the fantastic journey of Nichizō appear in such works as the Buddhist history *Fusō ryakki* (*Concise Chronicle of Japan*, early to mid-twelfth century), and the illustrated scrolls *Kitano Tenjin Engi* (*Origins of the Kitano Tenjin Shrine*, circa late twelfth/early thirteenth centuries).[46] The first of these versions is thought to date from the tenth century. Nichizō meets Michizane in a paradise atop Mount Kinpu and Emperor Daigo in hell. Daigo is considered guilty of unjustly exiling Michizane and indirectly causing the disease and natural disasters following his victim's death, brought on by the wrath of Michizane's spirit. Michizane appeals to Nichizō to help keep peace in Japan by encouraging people to worship him while Daigo repents his wrongdoings, and, in *Fusō ryakki*, seeks release from his suffering by requesting through Nichizō that reliquaries be constructed on his behalf for Michizane.[47] The information necessary to appease Michizane's spirit is thus conveyed through Nichizō. The *oni* in the mountains does not seek out just any mountain ascetic, but a man of influence and religious power.

The *oni* is described as having features which we associate with *gaki*: a thin neck, protruding chest bones, distended belly, and skinny shanks. Tall, with dark blue skin, he also has hair red as flames, as do some creatures in *Gaki zōshi* and *Jigoku zōshi*. For example, a redheaded *gaki* is central in Figure 7.4, from the Komoto Family *Gaki zōshi* in the Tokyo National Museum, contrasting with two terrifying *rasetsu/oni*. One of the 36 types of *gaki*, he squats between the *oni* as they brandish flaming swords, with his hands raised in a plea or submission. This type of sad-looking creature is thought to wander among tombs and funerary pyres eating the ashes of the cremated and the hot earth because, in human life, he (or she) "despoiled Buddhist temples for the sake of gain," for example, he "stole a flower offered to the Buddha and sold it."[48] While

---

45 See Robert Borgen, "Michizane as Tenjin," in *Sugawara no Michizane and the Early Heian Court* (Honolulu: University of Hawai'i Press, 1994), pp. 307–40.

46 Kuroita Katsumi (ed.), *Fusō ryakki*, Kokushi taikei 12 (Tokyo: Kokushitaikei kankōkai, 1932), pp. 219–22; Tyler, *Japanese Tales*, pp. 144–9; Hagiwara Tatsuo, Miyata Noboru, and Sakurai Tokutarō (eds), *Kitano Tenjin Engi*, in *Jisha engi*, Nihon shisō taikei 20 (Tokyo: Iwanami shoten, 1975), pp. 158–61; Conán Dean Carey, trans., *In Hell the One Without Sin is Lord*, Sino-Platonic papers 109 (October 2000), pp. 23–7.

47 Brian O. Ruppert, "Beyond Death and the Afterlife: Considering Relic Veneration in Medieval Japan," in Jacqueline I. Stone and Mariko Namba Walter (eds), *Death and the Afterlife in Japanese Buddhism* (Honolulu: University of Hawai'i Press, 2008), pp. 107–8. There may also be other versions mentioning the reliquaries.

48 Komatsu, *Gaki zōshi*, pp. 14–15. While the scroll has no text, Komatsu explains that the sutra illustrates some of the *gaki* described in *Shōbō nenjo kyō* (*Mindfulness of the Right Dharma*

Figure 7.4   Scene depicting one of three types of suffering of *gaki* who eat the
ashes of the cremated, as described in the *Sutra of Meditation on the
Correct Teaching* (*Zhengfa nianchu jing* in Chinese or *Shōbō nenjo kyō* in
Japanese). From *Scroll of Hungry Ghosts* (*Gaki zōshi*), twelfth century,
a National Treasure from the collection of Tokyo National Museum,
image provided by TNM Image Archives; source: http://www/tnm.jp/
modules/r_collection).

the *oni* in the tale physically resembles the *gaki* in this scene more than the fierce *oni*
who beat and cut the *gaki* with swords and sticks (one of the prescribed punishments),
his bellicose nature and unrelenting desire for revenge evoke *asura* (fighting spirits
usually motivated by anger or jealousy) in that realm of the six (*rokudō*), where cruel
and bloodthirsty individuals (martial figures) continue to fight. In this instance, we
see a blending of the posthumous possibilities.

Translator Royall Tyler renamed this tale "A Model Demon" in *Tales of Japan*
and, indeed, the *oni* sincerely appeals to Nichizō for help.[49] Four or five hundred
years ago, he died with a grudge against an enemy. He was subsequently able
to kill that man, a murder followed by numerous others of the sons, grandsons,
great grandsons, and great-great grandsons of the enemy, until no one was left.
However, far from being exemplary, he lacks remorse and would continue to kill,
were he able to trace the reincarnations of his enemies and their descendants. He is

Sutra) and other texts, and provides explanations of each scene based on the sutra. The
second quote comes from page 14, whereas the first is from an essay on *gaki* by Lafcadio
Hearn, in Louis Allen and Jean Watson (eds), *Lafcadio Hearn: Japan's Great Interpreter, A New
Anthology of his Writings: 1894–1904* (Sandgate, UK: Japan Library, 1992), p. 177.

49   Tyler, *Japanese Tales*, pp. 137–8.

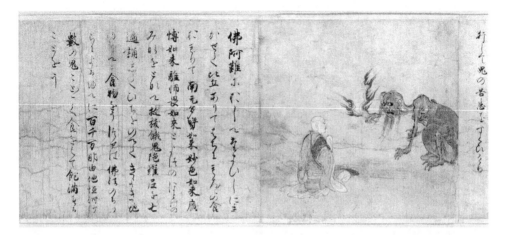

Figure 7.5   One of the Buddha's disciples, Ananda, listens to the suffering of a flaming-mouth *gaki*. From *Scroll of the Hungry Ghosts* (*Gaki zōshi*), twelfth century, a National Treasure from the collection of the Kyoto National Museum, used with permission.

left unable to relieve, even temporarily, his agony through action and suffers from "the scorching fires of his everlasting anger."[50]

The expectation that an *oni* would feel more than its own agony might be too high. In a second *Gaki zōshi* (in the Kyoto National Museum from the Sōgen Temple Collection), the Buddha preaches to *gaki* on the sin of gluttony (*kendon*), but their great suffering initially prevents his words from entering their hearts.[51] Only after he enables them to drink water are they able to heed his words and transform into bodhisattvas (those who postpone buddhahood to help others). As for Nichizō, his ability to help may be limited. Feeling pity for the *oni*, he performs rituals to nullify sins, but there is no indication that they work. While such rituals would probably have been seen as having an effect in the long term, the suggestion that the *oni* may continue to suffer even in the short term attests to the force of the transformation and the emotions behind it. (It took deification to appease the spirit of Michizane.)

The fantastic travels of Nichizō likely served as background for the *setsuwa* of the encounter of Nichizō and this *oni*. The creature has associative connections to the spirits of Michizane and Daigo: the deaths of Michizane's rivals, including Emperor Daigo, were attributed to Michizane's spirit, and both the *oni* and Emperor Daigo in hell long to escape the suffering caused by their pasts. Yet, as the encounter of Buddha with *gaki* in *Gaki zōshi* suggests, the Buddhist context of the *Uji shūi* tale, with an *oni* appealing to a holy man, has roots in Buddhist texts. In addition to the scene of the Buddha showing compassion for *gaki*, the sixth section of the same work (Figure 7.5) shows Ananda, a disciple of the Buddha, encountering a burning-mouth, lamenting *gaki*. The scene draws from *Foshuo jiuba yankou egui*

---

50   *Uji* 1:10; Miki, *Uji shūi, Kohon*, pp. 286–9; Mills, *Tales from Uji*, pp. 352–3.
51   Komatsu, *Gaki zōshi*, pp. 28–9.

tuoluoni jing (*Dhāraṇī Sūtra for the Salvation of the Burning-Mouth Preta*), translated into Chinese from Sanskrit in the eighth century.[52] While beliefs in restless spirits of the dead probably predate Buddhism, they are impossible to extract from Heian and medieval Buddhism.

In "How [a Priest of] Gyokusenbō of Mt Hiei Becomes an *Oni*," an *oni* is released from *kidō*, a term usually used as an abbreviation of *gakidō* (the realm of preta, or hungry ghosts). However, the tale most often refers to the spirit-creature as *oni* and never as *gaki*. It lacks details about the appearance of the *oni*, so we cannot know whether or not he, too, resembles a *gaki*. The important thing is not precisely into what realm he has fallen, but that he has fallen and can be helped.

Poetry, namely the classical Japanese verse known as *waka*, comes into play as the *oni* is released through the recitation of a poem.[53] The subtitle of the tale, "About How Gods and Demons Are Moved by Poetry," alludes to *Kokinshū*, an imperial anthology of poems that was created in the aristocratic tradition, not with Buddhist purposes. *Sangoku denki* is a late tale collection, likely compiled by a Tendai Buddhist novice, Gentō, around the early fifteenth century, when poetry had already long been accepted as a potential Buddhist practice. However, since the tale predates the collection, that fact does not fully explain the intermingling of Buddhist elements with a sense of the magical qualities of *waka*, threads typically distinct in earlier times. It falls into the category of *katoku setsuwa* or "tales of the wondrous benefits of poetry." Authors of two separate commentaries on the *Kokinshū* preface, Son'en Shinnō (1298–1356) and Ryōyo Shōgei (1341–1420), both employ the tale to illustrate the idea, expressed in the famous preface, of poetry enabling *oni* and gods to feel *aware*, or deep pathos, a sense of something touching or sad.[54]

The *setsuwa* first introduces a certain person of the Gyokusenbō residence. An arrogant holy man, he seeks to create a monk's residence so luxurious that it will give him "the glory of having the greatest pagoda of the three," referring to the three major divisions of the Tendai Buddhist complex Enryakuji. The construction materials include apricot wood for the beams and *katsura* wood for the pillars, as well as white or plain/pure clay, probably as part of a finish, and red boards. Carvings of mountains and seaweed lavishly decorate the room. The residence gets its name, literally "Jewel Fountain Quarters," from a tall fence inlaid with jewels and a fountain placed by the low wall.[55]

The narrative explains the death of the man with a quote from *Meibunshō* (late twelfth century), a compilation of quotations from Chinese classics: "The former

---

52   *Bussetsu kyūbatsu enku gaki darani kyō* in Japanese. Komatsu, *Gaki zōshi*, p. 32.

53   Narrowly defined, *waka* is a 31-syllable poem consisting of five units of 5–7–5–7–7 syllables.

54   The relevant passages are quoted in Konno Tōru, "Goen mankō 2: Nennen uta yurai: Urashima nisoku, Gyokusenbō no oni," *Yokohama kokudai kokugo kenkyū* 5 (March 1987), pp. 67–8. While the article focuses on the origins of certain lullabies, it quotes many versions of the Gyokusenbō tale.

55   Tale 27 in Ikegami Jun'ichi (ed.), *Sangoku denki* (Tokyo: Miyai shoten, 1982), 2:159–61.

kings despised arrogance. The Way Of Heaven diminishes superabundance."[56] Clinging emotionally to the beautiful quarters, the man dies and becomes a spirit-creature haunting it. He is not called *oni* at first. His spirit (*seishin*) becomes a *kiryō*, a neutral term referring to a deceased person. However, *oni* is used when he is visible. Before then, he makes his presence known by singing.

> ... the sound of a voice sang softly through the dust, accumulated thickly on the beams, and the vibrations of the pine eaves gradually [drying out] never ceased. As the grass grew deep in the garden, visitors rarely came to the gate. The splendid residence greatly deteriorated and was nothing like it had been in the old days. How the spring winds blew once the master had left.[57]

The residence remains abandoned, with no one willing to even approach the vicinity, until, one day, a certain monk reasons: "All beings and things on heaven and earth endowed with the energy of life are extremely precious. How can we fear the various *oni* and beasts?"[58] He visits the temple on the 15th of the eighth month (on the traditional, lunar calendar), the autumnal equinox, when the moon is fullest and brightest. A Buddhist festival centered on memorializing the dead is held around this time. Called Higan, meaning "the other shore," it emphasizes crossing from this side, the world of suffering, to the other side or enlightenment, and especially of assisting the spirits of the dead in that journey. Moreover, in Buddhist works, the moon is a metaphor for enlightenment. While it seems unlikely that the creature in this story becomes enlightened (the story does not indicate what new state the *oni* enters), the imagery supports the idea of a transmigration/transformation.

The once-splendid building now abandoned and haunted is a popular motif of *setsuwa*, whose influence extends even to *The Tale of Genji*. The Kawara Mansion—whose luxurious garden was designed to resemble the scenic site Shiogami, with its bay—appears in numerous tales as such. However, instead of describing a frightening atmosphere (as the audience might expect), the narrator introduces a poetic world: "On the night of the third five [the 15th], with the lake of the heavens full, the expanse of two thousand miles pains the monk's heart as he recalls the master of the residence from days gone by."[59] The sentence alludes to lines in a famous poem by Chinese poet Bai Juyi (772–846) about a friend in exile, included in the Heian collection *Wakan rōeishū* (*Collection of Japanese and Chinese Poems for Singing*, circa 1013):

> On the night of the third five
> colors of the newly risen moon;

---

56   The second sentence comes from several Chinese classics, including *Yijing* (*The Book of Changes*); Ikegami, *Sangoku denki*, p. 159, n. 8. It is also quoted in *Taiheiki/Chronicle of Great Pacification*, circa 1372.
57   Ikegami, *Sangoku denki*, vol. 2, p. 159.
58   Ibid.
59   Ibid., p. 160.

two thousand miles away,
the heart of my friend[60]
The visitor-monk in the story composes his own poem:

The former master
no longer lives
at Jewel Fountain
It is the high moon
who stays.[61]

Delighted, the *oni* rushes out from the study and, in a terrifying voice, says: "How interesting! You speak of the honorable monk's residence."[62] The visitor cannot get out through the gate fast enough, but the "violent *oni*" (*kijin*) chases after him. The monk falls and passes out, but the voice of the *oni* calls out softly and he revives: "Your fine words are truly mysterious. I have been released from the *Oni/Gaki* Realm. I turn over this residence to you, sir. From now on, you have no reason to fear the hindrance of *oni*." The creature then vanishes. The tale ends: "How mysterious that, after this, the monk's residence was peaceful: there was danger of neither fire nor thieves and now with the area tranquil came the very end of the struggle against the hindrances caused by mouth and tongue."

Here poetry promotes spiritual development. Since the image of the moon in Buddhist contexts connotes enlightenment, the poem composed by the visitor-monk suggests the supreme everlasting nature of enlightenment juxtaposed with the absence (death) of the priest with his worldly attachment. Additionally, the image of the jewel fountain can be reinterpreted within the context of the poem. Rather than suggesting luxury and attachment as it does in the narrative, "jeweled" in Buddhist texts can also imply sacredness. Jewel or *tama* can be written in more than one way, but the meanings of the different Chinese characters used are interrelated. The jewel, usually indicated by the character which can more precisely refer to a pearl, is sometimes used figuratively to refer to such things as Buddhist wisdom or Buddhahood inherent in everyone, as in one poem from a twelfth-century collection beginning with the line "the tripled-body Buddha nature is our jewel."[63] Moreover, the three main components of Buddhism, the Buddha, the teaching (the Dharma), and the community of Buddhist believers (*sangha*) are called the Three Treasures, indicated with a Chinese character also used to mean

---

60   Ibid., p. 60, n. 19 (includes the poem). Translation from J. Thomas Rimer and Jonathan Chaves (eds), *Japanese and Chinese Poems to Sing: The Wakan Rōei Shū* (New York: Columbia University Press, 1997), p. 242.

61   Ikegami, *Sangoku denki*, p. 160.

62   Ibid. The rest of the quotes from this tale come from the same page.

63   *Ryōjin hishō*, in Kobayashi Yoshinori (ed.), *Ryōjin hishō, Kanginshū, Kyōgen kayō*, Shin Nihon koten bungaku taikei 56 (Tokyo: Iwanami shoten, 1993), poem 137, p. 43; Yung-Hee Kim, *Songs to Make the Dust Dance: The Ryōjin Hishō of Twelfth-Century Japan* (Berkeley: University of California Press, 1994), p. 89. On the three bodies of the Buddha or trikāya, see Paul Williams, *Mahāyāna Buddhism: The Doctrinal Foundations*, 2nd edn (London: Routledge, 1989), pp. 179–82.

jewels.[64] Nor is the allusion to a poem by Bai Juyi coincidental, since both the fear that poetry might be "wild words and decorative phrases"[65] whose writing was a spiritual transgression, and the concept that poetry could serve as a form of religious practice and expression, initially come from him. Through the final comments in this story, poetry is contrasted with incorrect uses of speech, which in Buddhism means the false, malicious, harsh, and frivolous, and here, more specifically, argument (encompassing one or more of these types). Rather than being a form of frivolous speech, as poets often feared, poetry is the correct use of words. It frees the *oni*.

In the thirteenth century, an understanding of *waka* as a form of *dhāraṇi* (magical Buddhist incantations) emerged in certain circles, and this tale likely functioned to illustrate that concept.[66] The recitation of the *waka* here also has an effect similar to that of dedications of the *Lotus Sutra* in tales, copied or recited, to benefit the deceased. The *Lotus Sutra* enables spirits trapped in a lower realm, such as snakes, to progress after death to a higher state, whereas *dhāraṇi* in *setsuwa* are used mainly to protect against demonic beings whose fates are not considered.[67] Many stories tell of how the *Sonshō darani* ("Mystical Verse of the Honored and Victorious One") is used to ward off the Nocturnal Procession of One Hundred Demons. In one tale, the former wet nurse of a sexually active adolescent, who wanders out at night to meet his lover, has her brother, a Buddhist priest, write out the *dhāraṇi*, and then secretly sews the words into the boy's kimono collar. The *dhāraṇi* protects the boy from harm but does not render the *oni* friendly nor free them from their present state, as does the poem in this story or the *Lotus Sutra* for other creatures.[68]

---

64 There are additional meanings for "jewel" in the Buddhist context, including a wish-fulfilling gem or the relics of the Buddha. Also significant is that a homophone for "tama" (indicated with a different Chinese character) means "spirit," as in spirit of a person (alive or dead) or god.

65 This phrase comes from a poem on Buddhist matters in which the poet expresses his wish that his writing and errors of using "wild words and decorative phrases" as a poet will somehow be reversed so that instead his literary endeavors will become a form of Buddhist devotion. This idea had a major impact on Japanese poets. For the poem with comments, see Saeko Shibayama (trans.), "Japanese and Chinese Poems to Sing, *Wakan rōeishū*, ca. 1017–1021," in Shirane (ed.), *Traditional Japanese Literature*, p. 291, including n. 305. On the concern of Japanese medieval poets that literary arts were "sins of the language that would cause the unwary poet to be reincarnated in one of the lower, more hellish, of the Six Realms," see Susan Blakeley Klein, *Allegories of Desire: Esoteric Literary Commentaries of Medieval Japan* (Cambridge, MA: Harvard University, Asia Center for the Harvard-Yenching Institute, 2002), pp. 123–8. There are several ways to write Bai Juyi, including Bo Juyi and Po Chü-i.

66 On *katoku setsuwa*, see R. Keller Kimbrough, "Reading the Miraculous Powers of Japanese Poetry: Spells, Truth Acts, and a Medieval Buddhist Poetics of the Supernatural," *Japanese Journal of Religious Studies* 32/1 (2005), pp. 1–33; and Klein, *Allegories of Desire*, pp. 130–33.

67 On tales of snake spirits freed through dedications of the *Lotus Sutra*, see Li, *Ambiguous Bodies*, pp. 213–20.

68 Among the versions of this story are *Konjaku* 14:42; *Uchigiki* 213; *Kohon* 2:51.

While the tale apparently appealed to the medieval sensibility in part because of the magical role of *waka*, a very detailed version in *Taima mandara so* (*Commentary on the Taima Mandala*, 1436) demonstrates that there was also interest in the story for the plights of monks.[69] The commentary is thought to be a record of sermons by the Pure Land Buddhist abbot Yūyo Shōsō (1366–1440) and so the version is written with more specifically Buddhist vocabulary than others. While Yūyo acknowledges that the narrative illustrates the efficacy of *waka*, he also directs attention to the Buddhist practice of the monk who frees the *oni*. That man ultimately returns to his life as a mountain ascetic, rendering him a model for others, in contrast to the *oni*-turned-Gyokusenbō priest.

More commonly, monks would transform into *tengu*, a bird-like creature often impersonating monks and representing evil, because of their arrogance and attachment. The first five scrolls of *Tengu zōshi* (1296) address a problem suggested by the tale of Gyokusenbō: that of monks becoming too proud of their own temples and their sects.[70] The effort of the Gyokusenbō priest to build a grand temple residence is unproblematic in itself since the beauty might have inspired him and others toward enlightenment. Rather, his desire to outdo others and his attachment to his creation result in negative rebirth. In addition to *oni* being perceived as having human-like flaws, human flaws cause them to become *oni*. Their hunger for flesh sets them apart from the human, but that desire is inherent and, as with instinctual behavior, not something people expect them to control.

Both the Gyokusenbō *oni* and the *oni* who appeals to Nichizō Shōnin differ from *oni* who appear mainly as threats, either in non-Buddhist terms or as instruments of karma. *Oni* lacking personal histories can be easily objectified. The situation shifts when the idea strengthens that *oni*, too, have spiritual potential. The move toward humanizing *oni* has roots in the belief in *gui/oni* as spirits of the deceased, usually ancestors, a belief, however ancient, that persists through medieval and into modern and postmodern times.

The Gyokusenbō *oni* shows something akin to character when, after almost accidentally killing the monk through the chase, he speaks out in appreciation. The monster has a heart, something we see in medieval Japan. This element links him to an earlier, cheerful and humorous *oni*, who emerged in the classical or Heian period, dwelling at the gate to the capital, Rajōmon (later called Rashōmon), or the gate to the Greater Imperial Palace, Suzakumon, and whose tale appears in several versions in many collections. When a horseman recites a Chinese poem while passing the gate in one version, the *oni* responds with "*Aware, aware.*"[71] In another,

---

69   Yūyo Shōsō, *Taima mandara so*, in Jōdoshū Kaishū Happyakunen Kinen Keisan Jimukyoku (ed.), *Jōdoshū zensho* 13: Shūgi kenshō (Tokyo: Sankibō busshorin, 1971), pp. 125–6. See also Konno, "Nennen uta yurai," pp. 68–9.

70   Haruko Wakabayashi, "Tengu Images and the Buddhist Concepts of Evil in Medieval Japan," PhD dissertation, Princeton University, 1995, p. 90. See also Komatsu Shigemi, *Tengu zōshi*, in *Tsuchigumo zōshi, Tengu zōshi, Ōeyama ekotoba*, Zoku Nihon no emaki 26 (Tokyo: Chūō kōron sha, 1993), pp. 13–73.

71   *Gōdanshō* tale 4:20 in, among other editions, Gotō Akio, Ikegami Jun'ichi, and Yamane

the creature completes a *waka* recited by a passerby.[72] While the *oni* is linked to the human through poetry, no one wonders about his fate. He does not suffer. *Oni* change once views shift and a Buddhist sense of compassion becomes influential. The past and future existences of *oni*, and hence their spiritual development, matter. *Oni* remain monsters, then, but come to be increasingly like the people they menace.

Taisuke (eds), *Gōdanshō, Chūgaishō, Fuke go*, Shin Nihon koten bungaku taikei 32 (Tokyo: Iwanami shoten, 1997), pp. 114–15.

72   Tale 10:4 in Izumi Motohiro (ed.), *Jikkinshō: Daisan ruihon: Shōkōkan zō* (Osaka: Izumi shoin, 1984), p. 182.

The Maya "Cosmic Monster" as a Political and Religious Symbol

Matthew Looper

Like most cultures, the native peoples of Mesoamerica believed in a host of beings of "unnatural" aspect—human–animal hybrids, composite animals, and humanoids of frightful appearance. Prehispanic Mixtec manuscripts from Oaxaca tell of epic battles between heroic ancestors and the spirits of dead warriors in the form of skeletons and animal-headed men.[1] Aztec religion includes numerous deities of fearsome aspect such as Itzpapalotl, a star goddess also associated with slain warriors, who possesses a partly skeletal face, clawed limbs and joints, and bat wings sprouting obsidian blades.[2] The ancient Mesoamerican proclivity for human–animal hybrid imagery is rooted in very ancient shamanistic religious concepts. From early times, the fusion of the human form with various symbolic animals—especially predators—served as a central metaphor for the ritual transformation of humans into powerful spirits.[3] During the colonial period, these morally ambivalent figures were systematically suppressed and demoted to the status of demons or merged with the Devil, thereby complicating the study of their original Prehispanic significance.[4]

---

1   Zelia Nuttall (ed.), *Codex Nuttall* (New York: Dover, 1975), fol. 77–8.

2   Karl A. Taube, "Turquoise Hearth: Fire, Self-sacrifice, and the Central Mexican Cult of War," in Davíd Carrasco, Lindsay Jones, and Scott Sessions (eds), *Mesoamerica's Classic Heritage: Teotihuacán to the Aztecs* (Niwot: University Press of Colorado, 1999), pp. 325–7.

3   F. Kent Reilly III, "Art, Ritual, and Rulership in the Olmec World," in Jill Guthrie and Elizabeth P. Benson (eds), *The Olmec World: Ritual and Rulership* (Princeton: The Art Museum, Princeton University, 1995), pp. 30–2.

4   Modern Mayan languages preserve a number of terms translated in dictionaries as "demon" or "devil," such as *kisin, itzeel, laab', nawal,* and *pukuuj*. However, the meanings of these terms have often undergone considerable acculturation or are imperfectly translated. For example, *kisin* (literally, "flatulence") was a death god, and *itzeel, laab',* and *nawal* relate closely to witchcraft and spirit transformation. See Terrence Kaufman, "A Preliminary Mayan Etymological Dictionary," (2003), pp. 1364–8, electronic document: <http://www.famsi.org/reports/01051/index.html>, accessed July 1, 2009; J. Eric S. Thompson, *Maya History and Religion* (Norman: University of Oklahoma Press,

The Maya of the Classic period (250–900 CE) likewise depicted a host of beings with composite or so-called grotesque characteristics in their art and inscriptions. Early on, scholars recognized that many of these beings were in fact gods, or *k'uh*, as the ancient Maya called them.[5] Another class of spirits included flaming jaguars, bats, corpses, owls with bleeding bellies, deer with everted eyeballs, and louse-ridden monkeys.[6] Although we have known for some time that the ancient Maya referred to these beings as *way*, a term that also means "sleep" and "dream," scholars continue to call these beings "monsters" or "demons."[7] Nevertheless, as our understanding of ancient Maya religion grows, it seems desirable to employ native terminology in order to clarify conceptual categories that would otherwise be blurred by terms such as "monster," which have no recognized equivalent in Mayan languages or texts.

But there is another important reason why the term "monster" is problematic in the context of the study of Native American cultures, particularly by outsiders. This has to do with the historical connections of this term to the rhetoric of colonialism. During the early colonial period, European accounts commonly painted a picture of native peoples as savages more akin to animals than humans, in order to justify their subjugation.[8] The classic example is Columbus's slander of the Carib peoples as a fierce race of dog-faced man-eaters, a description that merges monstrosity with anthropophagy.[9] To the European chroniclers of the invasion of the Americas, it was only through the defeat of the sin of its native inhabitants that the riches of the "New World" could be exploited. Granted, some colonial authors evoked monstrosity in order to appeal to the readers' taste for the marvelous.[10] Still others

---

1970), p. 302. See also Cecelia F. Klein, "Devil and the Skirt: An Iconographic Inquiry into the Pre-Hispanic Nature of the Tzitzimime," *Ancient Mesoamerica* 11/1 (2000), pp. 1–26.

5   Stephen D. Houston and David Stuart, "Of Gods, Glyphs and Kings: Divinity and Rulership among the Classic Maya," *Antiquity* 70 (1996), pp. 289–312; Paul Schellhas, *Die Gottergestalten der Mayahandschriften* (Berlin: Verlag von A. Asher, 1904).

6   Nikolai Grube and Werner Nahm, "A Census of Xibalba: A Complete Inventory of 'Way' Characters on Maya Ceramics," in Justin Kerr (ed.), *The Maya Vase Book*, vol. 4 (New York: Kerr Associates, 1994), pp. 686–715.

7   Stephen D. Houston and David Stuart, *The Way Glyph: Evidence for "Co-essences" among the Classic Maya*, Research Reports on Ancient Maya Writing 30 (Washington, DC: Center for Maya Research, 1989); cf. Michael D. Coe, *Lords of the Underworld: Masterpieces of Classic Maya Ceramics* (Princeton: The Art Museum, Princeton University, 1978), p. 130; Andrea Stone and Marc Zender, *Reading Maya Art: A Hieroglyphic Guide to Ancient Maya Painting and Sculpture* (London: Thames and Hudson, 2011), p. 27; David Stuart, *Sourcebook for the 29th Maya Hieroglyph Forum, March 11–16, 2005* (Austin: Department of Art and Art History, University of Texas, 2005), pp. 161–2.

8   Tzvetan Todorov, *The Conquest of America: The Question of the Other* (New York: Harper and Row, 1984), p. 156.

9   Yobenj Aucardo Chicangana-Bayona, "El nacimiento del caníbal: un debate conceptual," *Historia crítica* 36 (2008), pp. 176–200. See also Davies and Steel, this volume.

10   Juan Francisco Maura, "Monstruos y bestias en las crónicas del nuevo mundo," *Espéculo* 19 (2001), electronic document: <http://www.ucm.es/info/especulo/numero19/

used monsters as a way to come to terms with creatures that were unfamiliar, such as Columbus's famous imagining of manatees as sirens.[11] Nevertheless, the use of "monsters" and related terms mainly served to vilify native religion. As scholars writing from a position of privilege and authority, we would do well to consider the legacy of racism and ethnocentrism that the term invokes when applied to Native Americans and their gods.

In ancient Maya art history, three beings are persistently referred to as "monsters."[12] One is the "cauac monster," now known to be a personification of hills and mountains (*witz*) and sometimes therefore called a "*witz* monster."[13] Another is the "waterlily monster" or "waterlily serpent," a god of terrestrial waters, wind, the moon, and caves.[14] The third, which is the subject of this essay, is the "cosmic monster," a composite crocodilian creature that exists in various manifestations or aspects (Figures 8.1–8.4). As personifications of the earth and (nocturnal) sky, crocodilians are frequently employed as supports or frames for rulers in order to sacralize the king and to signal his cosmological ritual identity. Further, contrary to Western expectations for monsters, these mythical creatures are not typically depicted as violent beings, but are the victims of sacrifice associated with episodes of cosmic renewal.

The identification of the cosmic crocodile in Maya art goes back more than a century to the pioneering archaeologist Alfred P. Maudslay, who sprinkled his writings with the term "dragon" to refer to various beings.[15] Maudslay's identification of a "two-headed dragon" at Copan and Palenque was foundational to the work of Herbert Spinden, who delineated most of the distinctive characteristics of this creature and pointed out many examples in Late Classic (600–800 CE) Maya courtly art, mainly from the sites of Copan, Palenque, Piedras Negras, and Quirigua.[16] Importantly, Spinden identified the body and limbs of the

---

monstruo.html>, accessed July 1, 2009.

11   See Davies, this volume.

12   See Linda Schele and Mary Ellen Miller, *The Blood of Kings: Dynasty and Ritual in Maya Art* (Fort Worth: Kimbell Art Museum, 1986), pp. 45–6.

13   David Stuart, *Ten Phonetic Syllables*, Research Reports on Ancient Maya Writing 14 (Washington, DC : Center for Maya Research, 1987), pp. 17–23; Dicey Taylor, "The Cauac Monster," in Merle Greene Robertson and Donnan C. Jeffers (eds), *Tercera Mesa Redonda de Palenque, 1978* (Monterrey: Pre-Columbian Art Research Center, 1978), pp. 79–90.

14   Matthew G. Looper, *To Be Like Gods: Dance in Ancient Maya Civilization* (Austin: University of Texas Press, 2009), p. 47; Karl A. Taube, *The Major Gods of Ancient Yucatan*, Studies in Pre-Columbian Art and Archaeology 32 (Washington, DC: Dumbarton Oaks, 1992), p. 59; Karl A. Taube, "Catalog Entry 1," in Daniel Finamore and Stephen D. Houston (eds), *Fiery Pool: The Maya and the Mythic Sea* (New Haven and London: Yale University Press, 2010), p. 45.

15   Alfred P. Maudslay, *Archaeology*, 5 volumes, Biologia Centrali-Americana (London: Porter, Dulau and Co., 1889–1902), vol. I, pp. 28, 52, 56, 57; vol. II, pp. 8–9, 18–19.

16   Maudslay, *Archaeology*, vol. IV, p. 37; Herbert J. Spinden, *A Study of Maya Art, Its Subject Matter and Historical Development*, Memoirs of the Peabody Museum of American

creature as reptilian and the "front" head of the creature as "shaped somewhat like that of a crocodile."[17] An analogous being depicted on page 74 of the Dresden Codex, a hieroglyphic book dating to the Post-classic period, was also identified as a crocodile by Ernst Förstemann.[18]

Building upon these early identifications, J. Eric S. Thompson emphasized the composite nature and cosmological symbolism of these "celestial monsters."[19] Noting their fusion of crocodile, iguana, snake, and deer characteristics, Thompson argued that these creatures represent the sky and earth. Although some of his specific identifications have not withstood the test of time, the notion that crocodilian supernaturals in ancient Maya art represent aspects of the sky and earth has endured. Later scholars frequently evoked Thompson's cosmological interpretation of these images, referring to them as "celestial monsters" or "cosmic serpents."[20]

Hybridizing this terminology, Andrea Stone referred collectively to these beings as "cosmic monsters."[21] Through a detailed structural analysis of the iconography, she was able to distinguish two major variants of the theme.[22] One variant has deer hooves rather than reptilian claws and is frequently associated with segmented bands that symbolize the sky (sky-bands). The second variant emphasizes aquatic imagery such as waterlily pads and water scrolls, and includes body or limb markings or personifications now known to represent mountains. The second variant also has a more prominent tail, often marked with dotted ovals and with leafy projections.

Stone argued that the distinction between these two configurations resulted from the adaptation of a cosmological image to certain artistic formats. The first, which she termed the "vertical model," is frequently extended along a vertical axis

Archaeology and Ethnology, Harvard University, vol. 6 (Cambridge, MA: Peabody Museum of American Archaeology and Ethnology, 1913), p. 53–6.

17   Spinden, *A Study of Maya Art*, p. 53.

18   Ernst W. Förstemann, "Commentary of the Maya Manuscript in the Royal Public Library of Dresden," in *Papers of the Peabody Museum of American Archaeology and Ethnology* 4/2 (Cambridge, MA: Harvard University, Peabody Museum of American Archaeology and Ethnology, 1906), p. 266.

19   J. Eric S. Thompson, *The Moon Goddess in Middle America, With Notes on Related Deities*, Carnegie Institution of Washington Publication 509, Contributions to American Anthropology and History 5/29 (Washington, DC: Carnegie Institution of Washington, 1939), pp. 152–61; Thompson, *Maya History and Religion*, pp. 212–33.

20   David A. Freidel and Linda Schele, "Symbol and Power: A History of the Lowland Maya Cosmogram," in Elizabeth P. Benson and Gillett G. Griffin (eds), *Maya Iconography* (Princeton, NJ: Princeton University Press, 1988), pp. 44–93; David Stuart, "Royal Auto-Sacrifice among the Maya," *RES: Anthropology and Aesthetics* 7/8 (1984), pp. 6–20.

21   Andrea Stone, "The Zoomorphs of Quirigua," unpublished PhD dissertation, Department of Art History, University of Texas at Austin (1983); Andrea Stone, "Variety and Transformation in the Cosmic Monster Theme at Quirigua, Guatemala," in Virginia Fields (ed.), *Fifth Palenque Round Table, 1983*, Palenque Round Table Series 7 (San Francisco: Pre-Columbian Art Research Institute, 1985), pp. 39–48.

22   Stone, "The Zoomorphs of Quirigua," p.162.

in order to emphasize the celestial domain. This type is prominent at Palenque and Piedras Negras. The second type of representation is associated with the horizontal format of boulder sculptures and thrones, particularly at Copan and Quirigua, and seems to emphasize the terrestrial and aquatic underworld level of the cosmos. This basic analysis of variation within the cosmic crocodilian theme in Maya art provides a departure point for the present analysis, which suggests the specific mythic prototypes and ritual contexts that link these two iconographic clusters. In fact, both of these manifestations of the sacred earth-sky, once dismissed as "monstrous," are closely connected to Maya lore of cosmogenesis.

The Starry Deer Crocodile

The celestial variant of the cosmic crocodile is represented in art more frequently than the terrestrial, and has therefore been studied more intensively. The cosmic crocodile in its celestial form was dubbed the Starry Deer Crocodile by David Stuart.[23] This being's diagnostic features include a saurian head, Venus-signs as eye-pupils, striated eyelids, deer ears with a bivalve shell below, a scaly crocodilian body with scutes and back ridges, water-scroll marked joints, and deer hooves rather than reptilian claws.[24] The creature's body is frequently rendered as a sky-band, or segments emblazoned with celestial symbols such as glyphs for sky, sun, moon, and darkness.[25] Some examples of the Starry Deer Crocodile also incorporate an important solar avian deity, the Principal Bird Deity, embedded in its back or carried on its tail.[26]

The Starry Deer Crocodile typically carries on its haunches a motif that also appears independently in Classic Maya art, the so-called Quadripartite Badge or Emblem.[27] This motif consists of a bowl marked with a "sun" glyph supported by a skeletal head. The bowl contains an erect stingray spine flanked by a *Spondylus* (spiny oyster) shell and a foliated element marked with crossed-bands.[28] The

23 David Stuart, "A Cosmological Throne at Palenque" (2003), electronic document: <www.mesoweb.com/stuart/notes/Throne.pdf>, accessed July 1, 2009; David Stuart, *The Inscriptions from Temple XIX at Palenque* (San Francisco: Pre-Columbian Art Research Institute, 2005), pp. 70–6.

24 Spinden, *A Study of Maya Art*, p. 53; Stone, "The Zoomorphs of Quirigua"; Stone, "Variety and Transformation."

25 See John B. Carlson and Linda Landis, "Bands, Bicephalic Dragons and Other Beasts: The Skyband in Maya Art and Iconography," in Merle Greene Robertson and Elizabeth P. Benson (eds), *Fourth Palenque Round Table, 1980* (San Francisco: Pre-Columbian Art Research Institute, 1985), pp. 115–40.

26 Stone, "The Zoomorphs of Quirigua."

27 Schele and Miller, *The Blood of Kings*, p. 45.

28 Merle Greene Robertson, "The Quadripartite Badge: A Badge of Rulership," in Merle Greene Robertson (ed.), *Primera Mesa Redonda de Palenque, Part I* (Pebble Beach, CA: Pre-Columbian Art Research, Robert Louis Stevenson School, 1974). pp. 77–94; Linda Schele,

Quadripartite Badge is interpreted as a personified burner for blood and incense offerings made by rulers in penance, as well as a headdress worn by an important deity known to Mayanists as GI ("God one").[29]

Although early scholars considered the Starry Deer Crocodile to be bicephalic, such cases are in fact rare. Yaxchilan Stela 1 (temple side) depicts a truly bicephalic Starry Deer Crocodile with a sky-band body, Venus-pupils, a Venus-marked deer ear, hoofed limbs, and water-scroll joint markings.[30] Deity heads emerge from the open jaws of the creature, while two more deity faces peer downward from a band of cartouches located beneath the sky-band. This image conflates the Starry Deer Crocodile with more conventional "vision serpent" iconography seen in other monuments.[31]

The Starry Deer Crocodile appears in Maya art from the Classic to Post-classic periods (about 450–1500 CE), in both iconographic and hieroglyphic contexts. In the Maya script, the front head of the Starry Deer Crocodile substitutes for the day sign Lamat, which is usually rendered as a Venus glyph, and also functions as the patron for the month Yax.[32] Current interpretations of the Starry Deer Crocodile as a celestial symbol owe much to the work of Thompson, who referred to it as a "sky monster," "Venus monster," or "celestial dragon."[33]

More recent scholars such as Linda Schele emphasized the celestial symbolism of the creature in its manifestations as door frames at Copan and Palenque.[34] In iconographic contexts, the Starry Deer Crocodile is frequently orientated on an east–west axis. The opposition of the Venus-marked front head and the sun-marked incense burner located on the rear of the creature suggests a symbolic association with the rising of the sun in relation to the cycles of Venus. Further, in several cases, including the Copan Margarita facade and the inner portal of Copan Structure 10L-22, the body of the Starry Deer Crocodile is studded with stars, indicating an association with the nocturnal sky. In the example from Copan Structure 10L-22, seven S-shaped cloud scrolls along the length of the creature's body led various

"Accession Iconography of Chan-Bahlum in the Group of the Cross at Palenque," in Merle Greene Robertson (ed.), *The Art, Iconography and Dynastic History of Palenque Part III* (Pebble Beach, CA: Pre-Columbian Art Research, Robert Louis Stevenson School, 1976), pp. 17–18.

29 Stuart, *The Inscriptions from Temple XIX*, pp. 167–70; Karl A. Taube, "The Jade Hearth: Centrality, Rulership, and the Classic Maya Temple," in Stephen D. Houston (ed.), *Function and Meaning in Classic Maya Architecture* (Washington, DC: Dumbarton Oaks, 1998), p. 464.

30 Spinden, *A Study of Maya Art*, p. 70.

31 For example, Yaxchilan Stela 10 temple side; Carolyn Tate, *Yaxchilan: The Design of a Maya Ceremonial City* (Austin: University of Texas Press, 1992), p. 63, figure 24b.

32 Martha J. Macri and Matthew G. Looper, *The New Catalog of Maya Hieroglyphs, Vol. 1: The Classic Period Inscriptions* (Norman: University of Oklahoma Press, 2003), p. 230.

33 Thompson, *The Moon Goddess*, pp. 154–60; J. Eric S. Thompson, *Maya Hieroglyphic Writing: An Introduction* (Norman: University of Oklahoma Press, 1960), p. 77.

34 Schele, "Accession Iconography of Chan-Bahlum," pp. 20–1; see also Schele and Miller, *The Blood of Kings*, p. 45; Stuart, "Royal Auto-Sacrifice," pp. 15–16.

scholars to propose that the Starry Deer Crocodile symbolizes the Milky Way in an east–west configuration.[35] The celestial symbolism of this image is also implied by a pair of Pawahtuns—sky-bearing gods—that support each end of the crocodile.

In addition to its basic celestial symbolism, the Starry Deer Crocodile is implicated in the lore of creation. In particular, Classic-period texts and imagery, as well as colonial-era documents, demonstrate the widespread Maya belief that the Starry Deer Crocodile was the source of a great flood that resulted in cosmic destruction and renewal.[36] Two colonial-period Maya documents, the Chilam Balam of Tizimín and Códice Pérez, state that the destruction of the universe was caused by the inversion of sky and earth, whereby the terrestrial crocodile Itzam Cab Ain ("Iguana Earth Crocodile") ascended into the sky, unleashing a flood.[37] The inundation came to an end when Bolon ti Ku ("Nine As God") cut the throat of the crocodile and formed the earth with the remains of its body, painting its back with the creature's blood. This imagery directly parallels the Aztec myth of cosmogenesis, in which the gods Quetzalcoatl and Tezcatlipoca dismember the body of the great caiman Tlaltecuhtli, and use the pieces to create the universe.[38] It also bears comparison to an eposide from the early colonial highland Maya document *Popol Vuh*, in which the Hero Twins defeat a crocodilian "maker of mountains" by entombing him within the earth and turning him to stone.[39] The deer imagery that forms a prominent aspect of the Classic period Starry Deer Crocodile may specifically symbolize the sacrificial aspect of this being, as the deer was a prime sacrificial animal to the ancient Maya.[40]

35　David Freidel, Linda Schele, and Joy Parker, *Maya Cosmos: Three Thousand Years on the Shaman's Path* (New York: William Morrow, 1993), p. 87; Susan Milbrath, *Star Gods of the Maya: Astronomy in Art, Folklore, and Calendars* (Austin: University of Texas Press, 1999); Stuart, "Royal Auto-Sacrifice," p. 15.

36　Stuart, *The Inscriptions from Temple XIX*, pp. 176–80; Karl A. Taube, *Aztec and Maya Myths* (Bath: British Museum Press, 1993); Karl A. Taube, "Where Earth and Sky Meet: The Sea in Ancient and Contemporary Maya Cosmology," in Daniel Finamore and Stephen D. Houston (eds), *Fiery Pool: The Maya and the Mythic Sea* (New Haven and London: Yale University Press, 2010), pp. 202–19; Erik Velásquez García, "The Maya Flood Myth and the Decapitation of the Cosmic Caiman," *The PARI Journal* 7/1 (2006), pp. 1–10, electronic document: <www.mesoweb.com/pari/publications/journal/701/Flood_e.pdf>, accessed July 1, 2009.

37　Timothy W. Knowlton, *Maya Creation Myths: Words and Worlds of the Chilam Balam* (Boulder: University Press of Colorado, 2010), pp. 70–5; Thompson, *The Moon Goddess*, pp. 153–4.

38　Taube, *Aztec and Maya Myths*, pp. 69–70, 73–4.

39　Dennis Tedlock, *Popol Vuh* (New York: Simon and Schuster, 1985), pp. 94–9. The *Popol Vuh* tale of the triumph of the Hero Twins over forces of chaos and disease has been widely viewed as a core Maya mythic cycle, equivalent in cultural and political symbolism to the Ramayana and Mahabharata of Hindu literature, or *The Iliad* and *Odyssey* of Homer.

40　Karl A. Taube, "A Study of Classic Maya Scaffold Sacrifice," in Elizabeth Benson and Gillett Griffin (eds), *Maya Iconography* (Princeton, NJ: Princeton University Press, 1988), pp. 331–51.

The inscription of the Palenque Temple XIX platform provides evidence of the specific conceptualization of this myth in the Classic period. This text relates a series of important events that laid the foundation for the current cosmic creation in 3114 BCE. In one of these episodes from 3297 BCE, the decapitation or dismemberment of the Starry Deer Crocodile released a torrent of blood.[41] This act is presumably the rationale for the common depiction of great streams of blood that flow from the mouth of the Starry Deer Crocodile and out of the incense burner which it carries on its posterior.[42] On page 74 of the Dresden Codex, the Starry Deer Crocodile unleashes a cataclysmic flood of water rather than blood, assisted by a pair of elderly deities.[43] The Temple XIX text refers to the "hole-back crocodile, painted back crocodile" as an agent of flooding and new fire, thereby tying the Starry Deer Crocodile to Maya and Mesoamerican mythic themes of apocalyptic floods, followed by the rebirth of the sun through the kindling of fire using a drill.[44] In colonial-period Yucatan, the cosmic flood and fire was recreated in rituals in which a painted caiman representing the flood was heaped with wood and burned to coals, over which the ritualists walked to remind them of the destruction of the world.[45]

Representations of the dismemberment of the cosmic crocodile are rare in ancient Maya art; however, an important example is perhaps preserved in the west facade stucco ornamentation of Margarita, a mid-fifth-century (Early Classic) temple in the Copan acropolis (Figure 8.1).[46] In this early example, the cosmic crocodile, in its manifestation as the Starry Deer Crocodile, frames a glyphic monogram of the Copan founding dynast, K'inich Yax K'uk' Mo', in the form of two intertwined birds. The segmented sky-band body of the Starry Deer Crocodile extends along the upper edge of the composition. On the right side of the panel, the head of the Starry Deer Crocodile hangs downward, releasing a stream of blood. On the left, instead of the usual haunches of the creature or Quadripartite Badge, is a square-snouted serpent, which pertains to blood iconography.[47]

41   Stuart, *The Inscriptions from Temple XIX*, pp. 68–77, 176–80.
42   Schele and Miller, *The Blood of Kings*, p. 45; Stuart, "Royal Auto-Sacrifice," p. 16; Velásquez García, "The Maya Flood Myth."
43   Förstemann, "Commentary of the Maya Manuscript," p. 266; Freidel, Schele, and Parker, *Maya Cosmos*, p. 107, figure 2:35; Spinden, *A Study of Maya Art*, pp. 67–8; Taube, "Where Earth and Sky Meet," p. 205.
44   Velásquez García, "The Maya Flood Myth," p. 4.
45   Thompson, *Maya History and Religion*, p. 217.
46   David W. Sedat, *Margarita Structure: New Data and Implications*, ECAP Paper No. 6 (Philadelphia: Instituto Hondureño de Antropología e Historia and the University of Pennsylvania Museum Early Copan Acropolis Program, 1997). In Post-classic Maya art, cosmic crocodiles are often depicted bound and pierced by darts, presumably with reference to the same mythic cycle. See Stuart, *The Inscriptions from Temple XIX*, pp. 178–9.
47   Freidel, Schele, and Parker, *Maya Cosmos*, p. 218, figure 4:29; David Stuart, "Blood Symbolism in Maya Iconography," in Elizabeth P. Benson and Gillett G. Griffin (eds), *Maya Iconography* (Princeton, NJ: Princeton University Press, 1988), p. 198.

Figure 8.1   Copan, Margarita facade, detail. Drawing by the author.

Clinging to the square-snouted blood serpent is the axe-wielding storm deity Chahk, who figures prominently in other episodes of cosmogenesis.[48] In this case, Chahk's role may be to chop the body of the Starry Deer Crocodile into segments, which appear below, in cartouches with scalloped edges, flanked by two X-marked bundle motifs. The central cartouche encloses a glyph composed of diagonal bands that is part of the sky-band repertoire. The two flanking cartouches inscribe glyphs for "stone," evoking the material substance of the nascent earth. A scalloped cartouche also appears along the body of the crocodile, just above the arm. The three scalloped cartouches in the lower register, therefore, seem to illustrate the process by which the Starry Deer Crocodile, hacked into rough chunks by Chahk, is transformed into the sacred stone of the earth. This image suggests that the colonial-period accounts of the dismemberment of the cosmic crocodile found in the Chilam Balam, *Popol Vuh*, and Aztec sources are relatively late manifestations of narratives current in the Maya area approximately a millennium earlier.

The specifics of the agency of the Starry Deer Crocodile in relation to cosmogenesis are important. The text from the Palenque Temple XIX platform emphasizes the role of the creature as a victim of decapitation, under the auspices of a creator god. Likewise, the colonial era Pérez manuscript states that the Bolon ti Ku god(s) thrust

---

48   Freidel, Schele, and Parker, *Maya Cosmos*, p. 94.

Figure 8.2   Piedras Negras Stela 6, drawing by David Stuart, *Corpus of Maya Hieroglyphic Inscriptions*, vol. 9, part 1, *Piedras Negras* (reproduced courtesy of the President and Fellows of Harvard College).

crocodile Itzam Cab Ain into the sky and then sacrificed it.[49] The Tizimín version of the myth mentions that the crocodilian's actions were in fulfillment of the prophesied destruction of the world.[50] Images of the Starry Deer Crocodile in Maya art likewise depict it as an object of violence, being dismembered or otherwise subdued by other gods in order to create the cosmos. The cosmic crocodile complex in Maya art therefore embodies a particular perspective on the universe as a dangerous, yet creative, vital entity that ritual practitioners may manipulate. This concept motivated the adaptation of the Starry Deer Crocodile image by ancient Maya kings as an instrument and emblem of power.

Numerous examples from the Late Classic period illustrate ancient Maya rulers' routine use of the astronomical and creation symbolism of the Starry Deer Crocodile to sanctify their authority. The most common formula was to frame the ruler's body or his visage with an image of the Starry Deer Crocodile.[51] An excellent example is found in stucco reliefs of the north terraces of the palace at Palenque.[52] These show large central portraits of the king K'inich K'an Joy Chitam II wearing a Principal Bird Deity headdress framed by a Starry Deer Crocodile, of which only the Quadripartite Badge of the lower two terraces survives.

Thrones or platforms emblazoned with Starry Deer Crocodile imagery were also used for royal accession ceremonies. This is prominently depicted on the Piedras Negras "niche" stelae (Stelae 6, 11, 14, 25, and 33), which show successive rulers of the city assuming office while seated atop scaffolds (Figure 8.2).[53] In each case, the upper platform of the scaffold is embellished with the Starry Deer Crocodile, above which the ruler is seated, framed by a sky-band. An effigy bundle in the form of a reptile lies immediately below the ruler's cushion, probably intended to be burned during the coronation ritual.[54] As usual, blood flows from the maw and Quadripartite Badge of the Starry Deer Crocodile, using the cosmic flood as a metaphor for the renewal of the cosmos under the auspices of the newly inaugurated king.

A similar ritual context may have motivated the elaborate stucco sculpture located above the northern interior doorway of Palenque House E. Built at the heart of the Palace complex, House E featured a throne with stuccoed and painted adornments that commemorated the accession of the ruler K'inich Janab' Pakal I in 615.[55] The building was used to celebrate other royal accessions during the Late

---

49   Eugene R. Craine and Reginald C. Reindorp, *The Codex Pérez and the Book of Chilam Balam of Mani* (Norman: University of Oklahoma Press, 1979), p. 118.
50   Knowlton, *Maya Creation Myths*, p. 73.
51   Stuart, "Royal Auto-Sacrifice," p. 15; Stuart, "Blood Symbolism in Maya Iconography," pp. 203–5.
52   Freidel and Schele, "Symbol and Power," pp. 78–80.
53   Taube, "A Study of Classic Maya Scaffold Sacrifice," pp. 331–51.
54   The imagery of rulers enthroned atop bound crocodiles and sky-bands persisted into the Post-classic period, as indicated by several illustrations from the Paris Codex. See Bruce Love, *The Paris Codex: Handbook for a Maya Priest* (Austin: University of Texas Press, 1994), pp. 25–6.
55   David Stuart and George Stuart, *Palenque: Eternal City of the Maya* (London: Thames and

Classic period, as recorded on the Tablet of the 96 Glyphs, in which rulers emerged from the subterranean chambers of the Palace, passing through the doorway to be enthroned.[56] The sculpture program of this portal, therefore, framed the ruler with an image of the Starry Deer Crocodile, analogously to the Piedras Negras stelae. The concept of a throne in the form of the Starry Deer Crocodile was also embodied at Palenque in Throne 1, a sculpted bench dedicated in circa 652 CE.[57] This monument features a low relief image of the Starry Deer Crocodile on its front face.

The use of the Starry Deer Crocodile as a symbol of royal accession was also traditional at Copan during the Late Classic period. For example, Structure 10L-22 featured a sculpted inner doorway frame in the form of the Starry Deer Crocodile, as described above. This monument was commissioned in 715, to mark the one-k'atun (7,200th day) anniversary of the coronation of the 13th king Waxaklajuun Ub'aah K'awiil in 695 CE. The altar of Stela M at Copan, dedicated in 756 CE, also depicts a Starry Deer Crocodile, though with prominent "stone" markings on the body, appropriate to its incarnation as a tufa boulder sculpture.[58] This sculpture and the stela before which it stands may have functioned as the inaugural monuments for the 15th Copan ruler, K'ahk' Yipyaj Chan K'awiil, who took office in 749 CE. Although several years had elapsed between this event and the dedication of these sculptures, no previous monumental commissions are known for this ruler. The subsequent ruler of Copan, Yax Pasaj Chan Yo'pat, who acceded in 763, may also have employed the same iconography for his inaugural monument, Structure 10L-11, dedicated in 773 CE.[59] The evidence for this includes colossal Pawahtun heads and serpent segments found in the rubble of the superstructure of the building.

Two other monuments at Copan featuring Starry Deer Crocodile iconography do not have a clear relationship to royal accession. One is Altar GI, dedicated by Yax Pasaj in 800 CE. This monument, however, includes only partial Starry Deer Crocodile iconography, with the front head of this being on its eastern end. The head on the west side is rendered as a skeletal serpent or centipede, which is not part of the standard Starry Deer Crocodile imagery. Moreover, because the text of this monument refers to it as a "great serpent" (*noh chan*) rather than a crocodile (*ahin*), the Starry Deer Crocodile imagery may have been of only minor significance to the overall theme. The other Copan monument with clear Starry Deer Crocodile imagery is the bench of the House of the Bacabs, Structure 9N-82, which bears a date of either September 10, 773 or July 10, 781.[60] However, the inscription of

---

Hudson, 2008), pp. 150, 157–8.

56   David A. Freidel and Charles K. Suhler, "The Path of Life: Toward a Functional Analysis of Ancient Maya Architecture," in Jeff Karl Kowalski (ed.), *Mesoamerican Architecture as a Cultural Symbol* (New York: Oxford University Press, 1999), pp. 250–73.

57   See Stuart, "A Cosmological Throne at Palenque."

58   Stone, "The Zoomorphs of Quirigua," pp. 170–3.

59   Linda Schele and David Freidel, *A Forest of Kings: The Untold Story of the Ancient Maya* (New York: William Morrow, 1990), pp. 325, 489.

60   Shannon E. Plank, "Monumental Maya Dwellings in the Hieroglyphic and Archaeological Records: A Cognitive-Anthropological Approach to Classic Maya

this bench defies full decipherment; therefore its relationship to accession ritual is unclear.

Andrea Stone observed that Copan Altar M served as the prototype for a series of cosmic crocodile sculptures at the nearby site of Quirigua; however, at that site, the sculptures were rendered on a colossal scale as boulder sculptures known to Mayanists as zoomorphs.[61] The sole example of a Starry Deer Crocodile at Quirigua is Zoomorph O, dedicated in 790 CE.[62] Although its front head is almost entirely obliterated, the imagery can be partly reconstructed from the surviving Fragment 1, which shows the eye of the creature with a typically striated lid and the traces of what may be a Venus sign on the eyeball.[63] A bivalve shell seems to be set into the forehead curl. The scaly legs of the creature, with reptile markings, cloven hooves, and water scrolls at the joints, are clearly visible on the west side, and an immense Quadripartite Badge appears on the south side, continuing onto the upper surface. Mountain masks adorn the limbs and upper surface, evoking the prototype of the altar of Stela M at Copan.

The Starry Deer Crocodile iconography of Zoomorph O may have commemorated a royal accession, in this case, the coronation of the king Sky Xul in 785 CE. Zoomorph O had a lengthy text, now largely eroded. Nevertheless, its well-preserved companion monument, Altar O prime, features the accession rites of Sky Xul in its initial series, rendered in full-figure glyphs. The only earlier monument associated with this ruler is Zoomorph G, dedicated in 785 CE. The text of this monument, however, is devoted mainly to the history of the previous king, K'ahk' Tiliw, who had died only 98 days prior to its dedication, and is located along the center line of the earlier king's main sculptural program, installed at the north end of the Great Plaza. Thus, Zoomorph G seems to have been conceived as a cenotaph for K'ahk' Tiliw, while Zoomorph O and its altar, located adjacent to the Acropolis, were designed to celebrate the inauguration of a new king. As I have argued elsewhere, zoomorphic sculptures at Quirigua were generally conceptualized as commemorative thrones of rulership.[64] Zoomorph O thus corresponds symbolically to the lower scaffold platform upon which the Piedras Negras rulers acceded to power, or to Palenque Throne 1.

In summary, the Starry Deer Crocodile, the most prominent manifestation of the cosmic crocodile concept in Maya art, was frequently employed to sanctify royal accessions. When seated upon or within an image of this creature, kings were presented as if they were primordial gods, manifesting their sacred duty of destroying, creating, and sustaining the universe.

Architecture," PhD dissertation, Boston University, 2003, pp. 326–7.

61 Stone, "The Zoomorphs of Quirigua," p. 173.

62 Matthew G. Looper, *Quiriguá: A Guide to an Ancient Maya City* (Guatemala City: Editorial Antigua, 2007), pp. 135–6.

63 Stone, "The Zoomorphs of Quirigua," figure 50.

64 Matthew G. Looper, "Quiriguá Zoomorph P: A Water-Throne and Mountain of Creation," in Andrea Stone (ed.), *Heart of Creation: Linda Schele and the Mesoamerican World* (Tuscaloosa: University of Alabama Press, 2002), pp. 185–200.

Terrestrial Crocodiles

A second variant of the cosmic crocodile theme shares the characteristics of a crocodilian head, water-scrolls on the joints, and a Quadripartite Badge carried on the tail, but unlike the Starry Deer Crocodile, this creature is not explicitly marked with celestial symbols. Nor does it possess deer attributes, but has fully reptilian claws and a head or tail studded with dotted ovals. It also usually has a crossed-bands infix in the eye and a lobed conch shell (sometimes glyphic *yax*) attached to the curled snout. As a glyph, the head of the crocodile (with crossed-bands eye) occurs simply as the standard sign for *ahin* ("crocodile").[65]

Symbolic interpretations of crocodilians as a metaphor for the living earth go back to Eduard Seler, who identified the earth crocodile in the Post-classic Dresden Codex (pages 4b–5b).[66] Other Post-classic representations of this being were later identified by Thompson and Taube.[67] Thompson lumped together an array of Classic-period zoomorphic creatures with water attributes under the designation as "earth monster," which he saw as analogous to the central Mexican *cipactli*, the crocodilian image of the earth.[68] Additional examples of earth crocodiles have been identified in Mixtec as well as Olmec art.[69]

Independent iconographic and contextual evidence supports identifying a distinct group of crocodilian beings in Classic Maya art as terrestrial metaphors. In several iconographic contexts the creature is marked with "stone" and "mountain" symbols, emphasizing its terrestrial associations. Two examples of crocodilians with reptilian feet are rendered in stucco relief in the subterranean passages of House E at Palenque.[70] Further, the Early Classic Yaxha Stela 6 employs a crocodilian as a basal register with the ruler standing upon its open mouth.[71] The earthbound context of these images is suggestive of a terrestrial symbolism.

In some examples, the earth crocodile stands head-downward with its body extending upward, transformed into a leafy tree, hence the term of reference to this beast as the Crocodile Tree. The fusion of the tree image with the earthly crocodile is rooted in the symbolism of the world tree, called *yaxche* in Yucatan. This cosmic tree is thought to penetrate the various layers of underworld, earth, and sky.[72] Hence, the Crocodile Tree specifically represents the world tree of the

---

65   Macri and Looper, *The New Catalog*, p. 64.
66   Eduard Seler, *Gesammelte Abhandlungen zur Amerikanischen Sprach- und Alterthumskunde*, 5 volumes (Berlin: A. Asher, 1902–23), vol. 4, p. 650.
67   Thompson, *Maya History and Religion*, p. 215; Karl A. Taube, *Itzam Cab Ain: Caimans, Cosmology, and Calendrics in Postclassic Yucatán*, Research Reports on Ancient Maya Writing 26 (Washington, DC: Center for Maya Research, 1989).
68   Thompson, *Maya Hieroglyphic Writing*, pp. 71–3.
69   Reilly, "Art, Ritual, and Rulership in the Olmec World," pp. 26–45.
70   Eduard Seler, *Observations and Studies in the Ruins of Palenque* (Pebble Beach, CA: Robert Louis Stevenson School, 1976), figures 116 and 117.
71   Stuart, "Blood Symbolism in Maya Iconography," p. 205–6.
72   See Thompson, *The Moon Goddess*, p. 156.

center.[73] The creature is related to other beings shown head-downward and with the trunk and legs transformed into trees, such as cacao gods and certain versions of the Maize God.[74]

A very early and well-known example of the Crocodile Tree appears on the Late Pre-classic Stela 25 from Izapa. This scene has elicited numerous conflicting interpretations; however, most scholars agree that it has some relation to a narrative sequence from the *Popol Vuh*. In this story, one of the Hero Twins loses his arm to the "false sun," Seven Macaw.[75] Another early representation of the Crocodile Tree is found on the Deletaille tripod, an Early Classic carved cylinder vessel.[76] In this extremely complex scene, two Starry Deer Crocodile heads appear adjacent to trees, even though their heads and bodies are discontinuous. A Quadripartite Badge is also visible, although the overall significance of the scene is elusive.

Several images suggest the association between the Crocodile Tree and solar rebirth. One example is Yaxchilan Structure 33, Stair 8, which depicts a ballplayer wearing the plaited headdress of the Sun God and carrying a Crocodile Tree effigy on his back. Another example is on Yaxchilan Structure 44, Step III (Figure 8.3). At the base of the composition is a glyphic compound which serves a locative function, indicating that the presentation of the captive depicted above takes place in Yaxchilan city center. The head of the Crocodile Tree appears on the left, with a netted headband and foliated snout. The haunch and upwardly extended tail are opposite, bearing the personified incense burner which is carried on a diagonal angle. Superimposed on the body of the Crocodile Tree is an oval cartouche framing a portrait of the Sun God. The location of a solar cartouche immediately above the glyph for Yaxchilan suggests that this entire basal register embodies the eastern horizon as viewed from the city center (Structure 44 faces toward the north-north-east), with the Crocodile Tree representing the earth. This image, therefore, constructs Yaxchilan as the central point of the earth, where the Crocodile Tree axis mundi joins diverse cosmic realms.

In Maya art, the Crocodile Tree has associations with earthly abundance and the regeneration of life, through a symbolic connection with the Maize God.[77] The connection between the Crocodile Tree and the Maize God is expressed in several images. Copan Altar 41, dedicated in 771 CE, features on one face a relief image of a crocodile, which has crossed-bands markings on the eyeball, reptilian claws, stone

---

73   Freidel, Schele, and Parker, *Maya Cosmos*, p. 137.

74   See Karl A. Taube, "The Symbolism of Jade in Classic Maya Religion," *Ancient Mesoamerica* 16 (2005), pp. 25–8; Looper, *To Be Like Gods*, pp. 98–9.

75   See Michael D. Coe, "The Hero Twins in Myth and Image," in Justin Kerr (ed.), *The Maya Vase Book*, vol. 1 (New York: Kerr Associates, 1989), pp. 161, 163; Constance Cortez, "The Principal Bird Deity in Preclassic and Early Classic Art," in Virginia M. Fields and Dorie Reents-Budet (eds), *Lords of Creation: The Origins of Sacred Maya Kingship* (London: Scala, 2005), pp. 62–6.

76   Nicholas M. Hellmuth, "Early Maya Iconography on an Incised Cylindrical Tripod," in Elizabeth P. Benson and Gillett Griffin (eds), *Maya Iconography* (Princeton: Princeton University Press, 1988), pp. 152–74; Freidel and Schele, "Symbol and Power," pp. 76–8.

77   Taube, "The Symbolism of Jade."

Figure 8.3   Yaxchilan Structure 44, Step III, drawing by Ian Graham, *Corpus of Maya Hieroglyphic Inscriptions*, vol. 3, part 3, *Yaxchilan* (reproduced courtesy of the President and Fellows of Harvard College).

markings, and the Quadripartite Emblem on its rear haunch. The head of the Maize God emerges from the mouth of the creature.

A precedent for this image is found in Copan Stela C, dedicated in 711 CE. The west face depicts the ruler as a bearded Maize God dancing before an altar rendered as a turtle. On the east face of this monument, the ruler wears a belt head in the form of a crocodile with its snout hanging downward. We are presumably meant to understand the torso and head of the king as embodiments of the trunk and branches of the world tree. This stela, therefore, contrasts the dancing Maize God with the Crocodile Tree on opposite faces of the monument. This image may be directly compared to a depiction of the resurrecting Maize God on a codex-style plate, in which the deity rises from a split turtle shell.[78] Even though the Crocodile Tree does not appear here, the adjacent glyphic caption names this being as *jun ixim ahin te'* ("One Maize Crocodile Tree").

In some cases, the terrestrial form of the cosmic crocodile may be tied specifically to the symbolism of creation. An important example of this is the appearance of a frontally orientated crocodilian with crossed-banded eyes, dotted oval body markings, glyphic signs for "stone," and additional aquatic iconography on the

---

78   Elizabeth Newsome, *Trees of Paradise and Pillars of the World: The Serial Stelae Cycle of "18-Rabbit-God K," King of Copan* (Austin: University of Texas Press, 2001), p. 112.

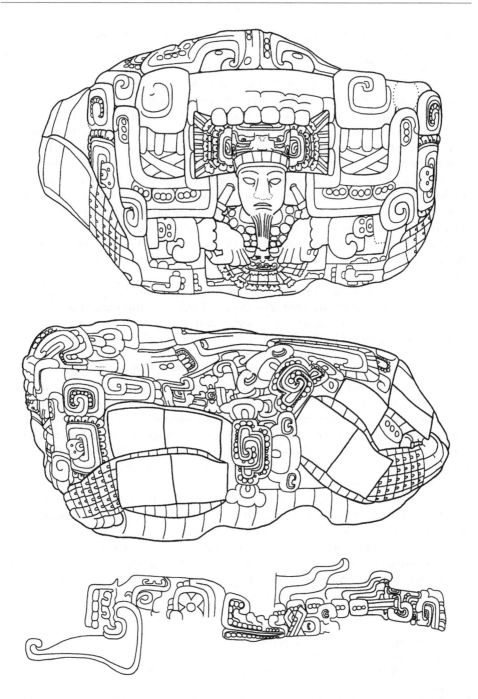

Figure 8.4   Quirigua Zoomorph B, views of south and east sides with rollout of
             tail. Drawings by the author; tail rollout adapted from drawing by
             Andrea Stone.

western entablature of the Palenque Temple of the Cross.[79] The temple bearing this image contains sanctuary texts that describe in detail the events associated with cosmogenesis.[80]

Two major monuments from Quirigua have long been recognized as terrestrial crocodiles, and both function as images of cosmic creation. These are Zoomorph B, dedicated in 780 (Figure 8.4), and Zoomorph P, dating to 795 CE. These two sculptures, commissioned by two successive kings, are almost perfectly preserved and demonstrate a strong iconographic correspondence.[81] Both include the standard cosmic crocodile iconography, as well as a crossed-bands motif in each eye, reptilian claws on the legs, and the tail rendered as branching hair-like strands marked with ovals that frame three dots arranged in a line. On Zoomorph B, the tail emerges from a Quadripartite Badge and wraps around the side of the monument, appearing on the west face. On Zoomorph P, the tail is visible on the south side, extending upward from the head of an unidentified god with a *Spondylus* shell in its mouth. The upward thrust of the tail on this monument specifically likens it to the Crocodile Tree.

Despite the horizontal position of its tail, the being depicted on Zoomorph B may in fact depict the Crocodile Tree. Zoomorph B was the culmination of a program of three monuments located in the north-west corner of the Great Plaza.[82] The program is introduced by the text of Stela C (dedicated in 775 CE), which contains a detailed description of the foundational Creation events of 3114 BCE. Featured are three monument dedications by the gods, with the climactic stone described as a "water throne-stone" and dedicated by Itzamnah. Zoomorph B is an effigy of this sacred throne, as its abundant water scrolls and general identification as a crocodile indicate. Thompson argued for an identification of cosmic crocodilians with the deity Itzamnah, citing the Dresden Codex image of this god peering out of the front maw of the terrestrial crocodile (pages 4b–5b).[83] However, in the Classic period, Itzamnah was specifically associated with the Crocodile Tree. On a codex-style vessel, the same deity is seated before an offering plate that is being used to conjure a diminutive Crocodile Tree.[84] Therefore, it is through the associations of Zoomorph B with the deity Itzamnah that we may identify it as a representation of the cosmic crocodile in the form of the Crocodile Tree.

Textual evidence for identifying Zoomorph P as the Crocodile Tree is more difficult to discern, but may be conveyed in the cartouches that appear to name the monument, located on the rear legs. The middle cartouche on the south-western leg includes glyphs for *jun ixim*, part of the name of the Crocodile Tree from

---

79   Maudslay, *Archaeology*, vol. 4, plate 68.

80   See Freidel, Schele, and Parker, *Maya Cosmos*, pp. 69–75.

81   Stone, "The Zoomorphs of Quirigua"; Stuart, "Blood Symbolism in Maya Iconography," pp. 205–6.

82   Matthew G. Looper, *Lightning Warrior: Maya Art and Kingship at Quirigua* (Austin: University of Texas Press, 2003), pp. 172–8.

83   Thompson, *The Moon Goddess*; Thompson, *Maya History and Religion*, p. 218.

84   Looper, *To Be Like Gods*, figure 3.26a.

the codex-style plate discussed above. Further, like its predecessor, Zoomorph P may have employed imagery of the Crocodile Tree as a reference to Creation. Zoomorph P was dedicated on a Four-Ajaw period ending, the same tzolk'in (260-day calendrical) position as cosmic creation. This event is commemorated in the text of Altar P prime, its companion monument, and the throne-stones may even be referenced in the text of the zoomorph itself.[85]

Both Zoomorphs B and P, therefore, employ Crocodile Tree iconography in order to connote their ritual associations with cosmogenesis. These monuments strengthen the case for identifying the Crocodile Tree with the symbolism of cosmogenesis in the context of Classic Maya art. While the Starry Deer Crocodile refers to the inversion of the sky and the great flood, the Crocodile Tree represents the fertility power of the nascent earth that is transformed into the world tree and Maize God, the personification of abundance.

For nearly five centuries, great crocodilian beings were rendered in Maya monumental art in order to invest rulers with the powers of periodic cosmic creation and destruction, as well as fertility. After the collapse of Classic-period kingship and the subsequent suppression of indigenous religion during the colonial period, these creatures were remembered through lore and manuscripts. As metaphors for the living earth and sky, cosmic crocodilians are one of the most enduring symbols of Mesoamerican religion.

The fundamental cosmological symbolism of composite crocodilians in Classic Maya art calls into question the traditional designation of these creatures as monsters. Generally serving as frames and supports for rulers, the creatures do not interact directly with humans and are never shown as agents of violence similar to monsters in other traditions. They are remarkably placid, especially compared to other supernaturals such as the *way*, whose iconography is characterized by burning, splattered blood, dismemberment, foul odors, putrefaction, and death. The feelings of fear and loathing that the *way* likely inspired in the ancient Maya audience almost certainly motivated rulers' frequent claims to possess and manipulate these spirit beings. Their patronage of *way* set the rulers apart from the rest of society and justified their moral prerogatives to commit personal bloodletting, captive sacrifice, and to maintain an elaborate funerary cult. The Maya elite may have similarly associated themselves with polymorphic creatures based on large predatory reptiles in order to intimidate enemies and reinforce status hierarchies. While it is unknown if the Maya in general feared these creatures, present data allow that if they were indeed considered monstrous beings, the Maya "cosmic monsters" were a force subdued, their considerable powers subjected to the will of divine kings.

---

85   Looper, "Quiriguá Zoomorph P," pp. 194–5.

Monsters Lift the Veil: Chinese Animal Hybrids and Processes of Transformation

Karin Myhre

While monsters are often conceived as freaks of nature or beings violating natural laws, this notion is a problematic one in traditional China as the inherent natural order (*dao*) was understood to be constantly transforming.[1] Nonetheless, animal hybrids and other chimera, common in tales and artistic depictions from earliest times, were known to breach normative categories. The category breaching invoked by monsters might involve both the transversal of ordinarily intact boundaries, as well as the transformation of monstrous beings themselves. Especially at the boundaries between familiar and unfamiliar forms of existence—human and animal, Chinese and foreign, life and death—there lurked monsters. Categories of all kinds could be traversed, but in order to maintain social and cultural stability, it was necessary that these traversals be controlled and proper. While in principle any set of distinctions might be breached, the purpose of rituals, institutions, and texts was to identify and control conventional transformations. Moreover, in traditional China, as in other locals, the strange and the monstrous were always especially close to the numinous.

Some of the earliest and most influential visual representations of hybrid figures in China are found in the monster masks (*taotie* 饕餮), which function as a central decorative motif in bronze vessels cast through the Shang (circa seventeenth century BCE–eleventh century BCE) and Zhou (1045 BCE–256 BCE) dynasties (Figure 9.1).[2]

---

1   In discussing differences in the development of science in China and the West, Joseph Needham has argued that traditional Chinese thought lacks the notion of natural law. See Needham, *Science and Civilization in China*, vol. 2 (Cambridge: Cambridge University Press, 1954), pp. 518–84. Derk Bodde has disputed this finding in the context of Qing legal practice. See Derk Bodde, Clarence Morris, and Jinqing Zhu, *Law in Imperial China: Exemplified by 190 Ch'ing Dynasty Cases*, Harvard Studies in East Asian Law 1 (Cambridge, MA: Harvard University Press, 1967).

2   See the classic Michael Loewe, "Man and Beast: The Hybrid in Early Chinese Art and Literature," *Numen* 25/2 (1978), pp. 97–117.

Figure 9.1   Diagram detailing part of the *Taotie* or monster mask motif after illustration in Edith Watts, Sue Koch, Metropolitan Museum of Art Great Bronze Age exhibition publication.

Though styles of depiction shifted, aspects of the *taotie* remained constant: round bulging eyes, swirling horns, ears, claws or tail, and a gaping mouth, often with only the upper jaw depicted. Across centuries, another habit of portrayal persists: while at first glance features of an animal face are clearly evident, with closer inspection the solid figures tend to break down. A monster's face may split into two birds in profile or the heads of two dragons. Parts detach from the whole and with horns or quills, for instance, become separate beings in their own right. Thus a gaping, jawless monster mask on a square-shaped *ding* vessel found in Fu Hao's tomb becomes two birds in profile. Within the detailed background's swirling, spiral designs, new forms emerge. On a ram *zun* from the Anyang period (circa 1300 BCE – circa 1030 BCE), what might otherwise be read as joints to the ram's forelegs, were these animals fully represented, are transformed into the circling plume of a bird (Figures 9.2, 9.3).

On an elephant-shaped *zun* wine vessel, also from Anyang, smaller creatures manifest on the legs of the larger one.[3] On the belly, back, and atop an upraised trunk of the larger beast are other gaping, bodiless mouths. Any attempt to finally resolve these figures finds them maddeningly ambiguous, with parts of bodies detaching and re-emerging as some other figure or form. Like optical illusions, figures on these bronzes shape and reshape into alternate forms. At multiple levels of vessel form, major image, background relief and line décor, different faces and bodies recede and re-emerge, producing in these solid metal objects a mass of movement.

The significance of the *taotie* motif and the meanings of the animals and animal features in the bronzes have been much debated among scholars, with art historians traditionally following the work of Max Loehr and tending to focus

---

3   Metropolitan Museum of Art (New York, NY), Wen Fong, Robert W. Bagley, Jenny F. So, and Maxwell K. Hearn, *The Great Bronze Age of China: An Exhibition from the People's Republic of China* (New York: Metropolitan Museum of Art, 1980), plate 34.

Figure 9.2   Detail of four-ram *fang zun*. Anyang. period. Source: *The Great Bronze Age of China*, plate 20, detail.

on formal aspects of design and its development, while historians and scholars of religion have looked instead for symbolic or practical meanings in these remarkable designs.[4]

Whatever the intentions or thoughts of those producing and using these vessels in the Shang, the notion that the eerie zoomorphic motifs represented monsters is evident as early as the late Zhou (1045 BCE–256 BCE) in mentions of *taotie* in a set of historical writings, the *Chunqiu Zuozhuan* 春秋左傳 (*Master Zuo's Commentary on the Spring and Autumn Annals*):

> *In the past when the Xia dynasty first possessed the Divine Virtue, the distant quarters made diagrams of the strange creatures, contributed metal*

4   Max Loehr's hypothesis of pure design was inspired by the work of Suzanne Langer. Loehr's perspective and analysis of the designs remain motivating concerns in the work of Robert Bagley. See Max Loehr, Asia Society and Asia House Gallery, *Ritual Vessels of Bronze Age China* (New York: Asia Society; distributed by New York Graphic Society [Greenwich, CT], 1968); Robert W. Bagley, Max Loehr, and Bernhard Karlgren, *Max Loehr and the Study of Chinese Bronzes: Style and Classification in the History of Art*, Cornell East Asia Series (Ithaca, NY: East Asia Program, Cornell University, 2008). For other interpretations, see, for instance, Sarah Allan, *The Shape of the Turtle: Myth, Art, and Cosmos in Early China* (Albany, NY: State University of New York Press, 1991); Elizabeth Childs-Johnson and Sajid Rizvi, *The Meaning of the Graph Yi and its Implications for Shang Belief and Art*, Eaj Monograph (London: Saffron, 2008).

to the Nine Herdsmen, and cast caldrons to replicate the strange creatures. Due to this the hundred spirit creatures were fully revealed, enabling the common people to recognize the machinations of the gods and the demons. Thus, when people went to the streams, marshes, mountains, and forests, they did not encounter the unseemly. None of the Chimei-goblins and the Wangliang monsters were able to waylay them. As a result, harmony was maintained between those above and those dwelling on Earth below while everywhere, the people received the protection of heaven.[5]

Here bronzes are thus taken as a kind of guidebook or map of dangerous creatures inhabiting the uncivilized wilds.[6]

About concurrent with the compilation of *Master Zuo's Commentary*, a volume was taking shape that would survive in later centuries as China's most well-known mythical geography and bestiary. The earliest textual layers of the *Classic of Mountains and Seas* (*Shanhai jing* 山海經) date to about the third century BCE. The text details and locates strange beings in the wilds beyond the borders of the middle kingdom.[7] By tradition, the authorship of the *Classic* was ascribed to the legendary figure Yu 禹, a great sage ruler who was said to have tamed floods, divided land into nine provinces and who is credited with establishing the Xia 夏 dynasty (circa 2200 BCE). The *Shanhai jing*, always closely associated with visual illustrations, was accepted prior to the modern period as comprising in part descriptions of the same monsters that appeared on the nine bronze tripods cast for the ruler Yu early in the Xia period.[8]

Despite its traditional classification as a set of notes for illustrations of monsters, the *Classic of Mountains and Seas* also effectively functioned as an attempt, through the mode of travelogue, progress, and geography, and as a move on the part of an increasingly text-oriented elite, to trace and manage the boundaries and periphery in parts of the world distinct from the settled, cultured Chinese center.[9] While

---

5   *Chronicles of Zuo*, Xuan 左傳宣 3, 21.15b–16b. Translation modified slightly and expanded from Donald Harper, "A Chinese Demonography of the Third Century BC," *Harvard Journal of Asiatic Studies* 45/2 (1985), p. 479, n. 56. Unless otherwise noted, translations are my own.

6   Here, as throughout traditional Chinese sources, depictions of a monster or demon can function apotropaically, either to magically repel malevolent forces, or as a kind of guide, helping humans to avoid trouble. These instructional and protective functions persist through centuries of traditional arts and letters.

7   The *Shanhai jing* was circulating by Han, then later lost. Recent scholarship suggests that the extant volume has been assembled from writings by a number of different authors over a period of six to eight centuries. Recent English translations of the *Classic of Mountains and Seas* include Anne Birrell, *The Classic of Mountains and Seas*, Penguin Classics (London and New York, NY: Penguin Books; Penguin Putnam, 1999); Richard E. Strassberg, *A Chinese Bestiary: Strange Creatures from the Guideways through Mountains and Seas* (Berkeley: University of California Press, 2002).

8   The third-century scholar Zuo Si 左思 noted that some of the beings described in the text had appeared on the nine tripods cast by Yu, the great sage king.

9   Michael Harbsmeier, "On Travel Accounts and Cosmological Strategies: Some Models

often treated as a bestiary or mythical geography, the volume also includes notes on medicine and directions for ritual behavior, as well as information on augury.[10] Later scholars have noted the heterogeneous nature of the text, and have identified it variously as a moral handbook, a collection of folklore, a travel guide, an encyclopedia of omens, and a sourcebook for later Chinese fictional accounts of the strange.

Anecdotes about the text also reveal aspects of its perceived significance and value. An oft-cited tale from the [Writings of] Master Guan (管子)

Figure 9.3   Four-ram *fang zun*. Source: *The Great Bronze Age of China*, plate 20.

mentions the famous prime minister Guan Zhong's (管仲) use of the information from the *Classic of Mountains and Seas* to identify a strange creature. When Guan Zhong's liege, the Duke of Qi, was out riding beyond the walls of the city, he came upon what looked like a tiger, though to the Duke's surprise, the animal did not attack. Guan Zhong explained that the Duke's horse must have resembled a *Bo* 左 傅, a being known for eating tigers and leopards. Thus the tiger had refrained from attacking, explained the minister, as it "was avoiding the duke's horse out of fear."[11] Knowledge of monsters, the periphery, and possible omens would have been essential to any ruler in early China, not simply because it was on occasion useful to be able to identify a strange creature, but because accurate understanding of the more unusual or subtle aspects of the phenomenal world was an indicator of access to all varieties of higher understanding. Thus discernible through the text is a concerted effort to determine, distinguish, and define the creatures and conditions of the periphery such that the information might be useful to rulers, scholars and others. Like the images of monsters on the nine bronze tripods from the Xia, the *Classic of Mountains and Seas* could serve as a guidebook in order to instruct, protect, and control the borderlands and their inhabitants.

---

in Comparative Xenology," *Ethnos* 3/4 (1985), pp. 273–312.

10   Strassberg, *A Chinese Bestiary*, pp. 3–7. Riccardo Fracasso, "Shan Hai Ching," in Michael Loewe (ed.), *Early Chinese Texts: A Bibliographical Guide* (Berkeley: University of California Press, 1993), pp. 357–67.

11   For a recounting of this tale, see Strassberg, *A Chinese Bestiary*, p. 1.

But certain elements of the periphery are difficult to pin down, and the transformations or essential instability of some creatures defy final definition or comprehensive description. Thus, the exuberant and long-lived work of tracking the borders, boundaries, and what lay beyond them underlines, on the one hand, the need for this enterprise and, on the other, the difficulty of ever successfully accomplishing the task. In other words, the presence of monsters not only marks boundaries, but also indicates where lines or demarcation are problematic, with weird hybrid bodies the sign of a breech or a crossing, or of some other uncommon connection between worlds. So the morphing figures on the early Chinese bronzes used as containers for food in mortuary rituals reflect both the challenge of bridging boundaries between life and death and the urgent necessity of feeding the ancestors. A guidebook to foreign lands and untamed wilds demonstrates persistent anxiety about others, the unknown, and untamed natural forces. In addition to boundaries delimiting the fields between life and death, local and foreign, human and animal, monsters also bridge ordinarily stable categories in thought and language. Not only are the bodies of monsters hybrid and complex, the very process of identifying uncommon beings may put pressure on the stability of documents, human powers of classification, and the possibilities of language. So stories of the *Classic of Mountains and Seas* being used to identify strange creatures may be contrasted with other cases in which knowledge about certain beings was complex, contradictory, and nearly impossible to untangle.

A case in point is a creature called the Yu 蜮. Whether the Yu is an ordinary animal or a monster, and what the particular characteristics of this creature might have been, are debated through hundreds of years of commentary. Briefly put, the word *yu* does not easily resolve into any concrete referent. Examples from texts coalescing through the Zhou and Han (circa 1000 BCE–200 CE) show a strong association between *yu* and "others," usually construed as foreign, animal, demonic, or deceased.[12] Commentaries on these same texts tend to relate the Yu back to a series of ordinary, but different, animals, most commonly foxes, turtles, and insects. Commentators on ancient texts do not consistently identify the Yu as an animal hybrid, though context often suggests a monster or possible demon. More striking in the collection of notes and definitions spanning roughly 2,000 years is a determination to identify *which* animal the word *yu* must have referred to. In the earliest textual notes, *yu* is glossed as a "short fox" *duanhu* 短狐. Where some try to square the word *duanhu* with a water creature, such as a turtle, others argue that the Yu is an insect. One scholar amends the term *duanhu* to *duanweihu* 短尾狐 "short-tailed fox."[13] In notes on the early ritual texts *Zhouli* 周禮 (traditionally mid-second century BCE) and *Dadai liji* 大戴禮繫 (traditionally second century BCE, probably second century CE), the same graph 蜮 (here pronounced *guo*, sometimes written 蟈) is understood to refer to toads. Zhu Junsheng's 朱駿聲 (1788–1858) note on a

---

12 For instance, the word *yu* is often collocated with the word *gui* 鬼 (other, demon, ghost).

13 "An Yu is a short fox, like a three legged water turtle. By means of shooting *qi*, it harms people." 蜮短狐也. 似鱉三足以氣射殺人. Xu Shen, *Shuowen jiezi* 說文解字 (Shanghai: Shanghai guji chuban she, 1981), p. 672.

commentary to a passage in the ritual text *Dadai liji* instead identifies the term Yu as "owl."[14] The common animals most frequently identified as the Yu (fox, turtle, insect) do not appear in combination as a common Chinese chimera. Despite the prevalence of animal and animal human hybrids through Chinese visual sources, at points where multiple commentaries on the same passage create discussion or debate, the reader encounters pointed critical back and forth through the notes, with some writers asserting that the Yu must be one entity, and others another.

Scholars through the ages cite each other with approbation or disagreement, but ultimately the meaning of the word *yu* remains unsettled. As if recalling from a textual point of view the identity and significance of *taotie*, the gaping jawless monster masks on Shang bronze vessels, what remains to us from years of commentary and exegesis is a failure to identify with any certainty the identity of a being called *yu*. Looking back from the perspective of nearly two centuries of notes, a short passage on Yu in the *Classic of Mountains and Seas* seems to poke fun at the whole enterprise of locating any specific meaning:

> There is an Yu Mountain, and there is a land of Yu people. Their last name is Sang (mulberry) and they eat millet and shoot Yu for food. There are people who draw back [their] bows to shoot yellow snakes, they are called Yu people.[15]

The *Classic of Mountains and Seas* passage deftly encompasses the whole protracted and contradictory debate about the creature Yu. The identification of the word *yu* as a place, a people, a creature, *and* a food recalls images of the shifting and illusionistic *taotie* as well as presaging critical thinking about "others": those beings definitively distinct which simultaneously express most perfectly the essential nature or values of the group from which they are circumscribed.

Identity between monsters and the humans who identify them as such echoes not only through the *Classic of Mountains and Seas* but also through the Han dynasty (206 BCE–220 CE) great exorcism (Han *danuo* 漢大儺), a regularly enacted state-sponsored ritual performed in the capital.[16] In period descriptions of the Han great exorcism, ritual officiants and government officials dressed up in animal furs, horns, and feathers and, brandishing shields and lances, paraded through the imperial palace, pronouncing a threatening chant in order to drive away malicious entities and forces.

---

14   Zhu Junsheng, *Shuowen tongxun dingsheng* 說文通訓定聲 (Wuhan: Wuhan shi guji shudian, 1983), p. 222.

15   Yuan Ke 袁珂 (ed.), *Shanhai jing jiaozhu* 山海經校注 (Shanghai: Shanghai guji chuban she, 1991), pp. 372–3.

16   On the Han Great Exorcism, see Derk Bodde, *Festivals in Classical China* (Princeton: Princeton University Press, 1975). On demon names in various descriptions of this rite in the Han, see William G. Boltz, "Philological Footnotes to the Han New Year Rites," *Journal of the American Oriental Society* 99/3 (1979), pp. 423–38. On archeological finds related to Han *nuo*, see Patricia Ann Berger, "Rites and Festivities in the Art of Eastern Han China: Shantung and Kiangsu Provinces," PhD dissertation, University of California, Berkeley, 1980.

A ritual specialist (*fangxiangshi* 方相氏) and a group from the office of palace attendants were central performers in a ceremony to dispel demons and evil influences:

> *One day before the New Year's feast (la 臘) there is the great exorcism, which is called "expulsion of pestilences" … They all wear red headcloths, black tunics, and hold large twirl-drums. The exorcist (fangxiangshi), [his head] covered with a bear skin having four eyes of gold, and clad in a dark upper garment and vermilion lower garment, grasps a lance and brandishes a shield … Palace attendants of the yellow gates act as twelve "animals," wearing fur, feathers and horns, and the supervisor of the retinue leads them to expel evil demons from the palace … [Meanwhile,] in the various official bureaus, each official wears a wooden animal mask with which he can act as a leader of those participating in the exorcism.*[17]

The physical attack on the malevolent beings and threats made to them of dismemberment are described in a rowdy chant in which the human performers threaten to eat the malicious interlopers.[18] Then the Palace Attendants of the Yellow Gates start a chant in which the troupe joins:

> *Jiazuo* 甲作, *devour the baneful* 凶!
> *Feiwei* 胇胃, *devour tigers* 虎![19]
> *Xiongbo* 雄伯, *devour the Mei monster* 魅!
> *Tengjian* 騰簡, *devour the inauspicious* 不祥!
> *Lanzhu* 攬諸, *devour calamities* 咎!
> *Boqi* 伯奇, *devour dreams* 夢!
> *Qiangliang* 強梁 *and Zuming* 祖明, *together devour the spirits which having been ripped from the dead, cling to the living* 磔死寄生![20]

---

17   See central section of section of Sima Biao's 司馬彪 (240-306) "Treatise on Ritual" 禮儀志 included in Fan Ye 范曄 History of the Latter Han 後漢書. Translation modified slightly from Bodde, *Festivals in Classical China*, pp. 81–2. The Palace Attendants of the Yellow Gates was a designation for palace eunuchs.

18   A bit further on, the description continues: "As this takes place the Exorcist and the twelve 'animals' dance and shout, going everywhere through the front and rear palace apartments." (Translation in Bodde, *Festivals in Classical China*, p. 82.) The twelve animals here refer to the twelve "eaters" in the ritual chant. Symbolically, the costumed and dancing exorcist and his troupe are consuming inauspicious and threatening beings and entities.

19   The original text uses the graph for "tiger" 虎, though Bodde makes a cogent case that the second of these devoured demons is the graphically similar "fever" 瘴.

20   Bodde's translation for *zhesi jisheng* 磔死寄生 is "those who, having suffered execution with public exposure, now cling to the living." *Zhezi* was "a recognized Han legal term for execution, normally by beheading, with the added penalty of public exposure; such exposure may be inflicted upon the still living criminal prior to public execution, or it may in addition include exposure of his corpse after death" (Bodde, *Festivals in Classical*

Weisui 委隨, *devour visions* 觀!
Cuoduan 錯斷, *devour giants* 巨!
Qiongqi 窮奇 *and Tenggen* 騰根, *together devour the magical gu* 蠱 *poisons!*
May all these twelve spirits drive away the evil and baneful.
Let them roast your bodies, break your spines and joints, tear off your flesh,
pull out your lungs and entrails.
If you do not leave at once, those who stay behind will become their food.[21]

Finally, blazing torches were carried out of the palace gates and hurled into the water to propel the evil influences to distant parts beyond the reaches of the middle kingdom.

Ritual participants, costuming themselves in bright colors, animal skins, and masks, brandishing weapons and chanting, proceeded through the palace. Thus the exorcism enacted the chaos it was meant to dispel and, in costuming government officials in monster masks and sending them through the most ordered residence of the empire shouting threats of destruction, order was meant to be reconstituted. By a force of sympathetic magic, humans impersonating animal-featured monsters, and threatening malevolent forces with destruction, malefactors could be engaged and conquered. This set of ontological inversions based in the imperial palace, from human to demon and order to chaos, was implicitly understood to act as a catalyst for a series of like reactions in spheres that could not be affected more directly. Driving off evil influences in the emperor's residence symbolically banished them from all of China. Monsters and other malevolent influences were expected to respond like human interlopers, running away in the face of a quasi-monster onslaught.

Transformed through costume, chant, and performance into animal-hybrid monsters, human officials in the great Han exorcism fought off malevolent forces. Here a ceremony enacted with monster bodies serves to break through the usual boundary between this world and the world of spirits. The other realm, conceived as existing in the same time and place as the everyday world, though not accessible by ordinary means, is also changed, and contained, through ritual performance. Other cultural productions, such as visual representations of demonic human–animal hybrids or strangely formed deities, are found through centuries of Chinese painting and sculpture and also serve both apotropaic and ritual functions. Like the costumed performers in the Han dynasty exorcism, monsters and strong men with animal attributes defended not only human communities, but also temples and tombs.

A set of guardian monsters made of clay and wood, found in an eighth-century tomb at Astana, are particularly fanciful (Figure 9.4).[22] These figures, echoing many

---

China, p. 98). Boltz translates "spirits which having been ripped from the dead, abide in the living." Spirits of people who had died by execution with public humiliation were understood to be particularly dangerous. Presumably "clinging to" or "abiding in" the living refers to a phenomenon now called *fushen*, when a spirit invades or takes over the body of a living being.

21 Translation modified slightly from Bodde, *Festivals in Classical China*, p. 82.
22 These figures were found by Aurel Stein in Astana tomb iii. 2; see *Innermost Asia*, vol. II

Figure 9.4   Painted stucco figures of monsters. Astana, tomb iii. 2. First half of
eighth century. Source: Sir Aurel Stein, *Innermost Asia*, vol. II. Fig. 325,
as reproduced in Whitfield and Farrer, *Caves of the Thousand Buddhas*,
p. 145.

literary descriptions of monsters, mix the body parts of various species. Three
animal bodies sit erect and alert, with muscles tensed and tails in the air. The beasts'
spotted fur is painted in a wild array of colors, unlike that of any living animal, and
each is given an incongruous head. The figure on the left, with a demonic, angry
face, is described by Aurel Stein as half-human and boar-like, with prominent green
eyebrows.[23] A long pair of canine fangs hangs over the lower lip, and bulging eyes
and flared nostrils are topped off with a pointed tasseled cap in rainbow colors. The
central figure has a human, though grotesque, face and obviously human ears. The
body, however, looks more like that of a large cat, and is painted in non-naturalistic
pink and blue with bright red spots. Not visible from the photo are the bushy blue
tail and the four wing feathers found broken next to the monster.[24] The figure on

---

(Oxford: Clarendon Press, 1928), p. 652, figure 325. Stein dates the whole set of tombs
in group iii to the first half of the eighth century on the basis of scrap paper found in
the tombs, which was believed to have been used to prop up the body in the coffin. See
Innermost Asia, pp. 657–8.

23   Information on colors is taken from Stein, *Innermost Asia*, p. 652.

24   The tomb in which these three were discovered had already been plundered before
Stein's arrival. Parts had broken off all but the monster on the right.

Figure 9.5   *Vaiśravaṇa and Retinue of Yakṣas*. Dunhuang, Five Dynasties, mid-tenth century. Ink and colors on silk. British Museum, Stein Painting 26. Source: Roderick Whitfield, *The Art of Central Asia: Paintings from Dunhuang*, vol. II, plate 15-1.

the right has a snout-like head, suggesting a dragon, with bulging eyes, as well as a gaping mouth displaying upper and lower fangs. Tendril-like feathers float up out of the figure's back, and a broader, variegated tail is extended in alarm.

Protector spirits in the retinue of other, more powerful, gods exhibit characteristics of animals as well as the features of foreign (non-Chinese) peoples. Buddhist deities are often displayed in groups or with an entourage. In the case of a major figure and attendant grouping, some of the retinue will be Hindu deities who, in the Buddhist context, have been converted to the true religion and serve to protect the major Buddhist figure. In visual depiction, these converted deities, though won over to the side of Buddhism, retain their original frightful shapes. Certainly the threatening stances and horrifying forms of these demonic defenders also serve to frighten the forces of evil that might endanger either the Buddhist pantheon or the human community.[25] Vaiśravaṇa 多聞天王, guardian

_____

25   As Buddhism traveled to China along the Silk Road from India, one might expect

Figure 9.6   *Vaiśravaṇa Riding Across the Waters*. Detail. Dunhuang, Five Dynasties, mid-tenth century. British Museum, Stein Painting 45. Source: Roderick Whitfield, *The Art of Central Asia: Paintings from Dunhuang*, vol. II, plate 16.

king of the north and one of the protectors of the Buddhist law, commonly appears with a group of both human and spirit attendants and warriors. In a mid-tenth-century painting preserved in Dunhuang, Vaiśravaṇa rides a white horse

Chinese depictions of Buddhist deities to have foreign (such as Indian or Middle Eastern) features. In fact, the highest ranking Buddhist deities have Chinese features, while heretics and the deities of other religions are represented with foreign and animal features. See Karin Myhre 麦瑞怡, "Picturing Spirits: Images of Gods, Ghosts and Demons in Chinese Painting 苗繪精神：描繪精神、鬼、妖的圖景," in Sarah E. Fraser (ed.), *Merit, Opulence, and the Buddhist Network of Wealth* 唐宋的佛教與社會－寺院財富與世俗供養 (Shanghai: Shanghai Fine Arts Publishers, 2003).

across the water, and is surrounded by a circular retinue of eleven little demon yakṣas (Figure 9.5).

The little yakṣas surrounding Vaiśravaṇa are round and muscular, and engaged in bouncy, romping motion. A figure at the lower left looks to be playing leapfrog over a friend's back; just to the right another demon runs off in the opposite direction, holding aloft a pronged stick shaped like a sling-shot. On either side of Vaiśravaṇa are fang-toothed, monkey-faced monsters. Orange and green hair rises in tufts above their heads; round white eyes bulge beneath bony, overhanging foreheads; squat noses sit atop split-lipped feline mouths displaying pointed threatening teeth. Two of the monsters look attentively, if not intelligently, towards Vaiśravaṇa upon his horse. Vaiśravaṇa is visually more closely aligned with the human figures that bring up the rear of his entourage. His almond eyes, delicate moustache, square, even teeth and dark hair distinguish him from the little demons. Though in movement through space, Vaiśravaṇa focuses the chaotic motion that encircles him. In contrast to the exuberant demon band, the guardian king of the north, in a composition recalling the construction of a mandala anchored by a still central deity, appears almost calm.

In addition to animal features, the characteristics of foreign (non-sinitic) peoples, such as either darker or pinkish light skin, round and colored rather than almond shaped and brown eyes, prominent noses or eyebrows, as well as, in some cases, unkempt and wildly colored hair, frequently accrue to spirit and demon figures. Protector spirits such as Vajrapāṇi金剛手菩薩and those in the retinue of deities guarding the directions are often shown with non-Chinese facial features and skin tone. The painting of figures in the entourage of Vaiśravaṇa in a mid-tenth-century painting on silk from Dunhuang contrasts the relatively spare visual representation of humans with the minutely detailed and more threatening faces of monsters (Figure 9.6). The eyes of the central dark-skinned strongman figure in elaborate orange headgear are nearly as round and wildly energetic as those of the three fanged monsters arrayed above and below him. The hair on the upper arms, chest, and face of this figure resembles fur, while an articulated upper lip echoes the feline-like split-lipped surrounding monsters. A prominent upturned nose and protruding eyebrows contrast with the more delicate faces of the Chinese figures at the upper right and lower left.[26]

A painting on silk of Virūpākṣa 廣目天王, guardian of the west, shows the god with striking and, for works in this genre, uncommon reddish pink skin, a bulging bony forehead and protruding eyebrows, fang-like front teeth, blue hair, and intense green eyes (Figure 9.7). A sense of movement in the painting is enhanced by the figure's focused and threatening expression, and also by the roiling struggle of the half-naked, fanged, snout-nosed green demon on which Virûpâksa stands.

---

26 The figure just to the right, holding a goblet, has been identified as the rishi Vasu, an Indian god who is the alternate aspect of Vaiśravaṇa. See Roderick Whitfield and Anne Farrer, *Caves of the Thousand Buddhas: Chinese Art from the Silk Route* (London: British Museum Publications, 1990), p. 34. His more prominent facial features suggest identification with Indians or Central Asians.

Figure 9.7 *Virūpākṣa, Guardian of the West*. Dunhuang, ninth–tenth century. Source: Roderick Whitfield, *The Art of Central Asia: Paintings from Dunhuang*, vol. I, plate 63.

While both Virūpākṣa and the demon beneath him have animal features, the god's pale skin and eyes also indicate non-Chinese descent.

Individual protector spirits are depicted as something between Chinese and foreign, human and animal, their liminal status marked by an amalgam of characteristics.[27] Other visual works used for ritual practice, such as mandalas and Ten Kings 十王 (*shiwang*) scrolls showing the courts of hell, demonstrate with greater clarity an elaborated hierarchy in which all beings, from netherworld denizens to the most celebrated Buddhas, are distinguished.[28] A multiplication of physical features is one indicator of spiritual efficacy, thus protector spirits appear with animal or non-Chinese features. By contrast, the more sanctified in the Buddhist pantheon may appear with a profusion of human features. A belief in karmic return and multiple rebirths places most beings somewhere on a continuum between the lowest hell demons and the highest Buddhas. Mandalas, diagrammatic paintings meant to provide visible representations of the ritual world, arrange groups of figures in registers around a prominent center. The figure in the center is the largest, and is understood to be the most powerful and the most holy. Moving progressively towards the outer edges of the painting, figures may have round angry eyes, wild hair, and other distinctive animal and foreign features. In a Womb Mandala executed in Japan according to Chinese models, the central figure of the Celestial Buddha Dainichi 大日 is absolutely still.[29] Surrounding registers are populated by

---

27 However, in some paintings, such as some Ming (1368–1644) works depicting another guardian deity, Erlang, malevolent forces are shown as simply animals.

28 On ten kings, see Stephen F. Teiser, *The Scripture on the Ten Kings and the Making of Purgatory in Medieval Chinese Buddhism* (Honolulu: University of Hawaii Press, 1994).

29 Womb Mandala, ink and colors on silk, second half of ninth century, at Tōji Temple 東寺. Tōji Hōbotsukan, *Tōji no mandara zu: mihotoke no gunzō* 東寺の曼荼羅図：みほとけの群像 (Kyoto: Toji Hōmotsukan, 1992), p. 30. In the ninth century, the Tōji Temple was the headquarters of the Shingon 真言 sect. The sect was established by the monk Kukai (774–835), who had traveled to China and returned to Japan in the year 805. The central figure in the Shingon sect is Dainichi, the Japanese name for Vairocana, a celestial Buddha prominent in Chinese Huayan 華嚴 and Japanese esoteric Buddhism.

Figure 9.8   The Six Ways, or Forms of Existence. Illustrations to the *Ten Kings Sutra*, detail, third section. Dunhuang, Five Dynasties, tenth century. British Museum, Stein Painting 80. Source: Roderick Whitfield, *The Art of Central Asia: Paintings from Dunhuang*, vol. II, plate 63-2.

darker skinned, mobile and more expressive figures, such as the group of four Myō-ō 明王 (Chinese: *mingwang*), the guardians of the four directions, sitting just below the central square. Their dark skin, bare chests, orange hair, fierce round eyes, and grimaces and, in the case of the figure on the far right, visible fangs, recall yakṣas and protector spirits in Chinese paintings from Dunhuang.[30]

---

30   Following Indian models, the multiplication of normal human body parts is used in artistic renderings of Buddhist deities to indicate divine powers.

Figure 9.9   Yan Geng 顏庚 (active circa 1300). *The Demon Queller Zhong Kui Giving His Sister Away in Marriage*, detail. Handscroll. Ink on silk. Metropolitan Museum of Art, New York. Source: Wen Fong, *Beyond Representation*, plate 82c, p. 372.

The Womb Mandala neatly maps out in visual terms a progress from the lowest levels of existence, as shown by the beings arrayed around the outside edge of a painting, to the highest, in the middle. In analogous fashion, ritual scrolls meant to help departed souls through the courts of the underworld depict in stark terms the range of possible routes for returning to the land of the living. Illustrations in a tenth-century scroll from Dunhuang show an ox-headed hell demon as the lowest possible form of rebirth, below hungry ghosts and ordinary animals (Figure 9.8). Arrayed above human beings are minor Buddhist deities and finally, Buddhas.

These Buddhist paintings from Dunhuang employ a consistent set of iconographic tools to indicate both spiritual powers and also moral status along the hierarchy of rebirth. Particular attention is drawn to the physical bodies of deities and demons, which all become monstrous, though in somewhat different ways. Where the human features of higher ranking Buddhas and bodhisattvas are emphasized, and deities are depicted with larger, sometimes mammoth, bodies and in some cases also multiple arms or eyes, lower ranking messengers and protectors are instead creatures: human bodies combined with the features of animals or non-Chinese foreigners. These monstrous bodies, strangely layered with odd incongruous elements, are drawn with such dense detail as to make the forms seem impossible to realize in real space. Where monsters have remarkable faces and bodies, for mortals, painterly attention is instead focused on clothing.[31]

---

31   Movement is also a consistent feature of beings who more properly inhabit another world. For those in lower orders of rebirth, physical movement and heightened or exaggerated emotion is evident. Images of Buddhas, by contrast, are solid and still, though surrounded with motion in the figures of followers and in wafting and

In later Chinese painting from about the twelfth through sixteenth centuries, protector spirits and ravaging monsters continue to be depicted as largely human figures embellished with animal or foreign features. Zhong Kui, the most well-known of demon quellers was said to have first appeared to one of the Tang dynasty (618–907) emperors in a dream and was regularly shown with fierce face and animal-like features.[32] Through the Tang and later, images of the demon queller Zhong Kui were given as gifts to imperial subjects and Zhong Kui remained a common subject of painting through the Song (960–1279) and Yuan (1271–1368) periods.[33]

Yan Geng's 顏庚 (active circa 1300) painting, *The Demon Queller Zhong Kui Giving His Sister Away in Marriage*, shows a band of particularly acrobatic and expressive demons leading off the nuptial procession of Zhong Kui's human sister (Figure 9.9). In the figures of Zhong Kui's helpers, the visual attributes of hungry ghosts and denizens of hell common in earlier Buddhist works—nearly naked bodies in ragged clothing with wild hair and animal features—combine. In each of the members of the demon band both muscles and bones are distinguished. The figures seem vibrant and lively at the same time as their physical bodies are virtually dissected by the painter's brush. Note the scamp who seems to have jumped back in gleeful surprise before a pot suspended in mid-air. The bulging muscles of his thighs, impossibly round and almost ham-like, narrow to tiny button-like knobby knees. Below this the calves explode on either side of the shin bones, and disappear again to dark lines indicating the tendons and bones of the ankle and foot. All of the figures have dark stripes across their chests, recalling the bony ribs of hungry demons; their upper chests and arms, however, are bulbous and powerfully muscular, similar to the typically heavy chested wardens and denizens of hell.

The gaping mouths of some of the fiends display rows of animal-like pointed teeth; these are most clearly evident in the little fellow hoisting a small mountain on the far right. Most of the demon attendants have snubby, snout-like noses, here visible in the profile of the figure holding a long staff turning to look backwards at the left. The imp jumping back from the pot has small pointy ears, a ragged spotted fur about his shoulders, and a spotted loincloth, with longer fur emerging from beneath his clothing. Other figures in this grouping show little horns emerging from a bumpy bald skull and cat-like slightly split lips. The hair of these beings is reminiscent of the hair in early representations of hungry ghosts: two tufts that rise

---

floating strips of cloth.

32   Stories about the origin of Zhong Kui from the Song period differ in detail. For more on Zhong Kui and paintings including Zhong Kui, see Chia Chi Jason Wang, "The Iconography of Zhong Kui in Chinese Painting," MA thesis, University of California, Berkeley, 1991, and Sherman E. Lee, "Yan Hui, Zhong Kui, Demons and the New Year," *Artibus Asiae* 53/1–2 (1992), pp. 211–27.

33   Though not a Buddhist deity, Zhong Kui is in some ways the analog of Vaiśravaṇa, the guardian king of the north. Both are understood to control demons; both share some of the physical attributes of demons and monsters. Paintings of Vaiśravaṇa and Zhong Kui find them both traveling with a little band of monsters that they have converted to the side of good, and both protect ordinary mortals from the ravages of more dangerous spirits.

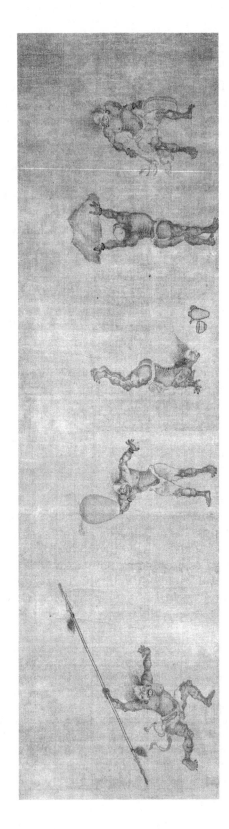

Figure 9.10 Yan Hui 顏輝 (active late 13th–early 14th centuries). Zhong Kui's *Excursion on the Night of the Lantern Festival*, detail. Handscroll. Ink and light colors on silk. The Cleveland Museum of Art. Source: *Eight Dynasties of Chinese Painting*, plate 91.

from behind the ears on either side of a balding pate. These little monsters, however, show no signs of the hungry ghosts' distress or longing for sustenance. They are invigorated, expressive, gleeful, and engaged with their immediate surroundings and activities in a manner so focused it is almost farcical.

Another processional painting, Yan Hui's 李輝 (active late 13th–early 14th centuries) *Zhong Kui's Excursion on the Night of the Lantern Festival*, also shows a motley band accompanying the demon catcher (Figure 9.10).[34]

The demon figures in this scroll, also unaccountably both overly muscular and markedly bony, barely clothed, and balding, are quite similar to those in the Yan Geng scroll, though this group of monsters is even more acrobatic than those that Yan Geng depicts. The central figure in the detail here is balancing on his hands as though about to somersault; another at the far left runs at full tilt, swinging an enormous lance. The creatures portrayed in the first sections of this painting are all turning, lifting, running, and leaping, as if the work were meant as a series of studies of the body in motion.

Visual attention is drawn to these beings, bursting with energy, in part through pronounced shading and dramatic poses. The physical bodies of the little monsters are infused with a wild sense of movement, vitality, and play. The romping motion of demi-god or demonic attendants, evident in some paintings from Dunhuang (see *Vaiśravaṇa and Retinue of Yakṣas*, above), is here transformed to acrobatics. Where other paintings represent the deity Zhong Kui, here we have instead a depiction of a Zhong Kui procession.[35] These monsters and demons, rather than invoking the presence of spirits through the powers of portraiture, instead show a group of actors. Period descriptions of life in both the Northern Song and Southern Song dynasty (960–1279) capitals give details of New Year's exorcisms related to the Han period *nuo* rites in which performers in the employ of the imperial palace would act as immortals, deities and protectors, including such figures as Zhong Kui and Zhong Kui's sister, to perform a New Year's *nuo* exorcism.[36] The paintings

---

34 Wen Fong has suggested a connection between Yan Geng and Yan Hui, as some of the figures in these two scrolls are so similar that the two may have belonged to the same workshop and used the same preparatory materials. See Wen Fong, *Beyond Representation: Chinese Painting and Calligraphy, 8th–14th Century* (New York: Metropolitan Museum of Art, and New Haven: Yale University Press, 1992), pp. 367–9. See also Lee, "Yan Hui, Zhong Kui, Demons and the New Year," p. 215.

35 Richard Von Glahn has suggested that processional paintings of Zhong Kui during this period were modeled on bands of beggars who would use the lunar New Year as an opportunity to dress up and go from house to house, demanding alms. While these practices may have influenced aspects of the composition, the muscular development and acrobatic skills of little monsters in the Yan Geng and Yan Hui scrolls make a depiction of professional actors more likely. See Von Glahn, *The Sinister Way: The Divine and the Demonic in Chinese Religious Culture* (Berkeley: University of California Press, 2004), pp. 122–8.

36 A description of the New Year's exorcism in the Northern Song capital is found in chapter (*juan*) 6 of Meng Yuanlao's 孟元老 *Dongjing menghua lu* 東京夢華錄, in *Dongjing menghua lu wai si zhong* 東京夢華錄外四種 (Taipei: Dali chubanshe, 1980), p. 62. For

by Yan Hui and Yan Geng are not depicting Zhong Kui the deity, but rather a *performance* of Zhong Kui and his band of rowdy impish demons. Futhermore, figures participating in the *nuo*, as well as those connected to other rituals and part of other popular beliefs, also appeared in narrative song dramas.[37] By the Ming and Qing periods (1368–1644, 1644–1911), Zhong Kui had become a regular character in performances of narrative drama.

In traditional Chinese sources, monsters emerge at the borders of a number of different domains and, as we have seen, hybrid figures can serve as both the indicators and means of boundary traversal: *taotie* invoke the possibility of communication between the living and the dead; a mythical geography depicts life beyond the known or knowable borders in the form of animal hybrids; and human actors ape, animal-like, the bodies, movements, and sounds so as to pass into the world of baleful and influential spirits. Paintings depicting processions of the demon queller Zhong Kui reflect broader historical and conceptual linkages between narrative drama and ritual performance, and further, between the world of spirits and the possibility of narrative imagination. In fact, all of the worlds inhabited by monsters, from geographically distant other cultures and races, to the sphere of spirits, the land of dreams, the distinct domains of other species, to the territories traced out through literary imaginings, share this: monsters, hybrids, and shape-changers lurk at the margins between those worlds and our own familiar world. In the negotiation between all of these worlds and our own, certain rules of engagement apply. It is possible, if not ordinary, to cross between worlds; the condition for and sometimes signs of such passages include the mixing and morphing of more familiar physical forms. Holding firm the boundaries between different domains—the between life and death, between this world and the realm of spirits as well as the land of dreams, between language that makes sense and the incursion of nonsense—is, of course, essential to the stability of both culture and meaning. And yet, it is just as necessary that these bounds be permeable and somehow traversable, that what lies beyond them—death, spirits, dreams, aliens, nonsense—can re-enter and impart vital significance to those living within the bounds of the ordinary.

English translation, see Wilt Idema and Stephen West, *Chinese Theater 1100–1450* (Wiesbaden: Steiner, 1982), pp. 122–3. A similar passage describing the ritual in the Southern Song capital is found in Wu Zimu 吳自牧, *Meng liang lu* 夢粱錄 in ibid., pp. 181–2. See also Wolfram Eberhard, *The Local Cultures of South and East China*, trans. Alide Eberhard (Leiden: E.J. Brill, 1968), p. 329, and Shih-Shan Susan Huang, "Summoning the Gods: Paintings of Three Officials of Heaven, Earth and Water and their Association with Daoist Ritual Performance in the Southern Song Period (1127–1279)," *Artibus Asiae* 61/1 (2001), pp. 5–52.

37 See, for instance, Qitao Guo, *Exorcism and Money: The Symbolic World of the Five-Fury Spirits in Late Imperial China* (Berkeley: Institute of East Asian Studies, University of California, Berkeley/Center for Chinese Studies, 2003), as well as David Johnson (ed.), *Ritual Opera, Operatic Ritual: Mu-Lien Rescues His Mother in Chinese Popular Culture* (Berkeley: Chinese Popular Culture Project, 1989). Readings in the collection by David Johnson, Andrew Nathan, and Evelyn Rawski (eds), *Popular Culture in Late Imperial China* (Berkeley: University of California Press, 1985) also remain useful.

From Hideous to Hedonist: The Changing Face of the Nineteenth-century Monster

Abigail Lee Six and Hannah Thompson

The nineteenth century can be characterized by political as well as literary upheaval. The French Revolution of 1789 radically changed the way that power relationships were understood and experienced, whilst differing modes of representation, such as the Gothic, Romanticism, Realism, and Decadence, opened up new ways of seeing and representing the world and our place in it. The figure of the monster is omnipresent throughout the nineteenth century as Romanticism's interest in the "grotesque" "initiated a cultural revaluation of monstrosity in all its forms."[1] This chapter will demonstrate how the monster's representation and meaning change in the course of the century to reflect—but also to comment on—the literature and society in which he or she is found.

The nineteenth century's political and literary revolutions did not completely redefine the monster. Rather they overlaid and inflected the monster's pre-existing connotations, which dated back to classical antiquity and beyond. Three key ideas from these long-standing notions remained relevant and form our starting point. Firstly, a monster stands as a visible symbol of something important and usually ominous, collapsing two Latin derivations in the popular imagination: *monere* "to warn" and *monstrare* "to show."[2] Thus, a monster is something put on display as a warning. This meaning is at the centre of Jeffery Jerome Cohen's "monster theory."[3] Secondly, monsters have a long-standing association with being enormous. This is hard to account for and not ubiquitous—conjoined twins used to be regarded by the medical establishment as well as the general public as monstrous, even when

---

1   Miranda Gill, *Eccentricity and the Cultural Imagination in Nineteenth-Century Paris* (Oxford: Oxford University Press, 2009), p. 211.

2   This etymology is discussed by Felton, Steel and Van Duzer in this collection.

3   Jeffery Jerome Cohen (ed.), *Monster Theory: Reading Culture* (London and Minneapolis, MN: University of Minnesota Press, 1996), p. 4.

their size was normal, for example[4]—but remains a persistent element. Thirdly, monstrosity has been connected with mixture since Greco-Roman antiquity, at least: mythological monsters combine the body parts of different animals, whilst creatures like the Minotaur mix human with animal elements. Mixture can also be understood as transgression of boundaries; indeed, many nineteenth-century monsters threaten to destabilize what had been seen as clear and normally uncrossable lines. In so doing, they also question the validity of binary pairs such as visible/concealed, moral/physical and internal/external.[5]

The present chapter will explore how these older ideas of monstrosity inflected newer applications of the concept and were articulated in a range of key French and British nineteenth-century texts. Its three main sections will consider: *Frankenstein* (1818), a foundational work early in the century; *Notre-Dame de Paris* (1831) and *L'Homme qui rit* (1868), a vital pair of works in the middle of the century; and a group of texts indicative of fin-de-siècle concerns. In this way, we will trace the evolution of representations of monstrosity from works appearing earlier in the century up to its final years, by which time authors have moved away from exploring physical deformity and have begun to pave the way for conceptualizations which we still recognize today, whereby monstrosity, disturbingly, has become invisible and potentially ubiquitous, for it lurks within seemingly normal, respectable people[6] and is grounded in anxieties concerning sexuality.

Mary Shelley, *Frankenstein or, The Modern Prometheus* (1818)

Frankenstein has influenced ideas on monstrosity to an extent that can hardly be overestimated, but it did not come out of a literary vacuum. The eighteenth century had seen the inauguration of the extremely popular Gothic novel, the mode to which *Frankenstein* belongs. This had produced the stock character of the Gothic villain, who was certainly morally monstrous but who tended to be at least normal in outward appearance and often decidedly good-looking. *Frankenstein*, then, marks a turning-point in the representation of monsters in the Gothic mode, for whilst it

---

4　See, for example, Laura Hartman et al., "From 'Monsters' to Modern Medical Miracles: Selected Moments in the History of Conjoined Twins from Medieval to Modern Times," on the website of the US National Library of Medicine: <http://www.nlm.nih.gov/hmd/conjoined/age.html>, accessed March 3, 2011.

5　Michel Foucault, *Abnormal: Lectures at the Collège de France 1974–1975*, trans. Graham Burchell, ed. Valerio Marchetti and Antonella Salomoni (London: Verso, 2003), p. 63. See also Lennard J. Davis, "Constructing Normalcy: The Bell Curve, the Novel, and the Invention of the Disabled Body in the Nineteenth Century," in Lennard J. Davis (ed.), *The Disability Studies Reader*, 2nd edn (New York and London: Routledge, 2006), pp. 3–16 for how the invention of the norm influenced nineteenth-century attitudes to "normality" and its opposites.

6　See Weinstock's essay in this collection for a discussion of the ramifications of these concepts in the twentieth and twenty-first centuries.

does not eliminate the morally monstrous villain—he is alive and well in the title character—it introduces and pits him against a physically monstrous being, rather than the hapless damsels who had been his victims previously.

Moreover, since the physical monster in *Frankenstein* has been brought into being by the moral one, the former can be read as a manifestation of the latter's inner monstrosity, sowing the seeds of analogous pairings of inner or moral with outer or physical monstrosity in later nineteenth-century characters, such as Jekyll with Hyde, or Dorian Gray with his picture. Thus, it is possible to analyze Shelley's monster as an autonomous being, as independent as anyone is of a parent, or as a dimension of Frankenstein's character, leading to an implicit debate still being played out today, which interrogates and problematizes the relationship between physical and moral—or visible and invisible—monstrosity.

Frankenstein's creature has impeccable credentials for a monster:[7] he transgresses two normally sacrosanct boundaries by mixing life and death, on the one hand, and the body parts of several individuals, on the other, as he is stitched together from cadavers. He is also over-sized, but, most obviously, most originally—and hence arguably most importantly of all—he is outside the range of normality because he is man-made rather than a product—however aberrant— of nature, the classical pantheon, or the Judaeo-Christian God.[8] This sense of being a completely new type of being leads the monster to identify with Milton's Adam when he reads *Paradise Lost*.[9]

The parallel with Adam goes further and deeper, however, when the monster's character development is considered, for he too is innocent and good in the first instance, a paradigm of the variety of monster whose hideous outer form imprisons a benevolent, even noble-spirited inner self. This combination places Frankenstein's monster initially in a category recognizable from numerous traditional narratives pre-dating Shelley, such as the Beast in "Beauty and the Beast," but which still has currency today. However, in the course of Shelley's novel, the monster becomes malevolent, vindictive, indeed murderous, and to that extent he is also the forerunner of innumerable evil creatures in fantasy and science fiction texts. The turning-point is clearly marked and explained by the monster himself:

---

7   This is also the term used for him most frequently in the novel, appearing 27 times, ahead of "fiend," "daemon," "creature," "wretch," "devil," "being," and "ogre." Chris Baldick, *In Frankenstein's Shadow: Myth, Monstrosity, and Nineteenth-century Writing* (Oxford: Clarendon Press, 1987), p. 10, n. 1.

8   This has struck a chord with the transgendered critic Susan Stryker, who compares the construction of her female body with Victor Frankenstein's assembly of the monster. "My Words to Victor Frankenstein Above the Village of Chamounix: Performing Transgender Rage," in Renée R. Curry and Terry L. Allison (eds), *States of Rage: Emotional Eruption, Violence, and Social Change* (New York: New York University Press, 1996).

9   "Like Adam, I was apparently united by no link to any other being in existence." Mary Shelley, *Frankenstein or, The Modern Prometheus*, ed. Maurice Hindle, revised edn (London: Penguin, 2003), vol. II, ch. vii, p. 132. Further references use the abbreviation *F*.

Finding myself unsympathised with, [I] wished to tear up the trees, spread havoc and destruction around me. ...

There was none among the myriads of men that existed who would pity or assist me; and should I feel kindness towards my enemies? No: from that moment I declared ever-lasting war against the species.[10]

In this development, Frankenstein's monster exemplifies a theory traceable to Francis Bacon's 1597 essay "Of Deformity," which argues that the scornful way in which deformed people are treated leads to the development of particular traits, and the wish to deliver themselves from that scorn spurs them either to great virtue or malice.[11] Thus, for Bacon as for Shelley, physical monstrosity is the indirect cause of moral monstrosity, because the latter is attributable to the cruelty unjustly meted out to those whose appearance falls outside what a particular society deems normal. Percy Shelley, indeed, considered that to be the key message of *Frankenstein*, writing: "the direct moral of the book consists [in]: Treat a person ill, and he will become wicked."[12]

At least, that is the reading suggested by an interpretation of the text which regards the monster as an independent being who can be analyzed in isolation from the character of his creator. However, an equally suggestive but different relationship between physical and moral monstrosity emerges if the monster is read as the embodiment of an aspect of Victor's nature. Then it is Victor's moral monstrosity—his excessive thirst for knowledge and the power which that promises, together with his readiness to sacrifice on such an altar those who love him (and whom he claims to love too); his Promethean arrogance in thinking he can steal the power of creation of a new species from God and the power to give birth from women—which is the cause of the creature's existence and that in turn, arguably, is inseparable from its physical monstrosity. This reading reverses the causal relationship between physical and moral monstrosity: the moral now is the cause of the physical, whether the monster is regarded as separate from Victor or his grotesque doppelgänger. In other words, visible monstrosity can then be read as a symptom, a betrayal of inner evil to the outer world, bringing us back to physical monstrosity as a sign and a warning.

Perhaps this is one reason why, unlike the monster-slayers of classical antiquity, Frankenstein's persecution of his monster is no entry ticket for him to heroic status, but rather forces the reader to ask which of the two is the greater monster: is it Frankenstein for rejecting and wanting to destroy his "child," no matter how ugly he

---

10   *F*, II, viii, p. 139.

11   Francis Bacon, "Of Deformity," in *Essays of Francis Bacon: The Essays or Counsels, Civil and Moral, of Francis Ld. Verulam Viscount St Albans*, <http://www.authorama.com/essays-of-francis-bacon-44.html>, accessed January 15, 2010.

12   Percy Bysshe Shelley, "On *Frankenstein*," in Harry Buxton Forman (ed.), *The Works of Percy Bysshe Shelley in Verse and Prose* (London: 1880), 7:11–14, cited in Mary Lowe-Evans, *Frankenstein: Mary Shelley's Wedding Guest* (New York: Twayne, 1993), p. 14.

is, or is it the monster for turning against the "parent" who gave him life, no matter how badly he treats him? However, Shelley does not stop there, in that closed dyad of mutual antagonism: by showing how others are implicated, a third candidate for monster status is posited. The fact that complete strangers attack the creature on sight[13] suggests that society's attitudes to those who look abnormal is also being critiqued, possibly to the extent that the charge of monstrosity can be laid at their door, too. This chimes with the collective application for the notion of the monster which was current in the wake of the French Revolution. Foucault has observed that those who sympathized with the revolutionary cause found the aristocracy to have deserved extermination for being monsters of sexual depravity as well as preying vampirically on the rest of the population, whilst those whose interests lay in demonizing the revolutionaries characterized their behavior as monstrously violent, animalistic, even cannibalistic.[14] On both sides of the political debate, in other words, the term was being used as a blaming strategy, justifying or critiquing violence against one group or another. To blame the aristocracy by labeling them collectively as monstrous and so justify the actions of the mob in violently exterminating them maps onto a reading of Shelley's novel that takes the monster's side; conversely, to indict the mob as monsters for turning on the aristocracy makes a case for incriminating the monster for turning on Frankenstein, his maker.[15]

Whilst suggestive as far as they go, however, these readings limit the debate on the nature and especially the slippery or arbitrary quality of monstrosity, notably because they exclude the important idea of the relationship between society collectively on the one hand, and the individual monster on the other, highlighted repeatedly in this text and others that will be discussed below. It appears not only in the aforementioned encounters between the monster and the general public, but also indirectly, when the monster incriminates Justine for a capital crime he has committed, leading to her conviction as a child-murderer and thus presenting the "monstrous" individual's relationship with the legal system; since we know Justine is innocent, we are implicitly invited to ask ourselves where to pin the monstrous label, echoing similar concerns already highlighted in *Caleb*

---

13   *F*, II, iii, pp. 108–9.
14   Foucault, *Abnormal*, pp. 97–8. See also, for example, on Marie-Antoinette, a pamphlet issued in the aftermath of her execution characterizing her as a monster, cited in Elizabeth Colwill, "Pass as a Woman, Act Like a Man: Marie-Antoinette as Tribade in the Pornography of the French Revolution," in Dena Goodman (ed.), *Marie-Antoinette: Writing on the Body of a Queen* (London: Routledge, 2003), pp. 139–70, at 160. For Louis XVI, see, for example, "Minutes of the Proceedings of the National Convention in France," where M. François Robert's speech calls him "a monster who disgraces humanity." Published in *The Gentleman's Magazine*, 62/2 (December 1792), p. 1138. For the mob characterized as "an out-of-control monster," see Robert Miles, "The 1790s: The Effulgence of Gothic," in Jerrold E. Hogle (ed.), *The Cambridge Companion to Gothic Fiction* (Cambridge: Cambridge University Press, 2002), pp. 41–62, at 55. For more on this topic, see also Ronald Paulson, "Gothic Fiction and the French Revolution," *English Literary History* 48 (1981), pp. 532–54.
15   For more on this, see Baldick, *In Frankenstein's Shadow*, pp. 16–25.

Williams (1794), by Shelley's father, William Godwin, to whom she dedicated the first edition of *Frankenstein*.[16]

Victor Hugo, *Notre-Dame de Paris* (1831) and *L'Homme qui rit* (1868)

Unlike Shelley's monster, Victor Hugo's most famous creation, Quasimodo, the hunchbacked bell-ringer of *Notre-Dame de Paris*, is not a man-made aberration but a human being whose congenital deformities lead to his vilification and alienation. Nevertheless, in accordance with Bacon's hypothesis and in common with *Frankenstein*, public reaction to Quasimodo's physical monstrosity causes him to embrace monstrous characteristics: he becomes nasty, aggressive, and violent in response to the way he is treated. However, Quasimodo's anti-social behavior does not make him a thoroughgoing moral monster. He has a strong sense of right and wrong, temporarily saves Esmerelda from her unmerited death-sentence by claiming refuge for her in the cathedral (an action diametrically opposed to Shelley's monster's deliberate incrimination of the innocent Justine), and, as his death from a broken heart demonstrates, is capable of love. Hugo's text is central to our discussion of monstrosity because its depictions of the monster go beyond the scientific detachment or lascivious fascination found in other nineteenth-century texts such as Émile Zola's 1890 novel *La Bête humaine* (*The Human Beast*) or Charles Baudelaire's 1857 poetry collection *Les Fleurs du Mal* (*The Flowers of Evil*). Instead, the intelligent and sensitive engagement with physical deformity manifested in *Notre-Dame de Paris*, as well as in Hugo's lesser known *L'Homme qui rit* (*The Laughing Man*) signals a redefinition of the notion of the monster and marks Hugo out as an advocate of difference and a forerunner of modern-day disability theorists.

Numerous film and television adaptations of Hugo's novel have enshrined Quasimodo in the popular imagination.[17] Unlike the inhabitants of Paris who cover their eyes as Quasimodo passes, (post)modern culture is fascinated by him. But the novel's narrator struggles to describe convincingly Quasimodo's monstrosity:

---

16 Pamela Clemit notes *Frankenstein*'s resonance with *Caleb Williams* in the mutually antagonistic relationship of Caleb and Falkland and the implicit question of which is more of a monster, but she does not focus on the striking parallel between the texts in their indictment of the general public and the social/legal system's monstrosity towards the individual lacking in standing or high birth. "*Frankenstein, Matilda*, and the Legacies of Godwin and Wollstonecraft," in Esther Schor (ed.), *The Cambridge Companion to Mary Shelley* (Cambridge: Cambridge University Press, 2003), pp. 26–44, at 32.

17 See Rachel Killick, "*Notre-Dame de Paris* as Cinema: From Myth to Commodity," in J.A. Hiddleston (ed), *Victor Hugo, romancier de l'abîme* (Oxford: Legenda, 2002), pp. 41–62.

Nous n'essaierons donc pas de donner au lecteur une idée de ce nez tétraèdre, de cette bouche en fer de cheval, de ce petit oeil gauche obstrué d'un sourcil roux en broussailles, tandis que l'œil droit disparaissait entièrement sous une énorme verrue, de ces dents désordonnées, ébréchées ça et là, comme les créneaux d'une forteresse, de cette lèvre calleuse sur laquelle une de ces dents empiétait comme la défense d'un éléphant, de ce menton fourchu, et surtout de la physionomie répandue sur tout cela, de ce mélange de malice, d'étonnement et de tristesse.[18]

[We shall not attempt to give the reader an idea of that tetrahedral nose, that horseshoe mouth, that tiny left eye obscured by a shaggy red eyebrow, while the right eye lay completely hidden beneath an enormous wart. Those irregular teeth, with gaps here and there like the battlements of a fortress, that calloused lip, over which one of those teeth protruded like an elephant's tusk, that cleft chin, and above all the facial expression extended over the whole, a mixture of malice, amazement and sadness.][19]

After alerting the reader to the impossibility of successfully depicting Quasimodo's features, the narrator demonstrates the allure of the monstrous by nonetheless attempting to put Quasimodo's appearance into words. He provides an overwhelming series of images that confuse rather than clarify the reader's image of Quasimodo. His use of similes such as "like the battlements of a fortress" and "like an elephant's tusk" distances us from Quasimodo, not only because we see him through a veil of comparative language, but also because the language used evokes ideas of impenetrability, fortitude, and defensiveness. By the end of the passage, the reader is unable to visualize the creature. Cohen has argued that the monster "lurks somewhere in that ambiguous, primal space between fear and attraction, close to the heart of what Kristeva calls 'abjection.'"[20] Like the abject, Quasimodo's deformity, which seems to fascinate and terrify in equal measure, is outside of language.

The lavish illustrations that accompany the 1850 edition of the novel demonstrate that illustrators also have trouble grasping the extent of Quasimodo's deformity. Most either hide or obscure his body. His face, with the one missing eye and protruding tooth, is depicted in more detail, but even when his body is shown he is not the shocking and repulsive monster we expect (Figures 10.1 and 10.2).[21] These representations of Quasimodo reveal that in the nineteenth century, despite realist novelists' desire to depict everything, physical monstrosity can only be fully envisaged in the reader's imagination.

---

18   Victor Hugo, *Notre-Dame de Paris 1482* (Paris: Pocket, 1998), I, v, p. 77. Further references use the abbreviation *NDP*.
19   Victor Hugo, *Notre-Dame de Paris*, trans. and intro. Alban Krailsheimer (Oxford: Oxford University Press, 1993), I, v, p. 58. Further references use the abbreviation *NDP* (trans).
20   Cohen, *Monster Theory*, p. 17.
21   Victor Hugo, *Notre-Dame de Paris, édition nouvelle illustrée* (Paris: Perrotin, 1850). See, for example, the illustrations "Audience au Grand Châtelet" (between pp. 188 and 189) and "Quasimodo au pilori" (between pp. 216 and 217).

AUDIENCE AU GRAND CHÂTELET

Figure 10.1 "Audience au Grand Châtelet," Victor Hugo, *Notre-Dame de Paris, édition nouvelle illustrée* (Paris, 1850).

It is tempting to agree with the inhabitants of Paris who see Quasimodo as an unproblematic manifestation of the grotesque and who celebrate his monstrous appearance by crowning him "Pope of Fools" (I, v). However, his association with the cathedral nuances our perception of him. It is impossible to distinguish Quasimodo completely from Notre-Dame. He inhabits it as a tortoise does its shell, becoming an integral part of it, like the stone gargoyles with which he is confused. This unity between man and monument invites the reader to rethink preconceived notions of the monstrous and rescue Quasimodo from the brink of abjection where the inhabitants of Paris push him. In his ground-breaking manifesto, the Preface to *Cromwell* (1827), Hugo argues that the truly beautiful, which characterizes the modern age, is formed of a combination of the grotesque and the sublime.[22] The logical consequence of this insistence that the sublime is rendered even purer through contact with the grotesque is that the splendor of the cathedral of Notre-Dame is more evident to the reader when it is juxtaposed with Quasimodo's monstrous body. However, in the novel it is Quasimodo, not Notre-Dame, who is elevated to the status of the beautiful. Quasimodo's appearance achieves a

---

22 Victor Hugo, "Preface" to *Cromwell* in *The Essential Victor Hugo*, trans. E.H. and A.M. Blackmore (Oxford: Oxford University Press, 2004), pp. 16–53, at 25 and passim.

QUASIMODO AU PILORI

Figure 10.2 "Quasimodo au Pilori," Victor Hugo, *Notre-Dame de Paris, édition nouvelle illustrée* (Paris, 1850).

harmony between the sublime and the grotesque not achieved by the monumental cathedral. His face is at once "cet idéal du grotesque" ("that grotesque ideal") that the spectators of the competition to choose the Pope of Fools are yearning for and "la grimace sublime qui venait d'éblouir l'assemblée"[23] ("the sublime grimace which had just dazzled the assembly.")[24] Quasimodo possesses a "perfection de ... laideur"[25] ("perfect ugliness")[26] that unites the sublime and the grotesque. His noble spirit and selfless sense of justice further serve to underline his beauty. The harmonious combination of the grotesque and the sublime embodied in the figure of Quasimodo reclaims the monstrous body from the realm of the abnormal by establishing the monster as an essential part of the ideal. In this striking move, Hugo reverses the binary differences between the monstrous and the beautiful that still haunt monster theory today. He argues for a kind of unity that allows differences to exist together. According to Cohen, "the monster is ... a code or a pattern or a presence or an absence that unsettles what has been constructed to be received as natural."[27] Hugo's monstrous images call for a re-evaluation of accepted realities. They ask the reader to rethink the hierarchical binary distinctions between the monstrous and the monumental, the ugly and the beautiful, the grotesque and the sublime, which traditionally give structure and meaning to nineteenth-century narratives.

In *Notre-Dame de Paris*, Hugo's challenge to his readers' preconceptions is not as wide-reaching as this comparison with Cohen's theories might suggest. Despite his figurative demolition of the monumental cathedral, and his suggestion that it is Quasimodo's beholders, rather than Quasimodo himself, who are truly monstrous because of the way they treat him and their inability to see beyond his appearance, Hugo maintains the kind of binary approach whereby the sublime and the grotesque remain locked in a dialectical relationship. He reverses them without questioning the validity of the terms of the pair. Quasimodo's monumental beauty cannot exist without the cathedral's monstrosity and the cathedral loses all meaning when its monumental monster dies.

In Hugo's later novel, *L'Homme qui rit*, the binary pairings reversed in *Notre-Dame de Paris* are dismantled to such an extent that the novel becomes a celebration of monstrosity. The eponymous hero of the novel, Gwynplaine, is artfully disfigured as a child by a band of traveling performers. The group intend to make money out of Gwynplaine's artificial deformity by displaying him as a freak for the paying public. Neither a hapless victim of nature like Quasimodo, nor a failed human attempt to create a beautiful being like Frankenstein's monster, Gwynplaine is a blank canvas on which deformity is crafted. Indeed, nature is incapable of creating the kind of perfect ugliness dreamed up by his deformers. Gwynplaine's designer face, although hideous, possesses an aesthetic completeness and an

---

23   *NDP*, I, v, p. 77.
24   *NDP* (trans), I, v, p. 57.
25   *NDP*, I, v, p. 78.
26   *NDP* (trans), I, v, p. 58.
27   Cohen, *Monster Theory*, p. ix.

artistic perfection that make him a work of art. His face is the perfect example of the "truly beautiful" theorized by Hugo in the Preface to *Cromwell*. It combines the grotesque, born of deviation from accepted norms of human appearance, with the sublime, created when an artist completes a task to perfection. In its combination of opposites, it transcends both and becomes the third, ideal term.

The way in which Gwynplaine is evoked throughout the narrative further emphasizes his status as pure beauty. The narrator of *L'Homme qui rit* does not struggle with descriptions of Gwynplaine as Quasimodo's narrator did. Gwynplaine's features are clearly and succinctly described with much less recourse to the allusions and metaphors deployed in *Notre-Dame de Paris*. Gwynplaine has: "une bouche s'ouvrant jusqu'aux oreilles, des oreilles se repliant jusque sur les yeux, un nez informe fait pour l'oscillation des lunettes de grimacier, et un visage qu'on ne pouvait regarder sans rire" ("A mouth opening up to his ears, ears bending over as far as his eyes, a shapeless nose made for the tricks of a joker's glasses and a face which one could not behold without laughing.")[28] This face can easily be expressed in language because its artificiality, whilst enhancing its beauty, also emphasizes the fact that he, like the prose used to describe him, is a work of artistic creation. When comparison is employed to further evoke his appearance, Gwynplaine is compared not to the monumental beauty of a building, but to that of his blind companion Déa.

Déa's blindness is significant for what it says about Hugo's understanding of disability. Déa is an undoubtedly positive force throughout the novel: she is beautiful, virtuous, and loving. Her disability has no negative impact on her depiction and she is never described as deformed. Just as Quasimodo's comparison with the monumental cathedral changes our understanding of his appearance, so Gwynplaine's association with Déa challenges our assumptions about his deformity. Like the Club of the Ugly (Part II, Book I, Chapter IV) which is "dédié à la difformité" ("dedicated to deformity") and whose members question traditional assumptions about the aesthetics of appearance, the descriptions of Déa and Gwynplaine shatter conventional understandings of disability.[29]

Unlike Quasimodo, Gwynplaine is not ashamed of his deformity and he does not hide it. Instead, he chooses the most public of occupations—*saltimbanque*—and proudly asserts the power of his deformity by using it to entertain thousands of spectators whilst making a comfortable living. In so doing, he challenges the assumption, prevalent in the nineteenth century, that freak-show performers were always pitiful victims exploited and objectified by paying spectators.[30]

---

28 Victor Hugo, *L'Homme qui rit* (Paris: Gallimard, 2002), p. 349. Further references use the abbreviation *LHQR*. Translations are by the authors.

29 *LHQR*, p. 286.

30 See Gill, *Eccentricity and the Cultural Imagination*, p. 131, and Rosemarie Garland Thomson, "Introduction: From Wonder to Error: A Genealogy of Freak Discourse in Modernity," in Rosemarie Garland Thomson (ed.), *Freakery: Cultural Spectacles of the Extraordinary Body* (New York, NY and London: New York University Press, 1996), pp. 1–19.

Gwynplaine's proud acceptance of his deformity, and the control he takes over his own status as subject, is reminiscent of Disability Studies' desire to deliberately recast the negativity traditionally associated with the disabled body in a positive way as a means of asserting the intrinsic cultural and political importance of physical difference. This move—which in turn reminds us of Queer Theory's reclaiming of the once insulting term "queer"—might be described as "an equivocal embrace of the 'insult' that examines the power of this status bequeathed from the outside."[31]

We might argue, nonetheless, that the narrator's description of the reaction which Gwynplaine provokes seems to undermine any possibility that he can reclaim or redefine the meaning of his deformity. Although he is able to make audiences laugh, this laughter quickly turns to horror and disgust. But unlike the freak-show monsters described by French fin-de-siècle writers Huysmans and Vallès, Gwynplaine does not have the same effect on the reader as on his audiences. The narrator's descriptions of him emphasize his humanity rather than his deformity and we do not turn away from him. Instead we regard his audiences, like Quasimodo's beholders and those who recoil from Frankenstein's monster on sight, as monstrous because of their inability to look beyond superficial appearance to the nobility that lies beneath. This emphasis on how Gwynplaine is received announces a shift in the way in which the monster was perceived which, as we shall see in the final section, is more fully articulated in the fin-de-siècle's interest in the inherent monstrosity of decadent society.

The Fin-de-Siècle

In the late nineteenth century, increased interest in teratology—understood here as the science of congenital deformity—as well as sexology, changed the way that monstrosity was depicted.[32] Rather than focusing on the story of the monster's suffering and the impact monstrosity has on the afflicted character and his beholders, as is the case in the works discussed thus far, fin-de-siècle texts are interested in the causes of physical or moral monstrosity and their ramifications for society more generally.

In the wake of France's disastrous defeat in the Franco-Prussian war and the subsequent collapse of the Second Empire, fin-de-siècle authors Joris-Karl Huysmans and Rachilde (Marguerite Vallette-Eymery) saw monstrosity as both

---

31 David T. Mitchell and Sharon L. Snyder, *Narrative Prosthesis: Disability and the Dependencies of Discourse* (Ann Arbor: University of Michigan Press, 2000), p. xii.

32 Evanghélia Stead provides a detailed appraisal of the fin-de-siècle obsession with the monster in *Le Monstre, le singe, et le fœtus: tératogonie et décadence dans l'Europe fin-de-siècle* (Geneva: Droz, 2004). Concerning the development of theories on sexology at this time, it is worth noting Richard von Krafft-Ebing's *Psychopathia Sexualis*, first published in 1886, and Jean-Martin Charcot's work on hysteria at La Salpêtrière hospital, where he started working in 1882.

a symptom of and a metaphor for France's moral degeneration. The heroine of Rachilde's *La Marquise de Sade* (1887) illustrates the impact of science on the fin-de-siècle understanding of the monster. After a violent and abusive childhood, Mary Barbe grows up into a sadistic and murderous man-hater. Whilst Mary's moral monstrosity, like that of Frankenstein's monster, might be explained by the way she is treated, the narrator's refusal to allow the reader any empathy with Mary encourages us to read her cruelty, as her scientist uncle does, as innate, predetermined by both a physical abnormality (according to her uncle, Mary's inordinately long thumbs predetermine her murderous inclinations) and the widespread degeneracy of the French population.[33]

If French fin-de-siècle monsters are pathologized by science, they are inspired by erotic fantasy and desire. Unlike the works by Shelley and Hugo, fin-de-siècle French texts overwhelmingly depict monstrous female heroines who prey upon effete and sensitive male protagonists. These heroines' sadistic and bloodthirsty behavior is rendered doubly monstrous by their subversion of gendered norms, which manifests itself in their sexual voraciousness and their dominant, even predatory actions. Mary Barbe is emblematic of this kind of monstrous woman who goes against the grain of nineteenth-century expectations by becoming financially independent, sexually dominant, and erotically liberated. In this way, *La Marquise de Sade* highlights contemporary anxieties concerning gender roles.

Where Mary differs from other fin-de-siècle female monsters is in her appearance. Unlike her male counterparts, Rachilde does not subscribe to the fin-de-siècle cult of female beauty. Mary is striking rather than devastatingly attractive and, although alluring, she does not have the sexual magnetism of other female monsters such as the vampire minions of Stoker's *Dracula*.[34] This fin-de-siècle obsession with women who combine a strong sexual appetite with a taste for sadism demonstrates the dangerous attraction that the female monster exerts. The figure of Salomé is the archetypal manifestation of the appeal of the monstrous woman. Salomé seduced Herod into giving her anything she wanted. Her request, the head of John the Baptist, testifies to her moral monstrosity.[35] The hero of Huysmans's decadent manifesto *À Rebours* (1884) encapsulates the Decadents' gleeful fascination with the monstrous in his description of Moreau's painting of Salomé:

---

33 Mary's uncle here can be seen to be subscribing to the belief in physiognomy prevalent in the nineteenth century, which held that a body's physical appearance could reveal its interior qualities. See Christopher Rivers, *Face Value: Physiognomical Thought and the Legible Body in Marivaux, Lavater, Balzac, Gautier, and Zola* (Madison: University of Wisconsin Press, 1994) for a more detailed discussion of this phenomenon.

34 Bram Dijkstra shows how the creation of female monsters such as vampires reflects the prevailing nineteenth-century attitude to, and fear of, women in *Idols of Perversity: Fantasies of Feminine Evil in Fin-de-siècle Culture* (New York and Oxford: Oxford University Press, 1986), pp. 333–51.

35 Salomé is a persistent presence at the fin-de-siècle. See Flaubert's "Hérodias" (1877), Oscar Wilde's *Salomé* (1893), and Gustave Moreau's eponymous painting (1876).

Elle devenait, en quelque sorte, la déité symbolique de l'indestructible Luxure, la déesse de l'immortelle Hystérie, la Beauté maudite, élue entre toutes ...; la Bête monstrueuse, indifférente, irresponsable, insensible, empoisonnant, de même que l'Hélène antique, tout ce qui l'approche, tout ce qui la voit, tout ce qu'elle touche.[36]

[She had become, as it were, the symbolic incarnation of undying Lust, the Goddess of Immortal Hysteria, the accursed Beauty exalted above all Beauties ...; the monstrous Beast, indifferent, impossible, insensible, poisoning, like the Helen of ancient myth, everything that approaches her, everything that sees her, everything that she touches.][37]

By describing Salomé as a "Beast," Huysmans positions her, and, by extension, the fin-de-siècle monster more generally, as uncontrollable, uncivilized and outside the realm of the human. This emphasis on the inherent animality of the monster reminds us of its associations with mixture, whilst also establishing a link with the assumptions behind the phenomenon of the Human Zoo. These exhibitions, evidence of the "popular craze for *monstrosity*" that swept through Paris and London in the nineteenth century, showcased natives of various colonized countries, positing them as freakish objects to be stared at and studied.[38] As well as being indicative of the unpalatable fact that "the exhibition of human beings for entertainment and profit was a central though until recently largely neglected feature of French cultural life," Human Zoos also implied that those who differed from the Western norm were physically, intellectually, and culturally abnormal.[39] The same implication may be drawn from Stoker's emphasis on the foreignness of Count Dracula, who, like Huysmans's Salomé, represents the threat of contagious monstrosity by virtue of his vampiric—read sexual—allure. Oscar Wilde, too, presents Dorian Gray's monstrosity as attributable, at least in part, to the contagious effect of others' ideas, even though, in his case, these are not necessarily foreign.[40]

---

36   J.-K. Huysmans, *À Rebours* [1884] (Paris: Gallimard, 1997), pp. 144–5.

37   J.-K. Huysmans, *Against Nature*, trans. Robert Baldick (Harmondsworth: Penguin, 1977), p. 66.

38   Pascal Blanchard, Nicolas Bancel, Gilles Boetsch, Éric Deroo, and Sandrine Lemaire, "Introduction," in Pascal Blanchard et al. (eds), *Human Zoos: Science and Spectacle in the Age of Colonial Empires* (Liverpool: Liverpool University Press, 2008), pp. 1–49, at 10 (italics in the original).

39   Gill, *Eccentricity and the Cultural Imagination*, p. 131.

40   Dorian's downward spiral into monstrosity is triggered by an Englishman, but one of the latter's key tools is a present of a French, which is to say foreign, book, referred to in the text as a "poisonous book" and containing "metaphors as monstrous as orchids" (Oscar Wilde, *The Picture of Dorian Gray* [London: Simpkin, Marshall, Hamilton, Kent, 1913], chapter 10, p. 141). In addition, Dorian's hedonism includes indulging in exotic products and artifacts such as oriental perfumes and furnishings. Thus, his monstrosity has a foreign patina, even though it is London-based. Future references use the abbreviation *DG*.

By placing colonial and deformed bodies alongside each other, such shows invited a problematic conflation of the ethnic and the disabled which encouraged the nineteenth-century interest in eugenics by presenting the monster as an impediment to national, social, political, and scientific progress.[41] The monster became a term used for anything that was different from the European norm, even though fin-de-siècle texts were increasingly suggesting that elements of monstrosity lurk within everyone.

Texts such as Robert Louis Stevenson's *Strange Case of Dr Jekyll and Mr Hyde* (1886) and Oscar Wilde's *The Picture of Dorian Gray* (1890/1891) disturb and problematize the notion of monstrosity as "other" by suggesting that it cannot be kept at such a psychologically safe distance. Both develop and make explicit certain ideas about monstrosity that *Frankenstein* had presented in a subtler, unstated form. Like Victor Frankenstein, Henry Jekyll experiments with the creation of human life and the being which he creates will also end in an antagonistic relationship with him; but instead of presenting this as the giving of life to a creature external to the scientist, now it is explicitly the giving of bodily form to inner monstrosity: the drug used by Jekyll brings forth "a second form and countenance," which are "the expression ... of lower elements in my soul."[42] So the reader has no choice but to see the embodied monster as the product and consequence of his creator's moral monstrosity; what was a possible metaphorical reading of secondary meaning in *Frankenstein* has become primary here.

Dorian Gray presents a more complicated pattern. Firstly, the eponymous character does not create his monster in the straightforward manner of Jekyll or Frankenstein; rather, it is Basil Hallward, who paints the portrait that becomes Dorian's monstrous double. Dorian is not the sole author of his own inner monstrosity either; this has a different creator, Lord Henry Wotton, who enjoys leading him astray. Nevertheless, these two men's activities coalesce to produce the moral monster that is Dorian and the picture that displays this.[43] So whilst Jekyll's inner evil is presented as a fundamental part of the human condition, Wilde comes closer to Shelley's presentation of human nature as turning monstrous due to the effects of the outside world upon the individual. What it is about the outside world that generates Dorian's monstrosity, though, is the opposite of that found in *Frankenstein* and *Notre-Dame de Paris*, where it was the cruelty which the creatures

---

41 See Davis, "Constructing Normalcy," for a demonstration that eugenics was a widespread and perfectly acceptable notion in the late nineteenth and early twentieth centuries.

42 Robert Louis Stevenson, *Strange Case of Dr Jekyll and Mr Hyde* in Roger Luckhurst (ed.), *Strange Case of Dr Jekyll and Mr Hyde and Other Tales* (Oxford: Oxford University Press, 2006), pp. 1–66, at 54. Further references use the abbreviation *JH*.

43 Judith Halberstam regards Lord Henry as "a kind of Frankenstein figure" because "he sees Dorian as a live experiment," but she also acknowledges that "Dorian is also Basil Hallward's creation," without, however, explaining where he fits into her parallel with Shelley. *Skin Shows: Gothic Horror and the Technology of Monsters* (Durham, NC and London: Duke University Press, 1995), pp. 54–5.

encountered that turned them from noble-spirited to malevolent, a factor too—if not the sole one—in Rachilde's depiction of the morally monstrous Mary. For Wilde's protagonist, it is the excessively privileged treatment that he receives on all sides, thanks to his beauty and wealth, combined with the temptation of hedonism spread before him by Lord Henry, which corrupts him.

A further key divergence between Stevenson's and Wilde's treatment of moral monstrosity is that *Jekyll and Hyde* rests upon the idea that people can conceal their inner evil. That is why Dr Jekyll is regarded as a pillar of respectable society, and only science fiction—the bringing into being of Mr Hyde—makes visible what would otherwise have remained undetectable to onlookers. By contrast, *Dorian Gray* posits, as Hallward says, that "sin is a thing that writes itself across a man's face. It cannot be concealed."[44] Here the supernatural needs to be evoked to make Dorian's monstrosity *in*visible, by transferring the signs of it to the picture.

So, unlike the fin-de-siècle's fatal women, whose inner character remains masked by physical attractiveness, moral monstrosity in Stevenson and Wilde is given a visible form. Two of the choices which Stevenson makes in this regard are telling. Firstly, in common with the description of Quasimodo, Mr Hyde is indescribable or, at least, what is monstrous about him is so:

> He must be deformed somewhere; he gives a strong feeling of deformity, although I couldn't specify the point. He's an extraordinary looking man, and yet I really can name nothing out of the way. ... I can't describe him. And it's not want of memory.[45]

Thus, the repugnance which he evinces cannot be traced to his face or physique, in a marked departure from Frankenstein's monster and many others before and since. This text, then, is not setting out to show how cruel people are towards those who look abnormal; such a message has apparently come off the literary agenda at the fin-de-siècle, perhaps because of the uneasy popularity of the freak show. Secondly, in the cultural context of anxieties around the degeneration of the human race, Stevenson opts for a physical appearance that is reminiscent of an earlier stage of human evolution: Hyde is smaller than Jekyll and described as "dwarfish,"[46] with hairy hands.[47] Utterson reflects: "The man seems hardly human! Something troglodytic,"[48] and Jekyll twice alludes to his being "apelike."[49] This implies that the vice which Hyde embodies is something animal, primitive, atavistic, with the logical corollary that virtue is a product of civilization. Such descriptions of Hyde are not dissimilar to those of the specimens of the Human Zoo, but the important difference is that Stevenson denies readers the comfort of conceptualizing such

---

44   *DG*, chapter 12, p. 167.
45   *JH*, p. 9.
46   *JH*, p. 15.
47   *JH*, p. 62.
48   *JH*, p. 16.
49   *JH*, pp. 65 and 66.

monstrosity as "other." And this is the opposite of the Rousseau-istic concept of the noble savage corrupted by civilization and echoed in Frankenstein's monster, as well as Dorian Gray.

Wilde's strategy is consistent with the converse logic of his narrative. If monstrosity for Stevenson derives from the vestiges of primitive savagery surviving in the civilized man and normally controlled by his maturity and spiritual and ethical education, it makes sense that Hyde should be smaller and younger than Jekyll. If Wilde, on the other hand, presents moral monstrosity as a product of the corruption of the cynical outside world, we should not be surprised that the picture blends the ageing process with the signs of vice, whilst the magically preserved human Dorian retains his beauty, presented as the quintessence of both innocence and youth. Thus, when Dorian stands before the portrait holding a mirror, he wonders which are "more horrible, the signs of sin or the signs of age."[50]

Flowing from this contrast between Shelley's, Stevenson's, and Wilde's presentation of the source of moral monstrosity comes the primary character's attitude to the monstrous creature in each case. Whilst Frankenstein rejects and flees in horror as soon as he successfully animates his monster, Jekyll embraces and accepts the "ugly idol"[51] which he sees in the mirror when he first metamorphoses into Hyde, significantly, because he recognizes it as part of himself. This is a realization which Victor could not be further from countenancing consciously, but which may well be the underlying explanation for the irrational violence of his reaction. Dorian, too, recognizes himself in the changing appearance of the picture, but his attitude is more ambivalent:

> He would sit in front of the picture, sometimes loathing it and himself, but filled, at other times, with that pride of individualism that is half the fascination of sin, and smiling with secret pleasure, at the misshapen shadow that had to bear the burden that should have been his own.[52]

Notwithstanding these important differences between Stevenson's and Wilde's presentation of monstrosity, it is played out on the same terrain and one which echoes not only Rachilde's configuration in *La Marquise de Sade*, fin-de-siècle portrayals of Salomé, Hugo's in *Notre-Dame de Paris* and Shelley's in *Frankenstein*, but also the earlier generation of Gothic novels in the eighteenth century. There, as here, the arena is—explicitly or implicitly—sexual. Whether we choose to read Frankenstein's monster as part of his creator or as an independent being, or, paradoxically, as both, it is striking that the monstrosity of the two characters is presented as inextricably bound up with their sexuality: as soon as the monster is animated, Frankenstein has a nightmare with overtly sexual connotations;[53] he postpones his marriage to complete his work and postpones going to his wife on

---

50   *DG*, chapter 11, p. 144.
51   *JH*, p. 55.
52   *DG*, chapter 11, p. 157.
53   *F*, I, v, p. 59.

their eventual wedding night, ostensibly to protect her from the monster, but in fact giving the latter the opportunity to kill her.[54] The monster, on the other hand, is driven to his extremes of murderous malevolence because Frankenstein has refused to make him a monster-wife, which is to say a sexual partner. Quasimodo's bitterness stems in part from his unrequited love for Esmerelda and the fact that his monstrosity is such that she cannot even look at him. Mary Barbe, as we have seen, is a sadistic sexual predator, embodying anxieties concerning femininity and female sexuality at the fin-de-siècle, which are also articulated in the fin-de-siècle hero's enthrallment to sexually alluring but sadistic heroines, whilst these two British texts from the same period evoke analogous fears concerning masculinity and male sexuality.

Although trampling a child and murdering a politician are the only crimes explicitly laid at Hyde's door, scholars have indicated that there is a strong undercurrent suggesting his sexual depravity. They link the child with under-age prostitution and find many more or less coded references to homosexuality in the text.[55] Similarly, Wilde avoids any explicit enumeration of Dorian's sexual proclivities. However, like Rachilde, who implies that Mary engages in all sorts of dubious and unnamed nocturnal practices, he feeds our imagination carefully: people have "heard the most evil things about him" and "strange rumours about his mode of life" are in circulation; he uses an assumed name and wears a disguise when he stays near the docks;[56] and when he reappears in society, some men "whisper to each other in corners," while others want nothing to do with him.[57]

It would seem, then, that fin-de-siècle moral monstrosity is tightly enmeshed with sexuality but that this resides in its very lack of definition or perhaps even definability, echoing Hugo's claim in the physical domain that Quasimodo evaded description too. Such nebulousness makes sense in the sociohistorical context, for if monstrosity of any kind can only be defined in contrast to normality, then in a period when beliefs concerning what constituted normal sexuality—for men as for women—were being profoundly shaken, its abnormal, monstrous obverse would necessarily remain beyond the reach of clarity. This, however, only increases the power of the motif: these texts haunt precisely because their characters' monstrosity lacks delineation; readers may imagine what they will, but are always left wondering if perhaps it may be something far worse, of which they are ignorant.

---

54   *F*, III, vi, p. 199.
55   For the link with child prostitution, see Linda Dryden, "'City of Dreadful Night': Stevenson's Gothic London," in Richard Ambrosini and Richard Dury (eds), *Robert Louis Stevenson, Writer of Boundaries* (Madison: University of Wisconsin Press, 2006), pp. 253–64, at 254–5). For the homosexual undertone, see Alan Sandison, *Robert Louis Stevenson and the Appearance of Modernism: A Future Feeling* (Basingstoke and London: Macmillan, 1996), pp. 252–3. Fred Botting notes the suggestion of a homosexual relationship between Jekyll and Hyde only as a misinterpretation by others within the narrative (*Gothic* [London and New York: Routledge, 1997], p. 142).
56   *DG*, chapter 11, p. 144.
57   *DG*, chapter 11, p. 158.

Thus, by the end of the century, monstrosity was no longer necessarily being viewed as an aberration of nature visited upon the very few, but as something residing within apparently normal, respectable, and respected individuals. The authors may present different hypotheses as to the reason for this monstrous element of the human condition, ranging from the degenerate nature of society, as in Dorian's case, to civilization's failure fully to annihilate the vestiges of primitive savagery, as in Jekyll's; alternately, like Rachilde, they may vacillate between presenting monstrosity as inborn for some—harking back to ideas of aberration— or inflicted from without through cruelty, echoing both of Hugo's monsters and Frankenstein's. Notwithstanding these divergences, however, what all these fin-de siècle monsters have in common is what, arguably, makes them more frightening than any visibly deformed character: they collectively pose the question of the extent to which monstrosity is containable and concealable. The answer is deeply disturbing either way, contributing no doubt to the enduring hold that these narratives have on our imagination: if we follow Stevenson's logic that, science fiction apart, monstrosity is concealed and contained within the normal and indeed virtuous, that means that we are surrounded by monsters who emphatically do not warn us of this by their appearance, belying the term's etymology. On the other hand, if we opt for Wilde's hypothesis, the implication is that sooner or later the poisonous world turns us all into monsters, and in our prosaic non-supernatural lives, we cannot prevent that seeping through our respectable outer selves and betraying our darkest secrets to all those whom we encounter.

Centaurs, Satyrs, and Cynocephali: Medieval Scholarly Teratology and the Question of the Human

Karl Steel

Medieval Scholarly Teratology: Key Features

In Jerome's late fourth-century *Life of Saint Paul, the First Hermit*, the nonagenarian monk Anthony searches the desert for the still older hermit Paul. Anthony prays for help, God sends a centaur, and, after crossing himself, Anthony asks it for directions. The centaur, "barbarum nescio quid infrendens, et frangens potius uerba quam proloquens inter horrentia ora" [gnashing out I don't know what foreignness, and with words broken rather than spoken through its bristly mouth],[1] extends its right hand and points out the way. A bewildered Anthony next meets a "homunculum … aduncis naribus, fronte cornibus asperata, cuius extrema pars corporis in caprarum pedes desinebat" [little man with a pointed nose, a forehead bristling with horns, whose extremities terminated in goat's feet].[2] Anthony girds himself in prayer, but instead of threatening him, the creature only offers him provisions. Anthony, "quisnam esset interrogans" [asking it what it was], receives this answer:

---

1   Jerome, *Trois vies de moines: Paul, Malchus, Hilarion*, ed. Edgardo Martín Morales, trans. [into French] Pierre Leclerc (Paris: Cerf, 2007), p. 158. Throughout, all translations are my own unless otherwise indicated. For a recent discussion of the range of meanings of "barbarus" in the ancient world—including among its connotations "subhuman," "bestial," "crude," and "irrational," and, in Roman rhetorical training, "solecistic"— see Ian Smith, *Race and Rhetoric in the Renaissance: Barbarian Errors* (New York: Palgrave Macmillan, 2009), pp. 25–43. I thank Alan Stewart for supplying this reference.

2   Jerome, *Trois vies de moines*, p. 160. Subsequent quotations from this episode are from this page and page 162.

> *Mortalis ego sum, et unus ex accolis eremi, quos uario delusa errore gentilitas*
> *Faunos, Satyrosque et Incubos colit. Legatione fungor gregis mei. Precamur*
> *ut pro nobis communem Dominum depreceris; salutem mundi olim uenisse*
> *cognouimus, et in uniuersam terram exiit sonus eius.*

> *[I am mortal, and one of those inhabitants of the desert which the gentiles,*
> *deluded by various errors, worship as Fauns, Satyrs, and Incubi. I am here as*
> *an ambassador of my flock. We plead with you to pray to our common Lord,*
> *whom we know to have come for the salvation of the world, and whose sound*
> *has gone out all over the world.]*

Anthony weeps, beats the ground with his staff, and berates Alexandria for worshiping monsters rather than Christ, since if "bestiae Christum loquuntur" [beasts speak of Christ], surely Alexandria's devotees of zoomorphic gods should do better.[3] Jerome ends the story with the authenticating claim that, during the reign of Constantine:

> *Alexandriam istiusmodi homo uiuus perductus magnum populo spectaculum*
> *praebuit, et postea cadauer exanime, ne calore aestatis dissiparetur, sale*
> *infusum, et Antiochiam, ut ab imperatore uideretur, adlatum est.*

> *[A living man of this kind was brought to Alexandria and shown as a great*
> *spectacle to the people; afterwards, its lifeless body, to prevent its dissolution*
> *in the Summer's heat, was salted, and carried to Antioch to be seen by the*
> *Emperor.]*

These two encounters represent in miniature most of the features of medieval scholarly teratology: traditional monsters; an exotic setting; an at least implicit presentation of monsters as embodied metaphors; a concern with whether monsters can be converted to Christianity or to some other norm; and finally an attempt to decide whether any given monster should be recognized as human or only as a kind of beast. The following pages explore each of these points before turning to another zoomorph, the cynocephalus, whose canine head, barking voice, and anthropomorphic, bipedal body compelled scholars to confront their own humanity as an uncertainty rather than as a *fait accompli*.

Jerome drew his monsters from the stock of his Mediterranean scholarly culture.[4] Other medieval teratologic traditions, such as those preserved and developed in

---

3   A similar complaint appears in the fourteenth-century *Letters to the Desert Brothers*, falsely attributed to Augustine of Hippo, which observes that, since the pagan priests of the blemmyae and cyclops keep chaste, abstain from meat, and drink very little water on holy days, then certainly human, Christian priests ought to do just as well; see Jacques Paul Migne (ed.), *Patrilogiae cursus completus: series latina*, 217 volumes (Paris: Garnier, 1844), vol. 40, pp. 1303–4 (hereafter *PL*).

4   Even after Jerome claimed to have abandoned the Latin classics, his library included

Breton lais, Old English epic poetry, and Norse sagas, might include werewolves and sometimes werebears, great serpents, serpentine or aquatic women who married and bred with human men, the green children of the otherworld, elves, trolls, the *draugar*—the unrestful dead of Icelandic sagas—and Cain's wicked, deformed descendants, most famously, Grendel and his mother.[5] But apart from the few monsters of the Bible (including Job's Leviathan and Behemoth; Isaiah and Jeremiah's *reguli*, or basilisks; and the giants of Genesis), only the monsters of classical legend—centaurs, cyclops, sirens, and the like—could claim universal representation throughout the medieval millennium. They can be distinguished by several key features. First, they tended not to be anomalous, singular beings; they were hybridized or hypertrophic species of animals, like the aspidochelone, an enormous, wily cetacean whose back resembled an island, or they were entire races of "homines" (men) or "gentes" (peoples), with their own habitats and regions, their own martial, religious, dietary, and burial practices, in short, their own culture.[6] Second, these monsters and their cultures were preserved in teratologic catalogs, which over the centuries both stabilized the tradition and generated new monsters within it by combining and splitting monstrous characteristics.[7] Influential examples

---

the works of Virgil, Horace, Terrence, and perhaps Sallust; Megan Hale Williams, *The Monk and the Book: Jerome and the Making of Christian Scholarship* (Chicago: University of Chicago Press, 2006), pp. 161–5. Jerome could have discovered satyrs in the *Eclogue VI* and centaurs in *Georgic II*, or both the satyr and centaur in either the wilderness monsters of Isaiah 34:14 or the dancing desert "pilosi" [hairy ones] of Isaiah 13:21, whose numbers included, per Jerome's Isaiah commentary (*PL* 24: 159B-C), fauns, centaurs, and sirens.

5 For werewolves, see Leslie Sconduto, *Metamorphoses of the Werewolf: A Literary Study from Antiquity through the Renaissance* (Jefferson, NC: McFarland & Co., 2008); for literary werewolves, see especially Leslie Sconduto (trans.), *Guillaume de Palerne* (Jefferson, NC: McFarland, 2004); "Bisclavret" in Marie de France, *Die Lais der Marie de France*, ed. Karl Warnke, 3rd edn (Halle: Max Niemeyer, 1925); and Amanda Hopkins (ed. and trans.), *Melion and Biclarel: Two Old French Werwolf Lays* (Liverpool: University of Liverpool Department of French, 2005). For werebears and several other monsters and marvels (including bellicose but honorable fish shaped like human knights), see Giles Roussineau (ed.), *Le Roman de Perceforest*, 9 volumes (Geneva: Droz, 1987–2007). For one example of an aquatic woman, see Geoffrey of Auxerre, *On the Apocalypse*, trans. Joseph Gibbons (Kalamazoo: Cistercian Publications, 2000), pp. 150–1. For elves, see Alaric Hall, *Elves in Anglo-Saxon England: Matters of Belief, Health, Gender and Identity* (Woodbridge, Suffolk: Boydell Press, 2007).

6 See, for example, the cynocephali in Mandeville's travels, which "riȝt as we say oure Pater Noster and oure Auez apon oure bedes, riȝt so þe kyng sayse ilk day apon his bedes ccc. praieres to his godd before he ete" [just as we say our "Our Father" and our "Hail Mary" with our rosaries, so does the king say 300 prayers to his god every day on his rosary before he eats]; George Warner (ed.), *The Buke of John Maundeuille* (Westminster: Nichols and Sons, 1889), p. 97.

7 John Block Friedman, *The Monstrous Races in Medieval Art and Thought* (Syracuse: Syracuse University Press, 2000), p. 23. For a typology of medieval monsters, see Claude-Clair Kappler, *Monstres, démons et merveilles à la fin du Moyen Age*, 2nd edn (Paris: Payot & Rivages, 1999), pp. 115–83.

Figure 11.1   Cynocephalus, Blemmya, and other monstrous humans, Jean de
Vignay, *Miroir historial*, J. Paul Getty Museum, Los Angeles, Ms.
Ludwig XIII 5, v1, fol. 67v, circa 1475

of the catalogs, which appear in encyclopedias of natural history, travel narratives, letters real and fabricated, and astrological commentary, include those found in Pliny's first-century *Natural History*, Solinus's third-century *Collection of Memorable Things*, Martianus Capella's fifth-century *Marriage of Philology and Mercury*, Isidore of Seville's seventh-century *Etymologies*, and the *Book of Monsters*, a Latin work produced perhaps in mid-seventh- or mid-eighth-century England.[8] These figures

---

8   Surveys of medieval catalogs of monsters and of medieval teratology include Friedman,
Monstrous Races; Kappler, *Monstres, démons et merveilles*; Claude Lecouteux, *Les monstres
dans la pensée médiévale européenne*, 3rd edn (Paris: Presses de l'Université de Paris-
Sorbonne, 1999); Claude Lecouteux, *Les monstres dans la littérature allemande du Moyen
Âge: contribution à l'étude du merveilleux médiéval* (Göppingen: Kümmerle, 1982); and
Rudolf Wittkower, "Marvels of the East: A Study in the History of Monsters," *Journal
of the Warburg and Courtauld Institutes* 5 (1942), pp. 159–97. Essay collections on the
topic include Karin E. Olsen and L.A.J.R. Houwen (eds), *Monsters and the Monstrous*

also appear in popular late medieval texts, like Jean de Vignay's *Miroir historial* (Figure 11.1). The catalogs' humanoid monsters included those of unusual size, such as giants and pygmies; those with strange bodies, including hermaphrodites, sciopods, which hop about on one enormous foot and in the noonday sun use it as a parasol, and blemmyae, whose faces are on their chests; those with strange diets, including those who ate only milk, apples, delectable odors, or human flesh; and centaurs, cynocephali, and other zoomorphs.

Jerome locates his monsters where the Middle Ages would have expected to find them, on the edges of what he construes as the civilized world, where nature becomes unfamiliar. As he explained, because the desert "solet ... monstruosorum ferax animalium" [customarily gives birth to monstrous wildlife], it may have "istam quoque gignat bestiam" [also birthed such a beast].[9] Medieval encyclopedias, as well as Alexander the Great's legendary encounters with cynocephali and other monsters as he traveled to and through India,[10] led people like the thirteenth-century friar William of Rubruck to expect things to become increasingly strange the further they traveled from home. William baffled the Mongols by asking them about "monstris sive de monstruosis hominibus de quibus narrat Ysidorus et Solinus" [the monsters or human monstrosities about which Isidore and Solinus speak].[11] Gerald of Wales, in a twelfth-century geographical and ethnographic study of Ireland, proposed that, like the East, the distant parts of the West have their

---

in Medieval Northwest Europe (Leuven: Peeters, 2001); Timothy S. Jones and David A. Sprunger (eds), *Marvels, Monsters, and Miracles: Studies in the Medieval and Early Modern Imaginations* (Kalamazoo: Medieval Institute Publications, 2002); and Bettina Bildhauer and Robert Mills (eds), *The Monstrous Middle Ages* (Cardiff: University of Wales Press, 2003). For a review of scholarship on the dating and provenance of the *Liber monstrorum,* see Andy Orchard, *Pride and Prodigies: Studies in the Monsters of the Beowulf-Manuscript* (Toronto: University of Toronto Press, 2003), pp. 86–7.

9   Jerome, *Trois Vies de moines*, p. 158. See also his letter to Rusticus (letter 125), which speaks of the "gryphas, et dracones, et immensorum corporum monstra" [griffins, dragons, and monsters with enormous bodies; *PL* 22: 1074] travelers are likely to encounter in India. Pliny the Elder, *Natural History*, ed. and trans. H. Rackham, vol. 3 (Cambridge: Harvard University Press, 1940), VIII.16, p. 33, famously asserted that "Africa is always producing some novelty." For more such notions in classical thought, see James Romm, *The Edges of the Earth in Ancient Thought: Geography, Exploration, and Fiction* (Princeton: Princeton University Press, 1992), pp. 82–120. For a survey of this intellectual tradition through the Middle Ages, see Mary Baine Campbell, *The Witness and the Other World: Exotic European Travel Writing, 400–1600* (Ithaca and London: Cornell University Press, 1988), pp. 47–86.

10 For example, the "Letter of Alexander to Aristotle" in Orchard, *Pride and Prodigies*, pp. 204–23.

11 Anastasius van den Wyngaert (ed.), *Itinera et relationes Fratrum Minorum saeculi XIII et XIV* (Florence: Colle S. Bonaventurae, 1929), p. 269. Translation in Christopher Dawson (ed.), *Mission to Asia* (Toronto: University of Toronto Press, 1980), p. 170. The missionary John de Marignollis recorded similar discussions in his *Chronicon Bohemorum*; see Robert Bartlett, *The Natural and the Supernatural in the Middle Ages* (New York: Cambridge University Press, 2008), p. 105.

own prodigies, where "Quociens quippe tanquam seriis et veris fatigata negociis paululum secedit et excedit, remotis his partibus quasi verecundis et occultis natura ludit excessibus" [Nature, as if worn out by serious and true labors, withdraws a little, and in these distant places plays with these shameful and secret excesses].[12] Other medieval writers placed their monsters in the far South, or, as Aethicus of Istria did in his seventh- or eighth-century *Cosmographia*, in the distant North.[13] In sum, medieval maps had no *terra incognita* awaiting the reports of explorers: when the twelfth-century monk Honorius of Auten wrote that "post paradisum sunt multa loca deserta et invia, ob diversa serpentum et ferarum genera"[14] [beyond paradise (in the far East) there are many wild and inaccessible places, on account of the hostile serpents and many kinds of wild beasts], the very inaccessibility of the far East argued for the existence of monsters. Nor were only the far edges so populated. Nearby lands might be imaginatively rewritten as strange wildernesses to justify a *mission civilisatrice*. Gerald of Wales gave Ireland this treatment in the twelfth century; the *Owl and the Nightingale* Scotland in the thirteenth; and *Sir Gawain and the Green Knight* Wales in the fourteenth: as Gawain traverses Wales, the object of centuries of imperialist longing by the English crown, a land only miles from the site of the poem's composition, he has to cut his way through dragons and "wodwos"[15] (wildmen). Only the wonder tradition itself limited what nature could do in these spaces. The tradition offered distant worlds unconstrained by familiar bodily forms or customs, worlds uncommitted to distinguishing between the categories of human, animal, or plant, organic or inorganic, life or non-life. Out there, in the wondrous beyond, travelers might gape at hordes of human-faced monkeys, trees whose fruit hatched sheep, or diamonds that mated and bred.[16]

---

12 Gerald of Wales, "Giraldus Cambrensis *In Topographia Hibernie*: Text of the First Recension," ed. John Joseph O'Meara, *Proceedings of the Royal Irish Academy* 52 (1949), p. 119; my translation relies upon Gerald of Wales, *The History and Topography of Ireland*, revised trans. John Joseph O'Meara (London: Penguin, 1982), p. 31. For other such statements, see *The Book of Monsters*, in Orchard, *Pride and Prodigies*, p. 254, on the "occulto orbis terrarum" [secret parts of the globe] where monsters flourish, and Ranulf Higden's fourteenth-century *Polychronicon*, which observes "that at the farthest reaches of the world often occur new marvels and wonders, as though Nature plays with greater freedom secretly at the edges of the world than she does openly and nearer us in the middle of it" (quoted in Friedman, *Monstrous Races*, p. 43).

13 Aethicus of Istria, *Die Kosmographie des Aethicus*, ed. Otto Prinz (Munich: Monumenta Germaniae Historica, 1993), p. 114. See also Adam of Bremen, *History of the Archbishops of Hamburg-Bremen*, trans. Francis J. Tschan (New York: Columbia University Press, 1893), pp. 200 and 206, and the ninth-century missionary Rimbert, discussed below, both of whom also set monsters in the far North.

14 *De Imagine Mundi*, in PL 172: 123b-c.

15 On Gerald and Ireland, see Jeffrey Jerome Cohen, *Hybridity, Identity, and Monstrosity in Medieval Britain: On Difficult Middles* (New York: Palgrave Macmillan, 2006), pp. 85–90; Neil Cartlidge (ed. and trans.), *The Owl and the Nightingale* (Exeter: University of Exeter Press, 2001), lines 1007–12; A.C. Cawley and J.J. Anderson (eds), *Sir Gawain and the Green Knight; Pearl; Cleanness; Patience* (London: Dent, 1991), line 722.

16 For human-faced monkeys and lamb-fruit, see the travels of the thirteenth-century

Readers of this literature might be frightened into staying at home or tempted to conquer. Thinking on and past the limits of their humanity, they might be enticed into letting themselves be transported entirely, like Marie de France's Lanval, who abandoned the mundane frustrations of King Arthur's court in favor of the delights and honors offered by a queen of an Elvish otherworld.[17]

Medieval teratologists might otherwise apply their exegetical training to make moral sense of monsters, wresting themselves from dangerous curiosity towards such a "mira diversarum formarum ... ubique varietas"[18] (plentiful and astonishing a variety of contradictory forms) by enclosing monsters into neat structures of significance. The supposed derivation of the word "monster" from "monitus" (admonition), "demonstrare" (indicate), or "monstrare" (show)[19] warrants such allegoresis, or interpretative special pleading,[20] whether in medieval or more recent readings, such as Jeffrey Jerome Cohen's argument that "the monstrous body is pure culture. A construct and a projection, the monster exists only to be read [and] signifies something other than itself."[21] Reading exegetically, Patricia Cox Miller argues that the affability and piety of Jerome's satyr and centaur, which contrast with their legendarily violent hedonism, might have been understood by Jerome's audience as demonstrating the desiccating powers of Christian desert asceticism.[22] Monsters function more overtly as moral

---

friar Odoric of Pordenone, included in Henry Yule (ed. and trans.), *Cathay and the Way Thither: Being a Collection of Medieval Notices of China* (London: Hakluyt Society, 1866), pp. 119 and 144; Odoric's travels are a key source text for the travels of John Mandeville (whose "longest journey was to the nearest library," C.W.R.D. Moseley (trans.), *The Travels of Sir John Mandeville* (London: Penguin, 1983), p. 12), who includes these stories as well as the material on the mating rituals of diamonds: Warner, *Buke of John Maundeville*, p. 79.

17   Marie de France, *Lais der Marie de France*.

18   Edition and translation of Bernard's *Apologia ad Guillelmum Abbatem*, in Conrad Rudolph, *The "Things of Greater Importance": Bernard of Clairvaux's Apologia and the Medieval Attitude toward Art* (Philadelphia: University of Pennsylvania Press, 1990), p. 283, where Bernard famously complains about the grotesque monsters of Cluniac architecture. For Rudolph's commentary on Bernard's passage on monstrous hybrids, see pp. 119–24 and 336–7, where Rudolph explains his translation of "diversarum" as "contradictory."

19   Isidore of Seville, *The Etymologies of Isidore of Seville*, ed. and trans. Stephen A. Barney et al. (New York: Cambridge University Press, 2006), p. 244.

20   For allegoresis as imposed allegory, as contrasted to "true allegory," see Maureen Quilligan, *The Language of Allegory: Defining the Genre* (Ithaca, NY: Cornell University Press, 1979), pp. 29–31.

21   Jeffrey Jerome Cohen, "Monster Culture (Seven Theses)," in Jeffrey Jerome Cohen (ed.), *Monster Theory: Reading Culture* (Minneapolis, MN: University of Minnesota Press, 1996), p. 4.

22   Patricia Cox Miller, "Jerome's Centaur: A Hyper-Icon of the Desert," *Journal of Early Christian Studies* 4 (1996), pp. 209–33. For further discussion, see Virginia Burrus, "Queer Lives of Saints: Jerome's Hagiography," *Journal of the History of Sexuality* 10 (2001), pp. 442–79.

signs in the *Cursor Mundi*, a late thirteenth-century versified Christian history, when four monstrous Saracens beg to see the wood that will become the True Cross. Immediately, "als milk þair hide becom sa quite, / and o fre blod þai had þe heu, / and al þair scapp was turnd neu"[23] [their skin became as white as milk, and they had the color of those of noble blood, and their shape was entirely made new], so demonstrating both the spiritual potency of Christianity and the symbolic, physiognomic understanding of the monstrous body as an outward sign of a degenerate spirit.[24] Many modern commentators, inspired as much by psychoanalysis as by medieval physiognomy, interpret monsters as at once threatening and erecting the boundaries of the self by generating, on the one side, the categories of the law and the symbolic order, both of which idealize limits and clear classification,[25] and on the other what Slavoj Žižek describes as the "shapeless, mucous stuff of the life-substance,"[26] "the crawling chaos" of H.P. Lovecraft's fiction, whose only imperative is to proliferate, mutate, and reaffiliate. Such readings, in a kind of post-symbolic symbology, understand monsters to embody "the conditions under which subjectivity disintegrates."[27] The monster eludes the grasp of any given interpretation; it embodies "all that the subject excludes in order to be what it is, to have the identity that it does";[28] it is the always unnamable *it*, the stranger.

---

23 Richard Morris et al. (eds), *Cursor mundi* (London: Kegan Paul, Trench, Trübner & Co., 1874), lines 8120–22.

24 For a classic treatment of monstrous Saracens, see C. Meredith Jones, "The Conventional Saracen of the Songs of Geste," *Speculum* 17 (1942), pp. 201–25, and more recently, Suzanne Conklin Akbari, *Idols in the East: European Representations of Islam and the Orient, 1100–1450* (Ithaca, NY: Cornell University Press, 2009), pp. 140–7 and 155–99. For a similar judgment, see Gerald of Wales, "*In Topographia Hibernie*," p. 192, which observes that "contra nature legem natura producat" [nature produces things contrary to the law of nature] among the Irish because of their sinfulness; for more on the monstrous body as a "legible sign of guilt," see Asa Simon Mittman, *Maps and Monsters in Medieval England* (New York and London: Routledge, 2006), pp. 89–92.

25 For articulations of similar points inspired by Cohen's "Monster Culture," see Mittman, *Maps and Monsters*, p. 6, "monsters ... through their extreme outlandishness, cast their creators as paragons of normality," and Elaine L. Graham, *Representations of the Post/Human: Monsters, Aliens and Others in Popular Culture* (Manchester: Manchester University Press, 2002), p. 39, where "monsters have a double function ... simultaneously marking the boundaries between the normal and the pathological but also exposing the fragility of the very taken-for-grantedness of such categories ... the horror of monsters rests in this capacity to destabilize axiomatic certitudes."

26 Slavoj Žižek and Mladen Dolar, *Opera's Second Death* (New York: Routledge, 2002), p. 192, among other places.

27 Barbara Creed, "Freud's Worst Nightmare: Dining with Dr Hannibal Lecter," in Steven Jay Schneider (ed.), *Horror Film and Psychoanalysis: Freud's Worst Nightmare* (New York: Cambridge University Press, 2004), p. 192.

28 Michael Grant, "Ultimate Formlessness: Cinema, Horror, and the Limits of Meaning," in Schneider (ed.), *Horror Film and Psychoanalysis*, p. 177.

The Question of the Human

Demythologizers derided reports of monsters as credulous misapprehensions. Some 40 years after Jerome, Palladius of Galatia adapted Jerome's story into Greek, and declared the centaur to be "Satan, who had taken the form of the creature in order that he might terrify the blessed man."[29] Isidore explained that centaurs were actually the "horsemen of Thessaly," so skilled in battle that "horses and men seemed to have one body";[30] Albert the Great identified cynocephali as great apes;[31] and, in the seventeenth century, François Hédelin argued that the salted satyr presented to the emperor was a monkey, and that which had spoken to Jerome, a demon.[32] Jerome's monsters, however, are neither symptoms of mistaken identity nor only moral signs. They possess an actual, material existence, though Jerome cannot quite decide how to classify them. He identifies the centaur as "hominem equo mixtum" [a man mixed with a horse] and "ille" [that one], before declaring his uncertainty as to whether it is a kind of living feature of the landscape itself or a demon; he calls the satyr "homunculum" [little man], "animal" [living thing], one of the "beastiae" [beasts], and "istiusmodi homo" [this kind of man], here too unable or unwilling to determine conclusively what the creature is. At stake in these varying classifications is the question of what should be done with monsters. Medieval Christianity numbers among many systems of thought that classify humans as the only worldly life to be treated as an end in itself; everything else God created for the sake of humans: animals were for food or labor or, in the case of dangerous beasts and vermin, to deflate human pride. In this anthropocentric system, monsters judged to be unclassifiable might be eradicated as unnatural scandals.[33] Those judged to be animals could be treated as unmournable, "nonlife," objects available for human use.[34] Those judged as human would be granted the privileges of humanity: potentially converted and baptized, protected in this mortal life as subjects of charity, and in the Last Judgment saved from the general destruction of creation and resurrected into bodies that would finally be made right.[35]

---

29 Ernest Alfred Wallis Budge (ed. and trans.), *The Paradise of the Holy Fathers* (London: Chatto & Windus, 1907), p. 199.
30 Isidore, *Etymologies*, XI.iii.37, p. 246.
31 Friedman, *Monstrous Races*, p. 215, n. 29.
32 François Hédelin, *Des satyres brutes, monstres et démons. De leur nature et adoration contre l'opinion de ceux qui ont estimé les satyres estre une espece d'hommes distincts & separez des adamicques* (Paris: Nicholas Buon, 1627), pp. 60–2. I thank Nicola Masciandaro for supplying this reference.
33 Like the wild man in an Alexander legend, immolated "because he lacked reason and was thus like a beast" (quoted in Friedman, *Monstrous Races*, p. 145).
34 See the questions in Judith Butler, *Precarious Life: The Powers of Mourning and Violence* (New York: Verso, 2004), p. 20: "Who counts as human? Whose lives count as lives? And, finally, What *makes for a grievable life*?" (original emphasis).
35 On the "correction" of human bodies, monstrous or otherwise, in the resurrection, see Augustine, *The City of God*, trans. Marcus Dods (New York: Modern Library, 1950),

A key medieval treatment of this problem appears in Augustine of Hippo's *City of God*, an enormous early fifth-century Christian doctrinal compendium. Several medieval texts hypothesized that monsters had descended from Cain, or from Noah's son Ham, or from those of Adam's children who, recapitulating the first sin, disobeyed their father by eating poisonous herbs.[36] Unconcerned with the corporeally evident culpability of monsters, Augustine sought only to determine what they were. He supposed that if monsters had descended from Adam, they should be understood to be as human as any of Adam's non-monstrous descendants. Augustine lists several monsters—cyclops, hermaphrodites, pygmies, sciopods, blemmyae—and finally the cynocephali, about which he professes himself particularly stymied: "What shall I say of the cynocephali, whose doglike head and barking proclaim them more beasts than men?" Augustine proposes incredulity as the proper response: "we are not bound to believe all we hear about all kinds of men [omnia genera hominum]."[37] He then reiterates his heuristic for distinguishing between humans and non-humans, namely, that *anyone* born from a human is a rational mortal, regardless of unusual shape, color, movement, sound—including, presumably, barking—and so forth. An unspoken but necessary correlative to this statement is that some creatures, human in shape, in fact may not be descended from Adam: what Augustine offers to monsters he takes away from the non-monstrous, stirring up a miasmic uncertainty around all creatures.

Genealogical arguments offered little immediate satisfaction to those trying to decide about the status of particular creatures that they encountered. Some thinkers simply refused to resolve the issue. Orosius's world history waffles over whether to speak of the minotaur "more aptly as a wild animal with the qualities of a man or as a human being with the qualities of a beast";[38] Honorius of Auten's *The Image of the World* observes inconclusively that "sunt ibi quaedam monstra, quorum quaedam hominibus, quaedam bestiis ascribuntur"[39] [there are certain monsters, some of which can be characterized as humans, and some as beasts]; more recently, Naomi Reed Kline classified the satyrs and centaurs of the thirteenth-century Hereford world map as both "animals" and as "strange races."[40] By contrast, Thomas of Cantimpré's preface to his encyclopedia's chapter on "The Monstrous Humans of the East" concludes "animalibus vero monstruosis animam inesse non credimus" [truly I do not believe that monstrous animals have a soul],

---

XXII.19, pp. 841–3; for a review of Christian scholastic doctrine on the non-resurrection of animals, see Francesco Santi, "Utrum Plantae et Bruta Animalia et Corpora Mineralia Remaneant post Finem Mundi: L'animale eterno," *Micrologus* 4 (1996), pp. 231–64.

36 Friedman, *Monstrous Races*, pp. 93–5.

37 Augustine, *City of God*, XVI.8, p. 531, translation modified by reference to Augustine, *De civitate Dei*, ed. Bernhard Dombart, 2 volumes (Leipzig: Teubner, 1909), vol. 2, p. 135.

38 Paulus Orosius, *The Seven Books of History against the Pagans*, trans. Roy Deferrari (Washington, DC: Catholic University of America Press, 1964), I.13, p. 34.

39 *De Imagine Mundi*, in *PL* 172: 172a-b.

40 See the discussion of Naomi Reed Kline, *Maps of Medieval Thought: The Hereford Paradigm* (Woodbridge, Suffolk: Boydell Press, 2001), pp. 95 and 143, in Mittman, *Maps and Monsters*, pp. 45–6.

asserting that if any such creature imitates human behavior, it does so only because its anthropomorphic aspects grant it that ability.[41]

The "soul" which Thomas references is the rational soul, a kind of soul which mainstream medieval Christianity argued that only humans possessed among mortal life.[42] In the absence of genealogical charts, thinkers had to develop some means to determine the presence of this immaterial, rational thing, essential for being human. Medieval arguments defined reason in several ways, most notably as the capacity to extract oneself mentally from one's immediate surroundings by, for example, making free choices or developing abstract concepts. Later generations, following the medieval groove, would argue that this extractive or reflective capacity granted the ability to "respond" rather than merely "react," or to apprehend things "as such" rather than to be *weltlos*, "world poor," wholly and unknowingly engulfed by one's environment.[43] Representative arguments for monstrous irrationality and therefore animality include Albert the Great's assertion that pygmies lack reason, since their language only mimics human language, and Peter of Auvergne's that pygmies only seem to worship the sun, because like flowers they are heliotropic.[44] However, the logic of these proofs finally turns against humans themselves: how could Alexander prove the authentic self-motivation of human language or Peter that of human piety? Firmer proof of human reason and particularity could be found in the human domination of animals, for, as Augustine and many others argued, whatever else humans had in common with animals, they could subjugate any animal without being subjugated in turn.[45] Thus in Chrétien de Troyes's twelfth-century romance *Yvain*, when the knight

---

41   Thomas of Cantimpré, *Liber de natura rerum: Editio princeps secundum codices manuscriptos,* ed. Helmut Boese (Berlin: W. De Gruyter, 1973), p. 97.

42   For a history of this concept of reason, see Richard Sorabji, *Animal Minds and Human Morals: The Origins of the Western Debate* (Ithaca, NY: Cornell University Press, 1995).

43   For an influential critique of Lacan's distinction between animal "reaction" and human "response," and of Heidegger's assertion of animal "world poverty," see Jacques Derrida, *The Animal That Therefore I Am,* ed. Marie-Louise Mallet, trans. David Wills (New York: Fordham University Press, 2008).

44   Friedman, *Monstrous Races,* pp. 190–6. For Peter of Auvergne, see Joseph Koch, "Sind die Pygmäen Menschen? Ein Kapitel aus der philosophischen Anthropologie der mittelalterlichen Scholastik," *Archiv für Geschichte der Philosophie* 40 (1931), pp. 209–13.

45   Augustine, *On Free Choice of the Will,* trans. Thomas Williams (Indianapolis: Hackett, 1993), p. 13. See also Adelard of Bath, *Questions on Natural Science,* Section 15, in *Conversations with His Nephew: On the Same and the Different; Questions on Natural Science; and, On Birds,* ed. and trans. Charles Burnett (Cambridge: Cambridge University Press, 1998), which explains how humans, without horns or great strength or swiftness, master animals: "For he has that which is much better and more worthy than these—I mean reason, by which he excels the very brute animals so much that they are tamed by it, and, once tamed, bridles are put on them, and once bridled, they are put to various tasks." Burnett's note, p. 230, n. 27, links Adelard's argument to Cicero, *De re publica* III.2 and Lactantius, *De opificio Dei* III, 16–19. See also Epictetus, *Discourses* 2.8.7–8 and Clement of Alexandria, *Paedagogus* 3.12, quoted and discussed in Janet E. Spittler, *Animals in the Apocryphal Acts of the Apostles: The Wild Kingdom of Early Christian Literature* (Tübingen: Mohr Siebeck, 2008), pp. 19 and 37.

Calogrenant encounters a giant peasant, its face a farrago of animal forms, speaking "nient plus c'une beste feïst" [no more than a beast would], Calogrenant demands: "Va, cor me di / se tu es boine chose ou non" [go on, tell me if you are a good thing or not]. The peasant's reply, "je sui uns hom" [I am a man], and its additional assurance that he is not a shapeshifter ("tes com tu voi. / Je ne sui autres nule fois" [I'm just as you see / I'm never anything else]), does not satisfy the knight. Only when the peasant brags about beating and terrifying his livestock into submission does Calogrenant accept the peasant's self-identification as human.[46] The monk Ratramnus of Corbie arrives at a similar solution in his mid-ninth-century *Letter on the Cynocephali*, apparently written in response to his fellow monk's question about whether he should preach to cynocephali. This letter, rare among scholarly texts for its focus on a single creature and for eschewing moralization in favor of practical missionary concerns, surveys the cynocephalic literature for evidence of their rationality. He presents the cynocephali as farming, dressing modestly, and organizing themselves into villages governed by law, and he recalls the existence of a cynocephalus, born "Reprobus" and renamed "Christopher" upon his conversion to Christianity, venerated as a saint.[47] With this evidence, Ratramnus declares that, despite cynocephalic barking, those who doubt cynocephalic rationality must themselves be irrational. In the course of his argument, Ratramnus abandons Augustine's genealogical approach to the question. Instead, he proves cynocephalic rationality by observing that they keep domestic animals, which "fieri posse, si bestialem et non rationalem animam haberent, nequaquam ... siquidem homini animantia terrae fuisse divinitus subjecta Geneseos lectione cognoscimus"[48] [could in no way be if they had a bestial and not a rational soul, since

---

46   Chrétien de Troyes, *Le Chevalier au Lion (Yvain)*, ed. David F. Hult, in Chrétien de Troyes, *Romans*, ed. Michel Zink (Paris: Le Livre de Poche, 1994), lines 322–31.

47   For the medieval cynocephalic tradition, see Friedman, *Monstrous Races*, pp. 70–5 and several works by Claude Lecouteux: "Les Cynocéphales: Étude d'une tradition tératologique de l'Antiquité au XIIe s," *Cahiers de civilisation médiévale* 24 (1981), pp. 117–29; *Les monstres dans la littérature allemande*, vol. 2, pp. 20–8; and *Les monstres dans la pensée médiévale européenne*, pp. 31–6. For background on Saint Christopher, see David Williams, *Deformed Discourse: The Function of the Monster in Mediaeval Thought and Literature* (Montreal: McGill-Queen's University Press, 1996), pp. 286–97, which considers Christopher's antecedents in Hermes, Anubis, and Herakles; also see Friedman, *Monstrous Races*, pp. 72–5; Venetia Newall, "The Dog-Headed Saint Christopher," in Linda Dégh et al. (eds), *Folklore on Two Continents: Essays in Honor of Linda Dégh* (Bloomington: Trickster Press, 1980), pp. 242–9; Joyce Tally Lionarons, "From Monster to Martyr: The Old English Legend of Saint Christopher," in Jones and Sprunger, *Marvels, Monsters, and Miracles*, pp. 167–74; and David Gordon White, *Myths of the Dog-Man* (Chicago: University of Chicago Press, 1991), chapter 2: "The Cynocephalic Saint." Eastern Orthodox iconography sometimes depicts the saint with a horse's head, while the iconography of the Roman church tends to imagine Christopher as merely a giant rather than as a dog-headed man. The saint first appeared in the fourth-century Egyptian *Acts of Bartholomew* and spread into France and Spain by the sixth century and Germany, England, and Ireland by the eighth.

48   For the letter, which survives in a single eleventh-century manuscript, see Ernst Dümmler (ed.), *Epistolae variorum XII*, MGH Epistolae 6 (Berlin: Weidmann, 1925),

the living things of the earth were subjected to men by heaven, as we know from reading Genesis]. Yet such arguments, however convincing they might be, effectively strip humans of any essential difference from animals. If humans rely on domination to distinguish themselves from animals, and to either include or exclude monsters from being recognized as human, then the category of the human becomes visible as a structural position, a retroactive, relative, and contingent effect of the action of dominating animals.[49] By seeking certainty, humans have lost it; they have had to think through the conditions of their human existence, discovering through the monster the speciousness of their claims for essential difference.[50]

Cynocephalic Gestures

The dog-like features of the cynocephali render them particularly resistant to classification as either familiar or strange, human or animal, because of the dog's taxonomic ambivalence. The dog is "the animal pivot of the human universe," as David Gordon White remarks, "lurking at the threshold between wildness and domestication and all of the valences that these two ideal poles of experience hold," or, as Laura Hobgood-Oster puts it, "the ultimate example of the excluded other who is and always has been present."[51] Relied upon for hunting and protection, and trusted as a household companion, the dog associates more intimately with humans than do other animals. At the same time, it resembles a wolf—recall the French idiom for twilight, "entre chien et loup," when the dog or wolf both become uncanny—whose carnivorousness presents, as Aleksander Pluskowski termed it, a "cosmological dilemma" to humans by challenging their dominance over other animals.[52] No wonder, then, that the cynocephalus often functioned as a limit case in the medieval teratological tradition. Ratramnus devoted an entire letter to the subject, extending reason to the cynocephali even while provisionally denying it to pygmies, the backwards-footed antipodes,

pp 155–7 (another edition is available in *PL* 121: 1153–6). My translation is guided by Paul Edward Dutton (ed. and trans.), *Carolingian Civilization: A Reader*, 2nd edn (Peterborough, Ontario: Broadview Press, 2004), pp. 452–5.

49   Karl Steel, "How to Make a Human," *Exemplaria* 20 (2008), pp. 3–27.

50   See Jacques Derrida and Elizabeth Weber, "Passages—from Traumatism to Promise," in Elizabeth Weber (ed.), *Points ...: Interviews, 1974–1994*, trans. Peggy Kamuf (Stanford: Stanford University Press, 1995), pp. 385–6: "Faced with a monster, one may become aware of what the norm is and when this norm has a history—which is the case with discursive norms, philosophical norms, socio-cultural norms, they have a history—any appearance of monstrosity in this domain allows an analysis of the history of norms."

51   White, *Myths of the Dog-Man*, p. 15; Laura Hobgood-Oster, *Holy Dogs and Asses: Animals in the Christian Tradition* (Urbana: University of Illinois Press, 2008), p. 84.

52   Aleksander Pluskowski, *Wolves and the Wilderness in the Middle Ages* (Woodbridge, Suffolk: Boydell Press, 2006), p. 15. For discussion of the biological and cultural resemblances—and enmities—between wolf and dog, see, in the same book, pp. 85–9.

Figure 11.2   Cynocephali, labeled "gigantes," Hereford World Map, detail.

Ethiopian giants, and short-lived Indian women, who potentially stem from Adam but who nonetheless might not be "homines ratione praeditos"[53] [humans gifted with reason]. The teratological list that begins Augustine's excursus on monsters in *City of God* concludes with the cynocephali, offering them as his knottiest problem. Cynocephali are the only monster that Isidore classifies as more bestial than human, even while he recognizes the humanity of the Artabatians, who "are said to walk on all fours, like cattle," and the Hippopodes, who "have a human form and horses' hooves."[54] The difficulty, for Ratramnus, Augustine, and Isidore, is not the fabled anthropophagy of the cynocephali, nor their odd shape, but their barking, which at once serves as their means of communication and obscures or occludes their rational expression.

The Hereford World Map concretely depicts this issue with its two pairs of cynocephali, one near Eden, the other in Scandinavia, both of whom are facing and apparently communicating with their mates (Figure 11.2 and see Figure 18.2).

---

53   Dümmler, *Epistolae*, p. 156.
54   Isidore, *Etymologies*, p. 245.

The map may be representing them as speaking in human voices marred by barking, as in the *Book of Monsters*, which declares that barks "corrumpunt" [contaminate] cynocephalic speech,[55] or perhaps their barking is only a slight impediment, as in a thirteenth-century moralized adaptation of Thomas of Cantimpré's *On the Nature of Things*, where cynocephali "com chien glatisent .../ mes sens de gens est lors savoirs" [bark like dogs, but human sense is their knowledge].[56] Alternately, the Hereford map may follow Isidore in depicting only irrational barking without language, exemplifying the virtually pleonastic old French phrase "mue beste" [mute beast].[57] There is, however, yet another possibility: barking that is intelligible as speech to the cynocephali but not to humans, that is, a non-human worldly language. If the barking of the Hereford map is not opposed to sense, but rather evidences sense as language, the "mes" of the adaptation of *On the Nature of Things* should perhaps become an "et" [and]—barking is not a perversion of speech, but only another language—or the passage might indeed be read "et sens *de chiens* [of dogs] est lors savoirs," as if dogs had a "sens" that humans might recognize as rational in its own right. If barking or any other animal noise can be speech, humans might have to reconsider other animals' noises as potentially, though incomprehensibly, linguistic. Animals may be incomprehensible not because they have nothing to say, but because humans have divided themselves from them by, so to speak, erecting a kind of Tower of Babel: this symbol of human arrogance, legendarily built by a "mighty hunter" (Genesis 10:9), is the largest detail on the Hereford map, significantly near the Edenic cynocephali. A key argument for human difference from other animals collapses.[58] The possibility of meaningful animal language already appears in the longstanding grammatical distinction between confused and distinct voices,[59] a definition that, rather than distinguishing

---

55 Orchard, *Pride and Prodigies*, I.16, p. 268.

56 Alfons Hilka (ed.), "Eine altfranzösische moralisierende Bearbeitung des Liber de Monstruosis Hominibus Orientis von Thomas von Cantimpré, De Naturis Rerum," in *Abhandundgen der Gesellschaft der Wissenschaften zu Göttingen: Philologisch-Historische Klasse 7* (Berlin: Weidmannsche Buchhandlung, 1933), lines 489–90.

57 Frédéric Godefroy, *Dictionnaire de l'ancienne langue française et de tous ses dialectes du IXe au XVe siècle*, 10 volumes (Paris: F. Vieweg, 1881), s.v. "mu."

58 See the allied point in H. Peter Steeves's engagement with Lévinas's well-known dismissal of dogs from any direct ethical concern in *The Things Themselves: Phenomenology and the Return to the Everyday* (Albany: State University of New York Press, 2006), p. 56: "If the dog barks, his contribution to the conversation will not be dull; he has something to say. And yet if we prepare ourselves to hear it—to hear it truly—we risk being harmed, risk injury from his ability to speak as much as from what he has to say. We risk our status."

59 A typical example appears in Thomas of Cantimpré, *Liber de natura rerum*, p. 26: "Omnis autem vox articulata est aut confusa: articulata hominum, confusa animalium. Articulata est, que scribi potest ut a, e; confusa, que scribi non potest ut gemitus infirmorum et voces volucrum aut bestiarum" [All voices are either distinct or indistinct: the human voice is distinct, and animal indistinct. A distinct voice is one that can be written, such as A or E; an indistinct voice is one that cannot be written, such as the moaning of the sick or the voices of birds and beasts].

between the rational and irrational, distinguishes between voices dividable into syllables and therefore writable, and non-syllabic and therefore unscriptable voices, like the crying of infants or the hissing of snakes. Such definitions focus not on the vocal content but on the tools for recording voices. They imply not that snakes lack language, but that human understanding has failed them; that any animal, any creature, including the centaur of Jerome's tale, might be understood by humans as well, if only humans could develop the capacity to construe or to transcribe its voice properly.

Even if barking was thought to have sense, one can still imagine a medieval thinker arguing that cynocephali lacked the full range of human communication. Abelard, for example, argued that dogs can signify emotions with their barking, but that they cannot make rational arguments.[60] The Hereford images offer no such comfort to pretensions of human communicative particularity, nor to the equally pernicious logocentric and anticorporeal prejudices that treat spoken, rather than gestural, language as the necessary evidence of reason: for the Hereford cynocephali form their hands into oratorical gestures recognizable to any trained viewer.[61] This is not the merely instrumental communication imputed to animals; rather, the cynocephalic postures suggest intellectual work or at least conviviality. Faced with the irresolvable possibility of cynocephalic rationality, humans could preserve the polar categories of human and animal only arbitrarily, by absorbing cynocephali into their humanity or by declaring them animal. Both responses simultaneously declare the ineffectiveness of using noise or other "animal" traits to classify cynocephali — or *any* creature, monstrous or otherwise — as either animal or human. The only certainty in such a scheme derives from a chauvinist tautology: if cynocephalic barking is irrational animal noise, or if it is human language, that is only because humans declare it to be so.

It is usual, as I have done above, to talk about monsters as establishing or blurring boundaries, as provoking or allaying anxiety, as rich symbolic sites

---

60   Peter Abelard, *Dialectica*, ed. Lambertus Marie de Rijk (Assen: Van Gorcum, 1956), p. 114. For an extended treatment of the medieval linguistic topos of the barking dog, whose bark thinkers assigned various degrees of naturalness, intentionality, and sometimes even cultural meaning, see Umberto Eco, Robert Lambertini, Constantino Marmo, and Andrea Tabarroni, "'Latratus Canis' or: The Dog's Barking," in John Deely, Brooke Williams, and Felicia E. Kruse (eds), *Frontiers in Semiotics* (Bloomington: Indiana University Press, 1986), pp. 63–73.

61   Other depictions of cynocephali making similar gestures include a thirteenth-century copy of Solinus's *Collectanea* (Milan, Ambrosian Library, MS cod. C. 246 inf., f. 57), reproduced in Kline, *Maps of Medieval Thought*, p. 109, and Sebastian Münster's sixteenth-century *Cosmographiae universalis*, Book VI, reprinted in Campbell, *The Witness and the Other World*, p. 46. For the pose of the gesturing cynocephalus near Eden, characterized by Mittman, *Maps and Monsters*, p. 186, as a "codified medieval gesture ... of speech," see Quintilian, *Institutes of Oratory*, trans. John Selby Watson, 2 volumes (London: G. Bell and Sons, 1902), XI.3.98, p. 367: "Sometimes we hold the two first fingers apart, without, however, inserting the thumb between them, but with the two lower fingers slightly curved inwards, and the two upper ones not quite straightened."

for thinking through, founding, disrupting, transgressing, and/or thickening various identitarian positions of gender, faith, race, sexuality, species, and so on. Of course, these approaches to teratology will continue to be useful, but before imputing anxiety, prejudice, and violence to encounters with monsters, we might allow ourselves to continue to be had by the curiosity for monsters responsible for this very volume, while also recognizing the communality of this feeling with medieval teratology itself. I am not recommending the grasping curiosity that inspired the transportation—kidnapping, perhaps—of the satyr from Alexandria and from thence as a corpse to Antioch; nor that which inspired Duke Ernst to return from a land of monsters bringing a cyclops, a panotius (whose ears were as long as his body), a pygmy, which he presented to the emperor, and a giant, which he kept for himself.[62] I recommend, rather, what inspired Yvain to follow his cousin Calogrenant's route, hoping that he too could behold the monstrous peasant.[63] Once Yvain meets the herdsman, his adventure begins, and he is never quite able to go home again. Curiosity is not directing at knowing the truth;[64] it does not anticipate where it will lead; by breaking the structures of what we know and what we can predict, curiosity might open us up to something entirely new, for "a future that would not be monstrous would not be a future; it would already be a predictable, calculable, and programmable tomorrow."[65] To be led by curiosity, to accept "the invitation to explore a spacious corporeality beyond the specious boundaries of the human,"[66] is to be in some sense "contra naturam," against nature, exceeding the useful, the rational, the predictable, the automatic and proper.

As a model for a curious encounter with monsters, consider the account of sheep-killing werewolves from an eleventh-century poem on Irish wonders by Bishop Patrick of Dublin. Patrick ends not with condemnation, nor with an attempt to determine whether the werewolves are criminal, human, animal, demonic, or some other, hitherto unimagined category. Instead, he ends with "nos miramur et omnes" [and we all wonder at the sight].[67] This is an ending that

---

62   Carolyn Dussère and J.W. Thomas, trans., *The Legend of Duke Ernst* (Lincoln, 1979), pp. 118–22; for a recent discussion of this work, see Debra Higgs Strickland, "The Sartorial Monsters of *Herzog Ernst*," *Different Visions* 2 (2010), http://differentvisions.org/two. html. For an account of a modern "monster" displayed in this way, see Clifton Crais and Pamela Scully, *Sara Baartman and the Hottentot Venus: A Ghost Story and a Biography* (Princeton, 2008).

63   Chrétien de Troyes, *Le Chevalier au Lion*, lines 708–11.

64   This is one of the reasons why curiosity is a vice; see Thomas Aquinas, *Summa Theologica*, trans. Fathers of the English Dominican Province (New York, 1947), 2a2ae, q. 167, art. 1.

65   Derrida and Weber, "Passages," p. 386.

66   Jeffrey Jerome Cohen, "Inventing with Animals in the Middle Ages," in Barbara A. Hanwalt and Lisa J. Kiser (eds.), *Engaging with Nature: Essays on the Natural World in Medieval and Early Modern Europe* (Notre Dame, Indiana, 2008), p. 55.

67   Aubrey Gwynn, ed. and trans., *The Writings of Bishop Patrick, 1074-1084* (Dublin, 1955), pp. 56-71. For Irish werewolves, see Kim R. McCone, "Werewolves, Cyclopes, Díberga

refuses to end. Bishop Patrick and his companions, amazed, let themselves linger in their curiosity, wondering as they look without knowing where they might be taken.

and Fíanna: Juvenile Delinquency in Early Ireland," *Cambrian Medieval Celtic Studies*, 12 (1986): pp. 1-22; John Carey, "Werewolves in Medieval Ireland," *Cambrian Medieval Celtic Studies*, 44 (2002): pp. 37–72; Catherine E. Karkov, "Tales of the Ancients: Colonial Werewolves and the Mapping of Postcolonial Ireland," in Patricia Clare Ingham and Michelle R. Warren (eds.), *Postcolonial Moves: Medieval Through Modern* (New York, 2003), pp. 99-100; and Matthieu Boyd, "Melion and the Wolves of Ireland," *Neophilologus*, 93 (2009): pp. 555–70.

Invisible Monsters: Vision, Horror, and Contemporary Culture

Jeffrey Andrew Weinstock

It takes a village to make a monster.

By this, I mean that nothing or no one is intrinsically or "naturally" monstrous. Instead, as Jeffrey Jerome Cohen points out in "Monster Culture (Seven Theses)," his introduction to his collection of academic essays on monstrosity, *Monster Theory: Reading Culture* (1996), the monster's body is always "pure culture," the embodiment of culturally specific fears, desires, anxieties, and fantasies.[1] What follows from this is that ideas of monstrosity and the forms that monsters take will differ across time and from place to place. This stands to reason—what scared people (and what they hoped for) in, say, twelfth-century Slovenia will obviously differ from what scares people (and what they hope for) in twenty-first-century America. We inevitably make our own monsters with the ingredients we have on hand, so the recipe keeps changing—even when the monsters themselves have been passed down from generation to generation.

The implications of the shifting social constructions of ideas of monstrosity are particularly significant when one bears in mind that what is monstrous is always defined in relation to what is human. The monster is, as Cohen appreciates, "difference made flesh";[2] it is the other, the "not us," that which a culture rejects, disowns, disavows, or, to borrow from Julia Kristeva, "abjects."[3] What this means is that to redefine monstrosity is simultaneously to rethink humanity. When our monsters change, it reflects the fact that we—our understanding of what it means to be human, our relations with one another and to the world around us, our conception of our place in the greater scheme of things—have changed as well.

This chapter will discuss a sequence of interrelated trends governing contemporary Western ideas and representations of monstrosity. While there is of

---

1   Jeffrey Jerome Cohen (ed.), *Monster Theory: Reading Culture* (Minneapolis, MN: University of Minnesota Press, 1996), p. 4.
2   Cohen, *Monster Theory*, p. 7.
3   Julia Kristeva, *The Powers of Horror: An Essay on Abjection*, trans. Leon S. Roudiez (New York: Columbia University Press, 1982), p. 1.

course some continuity between present-day representations of monstrosity and those of previous generations, the differences are telling and offer provocative insight into culturally specific anxieties and desires. To consider our current monsters is to reflect on how we think about ourselves and our relation to the world. I will begin by observing the contemporary disconnection of monstrosity from physical appearance. Beginning with the nineteenth-century Romantics and acquiring a substantial degree of momentum in the twentieth century—especially from post-Second World War reconsiderations of ethnic and racial difference—one significant trend in representing the monster has been to decouple physical abnormality from assumptions about intelligence, character, or morals. As presented in Mary Shelley's *Frankenstein* (1818) and elaborated on in Tim Burton's updated version of Shelley's seminal Gothic tale, *Edward Scissorhands* (1990), looking different is no longer sufficient to categorize a creature as monstrous. Instead, such narratives shift the emphasis onto oppressive cultural forces that unjustly ostracize or victimize those who are physically divergent. When the "monster" becomes the protagonist and culture becomes the antagonist, ideas of normality and monstrosity must be reconsidered. This trend of "sympathy for the devil" culminates in contemporary narratives such as the *Twilight* series (both book and film) in which one aspires toward monstrosity as an escape from the stultification of hegemonic social forces of normalization.

What follows from this decoupling of monstrosity from appearance is an important cultural shift that aligns monstrosity not with physical difference, but with antithetical moral values. Monstrosity thus is reconfigured as a kind of invisible disease that eats away at the body and the body politic, and manifests visibly through symptomatic behavior. I will suggest here that this reconfiguration of monstrosity surfaces in contemporary cultural narratives in four connected ways: (1) through the psychopath (and his first cousin, the terrorist) who lives among us and could be anyone; (2) through the faceless corporation or government agency that finds its impetus in greed and corruption, and sends forth its tendrils into the cracks and crevices of everyday life; (3) through the virus that silently infiltrates and infects the body; and (4) through the conceit of the revenge of an anthropomorphized nature that responds to human despoilment of the environment in dramatic and deadly ways. What links these four related manifestations of contemporary monstrosity is their invisibility and potential ubiquity, and the response that they elicit is a form of paranoia most evident in contemporary conspiracy theories.

I will then conclude this discussion of present-day monstrosity with some consideration of one form that the response to the fear that monsters are everywhere takes—what I will refer to as "rational irrationalism" or the construction of nonsensical origins. These are horror stories and monster movies that, to a certain extent circling around to my initial discussion of "sympathy for the devil," go back in time in the attempt to explain the origins of the monster. The attempt here is to offer a rational explanation for irrational behavior by inserting that behavior into a familiar narrative framework, be it childhood neglect and abuse, scientific hubris, or magic. These narratives, however, ultimately offer only a semblance of logic while in actuality failing to demystify anything. The monster, as Cohen notes, always escapes,[4] can never finally be known or captured fully—which is part of its monstrosity.

Sympathy for the Devil

Representations of monsters in mainstream media arguably vacillate back and forth between general cycles of identification and non-identification that develop out of and respond to specific cultural conditions. For example, many of the classic horror movies of the 1930s, such as *Frankenstein* (1931), *The Mummy* (1932), and *King Kong* (1933), offer the viewer sympathetic monsters victimized by cultural forces that reflect the shared senses of alienation and persecution felt by those traumatized by the Great Depression, while monster movies of the 1950s, giving shape to cultural anxieties about communism and atomic energy, offer creatures such as giant irradiated ants (*Them!* 1954) and the Blob (*The Blob*, 1958), for which it is difficult to feel anything other than loathing.[5] Despite these localized cycles, however, the overall trend in monstrous representation across the twentieth century and into the twenty-first has been toward not just sympathizing but empathizing with— and ultimately aspiring to be—the monster. Touchstone twentieth-century texts demonstrating this shift in response to established categories of monstrosity are John Gardner's novel *Grendel* (1971), a retelling of the Beowulf myth from the monster's perspective, and Anne Rice's *Vampire Chronicles* series, featuring her vampire heroes Louis and Lestat, which present to the reader a very attractive representation of the vampire. Twenty-first-century mainstream representations of monsters, most notably animated films oriented toward children such as *Shrek* (2001) and *Monsters, Inc.* (2001), and vampire narratives such as the Home Box Office (HBO) adaptation of the Charlaine Harris Sookie Stackhouse novels, *True Blood*, and the Stephenie Meyer *Twilight* franchise, forcefully develop this trend of asking the audience to identify with and even esteem the traditional monster while resisting or reviling the cultural forces that define monstrosity based on non-normative appearance or behavior. The result is a reversal of polarities in which evil is associated not with physical difference, but with cultural forces that constrain personal growth and expression.

John Gardner's 1971 novel *Grendel*, which arguably initiated the current trend of first-person monster narratives, is a retelling of the Anglo-Saxon epic poem, *Beowulf*, from the perspective of its antagonist, the monster Grendel. It is, however, much more than this, as it constitutes an extended meditation on the power and seduction of narrative, the pain of isolation, and what existentialist Jean-Paul Sartre refers to as our "monstrous freedom"—the fact that we alone are responsible for

---

4   Cohen, *Monster Theory*, p. 4.
5   Inasmuch as these monsters from the 1950s are thinly veiled metaphors for communism, they are on some level "human." Nevertheless, while we may recognize them as such, the films prevent us from overcoming our fundamental aversion to them.

our choices.[6] In contrast to many of the autobiographical accounts told by monsters that follow in its wake, *Grendel* arguably does not ask the reader to sympathize with its main character. The reader comes to understand Grendel and his evil nature more fully, but as Matthew Scott Winslow observes in his online review, his behavior is never justified and he is perhaps to be pitied but not liked.[7] What subsequent monster narratives rendered from the monster's point of view do tend to share with *Grendel*—and which Gardner's novel articulates more clearly than any of them—is a sense of the confusion and meaninglessness of existence. *Grendel* in essence asks the reader to consider not just what makes a monster, but if there is a difference between a man and a monster at all.

The attempts to understand what it means to exist and what the implications of existing are can also be found at the heart of Anne Rice's *Vampire Chronicles*, and these questions are emphasized most fully in the first novel in the series, *Interview with the Vampire* (1976), which introduces the reader to Louis, the angst-ridden vampire protagonist, and Lestat, his charismatic and devil-may-care companion. Rice, despite the commonly held misconception, was not the first author to feature the vampire telling his own story—that achievement arguably lies with Fred Saberhagen's *The Dracula Tape*, a novel published one year prior to *Interview* that features Dracula, depicted as the historical figure Vlad Tepes, telling his own story and coming off decidedly better than Van Helsing and the bungling vampire hunters whom he thwarts. Rice's achievement, however, is to create a rich, sensual world in which the traditional monster, the vampire, emerges as the complex and conflicted hero. Gifted with immortality, physical beauty, extraordinary speed and strength, and even the ability to fly, Rice's vampires are essentially transformed into superheroes. At the end of *Interview with the Vampire*, the young interviewer, Daniel, seduced by the power which the vampire possesses, encapsulates the thrust of much post-1970s monster fiction by desiring to *become* a vampire. He aspires to escape the world of the mundane by becoming monster.

Jumping ahead to the twenty-first century, this reversal of polarities, in which the traditional monster becomes the hero, is explicitly combined with an interrogation of the social construction of ideas of normality in works such as *Shrek, Monsters, Inc., Twilight,* and *True Blood*. *Shrek* and *Monsters, Inc.*, animated films ostensibly for children but appealing to adults, vigorously decouple monstrosity from physical appearance. The hero of *Shrek* is a traditional fairytale villain, an ogre. His eventual love-interest, Princess Fiona, is a sort of were-ogre—human during the day, ogre at night—and, running contrary to conventional narrative expectations, when presented with the option, she ultimately chooses to remain in her ogre form and to surrender her human one. The villain in the first *Shrek* film is the existing power structure as represented by Lord Farquaad, the diminutive ruler of the kingdom

---

6 On the idea of monstrous freedom, see Jean-Paul Sartre's *The Family Idiot: Gustave Flaubert 1821–1857* (Chicago: University of Chicago Press, 1989), p. 22.

7 Matthew Scott Winslow, review of John Gardner's *Grendel*, in *The Greenman Review* (online), <http://www.greenmanreview.com/book/book_gardner_grendel.html>, accessed June 27, 2010.

of Duloc. Conventional expectations are reversed even more fully in *Shrek 2* (2004) in which the villains are the physically attractive but morally bankrupt Fairy Godmother and Charming, her vain, spoiled, and egotistical son (who is also the villain in the third *Shrek* incarnation, *Shrek the Third* [2007]). *Monsters, Inc.* presents an even more straightforward disconnection of appearance from monstrosity and interrogation of normality as it presents a world of monsters—most notably kindly monsters Sully (voiced by John Goodman) and Mike (voiced by Billy Crystal)—who are scared of humans. *Monsters, Inc.* is thus entirely the product of contemporary cultural relativism—the awareness that what one culture considers normal may be considered exotic by another.

The *Shrek* films and *Monsters, Inc.* teach the lesson that it is moral values and behavior, not physical appearance, that define monstrosity. The hip HBO series *True Blood*, targeted at a more mature audience, adds to this contemporary awareness of cultural relativism attentiveness to the ways in which monstrosity is a socially constructed category used to police behavior and empower the arbiters of right and wrong. The premise of the series is that, co-opting a metaphor from the gay rights movement, vampires—who have always lived among humans—have decided to "come out of the coffin" and reveal their existence to the world. The push for "vampire rights" prompts a conservative backlash, as expressed in the opening credits of each episode by a billboard reading "God hates fangs," a tongue-in-cheek parody of evangelical homophobia. By paralleling vampires with homosexuals, each group unjustly demonized by a society with narrow ideas of socially correct behavior, the series prompts the awareness not just of the ways in which the term "monster" has functioned as a convenient catch-all rubric for any individual, group, race, or culture whose appearance, behavior, or values run contrary to prevailing social norms in a given time and place, but also of how the deployment of the term "monster" is a powerful political tool for the furthering of particular political designs. Expressed in *True Blood*, as in other contemporary revisions of traditional monster narratives, is the suspicion that it is those who refer to others as monsters who themselves are most deserving of the label.

The contemporary reversal of values, in which traditional monsters and individuals with non-normative appearances are recast as heroes, is at the center of any number of modern literary and cinematic narratives—most notably comic books and their cinematic adaptations, such as the *Hellboy* films (*Hellboy* [2004], *Hellboy II: The Golden Army* [2008]) featuring a demon fighting on behalf of good, the X-Men stories in which "mutants" advocate for their freedom from conservative forces of bigotry, *The League of Extraordinary Gentleman* (film, 2003) which features Mr Hyde cast in an heroic role and Mina Harker from Bram Stoker's *Dracula* (1897) as both a vampire and a hero, the Incredible Hulk stories, and so on—but nowhere is the attractiveness of monstrosity more vividly illustrated than in the novels and film adaptations of Stephenie Meyer's *Twilight* series, in which vampires and werewolves are presented as powerful and beautiful. As anyone with even a passing familiarity with these narratives is aware, at the center of the series is protagonist Bella, who falls in love with, essentially, the perfect man, Edward (played by Robert Pattinson in the films), who turns out to be a vampire—albeit a "vegetarian" one who resists drinking human blood. Although a monster as conceived of in traditional thinking, Edward in the *Twilight* narratives is represented as more angelic than demonic: he is powerful, immortal (barring certain forms of physical violation), handsome, caring, and faithful; and, as if that were not enough, he can read the minds of everyone except for Bella. He is the apotheosis of the modern sensitive man rather than a repellent monster, and he offers to Bella love, excitement, protection, and escape from the mundane.

The Monster Among Us: The Psychokiller

What first-person narrative accounts told from the monster's perspective and monster tales highlighting cultural relativism effectively assert is that, while we still recognize and refer to traditional monsters as such, the idea of monstrosity has been decoupled from physical appearance and today refers first and foremost to the intention and desire to do harm to the innocent. This redefinition of monstrosity, however, creates a conundrum for contemporary citizens: how does one remain safe in a world in which anyone could be a monster? This is the powerful epistemological anxiety underpinning the popularity of contemporary crime programs like the *CSI: Crime Scene Investigation* franchise, narratives of psychopaths and serial killers, and in a twist with very practical "real world" implications, paranoia concerning terrorists. What Shrek and Sully and Lestat and Edward Cullen present to us are traditional monsters that act humanely—that demonstrate the care and concern for others and the range of emotional responses which we currently define as characteristic of humanity; what *Psycho*'s Norman Bates (1960), and his figurative offspring, *American Psycho*'s Patrick Bateman (book, 1991; film, 2000), *The Silence of the Lambs*' Hannibal Lecter (book, 1988; film, 1991), to a certain extent the Showtime series *Dexter*'s eponymous antihero, and popular conceptualizations of terrorists such as the September 11 hijackers all have in common is that they look human while in reality being, from the contemporary perspective, monsters. Through his antisocial actions, the psychopath and the murderous terrorist make visible the internal lack of humanity obscured by their human facades—they are monsters on the inside.

Norman Bates, the antagonist of Alfred Hitchcock's film *Psycho*, famously played by Anthony Perkins, is arguably the poster boy for contemporary monstrosity. What is so disconcerting about Norman is just how *normal* and average he appears. Clean-cut, polite, and diffident, Norman disarms those whom he encounters with the appearance of wholesomeness. What the viewer dramatically discovers at the end of the film, however, is that Norman is not one person, but two—he suffers from multiple personality disorder and has internalized his "mother," who refuses to allow him to express adult male sexuality and instead orders him to kill any woman who arouses his lust. Norman thereby defies the conventional expectation that an individual personality be singular and coherent. He is in a sense possessed, compelled by a demonic force within to commit monstrous acts. The result is a disconnection between his external wholesomeness and his internal diseased state. He is a monster whose monstrousness only becomes visible through his actions.

The shock of *Psycho* is the revelation of Norman's mental disorder. Bret Easton Ellis tips his hat to *Psycho* both through the title of his novel, *American Psycho*, and through the name of his antihero protagonist, Patrick *Bate*man. Ellis, however, in curious ways inverts *Psycho*. To begin with, the narrative is a first-person account told from Bateman's perspective, in which he first reveals his obsessive materialist "yuppie" concerns with wealth and status, and then increasingly details his sadistic murders involving rape, torture, cannibalism, and necrophilia. Who the murderer is in *American Psycho* is not concealed and, as a result, the narrative suspense is shifted to when and whether he will be caught. In the end, though, Ellis undercuts the reader's expectations by raising questions as to whether Bateman has actually committed the horrendous acts that he narrates or rather if they were all in his mind—sick fantasies. Like Norman Bates, however, Patrick Bateman presents a facade of normality that obscures his monstrous, sadistic desires and, again like Norman, Patrick is clearly mentally deranged. Whether a murderer in fact or in fantasy, Patrick nevertheless is a Harvard-educated Wall Street monster whose monstrosity defies easy visual detection.

In contrast to Norman Bates and Patrick Bateman, who are made easy to revile in the end, Thomas Harris's creation, Hannibal Lecter, and Dexter of the Showtime series of the same name, based on the novels by Jeff Lindsay, are especially interesting—and troubling—manifestations of the psychopathic serial killer, as each is presented to varying degrees as simultaneously monstrous and heroic. Hannibal Lecter is a brilliant, soft-spoken, and cultured psychologist—which jars greatly with his murderous and cannibalistic impulses. As with Norman Bates and Patrick Bateman, one wouldn't know Lecter for the monster he is were his psychotic tendencies not explained to the viewer and then revealed through his actions. Nevertheless, despite knowing Lecter for a monster—indeed, in *Silence of the Lambs'* most brutal sequence the viewer observes Lecter reveal himself from beneath the flayed face of one of his guards that he has used to disguise himself— the narrative still manages to present Lecter as an attractive and compelling force. Because he is cultured; because his foil in villainy, Buffalo Bill, is so repulsive; because of the bond he forms with Detective Starling (Jodie Foster) whom he assists; and because he is so vastly more interesting than the repressive system of law and order that underestimates him, our sympathies are strangely enlisted on behalf of Lecter.

Showtime's Dexter, who is essentially Hannibal Lecter with a stricter moral system, engages those same sympathies. Dexter is the monster aware of his own monstrosity—he takes pains to hide it, but cannot suppress it entirely. As revealed in the series, Dexter is a sociopath who was taught by his adoptive police officer father to direct his murderous tendencies only toward other killers. Dexter must have proof that an individual is guilty of murdering an innocent person, lacks remorse, and intends to kill again before he murders the murderer. Dexter (who in interesting ways seems indebted to Kevin Spacey's character, John Doe, in *Se7en* [1995] who is a sociopath that kills those he considers reprehensible) is the dark side to the superhero narrative—he is essentially Batman if Batman did not only brutally apprehend villains but also intentionally killed them. And the trick of the series is to seduce the viewer into not just excusing but indeed sanctioning Dexter's "eye-for-an-eye" system of justice that allows him to be both hero and murderer. What Dexter, however, has in common with almost all accounts of serial killers and psychopaths is that, on the surface, he looks like a normal, average person. His monstrosity is an internal, irresistible force that compels him to harm others.

Monsters, as I have suggested above, give shape to culturally specific anxieties and desires. It is no surprise then that, in the wake of the contemporary decoupling of appearance from monstrosity, concerns that anyone could be a monster and monsters could be anywhere should find, in our post-9/11 world, especially compelling embodiment in the figure of the terrorist. The terrorist—more a convention of the action genre in film and literature than horror—is essentially the sociopath with a focused and often more political impetus for his monstrous desire to do harm and, as such, terrorist narratives are often more explicitly ideological than conventional monster narratives. When Jack Bauer (Kiefer Sutherland) saves the president and the United States from violent extremists on 24, he is supporting a particular set of beliefs and way of life. The problem for Jack Bauer and Homeland Security, and citizens riding the New York subway, however, is that—racial profiling notwithstanding—the terrorist, like the serial killer, presents no obvious external markers of his monstrosity. This is why old women and young children must go through metal detectors at airports. All of us are potentially psychopathic terrorists. We are subjected to these visual prostheses because vision is not enough to separate out the monsters from the rank and file of humanity. We no longer recognize a monster when we see one.

The Monster is Everywhere: Corporations, Governments, and Conspiracy Theories

It is really only a small step from the concern that anyone could be a monster and the monster could be anywhere to the paranoiac fantasy that *everyone* is a monster and the monster is *everywhere*. The invisibility of the monster allows it to infiltrate the city, the countryside, even the intimate domestic space of the home. In her recent study of monsters, *Pretend We're Dead: Capitalist Monsters in American Pop Culture*, Annalee Newitz surveys contemporary manifestations of a particular monster narrative, stories in which capitalism transforms human beings into monsters that cannot distinguish between commodities and people.[8] In the course of her analysis, she considers serial killers, mad doctors, the undead, robots, and—curiously—people involved in the media industry. What she omits from

---

8   Annalee Newitz, *Pretend We're Dead: Capitalist Monsters in American Pop Culture* (Durham, NC: Duke University Press, 2006), p. 2.

her discussion are corporate and government officers dedicated to furthering the greed-driven, insidious ambitions of power-hungry, capitalist organizations.

In the 1950s—as expressed in "Red Scare" monster movies such as *The Thing From Another World* (1951) and *Invasion of the Body Snatchers* (1956)—the anxiety that "communism" was infecting American democracy was rife. The problem with a communist—like a sociopath or terrorist—is that he is not immediately visually distinguishable. You could have Bolsheviks in your company washroom, as the famous propaganda poster states, and not even know it! Following the Vietnam War and the Watergate scandal—as well as the dissolution of the USSR and the fall of the Berlin Wall—social anxieties shifted from concerns about communist infiltration to concerns about corporate and government encroachment into everyday life, and these concerns have found expression in science fiction, fantasy, and horror narratives from *Alien* (1979) to *Avatar* (2009), and most notably in *The X-Files* television series which ran from 1993 until 2002, which are all linked by an emphasis on the monstrousness of capitalist corporations and corrupt government organizations.

The ostensible monster in *Alien* and its various sequels is obviously the nightmarish double-mouthed extraterrestrial designed by H.R. Giger. Just as monstrous and more insidious, however, is the corporation (unnamed in the first film, but subsequently identified in later films as the "Weyland-Yutani Corporation") that desires a specimen of the alien life form and considers the crew expendable in achieving this objective. In *Alien*, the agent of the corporation is the android, Ash (Ian Holm). In the 1986 sequel, *Aliens*, the corporate agent is Carter Burke (Paul Reiser at his most smarmy), a human. Both, however, have been "programmed" by the corporation to disregard human life and safety if it promotes the corporation's capitalist agenda. The *Alien* films thus essentially have two monsters—the alien itself and the bigger monster, the monstrous corporation, that just as clearly feeds off the lives of the human characters.

This monsterization of the corporation (with an eco-friendly twist) becomes the motor force propelling the blockbuster, *Avatar* (2009)—which, in keeping with the decoupling of appearance from monstrosity addressed above, casts the "traditional" monsters in the roles of sympathetic victims and heroes. *Avatar* is about a rapacious corporation conducting mining operations on the distant planet Pandora inhabited by the Na'vi, ten-foot tall, blue-skinned sapient humanoids who live in harmony with nature. When the RDA Corporation discovers a huge mineral deposit under the massive tree which constitutes the Na'vi home, the Na'vi are attacked and forced to leave, the tree is destroyed, and the area is despoiled. Eventually, the Na'vi—led by human Jake Sully, a paraplegic former marine whose consciousness animates an "avatar" Na'vi body—band together and, assisted by other Pandoran creatures, fight back and successfully repel the human invaders. The heroes in this film, upending the conventions of science fiction, are giant blue extraterrestrials. The monster is the human-run RDA Corporation—especially as represented by the head of RDA's private security force, Colonel Miles Quaritch (Stephen Lang)— which has no compunction about displacing and killing the Na'vi and destroying both their way of life and their planet.

Post-Watergate suspicion of the government as a monster furthering its own clandestine and menacing agenda without regard for the health or welfare of the general populace is the recurring theme of any number of films, including *Three Days of the Condor* (1976), *JFK* (1991), and *Enemy of the State* (1998), but finds its fullest expression through the hit 1990s television series, *The X-Files*. One of the primary slogans of the program (flashed during the opening credits of each episode), "Trust No One," clearly indicates the disposition of the program's primary detective, Fox Mulder (David Duchovny), who believes that a vast government conspiracy to hide evidence of extraterrestrial contact has occurred and that the US government is conspiring with aliens and other governments on a range of sinister projects. While approximately two out of every three *X-Files* episodes were stand-alone, in which Mulder, together with his partner, the skeptic Dana Scully (Gillian Anderson), investigated bizarre cases involving paranormal phenomena, the main story arc involving government conspiracy and a shadowy division of the government called "The Syndicate"—represented by the Smoking Man (William B. Davis), a merciless killer and masterful political strategist—effectively characterized the government itself as the series' most ruthless and craftiest monster.

As is the case in narratives about serial killers and terrorists, what is most unsettling in stories of corporate greed and government conspiracy is that the monster defies visual identification. And it is not just that hidden behind the facades of business executives and government officers lurk consuming lusts for power and wealth; beyond this, what is most disturbing about such narratives is the diffuse nature of the Kafka-esque monster that cannot be located, much less killed. Like a classical monster, the hydra, corporations and governments have many heads and if *The X-Files* teaches us anything, it is that for every "Smoking Man" apprehended, two more spring up in his place.

The Monster is Inside Us: The Virus

If the monster can be everywhere by virtue of its invisibility, if the snaky tendrils of corporate greed or government manipulation can bypass one's defenses and penetrate the intimate spaces of one's life, the logical final extension of this infiltration is the possibility that the invisible monster (invisible, at least, to the naked eye) is already within us. This fear is at the heart of the subgenre of film (also generalizable to literature) that Murray Pomerance has referred to as the "infection film"—films governed by the "omnipresent suggestion that the body (a body politic, a body of cultural wisdom, and most essentially, of course, of a protagonist's [usually beautiful] personal body) has been surreptitiously invaded, and that defenses treated in some central way as 'natural' and hegemonic have been outwitted, outmanned, outperformed, overrun, or bypassed."[9] The monster in

---

9   Murray Pomerance, "Whatever is *Happening* to M. Night Shyamalan: Meditation on an 'Infection' Film," in Jeffrey Andrew Weinstock (ed.), *Critical Approaches to the Films of*

such narratives is microscopic and the threat it presents is generally either death—often on a massive scale—or monstrous transformation. The virus as bringer of death is the underlying premise of films such as *The Andromeda Strain* (book, 1969; film, 1971) and *Outbreak* (1995). The virus as agent of monstrous transformation is the recurring premise of many zombie and vampire films such as *28 Days Later* (2002) and *I Am Legend* (1997).

The Andromeda Strain interestingly shares a basic conceit with the seminal zombie horror movie, *Night of the Living Dead*, released only one year prior to Michael Crichton's novel—that of extraterrestrial infection. In George A. Romero's *Night of the Living Dead*, the reanimation of the recently deceased and their cannibalistic appetite is credited to radiation released by the explosion of a returning space probe in the Earth's atmosphere. In *The Andromeda Strain*, the concern is over an extraterrestrial microorganism returned to Earth on a military satellite. The microorganism, dubbed the "Andromeda Strain," fatally clots human blood in most people, while causing suicidal or psychotic behavior in others, and the basic plot of both book and film is to isolate the organism, keep it from spreading, and develop a cure. In Wolfgang Petersen's *Outbreak*—which derives its impetus from the late twentieth-century AIDS pandemic—the culprit is a lethal virus originating in Africa. Combining the infection theme with the government conspiracy theme, the revelation in *Outbreak* is that the military discovered the virus 30 years prior to the California-based epidemic and has been experimenting with it as a form of germ warfare. *Outbreak*, like *Alien*, thus has two monsters: the virus itself and the military, especially as represented by Major General Donald McClintock (Donald Sutherland), who is willing to bomb the infected town of Cedar Creek to cover up his culpability in the viral epidemic and to continue his weapons development unimpeded.

In *28 Days Later* and *I Am Legend*, scientific experimentation goes horribly awry. In *28 Days Later*, animal rights activists break into a scientific research facility to free chimpanzees being used for medical research. In the process, they become infected with a disease referred to only as "Rage," which turns individuals psychotic. (While not technically a zombie film, the movie is often classified as such, given the resemblance of the infected to the living dead.) The virus spreads quickly throughout England and the plot centers on the struggle of the main characters to survive in a post-apocalyptic landscape. The plot of *I Am Legend*—the most recent adaptation of Richard Matheson's 1954 novel of the same name—is similar. A re-engineered strain of measles virus, developed as a treatment for cancer, mutates and becomes lethal, killing 90 percent of the world's population. Of those remaining, most are transformed into animalistic, aggressive creatures intolerant of sunlight. (Matheson's novel actually has vampires in it; the 2007 film adaptation does not.) The plot of the film concerns US Army virologist Lieutenant Colonel Robert Neville's (Will Smith) dual quests to stay alive and to develop a cure for the virus.

M. Night Shyamalan: Spoiler Warnings (New York: Palgrave Macmillan, 2010), p. 205.

All four films are representative of contemporary infection paranoia in which the virus takes center stage as a modern variant of the monster. Such films clearly reflect contemporary anxieties concerning both germ warfare and pandemics such as AIDS, the Ebola virus, Bird Flu, and Swine Flu. By virtue of its invisibility to the naked eye, not only does the virus have the potential to be everywhere and to bypass all boundaries, but the real concern is that we may already be infected without knowing it. The monster may not only be lurking without, but within, defying visibility until its horrific effects occur.

Reaping What We Have Sown: Nature as Monster

Closely related to the viral pandemic is the recurring contemporary nightmare of nature's revenge. Indeed, in monster virus narratives such as *I Am Legend*, the holocaust is often shown to be the product of man's tampering with nature—human hubris, sometimes with benevolent intentions, sometimes not, results in tragedy. In these instances, we literally make our own monsters. This is essentially the same story that gets played out in eco-disaster films in which human beings must contend for survival against an anthropomorphized mother nature. In films such as *The Day After Tomorrow* (2004) and most interestingly in M. Night Shyamalan's *The Happening* (2008), nature becomes monster as it actively—and with seeming intentionality—threatens human survival.

The Day After Tomorrow offers the most vivid representation of nature's revenge through its depiction of the catastrophic effects of global warming. What takes place in *The Day After Tomorrow* is a sequence of extreme weather events— including snowstorms in India, devastating hail in Japan, monster tornadoes in Los Angeles, and a massive super-hurricane that swamps New York with a 40-foot storm surge—all of which culminate in the ushering in of a new ice age. In this film, nature is the enemy—a monster of irresistible force seemingly punishing the human race for its failure to care for the environment. The thrust of the film, therefore, is that—just like any mad scientist in the typical "overreacher" horror film—humanity's overstepping of natural boundaries gives rise to the monster that wreaks its bloody revenge upon its arrogant creator. The nature-as-monster plot takes the idea of the monster being everywhere to its fullest possible expression: the world as monster bent on human destruction.

In *The Happening*, writer and director M. Night Shyamalan combines the themes of nature as monster and virus as monster to give us one of the most unsettling portrayals of the potential consequences of human alteration of the environment. The plot of the film is, in keeping with disaster films in general, the struggle for survival of a small group of people in a decimated landscape. In this instance, the struggle is against a mysterious neurotoxin that is carried by the wind and causes those infected to commit suicide. While there is no definitive explanation for the existence of the neurotoxin, the primary hypothesis presented in the film is that it is being released by trees and other plants that have developed a capacity to defend themselves against human encroachment. At the end of the film, the pandemic gripping the east coast of the United States abruptly abates, but an expert on television, comparing the outbreak to a red tide (aquatic algal blooms of harmful phytoplankton), warns that the epidemic may have just been a first sally, as plants respond to the human threat to the planet by releasing toxins. The film then concludes with a recurrence of the pandemic beginning in Paris.

What stands out about *The Happening* is the literal form of intentionality attributed to nature. The proposition presented in the film is that nature is aggressively responding to human desecration of the environment by fighting back in a particularly dramatic and perversely poetic way—we are literally killing ourselves, stresses the film, as a result of destroying nature. Of particular note within the film are shots that normally would be considered pastoral and soothing—of the wind blowing across fields of grass, for example, and of trees swaying in the breeze—that are infused by the plot with a sense of dread and fear. As Eliot (Mark Wahlberg), Alma (Zooey Deschanel), and Jess (Ashlyn Sanchez) attempt to flee nature's wrath, nature itself seems consciously to be pursuing them with the intention of killing them. But how does one run from the wind and where can one hide when the monster is the earth itself?

Rational Irrationalism or the Search for False Origins

The progression that this chapter has charted in terms of conceiving present-day monstrosity is one that has moved from the idea that, in the wake of decoupling monstrosity from appearance, anyone could be a monster (the psychopath), to the concern that everyone is a monster (the corporate or governmental conspiracy), to the concern that the monster is everywhere, including potentially within us (the virus and nature as antagonists). What links these four manifestations of contemporary monstrosity (psychopath, corporation, virus, nature) is epistemological anxiety related to visibility. We used to be able to recognize a monster when we saw one and therefore to act accordingly in the name of self-preservation. But how do you avoid a monster that you cannot see? How do you identify the monster when it could be anyone or anywhere? The recurring concern underlying contemporary monster narratives is that, through a sort of retroactive causality, we can now only determine the monster's presence through its effects. We know a serial killer is on the loose, that a corporation has prioritized wealth over health, that a deadly virus is spreading, or that nature is "angry," only after people start dying and the bodies begin to pile up—and the casualties then continue to mount as the protagonist is forced to determine who the monster is and how to combat it (assuming resistance is even possible).

I would like to suggest as a conclusion to this chapter that one cultural response to the epistemological barrier erected by invisibility and the anxiety attending it is the attempt to extend vision temporally and to augment it prosthetically so as to define, situate, and comprehend monstrosity and thus to be able to predict it. The attempt is to create narratives that allow us to see the invisible—to determine the origins of the monster and thus to understand—to see—what we are dealing with. More often than not, however, rather than producing actual understanding, the monster is inserted into a familiar, but nonsensical, narrative—an origin story that presents the semblance of logic, but under closer scrutiny is revealed to explain very little at all. Norman Bates's murderous inclinations in *Psycho* are revealed to be the product of a controlling mother, and the psychologist at the end of *Psycho* presents a compelling narrativization of Norman's psychoses, but what, in fact, is actually explained? Similarly, the hypothesis in *The Happening* is that nature is responding to human encroachment by producing deadly neurotoxins—an explanation that makes a kind of narrative sense, but very little from a scientific perspective. This is what I call "rational irrationalism"—a logical narration of nonsensical origins that has three significant effects: it responds to the reader or viewer's desire to make sense of what is taking place; however, it does not fully satisfy this desire, and it therefore leaves a residue of mystery and a sense of unease that allows for further elaboration in a sequel.

Vampire narratives in particular tend to be obsessed with making visible the invisible and providing origin stories that make no actual sense. One sees this in Rice's *Vampire Chronicles* when the origins of the vampire are traced back to ancient Egypt and demonic possession. One sees it repeatedly in vampire films such as *Blade* (1998) that attempt to offer a veneer of scientific plausibility, as well as in infection films, through the now-iconic shot of the scientist looking through the microscope and observing infected blood cells, indicating the presence of different or diseased blood. And one sees it in romantic horror films, such as Francis Ford Coppola's *Bram Stoker's Dracula* (1992), which trace the origins of the vampire back to heresy, magic, and the "true love conquers all" narrative; since this movie offers the most explicit example of what I am calling rational irrationalism, I would like to close by focusing on it in a bit more detail.

Bram Stoker's novel, *Dracula*, provides no explanation for the vampire's existence. In the 1992 film adaptation, however, Coppola felt the need to supply one and thus invented a beginning that, while explaining the vampire's existence, in actuality explains nothing. What the viewer learns is that, in 1462, Vlad Dracula, aka Vlad Ţepeş, returned from battling the Turks to discover that his wife and the love of his live, Elisabeta, had committed suicide after receiving false reports of his death. Enraged by this ironic twist of fate, Dracula desecrates a chapel and renounces God, as blood dramatically wells up from candles, the communion font, and the heart of a large cross that he stabs with his sword. Developing this thwarted love plot further, the film then has the infamous Count stalking Mina Harker because he believes her to be the reincarnation of his lost love, Elisabeta.

Despite being titled *Bram Stoker's Dracula*, this origin story for Dracula and the explanation of his pursuit of Mina finds no basis in Stoker's narrative. Rather, it is Coppola's invention and satisfies the modern desire for explanations. It tells the viewer how and why Dracula transformed into a monster, what animates him, and why he pursues Mina Harker in the way that he does. It makes the monster comprehensible by inserting him into the familiar narrative paradigm "love never dies." This is, of course, the same underlying explanatory framework that structures a large number of ostensible "monster" movies; from tales of the mummy, in which the animated mummy pursues the reincarnation of his ancient bride, to ghost stories such as the paradigmatic *Ghost* (1990), starring Patrick Swayze and Demi Moore, in which the murdered Sam Wheat (Swayze) hovers around his wife, Molly (Moore) until she is out of danger and his murderers are brought to justice, the desire to believe that departed loved ones are still "out there," looking out for us, is powerful indeed. The narrative is comforting because it is familiar, but in actuality it makes sense of nothing. The "logical" origin story that it conveys remains irrational, but it does powerful ideological work in supporting the cultural investment in the ideas of marriage, monogamous love, and divine justice, so it is received as making sense.

In *Bram Stoker's Dracula*, Mina recalls her previous life as Elisabeta; in *Ghost*, Molly "sees" Sam through the mediation of the psychic Oda Mae Brown (Whoopi Goldberg); in *Blade*, we see the vampire blood cells; in *Dexter*, we learn how Dexter became what he is. In other contemporary horror films centered on invisibility and vision—such as *Predator* (1987), in which the alien monster has a cloaking device, and *Pitch Black* (2000), in which the monsters only come out at night and when an eclipse is looming—the drive is toward visualization, both figurative and literal. Recalling the repeated mantra of *Avatar*, the "I see you" expression of love, the attempt is again and again to *see* our monsters for what they are, to bring them into view, to understand them, and thus to gain some control over them. Underlying this obsessive emphasis on the visual, including the rational irrationalism of familiar but illogical origin stories, is the deeply seated contemporary anxiety that our monsters are no longer visible until they kill. In the wake of the modern decoupling of monstrosity from appearance, the monster can be anyone and anywhere, and we only know it when it springs upon us or emerges from within us.

PART II
Critical Approaches to Monstrosity

Posthuman Teratology

Patricia MacCormack

Introduction

This chapter will explore ways of thinking posthuman teratology. Teratology has referred to the study of monsters and monstrosity in all epistemic incarnations, though most often in medicine and physiology. Two inclinations resonate with two effects encountered in relations with monsters. Irrefutable and irresistible wonder and terror have led, in the life sciences, to a compulsion to cure or redeem through fetishization, making sacred or simply sympathetic. The effect that monstrosity has upon the "non-monstrous" is an inherently ambiguous one, just as monsters themselves are defined, most basically, as ambiguities. The hybrid and the ambiguous hold fascination for the "non-monster" because they show the excesses, potentialities, and infinite protean configurations of form and flesh available in nature even while human sciences see them as unnatural. Human sciences' study of and quest for cures for monstrosity is less about monstrosity and more about preserving the myth and integrity of the base level zero, normal human.

Monsters are only ever defined contingent with their time and place; they are never unto themselves. It could be argued that monstrosity is only a failure of or catalyst to affirm the human. Can we even ask what a monster *is*? Configured as "subjects" who fail to fulfill the criteria of human subjects, monstrosity points out the human as the icon of what is normal, and thus the monster as what is not human. For this reason, the monster has an ideal and intimate relationship with the concept of the posthuman. Posthuman theory developed as a result of the deconstruction of meta-discourses such as science, history, and transcendental philosophy that had worked to attain and maintain the meaning, truth, and status of what defines the human.[1] It does not come after humanism

---

1   Critical key texts which introduce this concept in relation to technology, biology, and popular culture include the following: Ihab Hassan, "Prometheus as Performer: Toward a Postmodern Culture?" in Michel Benamou and Charles Caramello (eds), *Performance in Postmodern Culture* (Madison, WI: Coda Press, 1977); N. Katherine Hayles, *How We Became Posthuman: Virtual Bodies in Cybernetics, Literature, and Informatics* (Chicago: University of Chicago Press, 1999); Neil Badmington, *Posthumanism (Readers in Cultural*

but interrogates the conditions of possibility of being and knowing the human while offering examples from all discourses of how there is always something more in the human that delimits its parameters and possibilities. In this sense the posthuman emphasizes that we are all, and *must* be, monsters because none are template humans. The human is an ideal that exists only as a referent to define what deviates from it. Just as the monster is predicated on a judgment based upon what defines a normal human, so too, the human is a conceptualized idea which can be figured as a referent defined only through that which deviates from it. Through teratology we discover in the posthuman what can be thought as ethical, material, experimental, creative, and yet which escapes definition—the inhuman, the a-human, the non-human. In the most reduced sense then, through concepts of adaptability and evolution itself, all organisms are unlike—we are all, and must be monsters because nothing is ever like another thing, nor like itself from one moment to the next.

While immediately associated with human sciences, teratological studies frequently glean their names from both animality and myth—the Elephant Man/ Protean syndrome being one example that includes both animal and ancient monstrous-man figure. Myth, symbolic use of animals, fiction, and fable coalesce in hypertrichotic "werewolf" syndrome. These are two of many examples that show that the monster unifies disparate fields of study and the residue of myth, fantasy, fear, and hybrid aberration that is maintained in science. This chapter will explore ways in which monstrosity works alongside and inflects with the posthuman, and will also inflect science with myth and the actual with the fictive to emphasize the established relationship between these different orders of knowledge that seem to already form a hybrid—even monstrous—foundation of studies in monstrosity.

I consistently use the term "the monster." This tactical use should be qualified in two ways. First, it is clear that there is no single taxonomical category of monster; second, I use this term not to describe a thing but more to name a catalyst toward an encounter. "The monster" refers to the element outside the observer that sparks and creates an event of perception that necessitates the participation of two unlike entities. The monster can simultaneously refer to anything that refuses being "the human" and that which makes the person who encounters it posthuman. There are a number of ways by which we can conceive this kind of monster. Importantly it emphasizes that referring to a monster only ever refers to an encounter with alterity. This is so even if both entities could be described (or describe themselves) as monsters because monsters are as unlike each other as they are the non-monstrous.

Criticism) (Basingstoke: Palgrave Macmillan, 2000); *Cary Wolfe, What Is Posthumanism?* Posthumanities Series, no. 8 (Minneapolis, MN: University of Minnesota Press, 2010); Robert Pepperell, *The Posthuman Condition: Consciousness Beyond the Brain* (Exeter: Intellect, 1995); Judith Halberstam and Ira Livingston (eds), *Posthuman Bodies* (Bloomington: Indiana University Press, 1995); Donna Haraway, *Simians, Cyborgs and Women: The Reinvention of Nature* (New York and London: Routledge, 1991); and Francis Fukuyama, *Our Posthuman Future: Consequences of the Biotechnology Revolution* (New York: Farrar, Straus and Giroux, 2002).

Why a Posthuman Teratology?

Posthumanism has become a field of investigation that incites excitation due to its unapologetic refusal to quicken to a hermeneutic epistemology or an ontological project. Inherent in this play with the basic parameters and goals of discovery and analysis is the subject of the posthuman itself. Where humanism has sought to empirically and philosophically reduce the concept of being to a transcendental essence, so posthumanism seeks to open out the field of study of its "object" as an infinite refolding and metamorphic mobilization of its subject and thus its nature of enquiry. In spite of its name, the posthuman must not be understood as coming after the human. Inherent in posthumanism is the very notion of narrative time or causality as being arbitrary—both are taken as expressions of power rather than necessary elements of logic. The question for the posthuman becomes not "what is the posthuman" but "why is it necessary" and analyses ask "how does it emerge"? Before any exemplifications of the posthuman emerge, posthuman philosophy has taken as its task the ethical and creative need to rethink the category of human, both as an object of study and as a discursive technique of categorization where it is not so much what one is but *where* one is in the taxonomical hierarchy that matters and, indeed, where one's matter is created. Humanism allows investigation to collapse all differing systems of knowledge into an essentially unified consistency of value. The elements that measure value are deferred to an isomorphic system where alterity comes more from what one is not than what one is. Alterity is thus conceived as failure. The paradigmatic nature of philosophy, science, and other epistemologies means that certain qualities are consistently desired over others on the objects of analysis of each, but more so certain tendencies of modes of conception underpin the way that these objects are able to emerge at all.

The posthuman challenges not only qualities which make up the human—as an organism and a cultural, reflective, knowing subject (including knowledge of self)—but qualities which compel the paradigms by which things are perceived to be able to be known. These include organism or object discretion, the possibility of essence, the promise of investigation being exhausted when the object is known absolutely, belief in the myth of objectivity or the possibility of the observer being entirely extricated from the observed, and adherence to established, agreed modes of perception constituted by maintaining traditionally accepted techniques of experimentation and study. The posthuman does not therefore depose the human, nor come after it, but allows access to and celebrates the excesses, conundrums, jubilant failures, and disruptive events which are already inherent in any possibility of contemplation. Shifting possibility to potentiality, the posthuman spatially encourages an address to the multiple within a dividuated organism and the organism as part of a teeming series of relations with its inextricable environment, both conceptual and material (but of course no longer bifurcated). Temporally the posthuman is past, present, and future contracted into immanent entity, emergent without arrival and fled before it is complete. We can invoke certain words which persist in encounters with the

295

posthuman—the multiple, the transformative, the space between, the manifold, the other—but one term which is particularly resonant with the posthuman, sharing its tentative qualities, its failure to be majoritarian and most importantly, its ethical urgency, is the monster.

Majoritarian does not refer to the majority of people, nor the majority of beliefs, truths and such. Majoritarianism is a compulsion to reiterate certain modes of thinking rather than thoughts themselves. Majoritarian thinking is knowledge as absolute (or the possibility of it being such). Majoritarian knowledge anchors on a master discourse where it is not so much that things are monsters but certain traits, forms and ways of negotiating the world are considered the only ways, based on the privileging of concepts such as objectivity and logic. Historically, then, majoritarians have been white, able-bodied, heterosexual, educated males, but all people who participate in these ways of thinking are majoritarian in spite of their corporeal status.

Teras means both monster and marvel. Immediately one is struck with an inherent contradiction. The aberrant as marvellous points to the crucial role that desire plays in thinking both the posthuman and monsters. Where the posthuman is scary because it eviscerates absolute knowledge as an impossible goal, monsters are scary because they do not fit into the classifications we create in order for something to exist at all.[2] The monster is not a being unto itself; it is a failure to be a proper being. In 1831, Cambridge University Professor of Medicine W. Clark wrote a treatise based on transactions of the Cambridge Philosophical Society. Clark commented on the fascination which monsters elicit: "Of late years no subject has more incessantly occupied the labours of learned continental Anatomists than the investigation of the steps by which the rudimentary organs of embryos advance to their perfect form."[3] Here temporality is configured in an early heralding of evolution where the form at which one arrives, as well as the comparative place that form will occupy in relation to others, are "results" of stages toward perfection. Being a being is a finite goal in this configuration, creating resonances of the organic with the increments of knowledge which one must take to arrive at a concept of one's self philosophically and the ultimate arrival where man attains God, through access to truth, absolutism and, most importantly, likeness to God. The human template, the micro-God, is both that which nature seeks in order to create proper healthy, normal human life, and that which science seeks to know in order to match it elegantly with more esoteric or philosophical notions of what it means to be a living human. This template

---

2   For an elaboration of modes and purposes of teratological ontologies and their paradigmatic shift in contemporary culture, see Jeffrey Jerome Cohen, "Monster Culture (Seven Theses)," in Jeffrey Jerome Cohen (ed.), *Monster Theory: Reading Culture* (Minneapolis, MN: University of Minnesota Press, 1996), pp. 3–25 and Patricia MacCormack, "Perversion: Transgressive Sexuality and Becoming-monster," *Thirdspace* 3/2 (2004), <www.thirdspace.ca/articles/3_2_maccormack.htm, 2004>.

3   W. Clark, *A Case of Human Monstrosity*, Folio (Cambridge: Cambridge University Press, 1831), p. 2.

is seemingly basic and straightforward but actually an impossible concept of singularity, showing that any organism only ever exists as a version of an ideal that, by its very nature, is immaterial and phantasmatic. The focus on elements of disambiguation and temporal transformation is key in theories of the posthuman, where plethora replaces persona and being becomes becoming.

The monster reminds us of the ethical importance inherent in thinking about posthuman aberration. A key factor in posthumanism in relation to teratology is that teratology brings us back to history as a remembered present while it seeks the future-now upon which much posthuman theory focuses. Exchanging history for individual memories means that the past does not affirm the present and guarantee a future, as posthumanism opens up potentialities rather than repeating forms. However, it acknowledges the suffering, objectification, and effects of being named monster that cannot be denied. Remembered present asks "how does experience of the past effect present modes of being"? For the monster it validates experience as other; for the objectifier it demands accountability.

My positing posthuman teratology will not focus on the more obvious examples of the posthuman, the primary one of which is the techno-posthumanism. Perhaps the most famous theorist of the cyborg, Donna Haraway, created a connection between woman as the first step away from the "human" — correctly the Man masquerading gender specificity with all its associated powers of signification as neutrality — and technology. What she emphasized was that technology persists in the compulsion of majoritarian paradigms, which operate primarily through the production of meaning as "binary dichotomisation."[4] If the prehuman was nature to culture, the posthuman in the context of techno-biopolitics is culture to future while simultaneously a collapse between the most basic biology and the most refined technology. The persistence of the binary system is the issue here, as it shows that the quality of an event of the human cannot be posthuman if it stands in opposition to a less attractive, oppressed or suppressed other who both threatens to re-emerge in order to subsume it, but also reminds it of the irrefutable necessity for dominance in the quest for liberation from the flesh. It is the very flesh of the other that is usually subjugated (this is especially so for xeno-biology in animal organ harvest experiments for transplantation). A system of equivalence sits side by side with that of accumulation. As animal is to human, and woman is to man, so man is to cyborg. The first term in each dyad is one from which the majoritarian flees but also which it needs in order to operate a structure of proportion — definition based on difference as only success or failure at resemblance. In a seeming contradiction, the cyborg as a posthuman future reminds us that the "natural" flesh, particularly the animal and woman, is the most monstrous. A troubling appendix to this series of proportion is the current tendency to equate brains with computers, yet it is most often the computer system which is seen to offer an insight into the brain, while the brain's complexity finds its greatest power in its capacity to be synthetically constructed in cyborg consciousness. But neurophysiologist Rodney Cotterill emphasizes that it is:

---

4   Haraway, *Simians, Cyborgs and Women*, p. 209.

> *rather unlikely that computers as such could be given consciousness merely through the use of a specific type of software. There would have to be something that is likened to a body, equipped with counterparts of our muscle-moving apparatus ... Given that thought is essentially stimulation of the body's interactions with the environment, as I have said, this would mean that the computer would be simulating simulation ... we humans appear to be mesmerised by the prospect of artificially producing copies of ourselves.*[5]

Cyborg and simulated consciousness technology has come a long way since Cotterill's text; however, what remains the same is the desire to re-activate qualities associated with human-yet-transcendental subjectivity.

Is simulation empty copying, an elliptical compulsive return to the human, or is it a virtualization of potentiality which goes beyond the paradigms that allow traditional coveted qualities of idealized humanity to operate?[6] Two intriguing issues arise in Cotterill's lament—the first is the inextricability of identity from environment, the second the necessity of flesh or something akin to it. Consciousness is flesh and vice versa. A Cartesian extrication of consciousness from flesh compels many cyborg theories, while a more Spinozan understanding of expressions, relations, and affects between entities, environment, subject, thought, and (inter) act(ion) haunts its as yet impossibility. Spinoza states: "matter is everywhere the same, parts are distinguished in it only insofar as we conceive matter to be affected in different ways, so that its parts are distinguished only modally."[7] Robert Pepperell's seminal posthuman manifesto states: "The idealists think that the only things that exist are ideas, the materialists think that the only thing that exists is matter. It must be remembered that ideas are not independent of matter and that matter is just an idea."[8]

Pepperell emphasizes that posthumanity is liberated from binary dichotomization, anchoring of ideas into virtualities which must be actualized in order to be (that is, they are neither transcendental nor independent from other ideas from all fields, particularly the inextricability of science and philosophy). Yet there still resonates a fear of matter because, as will be explored below, through posthuman ethical philosophy, matter may be emergent as a negotiated concept through being an idea, but there is nonetheless matter beyond and independent of (because always within) simply being "just" an idea. Pain, actual suffering, experiments on non-consenting flesh, or the results of technologies of combat show us not an "idea" of matter but matter's ubiquitous all. I am not suggesting here

---

5   Rodney Cotterill, *Enchanted Looms* (Cambridge: Cambridge University Press, 1998), pp. 434–6.

6   In relation to the copy as a natural phenomenon and culture's fascination with both studying and creating copies, see Hillel Schwarz, *The Culture of the Copy* (New York: Zone Books, 1998).

7   Benedict Spinoza, *Ethics*, trans. Edwin Curley (London: Penguin, 1994), p. 12.

8   Robert Pepperell, *The PostHuman Condition: Consciousness Beyond the Brain* (Exeter: Intellect, 1997), p. 26.

that matter creates ideas, per se, or lurks beneath them, waiting to pounce out to destroy us by reminding us that we cannot be without a body, but in order to think an ethics of biopolitics, the future-now needs to acknowledge what we cannot get rid of, either through technology or through signification. Knowledge of matter is just matter as an idea, but matter for itself is not.

Disfunctional Cyborg Dreams

While the cyborg body is constituted by defining qualities of monstrosity—hybridity, negotiating binaries such as flesh/technology, nature/future and experimentation, on which an enormous amount has been written—I would argue this has been to the detriment of certain ways in which we can, or *should*, think posthumanism as now and as a field which should not place itself in a future without a past or residue. Critically, cyborgism can tend to a hyper-evolutionary obsession where the only way to be posthuman is to collapse the technology created by man to manipulate life with the organism, lamentably for cyborgs, as which we still persist to exist, with all our frailties and failures. Cyborgism has promises of enhancement toward immortality and a God-scientist who can create and extend life and become the ultimate self-authorizing identity, no longer in need of the physiology alienated from his will that threatens to destroy him through age and disease. Cyborgism can be experimental, playful, and hold much promise, but teratology reminds us that the negotiation of volition and self-expression which underpins cyborgism has too frequently been denied monsters, be they anatomical congenital aberrations, transgressives or bodies at the most basic level of alterity from the majoritarian understanding of the human. Additionally, perhaps contentiously, should not monsters in their posthuman incarnations, by their very aberrant definition, ethically and politically challenge the structures that underpin dominant powers? C. Ben Mitchell et al. write:

> Some individuals even call themselves "transhumanist", explicitly promoting the re-engineering of humankind into some form or forms of "posthuman" being. Even the US government has invested in a controversial project to re-engineer human beings.[9] Yet even if not adopting such an extreme view or goal it would seem a large number of individuals in the United States and around the world are enticed by all the potential technologies of "enhancement". The desires for modification may be rooted in wishes for fashioning oneself into a more socially acceptable image, attempting to improve self-esteem through reengineering, or making oneself more competitive in business, the professions,

---

9   The authors do not give examples of what they refer to here. They word their comment ominously, however, and so it is difficult to glean whether they are invoking eugenic projects, ultimate Frankensteinian man-making goals, or an extension of the human genome project.

academia, or athletics. Unfortunately the motivations behind these desires are usually socially driven fears, experiences of rejection or failure, or just plain greed, and they may reflect a social rather than biological pathology.[10]

While vaguely theological, this criticism elucidates the point that we cannot find the posthuman as a liberating concept in what it is, but in what it does to majoritarian systems of control, social hierarchies, and the obsessions with an extension or enhancement of the same old power enforcements taken to their longed-for eternity. The question with cyborgism is "enhancing what?" Artistic and conceptual-performance cyborgism, such as the work of Stelarc, which makes up a considerable component of cyborg incarnations and biotechnological experiments, may find itself aligned more with traditional teratology than with cyborg theory, per se. Stelarc's third arm project formed a disambiguation of the binarization of two arms (and even the healthy human baby as two arms, two legs) and the conceptualization of limb movement as volitional and organic, as the arm was manipulated by interface users. His third ear transplanted onto his forearm exhibited an organ with no use and redefined through its proximity with a non-compatible organ (itself relatively rudimentary, the forearm apprehended as a vista of skin rather than an organ with a function per se.)

Relationality as Hybridity

Covertly I could make the same argument against the fetishization of animality in certain becomings, where the posthuman collapses animality with human form brought out in experiments with body modification—the implantation of certain animal elements such as stripes, whiskers, fangs, and horns. Here, alterity has become over-signified as a liberatory regression or devolution. Such examples include Dennis Avner the Stalking Cat, and Eric Sprague the Lizard Man.[11] Rather than entering into their own becomings, however, both have rented themselves out, in that Sprague is a "freak show" performer and Avner performs personal narrativizations in public appearances, which suggests seeking to reify his being rather than explore his becomings. For this reason, while I invoke these figures, I use them as illustrative risks setting down a template as to what does or does not constitute a becoming-animal.[12] Where the cyborg is the future-human-now, the

---

10   C. Ben Mitchell, Edmund D. Pellegrino, Jean Bethke Elshtain, John F. Kilner, and Scott B. Rae, *Biotechnology and the Human Good* (Georgetown: Georgetown University Press, 2007), p. 11.

11   For their homepages, see <http://www.stalkingcat.net/> and <http://www.thelizardman.com/>.

12   For more on the problems of exemplification in discussions of body modification and animal-becomings, see Patricia MacCormack, "The Great Ephemeral Tattooed Skin," *Body and Society* 12/2 (May 2006), pp. 57–82.

becoming-animal of certain posthumans is the past-reclaimed.[13] Many teratological conditions have been named such because aberrant traits are perceived as animal qualities—elephant men, wolf children, mermaid (thus fish) syndrome. Becomings-animal in certain body modifications directly refuse being named as a failure by presenting as a volitional way to re-name oneself via qualities which are considered liberating rather than devolutionary. The power of naming and the myth of compulsory human-ness are taken from majoritarian systems, and so is the belief that being human is the most desirable state of subjectivity. Although offering fascinating examples of the inherent hybridity of any attempt to become something else, in a sense some of these animal-humans want to become, not animals, but irreducibly human perceptions of animals. An animal—and what is (or is not) an animal—is no less nor more "natural" than a human. The animal-human's seeking origin positions itself in a parabolic configuration with the cyborg's seeking eternity. Thinking the animal ethically—which may confess to not thinking it at all beyond thinking through grace as the pure allowance of the other to be, without intervention—gives way to idealizing and fetishizing.

More problematic than the animal aims of modifiers is the increasing collapse of possible resonances of biology, from testing to transplantation, where the subjugated element is not technically apprehended as living being but as living material. Theories of the posthuman are increasingly questioning the meaning of "life." The multiple in the singular may seem all-too posthuman—the pig's heart transplanted into the human body, the animal used for performances as some symbiotic claim (such as Monika Oeschler's Eagle Project)[14]—but these fail to encounter an animal as a consistency of (its own owned) life, let alone animality. It is fine for the human to question his own human status through experiments with hybridity, multiplicity, and symbiosis with alterity, but the seeking of these forms of the posthuman involves another element and that element, when animal, even in the most seemingly benevolent circumstances but certainly not those involving pain or death, is incapable of consent, is simply a return to the absolute power which the concept of being human perpetuates and vindicates. Beyond thinking that the impossibility of animal consent is something that comes solely from a linguistic system, the very notion of the right to "use" phantasizes that there is an appropriate field of operations where the human both has the right to intervene (including the symbolic or the performative) in animal life, or the opposing view that they do not. While the latter does acknowledge that the incapacity to consent should mean a refusal to compel, both impose an assimilating regime upon the animal

---

13   In reference to devolutionary alterity, I do not here invoke "modern primitives." In the context of a discussion of teratology, they do not represent the hybridity which the cyborg and human-animal illustrate.

14   This project can be understood as not only assimilative of animal behavior as it is distorted by humans, but it problematically involves the "domestication", tethering, and incarceration of birds of prey. From the perspective of a Spinozan consideration of the non-human this project is unethical. Monika Oechsler, *The Eagle Project*, performance at the James Hockney Gallery (2007), <http://monikaoechsler.co.uk/pages/eagle.html>.

nonetheless. The radical and uncomfortable issue is that we exist within purely human discourse, with all its ambiguities, temporal and spatial contingencies, and to attempt to operate outside these is itself a human project. The question is not one of purely linguistic or structural questioning of animal–human relations, though this is perhaps from whence it begins, but the right to consider difference at all if it is irreducible difference without negotiation.

Cary Wolfe states two factors that have made theories of animality become so prevalent in recent years. The first is the crisis in humanism in philosophy; the second, which inflects animality as a primal form of life toward the futures that techno-biopolitics promise, is that the animal has found its presence most in non-humanities epistemes.[15] Both are human-to-human tendencies, whatever that means beyond meaning incapable of encountering the extra-human. The question of who we are now that we are no longer human is counteracted by the question, what can we do with animals to make us live longer? Both uses of animals, however, persist in binary dichotomization, as they necessitate animals as nothing more than not human. Resemblance through metaphor and arrogant use through biological harvesting affirm that "it was as a comment on *human* nature that the concept of 'animality' [and so too monster] was devised."[16]

Cyborgism can facilitate our escape from just being animals, while using animals insinuates that we are not animals but a somehow higher form of life. Where, in post-structuralism, epistemes collide, these two claims cannot coexist. Giorgio Agamben calls this the ironic anthropomorphic machine of humanism: "You can degenerate into the lower things, which are brutes; you can regenerate, in accordance with your soul's decision, into the higher things which are divine ... The humanist discovery of man is the discovery that he lacks himself."[17] Posthumanism, neither a before nor after, is the *crisis* of the end of the myth of man. Questions such as what can we do to extend the human, or what does the animal mean, essentially ask one single question, which is the "what now" of the human?

While, once again, I am adamantly not claiming that cyborg and animal posthumans are always resonating with humanistic tendencies, what teratology reminds us is that the monster as aberration is that which is traditionally and historically denied volition or any sense of self-authorization. Defined through this word "marvel," teratology describes a study of *relation* more than of an object. Rather than I "am" a cyborg project or becoming-animal, monstrosity is an encounter. The subject in proximity with the monster must be accountable for subjects' mode of perception; the monster is nothing unto itself except aberrant to the other. The other is just as easily able to be monstrous to the monster. What is emphasized is the space between. Monstrosity is the event; thus teratologically speaking, posthumanism is neither a natural object nor a volitional refusal of the

---

15   Cary Wolfe, "Introduction," in Cary Wolfe (ed.), *Zoontologies* (Minneapolis, MN: University of Minnesota Press, 2003), p. x.

16   Keith Thomas, *Man and the Natural World* (New York: Pantheon, 1983), p. 41.

17   Giorgio Agamben, *The Open: Man and Animal*, trans. Kevin Attell (Stanford: Stanford University Press, 2004), pp. 29–30.

human, but the creation of a multiple through the desire to marvel at that which cannot be perceived via traditional modes of signification and apprehension. There is no resolution, no finality, no knowledge of, just the consistency of being as a being in relation with, and the incited thoughts, creative perceptions, and imagined potentiality which comes from this marvelous encounter where both and thus neither are aberrations except to one another, beyond scientific or philosophical humanist reduction or deferral to the already established categories of the human. "I find the other in me (it is always concerned with showing how the other, the distant, is always the near and the same.) It resembles exactly the invagination of a tissue in embryology, or the act of doubling in sewing: twist, fold, stop and so on."[18] Shifting the earlier critique of the manipulated posthuman, we can find in our most humble and ordinary bodies radical possibilities when we are liberated from taxonomy.

Monstrous Metamorphoses

The primary element that defines monsters is that they are not not-monsters, not us, not normal. They have no category of their own by which they may be recognized and thus removed. To have an object (monsters are objectified, never subjects unto themselves) which cannot be described and placed into a category alongside other like objects is the primary concept which structures all other elements of monstrosity—that is the ambiguous, the neither-neither—neither this, nor that, but not "not" these things. Monsters when they are formed from human matter are never entirely independent from the human form. The very problem comes from their uncanny redistribution of human elements into aberrant configurations. It is the part we recognize as made strange, or in proximity with a part with which it should not sit side by side, that makes monsters monstrous. Like the posthuman, the monster is neither before nor beyond the human, but an interrogation of the myths of human integrity, biologically and metaphysically. A monster is not a classified object nor a self-authorized subject but more the result of an act of being named such. So the next circle of ambiguity and relation after that which recognized the monster as familiar and unfamiliar is the relation between the monster and the non-monster who names it. Again this involves the element of the familiar, here normal, with the unfamiliar and indefinable, the monster. Both in itself and in its relation with the not-monster, the monster operates through this system of hybridity. We cannot speak of monsters. We speak only of examples of the plasticity and creativity that is inherent in all concepts, including those formed to describe and know biological phenomena. Ambiguous hybridity of form and encounter spatially locate the monster. Temporally, the monster is constituted through metamorphosis and distortion. While the form of a monster may not necessarily undergo perceptible alteration any more than all bodies are in constant

---

18   Gilles Deleuze, *Foucault*, trans. Sean Hand (London: Athlone Press, 1988), p. 98.

state of change, the way the monster is perceived does—historically, monsters have been encountered first as abominations, then with sympathy, then as projects to fix. Again we see that it is the structure of relation with the monster that creates its meaning, rather than the quality or nature of the monster itself.

Monsters in themselves are created through a bordering and create bordering encounters. Within monstrous "identity," therefore, there is already more-than-one and relating with the monster mirrors this multiplicity within the singular. There is no evidence of discrete identity, not even bad identity. Resonating with the turn to animality in posthuman theory, the monster is often a hybrid of "animal" and "human." But another way to utilize animality in posthuman teratology without assimilation or fetishization comes from fabulations of impossible combinations created not through sutured forms but intermingling intensities. For example, in fiction, myth, and popular culture we find the werewolf and the vampire. Werewolves are part–man, part-wolf without being examples of either. The werewolf is rather the "wolfing" of man. It is defined by its temporal transformations and instability. Additionally werewolves are frequently characterized by their tragic benevolence and horror at wolfing, so they cannot be reduced to a single expression of intent or nature. The vampire mingles dead with living undead, it becomes bat, wolf, even molecules of fog. The vampire does not metamorphosize, it is itself a metamorphosis. Covert to the tragically benevolent werewolf, the vampire is unapologetically horrifying and seductive precisely for being such. We cannot ask what a werewolf or vampire is as each is always changing. In a contradictive conundrum, they are defined by instability, mingling of different forms and invoking violent aggression in sympathy and irresistible desire in repulsion. "The abnormal can be defined only in terms of characteristics, specific or generic; but the anomalous is a position or set of positions in relation to a multiplicity ... It is always with the anomalous ... that one enters into alliance with becoming animal."[19]

In a posthuman project towards becoming-animal (where the venture, the becoming, is the focus, and the final form never arrives), ironically the fictive animal becomes more real than any becoming based on intimate knowledge of zoology. Just as teratology risks fetishizing the monster, as sacred, as victim, as repulsive, through claims that absolute knowledge will mean absolute capacity to name and describe the limits and meanings of the monster, so zoology's study of animals to the most refined molecular point creates a phantasy of understanding an animal and thus being ethically vindicated in co-opting one, be it through consumption, experimentation or just idealized symbolicization. The fictive fabulation animals which Deleuze and Guattari mention are those that demand creation and imagination—encounters which ignite thought rather than promise knowledge and its associated powers. As imaginary concepts, most frequently found in art, literature, and film, fabulation animal-monsters such as werewolves and vampires cannot be co-opted as they exist only as demands for relations of othering. We

---

19 Gilles Deleuze and Félix Guattari, *A Thousand Plateaus*, trans. Brian Massumi (Minneapolis, MN: University of Minnesota Press, 1987), p. 244.

can never "know" that which does not exist, but, like all art and fiction, it does not mean that our ideologies, paradigmatic tendencies, and responses are not affected by experiences of these entities. Posthuman tribal totems are not those of "primitive" culture, nor even of the use of animals as symbols in modernity, but strange, taxonomically impossible creatures that are us, and *not* us, which move us to different positions. The werewolf is man and beast, the vampire inherently metamorphic to the limit of being gaseous, a future of post-death rather than eternal, technologically facilitated life. Both are fleshy, furred, corroded, showing different conditions of the smooth, hard flesh of normal humanity and its ambition toward being impervious cyborg metal. Yet both are recognizably human. Most importantly, both infect and exist in packs. By very virtue of being infective, vampires must form packs, even if they are disparate. Indeed the idea that one belongs to a pack although one may never see one's fellow packmates exemplifies the oxymoronic status of these monstrous evocations. This means that the only way to access these monsters is to be part of them — the encounter is the concept itself. The enigmatic nature of these monsters is eternal but notably popular in contemporary culture. This shows that they are not abject abnormal creatures to be put away, made sacred or profane but always externalized. They are seductive present promises of extending thoughts of human potentiality, and we enter into an internal teratological realm. Emphasizing the marvellous, fascinating etymology of the word, fabulated monsters can only be encountered by becoming with them. While each emergence of werewolf and vampire is unique, the packs which they create are communities of those who are not common to each other, as much of a seeming contradiction as monsters themselves.

Toward an Ethics of Posthuman Monstrosity

There may seem to be a problem here with the possibility of ignoring "real-life" monsters, entities both human and animal that have been forced to suffer through oppression catalyzed by their alterity. The function of fiction here does not oppose that of reality, but it breaks down the binary itself. Fiction requires a belief in the unbelievable. While readers are aware of the fictive form, the affects and intensities incited in the imagination are real and have direct effects on the subjectivity of the reader, just as all fictive art affects the self beyond the fiction, and all science of the real operates via beliefs in what kinds of knowledge are possible and acceptable, the belief in which is its own fiction. Modes of perception are neither fictive nor true. They are constructs of possibilities of ideas. This means that all encounters with alterity will create a choice — to turn away by knowing the other as abnormal and therefore affirming the self as normal, or to enter into a bordering or pack with the monstrous, creating a revolutionary hybridity of two who were already hybrids, and so forth. This bordering is as relevant for political activism as it is for dreams of wolfing and vampirism. Foucault states of power: "That's just like you, always with the same *incapacity* to *cross the line*, to pass over to the other side ... it is always the same choice, for the side of power, for what power says or what it causes to be said."[20] It is just as easy for the fictive to incite reiterations of oppressive power—the hybrid must be punished, the abnormal is evil—as it is for the limitless potentials of fiction to exploit those elements that are unthinkable outside of literature and all art. As it is more difficult to imagine the becoming-vampire of everyday subjectivity, so it is more important in reference to the need to think the fact of everyday monstrosity as that which proves the infinite differentiations of the myth of the static human as a single possibility of expression whose only others are considered deviations rather than variations. Encounter and proximity refuse the distance required for one to objectify and name another. And both encountering entities alter within their own nature and as a single new hybrid manifestation. By this can be cured the most monstrous but repressed of animal functions which man operates in his oppressive regimes:

> History hides the fact that man is the universal parasite, that everything and everyone around him is hospitable space. Plants and animals are always his hosts; man is necessarily their guest. Always taking, never giving. He bends the logic of exchange and of giving in his favour when he is dealing with nature as a whole. When he is dealing with his kind he continues to do so: He wants to be the parasite of man as well.[21]

Michel Serres shows that it is not the monster who needs normal man to liberate it, but man who needs the monster to affirm himself and his status.

The monster is always liberated enough, too much, limitless. The monster's becomings with other monsters, already us as we are already them, is quelled by man's being as parasite. This relation, to know and name the monster, is an act of violence:[22]

> Consequently the basic combat situation reappears in knowledge. There. Just as we noted previously, a collectivity united by an agreement finds itself facing the world in a relation, neither dominated nor managed, of unconscious violence: Mastery and possession ... Science brings together fact and law: whence it is now decisive place. Scientific groups, in a position to control or do violence to the worldwide world, are preparing to take the helm of the worldly world.[23]

---

20 Michel Foucault, "The Subject and Power," in H.L. Dreyfus and P. Rabinow (eds), *Michel Foucault: Beyond Structuralism and Hermeneutics* (Brighton: Harvester, 1982), p. 220, original emphasis.

21 Michel Serres, *The Parasite*, trans. Lawrence Schehr (Minneapolis, MN: University of Minnesota Press, 2007), p. 24.

22 Derrida points out that "a monster is a species for which we do not have a name ... [However], as soon as one perceives a monster in a monster, one begins to domesticate it." In Jacques Derrida, *Points ...: Interviews, 1974–1994*, trans. Peggy Kamuf (Stanford: Stanford University Press, 1995), p. 386.

23 Michel Serres, *The Natural Contract*, trans. Elizabeth MacArthur and William Paulson (Ann Arbor: University of Michigan Press, 2001), p. 22.

Serres pleads for a natural contract, what Guattari would call an ecosophy of alterity and relations over law.[24] That science is law shows the fictitious nature of both, and monstrosity requires a certain lawlessness that, as a concept, is itself seen to be monstrous. It is not, it is simply not top-down. Traversal is active and activating. From abnormal thing to anomalous movement operates. Guattari names this the politics of traversal. Monsters show that all subjectivity must be considered pure singularity. Traversing domains of singularities, creating monstrous territories promotes:

> *innovatory practices, the expansion of alternative experiences centred around a respect for singularity and through the continuous production of an autonomising subjectivity that can articulate itself appropriately in relation to the rest of society ... Individuals must become both more united and increasingly different.*[25]

Teratology from taxonomy to traversal celebrates the singularity of each monster while showing that we are all monsters in our singularity. Collectivity comes from the unlike, to transform groups based on expressions of creativity through difference, not of power through knowledge. It also addresses the lived reality of monsters and their/our unique experiences of suffering and jubilance.

Conclusion

Guattari writes:

> *We can no longer sit idly by as others steal our mouths, our anuses, our genitals, our nerves, our guts, our arteries, in order to fashion parts and works in an ignoble mechanism of production which links capital, exploitation and the family. We can no longer allow others to turn our mucous membranes, our skin, all our sensitive areas, into occupied territory — territory controlled and regimented by others, to which we are forbidden access. We can no longer permit our nervous system to serve as a communications network for the system of capitalist exploitation, for the patriarchal state; nor can we permit our brains to be used as instruments of torture programmed by the powers that surround us. We can no longer allow others to repress our fucking, control our shit, our saliva, our energies, all in conformity with the prescriptions of the law and its carefully defined little transgressions. We want to see frigid,*

---

24   Félix Guattari, *The Three Ecologies*, trans. Ian Pindar and Paul Sutton (London: Athlone Press, 2000).

25   Guattari, *Three Ecologies*, pp. 59, 69.

> imprisoned, mortified bodies exploded to bits, even if capitalism continues to
> demand they be kept in check at the expense of our living bodies.[26]

Guattari emphasizes that the most monstrous bodies are those already available to us, from neither past nor future, and that are all that we are. The most basic and quiet of corporeal acts, if not enclosed in regimentation and signification, can cause horror, while grand experiments in posthumanism can reiterate the oppression and repression of bodies, depending on what symbolic values and by what means these bodies emerge and are encountered. "Pathology is not a general state of being, a disease which afflicts the whole system, but a local and readable lesion, a mappable topography ..."[27] Monsters are lesion bodies that must be extricated from the body politic, the corpus. They must be read before they can be encountered and removed, yet we could say that the encounter, which causes horror through aberration as ambiguity, is the catalyst for signification, where marveling converts to meaning. Marveling opens up the witness; meaning closes off the monster. It is a question of a revolutionary or reifying decision, the way the other is mapped. A lesion to be ablated, or a suppurating opening, what Guattari shows is that the way beyond the categorization of the human is what we have already repressed that is inherently part of and all that we are. And one could argue that cyborgs do not sweat, shit nor spit, while animals, including the human animal do, but we perceive it in either a ritualized or naturally innocent fashion.

Kristeva writes that: "experimental multiplicity is entirely different from the emptiness and destruction experienced in the loss of identity."[28] Monsters, multiple, hybridic and metamorphic, find their place—a no-place, an every-place—in postmodernity as proliferation. They offer a vitalistic foil to the sometimes cynical, even nihilistic, risks that the postmodern loss of identity may entail. The very nature of monsters as sicknesses of a failure to be human makes their dividuated corporeal aberrancies mirror their place in society as flaws or deformities of the social corpus. But when postmodernity facilitates posthumanity, monsters show the body already remapped. We are faced with our bodies as monstrous because the sites of what would be considered failures or flaws upon a human map, and signified as such, close off thinking the body differently, become openings toward life without and beyond humanity, actual lived experience, being without having to be a specified subject.

Monstrous "deformities" and symptoms traditionally punctuate a normal body as text to be read. These punctuative points can be encountered as *despositifs* which escape signification rather than functioning as an affirmation of the claimed necessity of normality. Lyotard states of the aberrant body that "the body is undone and its pieces are projected across libidinal space, mingling with other pieces in

---

26 Félix Guattari, *Soft Subversions*, trans. Jarred Becker (New York: Semiotext(e), 1996), p. 31.
27 Catherine Waldby, *Visible Human Project: Bodies and Posthuman Medicine* (London: Routledge, 2000), p. 24.
28 Julia Kristeva, *Revolt, She Said*, trans Brian O'Keeffe (New York: Semiotext(e), 2002), p. 131.

an inextricable patchwork."[29] Patching together despotic aberrations of the flesh, the genetic code connects points which are incommensurable with the normal human but which are also commensurable with each other. Where they are single points — conceptually and physically — which sully the smooth, sealed terrain of the human, they become multiple relations between other non-humans and each seam of the patchwork (and each despotic aberration has many sides, and thus many seams and many relations with others) is a unique connective tissue of creative singularity. It demands thought because it has never been encountered before. All bodies, perceived as formerly normal or not, have to think what relations they can make with multiple *despositifs*. Each body must therefore have more than one plane, side or aspect, and each specific connection exacerbates these multiplications. This operation involves:

> *opening the body to connections that presuppose an entire assemblage, circuits, conjunctions, levels and thresholds, passages and distributions of intensities and territories and deterritorialisations measured with the craft of a surveyor ... how can we unhook ourselves from the points of subjectification that secure us, nail us down to a dominant reality?*[30]

Teratological connectivity fulfills certain qualities of the posthuman — multiplicity in the one, singularity in the many, the death of reproduction for production of the unlike. This mode of teratological experimentation in thought and practice does not need an actual element of alterity that is not human — animal, machine — but reminds us all that humanity is made up of its own elements of otherness that are repressed, denied or catalogued. Teratological connectivity affirms that the category of human has never existed properly, but instead of co-opting elements opposed to the human, it celebrates and exploits that we already have everything we need to become posthuman monsters, without the need for fetishization or assimilation of those who cannot choose to become part of non-human assemblages, such as animals, or for access to overarching systems of modernity beyond the reach of most people, such as cyborg research. Teratological re-signification of all bodies should not involve a forgetting of the realities of the lived experiences of those named monsters by dominant epistemes. While connections involve opening futures as becomings to come, no single body comes from nowhere and the memories of suffering and oppression are part of the specificity of each *despositif* to which each connector will have its own relation, such as shared oppression and accountability. What matters most is that, by refusing regimes of signification, we all become accountable, while all acknowledging the urgency with which and the reasons why experiments in teratological connectivity are as political as they are interesting, artistic, liberating, and, hopefully, fun.

---

29   Jean-François Lyotard, *Libidinal Economy*, trans. Iain Hamilton Grant (Bloomington: Indiana University Press, 1993), p. 60.
30   Deleuze and Guattari, *A Thousand Plateaus*, p. 160.

Monstrous Sexuality: Variations on the *Vagina Dentata*

Sarah Alison Miller

Among the images which Plato chose to describe the human soul was a monster, a "many-headed beast, with a ring of tame and savage animal heads."[1] Imagine the soul, he asks, as a Chimera, a Scylla, a Cerberus, all creatures with mismatched body parts and sharp-toothed mouths.[2] Imprudence and acts of injustice feed this internal monster, as the "human" element of the soul grows weak and eventually starves. Plato broadly diagnosed the desires of this "appetitive" element of the soul: "food, drink, sex, and all the things that go along with them."[3] Early-Christian authorities, too, cautioned that indulging in carnal pleasures could generate monstrosities. In the late fourth century BCE, John Chrysostom warned that the wealthy crave such extravagance that, "if a person wishes to dream up one of their desires, nothing would materialise for that prodigy—neither Scylla nor Chimaera nor hippocentaur, but you will find that (their desire) contains all beasts at once."[4]

The excessive desire for carnal pleasures appeared on early lists of Deadly Sins as *luxuria*: luxury, excess, or extravagance, though conceived more broadly than in a strictly sexual sense. But by the early-medieval period, this sin came to be understood and cataloged as the excessive desire for sexual gratification: lust.[5]

---

1   Plato, *Republic,* trans. C.D.C. Reeve (Indianapolis: Hackett, 2004), 588c7–10, p. 292.

2   Ibid., 588c1–5, p. 292.

3   Ibid., 580e1–3, p. 281.

4   John Chrysostom, *On Colossians,* in Wendy Mayer and Pauline Allen (ed. and trans.), *John Chrysostom* (London: Routledge, 2000), 249F, p. 65.

5   The history of the Deadly Sins, and thus of the sin now known as "lust," is complicated and fragmentary. Evagrius of Pontus, a Christian ascetic of the late fourth century, is generally regarded as one of the earliest authors of a formal catalog of sins. Among these sins was *porneia,* which could refer to a range of sexual transgressions including fornication and incest (Bruce Malina, "Does *Porneia* Mean Fornication?" *Novum Testametum* 14/1 [January 1972], p. 17). In later lists, *porneia* was translated as *luxuria.* It has been suggested that the pairing of *castitas* (chastity) as the virtue opposed to *luxuria* in lists of virtues contributed to the eventual substitution of "lust" for *luxuria* (Rosemond Tuve, "Notes on the Virtues and Vices," *Journal of the Warburg and Courtauld*

Chaucer portrayed *luxuria* as "Lecherie" in "The Parson's Tale," and defined it even more narrowly, "to bireve a mayden of hir maydenhede."[6] The philosopher, holy man, and poet express the efforts of their communities to moderate sexual desires lest they grow into something monstrous and insatiably hungry. Sexuality—albeit inextricably bound to pleasure, fecundity, and reproduction—could, they warn, have you in the snares of its teeth.[7] That accounts of uncontrolled or perverse sexuality have repeatedly borrowed from the vocabulary of teratology suggests that a certain vigilance is required to keep sexual monsters and monstrous sex properly policed. Yet, at the same time, monstrous sexuality has proven to be irresistibly useful as a means of negotiating boundaries between what is desirable (whether that be a balanced soul or the promise of eternal salvation) and what is perilous (a deformed soul, corrupting desire, eternal damnation). This negotiation itself has periodically taken the form of sharp-toothed yet alluring monsters.

That iconic toothed monster, the vampire, sinks his teeth into the necks of women, piercing this sensuous flesh and thereby propagating his monstrous species. The biter's hunger satiated, the bitten herself then learns to use her teeth to satisfy her own needs. In the vampire's bite, there is violence, eroticism, and fertility. Anne Rice's erotic vampire and the heart-throb vampire of the *Twilight* series have ingrained in the imagination of modern readers and movie-goers the intersection of sex and monstrous teeth. But there are other monsters who like to bite. Although monstrous teeth generally appear in the mouth—itself an organ built to feed corporeal desires, nutritive and erotic—teeth sprout elsewhere in monstrous flesh, even in that other lipped organ equipped to stimulate and sate desire: the genitals of the female body. Perhaps more than any other toothed monster, the *vagina dentata*—the "vagina with teeth"—is monstrous sexuality incarnate. It is seductive, engulfing, treacherous, and transforming. Its bite, rooted in the female sexual organ and aimed at the male sexual organ, transforms sex, which is an amalgam of pleasure and vulnerability, into a dangerous, bloody, deadly affair. The object of pleasure becomes the agent of violence, the passive pleasurable body becomes the active punishing body, and that slippage of meaning is horrifying. This study of monstrous sexuality examines

---

Institutes 27 [1964], p. 58). For the close relationship between *luxuria* and gluttony in the Middle Ages, see Susan E. Hill, "'The Ooze of Gluttony:' Attitudes Toward Food, Eating and Excess in the Middle Ages," in Richard Newhauser (ed.), *The Seven Deadly Sins: From Communities to Individuals* (Leiden: Kinonklijke Brill NV, 2007), pp. 57–72.

6   Geoffrey Chaucer, *The Riverside Chaucer*, 3rd edn, ed. Larry D. Bensen (Oxford: Oxford University Press, 2008), p. 317. For a discussion of the Deadly Sins in Chaucer, see Frederick Tupper, "Chaucer and the Seven Deadly Sins," *PLMA* 29/1 (1914), pp. 93–128.

7   Anxieties about corrupt or insatiable sexuality is now less often directed towards one's own soul and more often toward others whom we avoid, fear, or prosecute for sex crimes—rapists, pedophiles. But Plato's warning nevertheless retains its poignancy when we question how human beings—sons, daughters, parents, neighbors, teachers, priests, upstanding citizens—become sexual "monsters." As I was formulating my initial thoughts about the subject of this chapter, I conducted an informal poll among my friends and colleagues: what comes to mind when you think of sexual monsters or monstrous sexuality? The most common responses by far were sex offenders.

several incarnations of the *vagina dentata*, some of which take the explicit form of dentate female genitals, and some of which borrow elements from this paradigmatic monster by reference, metaphor, or association. It aims to analyze what these instances communicate about the monstrosity inherent in sexuality and the sexuality inherent in monstrosity, and to consider how these exempla are shaped by the particular desires and fears of the cultures that produce them.

Although this study will focus primarily on examples of the *vagina dentata* found in Greco-Roman, late-medieval, early modern European, and modern American culture, the many iterations of the motif across a variety of folk, literary, and artistic traditions point to its semantic flexibility. Inasmuch as it is able to express a range of assumptions about sex, lust, reproduction, and the female body, the *vagina dentata* endures as a generic monster while remaining adept at articulating the esoteric fantasies of specific texts, persons, and communities. Anthropologists and ethnographers have located instances of the *vagina dentata* in Nahuatl and Pueblo tales from Mesoamerica, in Hopi Indian narratives, and among the tribes of central India.[8] A Baiga tale from the Mandla district of India describes a beautiful girl who, unbeknownst to her, had three teeth in her vagina. With these teeth, she cut into three pieces the penis of each of her many lovers. Despite this vicious reputation, the landlord of her village desired to marry her. He devised a plan to conquer her teeth by allowing four of his servants to have sex with her first. After one of them was maimed, the remaining three worked together—one covering the girl's face with a cloth, one holding her down, and the other thrusting a piece of flint into her vagina—to knock out a tooth. The other teeth were removed with tongs. Though "the girl wept with pain ... she was consoled when the landlord came in and said that he would now marry her immediately."[9] Some variations of the *vagina dentata*

---

8   See Pat Carr and Williard Gingerich, "The Vagina Dentata Motif in Nahuatl and Pueblo Mythic Narratives: A Comparative Study," in Brian Swann (ed.), *Smoothing the Ground: Essays on Native American Oral Literature* (Berkeley: University of California Press, 1983), pp. 187–203; Ekkehart Malotki, "The Story of the 'Tsimonmamant' or Jimson Weed Girls: A Hopi Narrative Featuring the Motif of the Vagina Dentata," in Swann (ed.), *Smoothing the Ground*, pp. 204–20; Stith Thompson, *Tales of the North American Indians* (Cambridge: Harvard University Press, 1929); Erich Neumann, *The Great Mother: An Analysis of the Archetype* (Princeton: Princeton University Press, 1955); and Verrier Elwin, "The Vagina Dentata Legend," *British Journal of Medical Psychology* 19 (1943), pp. 439–53.

9   Elwin, "Vagina Dentata Legend," pp. 439–40. According to Elwin, his research collecting folk tales in central India confirmed the existence of the *vagina dentata* motif in "every tribe" he examined: "I have found it among the Baiga, the Agaria and Asur, the Gond of Mandla and Bilaspur, the Dhoba of Mandla, the Korku, the primitive Lohar of Raipur, the wandering Doma of South Chhattisgarh and the Muria of Bastar." The motif had been previously attested among Native America tribes in north-west America, but had not, Elwin says, been established in South Asia (p. 439). Although Elwin insists that enthnographers should leave to psychologists the task of interpreting tales and dreams featuring toothed vaginas, he posits that the motif is "closely related to the primitive dread of castration," and a "related fear—the dread of impotence" (p. 451).

myth imagine the vagina to be inhabited by a carnivorous fish, fanged snake, or sharp-clawed crab; others imagine the clitoris as a tooth, barb, or saw.[10]

Depictions of menacing female genitals are not reserved to folk tales and myth, but also appear in philosophical and medical texts. In *Timaeus*, Plato describes the womb as an animal (*zōon*) that longs to conceive a child. When it remains barren for too long, it becomes distressed and wanders through the body where it may obstruct breathing and cause a variety of maladies.[11] According to the Hippocratic treatise, *Diseases of Women*, which was compiled between the late fourth and early third centuries BCE, the womb may move toward the liver, the head, the heart, the hip joint, and the breasts for a variety of reasons, among them: "menstrual suppression, exhaustion, insufficient food, sexual abstinence, and dryness or lightness of the womb."[12] These texts engineer female reproductive organs capable of experiencing needs and acting on their own behalf to satisfy them. The female body is often harmed in the process. As in mythical versions, masculine action is required to subdue wily female genitals.

The charge that alluring female genitals may harbor something painfully sharp appears, too, in the late-medieval text, *Women's Secrets*, once attributed to Albert the Great. This text warns of women who wound and infect the male genitals by placing pieces of iron in their vaginas.[13] The witch-trial manual, *Malleus Maleficarum*—which drew evidence for its misogynist claims from *Women's Secrets*—cites penis removal among the crimes of witches.[14] These representations of female reproductive organs

---

For a summary of the various psychoanalytical interpretations that have been applied to the *vagina dentata* motif in folklore, see Solimar Otero, "'Fearing Our Mothers': An Overview of the Psychoanalytic Theories Concerning the Vagina Dentata Motif," *American Journal of Psychoanalysis* 56/3 (September 1996), pp. 269–89.

10   Neumann, *Great Mother*, p. 168; Elwin, "Vagina Dentata Legend," pp. 440–3.

11   Plato, *Timaeus*, ed., Ioannes Burnet (Oxford: Oxford University Press, 1902), 91c. For more on animalistic references to both male and female reproductive organs in Greek and Roman gynecological literature, see Helen King, "Once Upon a Text: Hysteria from Hippocrates," in Sander L. Gilman et al. (eds), *Hysteria Beyond Freud* (Berkeley: University of California Press, 1993), pp. 25–8. In the second century CE, Soranus insisted in his *Gynecology* (3.9) that "the uterus does not issue forth like a wild animal (*therion*) from the lair, delighted by fragrant odors and fleeing bad odors: rather it is drawn together because of the stricture caused by the inflammation," *Soranus' Gynecology*, trans. Owsei Temkin (Baltimore: Johns Hopkins University Press, 1991), p. 153.

12   *Diseases of Women* 1.7, 2.127 (liver), 2.123 (head), 2.124 (heart), 2.133 (hip joint, breasts); see King, "Once Upon a Text," pp. 14, 18–21. For the many symptoms associated with womb movement in Greek and Roman gynecological texts, see ibid., pp. 18–19. Among the therapies suggested in the Hippocratic treatises are: "marriage and/or pregnancy, scent therapy, irritant pessaries, and various herbal concoctions administered by mouth, by nose, or direct to the vulva" (p.14).

13   Helen Rodnite Lemay, *Women's Secrets: A Translation of Pseudo-Albertus Magnus's 'De Secretis Mulierum' with Commentaries* (Albany, NY: State University of New York Press, 1992), p. 88.

14   For the use of *Women's Secrets* as a reference for *Malleus Maleficarum*, see Lemay, *Women's Secrets*, pp. 49–58. For the sexual crimes of witches, including penis theft, see Walter Stephens, *Demon Lovers: Witchcraft, Sex, and the Crisis of Belief* (Chicago: University

Figure 14.1 Scylla relief plaque from Melos, fifth century BCE (photo credit: Erich Lessing/Art Resource, NY).

portray the exigencies of sex and reproduction in the form of a feral, dangerous part of the female body and, by doing so, characterize female sexuality as something that should be feared and must be tamed: domesticated by intercourse, pregnancy, and childbirth. In this regard, the female reproductive apparatus materializes the slippage that so often occurs between the normative and the monstrous, the desirable and the abhorrent, and—inasmuch as the womb or vagina is an active agent over which women may or may not have control—the self and the other.

The following instances of the *vagina dentata* motif which I have chosen to explore in more detail map out a genealogy of toothed female genitals, beginning with one prototype, the ancient sea-monster, Scylla, whose loins often took the form of canine mouths. Scylla's body seems to speak expressively about the intersection

of Chicago Press, 2002), pp. 300–21; Walter Stephens, "Witches Who Steal Penises: Impotence and Illusion in *Malleus Maleficarum,*" *Journal of Medieval and Early Modern Studies* 28/3 (1998), pp. 495–529; Moira Smith, "The Flying Phallus and the Laughing Inquisitor: Penis Theft in the 'Malleus Maleficarum,'" *Journal of Folklore Research* 39/1 (January–April 2002), pp. 85–117; and Hans Peter Broedel, *The* Malleus Maleficarum *and the Construction of Witchcraft: Theology and Popular Belief* (Manchester: Manchester University Press, 2003), pp. 167–88.

of monstrosity and sexuality, for she has lent her shape to several creatures whose toothed genitals articulate the slippery borders between the allure of carnal pleasure and the horror of punishment, pain, and death. In her earliest incarnations, Scylla was a six-headed sea-monster who menaced Odysseus and his men on their voyage home to Ithaca after the Trojan War. Later classical accounts imagine her as a hybrid creature, beautiful woman on top and barking dogs below the waist.

In a fifth-century terra cotta relief plaque, the visual emphasis is on the alluring beauty of Scylla's human torso and face (Figure 14.1). Her full breasts are exposed to the viewer while she pensively places her hand to her chin. Her face follows classical standards for female beauty. A great sea serpent tail, crested with spines, emerges from beneath her skirts, making it almost possible to overlook the two snarling dogs that seem to pull her forward, their energy in great contrast to the calm repose of her human parts.

In *Paradise Lost*, John Milton drew from the Greco-Roman Scylla a model for his depiction of Sin, who is impregnated by Satan and gives birth to Death. The various versions of Scylla's story, her protean body, and the multiple interpretations of her monstrosity that have appeared from archaic Greece through seventeenth-century England, attest to the diverse forms of monstrous sexuality fashioned by cultures and authors invested in their own notions of normal, idealized, and perverse sexuality. Yet despite the fact that the monster is always a product of its particular environment and despite the vicissitudes of Scylla's body, she and her toothed sisters exemplify the ways in which female sexuality—both sexual physicality and erotic desire—is expressed monstrously. Scylla's lineage of figures bearing toothed female sexual organs continues today, both in imagination and, through modification, reality. The film *Teeth* (2007), for example, features a heroine who, after suffering a series of sexual violations, learns to exercise her feminine power through the gnashing of her vaginal teeth. This modern manifestation is rather different from its classical and medieval prototypes, in that the audience is encouraged to celebrate the heroine's empowerment, rather than demonizing female sexuality on account of it. The Rape-aXe (2010) female condom—armed with hidden plastic barbs positioned to maim rapists—was created to be marketed to women in South Africa, a country that has been called "the rape capital of the world."[15]

Scylla: Hungry for Heroic Men

In contemporary imagery, Scylla's identity has been largely disembodied. She has become a metaphor, her name paired with and juxtaposed to Charybdis—once a vicious whirlpool—to illustrate the mediation between two insurmountable threats, neither of which is notably toothed, voracious, or deadly. Yet for Odysseus's crew, Scylla was anything but a figure of speech. In Homer's *Odyssey* (circa eighth-

---

15   Rachel Jewkes and Naeema Abrahams, "The Epidemiology of Rape and Sexual Coercion in South Africa: An Overview," *Social Science & Medicine* 55/7 (2002), p. 1231.

century BCE), Circe warns Odysseus of a hungry, razor-toothed creature who lives inside a "yawning cave." Though "yelping, no louder than any suckling pup," Circe assures Odysseus that "she's a grisly monster":[16]

> *She has twelve legs, all writhing, dangling down*
> *and six long swaying necks, a hideous head on each,*
> *each head barbed with a triple row of fangs, thickset,*
> *packed tight—and armed to the hilt with black death!*
> *Holed up in the cavern's bowels from her waist down*
> *she shoots out her heads, out of that terrifying pit ...*[17]

As a *female* monster, Scylla is one of several dangerous or obstructing female creatures that plague Odysseus and his men on their journey. Though without sharp teeth, Circe, the Sirens, and Calypso demonstrate the alluring but perilous nature of feminine charms. Scylla, on the other hand, just seems hungry: she is, in *The Odyssey*, unlike on the relief plaque from Melos, ugly, scary, and without erotic charm. Yet despite Circe's counsel that heroic tactics are no match for this monster, Odysseus cannot bring himself to avoid her. He must bare his sword and confront her man-eating teeth to save the lives of his shipmates.[18] Scylla, however, snatches and devours six of his men. Later recounting the attack, Odysseus remembers the sight of their hands and feet flailing over his head, their screams, how they desperately shrieked his name.[19]

For Odysseus and his crew, Scylla's teeth, rooted in her six mouths rather than below her waist, represent the inevitable danger of the sea. She is a monster whose hunger cannot be conquered by heroic powers, and her teeth are supremely destructive for this reason: they cannot be tamed by Odysseus's wit, innovation, or sexual charm. This is the Odysseus whose name, throughout *The Odyssey*, is his heroic badge, the steady refrain of his fellow war veterans, his wife, and his son. It was Odysseus's refusal to be remembered as "Nobody" that impelled him to reveal his name to the blinded Cyclops, Polyphemous, thereby incurring the wrath of Poseidon.[20] In this encounter with Polyphemous, Odysseus's name is affirmed as a source of power, even if that power ultimately elicits divine punishment; but in his encounter with another man-eating monster, Scylla, Odysseus's name—screamed in desperation by his men as they are engulfed by her toothed maws—signals his impotence. Although Homer's Scylla is clearly a voracious female monster,

---

16   Homer, *The Odyssey*, trans. Robert Fagles (New York: Penguin, 1996), 12.89–91, p. 274.
17   Ibid., 12.99–104, p. 274.
18   Ibid., 12.128–30, p. 275.
19   Ibid., 12.267–70, p. 279; 12.280–82, p. 279.
20   Ibid., 9.455, p. 224. Part of Odysseus's strategy for blinding and escaping the imprisonment of Polyphemous was introducing himself as "Nobody" (*outis*), thereby rendering meaningless the blinded Polyphemous's cry for help: "Nobody is killing me!"

it would await her later incarnations to underscore the relationship between her teeth and her sexuality.

When Virgins Become Monsters: Ovid's Scylla

The Roman poet Ovid (b. 43 BCE) gives us another version of Scylla's monstrosity in his work on transforming bodies. In *Metamorphoses*, Ovid recounts the cause of Scylla's monstrous shape with attention to the psychological impact of this monstrosity on Scylla herself. He creates a narrative of her monstrous teeth, one that knits together the form of her genitals and her sexual history, but in this narrative Scylla is victimized by sexual voraciousness and suffers from the gnashing teeth that emerge from her own body. Ovid tells us that she was once a virgin nymph whose beauty aroused the lust of the sea-god, Glaucus, who spurns Circe in favor of Scylla. When Scylla flees the sexual advances of Glaucus, Circe punishes her for refusing the suitor whom she herself desires. In this version, Circe does not warn about the danger of Scylla's teeth, as she did in *The Odyssey*, but rather causes those teeth to sprout. In a fit of jealousy, she poisons the pool where Scylla is accustomed to bathe.

> Scylla came and had lowered herself up to the middle of her waist when she saw her own loins [inguina] disfigured by barking monsters. And at first, thinking that those parts did not belong to her own body, she shrinks back and tries to depart and fears the violent mouths of the dogs. But that which she flees, she drags along with her, and feeling for the body substance of her thighs, legs, and feet, she finds the gaping maws of Cerberus in place of those parts. She stands upon a frenzy of dogs and she restrains the backs of the beasts beneath her, her loins mutilated and her womb [uterus] visible.[21]

Almost as an afterthought, Ovid adds that Scylla eventually vented her hatred for Circe against Odysseus's company and would have destroyed Aeneas's shipmates, too, if she had not been transformed into a rock.[22] Ovid's Scylla may be avoided by sailors, but she, rather than heroic men, is most menaced by her teeth.

This alienation from her own body is an experience which Scylla shares with many characters in *Metamorphoses*, where physical transformation often preserves in unspecified ways the mind, memories, and impulses of the original body. Ovid's female characters often experience this corporeal estrangement after being raped or narrowly escaping rape, usually through physical transformation into something incapable of sexual penetration—plant, tree, constellation, stream. Scylla avoids the sexual advances of Glaucus, yet the "gaping maws" emerging from between her legs,

---

21   Ovid, *Ovidi Nasonis Metamorphoses*, ed. R.J. Tarrant (New York: Oxford University Press, 2004), 14.59–67, p. 412, my translation.
22   Ibid., 14.72–74, p. 412.

her disfigured loins, and her exposed womb are inescapable. Ovid gives us a Scylla who is victimized by the association of sexuality and fertility with monstrosity, who cowers at the sight of her own gnashing teeth, but drags them along with her. The message to be read in Scylla's monstrosity is that the female body that does not appropriately manage its sexuality teeters on the brink of becoming bestial.[23] Virginity, moreover, is cast as a precarious state that gives way to a female identity bound to the brutish antics of its sexual and reproductive anatomy.

The *Vagina Dentata* allegorized and Christianized

Ovid's Scylla is a clear literary ancestor of the figure of Sin in Milton's *Paradise Lost*. The suggestion that Scylla's teeth represent a punishment in the form of monstrous pregnancy and birth becomes fully developed in the tangle of "yelling Monsters … hourly conceiv'd / And hourly born," that torment Sin: "farr less abhorrd than these / Vexid Scylla."[24] By the time Milton wrote *Paradise Lost*, medieval and Renaissance readers of Ovid had drawn from Scylla's specific physicality universal implications concerning female monstrous sexuality. Of the many transforming bodies re-signified in this tradition that aimed to "moralize" Ovid by allegorizing his pagan tales of transformation within a Christian context, Scylla's body proved to be among the most popular and influential. In 1632, George Sandys published *Ovid's Metamorphoses, Englished, Mythologiz'd, and Represented in Figures* in which Scylla is said to represent a beautiful virgin who is "polluted with the sorceries of *Circe*" when she allows her "maiden honor to bee deflowered by bewitching pleasure" and "is transformed into an horrid monster."[25] Scylla is de-toothed in the process of allegorization, yet she

---

23   The textual record between Homer's *Odyssey* and Ovid's *Metamorphoses* offers further instances of Scylla's labile monstrosity. In his *Argonautica*, Apollonius of Rhodes (third century BCE) records Hera cautioning the Argonauts about the terrible jaws of Scylla, but without any mention of dogs' mouths (4.786 ff., 4.825). The second-century mythographer, Pseudo-Apollodorus, describes Scylla as a creature with the face and breast of a woman, but with six dog heads and twelve dog feet emerging from her thighs. Her canine teeth are said to have chewed up six of Odysseus's men (*Bibliotecha* [*Library*] Ep.7. 20–21). For the relationship between Greco-Roman material and literary representations of Scylla, see Mercedes Aguirre Castro, "Scylla: Hideous Monster or Femme Fatale? A Case of Contradiction Between Literary and Artistic Evidence," *Cuadernos de Filología Clásica: Estudios griegos e indoeuropeos* 12 (2002), pp. 319–28; and George M.A. Hanfmann, "The Scylla of Corvey and Her Ancestors,' *Dumbarton Oaks Papers* 41, *Studies on Art and Archeology in Honor of Ernst Kitzinger on His Seventy-Fifth Birthday* (1987), pp. 249–60.

24   John Milton, *Paradise Lost*, in Merrit Y. Hughes (ed.), *Complete Poems and Major Prose* (Upper Saddle River, NJ: Prentice Hall, 1957), 2.794–95, p. 251; 2.659–60, p. 248.

25   George Sandys, *Ovid's Metamorphoses, Englished, Mythologiz'd, and Represented in Figures*, ed. Karl Hulley and Stanley Vandersall (Lincoln, NE: University of Nebraska Press, 1970), pp. 645–6, italics in original.

remains dangerous by way of her erotic power, able to "shipwracke others ... upon those ruinous rocks, and make them share in the same calamities ... in regard of the impudency of lascivious women, hardened by custome."[26]

Sandys's allegory clearly links degrading carnal pleasures to female sexuality by reading in Scylla's transformation a message about virgins becoming whores. Yet there is also here a message about the monstrosity of the human condition:

> that the upper part of her body, is feigned to retaine humane figure, and the lower to be bestiall; intimates how man, a divine creature, endued with wisdom and intelligence, in whose superior parts, as in a high tower, that immortall spirit resideth, who only of all that hath life erects his looks unto heaven, can never so degenerate into a beast, as when he giveth himself over to the lowe delights of those baser parts of the body, Dogs and Wolves, the blind & savage fury of concupiscence ...[27]

Like Ovid's self-divided and alienated Scylla, the human being is a monstrous hybrid of heaven-striving spirit and pleasure-hungry body, its "baser parts" harassing its "superior parts." Recall that Plato had invoked Scylla to describe the disordered and deformed soul. The allegorized Scylla succumbs to monstrous sexual desire, and the fitting punishment for this corruption is a perpetual, cyclical feeding of lust upon itself. Her teeth represent a sexual appetite that threatens to transform humans into beasts. Scylla's monstrosity here signifies the ravages of concupiscence on humanity, while in *Paradise Lost*, the toothed-womb represents sin itself—now personified as Sin.

Born Athena-like from Satan's head when he conspired to rebel against the powers of Heaven, Sin—not yet a toothed monster—is soon impregnated by Satan himself. The "odious offspring" of that pregnancy is Death whose birth disfigures Sin's once-attractive body as he, in Sin's own words, "Tore through my entrails, that with fear and pain / Distorted, all my nether shape thus grew / Transform'd."[28] After his destructive emergence from Sin's body, Death promptly pursues her, and "Inflam'd with lust" overtook her "in embraces forcible and foule":[29]

> ... of that rape begot
> These yelling Monsters that with ceaseless cry
> Surround me, as thou saw'st, hourly conceived
> And hourly born, with sorrow infinite
> To me, for when they list, into the womb
> That bred them they return, and howl and gnaw
> My bowels, their repast; then bursting forth

---

26 Ibid., pp. 645–6.
27 Ibid., p. 646.
28 Milton, *Paradise Lost*, 2.783–5, p. 250.
29 Ibid., 2.2.790–93, p. 251. See Alexander A. Meyers, "'Embraces Forcible and Foul': Viewing Milton's Sin as a Rape Victim," *Milton Quarterly* 2/1 (1994), pp. 11–16.

Afresh with conscious terrors vex me round,
that rest or intermission none I find.[30]

In contradiction to the castrating *vagina dentata*, Sin—like Scylla—is victimized by her own body: she becomes, literally, the fodder for her own teeth as she suffers biting, howling mouths that are nevertheless indistinguishable from the anatomy of her female reproductive apparatus. The creatures that inhabit Sin's genitals take the form of parasitic offspring born only to chew their way back into her body to be born yet again. The polymorphous *vagina dentata* is a monster that may maim the reproductive male body during the act of sex, but it may also turn its teeth inward, to vex and bite the female reproductive body itself. It becomes a monster that cannot be conquered by male bravery, strength, or wit. Its teeth—whether they materialize punishment or recapitulate sexual violation—become a feature of female sexual and reproductive identity. This incarnation of the female genitals thus expresses Aristotle's summation of female identity: she is a deformity (*anapēria*), a monster (*teras*).[31] The legacy of Sin's suffering bears out this transformation of toothed genitals from the monstrous birth particular to a victim of sexual violation to the "natural" functions of the female reproductive body. Sin suffers the same fate that the Father promises to Eve and her daughters: "Thy sorrow I will greatly multiply / By thy Conception; Children thou shalt bring in sorrow forth."[32] After the Fall, the female reproductive process itself is marked by the monstrosity of Sin's *vagina dentata*.

The Fall also enables Sin to direct her teeth toward the world at large. Once the only fodder available to her "yelling Monsters," Sin now summons her "hell-hounds" to:

> ... *lick up the draff and filth*
> *Which man's polluting Sin with taint hath shed*
> *On what was pure, till cramm'd and gorg'd, nigh burst*
> *With suckt and glutted offal ...*[33]

By way of Sin's monstrosity, then, all of humankind becomes "Food for so foul a Monster," that is, Death, destined to "satisfy his Rav'nous Maw."[34] Eve laments that her descendants will be birthed in pain only to become "devour'd / by death at last."[35] In *Paradise Lost*, the teeth of Sin's womb—and by association the painful womb of the female reproductive body—become interlaced with the teeth of Death's mouth,

---

30   Milton, *Paradise Lost*, 2.794–802, p. 251. For a study of Milton's sources for the figure of Sin, see Catherine Gimelli Martin, "The Sources of Milton's Sin Reconsidered," *Milton Quarterly* 35/1 (2001), pp. 1–8.

31   Aristotle, *Generation of Animals*, trans. A.L. Peck (Cambridge, MA: Harvard University Press, 1979), 775a, II. 15–16 (4.6), and 767b, II. 7–9 (4.3).

32   Milton, *Paradise Lost*, 10.193–5, p. 411.

33   Ibid., 10.629–33, p. 421.

34   Ibid., 10.986–91, p. 429.

35   Ibid., 10.980–81, p. 429.

Figure 14.2 Illustration of Hildegard's apocalyptic vision, *Scivias* 3.11, Eibengen manuscript (photo credit: Erich Lessing/Art Resource, NY).

and the anatomical site of sex and childbirth becomes associated with the ultimate threshold of mortality: the gateway to hell. Perhaps drawing from Vergil's placement of "twi-formed Scyllas" at the mouth of the underworld in *The Aeneid*, Milton stations Sin as Portress of Hell Gate.[36] The hero, Herakles, who journeyed to the underworld to tame "the toothy hell-hound Cerberus," and medieval illustrations of the entrance

---

36 Vergil, *The Aeneid*, trans. Robert Fitzgerald (New York: Vintage Classics, 1990), 6.391, p. 169; Milton, *Paradise Lost*, 2.648–9, p. 248. Elsewhere in *The Aeneid*, "Weird Scylla" is described in this way: "Scylla lies immured in a rocky cave / In clefts of inky darkness, darting out / Her faces, pulling ships on to the reef. / First she looks human—a fair-breasted girl / Down to the groin [*pubis*]; but then, below, a monster / Creature of the sea [*pistrix*], a wolvish belly [*uterus*] / Merging in dolphins' tails" (3.570–76; pp. 80–81).

to hell as the "devouring mouth of a monstrous predator," bear witness to the menacing valence of teeth positioned at thresholds.[37] The *vagina dentata*, a "barred and dangerous entrance" nevertheless destined to be crossed by man, lends its shape to the darkest, deepest borderlands known to humanity.[38]

The twelfth-century mystic and polymath, Hildegard of Bingen, records in her *Scivias* a vision that graphically establishes this relationship between the hellmouth and female genitals. In this apocalyptic vision, Mother Church is assaulted by the Antichrist:

> *And from her waist to the place that denotes the female, she [Mother Church] had various scaly blemishes; and in that latter place was a black and monstrous head. It had fiery eyes, and ears like an ass', and nostrils and a mouth like a lion's; it opened wide its jowls and terribly clashed its horrible iron-colored teeth. And from this head down to her knees, the figure was white and red, as if bruised by many beatings; and from her knees to her tendons where they joined her heels, which appeared white, she was covered with blood. And behold! That monstrous head moved from its place with such a great shock that the figure of the woman was shaken through all her limbs. And a great mass of excrement adhered to the head; and it raised itself up upon a mountain and tried to ascend the height of heaven.*[39]

This vision was illustrated by a miniature in a—now lost, but reproduced—illuminated manuscript of *Scivias* (Figure 14.2).[40] In the lower register of the illustration, we see Mother Church, serene from the waist up, but in the place of her genitals appears a shaggy and pointy-toothed head. This monstrous figure simultaneously seems to emerge from and attack her body, leaving her legs marked with blemishes and blood. Mother Church is violated by the Antichrist, but Hildegard's meditations on this vision specify that this evil will come from within the Church, "raging with the arts he first used to seduce, in monstrous shamefulness, and blackest wickedness ... causing people to deny God and tainting

---

37 Aleksander Pluskowski, "Apocalyptic Monsters: Animal Inspirations for the Iconography of Medieval North European Devourers," in Bettina Bildhauer and Robert Mills (eds), *The Monstrous Middle Ages* (Toronto: University of Toronto Press, 2003), pp. 155–76. For more on medieval conceptualizations of hell as a hungry mouth, see G.D. Schmidt, *The Iconography of the Mouth of Hell: Eighth-Century Britain to the Fifteenth Century* (Selinsgrove, PA: Susquehanna University Press, 1995).

38 Wolfgang Lederer, *The Fear of Women* (New York: Harcourt, 1968), p. 47.

39 Hildegard of Bingen, *Scivias*, trans. Mother Columba Hart and Jane Bishop (Mahwah, NJ: Paulist Press, 1990), p. 493, italics in original.

40 The Rupertsberg manuscript of *Scivias* was created during Hildegard's lifetime (circa 1165–75), and was lost some time after 1945 when it was moved to Dresden for safekeeping. Fortunately, a facsimile based on a series of black and white photographs of the original miniatures had been made in Eibingen between 1927 and 1933. See Richard Kenneth Emmerson, "The Representation of Antichrist in Hildegard of Bingen's *Scivias*: Image, Word, Commentary, and Visionary Experience," *Gesta* 41/2 (2002), p. 95.

their minds and tearing the Church with the greed of rapine."[41] The Antichrist's own mother will "engage in vile fornication with men … And in the burning heat of this fornication, she will conceive the son of perdition without knowing which man's semen engendered him."[42] Both Mother Church and the mother of the Antichrist thus embody the effects of sexual desire in the fallen world: rape, painful childbirth, and sexual voraciousness merge under the image of this toothed creature in "the place that denotes the female."[43]

That mastering these toothed thresholds requires holy powers, heroic strength, a painful ordeal, rape, or death substantiates the notion that the *vagina dentata* is a monster that will maim unless it is mastered. But what do we make of Scylla and Sin, whose vaginal teeth appear to represent sexual violation and excruciating birth such that they threaten the integrity of the female body rather than the male body? Some recent incarnations of the *vagina dentata*—one fictional and the other factual—highlight the complicated relationship between monstrous female sexuality and female sexual vulnerability.

The Raped Body Bites Back

The film *Teeth* (2007), directed by Mitchell Lichtenstein, stars Jess Weixler as Dawn O'Keefe, a teenage virgin who discovers, through a series of bloody sexual encounters, that she has teeth in her vagina. Dawn is a chastity enthusiast with a talent for converting other teens to her Christian abstinence group. When she is raped by a member of this group, Tobey, her vaginal teeth bite for the first time. By the movie's end, Dawn has taken off three fingers of a gynecologist inappropriately performing a pelvic exam, and bitten off the penises of both a male acquaintance who had made wagers about her sexual availability, and of her licentious stepbrother. In the final scene of the film, Dawn has hitchhiked a ride out of town, and attempts to exit the car at a gas station, but the car's driver repeatedly locks the doors while licking his lips salaciously. Dawn appears briefly alarmed, but then deliberately arranges her face into a seductive smirk directed at the camera. The message she seems to communicate is that she will no longer be a sexual victim. Her body may be monstrous, but she has learned to wield her teeth to punish monstrous sexuality.

Teeth shares several features with a small genre of rape-revenge films analyzed by Barbara Creed in her book, *The Monstrous Feminine* (1993).[44] Creed argues that

---

41   Hildegard, *Scivias*, p. 498. For more on Hildegard's vision of the Antichrist, see Barbara Newman, *Sister of Wisdom: St Hildegard's Theology of the Feminine* (Berkeley: University of California Press, 1989), pp. 243–5, and Emmerson, "Representation of Antichrist," pp. 95–110.

42   Hildegard, *Scivias*, p. 502.

43   Emmerson, "Representation of Antichrist," p. 101.

44   Barbara Creed, *The Monstrous Feminine: Film, Feminism, Psychoanalysis* (London: Routledge, 1993), p. 128.

movies of this genre feature a female protagonist who subverts the cinematic paradigm of female victimization in horror films by killing, maiming, or torturing male victims. In particular, she analyzes *I Spit on Your Grave* (1978), which features a heroine who is brutally raped by four men and left for dead.[45] She ultimately punishes each of these men by drawing them into a sexual encounter, and then murdering them, some by actual castration. Although Creed grants that the representation of woman in *I Spit on Your Grave* is "still misogynist" inasmuch as she "signifies sex and death," she emphasizes the protagonist's transition from "battered, bleeding wound" into an "all-powerful, all-destructive, deadly *femme castratrice*" who, though monstrous, "appears to win, not lose, audience sympathy."[46] *Teeth* is a movie about Dawn's transformation from an abstinence-preaching virgin to a *femme castratrice* of the most literal sort, but it should be stressed that she overcomes her rigidity and naiveté, learning to use her vagina as an instrument of power, only by being sexually exploited, molested, and raped. Moreover, her sexual apparatus—though lethal to sexually voracious men—remains the alluring, but deceptive monster. The *vagina dentata* retains its ferocity, and the female body continues to signify sex and death.

Although she is the putative victor of the film, Dawn's sexuality is defined in terms of her vulnerability to sexual manipulation and assault. This fictive portrait of female sexuality is lamentably mirrored in the real lives of women today, especially in those parts of the world where rape is both rampant and virtually immune to legal prosecution. The so-called "anti-rape condom," Rape-aXe, was developed by a South African medical technician, Sonnet Ehlers, in 2005 in the hope of providing women with a weapon to defend themselves against rapists. Ehlers has said that she began thinking about the possibility of a real-life *vagina dentata* several decades ago when a rape victim confided to her the wish, "If only I had teeth down there."[47] The latex device, which is meant to be worn like a tampon, is fitted with "razor-sharp barbs" that attach themselves to the penis of the attacker. According to the official website for Rape-aXe, the "immense discomfort" experienced by the attacker paralyzes him long enough for the victim to escape. The barbs must be surgically removed, "which will result in the positive identification of the attacker and subsequent arrest."[48]

Though surely well intentioned, Ehlers's invention has garnered criticism on several grounds. As an "anti-rape" device, Rape-aXe is a misnomer. It functions only after the vagina has been penetrated, and may also put rape victims in increased danger of being beaten or killed by their rapists. As South Africa has one of the highest rape rates in the world, some critics worry that Rape-aXe may provide a false sense of security in this environment of fear, while actually serving

---

45 A remake was made by Steven R. Monroe in 2010, suggesting continued interest in the theme.

46 Creed, *Monstrous Feminine*, pp. 131, 129.

47 Sonnet Ehlers, *Rape-aXe: Take Back the Power*, January 16, 2011, <http://www.antirape.co.za/>.

48 Ibid.

Figure 14.3 "Medieval" chastity belt, Cluny Museum (photo credit: Wellcome Library, London).

as a constant reminder to the woman wearing it that she is a potential victim of sexual violence. Lisa Vetten of the Centre for the Study of Violence and Reconciliation of South Africa has, in this regard, warned that Rape-aXe forces women to "adapt to rape," and likened it to a modern chastity belt.[49] Ehlers has countered that "a medieval deed deserves a medieval consequence."[50] That Vetten and Ehlers both turned toward this medieval device to articulate their views about Rape-aXe—one to criticize it and the other to defend it—merits inspection. In his book, *The Medieval Chastity Belt: A Myth-Making Process*, Albrecht Classen has convincingly argued that the medieval chastity belt never existed, but was instead an invention of eighteenth- and nineteenth-century cultural historians. As such, it is an imaginary object that projects onto medieval men and women the fantasies of later minds.[51] Classen concludes that the so-called medieval chastity belts on display in museums today, many of which are fitted with metal teeth, "were deliberately produced in the nineteenth or twentieth century as objects to incite horror, curiosity, male pride, and to poke fun at a primitive, if not barbaric past" (Figure 14.3).[52]

The Cluny Museum chastity belt, which is arguably the most famous specimen, is equipped with a serrated vulva, lock, and key. It replaces the fantasy of desirable and pleasurable female genitals with a menacing mechanical replica that, despite its destructive capabilities, can be controlled by the man who possesses its key. The Cluny chastity belt thus represents a *vagina dentata* stationed to protect the threshold of the toothless vagina of the woman who is incapable or unwilling to police her own body boundaries.

Rape-aXe, by contrast, is an imaginary object—it currently exists as a prototype—that was created to combat a very real threat. And yet, it is an object that nevertheless projects sexual and violent fantasies onto the female body. Though the Rape-aXe condom was conceived as an empowering weapon, when the *vagina dentata* mutates from a creature born of misogynist myth into a creature of feminist retribution, monstrosity remains a necessary facet of a female sexuality, characterized as vulnerable and vicious.

49　Lauren Frayer, "South Africa Debuts Anti-Rape Female Condom," AOL News, June 21, 2010, <http://www.aolnews.com/2010/06/21/south-africa-debuts-anti-rape-female-condom/>.

50　Ehlers, *Rape-aXe: Take Back the Power*.

51　Albrecht Classen, *The Medieval Chastity Belt: A Myth-Making Process* (New York: Palgrave Macmillan, 2007).

52　Ibid., p. 61.

The sexually vulnerable and vicious heroine of *Teeth* is victimized, she is told more than once, because her body sends mixed messages. With her mouth, she demands sexual autonomy, but her rapist reads in her kisses sexual availability; she asks for a ride out of town, but the driver who picks her up assumes she is also willing to grant him sexual favors in return. In one scene, when she says she wants to end a sexual encounter, she is told: "Your mouth is saying one thing, babe, but your sweet pussy is saying something very different."[53] The message here is that the female body — with its lipped, and possibly toothed, orifices — is imagined as saying one thing, but meaning another, that it always speaks its sexual availability, even when it sets limits on that availability. The female voice, the one that consents to or refuses sexual acts, is thus stifled while the vagina is ventriloquized to speak the desires and fears of the other. Circe punishes Ovid's Scylla for being beautiful while refusing the erotic advances of Glaucus; the upper body of Sandys's Scylla longs for heaven, while the lower body longs to satisfy corporeal desires; Sin is raped by her son and tortured by the offspring she conceives. Dawn's toothed genitals and those manufactured by the Rape-aXe condom are similarly symptomatic of a female body that is presumed to be sexually exploitable, even when it violently protests. As a monster, the *vagina dentata* is a corporeal cipher made to express the conflicts of the cultures that produce it. It expresses the contradictory roles constructed for female sexuality by imagining the vagina to be a threshold that invites and threatens, that ushers new life into the world but also augurs death. Conquering, de-toothing, and raping the *vagina dentata* is, in part, an effort to stabilize the meaning of the sexual female body, which — to varying degrees in various cultures — is determined by the status of its reproductive system: virgins become wives who become mothers who become useless old women.[54] Sex is the process by which this body's narrowly conceived meaning becomes clear. When this sex is non-consensual, the inscription of that meaning becomes a vicious instrument of control.

The *vagina dentata* provides a paradigmatic illustration of how erotic desire, fear of the other, and the inexorable need to procreate become bound together in that threshold of the female body that other bodies cross. Sex and childbirth are processes wherein bodies are both joined and pulled apart, and this negotiation of corporeal boundaries entails a negotiation of corporeal meaning. The fantasy of toothed genitals aims to resolve the ambiguous implications of these negotiations by reifying female sexual identity as a monster. Under its various guises, the *vagina dentata* transforms the sexual and reproductive female body into a wild animal, a deformed virgin, a tortured mother, a rape victim. But the sexual and reproductive female body is such a frightening monster precisely because it is so viscerally attractive and utterly familiar. All human bodies cleave from the boundaries of the female body. In some sense, the *vagina dentata* represents the barred entrance to humanity's primordial home. As a paradigmatic illustration of

---

53   *Teeth*, Dir. Mitchell Lichtenstein, Mitchell Lichtenstein and Joyce Pierpoline, 2007, DVD.
54   For more on the relationship between these facets of female identity and notions of monstrosity, particularly in the Middle Ages, see Sarah Alison Miller, *Medieval Monstrosity and the Female Body* (New York: Routledge, 2010).

monstrous sexuality, it thus unevenly performs the monster's task of stabilizing the boundaries of what is normal, natural, and proper by locating what is aberrant, deformed, and threatening in the other. It also exemplifies how monstrosity erodes the boundaries between desire and dread, fertility and mortality.

Postcolonial Monsters: A Conversation with Partha Mitter

Partha Mitter, with Asa Simon Mittman and Peter Dendle

Editorial Introduction

In 1977, Partha Mitter published his landmark study *Much Maligned Monsters.*[1] Rooted in Postcolonial Studies, a field only just being developed—Edward Said's *Orientalism* would be published the following year[2]—this book seeks to explore the interpretations and misinterpretations of Indian art by Western scholars who often saw monsters where artists intended gods. The tremendous range of Hindu mythology, such fertile inspiration for the visual arts, reinforced Western preconceptions about the "exotic" East.

Mitter is a renowned scholar, a recipient of numerous fellowships and awards, who has lectured and taught throughout the world, including the Getty Research Institute in Los Angeles, Columbia, Princeton, Oxford and Cambridge universities, as well as the Institute for Advanced Study in Princeton. He is currently Emeritus Professor in Art History at the University of Sussex and a member of Wolfson College, Oxford University.

We asked Professor Mitter if, rather than writing a traditionally formatted essay, he would be interested in engaging with us in a dialogue about the issues and concerns that led him to write *Much Maligned Monsters*, and about his continued thinking on the subject of the role of the monstrous in South Asian culture, as seen from within and without. What follows is the transcript of our discussion, augmented with notes and bibliography for further reading.[3]

---

1   Partha Mitter, *Much Maligned Monsters: A History of European Reaction to Indian Art* (Oxford: Claredon Press, 1977) (further references use the abbreviation *MMM*). *MMM* was reissued by the University of Chicago Press in 1992 with a new preface covering some of the changes in Western interpretations of Indian art.
2   Edward Said, *Orientalism: Western Conceptions of the Orient* (London: Pantheon Books, 1978).
3   Our thanks to Sydney Williams for her assistance with these notes and sources.

Interview with Partha Mitter

1. Mittman and Dendle: Are there unique features that appear in Indian (or South Asian) art to denote that someone or something is "monstrous" (either physically or morally), that does not make sense to the Western eye? What do local particularities of monstrous forms tell us about this society, as opposed to more universal forms (serpentine forms, bat/insect forms, and so on)?

Partha Mitter: There is one unique feature of ancient Indian culture that disturbed Western visitors to India. The multiple arms and heads of Hindu gods that Westerners identified as monstrous,[4] a stereotypical image that drew upon two traditions: the classical one of monstrous races that were supposed to live in India,[5] and the terrifying Christian iconography of apocalyptic demons.[6] Here we have to ask ourselves: what does "monster" or "monstrous" mean in Western society? Behind this is a fundamental clash between Indian and Western rationalities. To the ancient Greeks, a figure with more than two heads or two arms was monstrous, namely, *contra naturam*, or against nature, but not necessarily ugly or hideous.[7] We know of course the homegrown monsters in Greece, especially the serpentine forms, Hydra or Medusa, but the Greeks also imagined monstrous races living far away in India, as a form of alterity or otherness.[8] Interestingly, these creatures were by no means malevolent and some, like the Cynocephali[9] or the Sciapod, were indeed quite harmless. This clash of competing rationalities continued down through the centuries in different guises. In the nineteenth century, Hegel, for instance, characterized Indian imagination as follows: India was "Non-Being," pure spirit, all imagination and fantastic irrationality, completely lacking in objectivity, the staggering contrast between the gross materiality of sacred eroticism and the highest abstraction of Indian philosophy.[10] This conclusion based on Hindu sculpture takes us back to the monster stereotypes of the pervious eras.

M&D Follow-up: Frequently, scholars discussing the so-called monstrous races work to find their "real" sources. These can be in the form of known beings (the dog-headed Cynocephalus is written off as a misunderstood baboon, the giant headless Blemmye is

---

4   Mitter, *MMM*, pp. 8–9, 25.
5   Ibid., p. 7. See also John Block Friedman, *The Monstrous Races in Medieval Art and Thought* (Cambridge, MA and London: Harvard University Press, 1981).
6   Mitter, *MMM*, pp. 9–10.
7   Ibid., pp. 3–31. See also Friedman, *Monstrous Races*, pp. 111 and 116, Lisa Verner, *The Epistemology of the Monstrous in the Middle Ages* (New York: Routledge, 2005), pp. 5–7. See also the essays by Karl Steel and Chet Van Duzer in this collection.
8   Rudolf Wittkower, "Marvels of the East: A Study in the History of Monsters," *Journal of the Warburg and Courtauld Institutes* 5 (1942), p. 159.
9   See Steel's essay in this collection for extended discussion of the Cynocephalus.
10   G.W.F. Hegel, *Vorlesungen über die Ästhetik*, published as *Ästhetik*, intro. G. Lukács (Berlin: Aufbau-Verlag, 1955). See also Hegel, *The Philosophy of Fine Art*, trans. P.B. Omaston (London: G. Bell & Sons, 1920).

explained via very tall Maasai warriors wearing large shoulder epaulets, and so on) or in the form of literary and artistic sources (the Panotii is "explained" by claiming it to be a descendant of the Karnapravarana of the Mahabharata). Do you give these explanations any credence? And if so, do connections exist between the monstrous races and textual accounts and images of Hindu gods? In essence, why is India so frequently cited as the location for these beings?

PM: You are right—there is arguably some basis in claims that creatures such as the Cynocephali, Martikhora, or the Panotii were distant, garbled versions of what the Greek travelers may have seen or most probably heard from their Indian informants.[11] As we know, Wittkower, in his seminal article,[12] had traced the ultimate or remote sources, often based on hearsay, of these monsters. But my point is very different and to explain this I will go back to the great scholar who writes: "The Greeks [rationalized] many instinctive fears ... by the invention of monstrous races and animals which they imagined to live at a great distance in the East, above all in India."[13] And it was these monsters inherited from the Greeks that dominated Western imagination from the Middle Ages until the eighteenth century and came to create the idea of India as the home of the fabulous and the bizarre, the true ingredient of the exotic. The most interesting question is not so much what the ultimate sources of these monsters were but what function these stereotypes had in Western thought and their necessity to the West. Strikingly, even when sixteenth-century travelers to India had a chance to check the veracity of what they had read in Pliny and so on, they preferred to believe what they had read rather than trust their eyes.[14] E.H. Gombrich speaks precisely of the role of mental sets or "schemata" in our perception of the visual world.[15] But why in the first place did Europeans imagine seeing these monsters, particularly the monstrous gods, in India, even though there is little truth in this? We do define ourselves by what the others are not. I have spoken of the clash of values, taste, and above all, the clash of two powerful rationalities in the case of Europe and India that has continued to dominate Western perceptions. Since the Middle Ages, the classical definitions of rationality and Christian morality have deeply colored Western representations of other cultures, especially with regard to India, which also has an equally evolved notion of rationality. In the West, unlike in India, a creature with more than two arms was *contra naturam*, in other words, irrational or monstrous.[16] In a different context, Edward Said has spoken of the construction of European self-identity through the projection of otherness in the imaginary Orient.[17]

---

11   Wittkower, "Marvels of the East," p. 160.
12   Wittkower, "Marvels of the East."
13   Ibid., p. 159.
14   Mitter, *MMM*, p. 23.
15   E.H. Gombrich, *Art and Illusion: A Study in the Psychology of Pictorial Representation* (Princeton: Princeton University Press, 2000), p. 75.
16   See note 7, above.
17   Said, *Orientalism*.

As to the connection between medieval monsters and Hindu gods, I can cite a striking example in the so-called *Nuremberg Chronicle* (1493), where the artist has placed a many-armed Hindu god next to congenital malformations as categories of abnormal beings,[18] but there are plenty of other examples. Why India? My answer can only be tentative and is to say that India has always offered an intriguing alternative to the West that challenges Western identity, whether it be monsters, wise Brahmans, fortitude of the widow to be burnt, or the daunting spirituality and vegetarianism of Indian sages. But surely this continues to hold true because even today India evokes the most extremes of reaction. Also let us not forget that, unlike, let us say, Africa which was too different or China as too remote, India always was the half-way house to the West, what someone once called an half-alien culture.[19] In addition, India, unlike China, was known to the Greco-Roman world, whereas China did not really loom large until the seventeenth and eighteenth centuries. This contact with India was lost once the Barbarians destroyed the Roman Empire and later Arabs cut off the West from India. The subcontinent lived on almost solely in medieval imagination.[20] As we know from medieval *mappa mundi*, India was a vague landmass stretching from the Levant to East Asia and conveniently the Earthly Paradise was also located in this amorphous region.[21]

M&D: You've given some examples of features that are natural and organic within Indian culture and not necessarily seen as threatening (for example, multiple arms/heads). Conversely, are there representational traits of Western gods, heroes, and the like that struck early (or even contemporary) Indians as monstrous, though they are non-threatening within the Western tradition?

This is a very interesting question. Of course, one must realize that cultures differ in their conceptual, intellectual, and imaginative priorities and even fears, and differ in the importance they ascribe to natural phenomena. I cannot think of any Greek gods or heroes that were seen to be threatening in the Indian context. On the other hand, one of the possible reasons why Hindu gods were described by travelers as "monstrous" was to sell their books by sensationalizing the exotic. To the Greeks, the Indian monstrous races were strange but harmless creatures. But even Greek homegrown monsters were not that frightening (perhaps Medusa is an exception?) This is because the classical tradition in art could not overcome the humanist ideal even in its portrayal of terrifying creatures. While in Indian art too the human ideal was important, it could release its imagination more effectively to create truly supra-human creatures.

---

18   Mitter, *MMM*, p. 9. See also Rodney W. Shirley, *The Mapping of the World: Early Printed World Maps 1472–1700* (London: Holland Press Cartographica, 1983).
19   Rudyard Kipling, *In the Vernacular: The English in India: Short Stories* (New York: Doubleday, 1963), p. xviii.
20   Ibid., p. 6.
21   Wittkower, "Marvels of the East," p. 166.

But to insist on my earlier point about "maligned monstrous gods," today do we really regard the beautiful many-armed dancing Shiva image as threatening? I do not think so.[22] The threat came from the fact that it belonged to a non-Christian religion. On a more general level, there are some universal features in our response to images that make us afraid. I do not know the full answer but my feeling is that these images go back to our primal sensations of the fear of death that often work on a subliminal level, though of course their cultural expressions can be very different. For example, vampires may have more specific Christian associations but they belong to a very primitive layer of mind. Think of the Lamia of the classical world.[23] Men are warned in India not to go under large tropical trees at night inhabited by the *pretini*, the ghostly female who has a partiality to the human male.

2. M&D: What word in Sanskrit comes closest to our modern English word "monster" and its European cognates? Are there some important semantic differences between it and "monster" or "the monstrous"? As a corollary, how do you define "monster" in the context of Indian art and culture? Does this European, Latinate term fit any Indian phenomena or not?

PM: There is no single word in Sanskrit that corresponds to the English word "monster," a fact that also reflects fundamental differences in outlook. The word "monster" is derived from the Latin, *monstrum*, and signifies a sign, an omen, a portent or an anomaly, once again incongruous or unnatural.[24] In Sanskrit, the words that closely correspond to "monster" are *danava, rakshasa*, and *pishacha*, which are more aesthetic or ethnological categories. Among these non-human mythical creatures, the *danavas* are closer to the European giants, while the *rakshasas* have physical attributes that were considered ugly by the ancient Indians. They have bulging eyes, large protruding teeth, snub noses, and black skin, and relish human flesh. In short these seem to be distorted and exaggerated descriptions of aboriginal peoples of India. The most familiar examples of *rakshasas* are in the epic *Ramayana* which tells the story of the battle between King Rama and the *rakshasa* King Ravana, who was supposed to have ruled what is modern Sri Lanka or Ceylon. *Pishachas* are ghouls and infernal beings. In the context of Indian art, the closest to "monsters" are the followers of King Mara, who came to tempt the Buddha. Some of the finest depictions of these creatures are at the Great Stupa at Sanchi where the sculptor has explored the art of caricature. But these are not monstrous in the European sense.[25]

M&D Follow-up: In his seminal 1942 study of the monsters of the Wonders of the East *tradition in the West, Rudolf Wittkower traces the Panotii, a common "monster" or*

---

22   Ananda K. Coomaraswamy, *The Dance of Siva* (New York: Sunwise Turn Press, 1918).
23   See Debbie Felton's essay in this collection.
24   Mitter, *MMM*, pp. 7–8. The etymology of *monstrum*, of great interest to classical and medieval authors, is taken up by several contributors to this volume. See Felton, Steel, Strickland, and Van Duzer.
25   Partha Mitter, *Indian Art* (Oxford: Oxford University Press, 2001).

"monstrous race" in medieval European texts and images, to "the Indian epics, particularly the Mahabharata, as Karnapravarana, i.e. people who cover themselves with their ears."[26] The Old English Wonders of the East *describes them as such:*

> *Then east from there people are born that are fifteen feet tall and ten feet broad. They have a great head and ears like fans. They spread one ear over themselves at night, and they cover themselves with the other. Their ears are very light, and their bodies are as white as milk. If they see or perceive anyone in that land, they take their ears in their hands and flee so quickly that one might imagine they were flying.[27]*

If such beings are borrowed from one culture to the other (from India to Greece, from Greek to Latin for the Romans, from Rome to the Western Middle Ages, and so on, but also from India to China and China to Japan, and so on, as these popular beings move throughout the globe), what is the significance of their retention and repetition? What factors explain their reuse by various cultures, and what cultural factors would impact their meaning in their new contexts?

PM: You raise here a very important, and at the moment evolving, notion that lies at the heart of postcolonial globalization. Cultural border crossings are a phenomenon that has gone on throughout human history. Style, concept, and technology freely circulated across societies, as they were adopted, adapted, reinterpreted, translated, sometimes assimilated, and transformed by the recipient society according to its needs, generating entirely new meanings from the original ones. However, the question of how some ideas from outside endure while others disappear is not easy to explain, except to reiterate a truism that their survival depends on their usefulness to the receiver. The generation of new meanings can be usefully studied in the case of Buddhism, which arose in India, and its afterlife in societies such as China and Japan. More recently, we know that the formal syntax of modernism has undergone very new and fecund interpretations outside the West.[28] Perhaps Wittkower's work on the migration and survival of symbols may offer us some answers here. He traces the transmission of motifs of monsters, hybrids, and mythical beasts from ancient Egypt and West Asia to the West via ancient trade routes and their transformations. Concepts, he writes, may often survive drained of their original meaning and significance, or the meaning may survive but the visual expression changes, or visual formula survives only as a decorative motif.[29]

---

26   Wittkower, "Marvels of the East," p. 164.

27   London, British Library, MS Cotton Vitellius A.xv (the *"Beowulf* Manuscript"), f. 101r, trans. Asa Simon Mittman and Susan Kim.

28   Partha Mitter, *The Triumph of Modernism: India's Artists and the Avant-garde, 1922–47* (Chicago: University of Chicago Press, 2007).

29   Rudolf Wittkower, *Selected Lectures of Rudolf Wittkower: The Impact of Non-European Civilizations on the Art of the West*, ed. Donald Martin Reynolds (Cambridge: Cambridge University Press, 1989).

M&D: You are right that monstrum *originally referred to omens or portents. The modern English (and European) word "monster" has lost that meaning, however. It means something more akin to unnatural, threatening, frightening, "not quite right." We say that people are monstrous (psychopathic killers), events are monstrous (the Holocaust), ideas are monstrous (eugenics), and so on, even while we still have movies and legends about "monsters"—actual creatures that are dangerous and not well understood. So is there no word in Sanskrit/Hindi that corresponds to this broad range of meanings? If not, does that tell us something fundamental about the relationship of these language groups with the world around them?*

PM: All cultures have their fears and anxieties and also what they wish to exclude from the normal and the comfortable. Even in the West, the word "monster," as you rightly say, means quite a few different things: portents as something miraculous or puzzling that appear as wondrous signs; anomalies like the harmless Indian monsters in Greek mythology. I agree, however, that there is something not only threatening but also inexplicable and enigmatic about monsters as covered by the meaning of monster as portent. Then, in all cultures, you have really terrifying or horrific beings that evoke fear and terror. The term "monster" for the Holocaust or eugenics or even for psychopaths is used, I think, metaphorically, as a figure of speech or as an adjective. The Holocaust is monstrous only in a very special sense in that its unimaginable cruelty and denigration of other human beings outrages our sense of decency and fairness. Of course the movie monsters are quite different and are deliberately created to evoke a sense of unease and wonder. Otherwise we would not flock to see them. To turn to India, all these different concepts such as a sense of wonder or the evocation of fear and horror or of feelings of outrage and disgust exist, but different words are used for these different concepts. Each of the words like *rakshasa, danava,* or *pishacha* relate to the actual context. Perhaps the Sanskrit word *danava* comes close to the threatening aspect of monsters while *rakshasa* often refers to monstrous races as a form of otherness. However, even in the West, for instance, the word "monster" is full of ambiguity and changes its meaning according to the context. Are ghouls actually monsters? We may hold that monsters are living creatures and unlike zombies or ghosts. But this is not always true, as demonstrated by the *Vetala* in the ancient Indian compendium of stories, the *Vetalapanchavimshati,* who hovers between the world of the living and the dead. Some of these universal creatures are part of our collective nightmares. In Sanskrit one could act in a *danaviya* manner (literally like a *danava*), which arouses *vibhatsa rasa,* or a feeling of fear mixed with disgust.

3. M&D: Why have Western authors from the Middle Ages to modernity perceived Indian culture as fundamentally monstrous? And how has this distorted Western perceptions of Indian culture?

PM: Interestingly, India evoked a sense of the marvelous and the fantastic since the end of the Middle Ages in the West, partly because the links set up by the ancient Greeks were broken and the notion of India lived on as a distant memory filled with mythical beings. India could not be located precisely on the map and stretched anywhere from beyond the Levant to the borders of China. Three powerful myths contributed to the image of India: the location of the Earthly Paradise,[30] the land of the Noble Savage Brahmans,[31] and the habitat of the harmless anomalous monsters of Greek legends. Following the fears of the millennium, a further set of demonic monsters made their appearance in Europe. Early travelers took this dual legacy to India. When confronted with many-armed pagan gods "inspired" by the devil, they preferred to trust what they had read rather than their eyes. Of course, as ethnography progressed, Hindu iconography became better known.[32] Nonetheless, what remained was this notion of the non-Christian, non-classical irrationality epitomized by ancient Indian art, a notion that entered art history and continued as late as the twentieth century.

M&D Follow-up: You say "continued as late as the twentieth century." Does this mean that you believe that, at least in the world of art historical scholarship, we have finally surpassed this 2,000-year-old trope?

PM: Perhaps I was being over-optimistic but it is nonetheless true that since the 1970s, critical assaults by postcolonial scholars have shaken faith in the dominance of the Western canon, which had distorted the perception of other artistic traditions for centuries. That of course doesn't mean that we have completely overcome the 2,000-year-old prejudice.[33]

4. M&D: In your survey text on Indian art and in your most recent work on Indian modernism, you take a decidedly postcolonialist approach, not only grappling with the art of India on its own terms but also explicitly considering the impacts of colonialism upon art and art history in India. In what ways has your early work on monsters impacted your research since?

PM: My two projects on the history of Indian art in the colonial period, *Art and Nationalism in Colonial India*[34] and *The Triumph of Modernism*,[35] followed on directly from *Much Maligned Monsters*. While much in sympathy with Edward Said, I also differed from him in seeing colonial discourse as an evolutionary process and not as a static idea, culminating in the high noon of empire. Working with E.H. Gombrich inspired me to seek the roots of the Western classical canon that stood in the way of understanding all non-classical styles. The body of knowledge called Orientalism

---

30   Wittkower, "Marvels of the East," p. 181.
31   Mitter, *MMM*, p. 49.
32   Ibid., pp. 115–16.
33   Ibid., p. 260.
34   Partha Mitter, *Art and Nationalism in Colonial India, 1850–1922* (Cambridge: Cambridge University Press, 1995).
35   Mitter, *Triumph of Modernism*.

by Said impacted greatly on the foundational writings of James Fergusson[36] and other colonial writers on Indian art and architecture. However, there were wider implications of the general view that Indian art was over-ornate, over-rich, and decadent (other names for monstrous or irrational). Fergusson and others were deeply imbued with the ideas of Winckelmann on classical taste.[37] Investigating these ideas in art history took me all the way back to the Middle Ages and the conflicting definitions of rationality, which I feel had a profound effect on taste and, *inter alia*, on the discipline of art history. Armed with these ideas, the colonial founders of Indian art schools in the 1850s formulated influential art policies predicated on the principle that Indians were wonderfully skilled at decorative art, but when it came to high art they were only capable of producing monsters, as stated memorably by George Birdwood.[38] These had an impact on nationalist thought, leading to art that resisted academic colonial art. In short, what I have been seeking in my works is to challenge the dominant Western artistic canon (classical and modernist), so *MMM* and the other two books are really two sides of the same coin. The resistance of Indian nationalist art consisted of challenging first the classical and then the modernist canon and their claims to teleological inevitability.

M&D Follow-up: As you quote in MMM, *Birdwood asserted that: "The monstrous shapes of the Puranic deities are unsuitable for the higher forms of artistic representation; and this is possibly why sculptures and painting are unknown, as fine arts, in India."[39] Of course, Birdwood's contemporaries in the West extolled the virtues of Greco-Roman sculptures of their mythological figures, many of which (for example, goat-legged Pan, one-eyed giant Cyclopes, cannibalistic Chronos) were as "monstrous" as those of Indian origin. To what degree is this colonial viewpoint based on religion, as opposed to on culture? To what degree can they be separated?*

PM: What Birdwood describes as "monstrous" is simply continuing the Western interpretation of the many-armed Hindu gods and goddesses as "anti-aesthetic" and irrational since the late medieval period (though by no means shared by everyone even in the early period). These Hindu gods were beautifully fashioned and considered to be beautiful by Indians and by some Westerners like the French sculptor Rodin.[40] Birdwood, like the average nineteenth-century educated, was deeply imbued with the specific "humanist" classical ideals of Greek sculpture reiterated by Winckelmann.[41] This taste was at odds with the very different Indian

---

36   See, for example, James Fergusson, *History of Indian and Eastern Architecture*, 2 volumes (New York: Dodd, Mead & Company, 1891).
37   Mitter, *MMM*, pp. 262–7.
38   Ibid., p. 237.
39   Ibid., p. 237.
40   Ibid., p. 253.
41   Johann Joachim Winckelmann, *Winckelmann: Selected Writings on Art*, ed. David Irwin (London: Phaidon, 1972).

humanist ideals as epitomized by the dancing Shiva Nataraja so admired by Rodin. The Greek mythological creatures, Pan, Chronos, or Cyclops, were in fact conceived as monsters, as opposed to Indian gods who were misinterpreted as monsters by the Europeans. We need to bear this important distinction in mind. Regarding the question as to whether European misinterpretation of Indian gods and monsters was inspired by religion or culture, I would say both. Initially, the classical monsters were considered harmless in the Middle Ages but they gradually acquired malevolent attributes derived from medieval demonology.[42] Classical monsters were a cultural expression, as opposed to the teaching of the Christian church that all pagan religions were invented by the devil, a definition of paganism later extended to the Indian gods.[43] By 1000 CE, as the terrors of the millennium gripped the age, the Church invented a series of powerful monsters that threatened Christianity, notably the Beast of the Apocalypse. The belief in the demonic origins of Hindu and other pagan gods were from then on simply reinforced. In short, by the end of the millennium, classical monsters, congenital malformations, apocalyptic demons, and classical and Hindu gods were all put in the all-embracing category of monsters. It becomes confused and messy.

M&D: You have referred a couple of times now to competing rationalities between East and West. Are there also competing rationalities within the Indian subcontinent (the way there were, for instance, between Mediterranean and Germanic cultures in the early European Middle Ages)? More specifically, are there some provocative or telling differences in perceptions of monstrosity between broad language or religion groups within internal Indian history?

First of all let me insist that the connection between the rational and the monstrous is an entirely Western construct and has little relevance in Indian, or I daresay, non-Western cultures in general. But of course India, being such a diverse multicultural society, there have been intersecting but parallel rationalities throughout history, which it is difficult to go into here.[44] Suffice to say, in ancient India around 1000 CE, there were vigorous debates about the nature of reality and rationality among a wide variety of intellectual positions, sometimes with irreconcilable differences.

5. M&D: East and West have a long history of accusing each other of monstrosity in various ways (for instance, ancient Greeks and Indians each accusing the other of being "barbarians"—people who can't speak correctly—while each using the same Indo-European term to do so). Is this changing in the face of a modern global economy, Internet communications, and the homogenizing of world culture in general?

PM: Very interesting question. Recently, I have in fact been involved in the question of the global and its implications on art in particular, especially the question of

---

42   Mitter, *MMM*, p. 9.
43   Ibid., p. 17.
44   Ibid., p. 17.

cosmopolitanism and crossing of cultural borders. You are quite right—people have always found ways of putting down the Other. However, until the colonial era, the West did not have a monopoly on this. Remember the contempt of the Chinese for people outside the Middle Kingdom, or the categorization of non-Hindus as *mleccha* (unclean). It is true, however, that the colonial order created a systematic hierarchical ideology of "difference," which was sustained by means of guns and Gramscian ideas of hegemony. Globalization has created an entirely new situation as it has given rise to a new form of postcolonial order and imbalance between the center and the periphery. There is a great deal of talk about Indian and Chinese artists having "arrived" in the world art market, but what does it really mean? If you look closely, it is still the Western canon that dominates the global art market.[45]

M&D Follow-up: Do you mean to say that the top-sellers remain works in the Western canon, or that those Indian and Chinese artists who have become financially successful in the global market have adopted or been co-opted or even corrupted by that Western canon to such a degree that you consider it no longer, in some sense, "authentic"?

I am not comfortable with the word "authentic" because I do not know what it means beyond the fact that it is often proclaimed by a particular community in order to exclude others. In fact this question about Indian and Chinese artists is a difficult one. While the actual integrity of these artists is not in doubt, they are simply co-opted by Western critics in the sense that they are often forced into the Western mold rather than being appreciated within their own context. But I do not want to be mechanical about this complicated issue, except to say that many Asian artists of striking originality and visually compelling work get ignored because their works are not compatible with the Western canon. My concern here is the monolithic teleology of the Western modernist canon, which is a closed discourse that is unable to accommodate plurality.[46]

M&D: While the economic dynamics are fairly clear, what explains the aesthetic colonization of the world by the Western canon?

PM: You have asked an intriguing but seldom probed issue here. I will state something unfashionable here, but there is evidence that naturalism or Renaissance illusionist art fascinated all those who first confronted it. In sixteenth-century India, the great Mughal emperor Akbar was totally taken with European naturalism, and his as well as his son Jahangir's artists copied European art out of avid curiosity and were deeply impressed with it. They thought these works were simply miraculous. Significantly, this was long before the colonization of India, at a time when European rulers, dazzled by the Grand Mogul, were courting him

---

45 Partha Mitter, "Decentering Modernism: Art History and Avant-Garde Art from the Periphery," *Art Bulletin* 90/4 (2008), pp. 531–48.

46 John Clark, "Open and Closed Discourses of Modernity in Asian Art," in *Modernity in Asian Art* (Sydney: Wild Peony Press, 1993), pp. 1–17.

assiduously and showering him with gifts. Secondly, Mughal emperors were great connoisseurs of Persian and Indian art. Akbar set up a large workshop consisting of some hundred artists. The Mughal emperors' art appreciation was on a high level of sophistication and they found European art deeply affecting.[47] A similar thing happened in Japan, I believe. I think the technical mastery of likeness is something that must affect people who are already visually alert. During the Victorian period, the colonial regime sought to inculcate "good taste" in Indians by Westernizing their art. But importantly, by the end of the nineteenth century, Indian taste, even of the unlettered, was solidly for naturalism.

M&D: In your Art Bulletin *essay, you suggest that "Perhaps we are witnessing the dissolution of the heroic modernism that prevailed during much of the twentieth century"[48] and that the "decolonization" of art history in the wake of the cultural shifts of the 1970s (including Edward Said's publication of* Orientalism *in 1978) challenged the canon by causing it to be seen as "complicit with the capitalist–colonialist patriarchy."[49] The notion of the monstrous has frequently been used to construct or reinforce colonial narratives, especially about India. Now that we are working toward the creation of new, allegedly more inclusive, narratives, does the monstrous still have a role to play?*

PM: Let us hope that monsters would no longer be used for stereotyping and misrepresenting other cultures, but one should not be too complacent about our own liberal age either. I think it is quite easy to fall into the habit, and I think this is a habit shared by all of us, of "demonizing" the Other, and this could apply equally to individuals and not simply to cultures. On the other hand, I do think that we need monsters to remain sane and vigorous in our thinking. However, they have to exist on a different plane and with a different function, and I hope that the monsters would continue to inhabit the world of imagination. Of course, nowhere is this more compelling than in the world of science fiction, where we continue to derive pleasure from being terrified and thrilled in turn, when we read, for instance, the classic *Frankenstein*[50] or watch the film *Alien* (1979). Without being able to imagine monsters, human society would be very poor indeed because "monsters" fulfill our deep-seated emotional needs.

M&D: Here you are presumably speaking of art mostly in academic/art community contexts — "high art." Can you speak to the role of increasingly global paradigms of mass produced, commercial monster representations (horror movies, monsters in video games, popular art, and so on)? Recently, Pakistan produced its first "slasher" film, Zibahkhana

---

47 Maurice S. Dimand, "Mughal Painting under Akbar the Great," *The Metropolitan Museum of Art Bulletin* 12/2 (1953), pp. 46–51.

48 Partha Mitter, "Interventions: The Author Replies," *Art Bulletin* 90/4 (2008), pp. 568–74, at 568.

49 Ibid., p. 569.

50 Mary Wollstonecraft Shelley, *Frankenstein; or, The Modern Prometheus*, first edn (London: Lackington, Hughes, Harding, Mavor & Jones, 1918).

(2007), a remake of The Texas Chainsaw Massacre *(1974, remake 2003). Industry-produced narratives, driven by profit, are arguably blind to cultural hierarchies and colonialism. Is there a different set of economic or ideological considerations for mass-produced depictions of the monstrous that makes it somewhat immune to historical or regional differences?*

As I just suggested, there is a deep-seated emotional need for monsters in our world of imagination. And we can push this idea further and say that in fact there is a need to enjoy vicariously the frisson produced in confronting terrifying monsters, albeit in the safe environment of the cinema or the television screen. This is surely a universal phenomenon. As you rightly point out, "slasher" films are as popular in the US as they are in Pakistan. Think of the enormous popularity of *Jurassic Park* (1993). But I would not see this as driven by profit. Rather the entertainment industry, in its constant search for box office hits, is simply tapping into this emotional need.[51] In South Asia, for instance, popular taste has simply graduated from demons and monsters of ancient epics, the *Ramayana* or the *Mahabharata*, to dinosaurs and sci-fi monsters. To me, this expresses a universal need that transcends local considerations. We cannot live by cold reality or social engineering alone.

---

51   See, for example, Robert Baird, "Animalizing 'Jurassic Park's' Dinosaurs: Blockbuster Schemata and Cross-Cultural Cognition in the Threat Scene," *Cinema Journal* 374 (1998), pp. 82–103.

Monstrous Gender: Geographies of Ambiguity

Dana Oswald

Monsters inhabit "geographies of ambiguity" and exhibit an "inherent instability of identity."[1] Their bodies are intermediate, interstitial, in transition, and the genders that they exhibit proceed from the ambiguous bodies and geographies that they inhabit. Yet, while the meaning of each monster depends on its context, geographical or otherwise—"its historical specificity"[2]—examining only each specific occurrence prevents us from understanding the monstrous as a "transhistorical phenomen[on]."[3] The purpose of this chapter is to understand monstrous gender through larger transhistorical trends, without suggesting a uniformity of meaning within each of these trends. It is a primary function of monsters to challenge and to confirm the boundaries of the societies that create and "encounter" them. They are, as Jeffrey Jerome Cohen has famously argued, "harbingers of category crisis,"[4] creatures who indicate the permeable limits of social and physical categories and boundaries. He argues that the monster always manages to escape (being caught, being killed) because its body cannot be easily categorized or understood—"the monster is dangerous, a form suspended between forms that threatens to smash distinctions."[5] It is their very indeterminacy, their ability to slide between existing cultural, physical, and social categories, that makes them dangerous and therefore fascinating. They call into question the order of daily life—they smash familiar

---

1   Judith Halberstam, *Female Masculinity* (Durham, NC: Duke University Press, 1998), pp. 163–4. Halberstam uses this language to describe the experience of the transsexual in transition. Though I do not wish to conflate the experience of transsexuals with monsters or to present transsexuals as monsters, I would note that, historically, they have been portrayed in similar theoretical spaces.

2   Jeffrey Jerome Cohen, *Of Giants: Sex, Monsters, and the Middle Ages* (Minneapolis: University of Minnesota Press, 1999), p. xv.

3   Ibid., p. xvi.

4   Jeffrey Jerome Cohen, "Monster Culture (Seven Theses)," in Jeffrey Jerome Cohen (ed.), *Monster Theory: Reading Culture* (Minneapolis: University of Minnesota Press, 1996), pp. 3–25, at 4.

5   Ibid., p. 6.

distinctions between reductive categories and reveal these structures to be flawed and inadequate.

And yet, the monstrous itself is a functional, if amorphous, category, which authors sub-divide and separate into tidy groupings: for example, many authors include the Plinian races, a familiar literary set-piece of monsters that appears consistently from the classical period through the Renaissance.[6] But monsters rarely remain neatly in these categories—for instance, how shall we class a monster with a man's torso and a horse's body—beast or man?[7] Or a serpent with a woman's face? These monsters have something to say about human qualities, certainly, but they also speak about the other categories that they span and exceed, and about the nature of categories in general. Just as monsters resist social and teleological order, so too do they challenge notions of the body and of gender, blurring the boundaries created by humans to exert some kind of control over the unwieldy world around them.

In this chapter, I will discuss the problematics of gender as they overlap with and are highlighted by the monstrous. This study will be organized thematically, rather than chronologically or by genre, tracing some common constructs and representational modes that have shown enduring cultural resonance. Much of my attention will be devoted to the Middle Ages, when many abiding constructs are formulated, but sources from the classical period through our contemporary moment will also be considered. I do not mean, in linking such disparate texts spanning some 2,000 years, to imply that these constructs are monovalent, or that they did not enjoy great variation in meaning and reception in their own social contexts. Indeed, I have in a number of places pointed outward to other chapters in this collection that provide greater contextualization for the figures under consideration. Nonetheless, certain patterns of continuity underlie many (though certainly not all) of these forms. Rather than arguing for archetypal universalism, I wish to draw attention to some recurring threads, out of the many possible entangled threads, that are evocative in their patterns as well as their variations, as they appear, for example, in medieval travel tales, early modern political and medical tracts, nineteenth-century novels, and twentieth- and twenty-first-century films. Many of the works discussed herein are discussed elsewhere in this collection with greater attention to historical context; there remains a need, however, to take a broader view, and elucidate representational patterns that seem to span many centuries with some continuity. I will begin with a basic discussion of contemporary gender theory, to present and define the terms and concepts that will be carried through the essay, and then will consider issues that arise from literary and artistic depictions of hypermasculinity, hypersexuality, transgender, and hermaphroditism.

---

6   See John Block Friedman, *The Monstrous Races in Medieval Art and Thought* (Cambridge, MA and London: Harvard University Press, 1981), and Rudolf Wittkower, "Marvels of the East: A Study in the History of Monsters," *Journal of the Warburg and Courtauld Institutes* 5 (1942), pp. 159–97.

7   See Asa Simon Mittman, *Maps and Monsters in Medieval England* (New York and London: Routledge, 2006), pp. 45–6.

The artificial division of the categories of sex, gender, and sexuality[8] attempts to separate out strands of identity in relation to physicality, function, and feeling. They signify, respectively, the biological nature of the body, the socially constructed role of the individual, and the desires experienced by the individual (perhaps enacted physically). However, Eve Sedgwick notes the complicated relationship among these "three terms whose usage relations and analytical relations are almost irremediably slippery."[9] By divorcing the terms from one another, we free gender and sexual identities from their forced association with physical sex characteristics; however, enforcing the division also diminishes the embodied natures of both social identity and desire. Moreover, such a division often suggests that sex itself is the simplest form, when in fact bodies, like genders, exist on a continuum rather than in a binary structure. Biologist and feminist scholar Anne Fausto-Sterling notes that:

> Our bodies are too complex to provide clear-cut answers about sexual difference. The more we look for a simple physical basis for "sex," the more it becomes clear that "sex" is not a pure physical category. What bodily signals and functions we define as male or female come already entangled in our ideas about gender.[10]

Therefore, assumptions about gender always already inform our understanding and identification of physiological sex. Gender and sex, then, are imbricated with one another—but gender is perhaps the trickiest of the three to pin down because of its complex admixture of body and behavior.

Gender is more than just the binary of masculinity and femininity, although, as Judith Butler argues, "Gender is the apparatus by which the production and normalization of masculine and feminine take place along with the interstitial forms of hormonal, chromosomal, psychic, and performative that gender assumes."[11] The binary may become normalized, but even as this happens, performances of gender disrupt the easy division by the very nature of repetition and imitation, which must always fail to repeat exactly. Gender is not merely performance, and it is not merely individual, but rather it proceeds from the body itself—although the relationship is not necessarily "natural." As transsexual theorist Jay Prosser argues, "it is through the suggestion of a possible transgendering that gender appears not simply constructed but radically contingent on the body."[12] In fact, the very nature

---

8   For a thorough discussion of monstrous sexuality, see Miller's chapter in this collection.

9   Eve Kosofsky Sedgwick, *Epistemology of the Closet* (Berkeley: University of California Press, 1990), p. 27.

10   Anne Fausto-Sterling, *Sexing the Body: Gender Politics and the Construction of Sexuality* (New York: Basic Books, 2000), p. 4. See also Judith Butler, *Bodies that Matter: On the Discursive Limits of Sex* (New York: Routledge, 1993).

11   Judith Butler, *Undoing Gender* (New York: Routledge, 2004), p. 42.

12   Jay Prosser, *Second Skins: The Body Narratives of Transsexuality* (New York: Columbia University Press, 1998), p. 29.

of transsex (or intersex) and transgender insists that we notice the body in which gender resides and through which it is constructed. Transsexual author Jane Fry asserts: "If people can't put a label on you they get confused … People have to know what you are … You categorise in your mind. One of the first things you do is determine the sex—if you can't do that, the whole system blows up."[13] To divorce gender from the body is just as limited as connecting masculinity only to the male body and femininity to the female body. In fact, gender is the playful intersection between body, behavior, and context.

If even human bodies transgress socially constructed categories of gender, then monstrous bodies articulate the means by which human bodies can do so. Krista Scott-Dixon argues that:

> the grotesque body crosses boundaries; it blurs distinctions and invents new forms for itself. If this concept is applied to gender, it becomes clear that the grotesque body can be constituted as that which interrupts static categories of gender. The grotesquely gendered body is that which calls attention to normative gender roles while it distorts, caricatures and blurs them.[14]

Thus, viable gender categories can be articulated by the monster—even as it exaggerates them. It is important to note that not all monsters exhibit monstrous gender. A great number seem to follow and even reify traditional gender codes, as we can see in the general practice of depicting the primary representative of a race as male in the texts and images of the monstrous races that accompany medieval works like the *Wonders of the East* or the very popular *Mandeville's Travels*, as discussed by several authors in this collection.[15] While the majority of male monsters who possess monstrous gender, for example, King Kong, fit into the category of hypermasculinity, a quality associated with excessive consumption, variations of gendered female monstrosity proliferate. Perhaps the reason for such a singular representation of masculine monstrosity is that:

> One of the greatest structural problems facing any patriarchal society is the control of the masculine aggressivity, violence, and self-assertion that constitute patriarchy's base. Although patriarchy depends on male homo-social ties and masculine aggressivity for its organization and enforcement, the masculine values inculcated by patriarchal societies can themselves pose a threat to patriarchal order.[16]

---

13   Robert Bogdan and Jane Fry, *Being Different: The Autobiography of Jane Fry* (New York: John Wiley, 1974), p. 96.

14   Krista Scott-Dixon, "The Bodybuilding Grotesque: The Female Bodybuilder, Gender Transgressions, and Designations of Deviance," *Mesomorphosis* 2/10 (December 15, 1998), para. 8.

15   See chapters by Davies, Braham, Van Duzer, Steel, and Strickland.

16   Ian Frederick Moulton, "'A Monster Great Deformed': The Unruly Masculinity of *Richard III*," *Shakespeare Quarterly* 47/3 (Autumn 1996), pp. 251–68, at 251.

As John Gardner writes, "humans are pattern-makers":[17] we seek to comprehend monsters by understanding the trends that they embody and inhabit, however incompletely they do so. Monsters operate as representations of human fears and desires. Their gender constructs human gender as stable, while revealing the fascination with genders that exceed boundaries and categories established, that show the endless possibilities and permutations of the monstrous—and also the *human*—form.

Hypermasculinity and Consuming Desires

Although not all male monsters are hypermasculine, some of the most familiar types of monster are constructed by this gender identity: the giant, the vampire, and the werewolf all exhibit traits of excessive masculine gender, a gender that is reinforced and sometimes necessitated by the nature of the monstrous body. Of course, other hypermasculine monsters exist; they are monsters who exceed the boundaries of civilized masculinity in their appetites for food, sex, and violence. Hypermasculinity is a category marked by inflated physical traits, as well as performances of aggression and domination: it is "the exaggeration of male stereotypical behavior ... [B]ody hair, strength, aggression, and outward appearance are expressed as male traits."[18] This ultra-virility is written on the body, but also performed by it, as hypermasculine monsters rape and consume, never to be satiated or incorporated themselves.

Those monsters occupied by excessive, particularly cannibalistic, consumption, often serve as metaphors for human greed or poor governance, but they also exhibit a kind of masculine tyranny and need for possession or inclusion. From the Anglo-Saxon *Donestre* and the giant of *Morte Arthure*, through to *An American Werewolf in London* and *Underworld*, the trope of hypermasculinity dominates. The *Donestre* of the Anglo-Saxon *Wonders of the East*, a medieval compendium of monstrous people, animals, and places, exemplifies excessive consumption, a transgressive behavior that is reflected by his hypermasculine body. In British Library, Cotton Tiberius B.V, an eleventh-century illuminated manuscript, he appears in the tripartite image as a creature with a lion-like head and bright red penis and testicles.[19] The illustrator obviously emphasizes his sexual excess, but this depiction of sensual indulgence also reflects his cannibalistic eating of human travelers, whom he lures by calling

---

17 John Gardner, *Grendel* (New York: Vintage, 1989), p. 27.
18 Claire M. Renzetti and Jeffrey L. Edleson, *Encyclopedia of Interpersonal Violence*, vol. 1 (Thousand Oaks, CA: Sage, 2008), p. 345.
19 For a color image, see Rosalyn Saunders, "Becoming Undone: Monstrosity, Leaslicam Wordum, and the Strange Case of the Donestre," *Different Visions: A Journal of New Perspectives on Medieval Art*, vol. 2 (2009), p. 10, figure 2, available at: <http://www.differentvisions.org/Issue2PDFs/Saunders.pdf>.

to them in their own language, "deceiv[ing them] with dishonest words."[20] In the second part of the image, we see the hypermasculine monster straddling and embracing the body of a vulnerable and supine human man, whose arm he has pulled into his mouth.[21] The sexual positioning of these two bodies emphasizes the masculinity of the monster and feminized state of the helpless human, for as Ruth Mazo Karras has shown, "to be active was to be masculine, regardless of the gender of one's partner, and to be passive was to be feminine."[22] Like the giant of Mont St-Michel in *The Alliterative Morte Arthure*—who roasts babies over a campfire while gnawing on a man's haunch[23]—by eating men, these monsters assert their own superior masculine gender, diminishing that of their victims, and demonstrating the authority that they hold over human bodies.

These medieval tropes invest the enduring tradition of the werewolf—popular from the Middle Ages to the present—and the now-popular vampire with extreme masculinity. In film, particularly, werewolves tear apart human bodies, dismantling the corporeal integrity of humans, an act which mimics their own divided identities. Their consumption of the human indicates their bestial status and primal appetites. In fact, the werewolf is perhaps the most fully hypermasculine figure, ironically because of its hybrid animal status: it is hairy, strong, aggressive, and driven by primal urges for food and sex. The prefix "wer-" itself derives from the Old English word for "man," not the general term for human or person.[24] In films from *An American Werewolf in London* (1981) to *Underworld* (2002) to the comic Michael J. Fox vehicle *Teen Wolf* (1985), the werewolf is uncontrollable, at least by humans (and often by the lingering human aspect that shares space with the werewolf within a single body), and operates completely outside the limits of civilization.[25] Charlotte

---

20 Andy Orchard, *Pride and Prodigies: Studies in the Monsters of the Beowulf-Manuscript* (Cambridge: D.S. Brewer, 1995), p. 196.

21 Cohen, *Of Giants*, p. 2, notes the contrast of the *Donestre's* "hypermasculine body" in comparison to the weak "ill proportioned" form of the traveler.

22 Ruth Mazo Karras, *Sexuality in Medieval Europe: Doing Unto Others* (New York: Routledge, 2005), p. 23.

23 Valerie Krishna (ed.), *The Alliterative Morte Arthure: A Critical Edition* (New York, 1976), line 1046, available at: <http://name.umdl.umich.edu/AllitMA>.

24 Joseph Bosworth, *An Anglo-Saxon Dictionary, Based on the Manuscript Collections of the Late Joseph Bosworth*, ed. T. Northcote Toller and Alistair Campbell (Oxford: Oxford University Press, 1838–1972), p. 1205: "wer, es; m. I. *a man, a male person.*" It should be noted that in contemporary fiction, authors have begun to bend this gender construct, with an increasing presence of female "were"-wolves.

25 It is important to note that in some narratives (like Stephenie Meyer's *Twilight* series) the wolves establish a pack-like social structure. Moreover, there are also anomalous narratives: Gerald of Wales, for example, features profoundly religious and non-violent werewolves, one of whom is a woman. See Caroline Walker Bynum, *Metamorphosis and Identity* (New York: Zone Books, 2001). Leslie Sconduto, like Bynum, notes the shift in the twelfth century, wherein there is a "radical departure from the traditional portrayal of the werewolf." Leslie Sconduto, *Metamorphosis of the Werewolf: A Literary Study from Antiquity through the Renaissance* (Jefferson, NC: McFarland & Co., 2008), p. 2. The werewolf is not only a male monster: "whilst in some countries it is restricted to

Otten claims that werewolf narratives of the medieval and Renaissance worlds look "honestly at violence, destructive urges that attack and devour the fabric of human life."[26] Certainly, this remains true of later werewolf narratives, as well. Andrea Gutenberg critiques the perceived masculine status of the werewolf: "Interestingly, despite the werewolf's obvious violation of the rules of respectable masculinity— self-mastery, restraint, discipline, and vigilance concerning bodily needs ... there seems to be no doubt in the minds of most (male) critics and theoreticians about the masculine gender of (were)wolves ..."[27] The werewolf does indeed violate the rules of masculinity—by exceeding them through hegemonic, violent hypermasculinity.

In contrast to the primal consumption of the werewolf, the vampire's primary affiliation is with sexualized violence. However, despite the proliferation of hypersexual female vampires in contemporary culture, Leah Wyman and George Dionisopoulos note that the origin and purpose of vampiric women, at least in Bram Stoker's genre-defining *Dracula* (and therefore in a great many of its offspring), derives from the central male figure:

> *This lethal sexuality is defined as inherently male, as evidenced in the story by the fact that all of the female vampires become vampires when they are attacked by the story's only male vampire, Dracula. In that vampirism is being shown as only passing from man to woman, the female vampires are only relevant to the story in terms of how they relate to Dracula.*[28]

Like the werewolf, the vampire's appetite is primal, but the means of hunting is radically different. Male sensuality is emphasized in the body of the vampire, as with Tom Cruise and Brad Pitt in the film adaptation of *Interview with a Vampire*

---

the male sex, in others it is confined to the female; and, again, in others it is to be met with in both sexes," in Elliott O'Donnell, *Werewolves* (Maryland: Wildside Press, 2008), p. 5. However, in Western culture, the werewolf is most often figured as male, or at least as masculinized. Alternatively, those featured in Charlaine Harris's *True Blood* series seem to be an uncomfortable part of a boys' club. However, female werewolves are not entirely absent in contemporary fiction; for example, Martin Millar's *Lonely Werewolf Girl* features several strong female werewolves who, nevertheless, are under the governance of even stronger male werewolves.

26   Charlotte F. Otten, *A Lycanthropy Reader: Werewolves in Western Culture* (Syracuse: Syracuse University Press, 1986), p. xiii.

27   Andrea Gutenberg, "Shape-Shifters from the Wilderness: Werewolves Roaming the Twentieth Century," in Konstanze Kutzbach and Monika Mueller (eds), *The Abject of Desire: The Aestheticization of the Unaesthetic in Contemporary Literature and Culture* (Amsterdam: Rodopi, 2007), pp. 149–80, at 151. See this essay for a discussion of the feminine resonances within this monstrous category. For further discussion of male and female vampires, see Lee Six and Thompson's chapter in this collection.

28   Leah M. Wyman and George N. Dionisopoulos, "Primal Urges and Civilized Sensibilities: The Rhetoric of Gendered Archetypes, Seduction, and Resistance in Bram Stoker's *Dracula*," *Journal of Popular Film and Television* 27/2 (Summer 1999), pp. 32–9, at 35.

(1994) and Robert Pattinson of *Twilight* (2008) tweener fame. Like the werewolf, these vampires are preternaturally strong, although notably less hairy, and ever-hungry. Their consumption, though, is affiliated with the exchange of fluids, a metaphor for sex and its attendant dangers, from plague to syphilis to the AIDS crisis. As James Hart, the screenplay writer of *Bram Stoker's Dracula* (1992) argues, "vampires seduce us and take us to dark places and awaken us sexually in ways that are taboo."[29] This sexual awakening, however, is based on the vampire's primary appetite for blood, and for the consumption of the human, normally figured as female.[30] Therefore, the conflation of food and sex, taken by violence, reasserts the gendered nature of the hypermasculine monster.

As Cohen reminds us, the hypermasculine giant "is a violently gendered body ... [he is] not reducible to some pure state of male identity because he incorporates ... sensuous physicality."[31] The appeal and threat of the giant, and of monstrously exaggerated masculinity, is that "if the giant is sometimes made to represent the masculine body's lost prehistory, that is precisely because he figures the dangerous instability of its present integrity."[32] The hypermasculine monster—giant, vampire, werewolf—reveals the fragility of the category of masculinity and the ways in which such masculinity may be feminized in its hypersexuality.

Hypersexuality and the Arts of Seduction

Although sexual potency, as figured in the bodies of male monsters like the rapist giant of Mont St-Michel, indicates a kind of super-masculinity, hypersexuality is a category more consistently associated with the feminine prior to the eighteenth century. As Thomas Laqueur claims, notions of sexual and gender division from antiquity to the pre-Enlightenment "equated friendship with men and fleshliness with women."[33] In this neatly bifurcated formulation, women were less capable of controlling their desires and bodies because they were more "fallen" from the state of original virtue associated with the Garden of Eden. Men, however, were above such lust and were able to reject or control the sexual advances of women. Therefore, the bodies of male monsters who are depicted as hypersexualized are

---

29   F.F. Coppola and J.V. Hart, *Bram Stoker's Dracula: The Film and the Legend* (New York: Newsmarket, 1992), p. 136.
30   Recent adaptations of the vampire narrative play with the fissures in the narrative, opening up spaces for queer elements and stronger female vampires. However, the same note regarding Meyer's female werewolves must be made: the feminine element of reproduction is erased from the bodies of female vampires. Both female and male vampires reformulate the nature of sex, gender, and appetite.
31   Cohen, *Of Giants*, p. xii.
32   Ibid., p. xv.
33   Thomas W. Laqueur, *Making Sex: Body and Gender from the Greeks to Freud* (Cambridge, MA: Harvard University Press, 1990), p. 4.

also, ironically, culturally feminized. While this formulation is inherently reductive, it functions effectively to undermine the category of masculinity itself, as those creatures whose bodies are the most male exceed its cultural descriptors.

The hypersexual is, then, a feminized category that includes both male and female monsters. Again, I will turn to two classical figures, and their enduring reinterpretations in the Middle Ages, to establish the paradigm: an image in a thirteenth-century Continental Bestiary depicts the dangers of each to the human male.[34] In this image, three men sit in a boat, under which swim a siren, complete with bare chest and scaled fish tail, and a centaur, drawn with exaggerated genitalia that, despite being located on his animal half, look pointedly human. Although only the siren reaches up to drag one of the men off the boat by his hair, "[b]oth the siren and the centaur are overtly sexual creatures ... who ensnare human souls with their powers of attraction."[35] The pairing of siren and centaur is a medieval commonplace, connecting both bodies as hybrid and bestial, but also sexually alluring and desirable.[36] As Elizabeth Lawrence notes, centaurs are "possessed of dangerously exaggerated masculinity in double portion resulting from the human male element being combined with the perceived strong sexual potency of stallions, and thus they were characterized by violent lust."[37] However, in addition to this hypermasculinity, and perhaps explicitly in relation to it, she argues that they "exemplify the testing of boundaries — as between man and beast, male and female, and culture and nature."[38] This depiction of the siren as seductress is unsurprising: from their appearance in early epics like *The Odyssey*, sirens act as lures to passing sailors:

> *Square in your ship's path are Seirênês, crying/beauty to bewitch men coasting by;/woe to the innocent who hears that sound!/He will not see his lady nor his children/in joy, crowding around him, home from sea;/the Seirênês will sing his mind away/on their sweet meadow lolling. There are bones/of dead men rotting in a pile behind them/and flayed skins shrivel around the spot.*[39]

---

34 This image is in London, British Library, MS Sloane 278, f.47r. For discussion of the Bestiary, see Debra Hassig (now Strickland, in this collection) (ed.), *The Mark of the Beast: The Medieval Bestiary in Art, Life, and Literature* (New York: Garland, 1999).

35 For a color image and discussion, see Alixe Bovey, *Monsters and Grotesques in Medieval Manuscripts* (Toronto: University of Toronto Press, 2002), pp. 25–7.

36 During the medieval period, "Centaurs represented the duplicitous nature of man as both pious and literally beastly in his behavior. Where this ... symbolism was employed, the Centaur was usually depicted along with a Siren or mermaid." Carol Rose, *Giants, Monsters, and Dragons: An Encyclopedia of Folklore* (New York: W.W. Norton, 2001), p. 72.

37 Elizabeth Atwood Lawrence, "The Centaur: Its History and Meaning in Human Culture," *Journal of Popular Culture* 27/4 (1994), pp. 57–68, at 63.

38 Ibid., p. 62.

39 Homer, *The Odyssey*, trans. Robert Fitzgerald (New York: Vintage Books, 1990), book 12, p. 210.

In classical depictions, like the Greek vase and Roman fresco in the British Museum, these figures are generally hybrid bird-women.[40] By the Middle Ages, the figure of the siren has transformed into the enduring mermaid figure, as in the eighth-century *Liber monstrorum*, which explains:

> Sirens are sea-girls, who deceive sailors with the outstanding beauty of their appearance and the sweetness of their song, and are most like human beings from the head to the navel, with the body of a maiden, but have scaly fishes' tails, with which they always lurk in the sea.[41]

Sirens, in both traditions, are always female, always alluring and dangerous, affiliated with the water and effluvia, but strangely absent of sexual capacity, as their nether regions are those of birds or fish, feathered or scaled, and impenetrable. Therefore, as in the Bestiary image, the centaur and the siren provoke desire for and warning about the destructive nature of sexual desire; in contrasting the sexes of these hybrid bodies, they are also aligned in a hypersexual monstrous gender. As Laqueur reminds us, medieval gender is as much about social status as about the body: "To be a man or a woman was to hold a social rank, a place in society, to assume a cultural role, not to *be* organically one or the other of two incommensurable sexes."[42] While we might find that few monsters hold any rank — aside from Other — within medieval society, the kind of excessive sexuality of both the centaur and the siren suggests an alternative gender category based not on their genitalia, but on their function as seducers.

In fact, the bodies of several female seducers continue to mark them as sex and gender hybrids — not just bestial ones — into the early modern and modern periods, within a range of representational contexts. Mary Arseneau characterizes many nineteenth-century literary characters, for example, including Geraldine, Melusine, Medusa, and Keats's Lamia, as "hybrid, ambiguous serpent-women,"[43] a tradition that springs from the classical figure of Medusa, the snake-haired murderous seductress. C.L. Moore keeps the classical hybrid seducer alive in her 1933 short story *Shambleau*, in which the protagonist, Smith, finds himself compelled to protect a mysterious female creature from an attacking mob. He is simultaneously attracted

---

40   The vase, a red-figure stamnos from circa 475 BCE, is British Museum GR 1843.11-3.31, Vase E440. The fresco can be found at British Museum, "Wall Painting of Ulysses and the Sirens, Roman, mid-1st century AD, from Pompeii, Italy," <http://www.britishmuseum.org/explore/highlights/highlight_objects/gr/w/wall_painting_of_ulysses_and_t.aspx>, accessed March 14, 2011.

41   "Sirenae sunt marinae puellae, quae nauigantes pulcherrima forma et cantu dulcedinis decipeunt, et a capite usque ad umbilicum sunt corpora uirginali et humano generi simillimae, squamosas tamen piscium causdas habent, quibus simper in gurgite latent." Orchard, *Pride and Prodigies*, pp. 262–3. For more on the *Liber monstrorum*, see Strickland and Van Duzer in this volume.

42   Laqueur, *Making Sex*, p. 8.

43   Mary Arseneau, "Madeline, Mermaids, and Medusas in 'The Eve of St Agnes,'" *Papers on Language and Literature* 33 (1997), pp. 227–43, at 237.

to and disgusted by the mysterious female monster, who hides her writhing worm-like hair in a turban. Indeed, it is through this hair, grotesque and sexualized, that the Shambleau consumes his life force.[44] In Thomas A. Bredehoft's analysis, Smith's masculinity is "'retooled'" by his encounter with Shambleau.[45] The danger of each of these seductresses is indicated through her snake-like hybridity, a quality that exceeds the boundaries of femininity in its phallic resonances.[46] Through these masculine appendages, in certain cases specifically used to penetrate men's bodies, the gender of these seductresses straddles typical categories of femininity and masculinity. In the combination of seductiveness, a feminine quality, and phallic elements, with which women might perform a traditionally masculine function, we can see the seducer as a class that exceeds the boundaries of binary gender.

Gender-benders: Masculine Women, Absent Men, and Political Allegory

Where centaurs and snaky seductresses possess bestial and phallic elements, other monsters take on human physical qualities of the opposite sex. While the bearded lady is an iconic resident of freak shows and monster texts, her male counterpart does not seem to exist in quite the same way. How might a man take on the physical qualities of a woman without becoming one? What markers of femininity can a man, in fact, take on—without, of course, hormone therapy and radical surgery? Hermaphroditism is an entirely different category, and transvestitism is an act that can be performed by both men and women. In medieval texts, which exhibit considerable gender anxieties, female saints frequently cross-dress to pass as men and thereby preserve their virginity, whereas male cross-dressers might not receive quite the same kind of social approbation—though they are generally not identified as monsters.[47] In terms of gender, those monsters who bend it are, typically, women.

---

44 C.L. Moore, *Shambleau* (Maryland: Wildside Press, 2009).

45 Thomas A. Bredehoft, "Origin Stories: Feminist Science Fiction and C.L. Moore's 'Shambleau,'" *Science Fiction Studies* 24 (1997), pp. 369–86, at 373.

46 We might also see the Poison Virgins as a part of this category, because of the vaginal snakes. However, they seem to be more representative of a different kind of fear of women's bodies and sexuality—through virginity—than that of women's powers of seduction. Moreover, their serpents are invisible and are not explicitly a part of their sexual appeal in the same way as these women upon whose bodies the serpents are clearly visible.

47 See, for example, *The Questioning of John Rykener, A Male Cross-Dressing Prostitute, 1395*, Medieval Sourcebook, <http://www.fordham.edu/halsall/source/1395rykener.html>, accessed July 28, 2010. As Vern Bullough suggests, female cross-dressing was more acceptable because "such women were striving to be more male-like and therefore better persons. Male impersonation of females, on the other hand, not only led to a lower status but was suspect because most male writers could find only one possible

As Laqueur posits: "Woman alone seems to have 'gender' since the category itself is defined as an aspect of social relations based on difference between sexes in which the standard has always been male."[48] Since the standard *is* male, we might suspect that the most dangerous monsters would be those that denude the category of its meaning or challenge its value, rather than propping it up by a desire to become it. However, it seems that this kind of monstrosity either is not very threatening (as a feminized man might be seen, simply, as weak), or is perhaps a step too far, even for monsters. Female monsters, in contrast, routinely take on male physical properties and adopt corresponding aspects of masculine gender. By doing so, they broaden the concept of gender by becoming, in a sense, transgender individuals. Susan Stryker claims that if we define contemporary transgender "broadly as anything that disrupts or denaturalises normative gender, and which calls our attention to the processes through which normativity is produced and atypicality achieves visibility, 'transgender' becomes an incredibly useful analytical concept."[49]

Women with beards or those, like the classical Amazons (popular through the so-called "Age of Exploration," and on),[50] without a breast who hunt are atypical and do denaturalize concepts of gender—but they do not become men; this makes them, for premodern audiences, monstrous. Early in *Mandeville's Travels*, the fictional narrator Sir John tells us that a monster is a "thing deformed against kind."[51] These women's bodies are hybrids, possessing the characteristics not of beasts and humans, but of men and women. In her illustration in the *Wonders of the East*, the bearded huntress looks very much like a man, bearded and squarely built, but she is drawn with delicate pink and white breasts that are clearly female and feminine.[52]

---

explanation for a man's adopting woman's guise, namely a desire to have easier access to women for sexual purposes." Vern Bullough, "Cross Dressing and Gender Role Change in the Middle Ages," in Vern Bullough and James Brundage (eds), *Handbook of Medieval Sexuality* (New York: Garland Publishing, 2000), pp. 223–42, at 225. Bullough notes that "male cross dressing was, however, permitted or at least tolerated under certain conditions," p. 234. Still, the *Liber monstorum* does open with an apparent male transvestite (Orchard, *Pride and Prodigies*, pp. 258–9).

48 Laqueur, *Making Sex*, p. 22.

49 Susan Stryker, "Transgender Feminism: Queering the Woman Question," in Stacy Gillis, Gillian Howie, and Rebecca Munford (eds), *Third Wave Feminism: A Critical Exploration* (London: Palgrave Macmillan, 2007), pp. 59–70, at 60.

50 See the chapters by Braham, Felton, Steel and Van Duzer for discussion of these popular figures.

51 "a monster is a þing difformed a3en kynde bothe of man or of best or of ony þing elles & þat is cleped a Monstre." P. Hamelius (ed.), *Mandeville's Travels, Translated from the French by Jean d'Outremeuse*, edited from MS Cotton Titus c. XVI, in the British Museum, 2 volumes, EETS, os 153–54 (London: Oxford University Press, 1919–23), p. 30.

52 Illustrations can be found in Dana Oswald, "Unnatural Women, Invisible Mothers: Monstrous Female Bodies in the Wonders of the East," *Different Visions: A Journal of New Perspectives on Medieval Art* 2 (2009), p. 10, figure 1, available at <http://www.differentvisions.org/Issue2PDFs/Oswald.pdf>, as well as in the facsimile, P. McGurk, D.N. Dumville, M.R. Godden, and Ann Knock (eds), *An Eleventh Century Anglo-Saxon Illustrated Miscellany*, Early English Manuscripts in Facsimile 21 (Baltimore: Johns

She seems to exist somewhere between categories, as she distorts the "normal" social order: women replace men in the hunt, cats replace dogs, horses are used as clothing instead of mounts.[53] It seems that, in taking on the masculine signifier of the beard, these women also adopt masculine behaviors while retaining qualities of the traditional feminine, like nurturing and making clothing. Similarly, the Amazons are skilled warriors whose bodies bear male attributes; however, instead of being born bearded, the Amazons adapt their own bodies by burning off one breast of all female children. Single-breastedness identifies these women as Amazons, confirming their social status and enabling physical prowess.[54] Through their physical alteration, the Amazons' bodies become, as Karma Lochrie frames the issue, "hard"; she states: "their hard, single-breasted bodies signify their masculinity, sexual subjectivity, rejection of femininity and the male gaze that consumes it."[55] I would posit that their removal of their own breasts and those of their daughters indicates more than just a masculinity, but rather a hybrid state that is also transitional, a state that Halberstam describes as being one of instability and ambiguity.[56] While they maintain the biological capability of women to reproduce, and they remain separate from people who define themselves as male, the Amazons clearly exceed the social and also the physical functions of medieval women. They fight and govern themselves, reconstituting how sex, gender, and sexuality function. And as Halberstam writes of Female to Male (FTM) transitions: "gender transition from female to male allows biological women to access male privilege within their reassigned genders ... the fact is that gender reassignment for FTMS does have social and political consequences."[57]

For contemporary people who choose to transition, the kinds of transitions that they make can affect their social and economic statuses in significant ways, beyond the achievement of personal identity. So too, by changing their bodies and becoming "monstrous" female–male hybrids, the mythical Amazons achieve political independence and the martial prowess necessary to maintain it.

Hopkins University Press, 1983), but both are unfortunately in black-and-white, and the delicately colored breasts are not visible.

53 "fore hundum tigras 7 leopardos þæt hi fedað þæt synda ða kenestan deor. 7 ealra ðæra wildeora kynn, 7 ealra ðæra wildeora kynn, þæra þe on þære dune akenda beoð, þæt gehuntigað" [instead of dogs, they bring up tigers and leopards, that are the fiercest beasts, and they hunt all kinds of wild beasts that are born on the mountain], Orchard, *Pride and Prodigies*, p. 198.

54 "And yf þei be of gentel blood, þei brenne of þe lyft pap for beryng of a schild; and yf þei be of oþer blood, þei brenne of þe ri3t pap for scheotyng of a bowe. For wymmen þere beþ goode werriouris" [And if they are of gentle blood, they burn off the left breast for the bearing of a shield, and if they are of other blood, they burn off the right breast for the shooting of a bow, because women there are good warriors], M.C. Seymour (ed.), *The Defective Version of Mandeville's Travels*, EETS, ns 319 (London: Oxford University Press, 2002), p. 69.

55 Karma Lochrie, "Amazons at the Gates," in *Heterosyncrasies: Female Sexuality When Normal Wasn't* (Minneapolis: University of Minnesota Press, 2005), pp. 103–38, at 137.

56 Halberstam, *Female Masculinity*, pp. 163–4.

57 Ibid., p. 143.

Alternatively, men who take on the properties of women's bodies must then lose privilege. Consequently, as I have suggested, gender-bending male monsters are rare. Perhaps social discomfort with this kind of monster limits its appearance in popular monster texts; it is difficult to find early examples,[58] and those that do appear often do so in an allegorical form. Gender-bending women are declared allegorically monstrous frequently—as is the case with John Knox's *The First Blast of the Trumpet Against the Monstrous Regiment of Women* (1558), wherein he draws the image of a monster, none of whose parts are where they ought to be, in order to demonstrate his objection to female rulers, whom he allegorizes as a deformation of the commonwealth.[59] For Knox, a woman in power is a "monster in nature: so I call a woman clad in the habit of a man, yea, a woman against nature reigning above man."[60] Like the Amazons and huntresses, the female ruler transgresses the boundaries of her proper gender role and becomes a monster. While Knox's allegory reveals a woman who takes on the properties of a man, Philip Melancthon's pamphlet *Of Two Wonderful Popish Monsters*, translated by John Brooke in 1579, depicts a feminized male monster in the figure of the Popish Ass (see Figure 2.1).[61] In the woodcut image, we see a basically human form, with an ass's head, a woman's torso, scaly skin, mismatched extremities, and two faces extruding from the buttocks. Although the most identifiable markers of gender are the feminine front of the body, the creature is referred to in masculine gender pronouns (admittedly, these are rare in the 17-page long explication of the allegory). Despite the rarity of gender pronouns, Melancthon makes clear the gendered monstrosity of the body, explaining that the front parts of the body:

> *which do resemble the belly and stomacke of a woman, signify the body of the Pope: That is to say the Cardinals, Archbishops [etc], and all the rest of his bawds, and fatte hogges, which have none other care all their lyfe time but to feede and pamper their paunches with delicious wynes and delicate dishes: to take their ease and all the allurements and enticements to whoredome, and to keepe themselves in al pleasures and jolenesse, and to give themselves unto all monstrous infamies ... As we do see this Popish Asse who sheweth before all mens eyes openly, and without any shame his belly of a woeman, naked and*

---

58 The figure in the *Liber monstrorum* mentioned above is a noteworthy exception.
59 "For who would not judge that body to be a monster, where there was no head eminent above the rest, but that the eyes were in the hands, the tongue and the mouth beneath in the belly, and the ears in the feet? Men, I say, should not only pronounce this body to be a monster, but assuredly they might conclude that such a body could not long endure. And no less monstrous is the body of that commonwealth where a woman bears empire; for either it does lack a lawful head (as in very deed it does), or else there is an idol exalted in the place of the true head," John Knox, *First Blast of the Trumpet* (Whitefish, MT: Kessinger Publishing, 2004), p. 19. Originally published in 1558 as *First Blast of the Trumpet Against the Monstrous Regiment of Women*.
60 Knox, *First Blast of the Trumpet*, p. 39.
61 For further discussion of this figure, see the chapters by Davies and Van Duzer in this collection.

bare: een to these, without any shame, does lead a dissolute and wanton lyfe, full of all filthinesse and wickednesse.[62]

The obvious message here is the corruption of the pope and his officers, in terms of lack of control demonstrated by the lusts and appetites of the female body. Therefore, the physical elements of the woman's body imbue the male figure with negative feminine gender characteristics. In this formulation, the body informs behavior, inasmuch as it represents this behavior allegorically. In the rest of the explication of this allegory of the Catholic church, monstrosity is described in terms of the animal parts (including those of an ass, an elephant, a griffin—itself a hybrid—and a fish), as well as the Antichrist; in essence, it would be difficult to make this body worse or more transgressive. To give this male monster elements of the female body makes him a truly incomprehensible form, a body gone wrong in fundamental ways. The political allegory of gender is one that corrupts a healthy, normal body, harming an entire nation (in Knox, of England, and in Melancthon, of Protestant Christians), in comparison to the more individual acts of violence undertaken by other monsters. It is the most taboo transgression, one that threatens to dismantle the monolith of masculinity. As Stryker claims:

> *transgender phenomena simultaneously threaten to refigure the basic conceptual and representational framework within which the category "woman" has been conventionally understood, deployed, embraced and resisted. Perhaps "gender," transgender tells us, is not related to "sex" in quite the same way that an apple is related to the reflection of a red fruit in the mirror; it is not a mimetic relationship.*[63]

Thus, the relationship between gender and the body is tested by the hermaphrodites and the transgendered; while gender and the body cannot be divorced entirely, the very nature of gender is hybridized by bodies that, while being primarily one, are also the other, and act accordingly.

This Sex Which is Not One: Hermaphrodites and the Balance of Gender

While Luce Irigaray's title (*This Sex Which is Not One*) evokes the multiple nature of womanhood, I use it here to indicate a different kind of duality.[64] The gender

---

62 Philip Melancthon, *Of Two Wonderful Popish Monsters*, trans. John Brooke (1579), *EEBO*, p. 5.
63 Stryker, "Transgender Feminism," pp. 59–60.
64 Luce Irigaray, *This Sex Which is Not One*, trans. Catherine Porter (Ithaca: Cornell University Press, 1985).

of the hermaphrodite is a question that very much concerns those writers who include it in their catalogs of monstrosity. They struggle to identify a primary gender, or to understand not just how such a body works, but how it performs. The hermaphrodite of the classical period was highly eroticized, but in the Middle Ages and early modern period was often seen as a portent, a warning or an indicator of God's displeasure at human behavior or power to create; however, the potent figure exceeds these simple meanings, just as it refuses to fit neatly into categories of sex or gender. As Halberstam notes of the difficulty of complete and unambiguous transsexual transition: "some bodies are never at home, some bodies cannot simply cross from A to B, some bodies recognize and live with the inherent instability of identity."[65] Like the transsexual, hermaphrodites inhabit geographies of ambiguity, destabilizing singular gender identities. Although great emphasis was—and perhaps still is—placed on the medical or legal designation of the hermaphrodite's primary sex, in truth, the hermaphroditic body is powerful because it is so dual. Even once a decision has been made, the gender of the body is never really stable; the trace of that other self is always present. The hermaphroditic body is viewed as monstrous because of its ambiguity; it is threatening precisely because it demonstrates the constructedness and arbitrary nature of the binary choice of gender.

The term "hermaphrodite" implies the possession of both male and female genitalia simultaneously. However, some medieval and early modern stories feature figures who have believed themselves to be young women until, upon physical activity, a penis emerges from the female genitals, and the sex and gender status of the person must be entirely reversed.[66] Ambroise Paré, chief surgeon to Charles IX and Henri III, affirms the one-sex model described by Thomas Laqueur when he includes "degenerative women" in his list of monsters, suggesting that "the reason why women can degenerate into men is because women have as much hidden within the body as men have exposed outside."[67] Although the gendered experience of these individuals is hermaphroditic—they live both as females and as males—they do not do so simultaneously. Such a genital configuration confirms gendered beliefs about the superiority and completeness of the male anatomy; however, most hermaphrodites described in monster texts have the physical capacities of both sexes, and therefore exist in intermediate or alternative genders. John Block Friedman cites the Roman author Pliny and influential seventh-century bishop Isidore of Seville in describing the Androgini, who "have the genitals of both sexes ... 'they both inseminate and bear.'"[68] Thus, the late classical or early

---

65   Halberstam, *Female Masculinity*, p. 164.
66   See Friedman's foreword (this collection) as well as Jeffrey Eugenides, *Middlesex* (New York: Picador, 2003).
67   Ambroise Paré, *On Monsters and Marvels*, trans. Janis L. Pallister (Chicago: University of Chicago Press, 1982), p. 32. Here, Paré is relying on the Galenic model of genitalia, in which the female genitals are essentially the inversion of the male, corresponding part for part.
68   Friedman, *Monstrous Races*, p. 10. Of them, Pliny reports: "androgynos esse utriusque naturae, inter se vicibus coeuntes, Calliphanes tradit" (Book 7, ch. 2) [androgini have a double nature and alternately cohabit with one another, according to Calliphanes].

medieval hermaphrodite was granted the ability to be both male and female and to perform the functions of each; their bodies are figured as divided, a means of attempting to confirm the binary even as it exists in a single body.

The early modern Paré carries this tradition forward, stating that hermaphrodites "take their pleasure first with one set of sexual organs and then with the other: first with those of a man, then with those of a woman, because they have the *natures* of man and of woman suitable to such an act."[69] In Paré's formulation, not only do hermaphrodites have the physical capacity to assume both roles, but they also have the nature to do so: their gender here is not quite so divided, even though they must shift between identities as they shift between sexual organs. Despite a desire in these descriptions to understand this multiple nature as binary in some ways, however, part of the appeal of the figure is its ambiguous and dual nature. In Ovid's classical poetry—and later attempts to translate its ambiguous Latin—"[r]ather than anatomizing the newly composite figure so that the reader can 'discern' its make-up, Hermaphroditus remains a blurred figure that can be 'taken two wayes'—as a boy or as a girl—depending on the preference of the reader."[70]

The idea of "taking the hermaphrodite two ways" suggests a kind of sexual fascination with the figure that is neither and both sexes at once. Jenny McCann argues: "early modern medical discourse on the hermaphrodite was not only a gendered but also a sexualized discourse, which led to the increasing association of the figure with pornography."[71] And yet, this tradition has a long history, as even within the classical period Hermaphrodite was the subject of erotic—if necessarily ambiguous—representations. The most famous example is the Louvre (or Sleeping) Hermaphroditos from second-century Rome, a work that emerges from a Hellenistic Greek context of emotionally and erotically charged imagery.[72] As

---

Isidore of Seville says: "Hermaphroditae autem nuncupati eo quod eis uterque sexus appareat ... Hi dexteram mamillam virilem, sinistram muliebrem habentes vicissim coeundo et gignunt et pariunt" (Book 11.3.9) [Hermaphrodites are so called because both sexes appear in them ... By coming together, having a man's breast on the right, and a woman's on the left, they engender and give birth] Priscilla Throop (trans.), *Isidore's Etymologies: Complete English Translation*, vol. 2 (Charlotte, VT: Lulu.com, 2005).

69 Paré, *On Monsters and Marvels*, p. 27.
70 Jenny C. McCann, "How to Look at a Hermaphrodite in Early Modern England," *Studies in English Literature 1500–1900* 46/1 (Winter 2006), pp. 67–91, at 75. McCann discusses English translations of Ovid, texts which approach the original Latin in a variety of ways. Ovid merely says "nec duo sunt et forma duplex, nec femina dici/ nec puer ut possit, neutrumque et utrumque videntur" (IV. 378–9) [they were not two, but a two-fold form, so that they could not be called male or female, and seemed neither or either]. Anthony Kline (trans.), *Ovid's Metamorphoses* (Virginia: University of Virginia Library, 2000).
71 McCann, "How to Look at a Hermaphrodite," p. 73.
72 Aileen Ajootian, "The Only Happy Couple: Hermaphrodites and Gender," in Ann Olga Koloski-Ostrow and Claire L. Lyons (eds), *Naked Truths: Women, Sexuality, and Gender in Classical Art and Archaeology* (London and New York: Routledge, 1997), pp. 220–42, at 220, discusses the possible Hellenistic original.

Aileen Ajootian argues, the figure "exploits the voyeuristic potential of a torsional pose to reveal its identity, relying on the back view of a vulnerable sleeping woman to engage the viewer in the process of discovery."[73] Indeed, there are seven largely complete classical variations on this work, as well as a number of more fragmentary survivals.[74] As Mary Beard and John Henderson write:

> These statues surely prompted all kinds of reaction: from learned curiosity, through credulous wonder and stunned disbelief, to prurient slavering. But as a group they inevitably focus attention not only on the nature of sexuality and desire (what constitutes gender division? How far does the difference between men and women reside in genital difference?), but also on the very basics of sexual arousal. No viewer can escape the question of whether that penis is erect; these statues invite you to home in on their genitalia—as if to fix the whole story of sex there. At the same time ... our first sight of this sleeping beauty cued us to signals of sexual arousal diffused from top to toe. Which signal is the stronger? And does the statue tell the same story of arousal to male and female viewers, whatever their different sexualities?[75]

Thus the hermaphrodite troubles notions of sex, gender, and even sexuality.

The indeterminate status of the hermaphrodite might have been rendered appealingly, at times, but it was also presented as dangerous and potentially deceptive. For the Greeks, whence the figure comes, "Hermaphroditos, embodying both male and female elements, was considered not a monstrous aberration, but a higher, more powerful form, male and female combining to create a third, transcendent gender."[76] On the other hand, "in Rome humans possessing physical traits of both sexes," like the female ruler of the early modern period, "constituted a state threat,"[77] and many Roman images present the figure as a subject of humor, scorn, or abjection, especially in images of Pan unveiling Hermaphroditos.[78]

Roman rejection of the duality of the figure is unsurprisingly carried into the early Christian context by Augustine and others. Augustine, noting that secondary sex characteristics should be considered, as well as primary, suggests that most hermaphrodites are identified as primarily male, adding that "customarily in speech they are assigned to the better sex, the masculine, for no one ever called them androgynesses or hermaphroditesses."[79] Returning to Paré, who consciously looks

---

73 Ibid., p. 231.
74 Mary Beard and John Henderson, *Classical Art: From Greece to Rome* (Oxford: Oxford University Press, 2001), p. 133.
75 Ibid., p. 134.
76 Ajootian, "The Only Happy Couple," p. 228.
77 Ibid., p. 229.
78 Beard and Henderson, *Classical Art*, p. 139.
79 "a meliore tamen, hoc est a masculine, ut appellarentur, loquendi consuetudo praevaluit. Nam nemo umquam Androgynaecas aut Hermaphroditas nuncupavit." Quoted in R.D. Fulk, "Male Homoeroticism in the Old English *Canons of Theodore*," in Carol Braun Pasternack and Lisa M.C. Weston (eds), *Sex and Sexuality in Anglo-Saxon*

back to classical conceptions, we find in his treatment of the subject echoes of the Roman rejection of the hermaphrodite. He states that the individuals themselves must choose how to identify, with severe punishment for any sexual violation of the decision:

> both the ancient and modern laws have obliged and still oblige the latter to choose which sex organs they wish to use, and they are forbidden on pain of death to use any but those they will have chosen, on account of the misfortunes that could result from such.[80]

While Paré recommends that doctors can help make the decision, their medical judgments were based on more than the nature of the genitals. They also took into account secondary sex characteristics like face shape and gendered notions of the body, like hair type, as well as gendered behaviors, such as "whether the whole disposition of the body is robust or effeminate; whether they are bold or fearful, and other actions like those of males or of females."[81] Neither the genitals alone, nor even the whole body, then, is the definitive means for choosing a sex identity for ambiguous people. This alternate sex and gender identity, however, does not serve only to disrupt the system, but rather:

> far from altering significantly androcentric structures, the acknowledgment of a separate hermaphroditic nature strengthened the need for the strict enforcement upon intersexed individuals of dichotomous legal classifications, as well as for the discipline of bodies in conformity with the expectations of binary gender.[82]

While for the Greeks, this seems to be a source for increased status and erotic potential, for the Romans onward, the ambiguity was cause for concern, condemnation, and medical or legal "remedies." Indeed, while contemporary approaches to intersex individuals do not regard them as monstrous, methods for understanding and treating ambiguous bodies are still defined by a legally validated sex binary of male and female.[83]

England (Tempe: Arizona Center for Medieval and Renaissance Studies, 2004), pp. 1–34, at 31, n. 84.

80 Paré, On Monsters and Marvels, p. 27.

81 Ibid., pp. 27–8.

82 Cary J. Nederman and Jacqui True, "The Third Sex: The Idea of the Hermaphrodite in Twelfth-Century Europe," Journal of the History of Sexuality 6/4 (1996), pp. 497–517, at 517.

83 Transsexual and transgender people are often reduced to their birth genders in terms of legal identification and social division, in ways that are both reductive and dangerous. See especially Anne Fausto-Sterling, Sexing the Body; Dean Spade, "Methodologies of Trans Resistance," in George E. Haggerty and Molly McGarry (eds), A Companion to Lesbian, Gay, Bisexual, Transgender, and Queer Studies (Oxford: Blackwell, 2007), pp. 237–61; and Elizabeth Loeb, "Cutting it Off: Bodily Integrity, Identity Disorders,

Conclusions

Monstrous bodies and genders reveal that all bodies and genders are somewhere in between rigidly constructed and patrolled categories of sex and gender. While the monstrous serves as a negative category, one meant to confirm boundaries and to warn people to stay within them, it reveals the very superficial nature of these imposed limits, and the uncomfortable ways in which we all fit within them. We might look to the body—to sex—as a place of security, a means of stabilizing flexible and performative gender, but monsters reveal that the slippery nature of gender derives from the body, which itself is contingent, dependent, derivative— always in some kind of transition, even if we do not seek to change sex or gender. As Prosser argues:

> transition represents the movement in between that threatens to dislocate our ties to identity places we conceive of as essentially (in every sense) secure. Transition provokes discomfort, anxiety … it pushes up against the very feasibility of identity. Yet transition is also necessary for identity's continuity; it is that which moves us on.[84]

While the monster presents us with the idea of ambiguity and unwillingness to reside in a single, fixed location, it can only do so because of our own competing social and individual human desires for home and the means to escape it.

External ambiguities can conceal—even signify—an underlying certainty, one committed to the hybrid, the interstitial, the in-between. Bodies that are monstrous are not "uncertain"—they exist in a very clear space, one that does not choose a side, but rather one that points out the futility and inadequacy of such divisions.[85] Judith/Jack Halberstam says that: "the borderlands are inhospitable for some transsexuals who imagine that home is just across the border because many transsexuals *do* transition to go somewhere, to be somewhere, and to

---

and the Sovereign Stakes of Corporeal Desire in US Law," *Women's Studies Quarterly* 36/3–4 (2008), pp. 44–63. Spade (p. 252) notes the wide variation in Department of Motor Vehicles policies, in which physiological sex binaries are privileged based on surgical status (p. 248), whereas homeless shelters rely on birth gender, sometimes with disastrous consequences: "Former shelter residents, particularly trans women, report rape and sexual harassment in men's shelters where they are placed." Similarly, Loeb (p. 51) notes pathologizing of surgical responses based on gender identity in relation to physiological sex: "If I have 'male' on my birth certificate and am troubled by fatty tissue atop my pectorals, not only will a licensed professional gladly perform the procedure without legal concern or additional medical cause … If, however, my birth certificate states 'female,' I must be diagnosed by a licensed psychiatrist with gender identity disorder and spend two years proving that I 'really have' this condition in order to obtain the exact same surgery."

84 Prosser, *Second Skins*, p. 3.
85 See MacCormack's discussion of the posthuman in this collection.

leave geographies of ambiguity behind."[86] It is not the geography of ambiguity that endangers us, however—it is the myth of certainty, of arrival, that undoes us. Whenever we insist on an identity—gender or otherwise—that is solid, that achieves personal, social, and cultural expectations, we simultaneously break those categories apart, learning that it is certainty, not ambiguity, that is untenable.

---

86   Halberstam, *Female Masculinity*, pp. 164 and 163.

Monstrosity and Race in the Late Middle Ages

Debra Higgs Strickland

There is no genetic basis for categorizing human beings into races, and it is a basic tenet of anthropological knowledge that all normal human beings have the capacity to learn any cultural behavior: nobody is born with a built-in culture or language.[1] And yet the concept of "race" as a genetically determined and permanent state identifiable on sight from external, physical characteristics has exerted a powerful influence on the ways in which Western cultures have perceived themselves in relation to others. Paramount among these is the literary and artistic tradition of the monstrous races, whose classificatory scheme for the world's more colorful pseudo-inhabitants served a multitude of cultural purposes. Inherited from Greek and Roman antiquity and developed throughout the Middle Ages and early modern period, as other chapters in this book detail,[2] scrutiny of this tradition perhaps more than any other can provide insight into the ideological infrastructure for the medieval, and ultimately, the modern rhetoric of what we might call "racism." Authors and artists, especially in the Middle Ages, created strong links between physical and non-physical characteristics among different human groups in a wide variety of written and visual arenas, sacred as well as secular. Concomitantly, medieval ideas about race also informed conceptions of monstrosity put to relentless service in late medieval representations of Jews, Mongols, Muslims, and "Ethiopians" that continued to influence images of these and still other groups far beyond the Middle Ages.

Semantic complications that haunt investigations like this one, however, include whether or not the use of the term "racism" in relation to the Middle Ages is anachronistic and inescapably misleading,[3] whether "ethnicity" is a better and

---

1   "AAA Statement on Race," *American Anthropologist* 100 (1998), pp. 712–13.
2   For discussions of the monstrous races in the Western tradition, see chapters in this collection by Surekha Davies, Debbie Felton, Chet Van Duzer, and, in their Eastern incarnation, Michael Dylan Foster.
3   As argued by William Chester Jordan, "Why 'Race'?"*Journal of Medieval and Early Modern Studies* 31 (2001), pp. 165–74.

more accurate designation for the medieval problem as well as the modern one,[4] and whether or not the term "racism," to whatever historical period it is applied, should incorporate anti-Semitism.[5] Although the Middle Ages is routinely excluded from discussions of racism by analysts who maintain that the use of the term "race" in something like its modern meaning did not occur until the late seventeenth century,[6] others have charted the far earlier origins of this concept and its attendant ideologies during the classical and medieval periods.[7] Beyond phenotypes, and in line with the recognition of multifarious historical formulations of racism,[8] an important and recent analysis of medieval Christian romance has identified the formulation of new racisms based on religious status.[9] From a linguistic perspective, Latin terms such as *gens* and *natio*, translatable in many contemporary medieval contexts as "race," pepper the parchment pages of many medieval manuscripts, including those that participate in the monstrous races tradition. Because so many of the basic ideas about monstrosity that developed in this tradition—such as physical deformity, aberrant dietary and sexual practices, lack of language or use of incomprehensible languages,[10] cannibalism, and "godlessness"—were repeatedly marshalled in Christian written and visual polemic against living Jews and Muslims, among others, I also incorporate Christian representations of non-Christians into this brief discussion of how medieval concepts of monstrosity intersected with those of what we refer to today as "race."

The purpose of the present chapter, then, is to explain how the monstrous races tradition contributed to the development of a medieval Christian concept of "race" and to examine how it subsequently provided an enduring blueprint for the condemnation and exclusion of real-world, non-Christian cultural outsiders.[11]

---

4   Robert Bartlett, "Medieval Concepts of Race and Ethnicity," *Journal of Medieval and Early Modern Studies* 31 (2001), pp. 39–56; his argument is based on the evidence of contemporary chronicles.

5   Les Back and John Solomos, "Introduction: Theories of Race and Racism: Genesis, Development and Contemporary Trends," in Les Back and John Solomos (eds), *Theories of Race and Racism: A Reader*, 2nd edn (London: Routledge, 2009), pp. 10–13; see also the individual chapters in Part Three of Back and Solomos's volume on "Racism and Anti-Semitism" (pp. 257–317).

6   Robert Bernasconi, "Who Invented the Concept of Race?" in Back and Solomos (eds), *Theories of Race and Racism*, pp. 83–103, at 84.

7   See especially David M. Goldenberg, "The Development of the Idea of Race: Classical Paradigms and Medieval Elaborations," *International Journal of the Classical Tradition* 5 (1999), pp. 561–84; and Goldenberg, *The Curse of Ham: Race and Slavery in Early Judaism, Christianity, and Islam* (Princeton: Princeton University Press, 2003).

8   David Theo Goldberg, *Racist Culture: Philosophy and the Politics of Meaning* (Oxford: Blackwell, 1993), especially pp. 41–60, 97–116.

9   Geraldine Heng, *Empire of Magic: Medieval Romance and the Politics of Cultural Fantasy* (New York: Columbia University Press, 2003), pp. 12–14.

10   See Karl Steel's chapter in this collection for extended discussion on incomprehensible languages among the cynocephali and centaurs.

11   I first introduced this thesis in Debra Hassig [Debra Higgs Strickland], "The Iconography of Rejection: Jews and Other Monstrous Races," in Colum Hourihane

The appellation "monstrous races," after all, suggests the intersection of two sets of ideas, monstrosity and race—which, besides apportioning the world's monsters into discrete races, also invites contemplation of race *as* monstrosity. Chronologically speaking, my focus will be on the later Middle Ages (circa 1000–circa 1500), as a period that drew on ancient traditions, experienced especially acute Christian/non-Christian tensions, and in turn established many tropes that have endured to the present day. Geographically, I shall concentrate primarily on medieval England, which, as Geraldine Heng notes, was excessively focused on the alien minority in its midst as attested by the overwhelming attention and surveillance accorded to English Jews, which set England apart from other places.[12] The intense interest in monsters and monster tales apparent in the cultural production of medieval England has been analyzed in relation to formative processes of self-identity, from the nation's mythical origins through the long period of the Crusades, providing another reason for locating my discussion here.[13] Most importantly, Anglo-Saxon England is the birthplace of the illustrated *Wonders of the East* tradition, which, grounded in classical traditions of ethnocentrism, is an especially fertile source in which to observe the literary and visual expression of medieval attitudes towards the alien and unknown, performed in word and picture as monstrosity. That works of art should figure prominently in this analysis follows from the fact that both monstrosity and racial differences are perceived visually.[14]

(ed.), *Image and Belief: Studies in Celebration of the Eightieth Anniversary of the Index of Christian Art* (Princeton: Princeton University Press, 1999), pp. 25–46. I examine it more fully in Debra Higgs Strickland, *Saracens, Demons, and Jews: Making Monsters in Medieval Art* (Princeton: Princeton University Press, 2003), especially pp. 29–59.

12   Geraldine Heng, "Jews, Saracens, 'Black Men,' Tartars: England in a World of Racial Difference," in Peter Brown (ed.), *A Companion to Medieval English Literature, c. 1350–c. 1500* (London: Blackwell Publishing, 2007), pp. 247–69, at 250–1. See also Heng, *Empire of Magic*, pp. 78–91. See also Colin Richmond, "Englishness and Medieval Anglo-Jewry," in T. Kushner (ed.), *The Jewish Heritage in British History* (London: Cass, 1992), pp. 42–59; and Richard C. Stacey, "Anti-Semitism and the Medieval English State," in J.R. Maddicott and D.M. Palliser (eds), *The Medieval State: Essay Presented to James Campbell* (London: Hambledon, 2000), pp. 153–78.

13   Jeffrey Jerome Cohen, *Of Giants: Sex, Monsters, and the Middle Ages* (Minneapolis: University of Minnesota Press, 1999), pp. 1–61; Asa Simon Mittman, "The Other Close at Hand: Gerald of Wales and the *Marvels of the West*," in Bettina Bildhauer and Robert Mills (eds), *The Monstrous Middle Ages* (Cardiff: University of Wales Press, 2003), pp. 97–112; and Mittman, *Maps and Monsters in Medieval England* (New York and London: Routledge, 2006), pp. 11–26.

14   On monstrosity as a primarily visual phenomenon, see Debra Higgs Strickland, "Introduction: The Future is Necessarily Monstrous," *Different Visions* 2 (2010), pp. 1–13. On race as visually perceived, see Ernst Mayr, "Darwin and the Evolutionary Theory in Biology," in Betty J. Meggars (ed.), *Evolution and Anthropology: A Centennial Appraisal* (Washington, DC: Anthropological Society of Washington, 1959), p. 3; and Herbert H. Odom, "Generalizations on Race in Nineteenth-Century Anthropology," *Isis* 58 (1967), pp. 4–18, at 5.

Figure 17.1 Monsters on the edge, Psalter Map. London, BL, MS Add. 28681, fol. 9r
© British Library Board

For medieval Christians, the monstrous races tradition and its rich symphony of physical and behavioral variety received its ultimate authority from the Genesis account of the aftermath of the flood, which describes the propagation of humanity via Noah's three sons, Shem, Japhet, and Ham (Genesis 9:18–19, Genesis 10). The belief that each son was assigned to procreate in particular parts of the world — Shem received Asia, Japhet inherited Europe and the islands of the sea, and Ham got Africa — informed not only the tripartite division of the world maps (*mappae mundi*), but also the common understanding that humanity was divided into different races, as articulated by "the Venerable" Bede (d. 735), among many others.[15] According to Bishop Isidore of Seville (560–636), there existed a total of 72 or 73 races, depending on how one counted them: 15 descended from Japhet, 27 from Shem, and 31 from Ham; they possessed an equal number of languages.[16] Additionally, Isidore repeated the important declaration made earlier by St Augustine of Hippo (354–430) in *The City of God* that just as monstrous progeny are occasionally born within a particular human race, so monstrous individuals can reproduce themselves to form entire races of monsters.[17] And so the notion of races as discrete groups descending from Noah's sons was extended to incorporate the physically aberrant, strange, dangerous, and distant; in other words, to embrace the monsters, whose remote locations were emblematized along the periphery of the late medieval Psalter, Hereford, and Ebstorf world maps (Figure 17.1).[18]

As Greta Austin has shown, the exotic Eastern peoples described in the Anglo-Saxon *Wonders of the East*, the ultimate armchair travel guide, were described as *genus* (in Latin) and *cyn* (in Old English), both of which may be translated as "race," although Austin herself considers this translation incorrect given its presumably irrelevant modern associations.[19] Isidore uses the word *gens* and its forms to designate both

15 See Bede, *De templo* 19.5, in Seán Connolly (trans.), *Bede: On the Temple* (Liverpool: Liverpool University Press, 1995), p. 86.

16 Isidore, *Etymologiae*, 9.2.2, in Stephen A. Barney et al. (eds and trans.), *The Etymologies of Isidore of Seville* (New York: Cambridge University Press, 2006), p. 192 and n. 5. The number of races was traditionally counted as 72, taking Eber (Heber) and Phaleg, both as described in Genesis 10, as progenitors of a single race.

17 Augustine, *De civitate Dei*, 16.8; in Marcus Dods (trans.), *St Augustin's City of God and Christian Doctrine*, Nicene and Post-Nicene Fathers 2 (1887; reprint Grand Rapids, MI: Eerdmans, 1983, pp. 314–15); Isidore, *Etymologiae*, 11.3.12 (Barney et al., *Etymologies*, p. 244).

18 In the form of inscriptions, if not images, monsters are also present along the periphery of earlier *mappae mundi*, such as the Cotton Map (circa 1050); see the excellent reproduction with explanatory apparatus available on *The Digital Mappaemundi Project* (directed by Martin K. Foys, Shannon Bradshaw, and Asa Simon Mittman), <http://bob.drew.edu/mappaemundi/mappa.swf>, accessed February 6, 2011. On further implications of the peripheral locations of monsters on the maps, see Mittman, *Maps and Monsters*, pp. 27–59.

19 Greta Austin, "Marvelous Peoples or Marvelous Races? Race and the Anglo-Saxon *Wonders of the East*," in Timothy S. Jones and David A. Sprunger (eds), *Marvels, Monsters, and Miracles: Studies in the Medieval and Early Modern Imaginations* (Kalamazoo, MI:

human and monstrous groups.[20] Whether translated as "race," "nation," or "people," the important point is that the words applied to the Sciopods, Panotii, Cynocephali, and other monsters are the same ones used to describe groups of human beings.[21] Without wishing to enter, much less attempt to settle, the contemporary medieval debate concerning whether or not the monstrous races were human,[22] we can at least observe that monsters were described using the same type of language that was applied to human groups, a factor that perhaps should be weighed into the debate's modern continuation. Both Augustine and Isidore otherwise imply a strong affinity between humans and monsters within the common framework of God's Creation by discussing monstrosities in the next breath after the Genesis roster of Noah's descendants. Whether or not this might represent an attempt to construct a hierarchy within nature, as Austin has argued with respect to the classified arrangement of the *Wonders* groups,[23] proximity of positioning suggests common conception.

Beginning with the earliest Indian and Greek sources and continuing with the Anglo-Saxon *Liber monstrorum* (Book of Monsters) and *Wonders*,[24] the thirteenth-century encyclopedias (such as Peter of Cornwall's *Pantheologus*) and bestiaries, to late medieval moralized collections (such as the *Gesta romanorum*) and travel literature (such as *Mandeville's Travels*), the main elements of monstrosity would appear to be (1) remote location, (2) unusual physical form, and (3) bizarre behavior. For example, the Cynocephali are located in India, have heads like dogs, and communicate only by barking. Some of them are also man-eaters.[25] While these points of distinction are simple enough to enumerate verbally, their implications are brought to fullest

---

Western Michigan University, 2002), pp. 25–51, at 26–7.

20 The translators of the new edition of Isidore's *Etymologiae* rarely translate either *gens* or *natio* as "race" but explain in a footnote that both terms may be translated variously as "nation," "race," "tribe," "people," or "family," depending on context (Barney et al., *Etymologies*, p. 192, n. 4). A corrected edition of Wallace M. Lindsay's 1911 Latin edition of the *Etymologies* is available online: <http://penelope.uchicago.edu/Thayer/E/Roman/texts/Isidore/home.html>.

21 Similarly, Austin ("Marvelous Peoples," p. 51) notes that both *genus* and *cyn* can designate "all human people."

22 On the terms of the medieval debate, see John Block Friedman, *The Monstrous Races in Medieval Art and Thought* (Cambridge, MA and London: Harvard University Press, 1981), pp. 178–96.

23 Austin, "Marvelous Peoples," pp. 28–48.

24 For a survey of the ancient and medieval sources, see the seminal article by Rudolf Wittkower, "Marvels of the East: A Study in the History of Monsters," *Journal of the Warburg and Courtauld Institutes* 5 (1942), pp. 159–97.

25 As noted, for example, in the Latin caption that accompanies the image of the Doghead (*Cinomolgus*) in the late thirteenth-century Getty Bestiary (Los Angeles, J.P. Getty Museum, MS Ludwig XV.4, fol. 117r) produced in Northern France. An earlier (ninth-century) description of Dogheads may be found in Ratramnus of Corbie (Ratramnus Corbeiensis), *Epistola de Cynocephalis* (Letter Concerning the Doghead) in Jacques Paul Migne (ed.), *Patrologia Latina* 121: cols 1153A–1156D (Paris: Garnier, 1844). See also David Gordon White, *Myths of the Dog-Man* (Chicago: University of Chicago Press, 1991).

Figure 17.2   Cynocephalus, *Wonders of the East*. London, BL, MS Cotton Tiberius
B.V, fol. 80r (detail) (© British Library Board).

vigor visually. The text that accompanies the Cynocephalus in the Tiberius *Wonders*
manuscript, for instance, states quite dispassionately that Cynocephali (*Conopeonas*)
are dog-headed, horse-maned, boar-tusked, and fire-breathing (Figure 17.2).[26]

To understand the monster's gigantic stature, ferocity, and rampant virility,
the reader-viewer requires the accompanying image, in which the dog-headed
figure fills the entire space of his frame, interrupting the narrative description
to allow time for contemplation of radical, hybrid strangeness, including the

---

26   London, British Library, MS Cotton Tiberius B.V, fol. 80r.

Figure 17.3   Mercantile Dogheads of Angaman pictured in an early fifteenth-century copy of Marco Polo's *Divisament dou monde. Livre des merveilles*, Paris, BNF, MS fr. 2810, fol. 76v (detail).

hyper-masculinity signaled by his prominent, red genitals.[27] Generally speaking, medieval representations of the one-legged Sciopods, the giant-eared Panotii, the tiny Pygmies, and especially the headless Blemmye and Epiphagi leave viewers in no doubt that they are looking at non-human monsters which, like the human "races," are recognizable by sight. They are monstrous phenotypes. Perhaps this is why so many of Western Europe's painted and sculpted Sciopods, Blemmye, Giants—but also "Ethiopians," Jews, and "Saracens"—do not require identifying inscriptions. In medieval art, one can tell a Blemmye or a "Saracen" just by looking: *monstrum* means "to show."

In many works of art, individual monstrous races are portrayed entirely nude or with minimal clothing, isolated like museum specimens or situated in a suitably hostile landscape. In others, they are depicted walking, wearing contemporary clothing, communicating, venerating idols, and enacting other recognizably human behaviors, such as in the image of the fashionably dressed, mercantile Dogheads of Angaman pictured in an early fifteenth-century French copy of Marco Polo's *Divisament dou monde* (Figure 17.3).[28]

---

27   On monstrous genitals, see Dana M. Oswald, *Monsters, Gender and Sexuality in Medieval English Literature* (Cambridge: D.S. Brewer, 2010), pp. 27–65.

28   Paris, Bibliothèque Nationale de France, MS fr. 2810, fol. 76v. For a color reproduction of this image and others from this manuscript, see Marie-Thèrese Gousset, *Il Milione,*

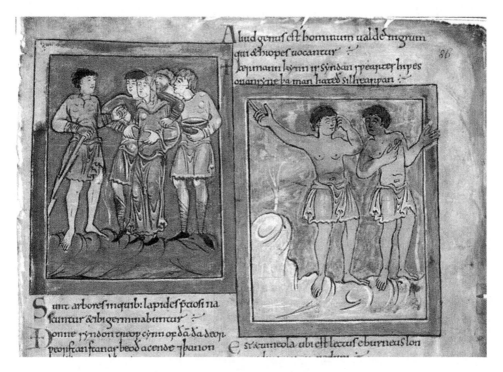

Figure 17.4   Wife-givers (left) and Ethiopians (right). *Wonders of the East*. London, BL, MS Cotton Tiberius B.V, fol. 86r (detail) (© British Library Board).

Stranger still, certain of the races pictured in the earlier *Wonders* manuscripts appear more human than monstrous, at least on physiognomical grounds. For example, again in the Tiberius manuscript, the Hospitable Kings, who rule over tyrants, are represented by an unprepossessing, crowned man wearing contemporary medieval garb (fol. 85vb). The Men Who Feed on Raw Flesh and Honey are represented by a clean-shaven man in a short tunic ingesting his favorite foods, and the Wife-givers are depicted as a group of four human males in medieval dress manhandling a woman wearing a contemporary gown (Figure 17.4).

For such as these, detecting monstrosity is more problematical, because while the geographical distance might be great, the *conceptual* distance between Us and Them, expressed as the phenotype, is not so. But the *Wonders'* taxonomical arrangement leaves the reader without any doubt that, although they look fairly familiar, such peoples as the Hospitable Kings and Wife-givers do form distinct races, as the accompanying texts indicate. Looking beyond the *Wonders* text and images, it is a relatively short conceptual step from the Wife-givers to multiple

---

Marco Polo (Paris: Bibliothèque de l'image, 2002). See also Debra Higgs Strickland, "Artists, Audience, and Ambivalence in Marco Polo's *Divisament dou monde*," *Viator* 36 (2005), pp. 493–529.

Figure 17.5   Dogheads worshiping an idol, *Travels of Sir John Mandeville*. London, BL, MS Harley 3954, fol. 40v (detail) (© British Library Board).

wife-keeping in actual distant Eastern cultures, such as that practiced by the Great Khan and others in "Tartary," detailed in *Mandeville's Travels*.[29]

It is an equally short conceptual step from walking, talking, well-dressed (if cannibalistic) Dogheads to medieval Christian characterizations of Muslims, known pejoratively as "Saracens," and characterized by some Christian chroniclers as "a race of dogs."[30] How this thought-pattern might have colored perceptions of the Mandeville author's polygamous and idol-worshiping "Tartars," the pejorative medieval designation for Mongols, is suggested in one English copy of this work,

---

29   See Malcolm Letts (ed.), *Mandeville's Travels: Texts and Transmissions*, 2 volumes (London: Hakluyt Society, 1953), vol. 2, pp. 150–1 and 170–1 (Egerton text). On the overlap between medieval conceptions of Tartars and monsters, see Strickland, *Saracens, Demons, and Jews*, pp. 192–209.

30   On this insult, see Strickland, *Saracens, Demons, and Jews*, pp. 159–60; and Strickland, "Meanings of Muhammad in Later Medieval Art," in Christiane J. Gruber and Avinoam Shalem (eds), *Picturing Prophetic Knowledge: The Prophet Muhammad in Cross-Cultural Literary and Artistic Traditions* (forthcoming).

which transforms Mongols into dog-headed monsters, clad only in loincloths, who kneel with hands clasped in prayer before an image of an ox positioned on an altar (Figure 17.5).[31]

It is perhaps also significant that the Mandeville author is at pains to explain that these "Tartars" are descended from Noah's son, Ham, identified in other medieval contexts as the dark-skinned progenitor of other "monstrous races," including black Africans and Jews.[32] Later in the same passage, the Mandeville author explains that the "Saracens" descended from Shem, and Europeans from Japhet. After Nimrod built the Tower of Babel, he continues, "there came many fiends in likeness of men and lay by women of his kindred and gat on them giants and other monsters of horrible figure, some without heads, some with hounds' heads, and many other disfigured and misshapen men." And so in a single paragraph, the genetic origins of Mongols, Muslims, and the strangest of Eastern monstrosities are all accounted for and, more importantly, conceived together as the independent racial components of God's vast creation. It is not at all clear where humanity stops and monstrosity begins.

The contemporary cultural reality in which "Saracens" and "Tartars" were excluded from medieval society based on both religious and physical differences invites us to consider not only the relationship between monstrosity and race, but also monstrosity and religion as a *surrogate* for race. It is true that both Muslims and Mongols were accused, among other aberrant behaviors, of the most atrocious crime of cannibalism, which linked them directly to the monstrous race of Anthropophagi (Man-eaters). The English monk Matthew Paris certainly described the Mongols along these lines in his mid-thirteenth-century *Chronica majora*, underscoring the supposed savagery of this group in his accompanying image of grotesque, man-eating "Tartars" roasting a human body over a spit (Figure 17.6).[33]

Such a characterization would seem to relegate Mongols to the same monstrous camp as the Anglo-Saxon *Wonders*. But as Geraldine Heng has argued, thirteenth-century England saw the development of *new* racisms based on differences of skin color, body, and religion.[34] She details the ways in which literary characterizations

---

31 London, British Library, MS Harley 3954, fol. 40v. For a fuller discussion of this image, see Strickland, *Saracens, Demons, and Jews*, pp. 203–4.

32 Letts, *Mandeville's Travels*, vol. 2, pp. 154–5 (Egerton text). On medieval beliefs concerning Ham's dark skin and God's curse upon his son Canaan as punishment for Ham's sinful regarding of his own father's (Noah's) nakedness (Genesis 9:20–25), see Goldenberg, *Curse of Ham*, especially pp. 141–77.

33 Cambridge, Corpus Christi College, MS 16, fol. 167r. On this image, see Suzanne Lewis, *The Art of Matthew Paris in the Chronica Majora* (Berkeley: University of California Press, 1987), pp. 285–7; and Strickland, *Saracens, Demons, and Jews*, pp. 192–4.

34 Heng, *Empire of Magic*, especially pp. 228–305. See also Jeffrey Jerome Cohen, "On Saracen Enjoyment: Some Fantasies of Race in Late Medieval France and England," *Journal of Medieval and Early Modern Studies* 31 (2001), pp. 113–46; and Madeline Caviness, "From the Self-Invention of the Whiteman to The Good, the Bad, and the Ugly," *Different Visions* 1 (2008).

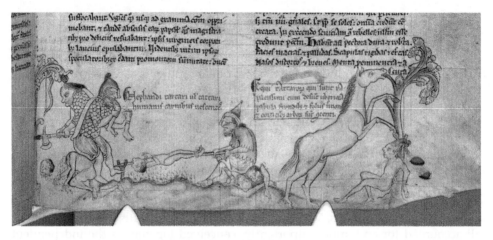

Figure 17.6 Man-eating Tartars, Matthew Paris, *Chronica Majora*. Cambridge, Corpus Christi College, MS 16, fol. 167r (detail) (photo: courtesy of the Master and Fellows of Corpus Christi College, Cambridge.

of Jews and Muslims in contemporary romance worked in cultural tandem with ecclesiastical and royal authorities who sought to subordinate, exclude, colonize, or murder these groups both within and outwith Christian society. More generally, in contemporary literary genres from romance to historical chronicle, monstrosity was conferred upon the defenders and practitioners of Judaism and Islam, largely because the religions they defended and practiced were considered the wrong ones. This is why figures of Muslims to some extent, and figures of Jews to a much greater one, are depicted in English medieval works of art from the twelfth century onwards as bestial and misshapen, engaged in sadistic behaviors. Sometimes they are rendered fully monstrous. While the great flood of medieval Christian literary and theological polemic against Jews created for this group an overwhelmingly negative identification, the all-important ideological transformation of Jews from sinful to monstrous was more fully accomplished visually. Passion imagery in late medieval devotional books (prayer books, psalters, Books of Hours) with depressing regularity includes grotesquely stereotyped figures of Jews, sometimes dark-skinned, cross-eyed or fanged, gleefully performing grisly tortures upon Christ's white, blameless body, as in the Winchester Psalter's depiction of the Betrayal and Flagellation of Christ (Figure 17.7), which even includes a Jewish tormentor with horns.[35]

---

35 These and other stereotyped characteristics were first identified and catalogued in Ruth Mellinkoff, *Outcasts: Signs of Otherness in Northern European Art of the Late Middle Ages*, 2 volumes (Berkeley: University of California Press, 1993). Medieval portrayals of horned Jews are rare, excepting the artistic tradition of the horned Moses that is generally interpreted in relation to St Jerome's famous translation mistake and therefore not considered pejorative, at least when it occurs in Old Testament illustration. But for an alternative analysis, see Stephen Bertman, "The Antisemitic Origin of Michelangelo's

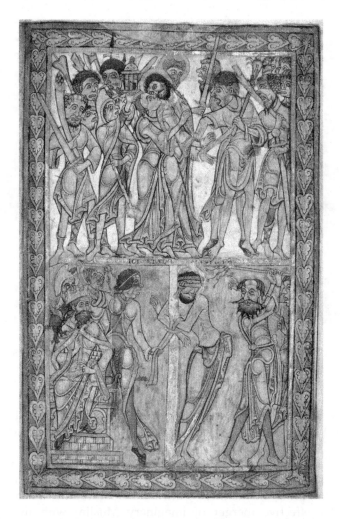

Figure 17.7 Betrayal and Flagellation of Christ, Winchester Psalter. London, BL,
MS Cotton Nero C IV, fol. 21r (© British Library Board).

Similarly, even if confined to literature, the shameful slanders directed
against the Prophet Muhammad and contemporary medieval followers of Islam
would have accomplished the goal of defaming Christianity's most successful
competitor. But the portrait of the Prophet as a hybrid fish monster drawn in red
ink in the margins of Peter the Venerable's twelfth-century copy of the Qur'an
spoke more directly and acutely of the supposed depravity of Islam, at this time
misunderstood by medieval Christians as a perverse form of Christianity, as a
heresy rather than a bona fide religion.[36]

Horned Moses," *Shofar* 27 (2009), pp. 95–106.

36   Paris, Bibliothèque de l'Arsenal, MS 1162, fol. 11r. See Walter B. Cahn, "The 'Portrait'

Figure 17.8   Alexander's army versus gigantic Saracen Cyclopes, *Romance of Alexander*. London, BL, MS Royal 20.B.xx, fol. 79v (detail) (© British Library Board).

Heresy or religion, medieval Christians wanted it silenced. The protracted, bloody project of the Crusades, believed sanctioned by God against the Muslim "heathen," was glorified in the *chansons des geste* and romance texts. It was also fuelled by pictorial images of Christian versus Muslim armies, in which the "Saracen" warriors are rendered as gigantic, dark, or otherwise physically distorted, and wearing the identifying attribute of a turban or a headband (*tortil*). One especially effective merger of imaginary Muslim with monster obtains in a vivid battle scene included in a fifteenth-century North French copy of the *Romance of Alexander*. In this image, Alexander's army, rendered in the guise of contemporary French crusaders, fights against the formidable force of one-eyed, gigantic Cyclopes rendered "Saracen" by their headbands (Figure 17.8).[37] Whether

of Muhammad in the Toledan Collection," in Elizabeth Sears and Thelma K. Thomas (eds), *Reading Medieval Images: The Art Historian and the Object* (Ann Arbor: University of Michigan Press, 2002), pp. 51–60; and Thomas E. Burman, *Reading the Qur'ān in Latin Christendom, 1140–1560* (Philadelphia: University of Pennsylvania Press, 2007), p. 60. On Islam as a Christian heresy, see John V. Tolan, *Saracens: Islam in the Medieval European Imagination* (New York: Columbia University Press, 2002), pp. 135–69.

37   London, British Library, MS Royal 20.B.xx, fol. 79v. On this image, see Debra Higgs Strickland, "Saracens, Eschatological Prophecies, and Later Medieval Art," in Veronika Weiser (ed.) *Occidental Apocalypticism: Compendium on the Genealogy of the End* (forthcoming).

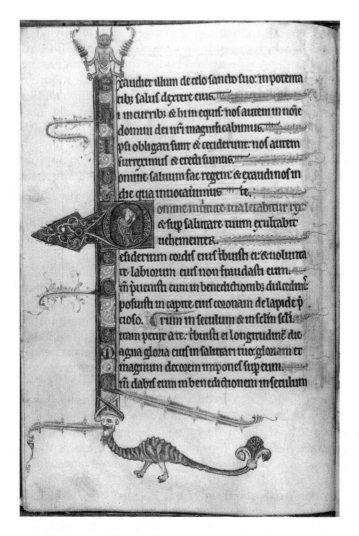

Figure 17.9 Monstrous, marginal Jew, Rutland Psalter. London, BL, MS Add. 62925, fol. 23v (detail) (© British Library Board).

identified primarily as Cyclopes or Muslim, the physical size and ferocity of the enemy signifies at a glance the perceived extent and nature of the danger posed to Christendom.

As a minority population in England until they were expelled in 1290, medieval Jews, with their equally "wrong religion," were another perceived threat to the Christian majority.[38] As the supposed descendants of "Christ-killers" looking for

38 For first person narratives and testimonies of the tensions born of social and religious intolerance, see Michael Goodich (ed.), *The Other Middle Ages: Witnesses at the Margins of Medieval Society* (Philadelphia: University of Pennsylvania Press, 1998).

opportunities to re-enact the crucifixion, Jews were additionally targets of crusader violence. In works of art produced in England from the twelfth century onwards, distortions of human physiognomy and bodily form that suggest or fully achieve monstrosity may be observed in images of hybrid Jewish monsters, identifiable by their ubiquitous hats, in marginal sculpture and manuscript illuminations. In a thirteenth-century English copy of the *Romance of Alexander*, for example, one member of a group of Giants representing the apocalyptic hoards of Gog and Magog is depicted eating a snake and wearing a knobbed, Jewish hat.[39] A fully monstrous Jew rendered as a hybrid, fire-breathing dragon appears in the lower margin of the Rutland Psalter (Figure 17.9); his Jewish identity is clear from his stereotyped features of grotesque physiognomy, long beard, and pointed Jewish hat.[40] These and other pictorial "Jewish monsters" may be viewed alongside contemporary chronicle and romance descriptions to provide another raft of evidence for medieval conflations of monstrosity, race, and religion.

The visual spectacle of monstrous Jewish hybrids in turn raises an interesting question about the Sciopods, Panotii, Giants, Cynocephali, and their ilk. Given medieval readings of exterior physical form as a sign of inner moral character,[41] are the physical deformities of the monstrous races signs of distance not only from human civilization, but also from God? There is another supporting analogy for this thesis in the medieval tradition of the Wild Folk, unfortunate persons who, having lost their human powers of reason, pursue a bestial existence in the woods, clothed only in a thick coat of body hair. But in the medieval romance tradition, such wildness is reversible: once the Wild Man *returns* to God, as the eponymous knight Yvain does in the twelfth-century Arthurian tale, he regains his power of mind and loses his excessive hair, hypersexuality, and ferality, so that he may re-enter the civilized spaces of Christendom.[42] As a visible sign of moral rectitude, outward, physical appearance inevitably improves when one embraces the Christian God. Elsewhere in medieval literature, this is also why black-skinned, "heathen" "Saracens" who convert to Christianity immediately turn white: whiteness is a physical manifestation of a moral turn from "pagan" sin to Christian virtue.[43]

The question of skin color also brings to mind the medieval invention of "Ethiopians," which is an especially rich source for the study of relationships

---

39   Cambridge, Trinity College, MS O.9.34, fol. 23v. The image is discussed and reproduced in Strickland, *Saracens, Demons, and Jews*, pp. 231–3 and figure 125.

40   London, British Library, MS Add. 62925, fol. 23v. On this image, see Hassig [Strickland], "Iconography of Rejection," pp. 36–7; and Strickland, *Saracens, Demons, and Jews*, pp. 128–30.

41   On the sources, see Strickland, *Saracens, Demons, and Jews*, pp. 29–41.

42   Chrétien de Troyes, *Yvain, the Knight of the Lion*, trans. Burton Raffel (New Haven: Yale University Press, 1987). See Richard Bernheimer, *Wild Men in the Middle Ages: A Study in Art, Sentiment, and Demonology* (Cambridge, MA: Harvard University Press, 1952); and Roger Bartra, *Wild Men in the Looking Glass: The Mythic Origins of European Otherness*, trans. Carol T. Berrisford (Ann Arbor: University of Michigan Press, 1994).

43   On this literary phenomenon, see Jacqueline de Weever, *Sheba's Daughters: Whitening and Demonizing the Saracen Woman in Medieval French Epic* (New York: Garland, 1998).

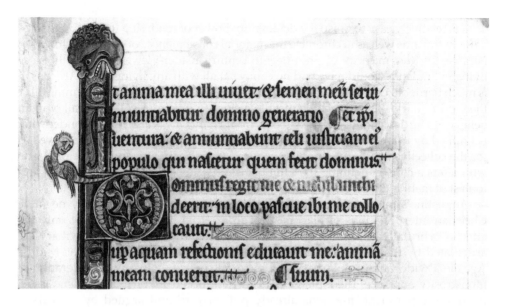

Figure 17.10   Ethiopian head and hybrid, Rutland Psalter. London, BL, MS Add. 62925, fol. 26r (detail) (© British Library Board).

between medieval concepts of monstrosity and race. Arguably, "Ethiopians"—a vague appellation used by medieval writers to designate African peoples living south of the Sahara—are uniquely expressive of ideas about race because representations of these imaginary, dark-skinned men with everted lips and woolly hair may be linked to an empirical reality, namely to the physiognomies of living black Africans.[44] For this reason, medieval descriptions and images of "Ethiopians," perhaps over those of all other human and monstrous groups, are likely to raise the spectre of race for modern reader-viewers. It is especially intriguing, therefore, that while the Anglo-Saxon *Wonders* text specifies that Ethiopians are "completely black," the accompanying images barely hint at darkened complexions (see Figure 17.4).[45] In other contexts, such as the Rutland Psalter, dark skin and exaggerated African physiognomical features function all on their own as a form of monstrosity; in this case, as a disembodied, black head gazing downward at an even more monstrous, miniature, Ethiopian hybrid (Figure 17.10).[46]

---

44   For an extended discussion of Christian definitions of "Ethiopians," see Gay L. Byron, *Symbolic Blackness and Ethnic Difference in Early Christian Literature* (London: Routledge, 2002). My thanks to Irina Metzler for this reference.

45   For black-and-white reproductions of the images (which are unsatisfactory for the present discussion), see Montague Rhodes James, *Marvels of the East: A Full Reproduction of the Three Known Copies* (Oxford: Printed for the Roxburghe Club by J. Johnson, at the University Press, 1929).

46   On this and other images of Ethiopians, see Strickland, *Saracens, Demons, and Jews*, pp. 79–93. Another English manuscript featuring several Ethiopian figures is the famous fourteenth-century Luttrell Psalter (London, British Library, MS Add. 42130). See

It is relatively easy to grasp the defamatory power of rendering Jews and Muslims as monstrous, as well as to chronicle the material consequences of doing so. However, because the vast majority of pre-fifteenth-century reader-viewers, especially those living in England, would have had no contact at all with any living black Africans, it is much harder to understand the cultural utility of conflating and transforming all of the world's dark-skinned inhabitants into a single, monstrous collective, all of them believed to be descended, as noted above, from Ham. One is also led to wonder what is implied by using the same name of "Ethiopian" for this particular race as well as for the collective of all other monstrous races. Once again, it is Augustine of Hippo who offers a clue by defining the Ethiopians of Psalm 72/71:9 as "the remotest and foulest of mankind," thereby coupling geographic and moral distance.[47]

Augustine's interpretation of the Ethiopians is heavily informed by negative Christian interpretations of blackness as an external, visual sign of not only the effects of a brutally sunny climate but also moral turpitude, interpretations that were articulated by the early Christian exegetes and repeated throughout the Middle Ages in a wide variety of literary and pictorial contexts.[48] In any consideration of monstrosity and race, then, blackness is an important literary and artistic issue. Among the pertinent questions already put forward and argued by scholars is whether, during the Middle Ages, white skin was normative or invented.[49] The exact definition of blackness has also been the subject of debate: was blackness something universal or was it defined as the greatest contrast to the skin color of whoever is looking?[50] The fact that black "pagans" turn miraculously white following their conversion to Christianity in medieval romance and the *chansons*, besides reinforcing the association between blackness and sin—and, concomitantly,

---

Michael Camille, *Mirror in Parchment: The Luttrell Psalter and the Making of Medieval England* (London: Reaktion, 1998), pp. 276–84.

47   Goldenberg, *Curse of Ham*, p. 22. See Augustin, *Ennarrationes in Psalmos* 21.12, in Philip Schaff (ed.), *Saint Augustine: Expositions on the Book of Psalms*, The Nicene and Post-Nicene Fathers, series 1, vol. 8 (New York: Christian Literature Publishing Co., 1888), pp. 330–1. It is interesting to consider that Augustine at the time of writing was living in North Africa (Roman province of Hippo) and, although legally a Roman, that his ethnicity is thought to reflect an intermingling of the North African peoples—Latins, Berbers, and Phoenicians. See Peter Brown, *Augustine of Hippo: A Biography*, 3rd rev. edn (Berkeley: University of California Press, 2000); and Calvin L. Troup, "Augustine the African: Critic of Roman Colonialist Discourse," *Rhetoric Society Quarterly* 25 (1995), pp. 91–106.

48   This tradition is succinctly explained by Irina Metzler, "Perceptions of Hot Climate in Medieval Cosmography and Travel Literature," in Joan-Pau Rubiés (ed.), *Medieval Ethnographies: European Perceptions of the World Beyond* (Farnham and Burlington, VT: Ashgate Variorum, 2009), pp. 379–415. See also Suzanne Conklin Akbari, "From Due East to True North: Orientalism and Orientation," in Jeffrey Jerome Cohen (ed.), *The Postcolonial Middle Ages* (New York: St Martin's Press, 2000), pp. 19–34.

49   Whiteness as normative: Heng, *Empire of Magic*, pp. 231–2; Lisa Lampert, "Race, Periodicity, and the (Neo) Middle Ages," *Modern Language Quarterly* 65 (2004), pp. 391–421, at 410. As invented: Caviness, "From the Self-Invention."

50   This question is explored by Goldenberg, *Curse of Ham*, especially pp. 113–28.

between whiteness and virtue—again suggests a strong link between race and religion, pithily summarized in the oft-quoted line from the ninth-century *Song of Roland*: "Pagans are wrong and Christians are right." Or to put it in visual terms: pagans are black and Christians are white.

I would like to end this discussion of monstrosity and race with the ominous figure for which an understanding of both concepts was crucial for his very recognition: Antichrist. Throughout the entire Middle Ages, the dreaded Son of Perdition was believed to be either already living on earth or else about to arrive and to rule as a tyrant for three and a half years in an attempt to annihilate Christendom until God annihilates him.[51] As the arch-enemy of Christendom, mentored by the Devil, Antichrist was monstrous by any medieval definition. He was also unequivocally identified as a Jew. Medieval Christian theological commentary, scriptural exegesis, popular legend, and pictorial imagery nearly always proclaim that Antichrist will be born a Jew from the tribe of Dan.[52] Written descriptions and pictorial renderings of Antichrist therefore display the ultimate merging of ideas about monstrosity and race-cum-religion characteristic of the later Middle Ages. The tradition reached its peak of popularity in England during the thirteenth century in dedicated pictorial cycles included in numerous illustrated Anglo-Norman Apocalypse manuscripts. It is notable that across this imagery, the figure of Antichrist is often identifiable by his ubiquitous Jewish hat and any of the other features comprising the contemporary visual caricature of a Jew, such as the beard, prominent nose, and grimacing expression of the cross-legged, seated Antichrist holding a huge falchion depicted in the Gulbenkian Apocalypse (Figure 17.11).

Even if otherwise rendered as a normally proportioned white man, as the would-be destroyer of Christendom, Antichrist would likely have been perceived by reader-viewers as the monstrous blasphemer, tyrant, sadist, and murderer that the contemporary written sources proclaimed him to be. In other devotional contexts, such as the sumptuously illustrated, thirteenth-century French *Bibles moralisées* (moralized Bibles) created for French royal patrons, Antichrist is depicted as a three-faced monster surrounded by stereotyped figures of Jews, who are explicitly named in the sources, including contemporary plays, as his first and most ardent supporters.[53] This is because Antichrist, as already noted, was slated to be born

---

51   On this tradition, see the seminal study by Richard Kenneth Emmerson, *Antichrist in the Middle Ages: A Study of Medieval Apocalypticism, Art, and Literature* (Manchester: Manchester University Press, 1981).

52   As articulated in the widely circulated version of the Antichrist legend compiled circa 1265 under the title, *Compendium of Theological Truth*, which during the Middle Ages was wrongly attributed to Albert the Great, Bonaventure, or Thomas Aquinas. See *Compendii theologicae veritatis*, in Étienne César Auguste Borgnet (ed.), *B. Alberti Magni Opera Omnia*, 38 volumes (Paris: Vives, 1890–99), vol. 34 (1895), pp. 241–7.

53   On images of Jews and their relationship to Antichrist, see Sara Lipton, *Images of Intolerance: The Representation of Jews and Judaism in the Bible moralisée* (Berkeley: University of California Press, 1999), especially pp. 38–43, 113–22; and Debra Higgs Strickland, "Antichrist and the Jews in Medieval Christian Art and Protestant Propaganda," *Studies in Iconography* 32 (2011), pp. 1–50.

Figure 17.11 Antichrist (far left) and henchmen, Gulbenkian Apocalypse. Lisbon, Museu Calouste Gulbenkian, MS L.A. 139, fol. 22v (detail) (photo: Conway Library, The Courtauld Institute of Art, London).

of the tribe—read "race"—of Dan, circumcize himself, rise to power, rebuild the Temple in Jerusalem, and occupy it as a counterfeit Messiah, supported by his Jewish followers, who in German tradition would include the monstrous Red Jews, for the time being confined by Alexander the Great somewhere deep in the Caspian Mountains.[54] The ultimate medieval Christian monster, then, was conceived along racial lines that exactly mimed the contemporary Jewish–Christian conflict that poisoned medieval English society. With the invention of the Antichrist tradition, Christians were able to bring this conflict to its imaginary, xenophobic conclusions. Perhaps partly in response to eschatological anxieties, Edward I expelled all of England's Jews in 1290.[55]

---

54 Andrew Gow, *The Red Jews: Antisemitism in an Apocalyptic Age, 1200–1600* (Leiden: Brill, 1995).

55 On the complexities of the English expulsion, see Robin R. Mundill, *England's Jewish*

Conclusion

While much attention has been devoted to medieval verbal and visual constructions of monstrosity in relationship to modern concepts of otherness, the relationship between monstrosity and race has been under-explored, apparently in the name of avoiding anachronism. The solution to this dilemma, it seems to me, is to rethink in still more detail the concept of race in light of contemporary medieval cultural concerns, as Geraldine Heng, Thomas Hahn,[56] Jeffrey Cohen and other scholars already cited have so effectively demonstrated. As these and other critics have clarified of late medieval England in particular, such concerns largely revolved around issues of self-definition and nationalism. To declare that *any* discussion of race and racism in relation to the Middle Ages is by definition impossible owing to temporal and cultural distance, and that to do so runs the risk of misinforming modern readers, is to sidestep the need to recognize the power and material consequences of medieval condemnatory systems apparently developed in all available cultural arenas. The medieval monstrous races tradition provided a foundational forum for the expression of Christian fears and fantasies about cultural outsiders, notions that were inevitably overlaid onto actual, human groups, to which the cases of Christian-constructed Jews, Muslims, Mongols, and black Africans clearly attest. The irony is that the medieval cultural work of sharply dividing groups of the world's inhabitants from each other was done with full knowledge of the equally fundamental Christian tenet that *all* races descended from the same parents—Adam and Eve. Augustine of Hippo famously argues in *The City of God* that for this reason, there can be only one human race to which even the monstrous races, if indeed they exist, must belong.[57] But I do not agree that we can interpret Augustine's argument as a display of cultural tolerance, as others have argued.[58] Explanation of difference is not the same thing as tolerance of it, and theory is not the same as practice. It was cultural and religious *conflict*, not tolerance, that drove medieval Christendom's obsessive creation of its many monsters, both real and imaginary, especially in late medieval England.

Solution: Experiment and Expulsion, 1262–1290 (Cambridge: Cambridge University Press, 1998); and Mundill, *The King's Jews: Money, Massacre and Exodus in Medieval England* (London: Continuum, 2010), pp. 145–66. As evidence of his eschatological interests, Edward I (then Prince Edward) commissioned the lavishly illustrated Douce Apocalypse (Oxford, Bodleian Library, MS Douce 180). See Nigel Morgan, *The Douce Apocalypse: Picturing the End of the World in the Middle Ages* (Oxford: Bodleian Library, 2007), p. 9.

56 Thomas Hahn, "The Difference the Middle Ages Makes: Color and Race Before the Modern World," *Journal of Medieval and Early Modern Studies* 31 (2001), pp. 1–37.

57 Augustine of Hippo, *De civitate Dei*, ed. Bernhard Dombart, 2 volumes (Leipzig: Teubner, 1909): 16.9.

58 For example, M.T. Hodgen, *Early Anthropology in the Sixteenth and Seventeenth Centuries*, 2nd edn (Philadelphia: University of Pennsylvania Press, 1971), pp. 213–14; Metzler, "Perceptions of Hot Climate," p. 394.

The genius of the medieval system was that it never required the monsters to change; indeed, the key to their diachronic utility was their constancy. That the fixed repertoire of monstrosity functioned so well and for so long complements a more general observation about racism articulated by Richard Hoffman:

> Racist ideologies are necessarily historical in that the constituent units exist in time and through time. With equal necessity, however, the units are ahistorical. They do not, they can not, change through time. They freeze. Momentary personal representatives simply stand for a permanent biological identity.[59]

In his study of racist ideologies in late medieval Europe, Hoffman notes a marked emphasis on biological definitions of race by medieval Christian authors writing about Europe's cultural frontiers: the Celtic north-west, the Iberian peninsula, and East-Central Europe. For the present discussion, it is suggestive that medieval chronicles and armchair travel guides alike locate the most aberrant of these races— human or monstrous—at the world's peripheries, and that the authors of both genres assume that abnormal bodies and inferior moral characters are biologically determined. Both traditions thereby suggest how crucial geographical location was for the characterization of the world's inhabitants that coalesced into a set of parameters equally applicable to the assessment of different groups *within* a given society, namely the non-Christian ones: the only prerequisite was that they *originate* elsewhere. The result was the creation, alongside Panotii, Sciopods, and Blemmye, of equally imaginary Jews, Muslims, black Africans, and Mongols, all of whom, in Christian eyes, were, to varying degrees, physically aberrant, culturally abhorrent, and, most importantly, ignorant of God. For all of these groups, presumed monstrosity brought grave, material results ranging from social subordination and exclusion to enslavement, expulsion, and murder. If racism is defined as "differences that are conceptualized in a strategically invoked essentialism as absolute and fundamental and that are used to distribute powers and positions differentially to human groups," then the term can be applied historically, and accurately describes what was happening in late medieval England.[60] For this reason, I am inclined to see the literary and pictorial rhetoric of monstrosity as a ubiquitous and powerful tool in the historical development of medieval racisms, not least in the common homeland of Grendel, Blemmye, and Edward I.

---

59   Richard C. Hoffman, "Outsiders by Birth and Blood: Racist Ideologies and Realities Around the Periphery of Medieval European Culture," *Studies in Medieval and Renaissance History* n.s. 6 (1983), pp. 1–34, at 22.
60   Heng, *Empire of Magic*, p. 253.

Hic sunt dracones: The Geography and Cartography of Monsters

Chet Van Duzer

So geographers, in Afric maps,
With savage pictures fill their gaps,
And o'er unhabitable downs
Place elephants for want of towns.
                    Jonathan Swift, *On Poetry*

In this chapter I will address Western ideas about the geographical distribution of monsters, and also the reflection of these ideas on maps,[1] from ancient Greece to the end of the sixteenth century. As almost no maps survive from classical antiquity, the emphasis in references to cartography will naturally fall on the medieval and Renaissance periods. Following a brief discussion of the belief that monsters were generated by extremes of climate, which tended to occur in regions distant from Europe, I will examine the pronounced tendency to locate monsters at the edges of the earth. Yet there are also "monsters among us," that is, monsters said to be located near where the writer or cartographer lived. I will discuss some examples of monsters of this type, and the characteristics that distinguish them from distant monsters. Finally I will give some examples of the transport of monsters from the edges of the earth to the center, which confirm the prevalence of monstrous habitations in distant regions.

The word "monster" is notoriously difficult to define, and indeed some of the definitions that have been offered over the centuries are contradictory. While many authors, both classical and medieval, including Marcus Cornelius Fronto, Pierre Bersuire, and Sir John Mandeville, define a monster as being in some way

---

1   On monstrous geography and cartography in other regions, see, for example, Anna Caiozzo, "L'image de l'Europe et des Européens dans les représentations de l'Orient médiéval," *Caietele Echinox* 10 (2006), pp. 84–120, especially 107–8; and Masayuki Sato, "Imagined Peripheries: The World and its Peoples in Japanese Cartographic Imagination," *Diogenes* 44/173 (1996), pp. 119–45, reprinted in Anthony Pagden (ed.), *Facing Each Other: The World's Perception of Europe and Europe's Perception of the World* (Aldershot, UK and Burlington, VT: Ashgate, 2000), vol. 2, pp. 367–94.

contra naturam or "against nature,"[2] for St Augustine and Isidore of Seville, a monster is part of God's plan, an adornment of the universe that can also teach about the dangers of sin.[3] Hybridity is often cited as a defining characteristic of monsters, but while this is perhaps a sufficient characteristic, it is not necessary.[4] For the purposes of this chapter, a monster will be defined as a creature that was thought astonishing and exotic (regardless of whether in fact it was real or mythical) in classical, medieval, or Renaissance times.[5] Most often the astonishing and exotic aspects of monsters imply physical deformity (defined in terms of then-current European norms), but I will also include cases of moral deformity (again, defined in terms of then-current European norms), such as cannibals. It is important to keep in mind that in the ancient, medieval, and Renaissance periods, a number of creatures—lions and whales, for example—were considered monstrous which we do not consider so today, and indeed one can tell a great deal about a culture by examining what creatures it defines as monsters.[6] Cicero and St Augustine defined monsters from the fact that they show (*monstrant* in Latin) signs or warnings from the gods or from God,[7] but this is one possible function of monsters rather than a defining characteristic.

---

2   See John Block Friedman, *The Monstrous Races in Medieval Art and Thought* (Cambridge, MA and London: Harvard University Press, 1981; reprinted with expanded bibliography Syracuse: Syracuse University Press, 2000), pp. 111 and 116; and on Mandeville's definition, Lisa Verner, *The Epistemology of the Monstrous in the Middle Ages* (New York: Routledge, 2005), pp. 5–7.

3   See St Augustine, *De civitate Dei* 16.8 and 21.8; and Isidore *Etymologiae* 11.3.1. For discussion, see Verner, *Epistemology of the Monstrous*, pp. 2–7. The passage from Isidore is quoted at the beginning of medieval bestiaries of the so-called Third Family. Also see the passage similar to Augustine's in Helen Rodnite Lemay, *Women's Secrets: A Translation of Pseudo-Albertus Magnus's "De secretis mulierum" with Commentaries* (Albany, NY: State University of New York Press, 1992), p. 113.

4   For discussion of different categories of monsters, see Peter Mason, "Half a Cow," *Semiotica* 85/1–2 (1991), pp. 1–39. Michel Foucault, in *Abnormal: Lectures at the Collège de France, 1974–75*, trans. Graham Burchell (New York: Picador, 2003), especially pp. 63 and 76, suggests that from the Middle Ages until the eighteenth century, monsters were essentially mixtures; for discussion of this idea, see Tom Tyler, "Deviants, Donestre, and Debauchees: Here be Monsters," *Culture, Theory and Critique* 49/2 (2008), pp. 113–31.

5   Paul Murgatroyd, *Mythical Monsters in Classical Literature* (London: Duckworth Publishing, 2007), p. 1, says that he will use the word "monster" to "cover mythical, fabulous and imaginary creatures which are extraordinary, alien and abnormal," but I do not agree that a monster must be mythical.

6   See Jeffrey Jerome Cohen, "Monster Culture (Seven Theses)," in Cohen (ed.), *Monster Theory: Reading Culture* (Minneapolis: University of Minnesota Press, 1996), pp. 3–25.

7   On monsters as warnings, see Cicero, *De divinatione* 1.42; St Augustine, *De civitate Dei* 21.8; Friedman, *Monstrous Races*, pp. 108–30; Robert Garland, "The Deformed and the Divine," in *The Eye of the Beholder: Deformity and Disability in the Graeco-Roman World* (Ithaca, NY: Cornell University Press, 1995), pp. 59–72; and A.W. Bates, *Emblematic Monsters: Unnatural Conceptions and Deformed Births in Early Modern Europe* (Amsterdam and New York: Rodopi, 2005), as well as other works cited below.

For many of us, when we think of the geography of the monstrous and monsters on maps, a medieval map with a legend reading *Hic sunt dracones*, "Here there are dragons," comes to mind. Somehow this mental image is much more common than it has any right to be, for in fact there is just one map[8] and one globe[9] on which this legend appears.[10] But while this specific legend is infrequent, monsters are common in geographical texts of all periods, and legends about and images of monsters appear on many of the more elaborate medieval and Renaissance maps.

The description and representation of distant monsters involves an intriguing tension between helplessness and control, between surrender and power. On the one hand, the far reaches of the earth are shown to be places of great danger, where human survival, except for a hero of the magnitude of Hercules or Alexander the Great, would be difficult or impossible: while confidence persisted in the eventual evangelization of the ends of the earth,[11] in many ways the edges of the world continued to be perceived as an unconquerable wilderness. On the

---

8   The map in question is a world map in a manuscript of Jean Mansel's *La Fleur des Histoires* that was created circa 1460–70, and is Brussels, Bibliothèque Royale de Belgique, MS 9260, f. 11r; the map is illustrated in Alessandro Scafi, *Mapping Paradise: A History of Heaven on Earth* (Chicago: University of Chicago Press, 2006), p. 203, figure 8.2, who discusses it briefly on pp. 202–3; and the texts are transcribed by Margriet Hoogvliet, *Pictura et scriptura: textes, images et herméneutique des Mappae Mundi (XIII–XVI siècles)* (Turnhout: Brepols, 2007), Appendix 1, p. 289: the legend reads *Hic sunt dragones*.

9   The globe is the Lenox globe of circa 1510 which is in the New York Public Library, where on the south-eastern coast of Asia there is the legend HC SVNT DRACONES. The globe is illustrated in A.E. Nordenskiöld, *Facsimile-Atlas to the Early History of Cartography* (Stockholm: P.A. Norstedt, 1889; New York: Dover Publications, 1973), p. 5; and see B.F. de Costa, "The Lenox Globe," *Magazine of American History* 3/9 (1879), pp. 529–40, reprinted in *Acta Cartographica* 4 (1969), pp. 120–34, who on p. 536/129 misinterprets this legend as referring to the Dragonians mentioned by Marco Polo.

10   On the rarity of this legend, see Erin C. Blake, "Where Be Dragons?" *Mercator's World* 4/4 (July 1999), p. 80, who, however, did not know that the legend occurs on the *mappamundi* in Brussels. Of course other similar phrases appear on many other medieval maps: for example, *hic abundant leones*, "here lions abound," on the tenth-century Cotton or Anglo-Saxon Map (London, British Library, MS Cotton Tiberius B.V, fol. 58v; and *hic grifes*, "here are griffons," *hic pannothi*, "here are panotii" (men with huge ears), and *Hic Pigmei et Fauni et reges gentium*, "here are pygmies and fauns and the kings of the nations," on Lambert of St-Omer's *mappamundi* in his *Liber Floridus*: see Danielle Lecoq, "La Mappemonde du *Liber Floridus* ou La Vision du Monde de Lambert de Saint-Omer," *Imago Mundi* 39 (1987), pp. 2 and 9–49, especially 17.

11   On evangelization to the ends of the earth, see Acts 13:47; Rainer Riesner, "Geographic Framework of the Mission," in *Paul's Early Period: Chronology, Mission Strategy, Theology*, trans. Doug Stott (Grand Rapids, MI: W.B. Eerdmans, 1998), pp. 241–56; and Ian Wood, "Missionaries and the Christian Frontier," in W. Pohl, I. Wood, and H. Reimitz (eds), *The Transformation of Frontiers from Late Antiquity to the Carolingians* (Leiden: Brill, 2001), pp. 209–18.

other hand, as Edward Said has written: "To have ... knowledge of a thing is to dominate it, to have authority over it, to deny autonomy to it."[12] The description and depiction of faraway monsters removed the edges of the earth from the realm of the entirely unknown, and the fact that knowledge of those regions and their monsters had been obtained entailed the unspoken implication that the regions could be visited again, this time with knowledge of their dangers.

The two most important geographical principles which have traditionally determined the regions inhabited by monsters are the idea that monsters are the product of climate, and the idea that they are located at the ends of the earth. The different expressions and consequences of these principles, the exceptions to them, and their reflection on maps will be explored in what follows.

Climate

In antiquity, the Middle Ages, and the early Renaissance, the world was thought to be divided into climatic zones:[13] in the simplest form of this theory, there was an uninhabitably hot Torrid Zone near the equator, habitable temperate zones to the north and south of the Torrid Zone, and uninhabitable frigid zones near the North and South Poles. These zones were often depicted on medieval maps, particularly on zonal maps,[14] the most common of which illustrate manuscripts of Macrobius's *Commentary on the Dream of Scipio*.[15] And extremes of climate, particularly heat, were thought to produce monsters. Pliny (6.35.187) says that

---

12   Edward W. Said, *Orientalism: Western Conceptions of the Orient* (New York and London: Pantheon Books, 1978), p. 32.

13   See D.R. Dicks, "The *Klimata* in Greek Geography," *Classical Quarterly* 49 (1955), pp. 248–55; Karlhans Abel, "Zone," in A. Pauly and G. Wissowa (eds), *Real-Encyclopädie der classischen Altertumswissenschaft*, Supplementband 14 (1974), cols 989–1188; Marian J. Tooley, "Bodin and the Mediaeval Theory of Climate," *Speculum* 28/1 (1953), pp. 64–83; Stefan Schröder, "Die Klimazonenkarte des Petrus Alfonsi. Rezeption und Transformation islamisch-arabischen Wissens im mittelalterlichen Europa," in Ingrid Baumgärtner, Paul-Gerhard Klumbies, and Franziska Sick (eds), *Raumkonzepte: Disziplinäre Zugänge* (Göttingen: V&R Unipress, 2009), pp. 257–77; Angelo Cattaneo, "Réflexion sur les climats et les zones face à l'expansion des XVe et XVIe siècles," *Bulletin du Comite Français de Cartographie* 199 (2009), pp. 7–21; and Craig Martin, "Experience of the New World and Aristotelian Revisions of the Earth's Climates during the Renaissance," *History of Meteorology* 3 (2006), pp. 1–15.

14   David Woodward, "Medieval *Mappaemundi*," in J.B. Harley and David Woodward (eds), *The History of Cartography* (Chicago: University of Chicago Press, 1987–), vol. 1, pp. 286–370, especially 353–5.

15   On Macrobian maps, see Marcel Destombes, *Mappemondes, A.D. 1200–1500* (Amsterdam: N. Israel, 1964), pp. 43–5 and 85–95; Leonid S. Chekin, *Northern Eurasia in Medieval Cartography: Inventory, Text, Translation, and Commentary* (Turnhout: Brepols, 2006), pp. 95–120; and Alfred Hiatt, "The Map of Macrobius before 1100," *Imago Mundi* 59/2 (2007), pp. 149–76.

it is not surprising that there are monstrous animals and men in the extreme reaches of Africa, because of the great heat there, and Diodorus Siculus (2.51.2–4) says that "hybrid creatures, in which parts of animals which differ widely by nature are combined," are particularly common in hot areas, particularly near the equator. Climate was also held to have created different races of men, particularly dark-skinned races and monstrous races;[16] this idea was first developed in detail by Hippocrates in his treatise *On Airs, Waters, and Places*, especially chapters 12 and 24, and continued during the Middle Ages, particularly in Albertus Magnus's *Liber de natura locorum*, part 2, chapter 3, and into the Renaissance.[17] However, as Europe was held to be in the temperate zone, the geographical implication of the zonal theory of monster creation was that monsters were in distant regions. Thus the two main principles which were held to govern monster location, namely their generation by climatic extremes and their tendency to be located in distant parts of the earth, both placed monsters in distant regions, and I will focus here on the tendency to locate monsters at the edges of the earth.

The Edges of the Earth

Since the ancient Greek period, what were perceived by Europeans to be the distant edges of the earth have been thought to be the realm of exotica—of treasures, strange animals, and monstrous beings. The Greek historian Herodotus (3.116) wrote that "the extreme regions of the earth, which surround and shut up within themselves all other countries, produce the things which are rarest," and he gives concrete expression to this idea in many stories he tells about wonders at the

---

16   For more on the monstrous races, see the articles in this collection by Debra Strickland, Karl Steel, and Debbie Felton.

17   For citations of classical authors on the effect of climate on human races, see Lloyd A. Thompson, *Romans and Blacks* (London and New York: Routledge; Norman, OK: Oklahoma University Press, 1989), pp. 100–4 and 208, n. 59; Clarence J. Glacken, "Airs, Waters, and Places," "Environmental Influences Within a Divinely Created World," and "Environmental Theories of Early Modern Times," in *Traces on the Rhodian Shore: Nature and Culture in Western Thought from Ancient Times to the End of the Eighteenth Century* (Berkeley: University of California Press, 1967), pp. 80–115, 254–87, and 429–60; Friedman, *Monstrous Races*, pp. 51–8; R.I. Meserve, "The Inhospitable Land of the Barbarians," *Journal of Asian History* 16 (1982), pp. 51–89; Jean Bergevin, *Déterminisme et géographie: Hérodote, Strabon, Albert le Grand et Sebastian Münster* (Sainte-Foy, Québec: Presses de l'Université Laval, 1992); Claude Lecouteux, *Les monstres dans la pensée médiévale européenne: essai de présentation* (Paris: Presses de l'Université de Paris-Sorbonne, 1993), pp. 75–85; and Irina Metzler, "Perceptions of Hot Climate in Medieval Cosmography and Travel Literature," *Reading Medieval Studies* 23 (1997), pp. 69–106, reprinted in Joan-Pau Rubiés (ed.), *Medieval Ethnographies: European Perceptions of the World Beyond* (Farnham, UK and Burlington, VT: Ashgate Variorum, 2009).

edges of the earth.[18] This idea was repeated by medieval authors. Gerald of Wales (circa 1146–circa 1223), for example, in his *Topography of Ireland*, emphasizes the presence of wonders in the far West:

> *For as the countries of the East are remarkable and preeminent for some prodigies peculiar to themselves and originating there, so also the Western parts are dignified by the miracles of nature performed within their limits. For sometimes, like one wearied with serious affairs and realities, she withdraws and retires for a little space, and, as it were, sportively employs herself with extraordinary freaks in secret parts reverently and mysteriously veiled.*[19]

Ranulf Higden (circa 1280–circa 1363), in his *Polychronicon* 2.1, also says that the furthest reaches of the earth, such as India, Ethiopia, and Africa, abound in wonders.[20] The tendency to locate marvels, including monsters, in the furthest reaches of the earth was so common that it attracted satire even in antiquity. The explorer Pytheas of Thule had reported various wonders in the northern Atlantic, and Antonius Diogenes (second century CE), in his *Wonders Beyond Thule*, reported having seen men and various wonders in the far north "which no-one … could have seen nor heard tell of nor imagined."[21] Lucian of Samosata (second century), in his

---

18   For discussion, see James Romm, "Dragons and Gold at the Ends of the Earth: A Folktale Motif Developed by Herodotus," *Marvels & Tales* 1/1 (1987), pp. 45–54; Klaus Karttunen, "Expedition to the End of the World: An Ethnographic Topos in Herodotus," *Studia Orientalia* 64 (1988), pp. 177–81; Karttunen, "Distant Lands in Classical Ethnography," *Grazer Beiträge* 18 (1992), pp. 195–204; and Heinz-Günther Nesselrath, "Herodot und die Grenzen der Erde," *Museum Helveticum* 52 (1995), pp. 20–44.

19   Gerald of Wales, *The Topography of Ireland*, trans. Thomas Forester (Cambridge, Ontario: In parenthesis Publications, 2000), 2nd preface, p. 6. For more on monsters in Gerald, see Asa Simon Mittman, "The Other Close at Hand: Gerald of Wales and the *Marvels of the West*," in Bettina Bildhauer and Robert Mills (eds), *The Monstrous Middle Ages* (Cardiff: University of Wales Press, 2003), pp. 97–112. For discussions of distant marvels in other medieval authors, see, for example, Christiane Deluz, "Des lointains merveilleux (d'après quelques textes géographiques et récits de voyage du Moyen Âge)," in *De l'étranger à l'étrange ou la conjointure de la merveille (en hommage à Marguerite Rossi et Paul Bancourt)* (Aix-en-Provence: CUERMA, Université de Provence, 1988), pp. 157–69; Lorraine Daston and Katharine Park, "The Topography of Wonder," in Daston and Park (eds), *Wonders and the Order of Nature, 1150–1750* (New York: Zone Books, 1998), pp. 21–66; and Juan Casas Rigall, "Razas humanas portentosas en las partidas remotas del mundo (de Benjamín de Tudela a Cristóbal Colón)," in Rafael Beltrán Llavador (ed.), *Maravillas, peregrinaciones y utopías: literatura de viajes en el mundo románico* (Valencia: Universidad de Valencia, 2002), pp. 253–90.

20   Ranulf Higden, *Polychronicon Ranulphi Higden monachi Cestrensis; Together with the English Translations of John Trevisa and of an Unknown Writer of the Fifteenth Century*, ed. Joseph Rawson Lumby (London: Longman & Co., 1865–86), vol. 2, p. 186.

21   Antonius Diogenes's work survives only in a summary written by Photius, which summary is translated by Gerald N. Sandy in B.P. Reardon (ed.), *Collected Ancient Greek*

facetiously titled *True Histories*, tells of being blown out into the Atlantic by a storm to an island with a river of wine, and then carried by a waterspout to the Moon, where he and his companions become involved in a war between the King of the Moon and the King of the Sun, in whose armies were exotic monstrous races such as the Cyanobalani or dog-faced men fighting on winged acorns, Psyllotoxotoe or flea-archers, and Nephelocentauri or cloud-centaurs; unfortunately the Hippogerani or horse-cranes did not join the battle.[22]

Lands distant from the teller are natural settings for stories of exotic and mythical wonders, not only because distance makes the stories difficult to refute, but also because distance creates possibilities: who knows what might be possible at the ends of the world, what unheard of things the earth might produce, or what bizarre customs might prevail? As Tacitus (*Agricola* 30) wrote, *omne ignotum pro magnifico* [Everything unknown is thought to be magnificent]. Another way to look at the issue of monsters at the edge of the world is through the prism of Richard Buxton's statement that "myths often fulfil the role of pathfinders, testing out boundaries, imagining the consequences of interfaces between categories."[23] Myths set at the edges of the world allow the teller to explore the consequences of interfaces between the known and the unknown, between things of this world and things beyond human ken.[24] On maps there is an additional factor favoring the placement of something at the edges of the world,[25] which is a *horror vacui* or discomfort at leaving empty spaces, and the resultant desire to place text or images in all parts of the world which are shown on a map.[26] The location of monsters at

---

    Novels (Berkeley: University of California Press, 1989), pp. 775–82; for discussion, see James S. Romm, *The Edges of the Earth in Ancient Thought: Geography, Exploration, and Fiction* (Princeton, NJ: Princeton University Press, 1992), pp. 205–11.

22   Lucian of Samosata, *True History and Lucius or the Ass*, trans. Paul Turner (Bloomington: Indiana University Press, 1974); for discussion of the relationship between Antonius Diogenes and Lucian, see J.R. Morgan, "Lucian's *True Histories* and the *Wonders Beyond Thule* of Antonius Diogenes," *Classical Quarterly* 35 (1985), pp. 475–90.

23   Richard Buxton, *Imaginary Greece: The Contexts of Mythology* (Cambridge and New York: Cambridge University Press, 1994), p. 204.

24   For discussion of the significance of monstrous races at the edge of the earth, with particular reference to maps, see Marina Münkler, "Experiencing Strangeness: Monstrous Peoples on the Edge of the Earth as Depicted on Medieval *Mappae Mundi*," *Medieval History Journal* 5 (2002), pp. 195–222; and Münkler, "*Monstra* und *mappae mundi*: die monströsen Völker des Erdrands auf mittelalterlichen Weltkarten," in Jürg Glauser and Christian Kiening (eds), *Text—Bild—Karte: Kartographien der Vormoderne* (Freiburg: Rombach Verlag, 2007), pp. 149–73.

25   For discussion of the monstrous races on maps, see Friedman, *Monstrous Races*, pp. 37–58; for mythical animals and the monstrous races on maps, see Hoogvliet, *Pictura et scriptura*, pp. 181–202 and 202–19, respectively.

26   On *horror vacui* as a motivation for adding illustrations to medieval maps, see Anna-Dorothee von den Brincken, "Weltbild der lateinischen Universalhistoriker und -kartographen," in *Popoli e paesi nella cultura altomedievale: 23–29 aprile 1981* (Spoleto: Presso la Sede del Centro, 1983), pp. 377–408, especially 403; and also von den Brincken, *Kartographische Quellen, Welt-, See-, und Regionalkarten* (Turnhout: Brepols, 1988), pp. 50

the ends of the earth might also be interpreted in psychological terms, as an attempt to keep monsters at a safe distance, or ban them to the realm of the subconscious. Certainly the tendency to locate monsters at the edges of the world, and the great interest in describing and illustrating them, reveal a deep ambivalence in our relationship with monsters: while repulsive and distant, they are also (as long as they are distant) attractive and fascinating. Distance enables a fascination which, if the monsters were close, would be replaced by terror.

There are a number of texts which refer not just to marvels at the ends of the earth, but specifically to monsters there. Diodorus Siculus (first century BCE), in his *Bibliotheca historica* 4.18.4, says that when Heracles set up his famous pillars at the western edge of the known world, he narrowed the Strait of Gibraltar to keep the sea monsters in the Atlantic from entering the Mediterranean:

> When Heracles arrived at the farthest points of the continents of Libya and Europe which lie upon the ocean, he decided to set up these pillars to commemorate his campaign. And since he wished to leave upon the ocean a monument which would be had in everlasting remembrance, he built out both the promontories, they say, to a great distance; consequently, whereas before that time a great space had stood between them, he now narrowed the passage, in order that by making it shallow and narrow he might prevent the great sea-monsters from passing out of the ocean into the inner sea, and that at the same time the fame of their builder might be held in everlasting remembrance by reason of the magnitude of the structures.

The anonymous author of the *Liber monstrorum*, a late seventh-or early eighth-century collection of monsters which was perhaps written in Britain, is very clear that monsters are found "in the hidden parts of the world, raised throughout the deserts and the islands of the Ocean and in the recesses of the farthest mountains."[27] Indeed, he goes on to suggest that the growth of the human population has pushed monsters to the edge of the lands and even into the seas, even though in the body of his book he mentions many monsters on land:

> ... because now, when humankind has multiplied and the lands of the earth have been filled, fewer monsters are produced under the stars, and we read that in most of the corners of the world they have been utterly eradicated and overthrown by them, and now, cast out from the shores, they are thrown

---

and 96–7; and von den Brincken, 'Fines Terrae': Die Enden der Erde und der vierte Kontinent auf mittelalterlichen Weltkarten (Hannover: Hahnsche Buchhandlung, 1992), p. 93.

27   This passage is from the Prologue to the *Liber monstrorum*; for the Latin text and an English translation, see Andy Orchard, *Pride and Prodigies: Studies in the Monsters of the Beowulf-Manuscript* (Cambridge: D.S. Brewer, 1995; Toronto: University of Toronto Press, 2003), pp. 254–316, especially 254–5. For discussion of the *Liber monstrorum*, see Orchard, *Pride and Prodigies*, pp. 86–115; and Brian McFadden, "Authority and Discourse in the *Liber monstrorum*," *Neophilologus* 89/3 (2005), pp. 473–93.

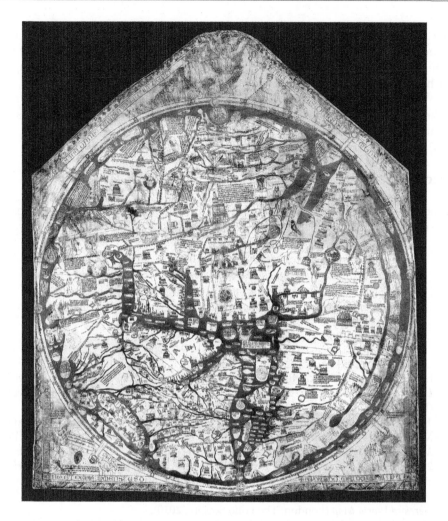

Figure 18.1   Hereford *Mappamundi*, circa 1300 (reproduced by kind permission of the Dean and Chapter of Hereford and the Hereford Mappa Mundi Trust).

down to the waves, and that by the churning from the steep summit of the
pole they turn from the edge of the entire circle and from every place on earth
towards this vast abyss of the flood.[28]

In the realm of medieval cartography,[29] one of the maps on which monsters and monstrous races are most clearly located at the edges of the world is the Hereford

28   Orchard, *Pride and Prodigies*, pp. 256–7.
29   For a general discussion of marvels and monsters at the edges of the earth on medieval *mappaemundi*, see Danielle Lecoq, "Les marges de la terre habitée. Géographie et

395

mappamundi of circa 1300 (Figure 18.1).[30] When the monsters and monstrous races on the map are highlighted, they almost form a ring around the map, albeit with some irregularities: there is a particularly large number of monsters along the southern edge of Africa, but very few in Western Europe.[31]

In what follows, I discuss the history and sources of the monsters in some of the regions distant from Western Europe: Africa, Asia,[32] the Antipodes, the Ocean, and the New World.

Africa

Herodotus 4.191 places a range of animal and human monsters in the distant western edge of Africa:

> It is here that huge snakes are found — and lions, elephants, bears, asps, and horned asses, not to mention dog-headed men, headless men with eyes in their breasts (I don't vouch for this, but merely repeat what the Libyans say), wild men and wild women, and a great many other creatures of by no means a fabulous kind.[33]

histoire naturelle des confines sur les mappemondes des XIIe et XIIIe siècles," in *L'Iconographie: Études sur les rapports entre textes et images dans l'Occident médiéval* (Paris: Le Léopard d'Or, 2001), pp. 99–186.

30   There is a good brief discussion of the Hereford *mappamundi* in Peter Barber, "Medieval Maps of the World," in P.D.A. Harvey (ed.), *The Hereford World Map: Medieval World Maps and their Context* (London: The British Library, 2006), pp. 1–44, especially 27–30; and a full treatment in Scott D. Westrem, *The Hereford Map: A Transcription and Translation of the Legends with Commentary* (Turnhout: Brepols, 2001). The map has now been published in a digitally restored color facsimile as *Mappa Mundi: The Hereford World Map* (London: The Folio Society, 2010).

31   On the location of the monsters and monstrous races on the Hereford *mappamundi*, see Naomi Reed Kline, *Maps of Medieval Thought: The Hereford Paradigm* (Woodbridge, UK, and Rochester, NY: Boydell Press, 2001), pp. 142–4, and also Kline, "The World of the Strange Races," in Leif Søndergaard and Rasmus Thorning Hansen (eds), *Monsters, Marvels and Miaracles: Imaginary Journeys and Landscapes in the Middle Ages* (Odense: University Press of Southern Denmark, 2005), pp. 27–40, especially 30–3; and Asa Simon Mittman, *Maps and Monsters in Medieval England* (New York and London: Routledge, 2006), p. 40.

32   In the fifth century BCE, Herodotus (4.42) mentions the division of the world into the continents of Europe, Asia, and Africa, though he himself is not certain of the divisions. For discussion of the history of the idea of the continents, see Martin W. Lewis and Kären E. Wigen, *The Myth of Continents: A Critique of Metageography* (Berkeley: University of California Press, 1997), especially pp. 21–6. Medieval "T-O" maps illustrate the division of the known world among Europe, Africa, and Asia.

33   Herodotus, *The Histories*, trans. Aubrey de Sélincourt (Harmondsworth, Middlesex, and Baltimore: Penguin Books, 1954), p. 306.

Africa, whose interior was poorly known, continued to attract this type of myth for centuries.[34] Aristotle, *On the Generation of Animals* 746b7–13, mentions the proverb that "Libya always nurtures some new thing," which alludes to the tendency of new heterogeneous creatures to appear there. Aristotle ascribes this tendency to the lack of water, which causes different species to encounter one another at water holes and there interbreed. Pomponius Mela, in his *De situ orbis*, locates some monsters in Africa which other authors place in Asia.[35] The Roman historian Pliny the Elder (*Naturalis historia* 7.2.21) remarks that India and Ethiopia were particularly abundant in marvels, and (8.17.42) that Africa was always producing something new;[36] and he describes a number of monstrous human hybrids resident in both of these regions, such as men with dogs' heads,[37] men whose faces are in their chests, men with giant ears, and so on. The number of monstrous races that Pliny places in Africa is not large: just the blemmyae, or headless men whose faces are in their chests;[38] satyrs (5.8.46); the himantopodes, who have long feet like leather thongs (5.8.46); the hermaphrodites (7.3.34); and the pygmies (6.35.188). Isidore, in his enumeration of the monstrous races in his *Etymologies* 11.3.12–39, locates several in Africa, and Solinus, in his *De mirabilibus mundi* 30, also places several monstrous races in the far reaches of Africa, beyond Ethiopia. These passages inspired a striking iconographic tradition in some *mappaemundi* of illustrating the monstrous races in a strip of land in southern Africa at the very edge of the earth. These maps include the Psalter Map of circa

---

34   The nickname "the Dark Continent," which refers to the lack of knowledge of the continent rather than to the skin color of many of its inhabitants, was perhaps first used in print by the explorer Henry M. Stanley in the title of his book *Through the Dark Continent*, first published in 1878.

35   See Rhiannon Evans, "Ethnography's Freak Show: The Grotesques at the Edges of the Roman Earth," *Ramus* 28/1 (1999), pp. 54–73.

36   Pliny *Naturalis historia* 7.2.21 runs *Praecipue India Aethiopumque tractus miraculis scatent*. Pliny 8.17.42 contains the famous line *vulgare Graeciae dictum semper aliquid novi Africam adferre*. For discussion of the history of this proverb from the fourth century BC to the eighteenth century AD, see A.V. Van Stekelenburg, "*Ex Africa semper aliquid novi* — A Proverb's Pedigree," *Akroteriòn* 33/4 (1988), pp. 114–20. Also see Italo Ronca, "*Semper aliquid novi Africam adferre*: Philological Afterthoughts on the Plinian Reception of a Pre-Aristotelian Saying," *Akroteriòn* 37/3–4 (1992), pp. 146–58; and Harvey M. Feinberg and Joseph B. Solodow, "Out of Africa," *The Journal of African History* 43/2 (2002), pp. 255–61.

37   For discussion of cynocephali, see Karl Steel's chapter in this collection.

38   On the blemmyae, see Ivar Hallberg, *L'Extrême Orient dans la littérature et la cartographie de l'Occident des XIIIe, XIVe, et XVe siècles; étude sur l'histoire de la géographie* (Göteborg: W. Zachrissons boktryckeri a.-b., 1907), pp. 78–9; Hans Barnard, "Sire, il n'y a pas de Blemmyes: A Re-Evaluation of Historical and Archaeological Data," in *People of the Red Sea: Proceedings of the Red Sea Project II, Held in the British Museum, October 2004* (Oxford: Archaeopress, 2005), pp. 23–40; and Mittman, *Maps and Monsters*, pp. 85–106 and passim. On these and other classical peoples of Inner Africa, see E. Schweder, "Die Angaben über die Völker von Innerafrika bei Plinius und Mela," *Philologus* 47 (1889), pp. 636–43, who discusses Pliny, *Naturalis historia* 5.43–46 and Pomponius Mela, *De situ orbis* 1.22–23, 1.43–48, and 3.103.

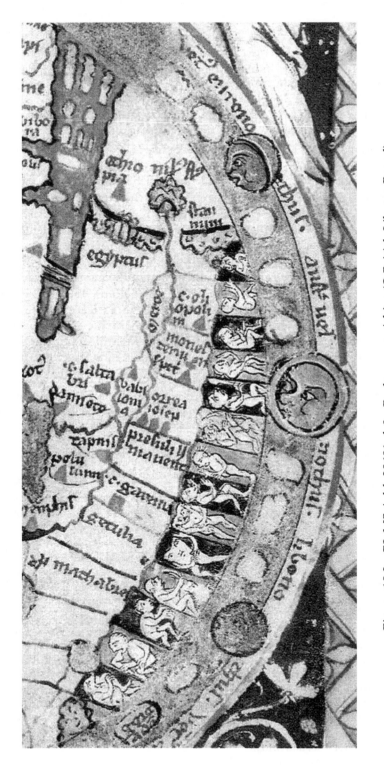

Figure 18.2   BL MS Add. 28681, f. 9r, Psalter map, Africa (© British Library Board).

1265, which illustrates 14 of the monstrous races in southern Africa (Figure 18.2; see also Figure 17.1),[39] the Duchy of Cornwall *mappamundi* fragment of circa 1290, which illustrates eight of the races,[40] the Ebstorf *mappamundi* of circa 1300, which illustrates 24 of the races,[41] the Hereford *mappamundi* of circa 1300, which illustrates 20,[42] and the Ramsey Abbey Ranulf Higden world map of circa 1350.[43] These striking images may have contributed to a tendency for modern scholars to think of Africa as the primary location of the monstrous races, even though the traditions locating them in Asia are just as strong.

The cartographic history of the blemmyae in Africa is complex and provides an interesting example of how the image of monsters in the same general area can develop over time. Martin Waldseemüller placed the blemmyae in eastern Africa on his world map of 1507, in accordance with Ptolemy's *Geography* 4.7; Johann Schöner, on his globe of 1515, places an illustration of a blemmya in the same spot. On his 1516 *Carta marina*, Waldseemüller has a legend about *cicloped[es] siue monoculi* [Cyclopes or monoculi] in western Africa, and somehow Lorenz Fries conflated the idea of the Cyclops and the blemmya in the illustration in the *Tab[ula] Mo[derna] Primae Partis Africae* in the 1522 Strasbourg edition of Ptolemy, so that Africa now has a one-eyed blemmya. This same illustration appears in the 1525 (Strasbourg), 1535 (Lyon), and 1541 (Vienna) editions of Ptolemy, and was copied from one of these editions by Pierre Desceliers on his world map of 1550,[44] who adds a six-armed man nearby from an unknown source.

---

39 The Psalter Map is London, British Library, MS Add. 28681, fol. 9r. The map is discussed, and the monstrous races identified, by Konrad Miller, *Mappaemundi: Die ältesten Welkarten* (Stuttgart: J. Roth, 1895–98), vol. 3, pp. 37–43; for a good recent discussion of the map, see Barber, "Medieval Maps of the World", pp. 15–19.

40 The Duchy of Cornwall *mappamundi* fragment is London, Duchy of Cornwall Office, Maps and Plans 1; for discussion, see Graham Haslam, "The Duchy of Cornwall Map Fragment," in Monique Pelletier (ed.), *Géographie du monde au Moyen Age et à la Renaissance* (Paris: Editions du C.T.H.S., 1989), pp. 33–44; and Barber, "Medieval Maps of the World", pp. 19–23.

41 The Ebstorf *mappamundi* was destroyed during the Second World War, but survives in facsimile; there is a good brief discussion in Barber, "Medieval Maps of the World", pp. 23–7, and a full reproduction and analysis in Hartmut Kugler, *Die Ebstorfer Weltkarte* (Berlin: Akademie Verlag, 2007).

42 For references on the Hereford *mappamundi*, see note 30 above.

43 The Ranulf Higden map in question is London, British Library, Royal MS 14.C.ix, fols 1v–2r; for a brief discussion, see Barber, "Medieval Maps of the World", pp. 32–5; for a transcription of all of the toponyms and legends, see Manuel Francisco de Barros y Sousa Santarem, *Essai sur l'histoire de la cosmographie et de la cartographie pendant le Moyen-Age* (Paris: Maulde et Renou, 1849–52), vol. 3, pp. 1–94. For discussion of the monstrous races indicated by legends but not depicted in southern Africa on Andreas Walsperger's world map of 1448 (Vatican City, Biblioteca Apostolica Vaticana, MS Pal. Lat. 1362 B), see Friedman, *Monstrous Races*, pp. 56–8.

44 Pierre Desceliers's 1550 map is London, British Library, MS Add. 24065, and is conveniently reproduced in Kenneth Nebenzahl, *Atlas of Columbus and the Great Discoveries* (Chicago: Rand McNally, 1990), pp. 114–15; and in twelve sheets in black-

The large medieval *mappaemundi* also have many non-human monsters in Africa. The Hereford *mappamundi*, for example, illustrates a phoenix, a crocodile, a poisonous salamander, and a monocerus which is probably intended for a rhinoceros.[45] The Ebstorf *mappamundi* has a leopard, a hyena, a mirmicaleon, monkeys, a camelopardalis, many types of snake, crocodiles, a flying lizard, and an elephant.[46]

When we think of monsters and maps of Africa, the famous lines of Jonathan Swift quoted at the beginning of this chapter come to mind, which mention the filling of blank spaces in Africa with "savage pictures" and elephants. And the African elephant, following its appearance on the Hereford *mappamundi*, had a long and distinguished career on maps. They are illustrated on nautical charts, for example, in Egypt on Angelino Dalorto's chart of 1330, together with a legend about the elephant and other monstrous animals of the Egyptian desert:

> *The desert of Egypt. Upper Egypt has many deserts in which there are many monstrous animals. There are leopards, tigers, basilisks, asps, horrible serpents, elephants, and many others which have not yet been described.*[47]

Illustrations of elephants with similar legends also appear on Angelino Dulcert's chart of 1339, and the Pizzigani chart of 1367; elephants without this legend appear on many later maps, for example, the Cantino chart of circa 1502, Martin

---

and-white as Map 3 in James Ludovic Lindsay Crawford and Charles Henry Coote, *Autotype Facsimiles of Three Mappemondes* (Aberdeen: Aberdeen University Press, 1898).

45 For discussion of the animals on the Hereford *mappamundi*, see R.K. French, "Putting Animals on the Map: The Natural History of the Hereford Mappa Mundi," *Archives of Natural History* 21 (1994), pp. 289–308; and Margriet Hoogvliet, "Animals in Context: Beasts on the Hereford Map and Medieval Natural History," in P.D.A. Harvey (ed.), *The Hereford World Map: Medieval World Maps and their Context* (London: British Library, 2006), pp. 153–65.

46 For discussion of the animals on the Ebstorf *mappamundi*, see Uwe Ruberg, "Die Tierwelt auf der Ebstorfer Weltkarte im Kontext mittelalterlicher Enzyklopädik," in Hartmut Kugler and Eckhard Michael (eds), *Ein Weltbild vor Columbus. Die Ebstorfer Weltkarte. Interdisziplinäres Colloquium 1988* (Weinheim: VCH, 1991), pp. 319–46.

47 Angelino Dalorto's chart is in Florence, in the Archivio Corsini, and is reproduced in Arthur R. Hinks, *The Portolan Chart of Angellino de Dalorto, MCCCXXV, in the Collection of Prince Corsini at Florence* (London: Royal Geographical Society, 1929); and in Ramon J. Pujades i Bataller, *Les cartes portolanes: la representació medieval d'una mar solcada* (Barcelona: Institut Cartogràfic de Catalunya, 2007), pp. 114–15 and on the accompanying DVD, number C7. For discussion of the elephants on this map and the Dulcert and Pizzigani maps which will be mentioned shortly, see Sandra Sáenz-López Pérez, "Imagen y conocimiento del mundo en la Edad Media a través de la cartografía hispana," PhD dissertation, Universidad Complutense de Madrid, 2007, vol. 1, pp. 688–92.

Waldseemüller's map of 1507,[48] and so on—the animal is essentially an emblem of the continent.[49]

The Nile itself was held to be a source of monsters. The anonymous ninth-century *Liber monstrorum* 2.21 says that "Nilus ... omnia monstra ferarum similia gignit" [the Nile ... begets all monsters similar to wild beasts].[50] The *Descriptio mappe mundi*, which has been attributed to Hugh of Saint-Victor (1096–1141), says of the Nile: "Hic igitur fluuius magna et mira monstra in Ethiopia gignit" [This river begets many large and astonishing monsters in Ethiopia], and proceeds to list several monstrous humanoid races and monstrous creatures which are found between the Nile, which runs west and east in southern Africa, and the southern Ocean. These monsters include men with two heads, men with four eyes (on one head), blemmyae, and the *prester*, a winged serpent with horns, a beard, and a long, knotted tail.[51] The *mappamundi* in an eleventh-century manuscript of Isidore (Munich, Bayerische Staatsbibliothek, CLM 10058, fol. 154v) shows a close relationship with the *Descriptio mappe mundi*, placing two of these winged serpents, one of them labeled *prester*, along the southern edge of Africa.[52] Indeed, a

48   Angelino Dulcert's chart is Paris, Bibliothèque nationale de France, Ge B 696 Rés., and is reproduced in Guglielmo Cavallo (ed.), *Cristoforo Colombo e l'apertura degli spazi: mostra storico-cartografica* (Rome: Istituto Poligrafico e Zecca dello Stato, 1992), vol. 1, pp. 164–5, with descriptive text on pp. 162–3; it is reproduced at a larger scale in Gabriel Marcel, *Choix de cartes et de mappemondes des XIVe et XVe siècles* (Paris: E. Leroux, 1896); and in Pujades i Bataller, *Les cartes portolanes*, pp. 120–1 and on the accompanying DVD, number C8. The 1367 Pizzigani chart is Parma, Biblioteca Palatina, Carta nautica no. 1612, and is reproduced in Cavallo, *Cristoforo Colombo e l'apertura degli spazi*, vol. 1, pp. 432–3. There is a good digital reproduction of the chart in Pujades i Bataller, *Les cartes portolanes*, on the accompanying DVD, number C13. The Cantino chart is Modena, Biblioteca Estense Universitaria, C.G.A.2, and is well reproduced in Nebenzahl, *Atlas of Columbus*, pp. 35–7. Martin Waldseemüller's world map of 1507 is in the Library of Congress, and excellent images of the map are available on the Library of Congress website.

49   For a discussion of elephants in other medieval artistic media, see G.C. Druce, "The Elephant in Medieval Legend and Art," *Archaeological Journal* 76 (1919), pp. 1–73.

50   See Franco Porsia (ed.), *Liber monstrorum* (Bari: Dedalo libri, 1976), pp. 244–5; and also the edition with English translation in Orchard, *Pride and Prodigies*, pp. 298–9. The idea that the Nile produces wild beasts probably comes from Orosius, *Historiae adversum paganos* 1.2.31.

51   The text is edited in Patrick Gautier Dalché, *La "Descriptio mappe mundi" de Hugues de Saint-Victor: texte inédit avec introduction et commentaire* (Paris: Études Augustiniennes, 1988), with this passage on p. 147; the description of the *prester* is as follows: "Est ibi serpens quidam, prester appellatus, alas habens et caput cornutum et barbatum quasi capra, habens caudam multis notis et flexuris tortuosam." The *prester* is mentioned by Lucan, *Pharsalia* 9.722, Isidore, *Etymologiae* 12.4.16, and Thomas of Cantimpré, *Liber de natura rerum* 8.27, but none of these authors specifies that it is winged or gives the other details in the *Descriptio mappe mundi*.

52   The Munich CLM 10058 map is reproduced in the frontispiece of Gautier Dalché's *La "Descriptio mappe mundi"*, and in P.D.A. Harvey, *Medieval Maps* (London: British Library, 1991), p. 22.

number of maps emphasize the serpents in Africa. On the *mappamundi* in a twelfth-century manuscript of Lambert of Saint-Omer's *Liber Floridus* (Wolfenbüttel, Herzog August Bibliothek, Cod. Gud. lat. 1.2, fols 69v–70r), a legend in south-eastern Africa reads "Locus draconum et serpentium et bestiarum crudelium" [Place of dragons and serpents and cruel beasts].[53]

In the late fifteenth century, the Portuguese explored to the south along the western coast of Africa, and in 1488 Bartholomew Dias rounded the Cape of Good Hope. Explorations of the coasts of Africa continued well into the sixteenth century, and the coasts of contemporary maps were updated in accordance with the new discoveries, but the interior of the continent remained largely unexplored,[54] and so cartographers still used Ptolemy and other ancient authors as sources for those regions. Thus, for example, Martin Waldseemüller, on his *Carta marina* of 1516, includes some basilisks in south-western Africa. Yet Waldseemüller includes a new Renaissance image of one of the traditional African monsters: in west Africa he has an image of a rhinoceros, which recalls the monocerus on the Hereford *mappamundi*, but Waldseemüller's image is much more lifelike, and is based on Albrecht Dürer's famous image of a rhinoceros made in 1515, just one year before the creation of Waldseemüller's map.[55] Waldseemüller's rhinoceros is an apt symbol of how, although the details were updated, Africa continued in its ancient role as a source of monsters into the sixteenth century and beyond.

Asia

The region most consistently associated with the monstrous races, monstrous animals, and other wonders over the centuries is India.[56] In classical antiquity, India was the edge of the known world: the only indications of anything beyond India were vague reports relating to the Seres, a race in the Far East associated with silk production and sometimes identified with the Chinese.[57] The stories of monstrous races and other wonders in India had their origin, at least in the West, in

---

53   See Lecoq, "La Mappemonde du *Liber Floridus* ", especially pp. 17 and 38.

54   For discussion of unexplored areas on maps, see Alfred Hiatt, "Blank Spaces on the Earth," *The Yale Journal of Criticism* 15/2 (2002), pp. 223–50.

55   See Wilma George, *Animals and Maps* (London: Secker and Warburg, 1969), pp. 147–8; and on Dürer's image, T.H. Clarke, *The Rhinoceros from Dürer to Stubbs, 1515–1799* (London: Philip Wilson for Sotheby's Publications; New York: Harper & Row, 1986).

56   There is an excellent account of the monsters of the east in Rudolf Wittkower, "Marvels of the East: A Study in the History of Monsters," *Journal of the Warburg and Courtauld Institutes* 5 (1942), pp. 159–97, reprinted in his *Allegory and Migration of Symbols* (Boulder, CO: Westview Press, 1977), pp. 45–74.

57   See S. Lieberman, "Who Were Pliny's Blue-Eyed Chinese?" *Classical Philology* 52 (1957), pp. 174–7; J.M. Poinsotte, "Les Romains et la Chine. Réalités et mythes," *Mélanges d'Archéologie et d'Histoire de l'École Française de Rome* 91 (1979), pp. 431–79; and Yves Janvier, "Rome et l'Orient lointain: le problème des Sères. Réexamen d'une question de géographie antique," *Ktèma* 9 (1984), pp. 261–303.

three works: the *Periplus* (that is, sailing directions) of Scylax,[58] the *Indica* of Ctesias of Cnidus, a Greek physician who stayed at the court of the Persian king Artaxerxes II Mnemon from 404 to 398/397 BCE, and the *Indica* of Megasthenes, who lived circa 350 to 290 BCE and was an ambassador of Seleucus I of Syria to the court of Sandrocottus in Pataliputra, India. Ctesias's work now survives only in quotations by classical authors and a summary made by the Byzantine scholar Photius (circa 815–897),[59] and Megasthenes also survives just in fragments cited by later authors,[60] particularly by Arrian in his description of India. Ctesias certainly did not travel to India, and his accounts of the monsters and monstrous races in that region derive either from myths and folktales he heard from Indian visitors to the Persian court, or from his own imagination.[61] Megasthenes's accounts of monsters in India derive with more probability from local sources, and in some cases his accounts are more accurate than those of Ctesias, though he also includes fantastic elements such as winged dragons.[62]

Ctesias's book was more influential than Megasthenes's, and its influence across the centuries and in various media clearly demonstrates that he was one of the most important mythographers in the Western tradition.[63] The most significant

---

58   On monstrous races in Scylax, see James Romm, "Belief and Other Worlds: Ktesias and the Founding of the 'Indian Wonders,'" in George E. Slusser and Eric S. Rabkin (eds), *Mindscapes: The Geography of Imagined Worlds* (Carbondale: Southern Illinois University Press, 1989), pp. 121–35, especially 121–2; Romm, *The Edges of the Earth*, pp. 84–5; Dmitri V. Panchenko, "Scylax' Circumnavigation of India and its Interpretation in Early Greek Geography, Ethnography and Cosmography," *Hyperboreus* 4/2 (1998), pp. 211–42, and 9/2 (2003), pp. 274–94; and Andrea Rossi-Reder, "Wonders of the Beast: India in Classical and Medieval Literature," in Timothy S. Jones and David A. Sprunger (eds), *Marvels, Monsters, and Miracles: Studies in the Medieval and Early Modern Imaginations* (Kalamazoo: Medieval Institute Publications, 2002), pp. 53–66.

59   See J.M. Bigwood, "Ctesias' *Indica* and Photius," *Phoenix* 43/4 (1989), pp. 302–16.

60   The fragments are collected in Megasthenes, *Indica: Fragmenta*, ed. E.A. Schwanbeck (Bonn, 1846; Amsterdam: Adolf M. Hakkert, 1966); translated in *Ancient India, as Described by Megasthenês and Arrian*, trans. J.W. McCrindle (Calcutta: Thacker, Spink, 1877; New Delhi: Today & Tomorrow's Printers & Publishers, 1972).

61   Earlier studies of Ctesias, such as F. Jacoby's article "Ktesias" in *Paulys Real-Encyclopädie der classischen Altertumswissenschaft* (Stuttgart: J.B. Metzler, 1894–1980), vol. 11, cols 2032–73, emphasized the idea that Ctesias was inventing what he recounted, while Andrew Nichols, "The Complete Fragments of Ctesias of Cnidus: Translation and Commentary with an Introduction," PhD dissertation, University of Florida, 2008, emphasizes Ctesias's reliance on oral sources to which he had access while he was in Persia.

62   See Truesdell S. Brown, "The Reliability of Megasthenes," *American Journal of Philology* 76/1 (1955), pp. 18–33.

63   See Wittkower, "Marvels of the East"; Albrecht Dihle, "The Conception of India in Hellenistic and Roman Literature," *Proceedings of the Cambridge Philological Society* 10 (1964), pp. 15–23, reprinted in Dihle, *Antike und Orient: gesammelte Aufsätze* (Heidelberg: C. Winter Universitätsverlag, 1984), pp. 83–93; Klaus Karttunen, "The Country of Fabulous Beasts and Naked Philosophers: India in Classical and Medieval Literature," *Arctos* 21 (1987), pp. 43–52; and Romm, "Belief and Other Worlds".

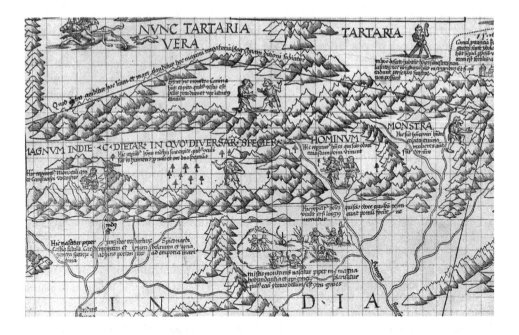

Figure 18.3   Martin Waldseemüller, *Carta marina* (1516), India monstrous races (courtesy of the Library of Congress).

avenues of transmission of his reports of monstrous races were by way of Pliny's *Naturalis historia* 7.2.9–32, and Isidore's *Etymologiae* 11.3; indeed these races are now often referred to as the "Plinian races."[64] Lists of the monstrous races of India appeared in Solinus's fourth-century *Collectanea rerum memorabilium* 53, and in chapter 16 of Pierre d'Ailly's *Imago mundi*, which was written in 1410, to mention just two examples; curiously, though many of these monstrous races appeared on medieval maps—for example, on the Hereford map there are pygmies, the monocoli or sciapods,[65] and Arimaspi or Cyclopes—there was no attempt at a systematic cartographic representation of the monstrous races of India until Martin Waldseemüller's *Carta marina* of 1516, where the monstrous races of Pierre d'Ailly's list are neatly represented in northern India (Figure 18.3).[66] These same

---

64   John Friedman, *Monstrous Races*, pp. 5–25. On these races, see also Claude-Clair Kappler, *Monstres, démons et merveilles à la fin du Moyen Age* (Paris: Payot, 1980), pp. 120–72; and the commentary on Pliny 7.2.9–32 in Mary Beagon (trans. and comm.), *The Elder Pliny on the Human Animal: Natural History: Book 7* (Oxford: Clarendon Press, 2005), pp. 120–62.

65   There is a good discussion of the history of the sciapods in Claude Lecouteux, "Herzog Ernst, les monstres dits 'sciapodes' et le problème des sources," *Etudes Germaniques* 34/1 (1979), pp. 1–21; and now see also Teresa Pàroli, "How Many are the Unipeds' Feet? Their Tracks in Texts and Sources," in Wilhelm Heizmann, Klaus Böldl, and Heinrich Beck (eds), *Analecta Septentrionalia: Beiträge zur nordgermanischen Kultur- und Literaturgeschichte* (Berlin and New York: Walter de Gruyter, 2009), pp. 281–327.

66   See Chet Van Duzer, "A Northern Refuge of the Monstrous Races: Asia on

monstrous races are depicted in Lorenz Fries's *Carta marina*, published in 1525, 1530, and 1531 (no copies of the 1525 edition survive), which is a close copy of Waldseemüller's work.[67]

Ctesias also included animal monsters in his account of India, among which are the manticore (section 15), which has a face like a man, is the size of a lion, has three rows of teeth, and a tail like that of a scorpion with a large stinger at the end;[68] a purple serpent (section 33) with a white head which, if hung up by its tail, discharges two kinds of poison, one yellow while it is alive, the other black when it is dead, and the first, if ingested, causes one's brain to flow out through one's nose, while the second causes death by consumption after a year; large thick worms (section 46) that live in the river Indus, which have two teeth, one in the upper jaw and the other in the lower, and emerge from the river mud at night to attack and eat camels or oxen. The manticore is represented on the Hereford *mappamundi*,[69] and is indicated by name, but without an image, on the fourteenth-century Aslake map.[70]

The Indian wonders gained a new life though accounts of the Indian campaign of Alexander the Great in 329–326 BCE. The *Alexander Romance*, a collection of Alexander's mythical exploits in India which was sometimes incorrectly attributed to Callisthenes, was probably compiled in the third century BCE, and includes descriptions of many monsters in India.[71] The *Epistola Alexandri Magni ad Aristotelem de miraculis Indiae* (or *Letter of Alexander to Aristotle about the Wonders of India*) is an expanded version of a letter included in the *Alexander Romance*, and it describes many monstrous beasts and races of men: Amazons,[72] blemmyae,

Waldseemüller's 1516 Carta Marina," *Imago Mundi* 62/2 (2010), pp. 221–31. There are also several monstrous races in northern Asia—at the northern edge of the map, in fact—on Sancho Gutierrez's map of 1551; for details on this map see note 170 below.

67   On Fries's *Carta marina*, see Hildegard Binder Johnson, *Carta marina: World Geography in Strassburg, 1525* (Minneapolis: University of Minnesota Press, 1963). Two copies of Fries's *Carta marina* survive, one of the 1530 edition in the Bayerische Staatsbibliothek, Munich, and one of the 1531 edition in the Museum zu Allerheiligen, Schaffhausen, on which, see Henry J. Bruman, "The Schaffhausen Carta Marina of 1531," *Imago Mundi* 41 (1989), pp. 124–32. A facsimile of the 1530 copy was published in Munich by the bookseller Ludwig Rosenthal in about 1926.

68   See Pierre Louis, "Les animaux fabuleux chez Aristote," *Revue des études grecques* 80 (1967), pp. 242–6, especially 244–5; and G.J.M. Bartelink, "Het fabeldier martichoras of mantichora," *Hermeneus* 43 (1972), pp. 169–74 and 225.

69   See Westrem, *The Hereford Map*, pp. 76–7, no. 157.

70   See Peter Barber and Michelle P. Brown, "The Aslake World Map," *Imago Mundi* 44/1 (1992), pp. 24–44, especially 28.

71   Richard Stoneman (trans.), *The Greek Alexander Romance* (New York: Penguin, 1991); for discussion of the monsters, see Stoneman, "Romantic Ethnography: Central Asia and India in the Alexander Romance," *Ancient World* 25 (1994), pp. 93–107.

72   For discussion, see Tobias Brandenberger, "El episodio amazónico del Libro de Alexandre. Fondo, fuentes, figuración," *Zeitschrift für romanische Philologie* 110/3–4 (1994), pp. 432–66; and Elizabeth Baynham, "Alexander and the Amazons," *Classical Quarterly* 51/1 (2001), pp. 115–26.

giants, strap-legged men,[73] cynocephali or dog-headed men, giant crabs, three-eyed lions, and the odontotyrannus, which had three horns and could devour an elephant.[74] The medieval literature about Alexander, based on this tradition of the wonders of India, is too large to survey here,[75] but some elements deriving from this literature, including the Amazons and giants, appear on medieval *mappaemundi*.[76]

But certainly the element derived from Alexander's story that is most frequently represented on medieval and Renaissance maps is his enclosure of the monstrous races of Gog and Magog in northern Asia. According to the *Alexander Romance*, Alexander reached a northern land devastated by barbarians, including the cannibalistic Gog and Magog, and he protected the land by building a huge wall between two mountains to contain the invaders until the end of history. According to Revelation 20:7–9, these peoples would come forth in the time of the Antichrist and devastate the earth; during the Middle Ages, Gog and Magog

---

73   For an interesting discussion of strap-legged men, see Natalia L.Tornesello, "From Reality to Legend: Historical Sources of Hellenistic and Islamic Teratology," *Studia Iranica* 31/2 (2002), pp. 163–92.

74   See Lloyd L. Gunderson, *Alexander's Letter to Aristotle about India* (Meisenheim am Glan: Hain, 1980), with an English translation of the *Letter* on pp. 140–56. For discussion of the monsters in the *Letter*, see Alexander Cizek, "Ungeheuer und magische Lebewesen in der *Epistola Alexandri ad magistratum suum Aristotelem de situ Indiae*," in Jan Goossens and Timothy Sodmann (eds), *Third International Beast Epic, Fable and Fabliau Colloquium, Münster 1979: Proceedings* (Cologne: Böhlau, 1981), pp. 78–94; and James Romm, "Alexander, Biologist: Oriental Monstrosities and the *Epistola Alexandri ad Aristotelem*," in Scott Westrem (ed.), *Discovering New Worlds: Essays on Medieval Exploration and Imagination* (New York: Garland, 1991), pp. 16–30, reprinted in Bill Readings and Bennet Schaber (eds), *Postmodernism Across the Ages: Essays for a Postmodernity that Wasn't Born Yesterday* (Syracuse, NY: Syracuse University Press, 1993), pp. 31–46. For illustrations of Alexander's Indian wonders, see D.J.A. Ross, *Illustrated Medieval Alexander-Books in Germany and the Netherlands: A Study in Comparative Iconography* (Cambridge, UK: Modern Humanities Research Association, 1971); Krystyna Secomska, "The Miniature Cycle in the Sandomierz *Pantheon* and the Medieval Iconography of Alexander's Indian Campaign," *Journal of the Warburg and Courtauld Institutes* 38 (1975), pp. 53–71; and Laurence Harf-Lancner, "From Alexander to Marco Polo, from Text to Image: The Marvels of India," in Donald Maddox and Sara Sturm-Maddox (eds), *The Medieval French Alexander* (Albany: State University of New York Press, 2002), pp. 235–57.

75   See George Cary, *The Medieval Alexander*, ed. D.J.A. Ross (Cambridge, UK: Cambridge University Press, 1956); and Richard Stoneman, *Alexander the Great: A Life in Legend* (New Haven: Yale University Press, 2008), pp. 199–216.

76   See Danielle Lecoq, "L'image d'Alexandre à travers les mappemondes médiévales (XIIe–XIIIe)," *Geographia Antiqua* 2 (1993), pp. 63–103; Hoogvliet, *Pictura et scriptura*, pp. 220–8; and Naomi Reed Kline, "Alexander Interpreted on the Hereford Mappamundi," in P.D.A. Harvey (ed.), *The Hereford World Map: Medieval World Maps and their Context* (London: British Library, 2006), pp. 167–83.

were quite anti-Semitically identified with the Ten Lost Tribes of Israel,[77] and the site of their enclosure was thought to be in north-eastern Asia.[78] On the Ebstorf *mappamundi* they are enclosed behind a wall at the north-eastern edge of the world, eating other people.[79] In the Catalan Atlas of 1375, Gog and Magog, and also the Antichrist and his followers, are enclosed behind mountains in north-eastern Asia.[80] The location of the enclosing mountains is similar, but somewhat easier to appreciate on the Catalan Estense *mappamundi* of circa 1460.[81] Fra Mauro, on his *mappamundi* of c. 1455, expressed doubt about the truth of the legend about Alexander's wall,[82] but later cartographers continued to indicate the enclosed nations in north-eastern Asia, for example, Martin Waldseemüller on his world map of 1507.[83]

---

77 On Gog and Magog as Jews, see Suzanne Lewis, *The Art of Matthew Paris in the Chronica Majora* (Berkeley: University of California Press, 1987), p. 349; and Scott D. Westrem, "Against Gog and Magog," in Sylvia Tomasch and Sealy Gilles (eds), *Text and Territory: Geographical Imagination in the European Middle Ages* (Philadelphia: University of Pennsylvania Press, 1998), pp. 54–75.

78 On Gog and Magog generally, see Andrew Runni Anderson, *Alexander's Gate, Gog and Magog, and the Inclosed Nations* (Cambridge, MA: The Medieval Academy of America, 1932); and Debra Higgs Strickland, *Saracens, Demons, and Jews: Making Monsters in Medieval Art* (Princeton, NJ: Princeton University Press, 2003), pp. 228–39; on their representation on maps, see Lecoq, "L'image d'Alexandre", pp. 92–103; Andrew Gow, "Gog and Magog on *Mappaemundi* and Early Printed World Maps: Orientalizing Ethnography in the Apocalyptic Tradition," *Journal of Early Modern History* 2/1 (1998), pp. 61–88; and Westrem, "Against Gog and Magog."

79 For a transcription of the legend and an illustration, see Kugler, *Die Ebstorfer Weltkarte*, vol. 1, pp. 58–9.

80 On the identification of the latter figure as the Antichrist, see Sandra Sáenz-López Pérez, "La representación de Gog y Magog y la imagen del Anticristo en las cartas náuticas bajomedievales," *Archivo Español de Arte* 78 (2005), pp. 263–76.

81 The Catalan Estense map is Modena, Biblioteca Estense Universitaria, C.G.A.1, and has been reproduced in facsimile, with transcription and commentary, in Ernesto Milano and Annalisa Batini, *Mapamundi Catalán Estense, escuela cartográfica mallorquina* (Barcelona: M. Moleiro, 1996), and the legend relating to Gog and Magog is transcribed on p. 157 of the commentary volume. There is also a high-resolution digital image of the map on the CD-ROM titled *Antichi planisferi e portolani: Modena, Biblioteca Estense Univesitaria* (Modena: Il Bulino; and Milan: Y. Press, 2004).

82 See Piero Falchetta, *Fra Mauro's World Map* (Turnhout: Brepols, 2006), pp. 617 and 619, no. *2403, and p. 685, no. *2752. Also see Andrew Gow, "Fra Mauro's World View: Authority and Empirical Evidence on a Venetian Mappamundi," in P.D.A. Harvey (ed.), *The Hereford World Map: Medieval World Maps and their Context* (London: The British Library, 2006), pp. 405–14.

83 Waldseemüller's 1507 map has been published in facsimile in Joseph Fischer and Franz Ritter von Wieser (eds), *Die älteste Karte mit dem Namen Amerika aus dem Jahre 1507 und die Carta marina aus dem Jahre 1516 des M. Waldseemüller (Ilacomilus)* (Innsbruck: Wagner'schen Universitäts-Buchhandlung, 1903; Amsterdam: Theatrum orbis terrarum, 1968); there are two excellent high-resolution scans of the map available on the internet site of the Library of Congress.

Many works later than the *Alexander Romance* continued the tradition of monsters in the East: the late seventh- or early eighth-century Anglo-Latin *Liber monstrorum*,[84] and the *Wonders of the East*, probably composed around the year 1000, a catalog of monstrous animals and men in various parts of the East, from Persia to India.[85]

Marvels and monsters in the East are very prominent in the *Letter of Prester John*, a forged letter purporting to be from a Christian monarch in the East which arrived in Europe about 1165. The letter proposed an alliance with the Christian West to fight the Saracens, and described Prester John's realm as being fabulously wealthy and full of wonders, including monstrous animals, pygmies, cynocephali, Cyclopes, and so on.[86] The legend of Prester John migrated from Asia to Africa,[87] and on medieval maps he is most often mentioned or represented on that continent: he is first mentioned in Africa on the map of Angelino Dulcert of 1339, and first represented there on the map of Mecia de Viladestes of 1413. The wonders of his kingdom are generally neither mentioned nor represented on maps, perhaps for lack of space.

---

84   On the *Liber monstrorum*, see the references cited above in note 27; on the monsters derived from the *Epistola Alexandri*, see Orchard, *Pride and Prodigies*, pp. 125–30.

85   On the *Wonders of the East*, see Orchard, *Pride and Prodigies*; Rossi-Reder, "Wonders of the Beast"; Mark Bradshaw Busbee, "A Paradise Full of Monsters: India in the Old English Imagination," *LATCH: A Journal for the Study of the Literary Artifact in Theory, Culture, or History* 1 (2008), pp. 49–70; and Alun James Ford, "The 'Wonders of the East' in its Contexts: A Critical Examination of London, British Library, Cotton MSS Vitellius A.xv and Tiberius B.v, and Oxford, Bodleian Library, MS Bodley 614," PhD dissertation, University of Manchester, 2009.

86   The text of Prester John's letter is edited by F. Zarncke, "Der Brief des Presters Johannes an den byzantinischen Kaiser Emanuel," *Abhandlungen der königlich sächsischen Gesellschaft der Wissenschaften, phil.-hist. Klasse* 7 (1879), pp. 873–934, reprinted in Charles F. Beckingham and Bernard Hamilton (eds), *Prester John, the Mongols, and the Ten Lost Tribes* (Aldershot, Hampshire; and Brookfield, VT: Variorum, 1996), pp. 40–102; it is translated into English in Michael Uebel, *Ecstatic Transformation: On the Uses of Alterity in the Middle Ages* (New York: Palgrave Macmillan, 2005), pp. 155–60. For discussion of Prester John's letter from a geographical point of view, see Rudolf Simek, *Heaven and Earth in the Middle Ages: The Physical World Before Columbus*, trans. Angela Hall (Woodbridge, Suffolk, and Rochester, NY: Boydell Press, 1997), pp. 69–72.

87   On the transfer of Prester John from Asia to Africa, see J. Richard, "L'Extrême-Orient Légendaire au Moyen Âge: Roi David et Prêtre Jean," *Annales d'Ethiopie* 12 (1957), pp. 225–44; Bernard Hamilton, "Continental Drift: Prester John's Progress through the Indies," in Charles F. Beckingham and Bernard Hamilton (eds), *Prester John, the Mongols, and the Ten Lost Tribes* (Aldershot, Hampshire; and Brookfield, VT: Variorum, 1996), pp. 237–69; Francesc Relaño, *The Shaping of Africa: Cosmographic Discourse and Cartographic Science in Late Medieval and Early Modern Europe* (Burlington, VT, and Aldershot, UK: Ashgate, 2002), pp. 51–72; and Manuel João Ramos, *Essays in Christian Mythology: The Metamorphosis of Prester John* (Lanham, MD: University Press of America, 2006), pp. 106–16.

Jacques de Vitry (circa 1160/70–1240), in his *Historia orientalis*, has a section on the monstrous races in India,[88] including giants, Amazons, cynocephali, men who live from the odor of apples, and women with long beards. He says that he took his information about these races from various written sources, including Augustine, Isidore, Pliny, and Solinus—and also from a *mappamundi*.[89] This passage provides interesting evidence for the existence of a twelfth- or early thirteenth-century map which contained information about the monstrous races in India.

Giovanni da Pian del Carpine, or John of Plano Carpini (circa 1180–1252), was one of the first Europeans to enter the court of the Great Khan of the Mongol Empire, and his *Ystoria Mongolorum* is the earliest important European account of northern and central Asia. Plano Carpini mentions some of the Plinian monstrous races of men in northern Asia; these are included in excerpts of his work in Book 32 of Vincent of Beauvais's *Speculum historiale*; and Martin Waldseemüller included representations of these races on his *Carta marina* of 1516 (one of these races is depicted in the upper right corner of Figure 18.3).[90]

Marco Polo (circa 1254–1324), in his enormously influential *Le devisament du monde*,[91] describes many marvels of the East, but contrary to popular opinion, describes very few indeed of the Plinian monstrous races of men.[92] Yet the tradition of monstrous races in the East was so strong that some illustrated manuscripts of his work include images of monstrous races.[93] For example, Paris, Bibliothèque nationale de France, MS fr. 2810, fol. 29v is an illustration of Siberia, and shows blemmyae, sciapods, and Cyclopes;[94] Polo says that the people in this region are wild, but does

---

88 For basic discussion of Jacques de Vitry's work, see Jessalynn Bird, "The *Historia Orientalis* of Jacques de Vitry: Visual and Written Commentaries as Evidence of a Text's Audience, Reception, and Utilization," *Essays in Medieval Studies* 20/1 (2004), pp. 56–74, with some mention of his treatment of alien peoples on page 59.

89 See Jacques de Vitry, *Iacobi de Vitriaco, primvm Acconensis, deinde Tvscvlani Episcopi ... libri dvo, quorum prior Orientalis, siue Hierosolymitanae, alter, Occidentalis historiae nomine inscribitur* (Douai: Ex officina typographica Balthazaris Belleri, 1597), p. 215.

90 See Van Duzer, "A Northern Refuge of the Monstrous Races".

91 The most copiously annotated English translation is *The Book of Ser Marco Polo, the Venetian: Concerning the Kingdoms and Marvels of the East*, trans. and ed. Henry Yule, 3rd edn (London: J. Murray, 1903).

92 Some discussion of Marco Polo's treatment of barbarous peoples is supplied by Marianne O'Doherty, "'They are like beasts, for they have no law': Ethnography and Constructions of Human Difference in Late-Medieval Translations of Marco Polo's Book," in Jean-François Kosta-Théfaine (ed.), *Travels and Travelogues in the Middle Ages* (New York: AMS Press, 2009), pp. 59–92.

93 See Rudolf Wittkower, "Marco Polo and the Pictorial Tradition of the Marvels of the East," in E. Balazs (ed.), *Oriente Poliano* (Rome: Istituto italiano per il Medio e Estremo Oriente, 1957), pp. 155–72; reprinted in Wittkower, *Allegory and the Migration of Symbols* (Boulder: Westview Press, 1977), pp. 76–92; and Debra Higgs Strickland, "Artists, Audience, and Ambivalence in Marco Polo's *Divisament dou monde*," *Viator* 36 (2005), pp. 493–529.

94 Paris, BnF, MS français 2810 is a famous, richly illustrated manuscript of Marco Polo's *Livre des merveilles*, John Mandeville's *Travels*, and other works; the manuscript was

not specify any of these monstrous races: these are the additions of the illuminator.[95] There is one case, however, in which Polo describes a monstrous race, which is in his account of the Andaman Islands: Polo says that the inhabitants are cannibals and have heads, eyes, and teeth very similar to those of dogs,[96] and the artist of BnF MS fr. 2810, fol. 76v quite justifiably represents a dog-faced race, relying on traditional images of cynocephali (see Figure 17.3).[97] This image was adopted by a number of later writers, including Friar Odoric of Pordenone and John Mandeville, and is illustrated on Pierre Desceliers's manuscript world map of 1550,[98] who has an image of a cynocephalus chopping up the body of another cynocephalus in preparation to eat it. Other maps depict the inhabitants of the Andaman Islands as cannibals, for example, the *Tabula Moder[na] Indiae Orientalis* in the 1522 (Strasbourg), 1525 (Strasbourg), 1535 (Lyon), and 1541 (Vienna) editions of Ptolemy's *Geography*.[99] As Laurence Goldman has remarked, cannibalism is the "quintessential symbol of alterity, an entrenched metaphor of cultural xenophobia."[100]

---

produced in the early fifteenth century for John the Fearless, Duke of Burgundy. The illustrations in this manuscript are reproduced in black-and-white in Henri Omont (ed.), *Livre des merveilles, Marco Polo, Odoric Pordenone, Mandeveille, Hayton, etc.* (Paris: Berthaud, 1907); all of the illustrations of Polo (fols 1–96) have been reproduced in a more recent color facsimile, Marco Polo, *Das Buch der Wunder [Le livre des merveilles]* (Lucerne: Faksimile Verlag, 1995), which is accompanied by a volume of commentary; all of the illustrations of Polo are more accessibly reproduced in Marie-Thérèse Gousset, *Le Livre des merveilles du monde* (Paris: Bibliothèque de l'image, 2002); and all of the images in the manuscript are available at <http://mandragore.bnf.fr>.

95   See Wittkower, "Marco Polo and the Pictorial Tradition," pp. 161–2; and Strickland, "Artists, Audience, and Ambivalence," p. 503. For discussion of a fifteenth-century Russian text titled *O chelovetsikh neznaemykh v vostochnei strane* (On Unknown Men in the Eastern Land), which coincidentally also locates some of the Plinian monstrous races in Siberia, see Janet Martin, *Treasure of the Land of Darkness: The Fur Trade and its Significance for Medieval Russia* (Cambridge: Cambridge University Press, 1986), pp. 80–1; the Russian text is supplied in D.N. Anuchin, "K istorii oznakomleniia s Sibiriu do Ermaka," *Drevnosti: Trudy Moskovskogo arkheologischeskogo obshchestva* 14 (1890), pp. 227–313.

96   Polo's description is cited by Martin Behaim on his globe of 1492: see E.G. Ravenstein, *Martin Behaim: His Life and his Globe* (London: G. Philip & Son, Ltd., 1908), p. 88.

97   Wittkower, "Marco Polo and the Pictorial Tradition," p. 160; and Strickland, "Artists, Audience, and Ambivalence," p. 505, suggest that the artist's interpretation is an exaggeration like his image of Siberia just mentioned, but Polo's text is quite clear: he says that the Andaman Islanders are "tuit senblable a chief de grant chienz mastin," that is, "entirely similar to the heads of large mastiffs." See Marco Polo, *Milione: il Milione nelle redazioni toscana e franco-italiana [Le divisament dou monde]*, ed. Gabriella Ronchi (Milan: A. Mondadori, 1982), p. 549.

98   On Pierre Desceliers's 1550 world map, see note 44 above.

99   For descriptions of these editions of Ptolemy, see Wilberforce Eames, *A List of Editions of Ptolemy's Geography 1475–1730* (New York: s.n., 1886), pp. 15–17, 17–18, 18–19, and 20–1.

100   Laurence R. Goldman, "From Pot to Polemic: Uses and Abuses of Cannibalism," in Goldman (ed.), *The Anthropology of Cannibalism* (Westport: Bergin and Garvey, 1999), pp. 1–26, at 1.

But if Polo does not speak of many of the Plinian races, he does describe some monsters, and he seems to locate more of them at the edge of the earth, on islands in the Indian Ocean, than elsewhere. He says that the men in the kingdom of Lambri on Java Minor (modern Sumatra) have tails,[101] speaks of cannibals in the kingdom of Dragoian on Java Minor,[102] and tells of a monstrous bird in Madagascar with a wingspan of 30 paces which is capable of carrying an elephant—this bird is usually known as the rukh or roc.[103] Marco Polo's account of the rukh had many literary descendants, and the monstrous bird also appears on several maps: it is mentioned in a legend on Fra Mauro's *mappamundi* of c. 1455,[104] is represented on the map of the Indian Ocean by Nuño Garcia de Toreno made in 1522,[105] is mentioned in a legend on the world map of Sebastian Cabot of 1544,[106] and Gerard Mercator's world map of 1569,[107] and is illustrated on three manuscript maps by Urbano Monte (1587 and 1590).[108]

101 See *The Book of Ser Marco Polo*, Book 3, chapter 11, vol. 2, p. 299, with Yule's commentary on pp. 301–2.

102 See *The Book of Ser Marco Polo*, Book 3, chapter 10, vol. 2, pp. 293–4, with Yule's commentary on p. 298.

103 See *The Book of Ser Marco Polo*, Book 3, chapter 33, vol. 2, p. 412, with Yule's commentary on p. 415–20. For discussion of the complicated history of this mythical bird, see Sandra Sáenz-López Pérez, "El vuelo de oriente a occidente del mítico pájaro Rujj y las transformaciones de su leyenda," in María Victoria Chico and Laura Fernández (eds), *La creación de la imagen en la Edad Media: de la herencia a la renovación*, Anales de Historia del Arte (2010), volumen extraordinario, pp. 325–41.

104 See Falchetta, *Fra Mauro's World Map*, pp. 179–82, no. *19.

105 The map by Nuño Garcia de Toreno is Turin, Biblioteca Reale, C. XVI. 2, and is reproduced in Cavallo, *Cristoforo Colombo e l'apertura degli spazi*, vol. 2, figure IV.38, p. 715.

106 Cabot's map is well reproduced in Nebenzahl, *Atlas of Columbus*, pp. 106–7; for the legend, see Charles Deane, "[Inscriptions on Cabot's Mappe-monde]," *Proceedings of the Massachusetts Historical Society* 6 (1890–91), pp. 305–39, especially 327 and 338; Deane's work is reprinted in H.R. Holmden, *Catalogue of Maps, Plans and Charts in the Map Room of the Dominion Archives* (Ottawa: Govt. Print. Bureau, 1912), pp. 568–88.

107 Three copies of Mercator's 1569 map survive: one in Paris at the Bibliothèque nationale de France, Cartes et Plans, Rés Ge. A 1064; another in Basel at the Universitätsbibliothek, Kartenslg AA 3–5; and a third in Rotterdam at the Maritiem Museum "Prins Hendrik," Atlas51. The third of these is hand colored and has been reproduced in facsimile as *Gerard Mercator's Map of the World (1569) in the Form of an Atlas in the Maritiem Museum "Prins Hendrik" at Rotterdam* (Rotterdam, 1961). There is a good reproduction of the whole map in Nebenzahl, *Atlas of Columbus*, pp. 128–9.

108 The 1587 copy of Urbano Monte's map was sold at Sotheby's on May 12, 1981, lot 53, and offered for sale at Christie's on May 20, 1998; it is described in *Cartography: Auction, Wednesday 20 May 1998 at approximately 11.30 a.m.* (London: Christie's, 1998), pp. 22–9. One of the 1590 manuscripts of Urbano Monte's maps is Milan, Biblioteca Ambrosiana, MS A. 260 Inf., and the other is Venegono, Biblioteca de Seminario Arcivescovile, FV.B-VII-56. The maps of the latter copy have been reproduced in Urbano Monte, *Descrizione del mondo sin qui conosciuto*, ed. Maurizio Ampollini (Lecco: Periplo, 1994), which also includes biographical details about Monte. Some other maps that have illustrations of the rukh are mentioned by Hoogvliet, *Scriptura et pictura*, pp. 200–1.

To write a complete history of monsters in the East would far exceed the bounds of this chapter, and would to some extent be superfluous as Wittkower has discussed this subject so ably, but I will mention one other author who discusses monsters in the East but who curiously was not used as a source by cartographers. The *Travels of Sir John Mandeville*, which is based largely on the works of other travelers such as Odoric of Pordenone, is an extravagant tale of travels in the East that enjoyed great popularity. The book mentions many monsters in both Africa and India,[109] and illustrated manuscripts of his work have abundant images of monsters and monstrous races.[110] Mandeville was viewed as an authority on geography by later writers,[111] and was used as a source by Martin Behaim in his terrestrial globe of 1492,[112] but not for material about monsters, and curiously Mandeville's descriptions of monsters do not seem to have attracted the attention of cartographers.

The Antipodes

The idea that there was a continent in the southern hemisphere corresponding to the *oikumene* or ecumene (the inhabited region) in the northern hemisphere goes back to Aristotle, and was elaborated by Crates of Mallos (fl. 180 BCE), Cicero (first century BCE), Geminus (first century CE), and Macrobius (early fifth century CE).[113] It was Geminus who first called the hypothetical inhabitants of this southern

---

109 For some discussion, see Suzanne Conklin Akbari, "The Diversity of Mankind in The Book of John Mandeville," in Rosamund Allen (ed.), *Eastward Bound: Travels and Travellers, 1050–1500* (Manchester: Manchester University Press, 2004), pp. 156–76. Mary B. Campbell, *The Witness and the Other World: Exotic European Travel Writing, 400–1600* (Ithaca and London: Cornell University Press, 1988), p. 153, notes that in Mandeville's narrative, "the farther we penetrate into the East, the weirder it gets."

110 For discussion of some of the illustrated manuscripts of Mandeville, see Andrea Kann, "Picturing the World: The Illustrated Manuscripts of *The Book of John Mandeville*," PhD Dissertation, University of Iowa, 2002; and on illustrations of the monstrous races, see Sarah Catherine Andyshak, "Figural and Discursive Depictions of the Other in the *Travels of Sir John Mandeville*," MA thesis, Florida State University, 2009.

111 See Christiane Deluz, "Le Livre Jehan de Mandeville, autorité géographique à la Renaissance," in Jean Céard and J.-Cl. Margolin (eds), *Voyager à la Renaissance: Actes du colloque de Tours 1983* (Paris: Maisonneuve et Larose, 1987), pp. 205–20.

112 See C.W.R.D. Moseley, "Behaim's Globe and 'Mandeville's Travels,'" *Imago Mundi* 33 (1981), pp. 89–91. For a full analysis of Behaim's globe, and transcription and translation of the legends, see Ravenstein, *Martin Behaim: His Life and his Globe*. Gerard Mercator also cites Mandeville as a source about Java and the southern hemisphere on his world map of 1569, but Mercator ends by saying that Mandeville is "an author unbelievable in other respects" —see Nicolas Crane, *Mercator: The Man Who Mapped the Planet* (New York: Henry Holt, 2002), p. 226.

113 For discussion of the history of the idea of the antipodal continent, see Armand Rainaud, *Le continent Austral; hypothèses et découvertes* (Paris: A. Colin, 1893; Amsterdam: Meridian, 1965); G. Boffito, "La leggenda degli Antipodi," in *Miscellanea di studi critici*

continent "antipodes," meaning those who had their feet opposed to the inhabitants of the known world.[114] Isidore of Seville (560–636), in his influential *Etymologiae*, summarized thinking about this southern continent, asserting the existence of a fourth continent in addition to Europe, Africa, and Asia, a continent beyond the ocean to the south, unknown to us because of the heat of the equatorial regions, in which continent the fabulous race called the antipodes was said to dwell (14.5.17). In another passage (*Etymologiae*, 11.3.24) Isidore says that the antipodes are a race in Africa with their feet pointing backwards, each with eight toes—curiously converting the antipodes into a monstrous race.[115] This idea is repeated and illustrated in one manuscript of the *Wonders of the East*, Oxford, Bodleian Library, MS Bodley 614, fol. 50r.[116]

The antipodal continent was usually held to be inaccessible, was generally thought to be beyond the limits of the inhabited world, and thus would seem to be an excellent location for monsters. Yet most of the medieval discussion of the antipodes addressed the question of whether the continent was inhabited, and if so, whether the people there were descendants of Adam, and whether they could be evangelized.[117] However, there are some maps which locate monsters in the antipodes.

---

edita in onore di Arturo Graf (Bergamo: Instituto italiano d'arti grafiche, 1903), pp. 583–601; and Romm, *The Edges of the Earth in Ancient Thought*, pp. 128–40. For discussion of medieval ideas and cartography of the antipodes, see John K. Wright, *The Geographical Lore of the Time of the Crusades* (New York: American Geographical Society, 1925), pp. 156–65; Anna-Dorothee von den Brincken, *"Fines Terrae": Die Enden der Erde und der vierte Kontinent auf mittelalterlichen Weltkarten* (Hannover: Hahnsche Buchhandlung, 1992); and Benjamin Olshin, "The Antipodes, the Antarctic Continent, and the Spherical Earth," in Olshin, "A Sea Discovered: Pre-Columbian Conceptions and Depictions of the Atlantic Ocean," PhD dissertation, University of Toronto, 1994, pp. 264–318.

114 Geminus, *Introduction aux phénomènes*, ed. Germaine Aujac (Paris: Les belles lettres, 1975), section 16.1.

115 On Isidore's confusion here, see Valerie I.J. Flint, "Monsters and the Antipodes in the Early Middle Ages and Enlightenment," *Viator* 15 (1984), pp. 65–80; reprinted in Flint, *Ideas in the Medieval West: Texts and their Contexts* (London: Variorum Reprints, 1988), pp. 65–80, especially 70–1; and Gabriella Moretti, "The Other World and the 'Antipodes': The Myth of the Unknown Countries between Antiquity and the Renaissance," in W. Haase and M. Reinhold (eds), *The Classical Tradition and the Americas*, vol. 1, part I, *European Images of the Americas and the Classical Tradition* (Berlin and New York: De Gruyter, 1994), pp. 241–84, especially 266–7. On the different senses of the word "antipodes" during the Middle Ages, see Alexander H. Krappe, "Antipodes," *Modern Language Notes* 59/7 (1944), pp. 441–7.

116 See Montague Rhodes James, *Marvels of the East: A Full Reproduction of the Three Known Copies* (Oxford: Printed for the Roxburghe Club by J. Johnson, at the University Press, 1929), who discusses the additions to Bodley 614 from Isidore on pp. 22–4 and 30–2, and illustrates fol. 50r in the facsimile section of the book.

117 In addition to the references cited in note 113, see Simek, *Heaven and Earth in the Middle Ages*, pp. 48–55; and John Carey, "Ireland and the Antipodes: The Heterodoxy of Virgil of Salzburg," *Speculum* 64 (1989), pp. 1–10. The antipodal continent is represented on the *mappaemundi* which illustrate manuscripts of Macrobius, but never with monsters.

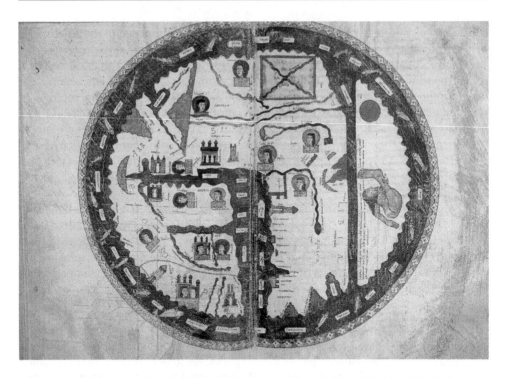

Figure 18.4   Burgo de Osma Beatus map, Cod. 1, ff. 34v-35r (Cabildo de la Catedral).

Some of the *mappaemundi* which illustrate the *Commentary on the Apocalypse* of Beatus of Liébana (circa 730–circa 800),[118] which date from the tenth to the thirteenth centuries, through a curious confusion indicate not antipodes but rather sciapods in the antipodal continent. Sciapods are also mentioned by Isidore (*Etymologiae* 11.3.23) and are said to live in Ethiopia, have one leg, be of great speed, and to shade themselves from the great heat with their large single foot. On the Burgo de Osma Beatus map (Figure 18.4), which dates from 1086, the legend in the antipodal continent says:

> *This region is unknown and uninhabitable to us because of the heat of the sun. The [race] of sciapods is said to live [here], with single legs and amazing speed, whom the Greeks call sciapods because in the summer they lie on their backs on the ground and are shaded by their wide feet.*[119]

---

118 On Beatus *mappaemundi* generally, see Destombes, *Mappemondes*, pp. 40–2; Gonzalo Menéndez-Pidal, "Mozárabes y asturianos en la cultura de la Alta Edad Media en relación especial con la historia de los conocimientos geográficos," *Boletín de la Real Academia de la Historia* 134 (1954), pp. 137–292; and Sáenz-López Pérez, "Imagen y conocimiento del mundo." My discussion of the sciapods on the Beatus maps is based on the analysis in Sáenz-López Pérez, vol. 1, pp. 215–24.

119 The Burgo de Osma map is Burgo de Osma (Spain), Cabildo de la Catedral de Burgo

The legend on the Lorvão Beatus of 1189 (Lisbon, Arquivo Nacional da Torre do Tombo, MS CXIII/247, fol. 34bis v) is very similar.[120] The eccentric *mappamundi* in the so-called Navarra Beatus from the end of the twelfth century (Paris, Bibliothèque nationale de France, MS nouv. acq. lat. 1366, fols 24v–25r)[121] does not show the antipodal continent and does not have a legend about sciapods there, but does illustrate a sciapod outside the ecumene, at the south-western edge of the world, near Ethiopia, and it seems likely that this sciapod alludes to the presence of sciapods in Ethiopia.

A much later map which shows some monsters in the southern continent is the 1513 map by the Ottoman admiral Piri Reis, which the cartographer claims is based on maps by Christopher Columbus.[122] This map seems to show the southern continent extending eastward from the southern tip of South America, and in that land there is an illustration of a large serpent, and a legend which runs: "This country is barren. Everything is desolate and in ruins and it is said that large serpents are found here. For this reason the Portuguese infidels did not land on these shores and these shores are said to be very hot."[123] Here the ends of the earth are a wasteland, which seems to have been inspired by ideas of the Torrid Zone.

Maps of the "Dieppe School" of cartography, which flourished from about 1540 to 1570,[124] typically have a large antipodal continent which extends north into Asia

---

de Osma, Cod. 1, fols 34v–35r. The best reproduction of the map is in the facsimile: Beatus of Liébana, *Expositio im Apocalisim* (Valencia: Vicent García, 1992). The Latin text of the legend runs: "Hec regio ab ardore solis incognita nobis et inhabitabilis manet. Sciopodum [gens] fertur habitare singulis cruribus et celeritate mirabili quos inde sciopodas greci vocant eo quod per estum in terra resupini iacentes pedum suorum magnitudine adumbrentur."

120 The legend is transcribed by Sáenz-López Pérez, "Imagen y conocimiento del mundo," vol. 1, p. 216; the manuscript has been reproduced in facsimile as *Beato de Liébana: Códice de San Mamede de Lorvao* (Valencia: Patrimonio, 2003).

121 The Navarra manuscript is reproduced in facsimile as Elisa Ruiz García and Soledad de Silva y Verástegui, *Beato de Navarra (ms. nouv. acq. Lat. 1366 de la Bibliothèque Nationale de France)* (Madrid: Millennium Liber, 2007).

122 The Piri Reis map is conveniently reproduced in Nebenzahl, *Atlas of Columbus*, p. 63; for discussion and translations of the legends, see Paul Kahle, "A Lost Map of Columbus," *Geographical Review* 23/4 (1933), pp. 621–38; and with greater precision by Gregory C. McIntosh, "Columbus and the Piri Reis Map of 1513," *The American Neptune* 53/4 (1993), pp. 280–94.

123 McIntosh, "Columbus and the Piri Reis Map of 1513," p. 292. There is good discussion of the southern continent on Piri Reis's map in Alfred Hiatt, *Terra Incognita: Mapping the Antipodes before 1600* (London: British Library, 2008), pp. 201–3.

124 On the "Dieppe School," see Henry Harrisse, "La cartographie Américano-Dieppoise," in Harrisse, *Découverte et évolution cartographique de Terre-Neuve et des pays circonvoisins, 1497–1501–1769* (London and Paris, 1900; Amsterdam: N. Israel, 1968), Part II, chapters 2–11; and Gayle K. Brunelle, "Dieppe School," in David Buisseret (ed.), *The Oxford Companion to World Exploration* (New York: Oxford University Press, 2007), pp. 237–8. There is a good brief list of all of the maps produced by the Dieppe School in William A.R. Richardson, *Was Australia Charted before 1606? The Java la Grande Inscriptions*

to include the island of Java, and which is usually called "Jave la Grande."[125] In two of the maps of this school, monstrous races are depicted in this southern continent. In Pierre Desceliers's world map of 1550,[126] the southern continent has images of idolaters worshipping an image of the sun and/or a statue of a bull-headed creature standing on its hind legs; and further to the south there is the image mentioned above of the cynocephalus chopping up the body of another cynocephalus in preparation to eat it (the corresponding legend applies to the Andaman Islands, but Desceliers represents the cynocephali in the southern continent). And Guillaume Le Testu's *Cosmographie universelle* of 1556 shows two panotii or men with enormous ears in fol. 36r of the atlas—one lying down to sleep in his ear as panotii are supposed to do—and on fol. 49r what seems to be a very long-necked cynocephalus.[127] These monstrous races in the southern continent in Le Testu's atlas offer a particularly clear case of monsters located in far-flung regions through the cartographer's *horror vacui*, and also a desire to delight the map's viewers with exotica, for Le Testu clearly states more than once that he does not believe that the southern continent he depicts in his atlas exists.[128]

Some later sixteenth-century maps also show monstrous creatures in the southern continent, apparently out of a hesitancy to leave blank spaces on the map and a taste for marvels. The nine-sheet printed world map by Giacomo Gastaldi, titled *Cosmographia universalis et exactissima iuxta postremam neotericorum tradition[n] em*, probably published in Venice by Matteo Pagano in about 1561,[129] has various

---

(Canberra: National Library of Australia, 2006), p. 96; there is a more detailed list in the Appendix to Sarah Toulouse, "Marine Cartography and Navigation in Renaissance France," in David Woodward (ed.), *The History of Cartography*, vol. 3, *Cartography in the European Renaissance*, Part II (Chicago: University of Chicago Press, 2007), pp. 1550–68.

125 For discussion of the southern continent on the Dieppe maps, see Helen Wallis, "Java la Grande: The Enigma of the Dieppe Maps," in Glyndwr Williams and Alan Frost (eds), *Terra Australis to Australia* (Melbourne: Oxford University Press, 1988), pp. 39–81.

126 For details on Pierre Desceliers's map of 1550, see note 44.

127 Le Testu's *Cosmographie universelle* is Paris, Bibliothèque du Service Historique de l'Armée de Terre (Château de Vincennes), MS D.L.Z.14. On the panotii, see Claude Lecouteux, "Les Panotéens: sources, diffusion, emploi," *Etudes germaniques* 35 (1980), pp. 253–66. The long-necked cynocephalus was perhaps inspired by the crane-headed men in Herzog Ernst, a German epic written in about 1180; for discussion, see Claude Lecouteux: "A propos d'un épisode de Herzog Ernst: La recontre des hommes-grues," *Etudes germaniques* 33 (1977), pp. 1–15; and Debra Higgs Strickland, "The Sartorial Monsters of Herzog Ernst," *Different Visions: A Journal of New Perspectives on Medieval Art* 2 (2010), pp. 1–35, <http://differentvisions.org/two.html>.

128 For Le Testu's assertion that the southern continent he depicts in his atlas is imaginary, see his *Cosmographie universelle* fols 34r, 35r, 37r, 39r, 40r, and 41r. The relevant texts on fols 35r and 39r are translated into English by Frank Lestringant, *Mapping the Renaissance World: The Geographical Imagination in the Age of Discovery* (Berkeley: University of California Press, 1994), pp. 133–4.

129 The only surviving copy of the map is in the British Library, with signature Maps C.18.n.1; there is also a photocopy of the map in the Newberry Library in Chicago. The map is well illustrated in Günter Schilder, *Monumenta cartographica Neerlandica* (Alphen

monsters in its southern continent, including two Cyclopes, dragons, a centaur, an elephant, a lion, and a manticore. Giovanni Francesco Camocio's world map of 1567 and 1569, titled *Cosmographia vniversalis et exactissima ivxta postremam neotericorvm traditionem*, which is derived from Gastaldi's, has a basilisk, elephant, unicorn, centaur, griffin, and other animals and monsters in its southern continent.[130] In addition, the Milanese cartographer Urbano Monte (1544–1613) created three surviving multisheet manuscript world maps on a north polar projection, one dated 1587,[131] and two dated 1590.[132] These maps, which were also influenced by Gastaldi, have a great variety of animal and humanoid monsters on their southern continent. These creatures, which seem not to derive from any specific text, illustrate with particular clarity our tendency to fill distant regions with monsters.

The Ocean—Sea Monsters

The sea was a dangerous and mysterious place in the classical and medieval periods: Pliny calls the sea "the most savage part of nature" (36.1.2), and both Pliny (19.1.6) and Propertius (1.17.13–14) curse the inventor of the ship, who brought such great danger to men.[133] How much more dangerous, then, was the distant ocean generally held to encircle the earth?[134] Pliny 9.1.2 has an interesting passage on the tendency of the open sea to produce sea monsters. In the quotation from Diodorus Siculus cited above, Heracles is said to narrow the Strait of Gibraltar in order to keep sea monsters from entering the Mediterranean, and a very evocative quotation from the Roman poet Albinovanus Pedo, which is preserved in Seneca's *Suasoriae* (1.15), conveys the terrors, including sea monsters, associated with sailing out into the Atlantic:

---

aan den Rijn, Holland: Uitgevermaatschappij Canaletto, 1986–), vol. 2, pp. 36–7; and is discussed in Rodney W. Shirley, *The Mapping of the World: Early Printed World Maps 1472–1700* (Riverside, CT: Early World Press, 2001), pp. 122–5.

130 A zoomable image of the copy of Camocio's map at the John Carter Brown Library is available through the Library's internet site; there is also a facsimile of this same copy of the map: Giovanni Francesco Camocio, *A Large World Map Dated 1569 Sold at the Sign of the Pyramid in Venice by Joan Franciscus Camotius, Now in the George H. Beans Library* (Philadelphia: George H. Beans Library, 1933).

131 On Urbano Monte's 1587 map, see note 108 above.

132 On Urbano Monte's 1590 world maps, see note 108 above. For discussion of Monte's maps see Roberto Almagià, "Un prezioso cimelio della cartografia italiana. Il Planisfero di Urbano Monte," *La Bibliofilia* 43 (1941), pp. 156–93.

133 For discussion, see Eugène de Saint-Denis, *Le rôle de la mer dans la poésie latine* (Paris: C. Klincksieck, 1935); Mary Beagon, *Roman Nature: The Thought of Pliny the Elder* (Oxford: Clarendon Press, 1992), especially pp. 177–80; and Rhiannon Evans, "The Cruel Sea?: Ocean as Boundary Marker and Transgressor in Pliny's Roman Geography," *Antichthon* 39 (2005), pp. 105–18.

134 On the circumfluent ocean, see, for example, Pliny 2.167 and Isidore 14.2.1, with discussion in Romm, *The Edges of the Earth*, pp. 124–71.

And now they see day and sun long left behind; banished from the familiar limits of the world they dare to pass through forbidden shades to the bounds of things, the remotest shores of the world. Now they think Ocean, that breeds beneath its sluggish waves terrible monsters, savage sea-beasts everywhere, and dogs of the sea, is rising, taking the ships with it (the very noise increases their fears): now they think the vessels are sinking in the mud, the fleet deserted by the swift wind, themselves left by indolent fate to the sea-beasts, to be torn apart unhappily.[135]

In a forthcoming book I will provide a full discussion of sea monsters on medieval and Renaissance maps,[136] and will confine myself here to some essential examples. The earliest surviving medieval maps which have substantial sea life in their circumfluent oceans are the world maps produced from the tenth to the thirteenth centuries which illustrate the *Commentary on the Apocalypse* of Beatus of Liébana.[137] One of the *mappaemundi* of this group displays several exotic sea creatures. On the Beatus map in Gerona, Spain, which is dated 975,[138] there are a number of sea creatures which seem to be more sea monsters than fish, including a hybrid creature which is perhaps a *canis marinus* or sea-dog, a curious marine chicken, a *serra* or "saw-fish" in the south-east with a serrated back,[139] and a man inside a huge sea creature, probably representing Jonah in the monster, in the west.

---

135 See Michael von Albrecht, *Roman Epic: An Interpretative Introduction* (Boston: Brill, 1998), Latin text and English translation on pp. 209–10, with discussion on pp. 210–15.

136 Chet Van Duzer, *Sea Monsters on Medieval and Renaissance Maps*, forthcoming from the British Library.

137 For references on Beatus *mappaemundi*, see note 118 above. My discussion of the sea creatures on these maps is based on the analysis in Sáenz-López Pérez, "Imagen y conocimiento del mundo,", vol. 1, pp. 78–87.

138 The signature of the Gerona Beatus map is Museu de la Catedral de Girona, Num. Inv. 7 (11), fols 54v–55r. This manuscript has been reproduced in facsimile twice: *Sancti Beati a Liebana in Apocalypsin Codex Gerundensis* (Olten: Urs Graf, 1962); and *Commentarium in Apocalypsim. Beati in Apocalipsin libri duodecim: Codex Gerundensis A.D. 975* (Madrid: Edilán, 1975). There is also a smaller reproduction of the map in John Williams, *The Illustrated Beatus: A Corpus of the Illustrations of the Commentary on the Apocalypse* (London: Harvey Miller, 1994–2003), vol. 1, figure 22, and vol. 2, figure 302. Sáenz-López Pérez, "Imagen y conocimiento del mundo,", vol. 2, figures 9 and 11, reproduces details of the *canis marinus* and the sea creature with a man inside.

139 On creatures like the sea-dog and sea-chicken, see Jacqueline Leclercq-Marx, "L'idée d'un monde marin parallèle du monde terrestre: émergence et développements," in Chantal Connochie-Bourgne (ed.), *Mondes marins du Moyen Âge: Actes du 30e colloque du CUER MA, 3, 4 et 5 mars 2005* (Aix-en-Provence: Université de Provence, 2006), pp. 259–71. On the *serra*, see G.C. Druce, "On the Legend of the Serra or Saw-Fish," *Proceedings of the Society of Antiquaries* 31 (1919), pp. 20–35; and Jacqueline Leclercq-Marx, "Drôles d'oiseaux. Le caladre, le phénix, la sirène, le griffon et la serre dans le Physiologus, les Bestiaires et les encyclopédies du XIIIe siècle. Mise en perspective," *Sénéfiance* 54 (2008), pp. 163–78, especially 172–3.

The Church of St Martin in Zillis, Switzerland, has a rectangular ceiling dating from the mid-twelfth century, consisting of 153 painted panels depicting scenes from the Bible and from the life of St Martin.[140] In each of the four corners there is an angel holding two trumpets, clearly inspired by St John's vision of "four angels standing on the four corners of the earth" (Revelation 7:1). Further, the water depicted along the four edges of the composition is certainly intended to represent the circumfluent ocean, so that the ceiling, though not a map in the modern sense of the word, is an image of the world as a stage for the playing out of Christian history.[141] The ocean surrounding the earth abounds with sea monsters, including sirens and many hybrid creatures such as a wolf-fish, horse-fish, elephant-fish, and so on. This is a gallery of monsters at the edge of the world quite as impressive, if not more so, than the row of monstrous races at the southern edge of Africa on the Ebstorf, Hereford, and other *mappaemundi* discussed above.

A *mappamundi* in a manuscript of circa 1180 in Munich (Bayerische Staatsbibliothek, CLM 7785, fol. 2v) presents a striking vision of the inhabited part of the earth surrounded by an enormous serpentine monster which is devouring its own tail (known as a *uroborus*, from the Greek for "tail-eater"), and beyond the uroborus in the ocean there are four hybrid sea monsters with human heads and piscine bodies and tails.[142] The monster encircling the earth is no doubt intended to represent the Biblical Leviathan.[143] In this case the edge of the earth *is* a sea monster: the monstrous holds the whole earth in its serpentine grasp (see Figure 18.5).

The so-called "Genoese" world map of 1457 (Florence, Biblioteca Nazionale Centrale, Portolano 1)[144] portrays four particularly impressive sea monsters in

---

140 There are several books about the ceiling of the Church of St Martin at Zillis; the best illustrated is Diether Rudloff, *Zillis: die romanische Bilderdecke der Kirche St. Martin* (Basel: P. Heman, 1989), also published under the title *Kosmische Bildwelt der Romanik: die Kirchendecke von Zillis* (Stuttgart: Urachhaus Johannes M. Mayer, 1989).

141 On the similarities between the Zillis ceiling and medieval *mappaemundi*, see Wolfgang Kemp, "Medieval Pictorial Systems," in Brendan Cassidy (ed.), *Iconography at the Crossroads: Papers from the Colloquium Sponsored by the Index of Christian Art, Princeton University, 23–24 March 1990* (Princeton, NJ: Index of Christian Art, Dept. of Art and Archaeology, Princeton University, 1993), pp. 121–37, especially 129–33; the essay is reprinted with some changes in Sylvie Deswarte-Rosa (ed.), *A travers l'image: Lecture iconographique et sens de l'oeuvre. Actes du Séminaire CNRS (G.D.R. 712) (Paris, 1991)* (Paris: Klincksieck, 1994), pp. 283–307, especially 292–6.

142 The *mappmamundi* in Munich is discussed in detail by Barbara Obrist, "Cosmological Iconography in Twelfth-Century Bavaria: The Earthly Zones and their Circling Serpent in Munich, Bayerische Staatsbibliothek, CLM 7785," *Studi medievali* 48/2 (2007), pp. 543–74, but she devotes almost no attention to the four hybrid sea monsters in the outer ocean.

143 See Obrist, "Cosmological Iconography," pp. 556–8.

144 The Genoese world map is reproduced in Cavallo, *Cristoforo Colombo e l'apertura degli spazi*, vol. 1, pp. 492–3. The legends are transcribed and translated by Edward L. Stevenson, *Genoese World Map, 1457* (New York: American Geographical Society and Hispanic Society of America, 1912), but with many errors; there is now a facsimile edition of the map, with a new transcription and translation of the legends by Angelo Cattaneo, in *Mappa mundi 1457* (Rome: Treccani, 2008).

Figure 18.5 *Mappamundi* (circa 1180), Munich, Bayerische Staatsbibliothek, CLM 7785, f. 2v (by permission of the Bayerische Staatsbibliothek).

the Indian Ocean. First there is a composite *porcus marinus*, or sea hog (a fish with a pig's head), off the eastern coast of Africa, and then a siren which is unaccompanied by a legend. Near the siren there is a creature which is a fish with a human head, behind which it has a large spiky red crest, and the legend explains that this *serra* attacks ships of the Indians, usually breaking them immediately, but its crest can get stuck in the ship's wood and as a result the fish, unable to escape, kills itself. The fourth monster, an impressive demon-like creature to be discussed below (see p. 432), is in the eastern Indian Ocean, in the region on the map most distant from Europe.

The Ocean—Islands

Islands, like distant parts of the world, are separated from the known and familiar, and for the same reasons as distant parts of the world, they are often settings for marvels and monsters.[145] The marvels and monsters on distant islands on medieval *mappaemundi* have already been studied to some extent,[146] but it is worth emphasizing here some of the monsters on islands in the Indian Ocean,[147] which is a well-known locus of marvels,[148] and in fact we have seen above how Marco Polo locates monsters on the Andaman Islands, Java Minor, and Madagascar, and also how Pierre Desceliers locates idolaters and cannibal cynocephali on Java and the Andaman Islands. The tradition of locating monsters on islands in the Indian Ocean is ancient, and in fact goes back to Ptolemy (second century CE). Ptolemy's eleventh map of Asia, which he describes in Book 7, chapters 2 and 3, contains a concentration of monstrous islands that has no equal elsewhere in his work.[149] The ten islands called the Maniolae are magnetic, and attract any boat with nails—and are inhabited by cannibals called Manioli.

---

145 See, for example, Francis Dubost, "Insularités imaginaires et récit médiéval: 'l'insularisation,'" in Jean-Claude Marimoutou and Jean-Michel Racault (eds), *L'insularité thématique et représentations: actes du colloque international de Saint-Denis de La Réunion, avril 1992* (Paris: L'Harmattan, 1995), pp. 47–57.

146 See Danielle Lecoq, "Les îles aux confins du monde," in Daniel Reig (ed.), *Ile des merveilles: mirage, miroir, mythe* (Paris: L'Harmattan, 1997), pp. 13–32.

147 On Islamic traditions of marvellous islands in the Indian Ocean, see A. Arioli, *Le isole mirabili. Periplo arabo medievale* (Turin: Einaudi, 1989), translated into Spanish as *Islario maravilloso: periplo arabe medieval*, trans. M. Rodriguez (Madrid: Ollero, 1992); María Mercedes Delgado Pérez, *Lo real y lo maravilloso en la ecúmene del siglo XIII. Las islas en el Ātār al-bilād de al-Qazwīnī* (Seville: El Alfar, 2003); and, for example, Shawkat M. Toorawa, "Wâq al-wâq: Fabulous, Fabular, Indian Ocean (?) Island(s)," *Emergences* 10/2 (2000), pp. 387–402.

148 Jacques Le Goff, "L'Occident médiéval et l'Océan indien: un horizon onirique," in *Mediterraneo e Oceano Indiano (Atti del VI Colloquio Internazionale di Storia Marittima)* (Florence: Olschki, 1970), pp. 243–63; translated into English by Arthur Goldhammer as "The Medieval West and the Indian Ocean: An Oneiric Horizon," in Le Goff, *Time, Work, and Culture in the Middle Ages* (Chicago: University of Chicago Press, 1980), pp. 189–200; reprinted in Anthony Pagden (ed.), *Facing Each Other: The World's Perception of Europe and Europe's Perception of the World* (Aldershot, UK, and Burlington, VT: Ashgate, 2000), vol. 1, pp. 1–19.

149 Although Ptolemy's *Geography* survives in many manuscripts, the maps in the medieval manuscripts of the work are probably not the result of a direct transmission from antiquity, but derive rather from reconstructions of the maps made by the Byzantine scholar Maximus Planudes around 1300. Planudes based his reconstructions on the co-ordinates in Ptolemy's text, but nonetheless we cannot be certain that his maps are precisely like Ptolemy's. For discussion, see J. Lennart Berggren and Alexander Jones, *Ptolemy's Geography: An Annotated Translation of the Theoretical Chapters* (Princeton: Princeton University Press, 2000), pp. 47–51. For our purposes here, however, it is enough that in his text Ptolemy places monstrous races on the islands of the Indian Ocean.

The Barussae, Sindae, and Sabadicae Islands are all inhabited by anthropophagi or cannibals, and further east are the Satyrorum Insulae, whose inhabitants have tails.[150] The rediscovery of Ptolemy's *Geography* in Europe in the early fifteenth century, and the acceptance of his work as an authority, entailed that these same islands appeared not only in fifteenth- and sixteenth-century manuscripts and editions of his *Geography*, but also in works dependent thereon, such as Martin Waldseemüller's world map of 1507.

An interesting episode in the Indian Ocean which combines the categories of island and monster is recounted in the *Alexander Romance*: Alexander sees an island in the ocean which he wishes to explore. His men suggest that they go first to see whether there is any danger:

> I was persuaded and allowed them to cross over. They disembarked, but after an hour the island dived into the depths, for it was a creature and not an island. We shouted out when the beast vanished and all the men perished, along with my best friend ... We remained eight days on the promontory, and on the seventh we saw the beast. It had tusks.[151]

The myth of the monster-island or whale-island neatly encapsulates the otherness of islands, and also appears in the *Physiologus*, an anonymous book of animals (but which also describes some stones and trees) written in Greek, probably in Alexandria in the third century CE, and later appears in the *Navigatio Sancti Brendani*, which describes the Atlantic wanderings of St Brendan of Ardfert and Clonfert (484–577).[152] Two maps show the Brendan version of the whale-island: Piri Reis's map of the Atlantic of 1513, and the map in Honorius Philoponus, *Nova typis transacta navigatio* (Linz: n.p., 1621), p. 12.

---

150 Alfred Stückelberger and Gerd Grasshoff's edition of Ptolemy's Greek text, *Klaudios Ptolemaios: Handbuch der Geographie* (Basel: Schwabe Basel, 2006) is the first in more than 150 years, and also includes a German translation; the English translation by Edward L. Stevenson, *Geography of Claudius Ptolemy* (New York: The New York Public Library, 1932); republished as *The Geography/Claudius Ptolemy* (Mineola, NY: Dover, 1991), is to be used with caution. For discussion of these islands with modern identification, see G.E. Gerini, *Researches on Ptolemy's Geography of Eastern Asia (Further India and Indo-Malay Archipelago)* (London: Royal Asiatic Society and Royal Geographical Society, 1909): on the Maniolae, pp. 420–4; on the Barussae, pp. 427–46; on the Sindae, pp. 449–58; on the Sabadicae, pp. 446–9; and on the islands of the satyrs, pp. 707–24.

151 See Richard Stoneman (trans.), *The Greek Alexander Romance* (New York: Penguin, 1991), p. 182.

152 See Cornelia C. Coulter, "The 'Great Fish' in Ancient and Medieval Story," *Transactions and Proceedings of the American Philological Association* 57 (1926), pp. 32–50; Dora Faraci, "*Navigatio Sancti Brendani* and its Relationship with *Physiologus*," *Romanobarbarica* 11 (1991), pp. 149–73; and Chet Van Duzer, "Floating Islands Seen at Sea: Myth and Reality," *Anuario do Centro de Estudos de História do Atlântico* 1 (2009), pp. 110–20.

The New World

The first-century Roman poet Seneca, in his *Medea* 375–379, predicted that one day new worlds would appear on the other side of the ocean: "There will come an age in the far-off years when Ocean shall unloose the bonds of things, when the whole broad earth shall be revealed, when Tethys shall disclose new worlds and Thule not be the limit of the lands."[153] The prophecy was often thought to have been fulfilled by the discovery of the New World.[154] The Americas, aside from being a distant new land across the ocean and beyond the edge of the previously known world, with its new landscapes, different vegetation, animals, peoples, and customs, naturally attracted many myths.[155] One issue raised by the New World had been discussed theoretically with regard to the antipodal southern continent, namely, whether the inhabitants of the New World were descended from Adam, and thus a true part of the human race.[156] Thus many thinkers considered all of the

---

153   Seneca, *Seneca's Tragedies*, with an English translation by Frank Justus Miller (London: William Heinemann, and Cambridge, MA: Harvard University Press, 1960), vol. 1, pp. 260–1.

154   See Diskin Clay, "Columbus' Senecan Prophecy," *American Journal of Philology* 113/4 (1992), pp. 617–20; James Romm, "New World and *novos orbes*: Seneca in the Renaissance Debate over Ancient Knowledge of the Americas," in W. Haase and M. Reinhold (eds), *The Classical Tradition and the Americas*, vol. 1, part I, *European Images of the Americas and the Classical Tradition* (Berlin and New York: De Gruyter, 1994), pp. 78–116; and Giuseppe Cardinali, "*Nec sit terris ultima Thule*: Echi della scoperta del Nuovo Mondo nei *Commentarii alla Medea* di Seneca," *Geographia Antiqua* 10–11 (2001–2002), pp. 155–62.

155   See, for example, Gordon Speck, *Myths and New World Explorations* (Fairfield, WA: Ye Galleon Press, 1979); Jean-Pierre Sánchez, "Myths and Legends in the Old World and European Expansionism on the American Continent," in W. Haase and M. Reinhold (eds), *The Classical Tradition and the Americas*, vol. 1, part I, *European Images of the Americas and the Classical Tradition* (Berlin and New York: Walter de Gruyter, 1994), pp. 189–240; Jean-Pierre Sánchez, *Mythes et légendes de la conquête de l'Amérique* (Rennes: Presses Universitaires de Rennes, 1996); and Neil L. Whitehead, "South America/Amazonia: The Forest of Marvels," in Peter Hulme and Tim Youngs (eds), *The Cambridge Companion to Travel Writing* (Cambridge, UK: Cambridge University Press, 2002), pp. 122–38.

156   On this question see Lewis Hanke, "Pope Paul III and the American Indians," *Harvard Theological Review* 30 (1937), pp. 65–102; Saul Jarcho, "Origin of the American Indian as Suggested by Fray Joseph de Acosta (1589)," *Isis* 50/4 (1959), pp. 430–8; Lee Eldridge Huddleston, *Origins of the American Indians: European Concepts, 1492–1729* (Austin: Published for the Institute of Latin American Studies by the University of Texas Press, 1967); Giuliano Gliozzi, *Adamo e il nuovo mondo: la nascità dell'antropologia come ideologia coloniale: dalle genealogie bibliche alle teorie razziali (1500–1700)* (Florence: La nuova Italia, 1977); Joan-Pau Rubiés, "Hugo Grotius's Dissertation on the Origin of the American Peoples and the Use of Comparative Methods," *Journal of the History of Ideas* 52/2 (1991), pp. 221–44; and Joachim Küpper, "The Traditional Cosmos and the New World," *MLN* 118/2 (2003), pp. 363–92.

inhabitants of the New World to be to some extent monstrous; the idea that they were something less than human was often used as a justification for enslaving or conquering them.[157]

Some creatures in the New World were so strange to European eyes that they were interpreted as monsters. For example, the opossum of South America was the first marsupial that Europeans had ever seen, and when Vicente Yáñez Pinzón described his discovery of the animal in 1499, he explicitly called it a monster, and described it as a composite, somewhat as one might describe a classical chimaera:

> *Between these Trees he saw a strange Monster, the foremost part resembling a Fox, the hinder a Monkey, the feet were like a Mans, with Ears like an Owl; under whose Belly hung a great Bag, in which it carry'd the Young, which they drop not, nor forsake till they can feed themselves.*[158]

The opossum was depicted as one of the marvels of the New World on Martin Waldseemüller's *Carta marina* of 1516 (Figure 18.6),[159] and on many maps influenced by his, such as the 1522 (Strasbourg), 1525 (Strasbourg), 1535 (Lyon), and 1541 (Vienna) editions of Ptolemy's *Geography*.[160]

But perhaps the most interesting aspect of the monstrous in the New World is the transfer thither of the Plinian monstrous races. One possible cause of this transfer was Christopher Columbus's belief that he was exploring Asia rather than a new territory, and in fact some maps showed the new lands joined to Asia well into the sixteenth century.[161] But there was certainly a more general force at work, namely

---

157 See particularly Patricia Seed, "'Are These Not Also Men?': The Indians' Humanity and Capacity for Spanish Civilisation," *Journal of Latin American Studies* 25/3 (1993), pp. 629–52.

158 See Charles R. Eastman, "Early Portrayals of the Opossum," *The American Naturalist* 49/586 (1915), pp. 585–94; and Susan Scott Parrish, "The Female Opossum and the Nature of the New World," *The William and Mary Quarterly* 54/3 (1997), pp. 475–514, especially 485.

159 Waldseemüller's legend about and image of the opossum are discussed in Gaetano Ferro, Luisa Faldini, Marica Milanesi, and Gianni Eugenio Viola, *Columbian Iconography* (Rome: Istituto poligrafico e Zecca dello Stato, Libreria dello Stato, 1996), pp. 546–7.

160 For more on strange animals in the New World, see, for example, Victoria Dickenson, *Drawn From Life: Science and Art in the Portrayal of the New World* (Toronto and Buffalo: University of Toronto Press, 1998); and Miguel de Asúa and Roger French, *A New World of Animals: Early Modern Europeans on the Creatures of Iberian America* (Aldershot, UK and Burlington, VT: Ashgate, 2005).

161 See George E. Nunn, "Did Columbus Believe that He Reached Asia on his Fourth Voyage?" in *The Geographical Conceptions of Columbus; A Critical Consideration of Four Problems* (New York: American Geographical Society, 1924), pp. 54–90; E.G.R. Taylor, "Idée fixe: The Mind of Christopher Columbus," *The Hispanic American Historical Review* 11 (1931), pp. 289–301; John H. Parry, "Asia-in-the-West," *Terrae Incognitae* 8 (1976), pp. 59–72; and Folker Reichert, "Columbus und Marco Polo—Asien in Amerika. Zur Literaturgeschichte der Entdeckungen," *Zeitschrift für historische Forschung* 15 (1988), pp. 1–63.

Figure 18.6   Martin Waldseemüller, *Carta marina* (1516), South America detail, cannibals, opossum (courtesy of the Library of Congress).

that European explorers and cartographers tended to interpret things they heard or saw in terms of familiar categories. On Pierre Desceliers's world map of 1550 there is an image of the pygmies fighting the cranes located in North America.[162] Their presence in North America is due to Jacques Cartier's report, in his account of his second voyage made in 1535–36, that Donnacona, "King of Canada," told him that there were "Picquemyans" or pygmies in Canada.[163] It is quite possible that Cartier himself interpreted something Donnacona said in familiar terms, as having to do with the pygmies, but Desceliers certainly did. To Cartier's hint about pygmies which supposedly came from a Native American king, Desceliers added a legend which derives from Albertus Magnus's discussion of the humanity of pygmies in *De animalibus* 7.1.6.62,[164] by way of the section titled "De Africa" in Sebastian Münster's *Typi cosmographici et declaratio et usus*, in the *Novus orbis regionum ac insularum ueteribus incognitarum*, edited by Simon Grynaeus and Johann Huttich

---

162 On the pygmies generally, see Pietro Janni, "I Pigmei dall'Antichità al Medioevo: le fortune di una favola," in Francesco Prontera (ed.), *Geografia e geografi nel mondo antico: guida storica e critica* (Rome: Editori Laterza, 1983), pp. 135–71—this is a reprint of Chapter 1 of Janni, *Etnografia e mito: la storia dei pigmei* (Rome: Edizioni dell'Ateneo & Bizzarri, 1978); and Bernd Roling, *Drachen und Sirenen: die Rationalisierung und Abwicklung der Mythologie an den europäischen Universitäten* (Leiden and Boston: Brill, 2010), pp. 481–549.

163 See Jacques Cartier, *Brief recit, & succincte narration, de la nauigation faicte es ysles de Canada, Hochelage & Saguenay & autres, auec particulieres meurs, langaige, & cerimonies des habitans d'icelles: fort delectable à veoir* (Paris: Roffet dict Faucheur & Anthoine le Clerc frères, 1545), fol. 40v; Henry P. Biggar, *The Voyages of Jacques Cartier* (Ottawa: F.A. Acland, 1924), pp. 121 and 221–2; and Jacques Cartier, *The Voyages of Jacques Cartier*, intro. Ramsay Cook (Toronto: University of Toronto Press, 1993), p. 82.

164 For discussion of the passage in Albertus Magnus, see Joseph Koch, "Sind die Pygmäen Menschen? Ein Kapitel aus der philosophischen Anthropologie der mittelalterlichen Scholastik," *Archiv für Geschichte der Philosophie* 40 (1931), pp. 195–213, and Friedman, *Monstrous Races*, pp. 190–6, especially 191.

(Basel: Johann Herwagen, 1532). Further, he illustrated this text with an image of the pygmies fighting the cranes, an image inspired by classical literature (the opening of Book 3 of the *Iliad*), though Cartier says not a word about cranes.

There are many other examples of the transfer of the Plinian races to the New World;[165] perhaps the most famous of these are the Amazons,[166] for whom the Amazon River was named. There were indigenous American legends about groups of aggressive women who lived apart from men, and these legends certainly contributed to the appearance, wide incidence, and persistence of the idea that there were Amazons in the New World.[167] Columbus, on his second voyage, in his diary entries for January 6 and 16, 1493, mentions an island called Matinio which was inhabited, according to the Native Americans with whom he spoke, only by women, and this was interpreted by Peter Martyr d'Anghiera as being an island of Amazons.[168] Later explorers sought Amazons in both Central and South America,

---

165 On the migration of the monstrous races to the New World, see Luis Weckmann, "The Middle Ages in the Conquest of America," *Speculum* 26/1 (1951), pp. 130–41, especially 132–3; Luigi de Anna, "Columbus and the *Mirabilia*," *Faravid* 16 (1992), pp. 133–40; Peter Mason, "Classical Ethnography and its Influence on the European Perception of the Peoples of the New World," in W. Haase and M. Reinhold (eds), *The Classical Tradition and the Americas*, vol. 1, part I, *European Images of the Americas and the Classical Tradition* (Berlin and New York: Walter de Gruyter, 1994), pp. 135–72; and Marion Steinicke, "Apokalyptische Heerscharen und Gottesknechte: Wundervölker des Ostens in abendländischer Tradition vom Untergang der Antike bis zur Entdeckung Amerikas," PhD dissertation, Freie Universität Berlin, Fachbereich Geschichts- und Kulturwissenschaften, 2002.

166 Georg Friederici, *Die Amazonen Amerikas* (Leipzig: Simmel & Co, 1910); Irving A. Leonard, "Conquerors and Amazons in Mexico," *The Hispanic American Historical Review* 24/4 (1944), pp. 561–79; Frank Lestringant, "De l'ubiquité des Amazones au siècle des grandes découvertes," in P.M. Martin and Ch.M. Ternes (eds), *La Mythologie, clef de lecture du monde classique: Hommage à R. Chevallier* (Tours: Centre de recherches A. Piganiol, 1986), pp. 297–319; Jean-Pierre Sánchez, *Le mythe des Amazones du Nouveau Monde* (Kassel: Edition Reichenberger, 1991); the excellent article by Kathleen M. March and Kristina M. Passman, "The Amazon Myth and Latin America," in W. Haase and M. Reinhold (eds), *The Classical Tradition and the Americas*, vol. 1, part I, *European Images of the Americas and the Classical Tradition* (Berlin and New York: Walter De Gruyter, 1994), pp. 285–338; and Alexandra M. Habershon, "Post-partum Nation: The Amazon Myth and Ideologies of Reproduction in the Conquest of the New World," PhD dissertation, Georgetown University, 2006. See also Persephone Braham's essay in this collection.

167 On indigenous legends of groups of women who live without men, see Alexander F. Chamberlain, "Recent Literature on the South American 'Amazons,'" *Journal of American Folklore* 24/91 (1911), pp. 16–20; and March and Passman, "The Amazon Myth and Latin America," pp. 325–32.

168 See Peter Martyr (Pietro Martire d'Anghiera), *De orbe novo, the Eight Decades of Peter Martyr d'Anghera*, trans. Francis Augustus MacNutt (New York: B. Franklin, 1970), 1.2.3, 7.8.1, and 7.10.3. For discussion, see Weckmann, "The Middle Ages in the Conquest of America," p. 132; A. Bognolo, "Geografia mitica e geografia moderna: le Amazonni nella scoperta dell'America," *Columbeis* 4 (1990), pp. 7–22; March and Passman, "The

particularly in Guyana, and Amazons are represented in South America on maps, beginning with Sebastian Cabot's world map of 1544[169] and on Sancho Gutierrez's map of 1551.[170]

Columbus also recorded native testimony of the existence of Cyclopes and cynocephali,[171] and Lorenz Fries's *Uslegung der Mercarthen oder Carta Marina* (Strasbourg: Johannes Grieninger, 1525), chapter 43, both recounts Columbus's tales of cynocephali and illustrates cannibalistic cynocephali. Cynocephali appear on the northern coast of South America on Piri Reis's map of 1513, which the cartographer claims is based on maps by Columbus, and also in Guillaume Le Testu's *Cosmographie universelle* of 1556, fol. 57r.

There are New World giants, particularly in Patagonia, which are those described by Antonio Pigafetta, the chronicler of Magellan's expedition (1519–22), and they had a long history of representation on maps, beginning with Sebastian Cabot's world map of 1544, and also appear on Pierre Desceliers's world map of 1550, for example.[172] Even the blemmyae, the "men whose heads / Do grow beneath their shoulders" (Shakespeare, *Othello* I, iii), managed to cross the Atlantic, and are located in Guyana by Sir Walter Raleigh in *The Discouerie of the Large, Rich, and Bevvtiful Empire of Guiana* (London: Robert Robinson, 1596), and subsequently appear on maps beginning with Jodocus Hondius's *Nieuwe caerte van het wonderbaer ende goudrijcke landt Guiana* (Amsterdam, 1598).[173]

The other and much more prominent human monster in the New World is the cannibal. Columbus spoke of cannibals during his first voyage to the New

Amazon Myth and Latin America," pp. 298–301. This island, with the legend *Matuina hanc solae mulieres inhabitant*, appears on Caspar Vopel's world map of 1558, the only surviving copy of which is in the Houghton Library at Harvard.

169 There are two surviving copies of Cabot's map, one in Paris at the Bibliothèque nationale de France (Rés. Ge AA 582), and the other at the Klassik Stiftung Weimar (Kt 020 - 31 S). The copy of Cabot's map in Paris is well reproduced in Nebenzahl, *Atlas of Columbus*, pp. 106–7. For further discussion of South American Amazons on maps, see Surekha Davies, "Representations of Amerindians on European Maps and the Construction of Ethnographic Knowledge, 1506–1624," PhD dissertation, Warburg Institute, School of Advanced Study, University of London, 2009, vol. 1, pp. 242–65.

170 Sancho Gutierrez's map is Vienna, Österreichische Nationalbibliothek, Map Department, K I 99.416; the best reproduction of the map is in Luisa Martín-Merás, *Cartografía marítima hispana: La imagen de América* (Barcelona and Madrid: Lunwerg, 1993), pp. 113–17; there is also an excellent reproduction in Ricardo Cerezo Martínez, *La cartografía náutica Española en los siglos XIV, XV y XVI* (Madrid: C.S.I.C., 1994), between pages 211 and 212.

171 Christopher Columbus, *A Synoptic Edition of the Log of Columbus's First Voyage*, ed. Francesca Lardicci (Turnhout: Brepols, 1999), p. 48.

172 See, for example, Jean-Paul Duviols, "The Patagonian 'Giants,'" in Colin McEwan, Luis A. Borrero, and Alfredo Prieto (eds), *Patagonia: Natural History, Prehistory and Ethnography at the Uttermost End of the Earth* (London: British Museum Press, 1997), pp. 127–39. For an account of representations of Patagonian giants on maps, see Davies, "Representations of Amerindians on European Maps," vol. 1, pp. 229–36.

173 See Davies, "Representations of Amerindians on European Maps,", vol. 1, pp. 244–58.

World,[174] and cannibalism was a constant theme of explorers' reports from the Caribbean and South America.[175] The first cartographic image of a cannibal on a map is on the anonymous "Kunstmann II" map of circa 1506, where a man roasts another on a spit in the western part of South America.[176] The bibliography on cannibalism in the Caribbean, Central America, and South America is vast, and the representations of these cannibals on maps (see, for example, Figure 18.6) have been studied in detail.[177] The truthfulness of European accounts of Caribbean and South American cannibalism has been disputed, particularly by William Arens and scholars inspired by his work.[178] Certainly, in addition to the reasons discussed

174 See Peter Hulme, "Columbus and the Cannibals: A Study of the Reports of Anthropophagy in the Journal of Christopher Columbus," *Ibero-Amerikanisches Archiv* 4 (1978), pp. 115–39; reprinted in Hulme, *Colonial Encounters: Europe and the Native Caribbean, 1492–1797* (London: Methuen, 1986), pp. 1–43; partial reprint in Bill Ashcroft, Gareth Griffiths, and Helen Tiffin (eds), *The Post-Colonial Studies Reader* (London and New York: Routledge, 1994), pp. 365–9; Yobenj Aucardo Chicangana-Bayona, "El nacimiento del Caníbal: un debate conceptual," *Historia Crítica* 36 (Bogotá, 2008), pp. 150–73; and Davies, "Representations of Amerindians on European Maps,", vol. 1, pp. 122–8; also see Nicolás Wey-Gómez, "Cannibalism as Defacement: Columbus's Account of the Fourth Voyage," *Journal of Hispanic Philology* 16/2 (1992), pp. 195–208.

175 See, for example, Samuel Roy Dunlap, "Among the Cannibals and Amazons: Early German Travel Literature on the New World," PhD dissertation, University of California, Berkeley, 1992; Philip P. Boucher, *Cannibal Encounters: Europeans and Island Caribs, 1492–1763* (Baltimore: The Johns Hopkins University Press, 1992); Yobenj Aucardo Chicangana-Bayona, "El festín antropofágico de los indios Tupinambá en los grabados de Theodoro de Bry, 1592," *Fronteras de la historia* 10 (2005), pp. 19–82.

176 The "Kunstmann II" map is Munich, Bayerische Staatsbibliothek, Cod. icon. 133; there is a tracing of the map in Konrad Kretschmer, *Die historischen Karten zur Entdeckung Amerikas: Atlas nach Konrad Kretschmer* (Frankfurt: Umschau, 1991), plate 8; it is reproduced at a large scale in black-and-white in Edward L. Stevenson, *Maps Illustrating Early Discovery and Exploration in America 1502–1530* (New Brunswick, NJ: n.p., 1903); and it is illustrated and discussed in Hans Wolff (ed.), *America: Early Maps of the New World* (Munich: Prestel-Verlag, 1992), pp. 134–6; and Ivan Kupčík, *Münchner Portolankarten: Kunstmann I–XIII und zehn weitere Portolankarten* [*Munich Portolan Charts: Kunstmann I–XIII and Ten Other Portolan Charts*] (Munich: Deutscher Kunstverlag, 2000), pp. 28–34.

177 See Cynthia A. Chambers, "Cannibalism in a Cultural Context: Cartographic Imagery and Iconography of the New World Indigenous Peoples During the Age of Discovery," PhD dissertation, The University of Texas at Arlington, 2006; and Davies, "Representations of Amerindians on European Maps,", vol. 1, pp. 122–82.

178 See William Arens, *The Man-Eating Myth: Anthropology and Anthropophagy* (New York: Oxford University Press, 1979); Erwin Frank, "'Sie fressen Menschen, wie ihr scheußliches Aussehen beweist ...': Kritische Überlegungen zu Zeugen und Quellen der Menschenfresserei," in Hans-Peter Duerr (ed.), *Authentizität und Betrug in der Ethnologie* (Frankfurt: Suhrkamp, 1987), pp. 199–224; Arens, "Rethinking Anthropophagy," in Francis Barker, Peter Hulme, and Margaret Iversen (eds), *Cannibalism and the Colonial World* (New York: Cambridge University Press, 1998), pp. 39–62; and Peter Hulme, "Introduction: The Cannibal Scene," in Barker, Hulme, and Iversen, *Cannibalism and the*

above for which monstrous races tend to be located in distant regions, the Europeans had a motive to invent or embellish stories of New World cannibalism, as such stories would help justify the conquest, enslavement, or conversion of the peoples of the New World.[179] Yet even Arens and, for example, his follower Gananath Obeyesekere concede that ritual cannibalism did occur in the New World,[180] and cogent arguments have been made supporting the existence of more extensive cannibalism.[181] Thus the real question, which still remains to be answered definitively, is not whether cannibalism existed in the New World, but whether or not it was always of a purely ritual nature.

Monsters Among Us

We have seen abundant evidence of the prevalence of monsters at the edges of the world, but although there is a tendency for monsters to be located in distant reaches of the earth, it is certainly also true that monsters are also found close to home—close to the teller of the story, the mythmaker, or the cartographer, or close to the perceived center of his or her world.[182] To mention two particularly striking

---

Colonial World (New York: Cambridge University Press, 1998), pp. 1–38.

179 Peter Hulme, "Caribs and Arawaks," in Hulme, Colonial Encounters: Europe and the Native Caribbean, 1492–1797 (London and New York: Methuen, 1986), pp. 44–87; and Mercedes López-Baralt, "La iconografía política de América: el mito fundacional en las imágenes católica, protestante y nativa," Nueva Revista de Filología Hispánica 32/2 (1983), pp. 448–61, especially 452.

180 Gananath Obeyesekere, Cannibal Talk: The Man-Eating Myth and Human Sacrifice in the South Seas (Berkeley: University of California Press, 2005), pp. 1–23.

181 See, for example, Donald W. Forsyth, "Three Cheers for Hans Staden: The Case for Brazilian Cannibalism," Ethnohistory 32/1 (1985), pp. 17–36; and Ercilio Vento Canosa, "Antropofagia en aborígenes de Cuba," Revista médica electrón 27/3 (2005), pp. 36–45. This article, though it addresses a different part of the New World, is also worth considering: Jennifer E. Marlar, "Biochemical Evidence of Cannibalism at a Prehistoric Puebloan Site in Southwestern Colorado," Nature 407/6800 (2000), pp. 74–8.

182 On the tendency to locate the center of the world near oneself, see the discussion of the "omphalos syndrome" in J.B. Harley, "Maps, Knowledge, and Power," in Denis Cosgrove and Stephen Daniels (eds), The Iconography of Landscape: Essays on the Symbolic Representation, Design and Use of Past Environments (Cambridge and New York: Cambridge University Press, 1988), pp. 277–312. In the Christian West, Jerusalem was generally held to be the center of the world: see Philip S. Alexander, "Jerusalem as the Omphalos of the World: On the History of a Geographical Concept," Judaism 46/182 (1997), pp. 147–59, reprinted in Lee I. Levine (ed.), Jerusalem: Its Sanctity and Centrality to Judaism, Christianity, and Islam (New York: Continuum, 1999), pp. 104–19; also see Rudolf Simek, "The Journey to the Centre of the Earth: Jerusalem as the Hub of the World," in Simek, Heaven and Earth in the Middle Ages: The Physical World Before Columbus, trans. Angela Hall (Woodbridge, UK: Boydell Press, 1996), pp. 73–81; Kerstin Hengevoss-Dürkop, "Jerusalem—Das Zentrum der Ebstorf-Karte," in Hartmut

examples, according to Genesis 3.1–6, Eden, the only land available to Adam and Eve, and therefore the center of their world, contained the serpent which tempted Eve to eat the fruit of the Tree of Knowledge, resulting in God's cursing of Adam and Eve and their expulsion from Eden. Indeed, in medieval art the serpent is often depicted as twined around the Tree, which was in the center of Eden (Genesis 2.9).[183] In ancient Greece, the omphalos at Delphi was held to be the center of the world, and was originally guarded by the serpent Python; Apollo killed Python and remade the oracle as his own.[184] And more generally, there are many Greek myths which involve monsters located in Greece: the Minotaur was believed to be in a labyrinth on Crete;[185] centaurs, composite men-horses, were said to inhabit Thessaly, Elis, and southern Laconia;[186] the Sphinx, though later accounts said it had come from Ethiopia, guarded the entrance to Thebes in Greece;[187] and satyrs were often depicted interacting with Greek women.

Further, although the geography of Odysseus's wanderings in Homer's *Odyssey* Books 9–12 is notoriously vague, and this vagueness has resulted in some modern interpretations which have Odysseus visiting locations as far away as the coast of South America, in antiquity the monstrous races of his wanderings—the cannibal Laestrygonians, Scylla and Charybdis, the Sirens, and the Cyclopes, among

---

Kugler and Eckhard Michael (eds), *Ein Weltbild vor Columbus: die Ebstorfer Weltkarte: Interdisziplinäres Colloquium 1988* (Weinheim: VCH, 1991), pp. 205–22; and Iain Macleod Higgins, "Defining the Earth's Center in a Medieval 'Multi-Text': Jerusalem in *The Book of John Mandeville*," in Sealy Gilles and Sylvia Tomasch (eds), *Text and Territory: Geographical Imagination in the European Middle Ages* (Philadelphia: University of Pennsylvania Press, 1998), pp. 29–53.

183   For discussion of the iconography of the serpent, see Henry Ansgar Kelly, "The Metamorphoses of the Eden Serpent During the Middle Ages and Renaissance," *Viator* 2 (1971), pp. 301–28.

184   See Hyginus, *Fabulae* 140; and Joseph Eddy Fontenrose, *Python: A Study of Delphic Myth and its Origins* (Berkeley: University of California Press, 1959). On Delphi as the center of the world in Greek thought, see Wilhelm Heinrich Roscher, "Omphalos, eine philologisch-archäologisch-volks-kundliche Abhandlung über die Vorstellungen der Griechen und anderer Völker vom 'Nabel der erde,'" in *Abhandlungen der philologisch-historischen Klasse der königlichen sächsischen Gesellschaft der Wissenschaften* 29/9 (1913), chapter 4.

185   See Ellen Young, "The Slaying of the Minotaur: Evidence in Art and Literature for the Development of the Myth, 700–400 B.C.," PhD dissertation, Bryn Mawr University, 1972; and Françoise Frontisi-Ducroux, "El minotauro, o la creación del híbrido," in Sappho Athanassopoulou (ed.), *Toros: imatge i culte a la Mediterrània antiga* [*Toros: imagen y culto en el Mediterráneo antiguo*] [*Bulls: Image and Cult in the Ancient Mediterranean*] (Barcelona: Museu d'Història de la Ciutat, 2002) pp. 222–35. Also see Euterpe Bazopoulou-Kyrkanidou, "Chimeric Creatures in Greek Mythology and Reflections in Science," *American Journal of Medical Genetics Part A* 100/1 (2001), pp. 66–80.

186   Alex Scobie, "The Origins of 'Centaurs,'" *Folklore* 89/2 (1978), pp. 142–7; and Elizabeth Atwood Lawrence, "The Centaur: Its History and Meaning in Human Culture," *Journal of Popular Culture* 27/4 (1994), pp. 57–68.

187   Lowell Edmunds, *The Sphinx in the Oedipus Legend* (Königstein im Taunus: Hain, 1981).

others—were usually located in the Mediterranean.[188] Indeed, Pliny 7.2.9 cites the Cyclopes and Laestrygonians as evidence that monsters occur even in the middle of the world. Odysseus's wanderings have been mapped many times, and the earliest of those maps, that by Abraham Ortelius in the *Parergon* in his *Theatrum Orbis Terrarum* beginning with editions of 1597, shows the places that Odysseus visited in the Mediterranean.[189]

In fact in almost every society there are monsters, especially folkloric monsters, but also moral monsters, which are close to home—goblins, beasts of the forest, lake monsters, schismatics, and so on,[190] and these examples raise the question of what it means to talk about a prevalence of monsters at the edges of the world. First I would suggest that implicit in most accounts of local monsters is the idea that the region near the teller is normal, and the knowledge from the experience of everyday life that monsters are not commonly encountered there. That is, in familiar areas, monsters are known to be a small percentage of the overall population, whereas at the edges of the world, we hear of little except monsters. In addition, many local monsters are ascribed to the distant past, when they were killed by "civilizing heroes,"[191] or are in one way or another elusive (they only appear under very restricted circumstances). Also, Jacqueline Leclercq-Marx has shown that monsters of the illiterate people of the Middle Ages (that is, folkloric monsters), tend to be close at hand, while the monsters of the educated tend to be located far away.[192]

---

188   On the Laestrygonians, see Thucydides 6.2 and Strabo 1.2.9; on Scylla and Charybdis, see Strabo 1.2.9 and 1.2.16; on the Sirens, see Strabo 1.2.12–13; and on the Cyclopes, see Thucydides 6.2 and Strabo 1.2.9. Unfortunately I have not been able to consult Alessandra Emilia Luisa Bonajuto, "Le antiche localizzazioni delle avventure di Odisseo narrate ai feaci," PhD dissertation, Università degli studi di Perugia, 1998.

189   Armin Wolf, "Mapping Homer's Odyssey," in George Tolias and Dimitris Loupis (eds), *Eastern Mediterranean Cartographies* (Athens: Institute for Neohellenic Research, 2004), pp. 309–34.

190   For discussion of other medieval examples of monsters in Europe, see Margriet Hoogvliet, "The Wonders of Europe: From the Middle Ages to the Sixteenth Century," in Ingrid Baumgärtner and Hartmut Kugler (eds), *Europa im Weltbild des Mittelalters, Kartographische Konzepte* (Berlin: Akademie Verlag, 2008), pp. 239–58. For discussion of alleged moral monsters within medieval Western human society, see Leon Neal McCrillis, "The Demonization of Minority Groups in Christian Society During the Central Middle Ages," PhD dissertation, University of California, Riverside, 1974; and Norman Cohn, *Europe's Inner Demons: The Demonization of Christians in Medieval Christendom* (Chicago: University of Chicago Press, 2000).

191   Hercules is the prototypical civilizing hero; for discussion of this aspect of him, see Diodorus Siculus 4.17.4–5; Léon Lacroix, "Heracles, heros voyageur et civilisateur," *Bulletin de la Classe des Lettres de l'Academie Royale de Belgique* 60 (1974), pp. 34–59; and Colette Jourdain-Annequin, *Héraclès aux portes du soir: mythe et histoire* (Besançon: Université de Besançon; Paris: Diffusion Les Belles Lettres, 1989), pp. 301–56.

192   Jacqueline Leclercq-Marx, "La localisation des peuples monstrueux dans la tradition savante et chez les *illitterati* (VIIe – XIIIe siècles). Une approche spatiale de l'Autre," *Studium Medievale: Revista de Cultura visual – Cultura escrita* 3 (2010), pp. 43–61.

Thus the density of monsters is indeed higher at the edges of the world, and it might also be argued that the monsters at the edges of the world are stranger, and more, well, monstrous than local monsters. But it is worth examining a few cases that run counter to this general tendency, cases where we find a greater density of monsters near the center of the world than at the edges, or where monsters which we would expect to see near the edges appear near the center.

One such example involves the sea monsters on the Hereford *mappamundi* of circa 1300. While the maker of the *mappamundi* placed many terrestrial monsters at the edges of the world, he locates almost no sea monsters in the circumfluent ocean, which he depicts as a narrow, de-emphasized band, but in the Mediterranean there is a prominent representation of a siren, as well as a swordfish (whose "sword" is curiously represented on its flank rather than projecting forward from its mouth), a sea serpent,[193] and also the monsters *Suilla* (Scylla) and *Caribdis* (Charybdis), which derive from Homer's *Odyssey*. Scylla is depicted as a head, and Charybdis as a coiled figure (intended to represent a whirlpool).[194] In fact, the only two sea monsters represented in the circumfluent ocean are two more or less canine heads spewing water, each labeled *Svilla*, that is, Scylla, which are evidently whirlpools, one to the north and one to the south of the British Isles—that is, near where the Hereford map was made.[195]

Another example is supplied by the *Carta marina* of the Swedish churchman and writer Olaus Magnus, which is a map of Northern Europe, Scandinavia, and Iceland published in 1539.[196] The map contains a remarkable number and variety of sea monsters in the north-eastern Atlantic, many of which are helpfully labeled. The map represents just the sort of density of exotic and dangerous monsters that we would expect to see at the ends of the earth in an area which, though not close

---

193 On the siren in the Mediterranean in the Hereford *mappamundi*, see Westrem, *The Hereford Map*, p. 404, no. 1028; on the fish and sea serpent, see ibid., p. 394, no. 999, p. 408, no. 1041, and p. 410, no. 1046.

194 On Scylla and Charybdis on the Hereford map, see Miller, *Mappaemundi*, vol. 4, p. 20; and Westrem, *The Hereford Map*, pp. 408–9, no. 1042, and pp. 416–17, no. 1063.

195 On the two heads labeled *Svilla* near the British Isles, see Westrem, *The Hereford Map*, pp. 220–1, no. 537, and pp. 324–5, no. 837; and also Mittman, *Maps and Monsters*, p. 23. The Hereford map does not include representations of other sea creatures in the circumfluent ocean, but does have an island in the south with the legend *Hic Sirenae abundant*. See Miller, *Mappaemundi*, vol. 4, p. 46; and Westrem, *The Hereford Map*, pp. 382–3, no. 972.

196 There are two surviving copies of Olaus Magnus's map, which are Munich, Bayerische Staatsbibliothek, 12 Mapp VII, and Uppsala University Library (no shelfmark). The map has been reproduced in facsimile, as Olaus Magnus, *Olai Magni Gothi Carta marina et descriptio septemtrionalium terrarum ac mirabilium rerum in eis contentarum* (Malmö: In officina J. Kroon, 1949), and as Olaus Magnus, *Die Wunder des Nordens*, ed. Elena Balzamo and Reinhard Kaiser (Frankfurt: Eichborn, 2006). For discussion of the map, see J. Granlund, "The *Carta Marina* of Olaus Magnus," *Imago Mundi* 8 (1951), pp. 35–43; and William B. Ginsberg, *Printed Maps of Scandinavia and the Arctic 1482–1601* (New York: Septentrionalium Press, 2006), pp. 39–44.

to the center of Europe, was for Olaus Magnus very close to his homeland—near the center of his world.

Finally, according to Christian eschatology, the end of time will change the geography of the monstrous: the end of Christian chronology will bring to the known and inhabited regions of the world monstrous peoples and creatures usually associated with the distant ends of the earth. With the advent of the Apocalypse, the monstrous peoples Gog and Magog, discussed above, will burst from the enclosure where Alexander the Great had confined them and overrun the earth. Locusts with human faces and teeth like those of lions (Revelation 9:7–10), the horsemen with heads of lions who breathe fire and have the tails of serpents (Revelation 9:15–19), the seven-headed beast from the sea (Revelation 13:1–4), the beast from the earth (Revelation 13:11–18), and, in medieval traditions, Behemoth and Leviathan, will plague mankind. Thus the end of time brings an end to standard monstrous geography.

The Transport of Monsters

There are monsters close to home, then, as well as at the distant edges of the world, but the higher frequency of monsters at the edges of the world can be confirmed by the tendency, which is traceable throughout history, to bring monsters from distant regions to more central areas as marvels and curiosities. The transport of elephants, tigers, lions, and so on to Rome for gladiatorial shows is well known,[197] but Romans were interested in more exotic creatures as well, and Roman emperors were said to have been presented with a phoenix, giants, hippocentaurs, satyrs, dwarves, and so on.[198] In 58 BCE, the curule aedile Scaurus put on extravagant public games which included hippopotami and crocodiles

---

197 On the variety of exotic animals put on show in Rome, see Pliny 8.64–71; also see J. Donald Hughes, "Europe as Consumer of Exotic Biodiversity: Greek and Roman Times," *Landscape Research* 28/1 (2003), pp. 21–31; George Jennison, *Animals for Show and Pleasure in Ancient Rome* (Philadelphia: University of Pennsylvania Press, 2005); and Marina Belozerskaya, *The Medici Giraffe: And Other Tales of Exotic Animals and Power* (Boston and London: Little, Brown, 2006). There is a fourth-century mosaic representation of hunting for exotic beasts in the distant reaches of the Roman Empire in the Corridor of the Great Hunt in the Villa Romana del Casale, Piazza Armerina, Sicily. For full illustration, see Andrea Carandini, Andreina Ricci, Mariette de Vos, and Maura Medri, *Filosofiana: The Villa of Piazza Armerina: The Image of a Roman Aristocrat at the Time of Constantine* (Palermo: S.F. Flaccovio, 1982).

198 See Mary Beagon, "Situating Nature's Wonders in Pliny's *Natural History*," in Ed Bispham and Greg Rowe (eds), *Vita vigilia est: Essays in Honour of Barbara Levick* (London: Institute of Classical Studies, 2007), pp. 19–40, especially 30–4 and 37–8; and Robert Garland, "The Roman Emperor in his Monstrous World," in Garland, *The Eye of the Beholder: Deformity and Disability in the Graeco-Roman World* (Ithaca, NY: Cornell University Press, 1995), pp. 45–58.

brought from Egypt, the first ever seen in Italy, and allegedly the bones of the sea monster which Perseus had slain in order to save Andromeda, which he had brought from Joppa (now part of Tel Aviv); the bones were "forty feet long, with ribs taller than an Indian elephant, and spines eighteen inches thick."[199] The ability to display the exotic wonders from distant realms symbolized the emperor's power over most of the known world.

Interest in exotic animals and monsters from faraway realms as symbols of power continued through the Middle Ages and the Renaissance.[200] A sea monster which was evidently transported from the Indian Ocean to Europe appears on a map: on the so-called Genoese world map of 1457, the imposing creature represented in the Indian Ocean with a humanoid head and upper body, large horns and ears, and wing-like red membranes joining its outstretched arms to its torso, was said to have been captured and mounted, and exhibited in Venice and elsewhere.[201] In addition, on Jodocus Hondius's wall map of Europe of 1595, there is an image of a walrus in the far north with a legend that explicitly calls the animal a monster (*monstrum*), and says that William Barentz caught one on his voyage of 1594 and brought it to Amsterdam.[202] Sadly, slaves from Africa and natives from the New World were counted among the exotica that were transported from distant regions to Europe,[203] and this particular taste for the exotic tore untold thousands of people from their homelands.

---

199 On this sea monster, see Pliny 9.5.11, Solinus 34.2.3, and Ammianus Marcellinus 22.15.24; Paul B. Harvey Jr, "The Death of Mythology: The Case of Joppa," *Journal of Early Christian Studies* 2/1 (1994), pp. 1–14, especially 11; and Adrienne Mayor, *The First Fossil Hunters: Paleontology in Greek and Roman Times* (Princeton: Princeton University Press, 2000), pp. 138–9.

200 In addition to Belozerskaya, *The Medici Giraffe*, see Lewis, *The Art of Matthew Paris*, pp. 212–16 (on the gift of an elephant from Louis IX to Henry III in 1264); Aleksander Pluskowski, "Narwhals or Unicorns? Exotic Animals as Material Culture in Medieval Europe," *European Journal of Archaeology* 7/3 (2004), pp. 291–313; Erik Ringmar, "Audience for a Giraffe: European Expansionism and the Quest for the Exotic," *Journal of World History* 17/4 (2006), pp. 353–97; and Christiane L. Joost-Gaugier, "Lorenzo the Magnificent and the Giraffe as a Symbol of Power," *Artibus et Historiae* 8/16 (1987), pp. 91–9.

201 For transcription and translation of the legend, see Stevenson, *Genoese World Map*, p. 25; for a more accurate version, see Cattaneo, *Mappa mundi 1457*, p. 180.

202 There are copies of Hondius's 1595 wall map of Europe in the Houghton Library at Harvard, *51-2509 PF, and in the Nürnberg Staatsarchiv, Reichsstadt Nürnberg, Karten und Pläne Nr. 1150; images of the former are available on the internet site of the Houghton Library.

203 See Núria Silleras-Fernández, "*Nigra sum sed formosa*: Black Slaves and Exotica in the Court of a Fourteenth-Century Aragonese Queen," *Medieval Encounters* 13/3 (2007), pp. 546–65; and Steven Mullaney, "Strange Things, Gross Terms, Curious Customs: The Rehearsal of Cultures in the Late Renaissance," *Representations* 3 (1983), pp. 40–67. Also see Merry Wiesner-Hanks, *The Marvelous Hairy Girls: The Gonzales Sisters and Their Worlds* (New Haven: Yale University Press, 2009).

Conclusion

During the Age of Exploration, even while the newly discovered lands attracted myths of monsters, more thorough investigation eventually conquered the purported strongholds of monsters and the monstrous races in distant realms. This transition is reflected in interesting ways. For example, in Jan van der Straet's *Venationes ferarum, auium, piscium*, first published in about 1566, and reprinted around 1630, plate 13 is an illustration of Ethiopia, a region in which sciapods were often represented using their outsized foot to shade themselves from the tropical sun—as they do on Martin Behaim's globe of 1492. And van der Straet's plate does include sciapods, but very small and in the distance, as if the artist was unsure of their existence.[204] The situation is similar on Caspar Vopel's world map of 1558 (*Nova et integra universalisque orbis totius ... descriptio*). The seas are full of exotic monsters, and on the land there are pygmies in North America and the opossum and a scene of cannibalism in South America, but off the eastern coast of South America there is a long legend about the anthropophagi or cannibals which had been reported to exist in South America. Vopel says that in fact the Spanish have searched the continent from the west, and the Portuguese from the east, and that no cannibals have been found—so that the words are contradicted by the images. Transitions are difficult and take time, but this legend was not a good sign for the survival of monsters on maps.

---

204 Also see, for example, Martín Fernández de Enciso's *Suma de geographía* (1519), who declares false the classical accounts of the Amazons, cynocephali, and blemmyae (fols 114, 151, and 156), while giving a detailed account of Alexander the Great's wonderstone. See Andrés Prieto, "Alexander and the Geographer's Eye: Allegories of Knowledge in Martín Fernández de Enciso's *Suma de Geographía* (1519)," *Hispanic Review* 78/2 (2010), pp. 169–88, especially 178. For citations of some earlier skeptics about the monstrous races, see Jana Valtrová, "Beyond the Horizons of Legends: Traditional Imagery and Direct Experience in Medieval Accounts of Asia," *Numen* 57/2 (2010), pp. 154–85.

Conclusion
Monsters and the Twenty-first Century: The Preternatural in an Age of Scientific Consensus

Peter J. Dendle

In 1977, Gary Gygax published the first edition of the *Monster Manual*, a compendium of demons, beasts, and mythical creatures for use with the fantasy role-playing game Advanced Dungeons and Dragons.[1] For millions of game enthusiasts, this was the first exposure to strange creatures such as the catoblepas, baluchitherium, and lammasu.[2] The encyclopedic approach to creatures real and imagined, familiar and strange, living and extinct, religious and scientific—as envisioned in this wide-selling product—has a flattening and demythologizing effect for creatures whose power ostensibly lies in their mystery: there are gorillas and kobolds, twelve types of dragon and 28 types of dinosaur, elves and djinnis, ghosts, goblins, trolls, tigers, and hydras, both pyro- and lernaean. In the space of a page or two, one passes from mammoths to manticores, medusas, and "men," then on to mermen, minotaurs, mules, and mummies. *Gods, Demi-Gods, and Heroes,* another Dungeons and Dragons game aid, lists statistics for Greek and Egyptian mythology (Zeus has an Armor Class of 4 and Ra has Psionic Ability Class 6); for Indian gods and monsters (Brahma has 300 hit points, while *rakshasa* demons can shapeshift and fight as 15th level fighters); and for a variety of world-historical pantheons and bestiaries.[3] The vocabulary of "hit points" and "Armor Class" are specific to the

---

1   Gary Gygax, *Monster Manual* (Lake Geneva, WI: TSR, 1977), p. 14.
2   The catoblepas is mentioned in Pliny the Elder, the baluchitherium is an extinct rhinoceros-like creature from the Eocine and Oligocene eras, and the lammasu is a Mesopotamian god with the body of a lion or bull and a human head.
3   Robert Kuntz and James Ward, *Gods, Demi-Gods, and Heroes* (Lake Geneva, WI: TSR, 1978). Interestingly, nowhere in these materials is the Judeo-Christian mythology demystified in the same way. Presumably the game makers and publishers were trying

game, but the general concept of quantifying the monstrous will be familiar to video game enthusiasts as well, who, for instance, note the "health bar" of their own persona and of the attacking monster diminish as each inflicts damage on the other. World folklore and mythology are collapsed into a practical reference manual for a leisure activity, implying some disposable income, and providing statistics for each creature and a brief description of behaviors and powers. There is little sense in any of this that the monster is frightening, unfamiliar, or uncanny. They are catalogued, controlled, and introduced into consciously created imaginative realms, for amusement.[4] In this sense, they are not so very unlike the giants of late medieval romance: props integrated for specific narrative purposes in a highly codified genre. Yet, when all the angels and demons, gods and ghosts of world religions and folklores are reduced to game pawns, where then is there room for a more authentic sense of the "monstrous" in the contemporary world?[5]

Monsters are commodity. Traditional monstrous forms have been rendered cute: "Barney," a purple dinosaur familiar to small children from a popular TV show, is a tamed caricature of the terrifying predator (or perhaps scavenger) *Tyrannosaurus rex*.[6] A person might own a Dirt Devil vacuum cleaner, a pair of Medusa footwear, a bottle of Kraken spiced rum, and a box full of cardboard cut-out ghosts and witch decorations to hang up in time for Halloween. Job seekers might frequent Monster. com, a popular resume-posting website, when not polishing their Rolls Royce Silver Ghost or their AMC Gremlin. In a largely secular and self-conscious age, the forms of monstrous past are infantilized, commoditized, and incorporated into the kitsch icons of leisure and entertainment. Monsters in horror movies trend according to the tastes of a given generation, with the vampire, the zombie, and the alien invader proving more enduring forms than, say, the goblin, the minotaur, or other less successful cinematic experiments, but no one mistakes any of these artistic representations as anything other than fiction (*almost* no one, in any event — more on this soon). The cultural and psychological space left open by the domestication of the pre-modern monstrous has given rise to new forms that are custom tailored for a global age of multiculturalism, media saturation, and unparalleled advances in information sharing.

Is the case so cut and dry, though, that people used to believe in monsters — especially in the pre-modern period — but that now we know better? Are "monsters"

---

to be sensitive to a Western, English language readership, in the promotion of a game that already came under suspicion in some communities as promoting the occult.

4   See Foster, this collection, pp. 133–50.

5   The "monstrous" could be studied by tracing the word "monster" itself, by delineating a set class of creatures which we agree count as "monsters" and then tracing the history of belief in those creatures, or by identifying set traits that define a "monster" contextually and then applying that definition to each historical society studied. The chapters in this collection, to a variety of degrees, approach the topic with all three of these methods.

6   See Maja Brzozowska-Brywczyńska, "Monstrous/Cute: Notes on the Ambivalent Nature of Cuteness," in Niall Scott (ed.), *Monsters and the Monstrous: Myths and Metaphors of Enduring Evil* (Amsterdam and New York: Rodopi, 2007), pp. 213–28.

the definitive provenance of the Other, and belief in them a hallmark of quaintness, superstition, or ignorance? The question is partially semantic and partially empirical, but it is anything but cut and dry. Many people, though not all, believed in monsters in the pre-modern world; many, though not all, believe in them today. Certainly, if society is losing most of its traditional monsters, some subcultures are not letting go of them without a fight. Semi-reductivist attempts to explain vampires or werewolves as people suffering from physiological conditions such as porphyria or hypertrichosis—people who were misunderstood by their own communities in earlier, more superstitious periods—do scant justice to the broader folkloric and literary accounts of the monsters in question. Harvard ethnobotanist Wade Davis, famous for *The Serpent and the Rainbow* (1985), made his career arguing that the Haitian zombie is a literally possible phenomenon, if one allows for the catatonia-inducing and brain-washing effects of a unique concoction of herbs and ingredients (especially tetrodotoxin, or puffer-fish poison).[7] All of these attempts to render the folkloric "rational" by providing scientific explanations have met with formidable criticism, but the more interesting point for our purposes is that for the modern secular world, there is still an apparent need for monsters to be "real." People devote significant attention to "saving" the deities of the monster pantheon, as it were, by euhemerizing them.

Contemporary monster hunters ("cryptozoology" is the term that has caught on popularly for the study of unconfirmed species) keep alive a sense of wonder in a world that has been very thoroughly charted, mapped, and tracked, and that is largely available for close scrutiny on Google Earth and satellite imaging.[8] There is perhaps moxie to be admired in amateur investigators' search expeditions for Bigfoot, the Loch Ness monster, and other sizeable species in well-trammeled territory, though on the whole the devotion of substantial resources for this pursuit betrays a lack of awareness of the basis for scholarly consensus (largely ignoring, for instance, the evidence of evolutionary biology and the fossil record). Indeed, widespread interest in the paranormal itself—including cryptozoology—exhibits resistance against the very notion of scholarly consensus. In a world where the mysteries of life and of the planet are being largely uncovered to a satisfying degree, the need for monsters is acute. What does or does not count as a "monster," however, reveals fault lines of religious difference, cultural and ideological presuppositions, and inherited folklore. This has been a recurring theme throughout the chapters of this collection. It is no less true today than it was in classical antiquity, the Middle Ages, or the early modern period, though

---

7   Wade Davis, *The Serpent and the Rainbow: A Harvard Scientist's Astonishing Journey into the Secret Societies of Haitian Voodoo, Zombis, and Magic* (New York: Touchstone, 1985), and Davis, *Passage of Darkness: The Ethnobiology of the Haitian Zombie* (Chapel Hill, NC: University of North Carolina Press, 1988).

8   "Cryptozoology" appears, perhaps a little tongue-in-cheek, in the name of the academic group MEARCSTAPA founded by Asa Mittman: Monsters: the Experimental Association for the Research of Cryptozoology through Scholarly Theory And Practical Application.

its shape and context are very different now in relatively educated, affluent communities of the twenty-first century.

A brief meditation on the word "monster" itself in contemporary usage can serve as a springboard to understanding its place in the contemporary world. Many of the scholars in this book have appealed to the "monster" as something that is large, imperfectly understood, and potentially threatening; this range of connotations recurs intermittently throughout references to the *monstrum* (portent) in the Western tradition. For most people speaking modern European languages, however, a "monster" (and its cognates) implies additionally a being that is fictional by definition.[9] In this sense our modern word is not the same as *monstrum*, and has no precise cognates in Greek or Latin. Monsters, as children are often proud to proclaim, are not real. Jacqueline D. Woolley summarizes:

> At some point, when the child has encountered and correctly classified enough instances, generalizations may develop and enable a stronger feeling of certainty that monsters and ghosts in general are not real ... Although speculative, it may be that it is important to children at a certain age to be very clear that monsters, by definition, are not real.[10]

This often happens before age eight or so, according to Liat Sayfan and Kristin Hansen Lagattuta:

> Between the ages of 4 and 7 years, children increasingly offered explanations that focused on the reality status of the stimulus (e.g., "There are no witches"), and all children provided this type of explanation significantly more often in stories about imaginary compared to real creatures ... These data reveal that with increasing age children evidence greater awareness of the ontological status of a stimulus.[11]

The anxieties of childhood gradually give way to those of adolescence and adulthood, a process in which the term "monster" serves as a dynamic yet vital border line. Consider a thought experiment: even if a colossal, hitherto unknown species suddenly rose from the oceans and began destroying coastal cities, it would only be called a "monster"—it could only have the ineffable, primordial

---

9 See Mittman, "Introduction: The Impact of Monsters and Monster Studies" in this collection, pp. 1–14, especially pp. 5–6. As Mittman astutely observes: "Whether we believe or disbelieve the existence of a phenomenon is not what grants it social and cultural force."

10 Jacqueline D. Woolley, "Thinking About Fantasy: Are Children Fundamentally Different Thinkers and Believers from Adults?" in Margaret E. Hertzig and Ellen A. Farber (eds), *Annual Progress in Child Psychiatry and Child Development* (Philadelphia: Brunner/Mazel, 1999): p. 80.

11 Liat Sayfan and Kristin Hansen Lagattuta, "Scaring the Monster Away: What Children Know about Managing Fears of Real and Imaginary Creatures," *Child Development* 80 (2009), pp. 1756–74, at 1769.

mystery of a monster—during the crisis and its immediate aftermath. Over time, once it was categorized, dissected, and integrated into contemporary taxonomies, it would simply be regarded as an animal. We would still tell our children that monsters don't exist.

But is this entirely true? For one thing, many of our monster movies do not include fictional creatures at all. The giant, irradiated insects of 1950s cinema are familiar (and frightening) enough, but often monster movies present an animal fairly similar to its natural state. Only a slight change in aggressiveness, habits, diet, numbers, or locale is enough to bring out the inherent strangeness of creatures we usually consider under control: ants (*It Happened at Lakewood Manor*, 1977); bees (*The Swarm*, 1978); spiders (*Arachnophobia*, 1990); cockroaches (*Bug*, 1975); ticks (*Infested*, 1993); snakes (*Sssssss*, 1973); rats (*Willard*, 1971, and remade in 2003); sharks (*Jaws*, 1975); crocodiles (*Lake Placid*, 1999); apes (*The Ape*, 1940); and even rabbits (*Night of the Lepus*, 1972). Some titles require nothing more than the animal's name itself to bring out our uneasy relationship with the natural world: *Frogs*, 1972; *Piranha*, 1978; *Orca*, 1977; *Scorpion*, 1989; and of course *The Birds*, 1963. Animals easily become "monsters" when they are of unusual size or savageness. The media, for instance, regularly calls unusually large sharks "monster sharks," even when they have not harmed anyone.[12] On the one hand, use of the word "monster" in these contexts is clearly figurative, deliberately intended to create a rhetorical sense of excitement or urgency—as when reporting on a "monster wave" or "monster storm." It is larger and more threatening than usual. On the other hand, it is still possible to experience surges of fear and wonder, faced with new species or encountering animals in a new environment. The first time that someone is made aware—perhaps in a documentary or online—of giant marine isopods of the cold Atlantic deeps, of the coconut crab of the Pacific Islands, or of the strange deep-sea creatures such as anglerfish and gulper eels, there is an immediate, visceral awareness of the monstrous. But just the first time, usually: then, over time, the creature can become normalized and integrated with the existing landscape of animals. Probably nothing comes closer to a core notion of the "monstrous" as an intimate and almost numinous sense of helplessness before the elemental and uncaring dangers of a savage world, such as unexpected animal attacks or instances of psychopathic violence. These are phenomenologically real.[13] The monstrous is known, as Asa Mittman writes, through its *impact*.[14] The

---

12   *The Daily Telegraph* put the word "monster" in quotation marks when running the headline "Tourists in Australia warned of 6m 'monster' shark," referring to the putative attacker of a three-meter shark who had been found with large bite marks, while in a similar headline a few weeks earlier *The Sydney Morning Herald*, referring to the sighting of a similarly large shark, also used the "monster" but did not put it in quotation marks (*The Telegraph*: November 28, 2010, <http://www.telegraph.co.uk/news/worldnews/australiaandthepacific/australia/6442974/Tourists-in-Australia-warned-of-6m-monster-shark.html>; *The Sydney Morning Herald*: October 24, 2010, <http://www.smh.com.au/national/swimmers-warned-of-monster-shark-20101024-16z0o.html>).

13   The word "monster" is a recurring trope in the first-hand accounts of shark attacks posted on jawshark.com, for instance.

14   See Mittman, "Introduction," p. 6.

monstrous can thus be seen as experience: an immediate relationship with the primordial, a wrenching from normal daylight consciousness and safety into a pre-rational awareness of vulnerability and mortality.

In more reflective moments, we accept that over-size sharks, bears, and crocodiles are not properly monsters—we may use the term loosely in headlines and casual conversation, but if pressed further, most people would readily concede that it is only a phrase. The existence of these creatures is fully confirmed and their traits thoroughly documented. But this insistence that monsters are things that by definition do not *really* exist is a distinctly modern usage of the term. The Plinian races, arguably monstrous by many criteria and discussed in many of the chapters in this collection, were rarely thought by the literary communities of the classical, medieval, and early modern world to be fictitious or metaphorical.[15] The births considered "monstrous" in the sixteenth and seventeenth centuries were demonstrably real. Throughout the periods covered in this collection, there were voices both credulous and skeptical concerning the ontological status of creatures such as ghosts, giants, and dragons, and concerning the meaning of anomalous specimens or monstrous births. It is somewhat arbitrary that we in the modern world catalog retrospectively the monsters of other time periods and non-Western cultures, when the term in its modern sense has a semantic range unique to our own culture. The meaning of the word "monster" is not stable: by definition, it remains at the boundary of epistemological comfort, even as science progresses and taxonomies continue to shift and evolve.

The front lines of epistemological slippage have shifted since earlier periods, but creatures still lurk among the crevices of those shifting boundaries. There are active, dynamic questions in society about what other sentient, liminal beings exist, beings potentially more powerful than we are and whose motives are not well understood.[16] Beyond known species or entities, the uncanny, unknown, and uncontrolled monsters of the imagination remain a very real part of many people's worldviews. Folklorists and other cultural interpreters of the future will have every right, retrospectively, to say that in the twentieth and twenty-first centuries many people still quaintly believed in "monsters," such as Bigfoot, lake monsters, aliens, and ghosts. Attempts to dismiss these beliefs as the eccentricities of the superstitious, the uneducated, or the provincial are not uniformly supported by data, and do not do justice to the scope and variety of beliefs in context.

Polls from the 1990s and 2000s have loosely tracked trends in popular belief for paranormal phenomena that occupy narrative and psychological functions once filled, arguably, by the monstrous (see Table C.1). Due to the limited nature of such polls,

---

15   See Peter Dendle, "Cryptozoology in the Medieval and Modern Worlds," *Folklore* 117 (2006), pp. 190–206, at 192–3.

16   Proponents of ghosts, alien visitors, lake monsters, or Bigfoot will often object to their subject being called a "monster," not unlike marine biologists who study sharks, but there is a broader cultural awareness that those creatures are all monsters in a general sense. A Google Image search of "monster" will soon turn up images of all of these, in caricatured clip art, Halloween costumes, and a variety of other contexts.

Table C.1   Cryptid Polls

	Gallup 1996[a]	Gallup 2001[b]	Gallup 2005[c]	CBS News 2010[d]
UFOs have visited the earth	45%	33%	24%	30%
Ghosts	—	38%	—	33%
Haunted Houses	—	42%	37%	—
Witches	—	26%	21%	—

Notes: [a] Frank Newport, "What if Government Really Listened to the People?" (October 15, 1997, reporting results of a 1996 survey; <http://www.gallup.com/poll/4594/What-Government-Really-Listened-People.aspx>). The results of a CNN/Time survey of 1,024 American adults, published June 15, 1997, seem anomalously high in their results: 64 percent are reported as believing that aliens have contacted humans, and 50 percent are reported as believing that aliens have abducted humans (<http://www.cnn.com/US/9706/15/ufo.poll/>).

[b] Frank Newport and Maura Strausberg, "Americans' Belief in Psychic and Paranormal Phenomena is Up Over Last Decade" (June 8, 2001, from 1,012 Americans polled; <http://www.gallup.com/poll/4483/Americans-Belief-Psychic-Paranormal-Phenomena-Over-Last-Decade.aspx>). The authors note that belief in extraterrestrials is up 6 percent, in ghosts is up 13 percent, and in witches is up 12 percent since a similar poll in 1990.

[c] Linda Lyons, "Paranormal Beliefs Come (Super)Naturally to Some" (November 1, 2005, from 1,002 American respondents; <http://www.gallup.com/poll/19558/Paranormal-Beliefs-Come-SuperNaturally-Some.aspx>). Women in this poll—just as in the 2001 survey—showed a greater propensity to believe in haunted houses, while men showed a higher tendency to believe in extraterrestrial contact.

[d] "The 60 Minutes/Vanity Fair Poll" (October 2010, from 847 adult respondents; <http://www.vanityfair.com/magazine/2010/10/60-minutes-poll-201010>).

and to the natural fluctuations that can be expected, one should not place too much stock in micro-trends of growth or decline. On the whole, though, it is fair to say that, for instance, at least a quarter to a third of respondents believe that extraterrestrials have visited the earth. Numbers are harder to report for more traditionally monstrous forms (that is, animals such as Bigfoot or the Loch Ness monster), because systematic polling has not been conducted as often for those phenomena, but when they are included in polls, they nonetheless maintain a notable presence. In the CBS News poll in Table C.1, for instance, around 60 people out of the 847 polled listed each of vampires, the Loch Ness monster, and Bigfoot as their first choice, in answering the question "which one of the following do you think is the most likely to actually exist?"[17] (The position of scientific consensus—"None of the Above"—came in last in this poll, trailing behind every other option.) A study conducted by Gallup in conjunction with the Institute for Studies of Religion at Baylor University in 2005 did address cryptids more directly: when asked, "Creatures such as Bigfoot and the Loch Ness monster will one day be discovered by science," responses were as follows: Strongly Agree/Agree—17%, Undecided—27%, and Strongly Disagree/Disagree—56%.[18] Even for creatures regularly dismissed as almost cartoonish in the normal course of civic, journalistic, and intellectual discourse, then, uncertainty or belief are self-reported in almost half the population.

The point is not to disparage popular beliefs; these are especially understandable in a time when The History Channel regularly runs shows on Area 51 (Roswell), ancient astronauts, and UFO encounters; when Syfy Channel sponsors a hit show, *Destination Truth*, that purports to track down cryptids in their natural habitats; when shows such as *Ghost Hunters* and *Most Haunted* enjoy enduring popularity; and when mainstream news sources report eagerly on alleged Bigfoot captures, even when they are quite obviously egregious hoaxes.[19] Alongside this implied imprimatur of major media sources, the internet provides compelling eye-witness testimonies, user-generated hubs for centralized reporting of sightings or encounters, readily available footage of all sorts, and ready-made communities of self-selected amateur enthusiasts.[20] These creatures retain some currency, then, not only despite the age of information, but because of it. The belief in such creatures is rightfully rejected by the scientific community, but just as interesting are the cultural meanings attached to such beliefs within the broader population.

Demographic differences in belief cohorts can be instructive. In the Baylor University surveys, men and women ranked almost equally for "monster" beliefs (18 percent versus 20 percent).[21] In the CBS poll, however, men ranked above

---

17   Results: ghosts 33%, UFOs 30%, vampires 7%, Loch Ness monster 7%, Big Foot 7%, and None of the Above 5%.

18   Rodney Stark, *What Americans Really Believe: New Findings from the Baylor Surveys of Religion* (Waco, TX: Baylor University Press, 2008), p. 127. The poll in question collected data from 1,721 American adults.

19   A case in 2008 involving a Bigfoot allegedly frozen solid in a freezer by Rick Dyer and Matthew Whitton was reported for several days by CNN, ABC, Fox News, and the BBC, in "real time," while the freezer was sold and then the thawing of the rubber creature inside commenced.

20   To name but a few, there is "Chapacabra Sightings" (*chupacabrasightings.com*), Bigfoot Field Researchers Organization (*bfro.net*), "Bigfoot Sightings" (*bigfootsightings.com*), Cyptozoology.com, Cryptomundo (*cryptomundo.com*), and "Mothman Sightings" (hosted by *mothmanmuseum.com*). Bigfoot especially lends itself to regional groups, such as the Pennsylvania Bigfoot Society (*pabigfootsociety.com*), the Texas Bigfoot Research Conservancy (*texasbigfoot.org*), and Florida Bigfoot Researchers (*floridabigfoot.com*).

21   Christopher D. Bader, F. Carson Mencken, and Joseph D. Baker, *Paranormal America: Ghost Encounters, UFO Sightings, Bigfoot Hunts, and Other Curiosities in Religion and Culture* (New York and London: New York University Press, 2010), p. 56. The surveys appear to show that both African-Americans and Other Race categories are more likely to believe

women significantly in picking Bigfoot or the Loch Ness monster as the most likely to exist (10 percent versus 6 percent, and 11 percent versus 4 percent respectively). In the Baylor surveys, the greatest predictive factors for whether or not someone is "likely to be interested in" cryptozoology (as opposed to "believing in" it) were as follows, in order: sex (male), income (lower), church attendance (lower), and age (younger). Bader, Mencken, and Baker summarize the findings of the Baylor surveys on gender and the paranormal thus: "If there is a trend here, it appears that men are somewhat more interested in 'concrete' paranormal subjects. In theory at least, it *would* be possible to capture, kill, or find concrete physical evidence for the existence of Bigfoot, lake monsters, or extraterrestrials—and men seem to enjoy the hunt. Women have greater interest in more ephemeral topics related to personal destiny and self-improvement."[22] These studies are useful in reminding us that society is a tapestry of sub-cultures, each with hallmarks of identity, heritage, and internally shared goals. Within the Bigfoot community, for instance, there are "shoot" versus "don't shoot" camps, as in the UFO community there are those who view the visitors as potentially threatening versus those who view them as benevolent mentors. In both of those cases, the alleged creatures are used to project social anxieties over our place in the natural world, either within our own ecosystem or within a solar system and galaxy that seem increasingly small. There are online communities of lycanthropes and vampires, which sometimes involve an elusive blend of role-play and sincerity that can be uncomfortable to the outside observer who tries to pin down what is going on too precisely. Belief and identity processes themselves are in constant flux; this is the provenance of monsters.

Joseph D. Andriano explores the impact of Darwinism on representations of fantastic beasts in literature and film, arguing that, since the nineteenth century, such representations track our anxiety over losing a privileged position of dominance over other animal species.[23] David Daegling portrays modern fascination with Bigfoot as a myth of the "Ecomessiah." Bigfoot signifies "wilderness and the power of nature," recapturing a sense of awe and humility, and serving as a parable for a wilderness rapidly disappearing.[24] Daegling surmises: "It is no accident that Bigfoot is perceived as existing between the realms of human and animal: How many Bigfoot encounters have ended when the hunter declared that he could not

---

in cryptids (White 18%, Black 27%, Other 21%), but the authors note: "the difference between whites and nonwhites on levels of belief in crypto-monsters disappears when we consider other factors such as education, income, and gender" (p. 58).

22 Bader, Mencken, and Baker, *Paranormal America*, p. 108.

23 He writes: "We need this monster to define ourselves, because we have always known that the Mark of the Beast is our own signature. Since Darwin and Mendel, however, the Mark has changed from a supernatural to a natural phenomenon: no god, no Circe or Comus, but a scientist or mutation—indeed the process of evolution itself—now creates the Beast" (Joseph D. Andriano, *Immortal Monster: The Mythological Evolution of the Fantastic Beast in Modern Fiction and Film* [Westport, CT and London: Greenwood Press, 1999], p. xi).

24 David J. Daegling, *Bigfoot Exposed: An Anthropologist Examines America's Enduring Legend* (Walnut Creek, CA: AltaMira Press, 2004), p. 249.

shoot the creature because it was simply too human? ... If we destroy Bigfoot, we kill part of ourselves."[25] Bigfoot encounters, furthermore, follow more detailed patterns than simply representing a perceived run-in with a hitherto unconfirmed great ape or hominid. There is greater significance: it is not just that Bigfoot is observed, but that he observes us. As with all monsters, Bigfoot embodies an archetype of humanity being seen from the outside, judged, evaluated, and used on terms outside of our own choosing:

> *A typical encounter in the heart of Bigfoot country is a chance occurrence, often on the edge of the wilderness but not necessarily deep within it. Bigfoot just stands there, contemplating the person, and after a time, turns and walks off. Seldom is there a violent display, no monstrous roars are brought forth, and the fear that the eyewitness feels is born of awe rather than any tangible threat behavior on the part of the Sasquatch ... Bigfoot seems altogether indifferent to the human presence. It is aware that someone is there, but its curiosity is muted much of the time.*[26]

In a world where no natural habitats remain undisturbed by human expansion and activity, there is something comforting in the idea that such a large species may remain intact, and something humbling in the idea that the human race is of such little concern to it. The apprehension and fear of unknown species implicit in the *Liber monstrorum* of the Middle Ages, for instance, is here reversed: the *de facto* position of cryptozoology enthusiasts is one of human incursion on a shrinking ecosystem, and of human disruption of natural processes perceived as intrinsically beautiful, harmonious, and in balance.[27]

Beyond the creatures who are thought by some to live, breathe, and die in the same way that other animals do, with more or less familiar physiognomies, a range of other entities can fairly be brought to the discussion as modern "monsters." Belief in alien visitors from other worlds via spacecrafts is a hallmark of the twentieth- and twenty-first centuries, especially in the post-war period: it is a signature folklore of the technological age. Aliens serve, in part, the same role that Bigfoot and ghosts and angels and gods do: to surround us and accompany us, and to keep us from the desperate conclusion that we are alone in the universe. The discourse surrounding alien visitation, moreover, is conspicuously intertwined with government conspiracy. The belief that alien visitations are frequent and have been ongoing for decades necessarily requires that central elements of the government, the military, and private industry sustain a conspiracy of secrecy, which itself raises questions about government motives.[28] It is not simply that belief in aliens requires a subsequent mistrust of government; rather, inherent mistrust for civil and military power structures can itself fuel questioning about why secrecy

---

25   Ibid., p. 250.
26   Ibid., p. 251.
27   Dendle, "Cryptozoology," p. 200.
28   See Jeffrey Weinstock, this collection.

exists and what it is that authorities are hiding. A feedback loop can be created within subcultures, just as feedback loops exist between media portrayals of the paranormal and media-consumer belief in the paranormal. As with many other subcultures associated with the paranormal, in this case the monster can become a vehicle for active resistance to authorities perceived as sole proprietors and disseminators of human knowledge. In a secular age in which scientific consensus drives the public discourse on what is and is not real, paranormal enthusiasts often take pride in considering themselves privy to a deeper truth, one unknown to the publicly hailed experts. Daegling writes: "Mistrust of institutional authority and perceptions of an elitist scientific community are persistent features of the American cultural landscape. It makes sense in a society that values the individualist."[29] Beyond this, speculation about other, more advanced races and about new eras of discovery and contact can lend a sense of trajectory and teleology to human history. Steven Spielberg's *Close Encounters of the Third Kind* (1977) presented alien visitation as ushering in a coming era of connection and harmony among sentient beings, a sentiment echoed in popular literature and online speculation.[30] As with all myths, these accounts give the world shape: they help frame it in time and space, and instill a sense of progress and direction.

The current discussion could be expanded organically, for instance, to an interpretation of the cultural significance of belief in ghosts, demons, or angels. Perhaps the semantic instability itself, however, is the most crucial point to be made here: whether or not one counts those as "monsters" will depend on the individual,

---

29   Daegling, *Bigfoot Exposed*, p. 256. See also Dendle: "The ubiquitous popular belief in ghosts, psychic ability, alien encounters, communication with the dead, and astrology, to name but a sampling of the 'paranormal,' documents a resistance to the canons of belief doled out by the orthodox structures of contemporary academic science. In an age when evolutionary scientists have all but robbed Judeo-Christians of their account of creation, genetic engineering appears to threaten the sanctity and individuality of human life, and medical authorities continuously make the general populace feel guilty about those very hallmarks of an affluent leisure-society that it apparently treasures most (high-fat and high-sugar diet, recreational use of tobacco, alcohol, and pharmaceuticals, and inactivity), it is natural that an undercurrent of resistance to beliefs imposed from above by an academic elite should flourish. In such an atmosphere, the para-sciences will inevitably thrive, not just *despite* evidence to the contrary from the scientific community, but—more to the point—actively *in spite* of it" (Dendle, "Cryptozoology," p. 200).

30   See John Mack, *Passport to the Cosmos: Human Transformation and Alien Encounters* (New York: Crown, 1999). Alien enthusiast Walter Shelburne writes on his blog, *Interdimensional Times*, that: "Alien disclosure will disrupt the sense of continuity we have with the past and usher in a new era" (<http://interdimensionaltimes.wordpress.com/2010/01/21/alien-dislcosure-2010-part-ii/>). Elsewhere on the blog he elucidates: "If a sufficiently critical mass of human beings choose transformation in the crisis of the 2012 time, we will experience an empowering reinvention of civilization and the world as we have known it will have come to an end." Crop circles, too, are often interpreted as signs of a great transition, including the end of the world or a new era of consciousness.

the community, and the context. For many people, the existence of ghosts or demons carries spiritual and religious overtones: they perceive them to be integral components of an inherited body of cultural beliefs, partaking of a spirit realm and thus outside of the provenance of scientific enquiry altogether.[31] For others, this is a doctrinal sort of quibbling, a case of believers attempting to legitimize their belief in certain monsters by appealing to cultural and religious heritage rather than demonstrable proof. Although discourse of this sort now enjoys the benefits of an interconnected global citizenry, of instant and rapid communication, and of unprecedented access to historically accumulated information, as other chapters in this collection have made clear, it is not different in kind from similar debates that have occurred historically in a number of cultures. It would not be fair to say, in that light, that societies used to believe in monsters but now in the modern world we know better. A variety of partially overlapping and partially conflicting belief systems have existed simultaneously in most societies for which we have substantial oral, literary, artistic, and archaeological records. It is true that many classical monsters such as the centaur or dragon have long been reduced to de-mythologized cultural commodity. But since it resides at the semantic and epistemological border between what society accepts as real and what it rejects as imaginary, and since it trespasses regularly and obstinately into both of those realms, the "monster" is well suited to explore those very boundaries, and to keep competing discourses of the real an active and open register, even in an age of transparency, technology, and information saturation.

---

31 Interestingly, whether or not people identify themselves as religious or non-religious does not determine whether they believe in entities such as Satan, hell, demons, angels, or ghosts as thoroughly as one might think: see Stark, *What Americans Really Believe*, pp. 141–6. Of those respondents identifying themselves as having "No Religion," for instance, 37 percent said they nonetheless believed in demons, 50 percent in angels, and 46 percent in ghosts (p. 144). It is important to recall that these are primarily folkloric entities, ones that are incidentally integrated within the local religious models of a wide variety of cultures globally and historically.

Postscript
The Promise of Monsters

Jeffrey Jerome Cohen

The animal looks at us, and we are naked before it. Thinking perhaps begins there.

Jacques Derrida, *The Animal That Therefore I Am*

As a child I was haunted by monsters.

A spirit dwelled in my basement, a drifting whiteness that might also have been the work of eyes adjusting to dark. A vampire inhabited my wall, and I could detect the scraping of his fingernails on plaster whenever sleep was distant. A Crooked Man once entered my bedroom to whisper *Listen to the night*. He told me that whenever I put my head to my pillow, I would hear his nearing footsteps. On the day he returned he would take me from my bed. Stone Giants dwelled beneath our house. They would surface to threaten earthquakes and tidal waves, or to bring me news of my grandfather in Maine. I was terrified of these inscrutable creatures. Yet as I grew older and their visits ceased, I felt the loss of their regard. How much wider, how filled with anxious possibility are nocturnal hours roamed by monsters. Although they threatened me, although they kept me awake while my family slumbered, I missed my companions. The world is diminished for their exorcism, their having been driven away by the plodding force of the ordinary.

Fortunately I have two children, and with them the arrival of new monsters. My son Alexander was long haunted by Mr Shadow, a phantom who lurked in the dim of his nursery, eyes a luminous green. Rather than allow Alex to sleep the night with his light burning, I suggested that he might talk to Mr Shadow: perhaps there was some story he wanted to impart. The next day Alex told me that he and his monster had had a nocturnal conversation. Mr Shadow, it seems, had once been a child named KidKid. This boy did not obey his parents, did not follow the instructions of his teacher, and was in every way therefore bad. The curse that he suffered was to become Mr Shadow: always present, filled with vague menace but incapable of doing much more than staring at young sleepers facing the same disciplinary regime against which he had lost his own battle. Another of my son's monsters was the Green Hand, known for scampering across the carpet whenever the lights dimmed. The Green Hand caused Alex to run many nights from his bed to that of his parents, until I asked if maybe sprinting to us wasn't such a good idea since the Green Hand might grab him along the way. (From then on he simply screamed for us to come to him). My daughter Katherine, a pixie of happiness, spent almost six years of her life free of anxiety, and of monsters. I was starting to worry at her cheerfulness: could it be healthy? Don't we need our nightmares to make us artists? Her first night terrors started soon after, and have mostly involved robots and dinosaurs—or sometimes (an ultimate paradox) robotic dinosaurs.

This monstrous genealogy illustrates, perhaps, how a parent has passed his distinctive fears along to his children, as if they were a family inheritance. The particularity of these monsters matters. Jacques Derrida writes compellingly of starting from "unsubstitutable singularity" when meditating upon the other-than-human. "The Animal That Therefore I Am (More to Follow)" begins with a specific animal entering a precise domestic space: Derrida's cat comes into his bedroom and beholds him unclothed.[1] This threshold-crossing animal is not, Derrida insists, "the *figure* of a cat," a sign or an emblem that might "silently enter the bedroom as an allegory for all the cats on earth."[2] Derrida's pet is not a generic animal "ambassador" which must shoulder "the immense symbolic responsibility with which our culture has always charged the feline race."[3] It is a real cat, a particular little kitty that enters Derrida's chamber, regards the naked philosopher and causes him to compose from the encounter an essay about the work of animals and autobiography. Its feline singularity is of consequence, rooting us in the specific, even if we do not know the cat's name (I would like to think that Derrida called his cat Hegel or Pharmakon, but I fear it bore something less exotic like Mr Whiskers). So I offer my own monsters, my own family bedrooms, to grant "unsubstitutable singularity" to them, to wonder what the monster, the animal, and the human share.

Autozōēgraphy ("labyrinthine, even aberrant")[4]

Family monsters are, like Derrida's cat, more than merely personal. Every monster is communal and historical. Take, for example, one of the best monster films yet made, Guillermo del Toro's *Pan's Labyrinth* (*El Laberinto del fauno*, 2006). Ofelia, its dreamy but doomed child heroine, encounters in subterranean and demonic form the human evil that saturates her surroundings, but which few around her

---

1   Jacques Derrida, "The Animal That Therefore I Am (More to Follow)," in *The Animal That Therefore I Am*, ed. Marie-Louise Mallet, trans. David Wills (New York: Fordham University Press, 2008).
2   Ibid., p. 6.
3   Ibid., pp. 7, 9.
4   Ibid., p. 23.

will acknowledge. In her fantastic labyrinth dwells the possibility of escaping the Fascist violence that suffocates her. This space offers a future beyond the present's horrors. So compelling is her dreaming that, as the film ends, we are not wholly certain if Ofelia enters the magic realm forever, or if she simply dies. Pan, the ambassador from that enchanted domain, declares in his last lines:

> And it is said that the Princess returned to her father's kingdom. That she reigned there with justice and a kind heart for many centuries. That she was loved by her people. And that she left behind small traces of her time on Earth, visible only to those who know where to look.

"Visible only to those who know where to look": has the film enabled us to discern these vestiges of a short life spent among monsters that now endures because of her love, or does this ending yield a future only to the brother Ofelia sacrifices herself to save? We suspect that Pan's words are a last gasp of fantasy as Ofelia's life recedes—and this possibility is heartbreaking, so compelling are her feats among the creatures of the labyrinth.

Ofelia's monsters intrude into her waking world from the fairy tales she loves. My childhood ghosts arrived from horror movies, offering access to forbidden realms. My vampire came from a Stephen King novel. The Crooked Man, whose approaching footsteps were my heartbeat in my ear, derived from a nursery rhyme. I suspect that when he arrived, if he arrived, the Crooked Man was not going to murder me, but whisper something I knew but did not want to hear: that the house in which I dwelled was not nearly as placid as I dreamed. The Stone Giants, with their natural catastrophes, were intimately related, I knew, to my grandfather's being a Jew in rural Maine. A gentle giant but a giant all the same, he stood between worlds. His life had been limned with peril, and I embodied within these monsters the shifting of the earth on which he had walked. Mr. Shadow and Kidkid were my son internalizing the docility-creating apparatuses of home and school. The Green Hand had crept out from a library book, and told stories about responsibilities that, when neglected, return to haunt. The dinosaur robots of my daughter speak of what it is to inhabit a world where you are smaller and less routine-driven than the ancient, mechanical adults who tower above you with their mindless rules, mechanical demands, tiresome threats, and alien desires.

Monsters are never as idiosyncratic as they seem. They are drawn from a shared vocabulary, even if this lexicon's expression takes on the contours of the location in which the monster's presence is felt. To the monster belongs a body both particular as well as transhistorical. The monster arrives in the present yearning to impart an old story, a narrative from the deep past. Though today often associated with science fiction and futurity, monsters are prehistoric, ahistoric, innate anachronisms. They arrive to recount a lesson in the complexity of temporality. History is a tangle, full of loops and doublings-back. Linear chronologies are a lie.

Le monstre que donc je suis

In 1996 I published a collection of essays entitled *Monster Theory*, about the cultural work that the monstrous accomplishes. My piece was entitled "Monster Culture: Seven Theses," and at several points within that essay I described the monster as a *messenger*.[5] At the time I did not know Michel Serres, whose messengers "always bring strange news" and connect unexpected times, knowledges, places.[6] I argued more simply that "The Monster is the Harbinger of Category Crisis" (Thesis III), embodying a relentless hybridity that resists assimilation into secure epistemologies. My closing thesis states that "The Monster Stands at the Threshold ... of Becoming" (Thesis VII), by which I meant that monsters open up more possibility than they foreclose. They also pose an insistent demand:

> *Monsters are our children. They can be pushed to the farthest margins of geography and discourse, hidden away at the edges of the world and in the forbidden recesses of our mind, but they always return. And when they come back, they bring not just a fuller knowledge of our place in history and the history of knowing our place, but they bear self-knowledge, human knowledge ... These monsters ask us how we perceive the world, and how we have misrepresented what we have attempted to place. They ask us to reevaluate our assumptions about race, gender, sexuality, our perception of difference, our tolerance towards its expressions. They ask us why we have created them.*[7]

The promise of the monster inheres within that question, that interrogative demand.

Before further journey down this haunted path, however, it is worth revisiting the "château of haunted friendship," the "haunted castle" in Normandy where Derrida delivered his lecture instigated by a cat. Derrida's title for the talk is "L'animal que donc je suis." That last verb, which he describes as "the powerful little word *suis*,"[8] can designate the first person singular of être or *suivre*, and so yields two meanings for his title: "The animal that therefore I am" as well as "The animal that therefore I follow." Like everything Derrida composes, his equivocal title is dense in allusion: to Descartes and his "I think therefore I am," to the conference's title of "The Autobiographical Animal," to the impossibility of being or capturing or coinciding with any stable entity. The trail which Derrida wanders begins by following a particular cat, and then many philosophers and

---

5   Jeffrey Jerome Cohen, "Monster Culture (Seven Theses)," in Cohen (ed.), *Monster Theory: Reading Culture* (Minneapolis: University of Minnesota Press, 1996), pp. 3–25.

6   Quotation from Michel Serres with Bruno Latour, *Conversations on Science, Culture, and Time,* trans. Roxanne Lapidus (Ann Arbor: University of Michigan Press, 1995), p. 66. See also Serres, *Angels: A Modern Myth,* trans. Francis Cowper (Paris: Flammarion, 1993).

7   Cohen, "Monster Culture," p. 20.

8   Derrida, "The Animal That Therefore I Am," p. 64.

many more cats. Although the essay published from this talk has become essential reading in critical animal studies, his topic is not the "general singular" of *animal* as a collective noun, but the hybrid beings that emerge from its analysis.[9] Beyond but not in opposition to the human, Derrida insists, exists:

> *a multiplicity of organizations of relations between living and dead, relations of organization or lack of organization among realms that are more and more difficult to dissociate by means of the figures of the organic and inorganic, of life and/or death. These relations are at once intertwined and abyssal, and they can never be totally objectified.*[10]

This pandemonic space resonates with what Michel Serres calls the multiple, a noisy and furious sea of non-individuated, non-harmonized relations: the necessary but neglected background of thought, of life.[11] By *objectified*, Derrida here means *named*: "Animal" cannot exist in separation, exteriority, or generality, cannot "corral a large number of living beings within a single concept."[12] Derrida forges the neologism *l'animot* to jar the ear in French, to bring together in disharmony the plural form of animal (*les animaux*) with the word for word (*le mot*), placing both behind a singular definite article: *l'animot* as the grammatically incoherent "animals-word":

> *Ecce animot. Neither a species nor a gender nor an individual, it is an irreducible living multiplicity of mortals, and rather than a double clone or a portmanteau word, a sort of monstrous hybrid, a chimera waiting to be put to death by its Bellerophon.*[13]

Derrida glosses the term by invoking the classical Chimaera, whose "monstrousness derived precisely from the multiplicity of the *animot* in it (head and chest of a lion, entrails of a goat, tail of a dragon)."[14] Although inaugurated by a household cat that regards Derrida and causes him to feel shame, an embarrassment at his own embarrassment, and an urge to write, the queer word *l'animot* is less *felis catus* than "monstrous hybrid."[15]

Between philosopher and cat was born *l'animot*. What neologism would Derrida have minted, what strange progeny would have arisen if, in the corner of his eye, he had seen not a familiar cat's cool gaze, but instead locked eyes with a demon, a ghost, some alien body that should not have been dwelling in his house and yet which he had long suspected had been making a home precisely there? If the

---

9   Ibid., p. 41.
10   Ibid., p. 31.
11   See, especially, Michel Serres, *Genesis*, trans. Geneviève James and James Nielson (Ann Arbor: University of Michigan Press, 1995).
12   Derrida, "The Animal That Therefore I Am," p. 32.
13   Ibid., p. 41.
14   Ibid., p. 41.
15   Ibid., p. 41.

monster is a messenger who delivers strange news, what would this household monster have announced? What presentiment would have arrived in that middle space, that messenger's space, in the communication between Jacques Derrida and the monster of being, of following, to follow?

It could be objected that a cat is real and a monster holds no materiality. It is true that some of us have never glimpsed a monster. Yet none of us have beheld time, or oxygen, or the wind. We vividly perceive their effects, and from this evidence we postulate agency and cause. The effects of the monster are undeniable: a spur to self-protection; an insistent impulsion to narrative; a catalyst to fear, to desire, and to art. Even if we never behold a monster striding the hinterlands or lurking in the basement of our house, we cannot deny that these creatures live full lives that have been well recorded in our literature, our visual arts, our dreams. The question of whether they exist is beside the point, since the monster perseveres regardless of our doubt, indifferent to our credulity.

The Monster Looks at Us (Thinking Begins There)

In the second portion of his *animot* essay ("But as for me, who am I?") Derrida raises the question of animal communication through what he calls "chimerical aphorisms":

> All the philosophers we will investigate … say the same thing: the animal is deprived of language. Or more precisely, of response, of a response that could be precisely and rigorously distinguished from a reaction … The animal that I am (following), does it speak? … Does it speak French?[16]

The animal poses philosophical questions, certainly, but can it pose these questions itself or only through a verbalizing intermediary? Can the animal deploy language, good French? Can it ask something unexpected, something I do not necessarily follow? The third portion of Derrida's *animot* meditation is dedicated to Jacques Lacan, who adamantly refused the possibility of animal language.[17] Derrida's title for this section is a resonant question: "And Say the Animal Responded?" If we continue glossing *l'animot* with *les monstres*, we can ask: And say the monster responded? What would that monster declare?

What passes between Derrida and his cat begins with the eyes. To understand the regard of an animal or a monster requires an attempt to inhabit their gaze, to see oneself being seen, and thereby exposed as fragile, a creature of uncertainty and ambivalence:

---

16   Ibid., pp. 32, 56.
17   Ibid., pp. 122–4.

> *The animal is there before me ... — I am who am (following) after it. And also,*
> *therefore, since it is before me, it is behind me. It surrounds me. And from the*
> *vantage point this being-there-before-me it can allow itself to be looked at, no*
> *doubt, but also — something that philosophy perhaps forgets, perhaps being*
> *this calculated forgetting itself — it can look at me. It has its point of view*
> *regarding me. The point of view of the absolute other, and nothing will ever*
> *give me more food for thinking through this absolute alterity of the neighbor*
> *or of the next(-door) than these moments when I see myself seen naked under*
> *the gaze of a cat.*[18]

Under the gaze of a cat ... or, worse, a vampire, or any of the demons who prefer to regard their victims nude in their bedroom. "Nudity is nothing other than that passivity," writes Derrida, "the involuntary exhibition of the self": the utter vulnerability of being seen and seeing oneself being seen, of realizing that "human" was not a very sturdy category under which to stake a claim to identity to begin with: "As with every bottomless gaze, as with the eyes of the other, the gaze called 'animal' offers to my sight the abyssal limit of the human: the inhuman or ahuman, the ends of man."[19] Perhaps this disquieting, disrobing power of the Other's gaze explains why monstrosity so often involves the ocular.[20] Think of Goya's giants, and their irresistible line of vision. Think of Polyphemos the Cyclops and his hideous monocularity. To behold Medusa is to be turned to stone. A dragon's eye can entrance. A baleful light shimmers from the eyes of Grendel in the Old English heroic poem *Beowulf*. The eyes are the entrance to the monster's soul, and point of view reveals the monsters that we are and follow.

Grendel's Story

Grendel may be more familiar internationally from a Robert Zemeckis film, *Beowulf* (2007, starring Angelina Jolie as Grendel's mom), than from the medieval heroic poem in which he first appears, written at least a millennium earlier. *Beowulf* is a lively Old English work that narrates how its eponymous hero slays three monsters: the troll-like Grendel; Grendel's vengeance-driven mother; and an ancient dragon guarding a hoard of treasure. The companion of demons and a ferocious anthropophage, Grendel is descended from Cain, the son of Adam and

---

18 Ibid., p. 11.
19 Ibid., p. 12.
20 Cf. "seeing oneself seen naked under a gaze behind which there remains a bottomlessness, at the same time innocent and cruel perhaps, perhaps sensitive and impassive, good and bad, uninterpretable, unreadable, undecidable, abyssal and secret ... And in these moments of nakedness, as regards the animal, everything can happen to me, I am like a child ready for the apocalypse, *I am (following) the apocalypse itself.*" (Ibid., p. 12).

Eve who murdered his own brother. Embodying everything contrary to the ethos of the heroic world, Grendel is a physical and moral monster. There are few moments when we are invited to sympathize with him. Yet the poem is structured to allow such a possibility twice, both times yielding a fleeting moment of identification through a sudden shift in point of view.[21] In these instances we see the world, for a moment, through a monster's eyes.

The first ocular shift occurs at Grendel's initial appearance. The warrior Hrothgar finds himself favored by fortune and rises to the status of king. He decides to house his growing retinue within a magnificent hall, an edifice that can express in soaring wood and lofty gables the stability he has brought to what had been a shifting political landscape. Hrothgar founds Heorot, a hall that becomes the "wonder of the world."[22] Initially, we view the interior of this resplendent space, where the king is dispensing treasure to reward his retainers. This segment ends with a flash forward, a proleptic scene of the hall incinerated because of squabbles among its dwellers. With a return to the present, the point of view changes completely, from the all-too-human interior to the sprawling, inhuman landscape of which the hall has declared itself to be the new center. We suddenly find ourselves companions to a monster discovering this architectural intrusion near his wilds. Perhaps carved from land he once wandered, the hall is unendurably noisy.[23] The din causes Grendel great pain (þrage geþolode [from geþolian, to suffer]): the ebullient clamor of a settled community causes the monster at its outskirts to ache.

Why should this joyful noise be so hurtful? Heorot's impressive timber safely encloses Hrothgar's people, demarcating a fire-warmed inside from an inimical world of fens and foes. Its gables announce to those who find themselves at the fortress walls the misery of their outsiderhood. What galls Grendel, perhaps, is his foundational exclusion from the solidarity which this architecture calls into being. He comes to the hall as an investigator, arrives just in time to hear not only "the din of the loud banquet" (as Seamus Heaney puts it in his contemporary translation of the poem), but the sweet notes of a harp, a poet performing a song of creation.[24] These are the words of the Book of Genesis translated from rhythmless Latin into undulating English—rendered through musical accompaniment, a radiant story of how God formed for humanity a world to inhabit:

> *how the Almighty had made the earth*
> *a gleaming plain girdled with waters;*
> *in His splendour He set the sun and the moon*

---

21   Andy Orchard has pointed out that there is "something deeply human" about all three of the monsters in *Beowulf: Pride and Prodigies: Studies in the Monsters of the Beowulf-Manuscript* (Cambridge: D.S. Brewer, 1995; Toronto: University of Toronto Press, 2003), p. 29.

22   Friedrich Klaeber (ed.), *Beowulf* (Lexington, MA: D.C. Heath and Company, 1950), and Seamus Heaney (trans.), *Beowulf: A Verse Translation* (New York: Norton, 2002), line 70.

23   Heaney, *Beowulf*, lines 88–9.

24   Ibid., line 88.

> *to be the earth's lamplight, lanterns for men,*
> *and filled the broad lap of the world*
> *with branches and leaves; and quickened life*
> *in every other thing that moved.*[25]

Placed immediately after an account of the building of the hall, God's work in fashioning the earth and arranging its elements into bounded expanses becomes the poem's second creation story: "Swa ða driht-guman dreamum lifdon," [so the men lived in joy.][26] Grendel will play the serpent who ruins everything, the fallen angel who spoils everyone else's enjoyment, perhaps because he has been so moved by the vision of harmonious unity he has overheard in the song, a vision denied him through his patrimony. We regard the hall through his joyless eyes; we listen to harp and voice from a vantage at which the pleasure of belonging can resound but not obtain. Both the creation song (*frumsceaft*) and the hall itself are aesthetic objects, transportive in their beauty. Yet Grendel knows that the Genesis story is just as demarcative, just as exclusionary as the walls of the hall. The poet with the harp narrates the origin of a world in which Grendel has no secure place. He is, after all, the progeny of Cain, eternal wanderer, cursed to exile:

> *For the killing of Abel*
> *the Eternal Lord had exacted a price:*
> *Cain got no good from committing that murder*
> *because the Almighty made him anathema*
> *and out of the curse of his exile there sprang*
> *ogres and elves and evil phantoms*[27]

Derrida writes sympathetically of Cain in "The Animal That Therefore I Am."[28] He argues that the farmer Cain is haunted by animality because he has fallen into a trap set by a divinity who loves animal sacrifice. Cain, "tiller of the ground," offers the fruit of his own agricultural labor instead of the flesh that his brother the herdsman provides. Cain kills Abel; God rebukes and curses Cain. Yet Cain then reproaches God, responding to the divine malediction with the complaint "My punishment is greater than I can bear" (Genesis 4:13). An outlaw, Cain fears being hunted like a beast. God marks the man and swears vengeance upon anyone who attacks him, rendering Cain at once animal and human, a wanderer and the founder of the first city, a singular being branded by God and the progenitor of a people.

The biblical narrative that bequeaths to Grendel his family inheritance is described by Derrida as offering a "double insistence upon nudity, fault and default at the origin of human history and within sight or perspective of the

---

25   Ibid., lines 92–8.
26   Ibid., line 99.
27   Ibid., lines 108–12.
28   Derrida, "The Animal That Therefore I Am," pp. 43–4.

animal."[29] The mark of Cain, in other words, is the mark of the *animot*, and thereby of the monster. Cain is ultimately excluded from the Genesis story, but haunts it; Grendel is excluded from the hall, excluded from the song about his progenitor sung within the hall, and smashes it. Grendel shatters the door of Hrothgar's building and wets its walls with blood because he is intent on breaking to pieces this place founded upon his absence, his exile. He attempts to restore the world to its aboriginal unboundedness, when he roamed its fens with his mother in an alien community of two that was never troubled by Danish kings and their lethal ambitions for secure kingdoms and delimiting architectures.[30]

Grendel is a murderer, an outcast, *feond on helle, rinc ... dreamum bedæled* ("a man deprived of joy.")[31] Even if we are given a glimmer of insight about his rage, we know that our cheers must be reserved for Beowulf, the warrior who will defeat him, who will tear away his arm and slice away his head. We must desire Grendel's dismemberment and death. It is surprising, then, that we are granted a second moment of regarding the world through his eyes, brought about once more through a sudden change of perspective and the forced inhabitation of his monstrous subjectivity. Grendel attacks Hrothgar's hall, not realizing that inside Beowulf patiently awaits his intrusion. The hero seizes the monster, binds him in an unbreakable grip. For the first time, Grendel feels himself overmatched: "Every bone in his body / quailed and recoiled, but he could not escape."[32] We are with Grendel as the terrible knowledge of his own mortality dawns. In panic and then in terror, he tries to pull his body from the inhuman grasp that holds him, to no avail. The two combatants destroy the hall's interior with their grappling, but still the monster is hopelessly bound. Grendel empties himself into a sound that harrows the hall:

> *Sweg up astag*
> *niwe geneahhe: Norð-Denum stod*
> *atelic egesa, anra gehwylcum*
> *þara þe of wealle wop gehyrdon,*
> *gryreleoð galan Godes andsacan*
> *sigeleasne sang, sar wanigean*
> *helle hæfton.*[33]

In Seamus Heaney's postcolonial, Irish-inflected version of the poem, these mournful lines read:

---

29   Ibid., p. 44.
30   Ultimately we will discover that Grendel abides with his mother in a *hrofsele* (roofed hall, line 1515). Like the dragon's *dryhtsele* (noble hall, line 2320; used of Heorot at lines 485 and 767), it is an architecture that humanizes the monsters rather than differentiates them.
31   *Beowulf*, 101, lines 720–1.
32   *Beowulf*, lines 752–3.
33   *Beowulf*, lines 782–8.

> Then an extraordinary
> wail arose, and bewildering fear
> came over the Danes. Everyone felt it
> who heard that cry as it echoed off the wall,
> a God-cursed scream and strain of catastrophe
> the howl of the loser, the lament of the hell-serf
> keening his wound. He was overwhelmed.

The "wail" (*sweg*) that pours from Grendel's mouth is, from one point of view, a mere scream, a visceral howl that signifies but holds no content. Yet *sweg* also means music. In the beautiful scene where the poet in the hall sings the creation of the world, his harp resonates with "sweg" (þær wæs hearpan sweg), the melodious accompaniment to sweet song (swutol sang).[34] The monster Grendel's scream is horrifying. Or it is like the resonance of a musical instrument. It communicates directly, implanting its vibration in the body, and exists outside of words.

To the fearful Danes, Grendel's noise is strange, unprecedented (*niwe geneahhe*), and therefore a source of "horrible awe" (*atelic egesa*). Yet these same men must recognize that this foreign sound, this monster's song, is a kind of weeping (*wop gehyrdon*)—in fact, a mournfulness with which the people of Heorot are intimately familiar. A similar noise gripped the hall when the evidence of Grendel's first gory foray was discovered long ago:

> Then as dawn brightened and the day broke
> Grendel's powers of destruction were plain:
> their wassail was over, they wept up to heaven
> and mourned under morning [morgensweg, lit. "morning song"].[35]

Like the wordless tears that flow at the first sight of ruined Heorot, Grendel's weeping is no bestial wail. His death-song is called a *gryreleoþ*: "*gryre*" means horror and "*leoþ*" is a song or lay.[36] Grendel's sound is thereby intimately connected to some of the poem's most moving moments of loss, memorialization, and elegy.

---

34   *Beowulf*, lines 89, 90. Cf. the song sung by Hrothgar's scop to honor Beowulf's triumph over Grendel, where we are told: "flær wæs sang ond sweg samod ætgædere" (line 1063). The sense is that words (sang) were accompanied by wordless melody (sweg).

35   Ibid., lines 126–9.

36   The same word appears later as part of the compound "fyrd-leoþ" ("war-song," line 1424), used to describe the noise of a guð-horn (war-horn) blown when the head of Æschere is discovered on a cliff above Grendel's mere; as "guð-leoð" ("battle song," line 1422) to convey the noise Beowulf's sword makes as it whirs toward the head of Grendel's mother; and "sorh-leoð" ("sorrow-song," line 2460), to describe the song intoned by the man who finds the earth has grown too large now that his son is dead ("The Father's Lament"). "Galan," the verb used to describe Grendel's action of singing, will reappear in two of these places: to describe the resounding of the horn at the discovery of Æschere's head (line 1432) and to convey the singing of the sorrow-song in "The Father's Lament" ("sorh-leoð gæleð," line 2460).

Grendel's song takes origin in the ending of his monster's life, in a mortal hurt that he can bemoan but never remedy. It is voice as well as instrument, word as well as music. Yet whatever content Grendel puts into his death-song is lost upon its auditors, who hear only a disturbingly alien noise. Because it issues from the mouth of "the enemy of God," its potential verbal signification disperses, transformed into a linguistic force that floods the hall in sonic barrage, as empty of language as it is replete with despair. Most translations of *Beowulf* miss the complexity of Grendel's song, the intimation that it might be full of a meaning that resonates profoundly with other moments in the poem. Translators tend to hear what the Danish men perceive, stressing the inhumanity of Grendel and his mother, rather than opening their ears to the words and music with which the monster here responds. Thus the best that Grendel can usually attain at his death is an inarticulate keen, wail, or scream.

Seamus Heaney is no exception. This celebrated translator found his "entry" into the poem through the fact that his Irish family possessed an Anglo-Saxon verb, þolian, "to suffer." When his grandmother uses a modern version of the Old English word, a poem that seemed to resist his art suddenly connects itself to him intimately. *Þolian*, Heaney fails to note, is the very verb used to describe Grendel's pain when he hears the noise inside Hrothgar's hall. Heaney does not love Grendel, will not listen to the monster's response, will not even grant to him his suffering. He describes Hrothgar's hall as a "bawn," writing:

> In Elizabethan English, bawn (from Irish bó-dhún, a fort for cattle) referred specifically to the fortified dwellings which the English planters built in Ireland to keep the dispossessed natives at bay ... every time I read the lovely interlude that tells of the minstrel singing in Heorot just before the attacks of Grendel, I cannot help thinking of Edmund Spenser in Kilcolman Castle, reading the early cantos of The Faerie Queene to Sir Walter Raleigh, just before the Irish burned the castle and drove Spenser out of Munster back to the Elizabethan court. Putting a bawn in Beowulf seems one way for an Irish poet to come to terms with that complex history of conquest and colony, absorption and resistance, integrity and antagonism.[37]

The hall of Heorot becomes a colonialist architecture; the poem becomes a displacement of English imperialism into a distant past, a history which suddenly takes on rich new meanings for the present. Heaney tells us that he modeled the poem's solemn diction on his father's relatives, "'big voiced Scullions'" from Ulster.[38] If the poet were true to his own historical parallel, he would have seen in Grendel the dispossessed native, hurling his fury against the structure that excludes him from a land once his. Grendel should be as Irish as Seamus Heaney, should be his postcolonial poetic forebear. He might have glimpsed in Grendel the monster that he follows. Yet Heaney discerns in Grendel's eyes no regard,

---

37 Heaney, "Introduction," in *Beowulf*, p. xxx.
38 Ibid., p. xxvii.

no query, just "a baleful light, / flame more than light."[39] Heaney, like the Danes, does not hear Grendel's song. He beholds in the monster a mere test of the hero's strength, terrible yet uncomplex.[40] Grendel and his mother are, in Seamus Heaney's words, "creatures of the physical world ... hardboned and immensely strong":[41] all body, a voiceless challenge of flesh to flesh. Thus Heaney translates Grendel's last utterances as "an extraordinary wail," an echoing "cry," "a God-cursed scream," a "howl." The closest Grendel gets to any human meaning is "the lament of the hell-serf / keening his wound."[42] Yet the monster's voice is also *song*, and resonates deeply with similar elegiac moments throughout this musical poem. What the baleful light of Seamus Heaney's Grendel illuminates is a lack of sympathy, a disregard for the monster's regard.

Heaney disavows the assemblage into which he has already entered.

A Creature, and the Creaturely

"Begone! Relieve me from the sight of your detested form."

With this dismissal, Victor Frankenstein attempts to rid himself of the monster he has brought into being, the monster who demands that Victor return his care. In Mary Shelley's novel *Frankenstein: or, The Modern Prometheus* (1818), the creature (as Victor calls his living handiwork) is fashioned from pieces of corpses, chemicals, and electricity.[43] Larger than any human and yet man-like in its form, the creature is abandoned by his creator at the moment when life animates his frame. The creature wanders the world, learning French, pondering natural and moral law, yearning for kindness and community, an end to his unchosen solitude. Unlike Grendel, Frankenstein's unnamed creature speaks insistently, his words full of reproach towards the unloving god who has renounced him: "I ought to be thy Adam, but I am rather the fallen angel, whom thou drivest from joy for no misdeed. Everywhere I see bliss, from which I alone am irrevocably excluded." Were Grendel a monster endowed by the author of *Beowulf* with the ability to speak during his life, these words of sorrowful reprimand might have issued from him. The complaint of Victor's creature, seeking nothing more than belonging and heed, haunts with its humane yearning. His words are devoid of the icy rancor to come.

---

39 *Beowulf*, lines 726–7.
40 See Heaney, "Introduction," p. xviii, where Heaney compares the Grendelcyn with some disappointment to the dragon, who possesses a "wonderful inevitability" and a "unique glamour."
41 Ibid., p. xviii.
42 *Beowulf*, lines 781–7.
43 All quotations are from Mary Wollstonecraft Shelley, *Frankenstein, or The Modern Prometheus*, unpaginated electronic edition, Project Gutenberg, <http://www.gutenberg.org/ebooks/84>, accessed 2011.

Patterned upon the diction of the King James translation of the bible, the creature's sentences are scriptural, weighty, Job-like. They are also heartbreaking. Yet Victor refuses to hear. He demands that his creature be not seen, as if visuality were the sole source of the monster's accusation. "Thus I relieve thee, my creator," the anguished creature responds, placing his hands over Victor's eyes, insisting all the same: "Still thou canst listen to me and grant me thy compassion." Compassion: *suffering-with*. The monster requests of his creator the possibility of an affective community, a companionship based upon mutual regard. "I demand this from you. Hear my tale; it is long and strange." The creature is met by closed eyes and unhearing ears. A self-absorbed and fearful divinity, Victor is never moved by his creation's pleas for long.

Why fashion a monster that you cannot love? Why not, once you engender a monster, once that monster insists upon persistent visitations, why not hail him as a companion (*com-panis*, someone to break bread with, someone with whom to form a mindful community)? For Victor Frankenstein and his creature are never separate, despite every protest Victor makes to the contrary. Enforced partition is Victor's undoing. His inability to behold this thing that is of him—the monster that he is and follows—denies the monstrous community already born. The creature demands of Victor his regard, yet he is met only by his retreat-inducing fears.

In this rejected progeny, we as readers perhaps discern not so much a monster as what Eric Santner calls the *creaturely*, a "caesura ... in the space of [human] meaning ... [an] uncanny loci of alterity within the order of meaning," at once inside and outside of the symbolic order. The creaturely demands a rethinking of the "radical otherness of the 'natural' world," its palpable if at times seemingly mute "thingness," the challenge it poses to human being as usual.[44] Although potentially exceeding all social order and alliable with the queer, Santner's idea of creatureliness is ultimately rather anthropocentric, "less a dimension that traverses the boundaries of human and nonhuman forms of life than a specifically human way of finding oneself caught in the midst of the antagonisms in and of the political field."[45] Victor's creature can be humane, but he (like every monster) is not exactly human. Merely to humanize the creature blunts his critique of the systems that exclude him. The creature is drawn to inhuman nature: glaciers, mountaintops, the roar of snow. His narration of his first arrival in the Alps includes a meditation upon a world that surrounds all creatures, but often works in thunderous indifference to them:

> *The icy wall of the glacier overhung me ... Imperial nature was broken only by the brawling waves or the fall of some vast fragment, the thunder sound of the avalanche or the cracking, reverberated along the mountains, of the accumulated ice, which, through the silent working of immutable laws, was ever and anon rent and torn, as if it had been but a plaything in their hands.*

---

44   Eric L. Santner, *On Creaturely Life: Rilke, Benjamin, Sebald* (Chicago: University of Chicago Press, 2006), p. xv.

45   Ibid., p. xix.

> *These sublime and magnificent scenes afforded me the greatest consolation that I was capable of receiving ... For some time I sat upon the rock that overlooks the sea of ice ... The surface is very uneven, rising like the waves of a troubled sea, descending low, and interspersed by rifts that sink deep ... I remained in a recess of the rock, gazing on this wonderful and stupendous scene ... My heart, which was before sorrowful, now swelled with something like joy.*

In such spaces of glacial beauty, where even the most stable of matter (mountainsides, ice sheets) is perpetually in sonorous motion, the creature finds not loneliness but joy. In such a wintry expanse will the creature, like his creator, meet his end. Victor perishes aboard an ice-locked ship, pushing as far north as the frozen waters allow. His monster boards the vessel to mourn, and declares that he will incinerate himself on a pyre in the snowbound wilderness, taking all trace of monster and maker to the blaze: "He is dead who called me into being; and when I shall be no more, the very remembrance of us both will speedily vanish. I shall no longer see the sun or stars or feel the winds play on my cheeks." Unlike Ofelia's story in *Pan's Labyrinth*, this narrative will leave behind no "small traces ... visible only to those who know where to look."

Except, of course, that it does. The narrative is imparted to an explorer on the ship. The story survives, and therefore so does remembrance of the creature. Victor's story, and Victor's monster's story, are about never discovering the place where one can find an everlasting home. Glaciers offer respite, but not the community for which both yearn. Julia Lupton notes that the word *creature* derives from the future participle of the Latin verb *creare*, so that *creatura* means "a thing always in the process of undergoing creation; the creature is actively passive or, better, *passionate*, perpetually becoming created, subject to transformations at the behest of the arbitrary commands of the Other."[46] And yet what the creature in Frankenstein reveals is that these demands do not necessarily arise from some distant Other at all. The space of transformation, becoming, passion, alterity, the uncanny, the utopian is in fact an interspace: between Grendel and the men in the hall; between an Irish poet and his disregarded Old English monster; between Victor and the thing he made which desires to unmake or remake him. The monster and its dreamer are not two entities inhabiting a divided world, but two participants in an open process, two components of a circuit that intermixes and disperses both within an open, vibrant, unstable expanse.

Gilles Deleuze and Félix Guattari would call such a machine of becoming an *agencement* or assemblage. So would Bruno Latour, another fan of the creature that Victor Frankenstein creates. In *Aramis, or The Love of Technology*, Latour quotes the rebuke that Victor's creature delivers upon the Alpine glacier, and then writes:

---

46 Julia Reinhard Lupton, "Creature Caliban," *Shakespeare Quarterly* 51/1 (2000), p. 1. Lupton writes movingly, on page 13, of Caliban's loneliness as a spur to reconsidering possible human relations.

If you did not want me, why did you keep me alive, year after year, in that glacial limbo, attaching to me dozens of poor devils who sacrificed their nights and their ardor to me? If I have been badly conceived, why not conceive me again? Why not take trouble to reshape me? ... Who has committed the inexpiable crime of abandoning a creature drawn out of the void? I, who did not ask to be born or to die? Or you, who insisted that I be born? Of all sins, unconsummated love is the most inexpiable. Burdened with my prostheses, hated, abandoned, innocent, accused, a filthy beast, a thing full of men, men full of things, I lie before you. Eloï, eloï, lama sabachthani.[47]

Though they sound uncannily similar, this aggrieved speech is not a continuation of the rebuke delivered by Victor Frankenstein's creature. So dramatic that its close quotes the dying words of Jesus upon the cross, the reproach is spoken by Aramis, a failed subway system that was supposed to have been built in Paris. Bruno Latour traces the assemblage of human and inhuman actors through which this idea took on a materiality, transformed itself, almost came into being. Aramis is at once a living concept, an incipient reality, and "a real monster."[48] Latour does not believe in metalanguages or external explanations: there are only networks and assemblages; the forces that animate and are catalyzed by these conglomerations of the organic and inorganic; the translations and hybridities that they foster. Even if the subway system never quite came into being, Latour grants to Aramis a life for the same reasons that monsters may not exactly live but certainly exist, move about, speak, regard us, make demands. Victor's creature may have felt "something like joy" in his glacial solitude, but that consolation came from his perceiving the connections that bound him, a technology, to a wider, ever-animate world. What the creature learns aboard a ship in the ice, what Grendel discovers at the bolted gate of a new wooden fortress, what Aramis declares as the engineers roll up their plans and declare him finished, is that identity is networked, hybrid, monstrous, fragile. Community of the posthuman kind is wide, and includes ice floes, vessels of exploration, subway systems, cadavers, scientists, authors, naked philosophers, animals, and buildings in relations of mutual regard.

And say the monster responded? What would that monster declare? Perhaps such a declaration inheres in the chaos of artistry that the monster might commit. Perhaps the monster will speak something chilling, like Grendel's unrecorded song, or "I will be with you on your wedding night" (as the creature states ominously to Victor). Or perhaps, most disconcertingly of all, the monster will state its love, its residence within the one whom it addresses, its ardor to be embraced rather than discarded, its future both with and following and as you.

---

47   Bruno Latour, *Aramis, or The Love of Technology*, trans. Catherine Porter (Cambridge: Harvard University Press, 1996), pp. 157–8.

48   Ibid., p. 174.

Bibliography

Manuscript Sources

Cambridge, Corpus Christi College, MS 16
Cambridge, Trinity College, MS O.9.34
London, British Library, MS Add. 28681
London, British Library, MS Add. 42130
London, British Library, MS Add. 62925
London, British Library, MS Cotton Tiberius B.V
London, British Library, MS Cotton Vitellius A.xv
London, British Library, MS Harley 3954
London, British Library, MS Royal 20.B.xx
London, British Library, MS Sloane 278
London, British Library, MS Add. 5246
Los Angeles, J.P. Getty Museum, MS Ludwig XV.4
Oxford, Bodleian Library, MS Douce 180
Paris, Bibliothèque de l'Arsenal, MS 1162
Paris, Bibliothèque nationale, MS Fr. 2810
Paris, Bibliothèque nationale, MS Fr. 22971

Primary and Secondary Sources

"AAA Statement on Race," *American Anthropologist* 100 (1998), pp. 712–13.
Abel, Karlhans, "Zone," in A. Pauly and G. Wissowa (eds), *Real-Encyclopädie der classischen Altertumswissenschaft*, Supplementband 14 (1974), cols 989–1188.
Abelard, Peter, *Dialectica*, ed. Lambertus Marie de Rijk (Assen: Van Gorcum, 1956).
Abulafia, David, *The Discovery of Mankind: Atlantic Encounters in the Age of Columbus* (New Haven, CT and London: Yale University Press, 2008).
Achebe, Chinua, *Girls at War and Other Stories* (London: Heinemann, 1972).
Ackermann, Hans-W., and Jeannine Gauthier, "The Ways and Nature of the Zombi," *The Journal of American Folklore* 104/414 (1991), pp. 466–94.
Acosta, Vladimir, *El continente prodigioso* (Caracas: Universidad Central de Venezuela, 1992).

Adair, Mark, "Plato's view of the 'Wandering Uterus,'" *The Classical Journal* 91/2 (December 1995–January 1996), pp. 153–63.

Adam of Bremen, *History of the Archbishops of Hamburg-Bremen*, trans. Francis J. Tschan (New York: Columbia University Press, 1893).

A declaration of a strange and wonderfull monster: born in Kirkham parish in Lancashire (the childe of Mrs. Haughton, a Popish gentlewoman) the face of it upon the breast, and without a head (after the mother had wished rather to bear a childe without a head then a Roundhead) and had curst the Parliamnet ... (London: Printed by Jane Coe, 1646).

Adelard of Bath, *Conversations with His Nephew: On the Same and the Different; Questions on Natural Science; and, On Birds*, ed. and trans. Charles Burnett (Cambridge: Cambridge University Press, 1998).

Aethicus of Istria, *Die Kosmographie des Aethicus*, ed. Otto Prinz (Munich: Monumenta Germaniae Historica, 1993).

Agamben, Giorgio, *The Open: Man and Animal*, trans. Kevin Attell (Stanford: Stanford University Press, 2004).

Ajootian, Aileen, "The Only Happy Couple: Hermaphrodites and Gender," in Ann Olga Koloski-Ostrow and Claire L. Lyons (eds), *Naked Truths: Women, Sexuality, and Gender in Classical Art and Archaeology* (London and New York: Routledge, 1997), pp. 220–42.

Akbari, Suzanne Conklin, "From Due East to True North: Orientalism and Orientation," in Jeffrey Jerome Cohen (ed.), *The Postcolonial Middle Ages* (New York: St. Martin's Press, 2000), pp. 19–34.

——, "The Diversity of Mankind in The Book of John Mandeville," in Rosamund Allen (ed.), *Eastward Bound: Travels and Travellers, 1050–1500* (Manchester: Manchester University Press, 2004), pp. 156–76.

——, *Idols in the East: European Representations of Islam and the Orient, 1100–1450* (Ithaca: Cornell University Press, 2009).

Aldrovandi, Ulisse, *Monstrorum historia* (Bologna, 1642).

Alexander, Philip S., "Jerusalem as the Omphalos of the World: On the History of a Geographical Concept," *Judaism* 46/182 (1997), pp. 147–59, reprinted in Lee I. Levine (ed.), *Jerusalem: Its Sanctity and Centrality to Judaism, Christianity, and Islam* (New York: Continuum, 1999), pp. 104–19.

Allan, Sarah, *The Shape of the Turtle: Myth, Art, and Cosmos in Early China* (Albany, NY: State University of New York Press, 1991).

Allen, Louis, and Jean Watson (eds), *Lafcadio Hearn: Japan's Great Interpreter, A New Anthology of his Writings: 1894–1904* (Sandgate, UK: Japan Library, 1992).

Allison, Anne, *Millennial Monsters: Japanese Toys and the Global Imagination* (Berkeley: University of California Press, 2006).

Almagià, Roberto, "Un prezioso cimelio della cartografia italiana. Il Planisfero di Urbano Monte," *La Bibliofilia* 43 (1941), pp. 156–93.

Alonso, Carlos J., *The Spanish American Regional Novel: Modernity and Autochthony* (New York: Cambridge University Press, 1990).

Al-Qazvini, Zakariyya b. Muhammad, *Kitab 'aja'ib al-makhluqat wa ghara'ib al-mawjudat* [1414] (Frankfurt: Jumhuriyya Almaniya al-Ittihadiyya, 1994).

Al-Tabari, Muhammad b. Jarir, *The History of al-Tabari. Volume One: General Introduction and From the Creation to the Flood*, trans. Franz Rosenthal (New York: State University of New York Press, 1989).

Altick, Richard D., *The Shows of London* (Cambridge, MA and London: Harvard University Press, 1978).

Anderson, Andrew Runni, *Alexander's Gate, Gog and Magog, and the Inclosed Nations* (Cambridge, MA: The Medieval Academy of America, 1932).

Anderson, Martha G., and Philip M. Peek (eds), *Ways of the Rivers: Arts and Environment of the Niger Delta* (Los Angeles: UCLA Fowler Museum of Cultural History, 2002).

Andrade, Osvaldo de, "The Anthropophagist Manifesto" [1928], trans. Alfred Mac Adam, *Latin American Literature and Arts* 51 (1995), pp. 65–8.

Andriano, Joseph D. *Immortal Monster: The Mythological Evolution of the Fantastic Beast in Modern Fiction and Film* (Westport, CT and London: Greenwood Press, 1999).

Andyshak, Sarah Catherine, "Figural and Discursive Depictions of the Other in the *Travels of Sir John Mandeville*," MA thesis, Florida State University, 2009.

Anna, Luigi de, "Columbus and the *Mirabilia*," *Faravid* 16 (1992), pp. 133–40.

Anon, "The 60 Minutes/Vanity Fair Poll," *Vanity Fair* online, <http://www.vanityfair.com/magazine/2010/10/60-minutes-poll-201010>, October 2010.

Antichi planisferi e portolani: Modena, Biblioteca Estense Univesitaria (Modena: Il Bulino, and Milan: Y. Press, 2004).

Anuchin, D.N., "K istorii oznakomleniia s Sibiriu do Ermaka," *Drevnosti: Trudy Moskovskogo arkheologischeskogo obshchestva* 14 (1890), pp. 227–313.

Aquinas, Thomas, *Summa Theologica*, trans. Fathers of the English Dominican Province, 3 volumes (New York: Benzinger Bros, 1947).

Arciniegas, Germán, *Amerigo and the New World*, trans. Harriet de Onís (New York: Alfred A. Knopf, 1955).

——, *Biografía del Caribe* (Buenos Aires: Sudamericana, 1963).

Arens, William, *The Man-Eating Myth: Anthropology and Anthropophagy* (New York: Oxford University Press, 1979).

——, "Rethinking Anthropophagy," in Francis Barker, Peter Hulme, and Margaret Iversen (eds), *Cannibalism and the Colonial World* (New York: Cambridge University Press, 1998), pp. 39–62.

Arioli, A., *Le isole mirabili: Periplo arabo medievale* (Turin: Einaudi, 1989), translated into Spanish as *Islario maravilloso: periplo arabe medieval*, trans. M. Rodriguez (Madrid: Ollero, 1992).

Aristotle, *Generation of Animals*, trans. A.L. Peck (London and Cambridge, MA: Harvard University Press, 1963 and 1979).

Arseneau, Mary, "Madeline, Mermaids, and Medusas in 'The Eve of St. Agnes,'" *Papers on Language and Literature* 33 (1997), pp. 227–43.

Asakura Kyōji, "Ano 'Kuchi-sake-onna' no sumika o Gifu sanchūni mita!" in Ishii Shinji (ed.), *Uwasa no hon* (Tokyo: JICC Shuppan kyoku, 1989).

Asheri, David, Alan Lloyd, and Aldo Corcella, *A Commentary on Herodotus Books I–IV* (Oxford: Oxford University Press, 2007).

Asma, Stephen T., *On Monsters: An Unnatural History of Our Worst Fears* (Oxford: Oxford University Press, 2009).

Astley, Thomas, *A New General Collection of Voyages and Travels* [1745], vol. 2 (New York: Barnes and Noble, 1968).

Aston, W.G. (trans.), *Nihongi: Chronicles of Japan from the Earliest Times to A.D. 697* (Rutland, VT: Charles E. Tuttle, 1972).

Asúa, Miguel de, and Roger French, *A New World of Animals: Early Modern Europeans on the Creatures of Iberian America* (Aldershot, UK and Burlington, VT: Ashgate, 2005).

Atherton, Catherine (ed.), *Monsters and Monstrosity in Greek and Roman Culture*, vol. 6, *Nottingham Classical Literature Series* (Bari: Levanti Editori, 1998).

Atsunobu, Inada, and Tanaka Naohi (eds), *Toriyama Sekien gazu hyakki yagyō* (Tokyo: Kokusho kankōkai, 1999).

Auerbach, Nina, *Woman and Demon: The Life of a Victorian Myth* (Cambridge: Harvard University Press, 1982).

Auge, M., *Le rivage alladian: Organisation et évolution des villages alladian* (Paris: ORSTOM, 1969).

Augustine of Hippo, *De civitate Dei*, in Marcus Dods (trans.), *St Augustin's City of God and Christian Doctrine*, Nicene and Post-Nicene Fathers 2 (1887; reprint Grand Rapids, MI: Eerdmans, 1983).

——, *Ennarrationes in Psalmos*, in Philip Schaff (ed.), *Saint Augustine: Expositions on the Book of Psalms*, The Nicene and Post-Nicene Fathers, series 1, vol. 8 (New York: Christian Literature Publishing Co., 1888).

——, *De civitate Dei*, ed. Bernhard Dombart, 2 volumes (Leipzig: Teubner, 1909).

——, *The City of God*, trans. Marcus Dods (New York: Modern Library, 1950).

——, *The City of God Against the Pagans*, trans. Eva Matthews Sanford and William McAllen Green, 7 volumes (London and Cambridge, MA: Heinemann and Harvard University Press, 1965).

——, *City of God*, The Loeb Classical Library, vol. 5 (Cambridge, MA: Harvard University Press 1966).

——, *On Free Choice of the Will*, trans. Thomas Williams (Indianapolis: Hackett, 1993).

Austin, Greta, "Marvelous Peoples or Marvelous Races? Race and the Anglo-Saxon *Wonders of the East*," in Timothy S. Jones and David A. Sprunger (eds), *Marvels, Monsters, and Miracles: Studies in the Medieval and Early Modern Imaginations* (Kalamazoo, MI: Western Michigan University, 2002), pp. 25–51.

Awn, Peter, *Satan's Tragedy and Redemption: Iblis in Sufi Psychology* (Leiden: Brill, 1983).

Baba Akiko, *Oni no kenkyū* (Tokyo: Sanichi shobō, 1971; reprint Chikuma shobō, 1988).

Back, Les, and John Solomos, "Introduction: Theories of Race and Racism: Genesis, Development and Contemporary Trends," in Les Back and John Solomos (eds), *Theories of Race and Racism: A Reader*, 2nd edn (London: Routledge, 2009).

Bacon, Sir Francis, *The Two Bookes of the Proficiencie and Advancement of Learning* (London, 1605).

——, "Of Deformity," in *Essays of Francis Bacon: The Essays or Counsels, Civil and Moral, of Francis Ld. Verulam Viscount St Albans*, <http://www.authorama.com/essays-of-francis-bacon-44.html>.

Bader, Christopher D., F. Carson Mencken, and Joseph D. Baker, *Paranormal America: Ghost Encounters, UFO Sightings, Bigfoot Hunts, and Other Curiosities in Religion and Culture* (New York and London: New York University Press, 2010).

Badmington, Neil, *Posthumanism (Readers in Cultural Criticism)* (Basingstoke: Palgrave Macmillan, 2000).

Bae, James H., *In a World of Gods and Goddesses: The Mystic Art of Indra Sharma* (Novato, CA: Mandala Publishing, 2003).

Bagley, Robert W., Max Loehr, and Bernhard Karlgren, *Max Loehr and the Study of Chinese Bronzes: Style and Classification in the History of Art*, Cornell East Asia Series (Ithaca, NY: East Asia Program, Cornell University, 2008).

Baird, Robert, "Animalizing 'Jurassic Park's' Dinosaurs: Blockbuster Schemata and Cross-Cultural Cognition in the Threat Scene," *Cinema Journal* 37/4 (1998), pp. 82–103.

Baldick, Chris, *In Frankenstein's Shadow: Myth, Monstrosity, and Nineteenth-century Writing* (Oxford: Clarendon Press, 1987).

Barber, Peter, "Medieval Maps of the World," in P.D.A. Harvey (ed.), *The Hereford World Map: Medieval World Maps and their Context* (London: The British Library, 2006), pp. 1–44.

Barber, Peter, and Michelle P. Brown, "The Aslake World Map," *Imago Mundi* 44/1 (1992), pp. 24–44.

Baring, Anne, and Jules Cashford, *The Myth of the Goddess: Evolution of an Image* (London: Arkana Penguin Books, 1991).

Barnard, Hans, "Sire, il n'y a pas de Blemmyes: A Re-Evaluation of Historical and Archaeological Data," in *People of the Red Sea: Proceedings of the Red Sea Project II, Held in the British Museum, October 2004* (Oxford: Archaeopress, 2005), pp. 23–40.

Bartelink, G.J.M., "Het fabeldier martichoras of mantichora," *Hermeneus* 43 (1972), pp. 169–74 and 225.

Bartlett, Robert, "Medieval Concepts of Race and Ethnicity," *Journal of Medieval and Early Modern Studies* 31 (2001), pp. 39–56.

——, *The Natural and the Supernatural in the Middle Ages* (New York: Cambridge University Press, 2008).

Barton, Carlin A., *The Sorrows of the Ancient Romans: The Gladiator and the Monster* (Princeton: Princeton University Press, 1993).

Bartra, Roger, *Wild Men in the Looking Glass: The Mythic Origins of European Otherness*, trans. Carol T. Berrisford (Ann Arbor: University of Michigan Press, 1994).

Bassani, Ezio, and William B. Fagg, *Africa and the Renaissance: Art in Ivory* (New York: The Center for African Art and Prestel, 1988).

Bates, A.W., *Emblematic Monsters: Unnatural Conceptions and Deformed Births in Early Modern Europe* (Amsterdam and New York: Rodopi, 2005).

Baynham, Elizabeth, "Alexander and the Amazons," *Classical Quarterly* 51/1 (2001), pp. 115–26.

Bazopoulou-Kyrkanidou, Euterpe, "Chimeric Creatures in Greek Mythology and Reflections in Science," *American Journal of Medical Genetics Part A*, 100/1 (2001), pp. 66–80.

Beagon, Mary, *Roman Nature: The Thought of Pliny the Elder* (Oxford: Clarendon Press, 1992).

—— (trans. and comm.), *The Elder Pliny on the Human Animal: Natural History Book 7* (Oxford: Clarendon Press, 2005).

——, "Situating Nature's Wonders in Pliny's *Natural History*," in Ed Bispham and Greg Rowe (eds), *Vita vigilia est: Essays in Honour of Barbara Levick* (London: Institute of Classical Studies, 2007), pp. 19–40.

Beal, Timothy K., *Religion and its Monsters* (New York: Routledge, 2002).

Beard, Mary, and John Henderson, *Classical Art: From Greece to Rome* (Oxford: Oxford University Press, 2001).

Beatus of Liébana, *Sancti Beati a Liebana in Apocalypsin Codex Gerundensis* (Olten: Urs Graf, 1962).

——, *Commentarium in Apocalypsim. Beati in Apocalipsin libri duodecim: Codex Gerundensis A.D. 975* (Madrid: Edilán, 1975).

——, *Expositio im Apocalisim* (Valencia: Vicent García, 1992).

——, *Beato de Liébana: Códice de San Mamede de Lorvao* (Valencia: Patrimonio, 2003).

Bede, *On the Temple*, trans. Seán Connolly (Liverpool: Liverpool University Press, 1995).

Belozerskaya, Marina, *The Medici Giraffe: And Other Tales of Exotic Animals and Power* (Boston and London: Little, Brown, 2006).

Bennett, Judith M., *History Matters: Patriarchy and the Challenge of Feminism* (Philadelphia: University of Pennsylvania Press, 2006).

Benninghof-Luhl, Sibylle, "Die Ausstellung der Kolonialsierten: Volkershauen von 1874–1932," in *Andenken an den Kolonialismus* (Tubingen: Attempto, 1984).

Berger, Patricia Ann, "Rites and Festivities in the Art of Eastern Han China: Shantung and Kiangsu Provinces," PhD dissertation, University of California, Berkeley, 1980.

Bergevin, Jean, *Déterminisme et géographie: Hérodote, Strabon, Albert le Grand et Sebastian Münster* (Sainte-Foy, Québec: Presses de l'Université Laval, 1992).

Berggren, J. Lennart, and Alexander Jones, *Ptolemy's Geography: An Annotated Translation of the Theoretical Chapters* (Princeton: Princeton University Press, 2000).

Bernasconi, Robert, "Who Invented the Concept of Race?" in Les Back and John Solomos (eds), *Theories of Race and Racism: A Reader*, 2nd edn (London: Routledge, 2009), pp. 83–103.

Bernatzik, Hugo Adolf, *Im Reich der Bidyogo: Geheimnisvolle Inseln in Westafrika* (Leipzig: Koehler and Voigtländer, 1944).

Bernheimer, Richard, *Wild Men in the Middle Ages: A Study in Art, Sentiment, and Demonology* (Cambridge, MA: Harvard University Press, 1952).

Bertman, Stephen, "The Antisemitic Origin of Michelangelo's Horned Moses," *Shofar* 27 (2009), pp. 95–106.

Bevan, William Latham, and H.W. Phillott, *Mediæval Geography. An Essay in Illustration of the Hereford Mappa Mundi* (London: E. Stanford, 1873; reprint Amsterdam: Meridian, 1969).

Bhattacharyya, N.N., *Indian Demonology: The Inverted Pantheon* (Delhi: Manohar, 2000).

Biblia Sacra: Iuxta Vulgatam Versionem, ed. Bonifatius Fisher, Robert Weber, and Roger Gryson (Stuttgart: Deutsche Bibelgesellschaft, 1994).

Biggar, Henry P., *The Voyages of Jacques Cartier* (Ottawa: F.A. Acland, 1924).

Bigwood, J.M., "Ctesias' *Indica* and Photius," *Phoenix* 43/4 (1989), pp. 302–16.

Bildhauer, Bettina, and Robert Mills (eds), *The Monstrous Middle Ages* (Cardiff: University of Wales Press, 2003).

Bird, Jessalynn, "The *Historia Orientalis* of Jacques de Vitry: Visual and Written Commentaries as Evidence of a Text's Audience, Reception, and Utilization," *Essays in Medieval Studies* 20/1 (2004), pp. 56–74.

Birdwood, G.C.M., *The Industrial Arts of India* (London: Chapman and Hall, 1879).

Birrell, Anne, *The Classic of Mountains and Seas*, Penguin Classics (London and New York, NY: Penguin Books; Penguin Putnam, 1999).

Bishop, Louise M., "The Myth of the Flat Earth," in Stephen J. Harris and Bryon Lee Grigsby (eds), *Misconceptions about the Middle Ages* (London and New York, NY: Routledge, 2008), pp. 97–101.

Bitterli, Urs, *Die "Wilden" und die "Zivilisierten"* [1976] (Munich: Beck. Benninghof-Luhl, 1984).

Blake, Erin C., "Where Be Dragons?" *Mercator's World* 4/4 (July 1999), p. 80.

Blanchard, Pascal, Nicolas Bancel, Gilles Boetsch, Éric Deroo, Sandrine Lemaire, and Charles Forsdick (eds), *Human Zoos: Science and Spectacle in the Age of Colonial Empires* (Liverpool: Liverpool University Press, 2008).

Blier, Suzanne Preston, "Imaging Otherness in Ivory: African Portrayals of the Portuguese ca. 1492," *Art Bulletin* 75 (1993), pp. 375–96.

Bloomfield, Morton W., *The Seven Deadly Sins: An Introduction to the History of a Religious Concept, With Special Reference to Medieval English Literature* (East Lansing, Michigan State College Press, 1952).

Blundell, Sue, *Women in Ancient Greece* (Cambridge, MA: Harvard University Press, 1995).

Blundeville, Thomas, *Exercises* (London, 1594).

Bodde, Derk, *Festivals in Classical China* (Princeton: Princeton University Press, 1975).

Bodde, Derk, Clarence Morris, and Jinqing Zhu, *Law in Imperial China: Exemplified by 190 Ch'ing Dynasty Cases*, Harvard Studies in East Asian Law 1 (Cambridge: Harvard University Press, 1967).

Boffito, G., "La leggenda degli Antipodi," in *Miscellanea di studi critici edita in onore di Arturo Graf* (Bergamo: Instituto italiano d'arti grafiche, 1903), pp. 583–601.

Bogdan, Robert, *Freak Show: Presenting Human Oddities for Amusement and Profit* (Chicago: University of Chicago Press, 1990).

Bogdan, Robert, and Jane Fry, *Being Different: The Autobiography of Jane Fry* (New York: John Wiley, 1974).

Bognolo, A., "Geografia mitica e geografia moderna: le Amazonni nella scoperta dell'America," *Columbeis* 4 (1990), pp. 7–22.

Bolívar, Simón, *Letter from Jamaica* (1815), trans. Lewis Bertrand, in *Selected Writings of Bolivar* (New York: Colonial Press, 1951).

Boltz, William G., "Philological Footnotes to the Han New Year Rites," *Journal of the American Oriental Society* 99/3 (1979), pp. 423–38.

Bonajuto, Alessandra Emilia Luisa, "Le antiche localizzazioni delle avventure di Odisseo narrate ai feaci," PhD dissertation, Università degli studi di Perugia, 1998.

Boone, Sylvia A., *Radiance from the Water: Ideals of Feminine Beauty in Mende Art* (New Haven: Yale University Press, 1986).

Borgatti, Jean M., "Tale of the Achikobo: It Is the Tail That is Mine," in Henry John Drewal (ed.), *Sacred Waters: Arts for Mami Wata and Other Water Divinities in Africa and the African Atlantic World* (Bloomington: Indiana University Press, 2008), pp. 105–13.

Borgen, Robert, *Sugawara no Michizane and the Early Heian Court* (Honolulu: University of Hawai'i Press, 1994).

Borges, Jorge Luis, *Libro de los seres imaginarios* (Buenos Aires: Kier, 1967).

Borgnet, Étienne César Auguste (ed.), *B. Alberti Magni Opera Omnia*, 38 volumes (Paris: Vives, 1890–99).

Bosworth, Joseph, *An Anglo-Saxon Dictionary, Based on the Manuscript Collections of the Late Joseph Bosworth*, ed. T. Northcote Toller and Alistair Campbell (Oxford: Oxford University Press, 1838–1972).

Botting, Fred, *Gothic* (London and New York: Routledge, 1997).

Boucher, Philip P., *Cannibal Encounters: Europeans and Island Caribs, 1492–1763* (Baltimore: The Johns Hopkins University Press, 1992).

Bourguignon, Erika, 'The Persistence of Folk Belief: Some Notes on Cannibalism and Zombis in Haiti', in *Journal of American Folklore* 72/283 (1959), pp. 36–46.

Bovey, Alixe, *Monsters and Grotesques in Medieval Manuscripts* (Toronto: University of Toronto Press, 2002).

Boyd, Matthieu, "Melion and the Wolves of Ireland," *Neophilologus* 93 (2009), pp. 555–70.

Brandenberger, Tobias, "El episodio amazónico del Libro de Alexandre. Fondo, fuentes, figuración," *Zeitschrift für romanische Philologie* 110/3–4 (1994), pp. 432–66.

Bredehoft, Thomas A., "Origin Stories: Feminist Science Fiction and C.L. Moore's 'Shambleau,'" *Science Fiction Studies* 24 (1997), pp. 369–86.

Bremmer, Jan, "Monsters en fabeldieren in de Griekse cultuur," *Vereniging van Vrienden Allard Pierson Museum Amsterdam: Mededelingenblad* 68 (1997), pp. 2–5.

Brend, Barbara, *Muhammad Juki's Shahnama of Firdausi* (London: The Royal Asiatic Society of Great Britain and Ireland and Philip Wilson Publishers, 2010).

British Museum and Roderick Whitfield, *The Art of Central Asia: The Stern Collection in the British Museum* (Tokyo/New York: Kodansha International, 1982).

Broedel, Hans Peter, *The* Malleus Maleficarum *and the Construction of Witchcraft: Theology and Popular Belief* (Manchester: Manchester University Press, 2003).

Brontë, Charlotte, *Jane Eyre* [1847] (New York: Relford, Clarke, & Co., 1885).

Brown, Peter, *Augustine of Hippo: A Biography*, 3rd rev. edn (Berkeley: University of California Press, 2000).

Brown, Truesdell S., "The Reliability of Megasthenes," *American Journal of Philology* 76/1 (1955), pp. 18–33.

Browning, Judith E., "Sin, Eve, and Circe: *Paradise Lost* and the Ovidian Circe Tradition," *Milton Studies* 26 (1990), pp. 135–57.

Bruman, Henry J., "The Schaffhausen Carta Marina of 1531," *Imago Mundi* 41 (1989), pp. 124–32.

Brundage, James, *Law, Sex, and Christian Society in Medieval Europe* (Chicago: University of Chicago Press, 1987).

Brunelle, Gayle K., "Dieppe School," in David Buisseret (ed.), *The Oxford Companion to World Exploration* (New York: Oxford University Press, 2007), pp. 237–8.

Brzozowska-Brywczyńska, Maja, "Monstrous/Cute: Notes on the Ambivalent Nature of Cuteness," in Niall Scott (ed.), *Monsters and the Monstrous: Myths and Metaphors of Enduring Evil* (Amsterdam and New York: Rodopi, 2007), pp. 213–28.

Bucher, Bernadette, *Icon and Conquest: A Structural Analysis of the Illustrations of de Bry's Great Voyages*, trans. Basia Miller Gulati (Chicago: University of Chicago Press, 1981).

Budge, Ernest Alfred Wallis (ed. and trans.), *The Paradise of the Holy Fathers* (London: Chatto & Windus, 1907).

Bullough, Vern, "Cross Dressing and Gender Role Change in the Middle Ages," in Vern Bullough and James Brundage (eds), *Handbook of Medieval Sexuality* (New York: Garland Publishing, 2000), pp. 223–42.

Bulwer, John, *Anthropometamorphosis: Man Transform'd; or, the Artificial Changeling* (London, 1650).

Burke, David G. "Translating *Hoi Ioudaioi* in the New Testament," *TIC Talk* 24 (1993).

Burman, Thomas E., *Reading the Qur'ān in Latin Christendom, 1140–1560* (Philadelphia: University of Pennsylvania Press, 2007).

Burnett, Mark Thornton, *Constructing "Monsters" in Shakespearean Drama and Early Modern Culture* (Basingstoke: Palgrave Macmillan, 2002).

Burns, William E., "The King's Two Monstrous Bodies: John Bulwer and the English Revolution," in Peter G. Platt (ed.), *Wonders, Marvels, and Monsters in Early Modern Culture* (Newark, DE and London: University of Delaware Press and Associated University Presses, 1999), pp. 187–202.

——, *An Age of Wonders: Prodigies, Politics and Providence in England, 1657–1727* (Manchester: Manchester University Press, 2002).

Burrus, Virginia, "Queer Lives of Saints: Jerome's Hagiography," *Journal of the History of Sexuality* 10 (2001), pp. 442–79.

Busbee, Mark Bradshaw, "A Paradise Full of Monsters: India in the Old English Imagination," *LATCH: A Journal for the Study of the Literary Artifact in Theory, Culture, or History* 1 (2008), pp. 49–70.

Butler, Judith, *Bodies that Matter: On the Discursive Limits of Sex* (New York: Routledge, 1993).

——, *Precarious Life: The Powers of Mourning and Violence* (New York: Verso, 2004).

——, *Undoing Gender* (New York: Routledge, 2004).

Buxton, Richard, *Imaginary Greece: The Contexts of Mythology* (Cambridge and New York: Cambridge University Press, 1994).

Bynum, Caroline Walker, *Metamorphosis and Identity* (New York: Zone Books, 2001).

Byron, Gay L., *Symbolic Blackness and Ethnic Difference in Early Christian Literature* (London: Routledge, 2002).

Cahn, Walter B., "The 'Portrait' of Muhammad in the Toledan Collection," in Elizabeth Sears and Thelma K. Thomas (eds), *Reading Medieval Images: The Art Historian and the Object* (Ann Arbor: University of Michigan Press, 2002), pp. 51–60.

Caiozzo, Anna, "L'image de l'Europe et des Européens dans les représentations de l'Orient médiéval," *Caietele Echinox* 10 (2006), pp. 84–120.

Calasso, Giovanna, "L'intervento di Iblis nella creazione dell'uomo: L'ambivalente figura del 'nemico' nelle tradizioni islamiche," *Rivista degli Studi Orientali* 45/1–2 (1971), pp. 71–90.

Caldwell, Richard, *The Origin of the Gods: A Psychoanalytic Study of Greek Theogonic Myth* (New York and Oxford: Oxford University Press, 1989).

Callan, Richard J., "The Archetype of Psychic Renewal in 'La Vorágine,'" in Carmello Virgillo and Naomi Lindstrom (eds), *Woman as Myth and Metaphor in Latin American Literature* (Columbia, MO: University of Missouri Press, 1985).

Camille, Michael, *Mirror in Parchment: The Luttrell Psalter and the Making of Medieval England* (London: Reaktion, 1998).

Camocio, Giovanni Francesco, *A Large World Map Dated 1569 Sold at the Sign of the Pyramid in Venice by Joan Franciscus Camotius, Now in the George H. Beans Library* (Philadelphia: George H. Beans Library, 1933).

Campbell, Mary Baine, *The Witness and the Other World: Exotic European Travel Writing, 400–1600* (Ithaca, NY and London: Cornell University Press, 1988).

——, *Wonder and Science: Imagining Worlds in Early Modern Europe* (Ithaca, NY: Cornell University Press, 1999).

Canosa, Ercilio Vento, "Antropofagia en aborígenes de Cuba," *Revista médica electrón* 27/3 (2005), pp. 36–45.

Caputi, Jane, *Goddesses and Monsters: Women, Myth, Power, and Popular Culture* (Madison: Popular Press, 2004).

Carandini, Andrea, Andreina Ricci, Mariette de Vos, and Maura Medri, *Filosofiana: The Villa of Piazza Armerina: The Image of a Roman Aristocrat at the Time of Constantine* (Palermo: S.F. Flaccovio, 1982).

Cardinali, Giuseppe, "*Nec sit terris ultima Thule*: Echi della scoperta del Nuovo Mondo nei *Commentarii alla Medea* di Seneca," *Geographia Antiqua* 10–11 (2001–2002), pp. 155–62.

Carey, Conán Dean, "In Hell the One Without Sin is Lord," *Sino-Platonic Papers* 109 (October 2000), pp. 23–7.

Carey, John, "Ireland and the Antipodes: The Heterodoxy of Virgil of Salzburg," *Speculum* 64 (1989), pp. 1–10.

——, "Werewolves in Medieval Ireland," *Cambrian Medieval Celtic Studies* 44 (2002), pp. 37–72.

Carlson, John B., and Linda Landis, "Bands, Bicephalic Dragons and Other Beasts: The Skyband in Maya Art and Iconography," in Merle Greene Robertson and Elizabeth P. Benson (eds), *Fourth Palenque Round Table, 1980* (San Francisco: Pre-Columbian Art Research Institute, 1985), pp. 115–40.

Carpentier, Alejo, "Prologue to *The Kingdom of this World*," trans. in Lois Parkinson Zamora and Wendy B. Faris (eds), *Magical Realism: Theory, History, Community* (Durham, NC: Duke University Press, 1995).

Carr, Pat, and Williard Gingerich, "The Vagina Dentata Motif in Nahuatl and Pueblo Mythic Narratives: A Comparative Study," in Brian Swann (ed.), *Smoothing the Ground: Essays on Native American Oral Literature* (Berkeley: University of California Press, 1983), pp. 187–203.

Carroll, Noël, *The Philosophy of Horror or Paradoxes of the Heart* (New York: Routledge, 1990).

Cartier, Jacques, *Brief recit, & succincte narration, de la nauigation faicte es ysles de Canada, Hochelage & Saguenay & autres, auec particulieres meurs, langaige, & cerimonies des habitans d'icelles: fort delectable à veoir* (Paris: Roffet dict Faucheur & Anthoine le Clerc frères, 1545).

——, *The Voyages of Jacques Cartier*, intro. Ramsay Cook (Toronto: University of Toronto Press, 1993).

Cartlidge, Neil (ed. and trans.), *The Owl and the Nightingale* (Exeter: University of Exeter Press, 2001).

Cary, George, *The Medieval Alexander*, ed. D.J.A. Ross (Cambridge, UK: Cambridge University Press, 1956).

Castro, Mercedes Aguirre, "Scylla: Hideous Monster or Femme Fatale? A Case of Contradiction between Literary and Artistic Evidence," *Cuadernos de Filología Clásica: Estudios griegos e indoeuropeos* 12 (2002), pp. 319–28.

Castro-Klaren, Sara, "What Does Cannibalism Speak? Jean de Léry and the Tupinamba Lesson," in Pamela Bacarisse (ed.), *Carnal Knowledge: Essays on the Flesh, Sex, and Sexuality in Hispanic Letters and Film* (Pittsburgh: Tres Ríos, 1993).

Cattaneo, Angelo, *Mappa mundi 1457* (Rome: Treccani, 2008).

——, "Réflexion sur les climats et les zones face à l'expansion des XVe et XVIe siècles," *Bulletin du Comite Français de Cartographie* 199 (2009), pp. 7–21.

Cavallo, Guglielmo (ed.), *Cristoforo Colombo e l'apertura degli spazi: mostra storico-cartografica* (Rome: Istituto Poligrafico e Zecca dello Stato, 1992).

Caviness, Madeline, "From the Self-Invention of the Whiteman to The Good, the Bad, and the Ugly," *Different Visions* 1 (2008).

Cawley, A.C., and J.J. Anderson (eds), *Sir Gawain and the Green Knight; Pearl; Cleanness; Patience* (London: Dent, 1991).

Céard, Jean, *La Nature et les prodiges: l'Insolite au XVIe siècle en France* (Geneva: Droz, 1977).

——, *La Nature et les prodiges: l'Insolite au XVIe siècle*, 2e édition revue et augmentée (Geneva: Droz, 1996).

Cerezo Martínez, Ricardo, *La cartografía náutica Española en los siglos XIV, XV y XVI* (Madrid: C.S.I.C., 1994).

Chamberlain, Alexander F., "Recent Literature on the South American 'Amazons,'" *Journal of American Folklore* 24/91 (1911), pp. 16–20.

Chambers, Cynthia A., "Cannibalism in a Cultural Context: Cartographic Imagery and Iconography of the New World Indigenous Peoples During the Age of Discovery," PhD dissertation, The University of Texas at Arlington, 2006.

Chaucer, Geoffrey, *The Riverside Chaucer*, 3rd edn, ed. Larry D. Bensen (Oxford: Oxford University Press, 2008).

Chekin, Leonid S., *Northern Eurasia in Medieval Cartography: Inventory, Text, Translation, and Commentary* (Turnhout: Brepols, 2006).

Chicangana-Bayona, Yobenj Aucardo, "El festín antropofágico de los indios Tupinambá en los grabados de Theodoro de Bry, 1592," *Fronteras de la historia* 10 (2005), pp. 19–82.

——, "El nacimiento del caníbal: un debate conceptual," *Historia crítica* 36 (2008), pp. 150–73.

Childs-Johnson, Elizabeth, and Sajid Rizvi, *The Meaning of the Graph Yi and its Implications for Shang Belief and Art*, Eaj Monograph (London: Saffron, 2008).

Chrétien de Troyes, *Yvain, the Knight of the Lion*, trans. Burton Raffel (New Haven: Yale University Press, 1987).

——, *Romans*, ed. Michel Zink (Paris: Le Livre de poche, 1994).

Chrysostom, John, *John Chrysostom*, ed. Wendy Mayer and Pauline Allen (London: Routledge, 2000).

Cicero, *De senectute; De amicitia; De divinatione*, trans. William Armistead Falconer (London and Cambridge, MA: Heinemann and Harvard University Press, 1971).

Cizek, Alexander, "Ungeheuer und magische Lebewesen in der *Epistola Alexandri ad magistratum suum Aristotelem de situ Indiae*," in Jan Goossens and Timothy Sodmann (eds), *Third International Beast Epic, Fable and Fabliau Colloquium, Münster 1979: Proceedings* (Cologne: Böhlau, 1981), pp. 78–94.

Clare, R.J., "Representing Monstrosity: Polyphemus in the *Odyssey*," in Catherine Atherton (ed.), *Monsters and Monstrosity in Greek and Roman Culture*, vol. 6, *Nottingham Classical Literature Series* (Bari: Levanti Editori, 1998), pp. 1–17.

Clark, John, "Open and Closed Discourses of Modernity in Asian Art," in *Modernity in Asian Art* (Sydney: Wild Peony Press, 1993), pp. 1–17.

Clark, W., *A Case of Human Monstrosity*, Folio (Cambridge: Cambridge University Press, 1831).

Clarke, T.H., *The Rhinoceros from Dürer to Stubbs, 1515–1799* (London: Philip Wilson for Sotheby's Publications; New York: Harper & Row, 1986).

Classen, Albrecht, *The Medieval Chastity Belt: A Myth-Making Process* (New York: Palgrave Macmillan, 2007).

Clay, Diskin, "Columbus' Senecan Prophecy," *American Journal of Philology* 113/4 (1992), pp. 617–20.

Clemit, Pamela, "*Frankenstein, Matilda*, and the Legacies of Godwin and Wollstonecraft," in Esther Schor (ed.), *The Cambridge Companion to Mary Shelley* (Cambridge: Cambridge University Press, 2003), pp. 26–44.

Clifford, James, "On Ethnographic Surrealism," *Comparative Studies in Society and History* 23 (1981), pp. 539–64.

Coe, Michael D., *Lords of the Underworld: Masterpieces of Classic Maya Ceramics* (Princeton: The Art Museum, Princeton University, 1978).

——, "The Hero Twins in Myth and Image," in Justin Kerr (ed.), *The Maya Vase Book,* vol. 1 (New York: Kerr Associates, 1989), pp. 161–84.

Cohen, Jeffrey Jerome, "Monster Culture (Seven Theses)," in Jeffrey Jerome Cohen (ed.), *Monster Theory: Reading Culture* (London and Minneapolis: University of Minnesota Press, 1996), pp. 3–25.

——, "Preface: In a Time of Monsters," in Jeffrey Jerome Cohen (ed.), *Monster Theory: Reading Culture* (London and Minneapolis: University of Minnesota Press, 1996).

——, (ed.), *Monster Theory: Reading Culture* (London and Minneapolis: University of Minnesota Press, 1996).

——, *Of Giants: Sex, Monsters, and the Middle Ages* (Minneapolis: University of Minnesota Press, 1999).

——, *Hybrids, Monsters, Borderlands: The Bodies of Gerald of Wales* (New York: St Martin's Press, 2000).

——, "On Saracen Enjoyment: Some Fantasies of Race in Late Medieval France and England," *Journal of Medieval and Early Modern Studies* 31 (2001), pp. 113–46.

——, *Hybridity, Identity and Monstrosity in Medieval Britain: On Difficult Middles* (New York: Palgrave Macmillan, 2006).

——, "Inventing with Animals in the Middle Ages," in Barbara A. Hanawalt and Lisa J. Kiser (eds), *Engaging with Nature: Essays on the Natural World in Medieval and Early Modern Europe* (Notre Dame, Indiana: University of Notre Dame Press, 2008).

Cohn, Norman, *Europe's Inner Demons: The Demonization of Christians in Medieval Christendom* (Chicago: University of Chicago Press, 2000).

Cole, H.H., *Catalogue of the Objects of Indian Art Exhibited in the South Kensington Museum* (London: G.E. Eyre and W. Spottiswoode, 1874).

Columbus, Christopher, *The Journal of Christopher Columbus* [1493], trans. Clements R. Markham (London: Hakluyt Society, 1893; reprint Boston: Adamant Media Corporation, 2001).

——, *Letters from America: Columbus's First Accounts of the 1492 Voyage,* ed. and trans. B.W. Ife (London: King's College London, School of Humanities, 1992).

——, *A Synoptic Edition of the Log of Columbus's First Voyage,* ed. Francesca Lardicci (Turnhout: Brepols, 1999).

Colwill, Elizabeth, "Pass as a Woman, Act Like a Man: Marie-Antoinette as Tribade in the Pornography of the French Revolution," in Dena Goodman (ed.), *Marie-Antoinette: Writing on the Body of a Queen* (London: Routledge, 2003), pp. 139–70.

Coomaraswamy, Ananda K., *The Dance of Siva* (New York: Sunwise Turn Press, 1918).

——, *The Transformation of Nature in Art* (Cambridge, MA: Harvard University Press, 1934).

Coote, Jeremy, and Jill Salmons, "Mermaids and Mami Wata on Brassware from Old Calabar," in Henry John Drewal (ed.), *Sacred Waters: Art for Mami Wata and Other Water Divinities in Africa and the African Atlantic World* (Bloomington: Indiana University Press, 2008), pp. 259–75.

Coppola, F.F., and J.V. Hart, *Bram Stoker's Dracula: The Film and the Legend* (New York: Newsmarket, 1992).

Coquilhat, Camille, *Sur le Haut-Congo* (Paris: J. Lebegue, 1888).

Corfis, Ivy A., "Beauty, Deformity, and the Fantastic in the Historia de la linda Melosina," *Hispanic Review* 55/2 (1987), pp. 181–93.

——, "Empire and Romance: Historia de la linda Melosina," *Neophilologus* 82/4 (1998), pp. 559–75.

Cortez, Constance, "The Principal Bird Deity in Preclassic and Early Classic Art," in Virginia M. Fields and Dorie Reents-Budet (eds), *Lords of Creation: The Origins of Sacred Maya Kingship* (London: Scala, 2005), pp. 62–6.

Cotterill, Rodney, *Enchanted Looms* (Cambridge: Cambridge University Press, 1998).

Coulter, Cornelia C., "The 'Great Fish' in Ancient and Medieval Story," *Transactions and Proceedings of the American Philological Association* 57 (1926), pp. 32–50.

Craige, John Houston, *Cannibal Cousins* (New York: Minton, Balch & Co., 1934).

Craine, Eugene R., and Reginald C. Reindorp, *The Codex Pérez and the Book of Chilam Balam of Maní* (Norman: University of Oklahoma Press, 1979).

Crais, Clifton, and Pamela Scully, *Sara Baartman and the Hottentot Venus: A Ghost Story and a Biography* (Princeton: Princeton University Press, 2008).

Crane, Nicolas, *Mercator: The Man Who Mapped the Planet* (New York: Henry Holt, 2002).

Crawford, James Ludovic Lindsay, and Charles Henry Coote, *Autotype Facsimiles of Three Mappemondes* (Aberdeen: Aberdeen University Press, 1898).

Crawford, Julie, *Marvelous Protestantism: Monstrous Births in Post-Reformation England* (Baltimore, MD and London: The Johns Hopkins University Press, 2005).

Creed, Barbara, *The Monstrous Feminine: Film, Feminism, Psychoanalysis* (London: Routledge, 1993).

——, "Freud's Worst Nightmare: Dining with Dr. Hannibal Lecter," in Steven Jay Schneider (ed.), *Horror Film and Psychoanalysis: Freud's Worst Nightmare* (New York: Cambridge University Press, 2004).

Cressy, David, "Lamentable, Strange, and Wonderful: Headless Monsters in the English Revolution," in Laura Lunger Knoppers and Joan B. Landes (eds), *Monstrous Bodies/Political Monstrosities in Early Modern Europe* (Ithaca, NY: Cornell University Press, 2004), pp. 40–63.

Crone, Gerald R., *The Voyages of Cadamosto and Other Documents on Western Africa in the Second Half of the Fifteenth Century* (London: Hakluyt Society, 1937).

Curran, Andrew, *Sublime Disorder: Physical Monstrosity in Diderot's Universe* (Oxford: Voltaire Foundation, 2001).

——, "Afterword," in Laura Lunger Knoppers and Joan B. Landes (eds), *Monstrous Bodies/Political Monstrosities in Early Modern Europe* (Ithaca, NY and London: Cornell University Press, 2004), pp. 227–45.

Curran, Andrew, and Patrick Graille, "The Faces of Eighteenth-Century Monstrosity," introduction to Andrew Curran, Robert P. Maccubbin, and David

F. Morrill (eds), *Faces of Monstrosity in Eighteenth-Century Thought, Eighteenth-Century Life* 21, n.s., 2 (1997), pp. 1–15.

Cussans, John, "Voodoo Terror: (Mis)Representations of Vodu and Western Cultural Anxieties," presented for "Feels Like Voodoo Spirit–Haitian Art, Culture, Religion," *The October Gallery* (London, 2000), <http://codeless88. wordpress.com/voodoo-terror>, 2000.

Daegling, David J., *Bigfoot Exposed: An Anthropologist Examines America's Enduring Legend* (Walnut Creek, CA: AltaMira Press, 2004).

Daniel, Elton L., "Manuscripts and Editions of Bal'ami's 'Tarjamah-i Tarikh-i Tabari,'" *Journal of the Royal Asiatic Society of Great Britain and Ireland* 2 (1990), pp. 282–321.

Dash, J. Michael, "The (Un)kindness of Strangers: Writing Haiti in the 21st Century," *Caribbean Studies* 36/2 (2008), pp. 171–8.

Daston, Lorraine, and Katharine Park, "Unnatural Conceptions: The Study of Monsters in Sixteenth- and Seventeenth-Century France and England," *Past and Present* 92 (1981), pp. 20–54.

——, "The Topography of Wonder," in Lorraine Daston and Katharine Park (eds), *Wonders and the Order of Nature, 1150–1750* (New York, NY: Zone Books, 1998), pp. 21–66.

——, *Wonders and the Order of Nature, 1150–1750* (New York, NY: Zone Books, 1998).

Davies, Surekha, "Representations of Amerindians on European Maps and the Construction of Ethnographic Knowledge, 1506–1624," PhD dissertation, University of London, 2009.

——, "The Wondrous East in the Renaissance Geographical Imagination: Marco Polo, Fra Mauro and Giovanni Battista Ramusio", *History and Anthropology* 23/2, near n. 56 (2012, forthcoming).

Davis, Lennard J., "Constructing Normalcy: The Bell Curve, the Novel, and the Invention of the Disabled Body in the Nineteenth Century," in Lennard J. Davis (ed.), *The Disability Studies Reader*, 2nd edn (New York and London: Routledge, 2006), pp. 3–16.

——, (ed.), *The Disability Studies Reader*, 2nd edn (New York and London: Routledge, 2006).

Davis, Wade, *The Serpent and the Rainbow: A Harvard Scientist's Astonishing Journey into the Secret Societies of Haitian Voodoo, Zombis, and Magic* (New York: Touchstone 1985).

——, *Passage of Darkness: The Ethnobiology of the Haitian Zombie* (Chapel Hill, NC: University of North Carolina Press, 1988).

Dawson, Christopher (ed.), *Mission to Asia* (Toronto: University of Toronto Press, 1980).

Dayan, Joan, *Haiti, History, and the Gods* (Berkeley: University of California Press, 1998).

Deane, Charles, "[Inscriptions on Cabot's Mappe-monde]," *Proceedings of the Massachusetts Historical Society* 6 (1890–91), pp. 305–39, reprinted in H.R. Holmden, *Catalogue of Maps, Plans and Charts in the Map Room of the Dominion Archives* (Ottawa: Govt. Print. Bureau, 1912), pp. 568–88.

Debrunner, H.C., *Presence and Prestige: Africans in Europe* (Basel: Basler Afrika Bibliographien, 1979).

de Costa, B.F., "The Lenox Globe," *Magazine of American History* 3/9 (1879), pp. 529–40, reprinted in *Acta Cartographica* 4 (1969), pp. 120–34.

De Fouchécour, Charles-Henri, *Moralia: Les notions morales dans la litterature persane du 3/9 au 7/13 siècle* (Paris: Editions Recherche sur les civilisations, 1986).

Deleuze, Gilles, *Foucault*, trans. Sean Hand (London: Athlone Press, 1988).

Deleuze, Gilles, and Félix Guattari, *A Thousand Plateaus*, trans. Brian Massumi (Minneapolis, MN: University of Minnesota Press, 1987).

Delgado Pérez, María Mercedes, *Lo real y lo maravilloso en la ecúmene del siglo XIII: Las islas en el Ātār al-bilād de al-Qazwīnī* (Seville: El Alfar, 2003).

Deluz, Christiane, "Le Livre Jehan de Mandeville, autorité géographique à la Renaissance," in Jean Céard and J.-Cl. Margolin (eds), *Voyager à la Renaissance: Actes du colloque de Tours 1983* (Paris: Maisonneuve et Larose, 1987), pp. 205–20.

——, "Des lontains merveilleux (d'après quelques textes géographiques et récits de voyage du Moyen Âge)," in *De l'étranger à l'étrange ou la conjointure de la merveille (en hommage à Marguerite Rossi et Paul Bancourt)* (Aix-en-Provence: CUERMA, Université de Provence, 1988), pp. 157–69.

Dendle, Peter, "Cryptozoology in the Medieval and Modern Worlds," *Folklore* 117 (2006), pp. 190–206.

De Puma, Richard, "The Tomb of Fastia Velsi from Chiusi," *Etruscan Studies* 11/1 (2008), pp. 135–49.

Derrida, Jacques, *Points ...: Interviews, 1974–1994*, trans. Peggy Kamuf (Stanford: Stanford University Press, 1995).

——, *The Animal That Therefore I Am*, ed. Marie-Louise Mallet, trans. David Wills (New York: Fordham University Press, 2008).

——, "The Animal That Therefore I Am (More to Follow)," in *The Animal That Therefore I Am*, ed. Marie-Louise Mallet, trans. David Wills (New York: Fordham University Press, 2008).

Derrida, Jacques, and Elizabeth Weber, "Passages—from Traumatism to Promise," in Elizabeth Weber (ed.), *Points ...: Interviews, 1974–1994*, trans. Peggy Kamuf (Stanford: Stanford University Press, 1995).

Destombes, Marcel, *Mappemondes, A.D. 1200–1500* (Amsterdam: N. Israel, 1964).

de Weever, Jacqueline, *Sheba's Daughters: Whitening and Demonizing the Saracen Woman in Medieval French Epic* (New York: Garland, 1998).

Dewisme, C.H., *Les zombis; ou, Le secret des morts-vivants* (Paris: Bernard Grasset, 1957).

DeYoung, Rebecca Konyndyk, *Glittering Vices: A New Look at the Seven Deadly Sins and their Remedies* (Grand Rapids, MI: Brazos Press, 2009).

Díaz Rodríguez, Manuel, "Sobre el modernismo," in *Narrativa y ensayo* (Caracas: Biblioteca Ayacucho, 1982).

——, *Sangre patricia* [1902] (Caracas: Ayacucho, 1992).

Dickenson, Victoria, *Drawn From Life: Science and Art in the Portrayal of the New World* (Toronto and Buffalo: University of Toronto Press, 1998).

Dicks, D.R., "The *Klimata* in Greek Geography," *Classical Quarterly* 49 (1955), pp. 248–55.

Dickson, Martin B., and Stuart C. Welch, *The Houghton Shahnama* (Cambridge, MA: Harvard University Press, 1981).

Diemeringen, O. von, *Johannes von Montevilla Ritter* (Sir John Mandeville) (Strausburg, 1484).

Dihle, Albrecht, "The Conception of India in Hellenistic and Roman Literature," *Proceedings of the Cambridge Philological Society* 10 (1964), pp. 15–23, reprinted in Dihle, *Antike und Orient: gesammelte Aufsätze* (Heidelberg: C. Winter Universitätsverlag, 1984), pp. 83–93.

Dijkstra, Bram, *Idols of Perversity: Fantasies of Feminine Evil in Fin-de-siecle Culture* (New York and Oxford: Oxford University Press, 1986).

Dimand, Maurice S., "Mughal Painting under Akbar the Great," *The Metropolitan Museum of Art Bulletin* 12/2 (1953), pp. 46–51.

Douglas, Mary, *Purity and Danger: An Analysis of Concepts of Pollution and Taboo* (New York: Praeger, 1966).

Drewal, Henry John, "Interpretation, Invention, and Re-Presentation in the Worship of Mami Wata," *Journal of Folklore Research* 25 (1988), pp. 101–39. (Reprinted in R. Stone (ed.), *Performance in Contemporary African Arts* [Bloomington: African Studies Program, Indiana University, 1988], pp. 101–39).

——, "Mermaids, Mirrors, and Snake Charmers: Igbo Mami Wata Shrines," *African Arts* 21 (1988), pp. 38–45.

——, "Performing the Other: Mami Wata Worship in West Africa," *The Drama Review* T118 (1988), pp. 160–85.

——, *Mami Wata: Arts for Water Spirits in Africa and Its Diasporas* (Los Angeles: Fowler Museum-UCLA, 2008).

——, *Sacred Waters: Arts for Mami Wata and Other Divinities in Africa and the Diaspora* (Bloomington: Indiana University Press, 2008).

Drewal, Henry John, with Charles Gore and Michelle Kisliuk,"Siren Serenades: Music for Mami Wata and Other Water Spirits in Africa," in Linda Phyllis Austern and Inna Naroditskaya (eds), *Music of the Sirens* (Bloomington: Indiana University Press, 2006), pp. 294–316.

Druce, G.C., "The Elephant in Medieval Legend and Art," *Archaeological Journal* 76 (1919), pp. 1–73.

——, "On the Legend of the Serra or Saw-Fish," *Proceedings of the Society of Antiquaries* 31 (1919), pp. 20–35.

Dryden, Linda, "'City of Dreadful Night': Stevenson's Gothic London," in Richard Ambrosini and Richard Dury (eds), *Robert Louis Stevenson, Writer of Boundaries* (Madison: University of Wisconsin Press, 2006), pp. 253–64.

Dubost, Francis, "Insularités imaginaires et récit médiéval: 'l'insularisation,'" in Jean-Claude Marimoutou and Jean-Michel Racault (eds), *L'insularité thématique et représentations: actes du colloque international de Saint-Denis de La Réunion, avril 1992* (Paris: L'Harmattan, 1995), pp. 47–57.

Dümmler, Ernst (ed.), *Epistolae variorum XII*, MGH Epistolae 6 (Berlin: Weidmann, 1925).

Dunlap, Samuel Roy, "Among the Cannibals and Amazons: Early German Travel Literature on the New World," PhD dissertation, University of California, Berkeley, 1992.

Dussère, Carolyn, and J.W. Thomas (trans.), *The Legend of Duke Ernst* (Lincoln: University of Nebraska Press, 1979).

Dutton, Paul Edward (ed. and trans.), *Carolingian Civilization: A Reader*, 2nd edn (Peterborough, Ontario: Broadview Press, 2004).

Duviols, Jean-Paul, "The Patagonian 'Giants,'" in Colin McEwan, Luis A. Borrero, and Alfredo Prieto (eds), *Patagonia: Natural History, Prehistory and Ethnography at the Uttermost End of the Earth* (London: British Museum Press, 1997), pp. 127–39.

Dykstra, Yoshiko K. (trans.), *Miraculous Tales of the Lotus Sutra: The Dainihonkoku Hokekyōkenki of Priest Chingen* (Honolulu: University of Hawai'i Press, 1984).

Eames, Wilberforce, *A List of Editions of Ptolemy's Geography 1475–1730* (New York: s.n., 1886).

Eastman, Charles R., "Early Portrayals of the Opossum," *The American Naturalist* 49/586 (1915), pp. 585–94.

Eberhard, Wolfram, *The Local Cultures of South and East China*, trans. Alide Eberhard (Leiden: E.J. Brill, 1968).

Eco, Umberto, Robert Lambertini, Constantino Marmo, and Andrea Tabarroni, "'Latratus Canis' or: The Dog's Barking," in John Deely, Brooke Williams, and Felicia E. Kruse (eds), *Frontiers in Semiotics* (Bloomington: Indiana University Press, 1986).

Edmunds, Lowell, *The Sphinx in the Oedipus Legend* (Königstein im Taunus: Hain, 1981).

Ehlers, Sonnet, *Rape-aXe: Take Back the Power*, January 16, 2011, <http://www.antirape.co.za/>.

Elwin, Verrier, "The Vagina Dentata Legend," *British Journal of Medical Psychology* 19 (1943), pp. 439–53.

Emmerich, Michael (trans.), "How a Deeply Resentful Woman Became a Living Demon," in Haruo Shirane (ed.), *Traditional Japanese Literature: An Anthology, Beginnings to 1600* (New York: Columbia University Press, 2007), pp. 692–3.

Emmerson, Richard Kenneth, *Antichrist in the Middle Ages: A Study of Medieval Apocalypticism, Art, and Literature* (Manchester: Manchester University Press, 1981).

——, "The Representation of Antichrist in Hildegard of Bingen's *Scivias*: Image, Word, Commentary, and Visionary Experience," *Gesta* 41/2 (2002), pp. 95–110.

Eubanks, Charlotte, *Miracles of Book and Body: Buddhist Textual Culture and Medieval Japan* (Berkeley: University of California Press, 2010).

Eugenides, Jeffrey, *Middlesex* (New York: Picador, 2003).

Evans, Rhiannon, "Ethnography's Freak Show: The Grotesques at the Edges of the Roman Earth," *Ramus* 28/1 (1999), pp. 54–73.

——, "The Cruel Sea?: Ocean as Boundary Marker and Transgressor in Pliny's Roman Geography," *Antichthon* 39 (2005), pp. 105–18.

Falchetta, Piero, *Fra Mauro's World Map* (Turnhout: Brepols, 2006).

Faraci, Dora, "*Navigatio Sancti Brendani* and its Relationship with *Physiologus*," *Romanobarbarica* 11 (1991), pp. 149–73.

Farhad, Massumeh, with Serpil Bağcı, *Falnama: The Book of Omens* (Washington, DC: Arthur Sackler Gallery, Smithsonian Institution, 2009).

Fausto-Sterling, Anne, *Sexing the Body: Gender Politics and the Construction of Sexuality* (New York: Basic Books, 2000).

Fay, Jennifer, "Dead Subjectivity: *White Zombie*, Black Bagdad," *The New Centennial Review* 8/1 (2008), pp. 81–101.

Feinberg, Harvey M., and Joseph B. Solodow, "Out of Africa," *The Journal of African History* 43/2 (2002), pp. 255–61.

Fergusson, James, *The Rock Cut Temples of India* (London: John Murray, 1864).

——, *On the Study of Indian Architecture* (London: John Murray, 1867).

——, *The History of Indian and Eastern Architecture* (London: John Murray, 1876).

——, *History of Indian and Eastern Architecture*, 2 volumes (New York: Dodd, Mead & Company, 1891).

Ferro, Gaetano, Luisa Faldini, Marica Milanesi, and Gianni Eugenio Viola, *Columbian Iconography* (Rome: Istituto poligrafico e Zecca dello Stato, Libreria dello Stato, 1996).

Figal, Gerald, *Civilization and Monsters: Spirits of Modernity in Modern Japan* (Durham, NC: Duke University Press, 1999).

Findlen, Paula, *Possessing Nature: Museums, Collecting, and Scientific Culture in Early Modern Italy* (Berkeley: University of California Press, 1994).

Firdawsi, Abu'l Qasim, *The Shahnama of Firdousi Done into English*, trans. Arthur G. Warner and Edmund Warner, 9 volumes (London: K. Paul, Trench, Trübner & Co., 1905–25).

——, *Shahnameh*, ed. Djalal Khaleghi-Motlagh, 8 volumes (New York: Bibliotheca Persica, 1988–2008).

Fischer, Joseph, and Franz Ritter von Wieser (eds), *Die älteste Karte mit dem Namen Amerika aus dem Jahre 1507 und die Carta marina aus dem Jahre 1516 des M. Waldseemüller (Ilacomilus)* (Innsbruck: Wagner'schen Universitäts-Buchhandlung, 1903; Amsterdam: Theatrum orbis terrarum, 1968).

Fleming, William, *Arts and Ideas* (New York: Holt, Rinehart and Winston, 1980).

Flint, Valerie I.J., "Monsters and the Antipodes in the Early Middle Ages and Enlightenment," *Viator* 15 (1984), pp. 65–80; reprinted in Valerie I.J. Flint, *Ideas in the Medieval West: Texts and their Contexts* (London: Variorum Reprints, 1988), pp. 65–80.

Fong, Wen, *Beyond Representation: Chinese Painting and Calligraphy, 8th–14th Century* (New York: Metropolitan Museum of Art, and New Haven: Yale University Press, 1992).

Fontenrose, Joseph Eddy, *Python: A Study of Delphic Myth and its Origins* (Berkeley: University of California Press, 1959).

Fontes da Costa, Palmira, *The Singular and the Making of Knowledge at the Royal Society of London in the Eighteenth Century* (Newcastle Upon Tyne: Cambridge Scholars Publishing, 2009).

Ford, Alun James, "The 'Wonders of the East' in its Contexts: A Critical Examination of London, British Library, Cotton MSS Vitellius A.xv and Tiberius B.v, and Oxford, Bodleian Library, MS Bodley 614," PhD dissertation, University of Manchester, 2009.

Ford, Simon, *A Discourse Concerning Gods Judgements* (London, 1678).

Förstemann, Ernst W., "Commentary of the Maya Manuscript in the Royal Public Library of Dresden," in *Papers of the Peabody Museum of American Archaeology and Ethnology* 4/2 (Cambridge, MA: Harvard University, Peabody Museum of American Archaeology and Ethnology, 1906), pp. 53–266.

Forsyth, Donald W., "Three Cheers for Hans Staden: The Case for Brazilian Cannibalism," *Ethnohistory* 32/1 (1985), pp. 17–36.

Foster, Michael Dylan, "The Question of the Slit-Mouthed Woman: Contemporary Legend, the Beauty Industry, and Women's Weekly Magazines in Japan," *Signs: Journal of Women in Culture and Society* 32/3 (Spring 2007), pp. 699–726.

——, "Haunted Travelogue: Hometowns, Ghost Towns, and Memories of War," *Mechademia* 4 (2009), pp. 164–81.

——, *Pandemonium and Parade: Japanese Monsters and the Culture of Yōkai* (Berkeley: University of California Press, 2009).

Foucault, Michel, "The Subject and Power," in H.L. Dreyfus and P. Rabinow (eds), *Michel Foucault: Beyond Structuralism and Hermeneutics* (Brighton: Harvester, 1982).

——, *Abnormal: Lectures at the Collège de France 1974–1975*, trans. Graham Burchell, ed. Valerio Marchetti and Antonella Salomoni (London: Verso, and New York: Picador, 2003).

Fouchécour, Charles-Henri de, *Moralia: Les notions morales dans la litterature persane du 3/9 au 7/13 siècle* (Paris: Editions Recherche sur les civilisations, 1986).

Foys, Martin K., Shannon Bradshaw, and Asa Simon Mittman, *The Digital Mappaemundi Project*, <http://bob.drew.edu/mappaemundi/mappa.swf>, accessed February 6, 2011.

Fracasso, Riccardo, "Shan Hai Ching," in Michael Loewe (ed.), *Early Chinese Texts: A Bibliographical Guide* (Berkeley: University of California Press, 1993), pp. 357–67.

Frank, Erwin, "'Sie fressen Menschen, wie ihr scheußliches Aussehen beweist ...': Kritische Überlegungen zu Zeugen und Quellen der Menschenfresserei," in Hans-Peter Duerr (ed.), *Authentizität und Betrug in der Ethnologie* (Frankfurt: Suhrkamp, 1987), pp. 199–224.

Frantzen, Allen, *Before the Closet: Same-Sex Love from Beowulf to Angels in America* (Chicago: University of Chicago Press, 1998).

Fraser, Douglas, "The Fish-Legged Figure in Benin and Yoruba Art," in Douglas Fraser and Herbert M. Cole (eds), *African Art and Leadership* (Madison: University of Wisconsin Press, 1972), pp. 261–94.

Frayer, Lauren, "South Africa Debuts Anti-Rape Female Condom," AOL News, June 21, 2010, <http://www.aolnews.com/2010/06/21/south-africa-debuts-anti-rape-female-condom/>.

Freidel, David A., and Linda Schele, "Symbol and Power: A History of the Lowland Maya Cosmogram," in Elizabeth P. Benson and Gillett G. Griffin (eds), *Maya Iconography* (Princeton, NJ: Princeton University Press, 1988), pp. 44–93.

Freidel, David, Linda Schele, and Joy Parker, *Maya Cosmos: Three Thousand Years on the Shaman's Path* (New York: William Morrow, 1993).

Freidel, David A., and Charles K. Suhler, "The Path of Life: Toward a Functional Analysis of Ancient Maya Architecture," in Jeff Karl Kowalski (ed.), *Mesoamerican Architecture as a Cultural Symbol* (New York: Oxford University Press, 1999), pp. 250–73.

French, R.K., "Putting Animals on the Map: The Natural History of the Hereford Mappa Mundi," *Archives of Natural History* 21 (1994), pp. 289–308.

Freud, Sigmund, *Three Contributions to the Theory of Sex*, 2nd edn, trans. A.A. Brill (Washington, DC: Nervous and Mental Disease Publishing Company, 1930; reprint Mineola, NY: Dover, 2001).

Friederici, Georg, *Die Amazonen Amerikas* (Leipzig: Simmel & Co, 1910).

Friedman, John Block, (ed.), *John de Foxton's Liber Cosmographiae (1408)* (Leiden: J.J. Brill, 1988).

——, *The Monstrous Races in Medieval Art and Thought* (Cambridge, MA and London: Harvard University Press, 1981; reprinted with expanded bibliography Syracuse: Syracuse University Press, 2000).

Fries, Lorenz, *Uslegung der Mercarthen oder Carta Marina* (Strasbourg: Johannes Grieninger, 1525).

Frisch, Andrea, *The Invention of the Eyewitness: Witnessing and Testimony in Early Modern France* (Chapel Hill, NC: University of North Carolina Press, 2004).

Frontisi-Ducroux, Françoise, "El minotauro, o la creación del híbrido," in Sappho Athanassopoulou (ed.), *Toros: imatge i culte a la Mediterrània antiga* [*Toros: imagen y culto en el Mediterráneo antiguo*] [*Bulls: Image and Cult in the Ancient Mediterranean*] (Barcelona: Museu d'Història de la Ciutat, 2002), pp. 222–35.

Fukuyama, Francis, *Our Posthuman Future: Consequences of the Biotechnology Revolution* (New York: Farrar, Straus and Giroux, 2002).

Fulk, R.D., "Male Homoeroticism in the Old English *Canons of Theodore*," in Carol Braun Pasternack and Lisa M.C. Weston (eds), *Sex and Sexuality in Anglo-Saxon England* (Tempe: Arizona Center for Medieval and Renaissance Studies, 2004), pp. 1–34.

Fulk, R.D., Robert Bjork, and John Niles (eds), *Klaeber's Beowulf*, 4th edn (Toronto: University of Toronto Press, 2008).

Gallegos, Rómulo, *Doña Bárbara* [1929] (Mexico: Porrúa, 1981).

Gardner, John, *Grendel* (New York: Vintage, 1989).

Garland, Robert, *The Eye of the Beholder: Deformity and Disability in the Graeco-Roman World* (Ithaca: Cornell University Press, 1995).

Garland Thomson, Rosemarie, "Introduction: From Wonder to Error: A Genealogy of Freak Discourse in Modernity," in Rosemarie Garland Thomson (ed.), *Freakery: Cultural Spectacles of the Extraordinary Body* (New York and London: New York University Press, 1996), pp. 1–23.

———, "Integrating Disability, Transforming Feminist Theory," in Bonnie Smith and Beth Hutchison (eds), *Gendering Disability* (New Brunswick: Rutgers University Press, 2004).

Garrard, Timothy, "Figurine Cults of the Southern Akan," in Christopher Roy (ed.), *Iowa Studies in African Art* (Iowa City: The School of Art and Art History, University of Iowa, 1984), pp. 167–90.

Gautier Dalché, Patrick, *La "Descriptio mappe mundi" de Hugues de Saint-Victor: texte inédit avec introduction et commentaire* (Paris: Études Augustiniennes, 1988).

Geminus, *Introduction aux phénomènes*, ed. Germaine Aujac (Paris: Les belles lettres, 1975).

Geoffrey of Auxerre, *On the Apocalypse*, trans. Joseph Gibbons (Kalamazoo: Cistercian Publications, 2000).

George, Wilma, *Animals and Maps* (London: Secker and Warburg, 1969).

Georgiadou, Aristoula, and David H.J. Larmour, *Lucian's Science Fiction Novel* True Histories: *Interpretation and Commentary* (Leiden: Brill, 1998).

Gerald of Wales, "Giraldus Cambrensis *In Topographia Hibernie*: Text of the First Recension," ed. John Joseph O'Meara, *Proceedings of the Royal Irish Academy* 52 (1949), pp. 113–78.

———, *The History and Topography of Ireland*, trans. John Joseph O'Meara (London: Penguin, 1982).

———, *The Topography of Ireland*, trans. Thomas Forester (Cambridge, Ontario: In parenthesis Publications, 2000).

Gerini, G.E., *Researches on Ptolemy's Geography of Eastern Asia (Further India and Indo-Malay Archipelago)* (London: Royal Asiatic Society and Royal Geographical Society, 1909).

Geschiere, Peter, *The Modernity of Witchcraft: Politics and the Occult in Postcolonial Africa* (Charlottesville, VA: University of Virginia Press, 1997).

Gilbert, Michelle, "Shocking Images: Ghanaian Painted Posters," in *Ghana Yesterday and Today* (Paris: Musée Dapper, 2003).

Gill, Miranda, *Eccentricity and the Cultural Imagination in Nineteenth-Century Paris* (Oxford: Oxford University Press, 2009).

Gillies, John, "Posed Spaces: Framing in the Age of the World Picture," in Paul Duro (ed.), *The Rhetoric of the Frame: Essays on the Boundaries of the Artwork* (Cambridge: Cambridge University Press, 1996).

Gilmore, David D., *Monsters: Evil Beings, Mythical Beasts, and All Manner of Imaginary Terrors* (Philadelphia: University of Pennsylvania Press, 2003).

Ginsberg, William B., *Printed Maps of Scandinavia and the Arctic 1482–1601* (New York: Septentrionalium Press, 2006).

Glacken, Clarence J., "Airs, Waters, and Places," "Environmental Influences Within a Divinely Created World," and "Environmental Theories of Early Modern Times," in *Traces on the Rhodian Shore: Nature and Culture in Western Thought from Ancient Times to the End of the Eighteenth Century* (Berkeley: University of California Press, 1967).

Gliozzi, Giuliano, *Adamo e il nuovo mondo: la nascita dell'antropologia come ideologia coloniale: dalle genealogie bibliche alle teorie razziali (1500–1700)* (Florence: La nuova Italia, 1977).

Godefroy, Frédéric, *Dictionnaire de l'ancienne langue française et de tous ses dialectes du IXe au XVe siècle*, 10 volumes (Paris: F. Vieweg, 1881).

God's Word to the Nations Bible Mission Society, *God's Word* (Grand Rapids: World Publisher, 1995).

Goldberg, David Theo, *Racist Culture: Philosophy and the Politics of Meaning* (Oxford: Blackwell, 1993).

Goldenberg, David M., "The Development of the Idea of Race: Classical Paradigms and Medieval Elaborations," *International Journal of the Classical Tradition* 5 (1999), pp. 561–84.

——, *The Curse of Ham: Race and Slavery in Early Judaism, Christianity, and Islam* (Princeton: Princeton University Press, 2003).

Goldman, Laurence R., "From Pot to Polemic: Uses and Abuses of Cannibalism," in Laurence R. Goldman (ed.), *The Anthropology of Cannibalism* (Westport: Bergin and Garvey, 1999), pp. 1–26.

Gombrich, E.H., *Art and Illusion: A Study in the Psychology of Pictorial Representation* (Princeton: Princeton University Press, 2000).

González Echevarría, Roberto, *Myth and Archive: A Theory of Latin American Narrative* (Durham, NC: Duke University Press, 1998).

Goodich, Michael (ed.), *The Other Middle Ages: Witnesses at the Margins of Medieval Society* (Philadelphia: University of Pennsylvania Press, 1998).

Gore, Charles, "Mami Wata: An Urban Presence or the Making of a Tradition in Benin City, Nigeria," in Henry John Drewal (ed.), *Sacred Waters: Arts for Mami Wata and Other Water Divinities in Africa and the African Atlantic World* (Bloomington: Indiana University Press, 2008), pp. 361–81.

Gotō Akio, Ikegami Jun'ichi, and Yamane Taisuke (eds), *Gōdanshō, Chūgaishō, Fuke go*, Shin Nihon koten bungaku taikei 32 (Tokyo: Iwanami shoten, 1997).

Gousset, Marie-Thérèse, *Le Livre des merveilles du monde* (Paris: Bibliothèque de l'image, 2002).

——, *Il Milione, Marco Polo* (Paris: Bibliothèque de l'image, 2002).

Gow, Andrew, *The Red Jews: Antisemitism in an Apocalyptic Age, 1200–1600* (Leiden: Brill, 1995).

——, "Gog and Magog on *Mappaemundi* and Early Printed World Maps: Orientalizing Ethnography in the Apocalyptic Tradition," *Journal of Early Modern History* 2/1 (1998), pp. 61–88.

——, "Fra Mauro's World View: Authority and Empirical Evidence on a Venetian Mappamundi," in P.D.A. Harvey (ed.), *The Hereford World Map: Medieval World Maps and their Context* (London: The British Library, 2006), pp. 405–14.

Graham, Elaine L., *Representations of the Post/Human: Monsters, Aliens and Others in Popular Culture* (Manchester: Manchester University Press, 2002).

Graham, Ian, *Corpus of Maya Hieroglyphic Inscriptions*, vol. 3, part 3 (Cambridge, MA: Peabody Museum of Archaeology and Ethnology, Harvard University, 1982).

Granlund, J., "The *Carta Marina* of Olaus Magnus," *Imago Mundi* 8 (1951), pp. 35–43.

Grant, Michael, "Ultimate Formlessness: Cinema, Horror, and the Limits of Meaning," in Steven Jay Schneider (ed.), *Horror Film and Psychoanalysis: Freud's Worst Nightmare* (New York: Cambridge University Press, 2004).

Gravestock, Pamela, "Did Imaginary Animals Exist?" in Debra Hassig (ed.), *The Mark of the Beast: The Medieval Bestiary in Art, Life, and Literature* (New York: Garland, 1999).

Greenblatt, Stephen, *Marvelous Possessions* (Chicago: University of Chicago Press, 1991).

Gregory, Steven, "Voodoo, Ethnography, and the American Occupation of Haiti: William B. Seabrook's *The Magic Island,*" in Christine Ward Gailey (ed.), *Dialectical Anthropology: Essays in Honor of Stanley Diamond, II: The Politics of Creativity: A Critique of Civilization* (Gainesville: University Press of Florida, 1992).

Grube, Ernst J., "The Problem of the Istanbul Paintings," in Ernst J. Grube and Eleanor Sims (eds), *Between China and Iran: Paintings from Four Istanbul Albums* (London: University of London, 1985), pp. 1–30.

Grube, Nikolai, and Werner Nahm, "A Census of Xibalba: A Complete Inventory of 'Way' Characters on Maya Ceramics," in Justin Kerr (ed.), *The Maya Vase Book*, vol. 4 (New York: Kerr Associates, 1994), pp. 686–715.

Gruber, Christiane J., *The Timurid "Book of Ascension" (Mi'rajnama): A Study of Text and Image in a Pan-Asian Context* (Valencia: Ediciones Patrimonio, 2009).

Grynaeus, Simon, and Johann Huttich (eds), *Novus orbis regionum ac insularum ueteribus incognitarum* (Basel: Johann Herwagen, 1532).

Guattari, Félix, *Soft Subversions*, trans. Jarred Becker (New York: Semiotext(e), 1996).

——, *The Three Ecologies*, trans. Ian Pindar and Paul Sutton (London: Athlone Press, 2000).

Güiraldes, Ricardo, *Don Segundo Sombra*, trans. Harriet de Onís (New York: New American Library, 1966).

——, *Don Segundo Sombra* (Madrid: Alianza, 1982).

Gunderson, Lloyd L., *Alexander's Letter to Aristotle about India* (Meisenheim am Glan: Hain, 1980).

Guo, Qitao, *Exorcism and Money: The Symbolic World of the Five-Fury Spirits in Late Imperial China* (Berkeley: Institute of East Asian Studies, University of California, Berkeley/Center for Chinese Studies, 2003).

Gutenberg, Andrea, "Shape-Shifters from the Wilderness: Werewolves Roaming the Twentieth Century," in Konstanze Kutzbach and Monika Mueller (eds), *The Abject of Desire: The Aestheticization of the Unaesthetic in Contemporary Literature and Culture* (Amsterdam: Rodopi, 2007), pp. 149–80.

Gutierrez, Fernando G., "Emakimono Depicting the Pains of the Damned," *Monumenta Nipponica* 22/3–4 (1967), pp. 278–89.

Gwynn, Aubrey (ed. and trans.), *The Writings of Bishop Patrick, 1074–1084* (Dublin: Dublin Institute for Advanced Studies, 1955).

Gygax, Gary, *Monster Manual* (Lake Geneva, WI: TSR, 1977).

Habershon, Alexandra M., "Post-partum Nation: The Amazon Myth and Ideologies of Reproduction in the Conquest of the New World," PhD dissertation, Georgetown University, 2006.

Hackett, Rosalind I., "Mermaids and End-Time Jezebels: New Tales from Old Calabar," in Henry John Drewal (ed.), *Sacred Waters: Arts for Mami Wata and Other Water Divinities in Africa and the African Atlantic World* (Bloomington: Indiana University Press, 2008), pp. 405–12.

Hagenbeck, Carl, *Von Tieren und Menschen: Erlebnisse und Erfahrungen* [1909] (Leipzig: Paul List, 1925).

Hagiwara Tatsuo, Miyata Noboru, and Sakurai Tokutarō (eds), *Kitano Tenjin Engi*, in *Jisha engi*, Nihon shisō taikei 20 (Tokyo: Iwanami shoten, 1975), pp. 158–61.

Hahn, Thomas, "The Difference the Middle Ages Makes: Color and Race Before the Modern World," *Journal of Medieval and Early Modern Studies* 31 (2001), pp. 1–37.

Halberstam, Judith, *Skin Shows: Gothic Horror and the Technology of Monsters* (Durham, NC and London: Duke University Press, 1995).

——, *Female Masculinity* (Durham, NC: Duke University Press, 1998).

Halberstam, Judith, and Ira Livingston (eds), *Posthuman Bodies* (Bloomington: Indiana University Press, 1995).

Hall, Alaric, *Elves in Anglo-Saxon England: Matters of Belief, Health, Gender and Identity* (Woodbridge, Suffolk: Boydell Press, 2007).

Hallberg, Ivar, *L'Extrême Orient dans la littérature et la cartographie de l'Occident des XIIIe, XIVe, et XVe siècles; étude sur l'histoire de la géographie* (Göteborg: W. Zachrissons boktryckeri a.-b., 1907).

Hamelius, P. (ed.), *Mandeville's Travels, Translated from the French by Jean d'Outremeuse*, 2 volumes, EETS, os 153–54 (London: Oxford University Press, 1919–23).

Hamilton, Bernard, "Continental Drift: Prester John's Progress through the Indies," in Charles F. Beckingham and Bernard Hamilton (eds), *Prester John, the Mongols, and the Ten Lost Tribes* (Aldershot, Hampshire and Brookfield, VT: Variorum, 1996), pp. 237–69.

Hanafi, Zakiya, *The Monster in the Machine: Magic, Medicine, and the Marvelous in the Time of the Scientific Revolution* (Durham, NC: Duke University Press, 2000).

Hanfmann, George M.A., "The Scylla of Corvey and Her Ancestors," *Dumbarton Oaks Papers* 41, *Studies on Art and Archeology in Honor of Ernst Kitzinger on His Seventy-Fifth Birthday* (1987), pp. 249–60.

Hanke, Lewis, "Pope Paul III and the American Indians," *Harvard Theological Review* 30 (1937), pp. 65–102.

Hansen, William (trans. and comm.), *Phlegon of Tralles' Book of Marvels* (Exeter: University of Exeter Press, 1996).

Haraway, Donna, *Simians, Cyborgs and Women: The Reinvention of Nature* (New York and London: Routledge, 1991).

Harbsmeier, Michael, "On Travel Accounts and Cosmological Strategies: Some Models in Comparative Xenology," *Ethnos* 3/4 (1985), pp. 273–312.

Harding, Davis P., *Milton and the Renaissance Ovid* (Urbana: University of Illinois, 1946).

Harf-Lancner, Laurence, "From Alexander to Marco Polo, from Text to Image: The Marvels of India," in Donald Maddox and Sara Sturm-Maddox (eds), *The Medieval French Alexander* (Albany: State University of New York Press, 2002), pp. 235–57.

Harley, J.B., "Maps, Knowledge, and Power," in Denis Cosgrove and Stephen Daniels (eds), *The Iconography of Landscape: Essays on the Symbolic Representation, Design and Use of Past Environments* (Cambridge and New York: Cambridge University Press, 1988), pp. 277–312.

Harper, Donald, "A Chinese Demonography of the Third Century BC," *Harvard Journal of Asiatic Studies* 45/2 (1985), pp. 459–98.

Harriot, Thomas, *A briefe and true report of the new found land of Virginia* (Frankfurt am Main, 1590).

Harris, Marvin, *Good to Eat: Riddles of Food and Culture* (New York: Simon and Schuster, 1985).

Harris, Stephen L., and Gloria Platzner, *Classical Mythology: Images and Insights*, 6th edn (New York: McGraw-Hill, 2012).

Harrisse, Henry, "La cartographie Américano-Dieppoise," in Henry Harrisse, *Découverte et évolution cartographique de Terre-Neuve et des pays circonvoisins, 1497–1501–1769* (London and Paris, 1900; Amsterdam: N. Israel, 1968).

Hartman, Laura, et al., "From 'Monsters' to Modern Medical Miracles: Selected Moments in the History of Conjoined Twins from Medieval to Modern Times," <http://www.nlm.nih.gov/hmd/conjoined/age.html>.

Harvey, P.D.A., *Medieval Maps* (London: British Library, 1991).

Harvey, Paul B., Jr, "The Death of Mythology: The Case of Joppa," *Journal of Early Christian Studies* 2/1 (1994), pp. 1–14.

Haslam, Graham, "The Duchy of Cornwall Map Fragment," in Monique Pelletier (ed.), *Géographie du monde au Moyen Age et à la Renaissance* (Paris: Editions du C.T.H.S., 1989), pp. 33–44.

Hassan, Ihab, "Prometheus as Performer: Toward a Postmodern Culture?" in Michel Benamou and Charles Caramello (eds), *Performance in Postmodern Culture* (Madison, WI: Coda Press, 1977).

Hassig, Debra (ed.), *The Mark of the Beast: The Medieval Bestiary in Art, Life, and Literature* (New York: Garland, 1999).

Haydaroğlu, Mine (ed.), *Ben Mehmed Siyah Kalem, Insanlar ve Cinler Ustasi* (Istanbul: T.C. Kültür ve Turizm Bakanligi, 2004).

Hayles, N. Katherine, *How We Became Posthuman: Virtual Bodies in Cybernetics, Literature, and Informatics* (Chicago: University of Chicago Press, 1999).

Heaney, Seamus (trans.), *Beowulf: A Verse Translation* (New York: Norton, 2002).

Hédelin, François, *Des satyres brutes, monstres et démons. De leur nature et adoration contre l'opinion de ceux qui ont estimé les satyres estre une espece d'hommes distincts & separez des adamicques* (Paris: Nicholas Buon, 1627).

Hegel, G.W.F., *The Philosophy of Fine Art*, trans. P.B. Omaston (London: G. Bell & Sons, 1920).

——, *Ästhetik* (Berlin: Aufbau-Verlag, 1955).

Hellmuth, Nicholas M., "Early Maya Iconography on an Incised Cylindrical Tripod," in Elizabeth P. Benson and Gillett Griffin (eds), *Maya Iconography* (Princeton: Princeton University Press, 1988), pp. 152–74.

Helms, Mary W., *Ulysses' Sail: An Ethnographic Odyssey of Power, Knowledge and Geographical Distance* (Princeton, NJ: Princeton University Press, 1988).

Heng, Geraldine, *Empire of Magic: Medieval Romance and the Politics of Cultural Fantasy* (New York: Columbia University Press, 2003).

——, "Jews, Saracens, 'Black Men,' Tartars: England in a World of Racial Difference," in Peter Brown (ed.), *A Companion to Medieval English Literature, c. 1350–c. 1500* (London: Blackwell Publishing, 2007), pp. 247–69.

Hengevoss-Dürkop, Kerstin, "Jerusalem—Das Zentrum der Ebstorf-Karte," in Hartmut Kugler and Eckhard Michael (eds), *Ein Weltbild vor Columbus: die Ebstorfer Weltkarte: Interdisziplinäres Colloquium 1988* (Weinheim: VCH, 1991), pp. 205–22.

Hernández, Elizabeth, and Consuelo López Springfield, "Women and Writing in Puerto Rico: An Interview with Ana Lydia Vega," *Callaloo: A Journal of African American and African Arts and Letters* 17/3 (Summer 1994), pp. 816–25.

Herodotus, *The Histories*, trans. Aubrey de Sélincourt (Harmondsworth, Middlesex, and Baltimore: Penguin Books, 1954).

Herrera-Sobek, Maria, *The Mexican Corrido: A Feminist Analysis* (Bloomington: Indiana University Press, 1993).

Hiatt, Alfred, "Blank Spaces on the Earth," *The Yale Journal of Criticism* 15/2 (2002), pp. 223–50.

——, "The Map of Macrobius before 1100," *Imago Mundi* 59/2 (2007), pp. 149–76.

——, *Terra Incognita: Mapping the Antipodes before 1600* (London: British Library, 2008).

Hiddleston, J.A. (ed.), *Victor Hugo, romancier de l'abîme* (Oxford: Legenda, 2002).

Higden, Ranulf, *Polychronicon Ranulphi Higden monachi Cestrensis; Together with the English Translations of John Trevisa and of an Unknown Writer of the Fifteenth Century*, ed. Joseph Rawson Lumby (London: Longman & Co., 1865–86).

Higgins, Iain Macleod, "Defining the Earth's Center in a Medieval 'Multi-Text': Jerusalem in *The Book of John Mandeville*," in Sealy Gilles and Sylvia Tomasch (eds), *Text and Territory: Geographical Imagination in the European Middle Ages* (Philadelphia: University of Pennsylvania Press, 1998), pp. 29–53.

Hildegard of Bingen, *Scivias*, trans. Mother Columba Hart and Jane Bishop (Mahwah, NJ: Paulist Press, 1990).

Hilka, Alfons (ed.), "Eine altfranzösische moralisierende Bearbeitung des Liber de Monstruosis Hominibus Orientis von Thomas von Cantimpré, De Naturis Rerum," in *Abhandundgen der Gesellschaft der Wissenschaften zu Göttingen: Philologisch-Historische Klasse* 7 (Berlin: Weidmannsche Buchhandlung, 1933).

Hill, Susan E., "'The Ooze of Gluttony': Attitudes Toward Food, Eating and Excess in the Middle Ages," in Richard Newhauser (ed.), *The Seven Deadly Sins: From Communities to Individuals* (Leiden: Kinonklijke Brill NV, 2007), pp. 57–72.

Hilton, Anne, *The Kingdom of Kongo* (Oxford: Clarendon, 1985).

Hinks, Arthur R., *The Portolan Chart of Angellino de Dalorto, MCCCXXV, in the Collection of Prince Corsini at Florence* (London: Royal Geographical Society, 1929).

Hobby, Teresa Santerre, "*Independence Day*: Reinforcing Patriarchal Myths about Gender and Power," *Journal of Popular Culture*, 34/2 (2000), pp. 39–55.

Hobgood-Oster, Laura, *Holy Dogs and Asses: Animals in the Christian Tradition* (Urbana: University of Illinois Press, 2008).

Hodgen, M.T., *Early Anthropology in the Sixteenth and Seventeenth Centuries*, 2nd edn (Philadelphia: University of Pennsylvania Press, 1971).

Hoffman, Richard C., "Outsiders by Birth and Blood: Racist Ideologies and Realities Around the Periphery of Medieval European Culture," *Studies in Medieval and Renaissance History*, n.s. 6 (1983), pp. 1–34.

Holas, Bohumil, *Mission dans l'est libérien* (Dakar: IFAN, 1952).

Holland, Philemon (trans.), *C. Plinius Secundus: The Historie of the World* (1601).

Homer, *The Odyssey*, trans. Robert Fitzgerald (New York: Vintage Books, 1990).

Homer, *The Odyssey*, trans. Robert Fagles (New York: Penguin, 1996).

Hoogvliet, Margriet, "Animals in Context: Beasts on the Hereford Map and Medieval Natural History," in P.D.A. Harvey (ed.), *The Hereford World Map: Medieval World Maps and their Context* (London: British Library, 2006), pp. 153–65.

——, *Pictura et scriptura: textes, images et herméneutique des Mappae Mundi (XIII–XVI siècles)* (Turnhout: Brepols, 2007).

——, "The Wonders of Europe: From the Middle Ages to the Sixteenth Century," in Ingrid Baumgärtner and Hartmut Kugler (eds), *Europa im Weltbild des Mittelalters, Kartographische Konzepte* (Berlin: Akademie Verlag, 2008), pp. 239–58.

Hopkins, Amanda (ed. and trans.), *Melion and Biclarel: Two Old French Werwolf Lays* (Liverpool: University of Liverpool Department of French, 2005).

Horsfall, Nicholas, *Vergil, Aeneid 3: A Commentary* (Leiden: Brill, 2006).

Houston, Stephen D., and David Stuart, *The Way Glyph: Evidence for "Co-essences" among the Classic Maya*, Research Reports on Ancient Maya Writing 30 (Washington, DC: Center for Maya Research, 1989).

——, "Of Gods, Glyphs and Kings: Divinity and Rulership among the Classic Maya," *Antiquity* 70 (1996), pp. 289–312.

Huang, Shih-Shan Susan, "Summoning the Gods: Paintings of Three Officials of Heaven, Earth and Water and their Association with Daoist Ritual Performance in the Southern Song Period (1127–1279)," *Artibus Asiae* 61/1 (2001), pp. 5–52.

Huddleston, Lee Eldridge, *Origins of the American Indians: European Concepts, 1492–1729* (Austin: Published for the Institute of Latin American Studies by the University of Texas Press, 1967).

Huet, Marie-Hélène, *Monstrous Imagination* (Cambridge, MA: Harvard University Press, 1993).

——, "Monstrous Medicine," in Laura Lunger Knoppers and Joan B. Landes (eds), *Monstrous Bodies/Political Monstrosities in Early Modern Europe* (Ithaca, NY and London: Cornell University Press, 2004), pp. 127–47.

Hughes, J. Donald, "Europe as Consumer of Exotic Biodiversity: Greek and Roman Times," *Landscape Research* 28/1 (2003), pp. 21–31.

Hugo, Victor, *Notre-Dame de Paris, édition nouvelle illustrée* (Paris: Perrotin, 1850).

——, *Notre-Dame de Paris*, trans. Alban Krailsheimer (Oxford: Oxford University Press, 1993).

——, *Notre-Dame de Paris 1482* (Paris: Pocket, 1998).

——, *L'Homme qui rit* (Paris: Gallimard, 2002).

——, "Preface" to *Cromwell* in *The Essential Victor Hugo*, trans. E.H. Blackmore and A.M. Blackmore (Oxford: Oxford University Press, 2004), pp. 16–53.

Hulme, Peter, "Columbus and the Cannibals: A Study of the Reports of Anthropophagy in the Journal of Christopher Columbus," *Ibero-Amerikanisches Archiv* 4 (1978), pp. 115–39; reprinted in Peter Hulme, *Colonial Encounters: Europe and the Native Caribbean, 1492–1797* (London: Methuen, 1986), pp. 1–43.

——, *Colonial Encounters: Europe and the Native Caribbean, 1492–1797* (London: Methuen, 1986).

——, "Columbus and the Cannibals," in Bill Ashcroft, Gareth Griffiths, and Helen Tiffin (eds), *The Post-Colonial Studies Reader* (London: Routledge, 1995), pp. 365–9.

——, "Introduction: The Cannibal Scene," in Francis Barker, Peter Hulme, and Margaret Iversen (eds), *Cannibalism and the Colonial World* (New York: Cambridge University Press, 1998), pp. 1–38.

Humboldt, Alexander von, *Personal Narrative of a Journey into the Equinoctial Regions of the New Continent*, trans. Jason Wilson (New York: Penguin, 1995).

Hunter-Hindrew, Mamaissii Vivian (Mama Zogbé, Hounon-Amengansie), *Mami Wata: Africa's Ancient God/dess Unveiled*, 2 volumes (Augusta, GA: Mami Wata Healing Society, 2004).

Hurston, Zora Neale, *Tell My Horse: Voodoo and Life in Haiti and Jamaica* (Philadelphia: Lippincott, 1938).

Huysmans, J.-K., *Against Nature*, trans. Robert Baldick (Harmondsworth: Penguin, 1977).

——, *À Rebours* (Paris: Gallimard, 1997).

Ian, Marcia, *Remembering the Phallic Mother: Psychoanalysis, Modernism and the Fetish* (Ithaca: Cornell University Press, 1996).

Idema, Wilt, and Stephen West, *Chinese Theater 1100–1450* (Wiesbaden: Steiner, 1982).

Ikegami Jun'ichi (ed.), *Sangoku denki*, vol. 2 (Tokyo: Miyai shoten, 1982).

——, "'Oni' no kanashimi: chūsei no 'ningen' rikai," *Kokugo tsūshin, tokushū: chūsei o ikiru hitobito* 266 (June 1984), pp. 12–18.

Ingemark, Camilla Asplund, "The Octopus in the Sewers: An Ancient Legend Analogue," *Journal of Folklore Research* 45/2 (2008), pp. 145–70.

Inoue Mitsusada, and Ōsone Shōsuke (eds), *Ōjōden, Hokkegenki*, Nihon shisō taikei 7 (Tokyo: Iwanami shoten, 1974).

Ipširoglu, Mazhar S., *Siyah Qalem* (Graz: Akademische Druck- u. Verlagsanstalt, 1976).

Irigaray, Luce, *This Sex Which is Not One*, trans. Catherine Porter (Ithaca: Cornell University Press, 1985).

Ishikawa Juni'ichirō, *Shinpan kappa no sekai* (Tokyo: Jiji tsūshinsha, 1985).

Isidore of Seville, *Etymologiarum*, The Latin Library, <thelatinlibrary.com/isidore.html>.

——, *The Etymologies of Isidore of Seville*, ed. and trans. Stephen A. Barney, W.J. Lewis, Oliver Berghof, and J.A. Beach (New York: Cambridge University Press, 2006).

Iwata Noriko, "Bakemono to asobu: Nankenkeredomo bakemono sugoroku," *Tōkyō-to Edo-Tōkyō hakubutsukan hōkoku* 5 (February 2000), pp. 39–52.

Izumi Motohiro (ed.), *Jikkinshō: Daisan ruihon: Shōkōkan zō* (Osaka: Izumi shoin, 1984).

Jacoby, F., "Ktesias," in *Paulys Real-Encyclopädie der classischen Altertumswissenschaft* (Stuttgart: J.B. Metzler, 1894–1980).

Jacques de Vitry, *Iacobi de Vitriaco, primvm Acconensis, deinde Tvscvlani Episcopi ... libri dvo, quorum prior Orientalis, siue Hierosolymitanae, alter, Occidentalis historiae nomine inscribitur* (Douai: Ex officina typographica Balthazaris Belleri, 1597).

James, Montague Rhodes, *Marvels of the East: A Full Reproduction of the Three Known Copies* (Oxford: Printed for the Roxburghe Club by J. Johnson, at the University Press, 1929).

——, *The Romance of Alexander* (Oxford: Clarendon Press, 1933).

Janni, Pietro, *Etnografia e mito: la storia dei pigmei* (Rome: Edizioni dell'Ateneo & Bizzarri, 1978).

——, "I Pigmei dall'Antichità al Medioevo: le fortune di una favola," in Francesco Prontera (ed.), *Geografia e geografi nel mondo antico: guida storica e critica* (Rome: Editori Laterza, 1983), pp. 135–71.

Jansen, Sharon, *The Monstrous Regiment of Women: Female Rulers in Early Modern Europe* (Basingstoke: Palgrave Macmillan, 2002).

Janvier, Yves, "Rome et l'Orient lointain: le problème des Sères. Réexamen d'une question de géographie antique," *Ktèma* 9 (1984), pp. 261–303.

Jarcho, Saul, "Origin of the American Indian as Suggested by Fray Joseph de Acosta (1589)," *Isis* 50/4 (1959), pp. 430–38.

Jáuregui, Carlos, *Canibalia: Canibalismo, calibanismo, antropofagia cultural y consumo en América Latina* (Madrid/Frankfurt: Iberoamericana/Vervuert, 2008).

Jayne, K.G., *Vasco da Gama and His Successors* [1910] (New York: Barnes and Noble, 1970).

Jell-Bahlsen, Sabine, "Dada-Dreadlock-Hair: The Hidden Messages of Mammy Water in Southeastern Nigeria," in Henry John Drewal (ed.), *Sacred Waters: Arts for Mami Wata and Other Water Divinities in Africa and the African Atlantic World* (Bloomington: Indiana University Press, 2008), pp. 245–57.

Jennison, George, *Animals for Show and Pleasure in Ancient Rome* (Philadelphia: University of Pennsylvania Press, 2005).

Jerome, *Trois vies de moines: Paul, Malchus, Hilarion*, ed. Edgardo Martín Morales, trans. [into French] Pierre Leclerc (Paris: Cerf, 2007).

Jewkes, Rachel, and Naeema Abrahams, "The Epidemiology of Rape and Sexual Coercion in South Africa: An Overview," *Social Science & Medicine* 55/7 (2002), pp. 1231–44.

Johnson, David (ed.), *Ritual Opera, Operatic Ritual: Mu-Lien Rescues His Mother in Chinese Popular Culture* (Berkeley: Chinese Popular Culture Project, 1989).

Johnson, David, Andrew J. Nathan, and Evelyn S. Rawski (eds), *Popular Culture in Late Imperial China* (Berkeley: University of California Press, 1985).

Johnson, Hildegard Binder, *Carta marina: World Geography in Strassburg, 1525* (Minneapolis: University of Minnesota Press, 1963).

Jones, C. Meredith, "The Conventional Saracen of the Songs of Geste," *Speculum* 17 (1942), pp. 201–25.

Jones, G.I., "Mbari Houses," *Nigerian Field* 6 (1937), pp. 77–9.

——, *The Art of Eastern Nigeria* (Cambridge: Cambridge University Press, 1984).

Jones, Timothy S., and David A. Sprunger (eds), *Marvels, Monsters, and Miracles: Studies in the Medieval and Early Modern Imaginations* (Kalamazoo: Medieval Institute Publications, 2002).

Joost-Gaugier, Christiane L., "Lorenzo the Magnificent and the Giraffe as a Symbol of Power," *Artibus et Historiae* 8/16 (1987), pp. 91–9.

Jordan, William Chester, "Why 'Race'?" *Journal of Medieval and Early Modern Studies* 31 (2001), pp. 165–74.

Jordanus, Friar, *Mirabilia Descripta*, trans. H. Yule, *The Wonders of the East* (London: Hakluyt Society, 1863).

Joseph, May, *Nomadic Identities: The Performance of Citizenship* (Minneapolis: University of Minnesota Press, 1999).

Jourdain-Annequin, Colette, *Héraclès aux portes du soir: mythe et histoire* (Besançon: Université de Besançon; Paris: Diffusion Les Belles Lettres, 1989).

Junsheng, Zhu, *Shuowen tongxun dingsheng* (Wuhan: Wuhan shi guji shudian, 1983).

Kabat, Adam, *Edo bakemono zōshi* (Tokyo: Shōgakkan, 1999).

——, "Bakemono zukushi no kibyōshi no kōsatsu: Bakemono no gainen o megutte," in Komatsu Kazuhiko (ed.), *Yōkai* (Tokyo: Kawade shobō shinsha, 2000), pp. 141–64.

——, *Ōedo bakemono saiken* (Tokyo: Shōgakkan, 2000).

Kagawa Masanobu, "Yōkai to goraku," *Kai* 11 (August 2001), pp. 306–7.

——, *Edo no yōkai kakumei* (Tokyo: Kawade shobō shinsha, 2006).

Kahle, Paul, "A Lost Map of Columbus," *Geographical Review* 23/4 (1933), pp. 621–38.

Kann, Andrea, "Picturing the World: The Illustrated Manuscripts of *The Book of John Mandeville*," PhD dissertation, University of Iowa, 2002.

Kappler, Claude-Clair, *Monstres, démons et merveilles à la fin du Moyen Age*, 2nd edn (Paris: Payot & Rivages, 1980 and 1999).

Karkov, Catherine E., "Tales of the Ancients: Colonial Werewolves and the Mapping of Postcolonial Ireland," in Patricia Clare Ingham and Michelle R. Warren (eds), *Postcolonial Moves: Medieval Through Modern* (New York: Palgrave Macmillan, 2003).

Karras, Ruth Mazo, *Sexuality in Medieval Europe: Doing Unto Others* (New York: Routledge, 2005).

Karttunen, Klaus, "The Country of Fabulous Beasts and Naked Philosophers: India in Classical and Medieval Literature," *Arctos* 21 (1987), pp. 43–52.

——, "Expedition to the End of the World: An Ethnographic Topos in Herodotus," *Studia Orientalia* 64 (1988), pp. 177–81.

——, "Distant Lands in Classical Ethnography," *Grazer Beiträge* 18 (1992), pp. 195–204.

Kawashima, Terry, *Writing Margins: The Textual Construction of Gender in Heian and Kamakura Japan* (Cambridge, MA: Harvard University Asia Center, 2001).

Ke, Yuan (ed.), *Shanghai jing jiaozhu* (Shanghai: Shanghai guji chuban she, 1991).

Kelly, Henry Ansgar, "The Metamorphoses of the Eden Serpent During the Middle Ages and Renaissance," *Viator* 2 (1971), pp. 301–28.

Kemp, Wolfgang, "Medieval Pictorial Systems," in Brendan Cassidy (ed.), *Iconography at the Crossroads: Papers from the Colloquium Sponsored by the Index of Christian Art, Princeton University, 23–24 March 1990* (Princeton, NJ: Index of Christian Art, Dept. of Art and Archaeology, Princeton University, 1993), pp. 121–37; reprinted with some changes in Sylvie Deswarte-Rosa (ed.), *A travers l'image: Lecture iconographique et sens de l'oeuvre. Actes du Séminaire CNRS (G.D.R. 712) (Paris, 1991)* (Paris: Klincksieck, 1994), pp. 283–307.

Killick, Rachel, "*Notre-Dame de Paris* as Cinema: From Myth to Commodity," in J.A. Hiddleston (ed.), *Victor Hugo, romancier de l'abîme* (Oxford: Legenda, 2002), pp. 41–62.

Kim, Yung-Hee, *Songs to Make the Dust Dance: The Ryōjin Hishō of Twelfth-Century Japan* (Berkeley: University of California Press, 1994).

Kimbrough, R. Keller, "Reading the Miraculous Powers of Japanese Poetry: Spells, Truth Acts, and a Medieval Buddhist Poetics of the Supernatural," *Japanese Journal of Religious Studies* 32/1 (2005), pp. 1–33.

—— (trans.), "The Demon Shuten Dōji," in Haruo Shirane (ed.), *Traditional Japanese Literature: An Anthology, Beginnings to 1600* (New York: Columbia University Press, 2007), pp. 1123–38.

King, Helen, "Once Upon a Text: Hysteria from Hippocrates," in Sander L. Gilman, Helen King, Roy Porter, G.S. Rousseau, and Elaine Showalter (eds), *Hysteria Beyond Freud* (Berkeley: University of California Press, 1993), pp. 3–90.

Kipling, Rudyard, *In the Vernacular: The English in India: Short Stories* (New York: Doubleday, 1963).

Kircher, A., *China Monumentis qua Sacris qua Profanis ... Illustrata* (Amsterdam, 1667).

Klaeber, Friedrich (ed.), *Beowulf* (Lexington, MA: D.C. Heath and Company, 1950).

Klein, Cecelia F., "Devil and the Skirt: An Iconographic Inquiry into the Pre-Hispanic Nature of the Tzitzimime," *Ancient Mesoamerica* 11/1 (2000), pp. 1–26.

Klein, Susan Blakeley, *Allegories of Desire: Esoteric Literary Commentaries of Medieval Japan* (Cambridge, MA: Harvard University, Asia Center for the Harvard-Yenching Institute, 2002).

Kline, Anthony (trans.), *Ovid's Metamorphoses* (Virginia: University of Virginia Library, 2000).

Kline, Naomi Reed, *Maps of Medieval Thought: The Hereford Paradigm* (Woodbridge, UK, and Rochester, NY: Boydell Press, 2001).

——, "The World of the Strange Races," in Leif Søndergaard and Rasmus Thorning Hansen (eds), *Monsters, Marvels and Miracles: Imaginary Journeys and Landscapes in the Middle Ages* (Odense: University Press of Southern Denmark, 2005), pp. 27–40.

——, "Alexander Interpreted on the Hereford Mappamundi," in P.D.A. Harvey (ed.), *The Hereford World Map: Medieval World Maps and their Context* (London: British Library, 2006), pp. 167–83.

Klingender, Francis Donald, *Animals in Art and Thought to the End of the Middle Ages* (Cambridge, MA: MIT Press, 1971).

Knoppers, Laura Lunger, "'The Antichrist, the Babilon, the great dragon': Oliver Cromwell, Andrew Marvell, and the Apocalyptic Monstrous," in Laura Lunger Knoppers and Joan B. Landes (eds), *Monstrous Bodies/Political Monstrosities in Early Modern Europe* (Ithaca, NY and London: Cornell University Press, 2004), pp. 93–123.

Knoppers, Laura Lunger and Joan B. Landes (eds), *Monstrous Bodies/Political Monstrosities in Early Modern Europe* (Ithaca, NY and London: Cornell University Press, 2004).

Knowlton, Timothy W., *Maya Creation Myths: Words and Worlds of the Chilam Balam* (Boulder: University Press of Colorado, 2010).

[Knox, John], *The First Blast of the Trumpet against the Monstrous Regiment of Women* (Geneva, 1558).

——, *First Blast of the Trumpet* (Whitefish, MT: Kessinger Publishing, 2004).

Kobayashi Yoshinori (ed.), *Ryōjin hishō*, in *Ryōjin hishō, Kanginshū, Kyōgen kayō*, Shin Nihon koten bungaku taikei 56 (Tokyo: Iwanami shoten, 1993).

Koch, Joseph, "Sind die Pygmäen Menschen? Ein Kapitel aus der philosophischen Anthropologie der mittelalterlichen Scholastik," *Archiv für Geschichte der Philosophie* 40 (1931), pp. 194–213.

Koizumi Hiroshi, Yamada Shōzen, Kojima Takayuki, and Kinoshita Motoichi (eds), *Kankyo no tomo*, in *Hōbutsu shū, Kankyo no tomo, Hirasan kojin reitaku*, Shin Nihon koten bungaku taikei 40 (Tokyo: Iwanami shoten, 1993).

Kojima Noriyuki, Naoki Kōjirō, Kuranaka Susumu, Mōri Masamori, and Nishimiya Kazutami (eds), *Nihon Shoki*, Nihon koten bungaku zenshū 2, vol. 1 (Tokyo: Shōgakkan, 1994).

Komatsu Kazuhiko, *Yōkaigaku shinkō: Yōkai kara miru Nihonjin no kokoro* (Tokyo: Shōgakkan, 1994).

——, *Shutendōji no kubi* (Tokyo: Serika shobō, 1997).

——, "Yōkai: Kaisetsu," in Komatsu Kazuhiko (ed.), *Yōkai* (Tokyo: Kawade shobō shinsha, 2000), pp. 435–6.

Komatsu Shigemi (ed.), *Gaki zōshi* and *Jigoku zōshi*, in *Gaki zōshi, Jigoku zōshi, Yamai zōshi, Kusō shi emaki*, Nihon no emaki 7 (Tokyo: Chūō kōron sha, 1987).

——, *Tengu zōshi*, in *Tsuchigumo zōshi, Tengu zōshi, Ōeyama ekotoba*, Zoku Nihon no emaki 26 (Tokyo: Chūō kōron sha, 1993).

Konishi Jin'ichi (ed.), "Shūgyoku tokka," in *Zeami shū*, Nihon no shisō 8 (Tokyo: Chikuma shobō, 1970).

Konno Tōru, "Goen mankō 2: Nennen uta yurai: Urashima nisoku, Gyokusenbō no oni," *Yokohama kokudai kokugo kenkyū* 5 (March 1987), pp. 67–8.

Kovacs, Maureen Gallery, *The Epic of Gilgamesh* (Stanford: Stanford University Press, 1989).

Kramer, Heinrich, and James Sprenger, *Malleus Maleficarum*, trans. Montague Summers (New York: Dover, 1971).

——, *Malleus Maleficarum*, ed. Andre Schnyder (Goppingen: Kummerle, 1991).

Krappe, Alexander H., "Antipodes," *Modern Language Notes* 59/7 (1944), pp. 441–7.

Kretschmer, Konrad, *Die historischen Karten zur Entdeckung Amerikas: Atlas nach Konrad Kretschmer* (Frankfurt: Umschau, 1991).

Kripal, Jeffrey J., "Psychoanalysis and Hinduism," in Diane Jonte-Pace and William B. Parsons (eds), *Religion and Psychology: Mapping the Terrain* (London: Routledge, 2001).

Krishna, Valerie (ed.), *The Alliterative Morte Arthure: A Critical Edition* (New York, 1976), available at: <http://name.umdl.umich.edu/AllitMA>.

Kristeva, Julia, *The Powers of Horror: An Essay on Abjection*, trans. Leon S. Roudiez (New York: Columbia University Press, 1982).

——, *Revolt, She Said*, trans. Brian O'Keeffe (New York: Semiotext(e), 2002).

Kugler, Hartmut, *Die Ebstorfer Weltkarte* (Berlin: Akademie Verlag, 2007).

Kuntz, Robert, and James Ward, *Gods, Demi-Gods, and Heroes* (Lake Geneva, WI: TSR, 1978).

Kunze, Max, *The Pergamon Altar: Its Rediscovery, History, and Reconstruction* (Mainz: Verlap Philipp von Zabern, 1995).

Kupčík, Ivan, *Münchner Portolankarten: Kunstmann I–XIII und zehn weitere Portolankarten [Munich Portolan Charts: Kunstmann I–XIII and Ten Other Portolan Charts]* (Munich: Deutscher Kunstverlag, 2000).

Küpper, Joachim, "The Traditional Cosmos and the New World," *MLN* 118/2 (2003), pp. 363–92.

Kuroita Katsumi (ed.), *Fusō ryakki*, Kokushi taikei 12 (Tokyo: Nichiyō shobō, 1932).

Kyōgoku Natsuhiko, "Yōkai to iu kotoba ni tsuite (sono 2)," *Kai* 12 (December 2001), pp. 296–307.

Lacroix, Léon, "Heracles, heros voyageur et civilisateur," *Bulletin de la Classe des Lettres de l'Academie Royale de Belgique* 60 (1974), pp. 34–59.

LaFleur, William, *The Karma of Words: Buddhism and the Literary Arts of Medieval Japan* (Berkeley: University of California Press, 1983).

Lamp, Frederick, "Cosmos, Cosmetics, and the Spirit of Bondo," *African Arts* 18 (1985), pp. 28–43, 98–9.

Lampert, Lisa, "Race, Periodicity, and the (Neo) Middle Ages," *Modern Language Quarterly* 65 (2004), pp. 391–421.

Laqueur, Thomas W., *Making Sex: Body and Gender from the Greeks to Freud* (Cambridge, MA: Harvard University Press, 1990).

Latour, Bruno, *Aramis, or The Love of Technology*, trans. Catherine Porter (Cambridge: Harvard University Press, 1996).

Lawless, Andrew, "Gendered Monsters: Art and Politics in the Representation of St George and the Dragon," review of Samantha Riches, *Pawns or Players: Studies on Medieval and Early Modern Women* [Four Courts Press, 2003], Three Monkeys Online, <http://www.threemonkeysonline.com/als/_gendered_dragons_st_george.html> (October 2005), accessed July 24, 2010.

Lawrence, Elizabeth Atwood, "The Centaur: Its History and Meaning in Human Culture," *Journal of Popular Culture* 27/4 (1994), pp. 57–68.

Lea, H.C., *Material Toward a History of Witchcraft* (London: Thomas Yoseloff, 1957).

Leclercq-Marx, Jacqueline, *La Sirène dans la pensée et dans l'art de l'Antiquité et du Moyen Âge: du mythe païen au symbole chrétien* (Brussels: Académie Royale de Belgique, 1997).

——, "L'idée d'un monde marin parallèle du monde terrestre: émergence et développements," in Chantal Connochie-Bourgne (ed.), *Mondes marins du Moyen Âge: Actes du 30e colloque du CUER MA, 3, 4 et 5 mars 2005* (Aix-en-Provence: Université de Provence, 2006), pp. 259–71.

——, "Drôles d'oiseaux. Le caladre, le phénix, la sirène, le griffon et la serre dans le *Physiologus*, les Bestiaires et les encyclopédies du XIIIe siècle. Mise en perspective," *Sénéfiance* 54 (2008), pp. 163–78.

——, "La localisation des peuples monstrueux dans la tradition savante et chez les *illitterati* (VIIe – XIIIe siècles). Une approche spatiale de l'Autre," *Studium Medievale: Revista de Cultura visual – Cultura escrita* 3 (2010), pp. 43–61.

Le Compatriote [Democratic Republic of the Congo], no. 231, July 15, 1995.

Lecoq, Danielle, "La Mappemonde du *Liber Floridus* ou La Vision du Monde de Lambert de Saint-Omer," *Imago Mundi* 39 (1987), pp. 9–49.

——, "L'image d'Alexandre à travers les mappemondes médiévales (XIIe–XIIIe)," *Geographia Antiqua* 2 (1993), pp. 63–103.

——, "Les îles aux confins du monde," in Daniel Reig (ed.), *Ile des merveilles: mirage, miroir, mythe* (Paris: L'Harmattan, 1997), pp. 13–32.

——, "Les marges de la terre habitée. Géographie et histoire naturelle des confines sur les mappemondes des XIIe et XIIIe siècles," in *L'Iconographie: Études sur les rapports entre textes et images dans l'Occident médiéval* (Paris: Le Léopard d'Or, 2001), pp. 99–186.

Lecouteux, Claude, "A propos d'un episode de Herzog Ernst: La recontre des hommes-grues," *Etudes germaniques* 33 (1977), pp. 1–15.

——, "Herzog Ernst, les monstres dits 'sciapodes' et le problème des sources," *Etudes Germaniques* 34/1 (1979), pp. 1–21.

——, "Les Panotéens: sources, diffusion, emploi," *Etudes germaniques* 35 (1980), pp. 253–66.

——, "Les Cynocéphales: Étude d'une tradition tératologique de l'Antiquité au XIIe s.," *Cahiers de civilisation médiévale* 24 (1981), pp. 117–29.

——, *Les monstres dans la littérature allemande du Moyen Âge: contribution à l'étude du merveilleux médiéval* (Göppingen: Kümmerle, 1982).

——, *Les monstres dans la pensée médiévale européenne: essai de présentation* (Paris: Presses de l'Université de Paris-Sorbonne, 1993 and 1999).

Lederer, Wolfgang, *The Fear of Women* (New York: Harcourt, 1968).

Lee, Sherman E., "Yan Hui, Zhong Kui, Demons and the New Year," *Artibus Asiae* 53/1–2 (1992), pp. 211–27.

Le Goff, Jacques, "L'Occident médiéval et l'Océan indien: un horizon onirique," in *Mediterraneo e Oceano Indiano (Atti del VI Collequio Internazionale di Storia Marittima)* (Florence: Olschki, 1970), pp. 243–63; translated into English by Arthur Goldhammer as "The Medieval West and the Indian Ocean: An Oneiric Horizon," in Jacques Le Goff, *Time, Work, and Culture in the Middle Ages* (Chicago: University of Chicago Press, 1980), pp. 189–200; reprinted in

Anthony Pagden (ed.), *Facing Each Other: The World's Perception of Europe and Europe's Perception of the World*, vol. 1 (Aldershot, UK and Burlington, VT: Ashgate, 2000), pp. 1–19.

Leitch, Stephanie, "The Wild Man, Charlemagne and the German Body," *Art History* 31/3 (2008), pp. 283–302.

Lemay, Helen Rodnite, *Women's Secrets: A Translation of Pseudo-Albertus Magnus's "De secretis mulierum" with Commentaries* (Albany, NY: State University of New York Press, 1992).

Lentz, Thomas W., and Glenn D. Lowry, *Timur and the Princely Vision: Persian Art and Culture in the Fifteenth Century* (Los Angeles: Los Angeles County Museum of Art; Washington, DC: Arthur M. Sackler Gallery, Smithsonian Institution, 1989).

Leoderer, Richard, *Voodoo Fires in Haiti*, ed. Lois Wilcken (Gretna, LA: Pelican, 2005).

Leonard, Irving A., "Conquerors and Amazons in Mexico," *The Hispanic American Historical Review* 24/4 (1944), pp. 561–79.

Leone, Massimo, "Literature, Travel, and Vertigo," in Jane Conroy (ed.), *Cross-Cultural Travel: Papers from the Royal Irish Academy Symposium on Literature and Travel, National University of Ireland, Galway, November 2002* (New York: Peter Lang, 2003).

——, *Religious Conversion and Identity: The Semiotic Analysis of Texts* (New York: Routledge, 2004).

Leoni, Francesca, "The Revenge of Ahriman: Images of *Div*s in the *Shahnama*, 1300–1600," PhD dissertation, Princeton University, 2008.

Léry, Jean de, *Histoire d'un voyage fait en la terre du Brésil, 1557 [1580]*, ed. Frank Lestringant (Montpellier: Max Chaleil, 1992).

Lestringant, Frank, "De l'ubiquité des Amazones au siècle des grandes découvertes," in P.M. Martin and Ch.M. Ternes (eds), *La Mythologie, clef de lecture du monde classique: Hommage à R. Chevallier* (Tours: Centre de recherches A. Piganiol, 1986), pp. 297–319.

——, *Mapping the Renaissance World: The Geographical Imagination in the Age of Discovery* (Berkeley: University of California Press, 1994).

Letts, Malcolm (ed.), *Mandeville's Travels: Texts and Transmissions*, 2 volumes (London: Hakluyt Society, 1953).

Lewis, Martin W., and Kären E. Wigen, *The Myth of Continents: A Critique of Metageography* (Berkeley: University of California Press, 1997).

Lewis, Suzanne, *The Art of Matthew Paris in the Chronica Majora* (Berkeley: University of California Press, 1987).

——, "Encounters with Monsters at the End of Time: Some Early Medieval Visualizations of Apocalyptic Eschatology," *Different Visions: A Journal of New Perspectives on Medieval Art* 2 (2010), pp. 1–76.

Lewis-Williams, J.D., *Believing and Seeing: Symbolic Meaning in Southern San Rock Paintings* (London: Academic Press, 1981).

Li, Michelle Osterfeld, *Ambiguous Bodies: Reading the Grotesque in Japanese Setsuwa Tales* (Stanford: Stanford University Press, 2009).

Lichtenstein, Mitchell (dir.), *Teeth* (Momentum Pictures, 2007).

Lieberman, S., "Who Were Pliny's Blue-Eyed Chinese?" *Classical Philology* 52 (1957), 174–7.

Lin, Irene H., "The Ideology of Imagination: The Tale of Shuten Dōji as a *Kenmon* Discourse," in Bernard Faure and François Lachaud (eds), *Buddhist Priests, Kings, and Marginals: Studies on Medieval Japanese Buddhism*, Cahiers d'Extrême Asie 13 (2002–2003), pp. 379–410.

Lionarons, Joyce Tally, "From Monster to Martyr: The Old English Legend of Saint Christopher," in Timothy S. Jones and David A. Sprunger (eds), *Marvels, Monsters, and Miracles: Studies in the Medieval and Early Modern Imaginations* (Kalamazoo: Medieval Institute Publications, 2002).

Lipton, Sara, *Images of Intolerance: The Representation of Jews and Judaism in the Bible moralisée* (Berkeley: University of California Press, 1999).

Lochrie, Karma, "Amazons at the Gates," in *Heterosyncrasies: Female Sexuality When Normal Wasn't* (Minneapolis: University of Minnesota Press, 2005), pp. 103–38.

Loe, Thomas, "Patterns of the Zombie in Jean Rhys's *Wide Sargasso Sea*," *Journal of Postcolonial Writing* 31/1 (1991), pp. 34–42.

Loeb, Elizabeth, "Cutting it Off: Bodily Integrity, Identity Disorders, and the Sovereign Stakes of Corporeal Desire in U.S. Law," *Women's Studies Quarterly* 36/3–4 (2008), pp. 44–63.

Loehr, Max, *Ritual Vessels of Bronze Age China* (New York: Asia Society, distributed by New York Graphic Society [Greenwich, CT], 1968).

Loewe, Michael, "Man and Beast: The Hybrid in Early Chinese Art and Literature," *Numen* 25/2 (1978), pp. 97–117.

Looper, Matthew G., "Quiriguá Zoomorph P: A Water-Throne and Mountain of Creation," in Andrea Stone (ed.), *Heart of Creation: Linda Schele and the Mesoamerican World* (Tuscaloosa: University of Alabama Press, 2002), pp. 185–200.

——, *Lightning Warrior: Maya Art and Kingship at Quirigua* (Austin: University of Texas Press, 2003).

——, *Quiriguá: A Guide to an Ancient Maya City* (Guatemala City: Editorial Antigua, 2007).

——, *To Be Like Gods: Dance in Ancient Maya Civilization* (Austin: University of Texas Press, 2009).

López-Baralt, Mercedes, "La iconografía política de América: el mito fundacional en las imágenes católica, protestante y nativa," *Nueva Revista de Filología Hispánica* 32/2 (1983), pp. 448–61.

Louis, Pierre, "Les animaux fabuleux chez Aristote," *Revue des études grecques* 80 (1967), pp. 242–6.

Love, Bruce, *The Paris Codex: Handbook for a Maya Priest* (Austin: University of Texas Press, 1994).

Lowe-Evans, Mary, *Frankenstein: Mary Shelley's Wedding Guest* (New York: Twayne, 1993).

Lucian of Samosata, *True History and Lucius or the Ass*, trans. Paul Turner (Bloomington: Indiana University Press, 1974).

Lupton, Julia Reinhard, "Creature Caliban," *Shakespeare Quarterly* 51/1 (2000), pp. 1–23.

Lyons, Linda, "Paranormal Beliefs Come (Super)Naturally to Some," Gallup, <http://www.gallup.com/poll/19558/Paranormal-Beliefs-Come-SuperNaturally-Some.aspx>, November 1, 2005.

Lyotard, Jean-François, *Libidinal Economy*, trans. Iain Hamilton Grant (Bloomington: Indiana University Press, 1993).

Mabuchi Kazuo, Kunisaki Fumimaro, and Inagaki Taiichi (eds), *Konjaku Monogatarishū*, Shinpen Nihon koten bungaku zenshū 35 (Tokyo: Shōgakkan, 1999).

MacCormack, Carol P., "Proto-Social to Adult: A Sherbro Transformation," in Carol P. MacCormack and M. Strathern (eds), *Nature, Culture, and Gender* (Cambridge: Cambridge University Press, 1980), pp. 95–118.

MacCormack, Patricia, "Perversion: Transgressive Sexuality and Becoming-monster," *Thirdspace* 3/2 (2004), <www.thirdspace.ca/articles/3_2_maccormack.htm>.

——, "The Great Ephemeral Tattooed Skin," *Body and Society* 12/2 (May 2006), pp. 57–82.

Mack, John, *Passport to the Cosmos: Human Transformation and Alien Encounters* (New York: Crown, 1999).

Macri, Martha J., and Matthew G. Looper, *The New Catalog of Maya Hieroglyphs, Vol. 1: The Classic Period Inscriptions* (Norman: University of Oklahoma Press, 2003).

Magasich-Airola, Jorge, and Jean-Marc de Beer, *America Magica: When Renaissance Europe Thought It Had Conquered Paradise*, trans. Monica Sandor (London: Anthem Press, 2006).

——, *America Magica: When Renaissance Europe Thought It Had Conquered Paradise*, 2nd edn (New York and London: Anthem Press, 2007).

Malhotra, Ruth, *Manege Frei! Artisten-und Circusplakate von Adolf Friedlander* (Dortmund: Harenberg Kommunikation, 1979).

Malina, Bruce, "Does *Porneia* Mean Fornication?" *Novum Testamentum* 14/1 (January 1972), pp. 10–17.

Malotki, Ekkehart, "The Story of the 'Tsimonmamant' or Jimson Weed Girls: A Hopi Narrative Featuring the Motif of the Vagina Dentata," in Brian Swann (ed.), *Smoothing the Ground: Essays on Native American Oral Literature* (Berkeley: University of California Press, 1983), pp. 204–20.

Mappa Mundi: The Hereford World Map (London: The Folio Society, 2010).

Marcel, Gabriel, *Choix de cartes et de mappemondes des XIVe et XVe siècles* (Paris: E. Leroux, 1896).

March, Kathleen M., and Kristina M. Passman, "The Amazon Myth and Latin America," in W. Haase and M. Reinhold (eds), *The Classical Tradition and the Americas*, vol. 1, part I, *European Images of the Americas and the Classical Tradition* (Berlin and New York: Walter De Gruyter, 1994), pp. 285–338.

Marie de France, *Die Lais der Marie de France*, ed. Karl Warnke, 3rd edn (Halle: Max Niemeyer, 1925).

Markham, Clements R. (trans.), *The Letters of Amerigo Vespucci and Other Documents Illustrative of His Career* (London: Printed for the Hakluyt Society, 1894).

Marlar, Jennifer E., "Biochemical Evidence of Cannibalism at a Prehistoric Puebloan Site in Southwestern Colorado," *Nature* 407/6800 (2000), pp. 74–8.

Marlowe, Michael, "Against the Theory of 'Dynamic Equivalence,'" revised, August 2009, <http://www.bible-researcher.com/dynamic-equivalence.html#nota41>, accessed March 12, 2011.

Márquez, Luis Cuervo, *Geografía médica y patológica de Colombia: Contribución al estudio de las enfermedades intertropicales* (Bogotá: Librería Colombiana, 1915).

Martin, Catherine Gimelli, "The Sources of Milton's Sin Reconsidered," *Milton Quarterly* 35/1 (2001), pp. 1–8.

Martin, Craig, "Experience of the New World and Aristotelian Revisions of the Earth's Climates during the Renaissance," *History of Meteorology* 3 (2006), pp. 1–15.

Martin, Janet, *Treasure of the Land of Darkness: The Fur Trade and its Significance for Medieval Russia* (Cambridge: Cambridge University Press, 1986).

Martín-Merás, Luisa, *Cartografía marítima hispana: La imagen de América* (Barcelona and Madrid: Lunwerg, 1993).

Martyr, Peter (Pietro Martire d'Anghiera), *De orbe novo, the Eight Decades of Peter Martyr d'Anghera*, trans. Francis Augustus MacNutt (New York: B. Franklin, 1970).

Mason, Peter, *Deconstructing America: Representations of the Other* (London: Routledge, 1990).

——, "Half a Cow," *Semiotica* 85/1–2 (1991), pp. 1–39.

——, "Classical Ethnography and its Influence on the European Perception of the Peoples of the New World," in W. Haase and M. Reinhold (eds), *The Classical Tradition and the Americas*, vol. 1, part I, *European Images of the Americas and the Classical Tradition* (Berlin and New York: Walter de Gruyter, 1994), pp. 135–72.

Matthews, John, and Caitlin Matthews, *The Element Encyclopedia of Magical Creatures* (London: Harper Element, 2005).

Maudslay, Alfred P., *Archaeology*, 5 volumes, Biologia Centrali-Americana (London: Porter, Dulau and Co., 1889–1902).

Maura, Juan Francisco, "Monstruos y bestias en las crónicas del nuevo mundo," *Espéculo* 19 (2001), <http://www.ucm.es/info/especulo/numero19/monstruo.html>, accessed July 1, 2009.

Maximilianus Transylvanus, *De Moluccis Insulis* (Rome, 1523).

Mayor, Adrienne, *The First Fossil Hunters: Paleontology in Greek and Roman Times* (Princeton: Princeton University Press, 2000).

Mayr, Ernst, "Darwin and the Evolutionary Theory in Biology," in Betty J. Meggars (ed.), *Evolution and Anthropology: A Centennial Appraisal* (Washington, DC: Anthropological Society of Washington, 1959).

McCann, Jenny C., "How to Look at a Hermaphrodite in Early Modern England," *Studies in English Literature 1500–1900* 46/1 (Winter 2006), pp. 67–91.

McCone, Kim R., "Werewolves, Cyclopes, Díberga and Fíanna: Juvenile Delinquency in Early Ireland," *Cambridge Medieval Celtic Studies* 12 (1986), pp. 1–22.

McCrillis, Leon Neal, "The Demonization of Minority Groups in Christian Society During the Central Middle Ages," PhD dissertation, University of California, Riverside, 1974.

McCrindle, J.W., *Indika of Ktesias* (London, 1882).

——, *Ancient India as Described in Megasthenes and Arrian* (Calcutta: Chuckervertty, Chatterjee, 1960).

McFadden, Brian, "Authority and Discourse in the *Liber monstrorum*," *Neophilologus* 89/3 (2005), pp. 473–93.

McGurk, P., D.N. Dumville, M.R. Godden, and Ann Knock (eds), *An Eleventh Century Anglo-Saxon Illustrated Miscellany*, Early English Manuscripts in Facsimile 21 (Baltimore: Johns Hopkins University Press, 1983).

McIntosh, Gregory C., "Columbus and the Piri Reis Map of 1513," *The American Neptune* 53/4 (1993), pp. 280–94.

Megasthenes, *Indica: Fragmenta*, ed. E.A. Schwanbeck (Bonn: Sumptibus Pleimesii, 1846; Amsterdam: Adolf M. Hakkert, 1966); translated in *Ancient India, as Described by Megasthenês and Arrian*, trans. J.W. McCrindle (Calcutta: Thacker, Spink, 1877; New Delhi: Today & Tomorrow's Printers & Publishers, 1972).

Meisami, Julie Scott, "The Past in Service of the Present: Two Views of History in Medieval Persia," *Poetics Today* 14/2 (1993), pp. 247–75.

——, "The *Shahname* as a Mirror for Princes: A Study in Reception," in Christophe Balaÿ, Claire Kappler, and Ziva Vesel (eds), *Pand-o Sokhan: Mélanges Offerts à Charles-Henri de Fouchécour* (Tehran: Institut Français de Recherche en Iran, 1995).

Melancthon, Philip, *Of Two Wonderful Popish Monsters*, trans. John Brooke (1579), *EEBO*.

Mellinkoff, Ruth, *Outcasts: Signs of Otherness in Northern European Art of the Late Middle Ages*, 2 volumes (Berkeley: University of California Press, 1993).

Menéndez-Pidal, Gonzalo, "Mozárabes y asturianos en la cultura de la Alta Edad Media en relación especial con la historia de los conocimientos geográficos," *Boletín de la Real Academia de la Historia* 134 (1954), pp. 137–292.

Meng Yuanlao, *Dongjing menghua lu*, in *Dongjing menghua lu wai si zhong* (Taipei: Dali chubanshe, 1980).

Mercator, Gerard, *Gerard Mercator's Map of the World (1569) in the Form of an Atlas in the Maritiem Museum 'Prins Hendrik' at Rotterdam* (Rotterdam: Maritiem Museum, 1961).

Meserve, R.I., "The Inhospitable Land of the Barbarians," *Journal of Asian History* 16 (1982), pp. 51–89.

Métraux, Alfred, *Le Vaudou Haitien* (Paris: Gallimard, 1968).

Metropolitan Museum of Art, Jenny F. So, Robert W. Bagley, Wen Fong, and Maxwell K. Hearn, *The Great Bronze Age of China: An Exhibition from the People's Republic of China* (New York: Metropolitan Museum of Art, 1980).

Metzler, Irina, "Perceptions of Hot Climate in Medieval Cosmography and Travel Literature," *Reading Medieval Studies* 23 (1997), pp. 69–106, reprinted in Joan-Pau Rubiés (ed.), *Medieval Ethnographies: European Perceptions of the World Beyond* (Farnham, UK and Burlington, VT: Ashgate Variorum, 2009), pp. 379–415.

Meyer, Birgit, "Mami Water as a Christian Demon: The Eroticism of Forbidden Pleasures in Southern Ghana," in Henry John Drewal (ed.), *Sacred Waters: Arts for Mami Wata and Other Water Divinities in Africa and the African Atlantic World* (Bloomington: Indiana University Press, 2008), pp. 383–98.

Meyers, Alexander A., "'Embraces Forcible and Foul': Viewing Milton's Sin as a Rape Victim," *Milton Quarterly* 2/1 (1994), pp. 11–16.

Michalko, Rod, *The Difference that Disability Makes* (Philadelphia: Temple University Press, 2002).

Migne, Jacques Paul (ed.), *Patrilogiae cursus completus: series latina*, 217 volumes (Paris: Garnier, 1844).

Miki Sumito, Asami Kazuhiko, Nakamura Yoshio, and Kouchi Kazuaki (eds), *Uji shūi monogatari. Kohon setsuwa shū*, Shin Nihon koten bungaku taikei 42 (Tokyo: Iwanami shoten, 1990).

Milano, Ernesto, and Annalisa Batini, *Mapamundi Catalán Estense, escuela cartográfica mallorquina* (Barcelona: M. Moleiro, 1996).

Milbrath, Susan, *Star Gods of the Maya: Astronomy in Art, Folklore, and Calendars* (Austin: University of Texas Press, 1999).

Miles, Robert, "The 1790s: The Effulgence of Gothic," in Jerrold E. Hogle (ed.), *The Cambridge Companion to Gothic Fiction* (Cambridge: Cambridge University Press, 2002), pp. 41–62.

Miller, Konrad, *Mappaemundi: Die ältesten Welkarten* (Stuttgart: J. Roth, 1895–98).

Miller, Patricia Cox, "Jerome's Centaur: A Hyper-Icon of the Desert," *Journal of Early Christian Studies* 4 (1996), pp. 209–33.

Miller, Sarah Alison, *Medieval Monstrosity and the Female Body* (New York: Routledge, 2010).

Mills, D.E., *A Collection of Tales from Uji: A Study and Translation of Uji Shūi Monogatari* (Cambridge: Cambridge University Press, 1970).

Milstein, Rachel, "The Battle of Good and Evil in Islamic Painting," *Jerusalem Studies in Arabic and Islam* 18 (1994), pp. 198–216.

Milstein, Rachel, Karin Rührdanz, and Barbara Schmitz, *Stories of the Prophets: Illustrated Manuscripts of the Qisas al-Anbiya'* (Costa Mesa, CA: Mazda Publishers, 1999).

Milton, John, *Paradise Lost*, in Merrit Y. Hughes (ed.), *Complete Poems and Major Prose* (Upper Saddle River, NJ: Prentice Hall, 1957).

Minorsky, Vladimir, "The Older Preface to the *Shah-nama*," in *Studi orientalistici in onore di Giorgio Levi della Vida* 2 (Roma: Istituto per l'Oriente, 1956), pp. 159–79.

Mitchell, C. Ben, Edmund D. Pellegrino, Jean Bethke Elshtain, John F. Kilner, and Scott B. Rae, *Biotechnology and the Human Good* (Georgetown: Georgetown University Press, 2007).

Mitchell, David T., and Sharon L. Snyder, *Narrative Prosthesis: Disability and the Dependencies of Discourse* (Ann Arbor: University of Michigan Press, 2000).

Mitter, Partha, *Much Maligned Monsters: A History of European Reaction to Indian Art* (Oxford: Clarendon Press, 1977; reprint University of Chicago Press, 1992).

——, *Art and Nationalism in Colonial India, 1850–1922* (Cambridge: Cambridge University Press, 1995).

——, *Indian Art* (Oxford: Oxford University Press, 2001).

——, *The Triumph of Modernism: India's Artists and the Avant-garde, 1922–47* (Chicago: University of Chicago Press, 2007).

——, "Decentering Modernism: Art History and Avant-Garde Art from the Periphery," *Art Bulletin* 90/4 (2008), pp. 531–48.

——, "Interventions: The Author Replies," *Art Bulletin* 90/4 (2008), pp. 568–74.

Mittman, Asa, "The Other Close at Hand: Gerald of Wales and the *Marvels of the West*," in Bettina Bildhauer and Robert Mills (eds), *The Monstrous Middle Ages* (Cardiff: University of Wales Press, 2003), pp. 97–112.

——, *Maps and Monsters in Medieval England* (New York and London: Routledge, 2006).

Mittman, Asa Simon, and Susan Kim, *Inconceivable Beasts: The Wonders of the East in the Beowulf Manuscript* (Tempe, AZ: ACMRS, forthcoming).

Mizuki Shigeru, *Zoku yōkai jiten* (Tokyo: Tokyo-dō Shuppan, 1984).

——, *Zusetsu Nihon yōkai taizen* (Tokyo: Kōdansha, 1994).

Moerman, D. Max, "Demonology and Eroticism: Islands of Women in the Japanese Buddhist Imagination," *Japanese Journal of Religious Studies* 36/2 (2009), pp. 351–80.

Monte, Urbano, *Descrizione del mondo sin qui conosciuto*, ed. Maurizio Ampollini (Lecco: Periplo, 1994).

Montero, Mayra, *Tú, la oscuridad* (Barcelona: Tusquets, 1995).

Moor, E., *The Hindu Pantheon* (London: J. Johnson, 1810).

Moore, C.L., *Shambleau* (Maryland: Wildside Press, 2009).

Moretti, Gabriella, "The Other World and the 'Antipodes': The Myth of the Unknown Countries between Antiquity and the Renaissance," in W. Haase and M. Reinhold (eds), *The Classical Tradition and the Americas*, vol. 1, part I, *European Images of the Americas and the Classical Tradition* (Berlin and New York: De Gruyter, 1994), pp. 241–84.

Morgan, J.R., "Lucian's *True Histories* and the *Wonders Beyond Thule* of Antonius Diogenes," *Classical Quarterly* 35 (1985), pp. 475–90.

Morgan, Nigel, *The Douce Apocalypse: Picturing the End of the World in the Middle Ages* (Oxford: Bodleian Library, 2007).

Morris, Richard, Hugo Carl Wilhelm Haenisch, Heinrich Hupe, and Max Kaluza (eds), *Cursor mundi* (London: Kegan Paul, Trench, Trübner & Co., 1874).

Moseley, C.W.R.D., "Behaim's Globe and 'Mandeville's Travels,'" *Imago Mundi* 33 (1981), pp. 89–91.

—— (trans.), *The Travels of Sir John Mandeville* (London: Penguin, 1983).

Moulton, Ian Frederick, "'A Monster Great Deformed': The Unruly Masculinity of *Richard III*," *Shakespeare Quarterly* 47/3 (Autumn 1996), pp. 251–68.

Moyer, Eileen, "Death of the Mermaid and Political Intrigue in the Indian Ocean," in Henry John Drewal (ed.), *Sacred Waters: Arts for Mami Wata and Other Water Divinities in Africa and the African Atlantic World* (Bloomington: Indiana University Press, 2008), pp. 451–65.

Münster, Sebastian, *Cosmographiae introductio* (Basle, 1550).

Mullaney, Steven, "Strange Things, Gross Terms, Curious Customs: The Rehearsal of Cultures in the Late Renaissance," *Representations* 3 (1983), pp. 40–67.

Mundill, Robin R., *England's Jewish Solution: Experiment and Expulsion, 1262–1290* (Cambridge: Cambridge University Press, 1998).

——, *The King's Jews: Money, Massacre and Exodus in Medieval England* (London: Continuum, 2010).

Münkler, Marina, "Experiencing Strangeness: Monstrous Peoples on the Edge of the Earth as Depicted on Medieval *Mappae Mundi*," *Medieval History Journal* 5 (2002), pp. 195–222.

——, "*Monstra* und *mappae mundi*: die monströsen Völker des Erdrands auf mittelalterlichen Weltkarten," in Jürg Glauser and Christian Kiening (eds), *Text — Bild — Karte: Kartographien der Vormoderne* (Freiburg: Rombach Verlag, 2007), pp. 149–73.

Murakami Kenji, *Yōkai jiten* (Tokyo: Mainichi shinbunsha, 2000).

Murgatroyd, Paul, *Mythical Monsters in Classical Literature* (London: Duckworth Publishing, 2007).

Myhre, Karin, "Picturing Spirits: Images of Gods, Ghosts and Demons in Chinese Painting," in Sarah E. Fraser (ed.), *Merit, Opulence, and the Buddhist Network of Wealth* (Shanghai: Shanghai Fine Arts Publishers, 2003).

Nagazumi Yasuaki and Shimada Isao (eds), *Kokon chomonjū*, vol. 2, Nihon koten bungaku taikei 84 (Tokyo: Iwanami shoten, 1966).

Nakamura, Kyoko Motomochi (trans.), *Miraculous Stories from the Japanese Buddhist Tradition: The Nihon ryōiki of the Monk Kyōkai* (Cambridge, MA: Harvard University Press, 1973; reprint, Richmond, Surrey: Curzon Press, 1997).

Nakamura Teiri, *Kappa no Nihonshi* (Tokyo: Nihon editâsukūru shuppanbu, 1996).

Nakazawa Shin'ichi, *Poketto no naka no yasei* (Tokyo: Iwanami shoten, 1997).

Nebenzahl, Kenneth, *Atlas of Columbus and the Great Discoveries* (Chicago: Rand McNally, 1990).

Nederman, Cary J., and Jacqui True, "The Third Sex: The Idea of the Hermaphrodite in Twelfth-Century Europe," *Journal of the History of Sexuality* 6/4 (1996), pp. 497–517.

Needham, Joseph, *Science and Civilization in China*, vol. 2 (Cambridge: Cambridge University Press, 1954).

Nesselrath, Heinz-Günther, "Herodot und die Grenzen der Erde," *Museum Helveticum* 52 (1995), pp. 20–44.

Neumann, Erich, *The Great Mother: An Analysis of the Archetype* (Princeton: Princeton University Press, 1955).

——, *The Great Mother*, trans. Ralph Mannheim (Princeton: Princeton University Press, 1972).

Nevadomsky, Joseph, "Mami Wata, Inc.," in Henry John Drewal (ed.), *Sacred Waters: Arts for Mami Wata and Other Water Divinities in Africa and the African Atlantic World* (Bloomington: Indiana University Press, 2008), pp. 351–9.

Newall, Venetia, "The Dog-Headed Saint Christopher," in Linda Dégh, Nikolai Burlakoff, Carl Lindahl, and Harry Gammerdinger (eds), *Folklore on Two Continents: Essays in Honor of Linda Dégh* (Bloomington: Trickster Press, 1980).

Newitz, Annalee, *Pretend We're Dead: Capitalist Monsters in American Pop Culture* (Durham, NC: Duke University Press, 2006).

Newman, Barbara, *Sister of Wisdom: St. Hildegard's Theology of the Feminine* (Berkeley: University of California Press, 1989).

New Oxford Annotated Bible, ed. Bruce M. Metzger and Roland E. Murphy, new revised standard version (Oxford: Oxford University Press, 1994).

Newport, Frank, "What if Government Really Listened to the People?" Gallup, <http://www.gallup.com/poll/4594/What-Government-Really-Listened-People. aspx>, October 15, 1997.

Newport, Frank, and Maura Strausberg, "Americans' Belief in Psychic and Paranormal Phenomena is Up Over Last Decade," Gallup, <http://www.gallup. com/poll/4483/Americans-Belief-Psychic-Paranormal-Phenomena-Over-Last-Decade.aspx>, June 8, 2001.

Newsome, Elizabeth, *Trees of Paradise and Pillars of the World: The Serial Stelae Cycle of "18-Rabbit-God K," King of Copan* (Austin: University of Texas Press, 2001).

Niccoli, Ottavia, *Prophecy and People in Renaissance Italy*, trans. Lydia G. Cochrane (Princeton, NJ: Princeton University Press, 1990).

Nichols, Andrew, "The Complete Fragments of Ctesias of Cnidus: Translation and Commentary with an Introduction," PhD dissertation, University of Florida, 2008.

Niemeyer, Guenter H.W., *Hagenbeck* (Hamburg: H. Christians, 1972).

Nordenskiöld, A.E., *Facsimile-Atlas to the Early History of Cartography* (Stockholm: P.A. Norstedt, 1889; New York: Dover Publications, 1973).

Nunn, George E., "Did Columbus Believe that He Reached Asia on his Fourth Voyage?" in *The Geographical Conceptions of Columbus: A Critical Consideration of Four Problems* (New York: American Geographical Society, 1924), pp. 54–90.

Nuttall, Zelia (ed.), *Codex Nuttall* (New York: Dover, 1975).

Obeyesekere, Gananath, *Cannibal Talk: The Man-Eating Myth and Human Sacrifice in the South Seas* (Berkeley: University of California Press, 2005), pp. 1–23.

Obregón, Diana, "Building National Medicine: Leprosy and Power in Colombia, 1870–1910," *Social History of Medicine* 15/1 (2002), pp. 89–108.

Obrist, Barbara, "Cosmological Iconography in Twelfth-Century Bavaria: The Earthly Zones and their Circling Serpent in Munich, Bayerische Staatsbibliothek, CLM 7785," *Studi medievali* 48/2 (2007), pp. 543–74.

O'Doherty, Marianne, "'They are like beasts, for they have no law': Ethnography and Constructions of Human Difference in Late-Medieval Translations of Marco Polo's Book," in Jean-François Kosta-Théfaine (ed.), *Travels and Travelogues in the Middle Ages* (New York: AMS Press, 2009), pp. 59–92.

Odom, Herbert H., "Generalizations on Race in Nineteenth-Century Anthropology," *Isis* 58 (1967), pp. 4–18.

O'Donnell, Elliott, *Werewolves* (Maryland: Wildside Press, 2008).

Odoric of Pordenone, "Travels," trans. H. Yule, in *Cathay and the Way Thither*, vol. 2 (London: Hakluyt Society, 1913).

Oechsler, Monika, *The Eagle Project*, performance at the James Hockney Gallery (2007), <http://monikaoechsler.co.uk/pages/eagle.html>.

Olaus Magnus, *Olai Magni Gothi Carta marina et descriptio septemtrionalium terrarum ac mirabilium rerum in eis contentarum* (Malmö: In officina J. Kroon, 1949).

———, *Die Wunder des Nordens*, ed. Elena Balzamo and Reinhard Kaiser (Frankfurt: Eichborn, 2006).

Olschki, L., *Marco Polo's Asia* (Cambridge: Cambridge University Press, 1960).

Olsen, Karin E., and L.A.J.R. Houwen (eds), *Monsters and the Monstrous in Medieval Northwest Europe* (Leuven: Peeters, 2001).

Olshin, Benjamin, "A Sea Discovered: Pre-Columbian Conceptions and Depictions of the Atlantic Ocean," PhD dissertation, University of Toronto, 1994.

Olson, Julius E., and Edward Gaylord Bourne (eds), *The Northmen, Columbus, and Cabot, 985–1503: The Voyages of the Northmen* (New York: Charles Scribner's Sons, 1906).

Omont, Henri (ed.), *Livre des merveilles, Marco Polo, Odoric Pordenone, Mandeveille, Hayton, etc.* (Paris: Berthaud, 1907).

Orchard, Andy, *Pride and Prodigies: Studies in the Monsters of the Beowulf-Manuscript* (Cambridge: D.S. Brewer, 1995; Toronto: University of Toronto Press, 2003).

Orosius, Paulus, *The Seven Books of History against the Pagans*, trans. Roy Deferrari (Washington, DC: Catholic University of America Press, 1964).

Ortega, Julio, "The Discourse of Abundance," *American Literary History* 4/2 (1992), pp. 369–85.

Osamu Izumoji (ed.), *Nihon ryōiki*, Shin Nihon bungaku taikei 30 (Tokyo: Iwanami, 1996).

Oswald, Dana, "Unnatural Women, Invisible Mothers: Monstrous Female Bodies in the Wonders of the East," *Different Visions: A Journal of New Perspectives on Medieval Art* 2 (2009), <http://www.differentvisions.org/Issue2PDFs/Oswald.pdf>.

———, *Monsters, Gender, and Sexuality in Medieval English Literature* (Cambridge: D.S. Brewer, 2010).

Otero, Solimar, "'Fearing Our Mothers': An Overview of the Psychoanalytic Theories Concerning the Vagina Dentata Motif," *American Journal of Psychoanalysis* 56/3 (September 1996), pp. 269–89.

Otten, Charlotte F., *A Lycanthropy Reader: Werewolves in Western Culture* (Syracuse: Syracuse University Press, 1986).

Ovid, *Ovidi Nasonis Metamorphoses*, ed. R.J. Tarrant (New York: Oxford University Press, 2004).

Ovington, J., *A Voyage to Suratt in the Year 1689* (London: 1696).

Ōwa Iwao, *Oni to tennō* (Tokyo: Hakusuisha, 1992).

Pacques, Viviana, *L'arbre cosmique* (Paris: Institut d'Ethnologie, Travaux et Mémoires 70, 1964).

Pagden, Anthony, *The Fall of Natural Man: The American Indian and the Origins of Comparative Ethnology* (Cambridge: Cambridge University Press, 1986).

———, *European Encounters with the New World from Renaissance to Romanticism* (New Haven: Yale University Press, 1993).

Palencia-Roth, Michael, "Cannibalism and the New Man of Latin America in the 15th- and 16th-Century European Imagination," *Comparative Civilizations Review* 12 (1985), pp. 1–27.

Panchenko, Dmitri V., "Scylax' Circumnavigation of India and its Interpretation in Early Greek Geography, Ethnography and Cosmography," *Hyperboreus* 4/2 (1998), pp. 211–42, and 9/2 (2003), pp. 274–94.

Pandey, Rajyashree, "Women, Sexuality, and Enlightenment: *Kankyo no Tomo*," *Monumenta Nipponica* 50/3 (Autumn 1995), pp. 325–56.

Paravisini-Gebert, Lizabeth, "Women Possessed: Eroticism and Exoticism in the Representation of Woman as Zombie," in Margarite Fernandez Olmos and Lizabeth Paravisini-Gebert (eds), *Sacred Possessions: Vodou, Santeria, Obeah, and the Caribbean* (New Brunswick, NJ: Rutgers University Press, 1997), pp. 37–58.

Paré, Ambroise, *Des Monstres et prodiges* (Paris, 1573).

——, *Les Oeuvres d'Ambroise Paré* (Paris, 1579).

——, *Des Monstres et prodiges*, ed. Jean Céard (Geneva: Droz, 1971).

——, *On Monsters and Marvels*, trans. Janis L. Pallister (Chicago: University of Chicago Press, 1982).

Parman, Talat, "The Demon as a Human Double," in Mine Haydaroğlu (ed.), *Ben Mehmed Siyah Kalem, Insanlar ve Cinler Ustasi* (Istanbul: T.C. Kültür ve Turizm Bakanligi, 2004), pp. 129–34.

Pàroli, Teresa, "How Many are the Unipeds' Feet? Their Tracks in Texts and Sources," in Wilhelm Heizmann, Klaus Böldl, and Heinrich Beck (eds), *Analecta Septentrionalia: Beiträge zur nordgermanischen Kultur- und Literaturgeschichte* (Berlin and New York: Walter de Gruyter, 2009), pp. 281–327.

Parrish, Susan Scott, "The Female Opossum and the Nature of the New World," *The William and Mary Quarterly* 54/3 (1997), pp. 475–514.

Parry, John H., "Asia-in-the-West," *Terrae Incognitae* 8 (1976), pp. 59–72.

Pasternack, Carol Braun, "The Sexual Practices of Virginity and Chastity in Aldhelm's *De Virginitate*," in Carol Braun Pasternack and Lisa M.C. Weston (eds), *Sex and Sexuality in Anglo-Saxon England* (Tempe: Arizona Center for Medieval and Renaissance Studies, 2004), pp. 93–120.

Pasternack, Carol Braun, and Lisa M.C. Weston, "Introduction," in Carol Braun Pasternack and Lisa M.C. Weston (eds), *Sex and Sexuality in Anglo-Saxon England* (Tempe: Arizona Center for Medieval and Renaissance Studies, 2004).

Pastor Bodmer, Beatriz, *The Armature of Conquest: Spanish Accounts of the Discovery of America, 1492–1589*, trans. Lydia Longstreth Hunt (Stanford: Stanford University Press, 1992).

Paulson, Ronald, "Gothic Fiction and the French Revolution," *English Literary History* 48 (1981), pp. 532–54.

Paxon, Barbara, "Mammy Water: New World Origins?" *Baessler-Archiv* 31 (1983), pp. 407–46.

Peacock, A.C.S., *Medieval Islamic Historiography and Political Legitimacy: Bal'ami's Tarikhnama* (London and New York: Routledge, 2007).

Pepperell, Robert, *The Posthuman Condition: Consciousness Beyond the Brain* (Exeter: Intellect, 1995 and 1997).

Pepys, Samuel, *The Diary of Samuel Pepys: A New and Complete Transcription*, ed. Robert Latham and William Matthews, 11 volumes (London etc., 1970–83 [2000 printing]).

Peucer, Caspar, *Commentarius de paecipuis generibus divinationum* (Wittemberg, 1560).

Philippi, Donald L. (trans.), *Kojiki* (Tokyo: University Press, 1968).

Phillips, Ruth B., *Representing Woman: Sande Masquerades of the Mende of Sierra Leone* (Los Angeles: UCLA Fowler Museum of Cultural History, 1995).

Pigafetta, Antonio, *Magellan's Voyage: A Narrative Account of the First Circumnavigation*, ed. and trans. R.A. Skelton (New York: Dover Publications, 1994).

Pigafetta Antonio, and Maximilianus Transylvanus, *First Voyage Around the World by Antonio Pigafetta and "De Moluccis Insulis" by Maximilianus Transylvanus*, ed. and trans. Carlos Quirino (Manila: Filipiniana Book Guild, 1969).

Pinckney, P., *American Figureheads and Their Carvers* (New York: W.W. Norton, 1940).

Plank, Shannon E., "Monumental Maya Dwellings in the Hieroglyphic and Archaeological Records: A Cognitive-Anthropological Approach to Classic Maya Architecture," PhD dissertation, Boston University, 2003.

Plato, *Republic*, trans. C.D.C. Reeve (Indianapolis: Hackett, 2004).

——, *Timaeus*, ed. Ioannes Burnet (Oxford: Oxford University Press, 1902).

Pliny the Elder, *Naturalis Historia*, ed. Karl Friedrich Theodor Mayhoff (Leipzig: Teubner, 1906).

——, *Natural History*, ed. and trans. H. Rackham, 10 volumes (Cambridge: Harvard University Press, 1940, 1958 and 1969).

Pluskowski, Aleksander, "Apocalyptic Monsters: Animal Inspirations for the Iconography of Medieval North European Devourers," in Bettina Bildhauer and Robert Mills (eds), *The Monstrous Middle Ages* (Toronto: University of Toronto Press, 2003), pp. 155–76.

——, "Narwhals or Unicorns? Exotic Animals as Material Culture in Medieval Europe," *European Journal of Archaeology* 7/3 (2004), pp. 291–313.

——, *Wolves and the Wilderness in the Middle Ages* (Woodbridge, Suffolk: Boydell Press, 2006).

Po-Chia Hsia, R., "A Time for Monsters," in Laura Lunger Knoppers and Joan B. Landes (eds), *Monstrous Bodies/Political Monstrosities in Early Modern Europe* (Ithaca, NY and London: Cornell University Press, 2004), pp. 67–92.

Poesch, Jessie, "The Beasts from Job in the *Liber Floridus* Manuscripts," *Journal of the Warburg and Courtauld Institutes* 33 (1970), pp. 41–51.

Poinsotte, J.M., "Les Romains et la Chine: Réalités et mythes," *Mélanges d'Archéologie et d'Histoire de l'École Française de Rome* 91 (1979), pp. 431–79.

"Pokemon Black Version and Pokemon White Version Coming to North America in Spring 2011," *Business Wire* (May 28, 2010) ABI/INFORM Dateline, ProQuest, Web, June 23, 2010.

Polo, Marco, *The Book of Ser Marco Polo, the Venetian: Concerning the Kingdoms and Marvels of the East*, trans. and ed. Henry Yule, 3rd edn (London: J. Murray, 1903).

——, *Milione: il Milione nelle redazioni toscana e franco-italiana* [*Le divisament dou monde*], ed. Gabriella Ronchi (Milan: A. Mondadori, 1982).

——, *Das Buch der Wunder* [*Le livre des merveilles*] (Lucerne: Faksimile Verlag, 1995).

Pomerance, Murray, "Whatever is *Happening* to M. Night Shyamalan: Meditation on an 'Infection' Film," in Jeffrey Andrew Weinstock (ed.), *Critical Approaches to the Films of M. Night Shyamalan: Spoiler Warnings* (New York: Palgrave Macmillan, 2010), pp. 203–18.

Pomeroy, Sarah B., *Goddesses, Whores, Wives, and Slaves: Women in Classical Antiquity* (New York: Schocken Books, 1975).

Porsia, Franco (ed.), *Liber monstrorum* (Bari: Dedalo libri, 1976).

Prado Bellei, Sérgio Luiz, "Brazilian Anthropophagy Revisited," in Francis Barker, Peter Hulme, and Margaret Iversen (eds), *Cannibalism and the Colonial World* (New York: Cambridge University Press, 1998).

Pratt, Mary Louise, *Imperial Eyes: Travel Writing and Transculturation*, 2nd edn (New York/London: Routledge, 2008).

Prieto, Andrés, "Alexander and the Geographer's Eye: Allegories of Knowledge in Martín Fernández de Enciso's *Suma de Geographía* (1519)," *Hispanic Review* 78/2 (2010), pp. 169–88.

Prosser, Jay, *Second Skins: The Body Narratives of Transsexuality* (New York: Columbia University Press, 1998).

Pseudo-Albertus Magnus, *Women's Secrets: A Translation of Pseudo-Albertus Magnus's* De Secretis Mulierum *with Commentaries*, ed. Helen Rodnite Lemay (New York: State University of New York Press, 1992).

Pujades i Bataller, Ramon J., *Les cartes portolanes: la representació medieval d'una mar solcada* (Barcelona: Institut Cartogràfic de Catalunya, 2007).

Purchas, Samuel, *Microcosmus or The Historie of Man* (London, 1619).

The Questioning of John Rykener, A Male Cross-Dressing Prostitute, 1395, Medieval Sourcebook, <http://www.fordham.edu/halsall/source/1395rykener.html>, accessed July 28, 2010.

Quilligan, Maureen, *The Language of Allegory: Defining the Genre* (Ithaca: Cornell University Press, 1979).

Quintilian, *Institutes of Oratory*, trans. John Selby Watson, 2 volumes (London: G. Bell and Sons, 1902).

Qur'an, The, trans. Muhammad A.S. Abdel Haleem (Oxford: Oxford University Press, 2004).

Raby, Peter, *Oscar Wilde* (Cambridge: Cambridge University Press, 1988).

Rainaud, Armand, *Le continent Austral; hypothèses et découvertes* (Paris: A. Colin, 1893; Amsterdam: Meridian, 1965).

Raitt, Jill, "The Vagina Dentata and the immaculatus uterus divini fontis," *Journal of the American Academy of Religion* 48/3 (1980), pp. 415–31.

Raleigh, Walter, *The Discouerie of the Large, Rich, and Bevvtiful Empire of Guiana* (London: Robert Robinson, 1596).

Ramos, Manuel João, *Essays in Christian Mythology: The Metamorphosis of Prester John* (Lanham, MD: University Press of America, 2006).

Ravenstein, E.G., *Martin Behaim: His Life and his Globe* (London: G. Philip & Son, 1908).

Reardon, B.P. (ed.), *Collected Ancient Greek Novels* (Berkeley: University of California Press, 1989).

Reichert, Folker, "Columbus und Marco Polo—Asien in Amerika. Zur Literaturgeschichte der Entdeckungen," *Zeitschrift für historische Forschung* 15 (1988), pp. 1–63.

Reider, Noriko T., "Shuten Dōji: Drunken Demon," *Asian Folklore Studies* 64 (2005), pp. 207–31.

——, *Japanese Demon Lore: Oni from Ancient Times to the Present* (Logan: Utah State University Press, 2010).

Reilly, F. Kent III, "Art, Ritual, and Rulership in the Olmec World," in Jill Guthrie and Elizabeth P. Benson (eds), *The Olmec World: Ritual and Rulership* (Princeton: The Art Museum, Princeton University, 1995), pp. 26–45.

Relaño, Francesc, *The Shaping of Africa: Cosmographic Discourse and Cartographic Science in Late Medieval and Early Modern Europe* (Burlington, VT and Aldershot, UK: Ashgate, 2002).

Renda, Mary A., *Taking Haiti: Military Occupation and the Culture of U.S. Imperialism, 1915–1940* (Chapel Hill: University of North Carolina Press, 2001).

Renzetti, Claire M., and Jeffrey L. Edleson, *Encyclopedia of Interpersonal Violence*, vol. 1 (Thousand Oaks, CA: Sage, 2008).

Rhys, Jean, *Wide Sargasso Sea* [1966], intro. Francis Wyndham (New York: Norton, 1982).

Richard, J., "L'Extrême-Orient Légendaire au Moyen Âge: Roi David et Prêtre Jean," *Annales d'Ethiopie* 12 (1957), 225–44.

Richardson, William A.R., *Was Australia Charted before 1606? The Java la Grande Inscriptions* (Canberra: National Library of Australia, 2006).

Riesner, Rainer, "Geographic Framework of the Mission," in *Paul's Early Period: Chronology, Mission Strategy, Theology*, trans. Doug Stott (Grand Rapids, MI: W.B. Eerdmans, 1998), pp. 241–56.

Rigall, Juan Casas, "Razas humanas portentosas en las partidas remotas del mundo (de Benjamín de Tudela a Cristóbal Colón)," in Rafael Beltrán Llavador (ed.), *Maravillas, peregrinaciones y utopías: literatura de viajes en el mundo románico* (Valencia: Universitad de Valencia, 2002), pp. 253–90.

Rimer, J. Thomas, and Jonathan Chaves (eds), *Japanese and Chinese Poems to Sing: The Wakan rōeishū* (New York: Columbia University Press, 1997).

Rimer, J. Thomas, and Yamazaki Masakazu (trans.), *On the Art of Nō Drama: The Major Treatises of Zeami* (Princeton, NJ: Princeton University Press, 1984).

Ringmar, Erik, "Audience for a Giraffe: European Expansionism and the Quest for the Exotic," *Journal of World History* 17/4 (2006), pp. 353–97.

Rivera, José Eustasio, *La vorágine* (Caracas: Biblioteca Ayacucho, 1976).

Rivera, José Eustasio, *The Vortex*, trans. Earle K. James (New York: Putnam, 1935).

Rivera Villegas, Carmen, "Nuevas rutas hacia Haití en la cartografía de Mayra Montero," *Revista Hispánica Moderna* 54/1 (2001), pp. 154–65.

Rivers, Christopher, *Face Value: Physiognomical Thought and the Legible Body in Marivaux, Lavater, Balzac, Gautier, and Zola* (Madison: University of Wisconsin Press, 1994).

Robert, François, in "Minutes of the Proceedings of the National Convention in France," *The Gentleman's Magazine* 62/2 (December 1792), p. 1138.

Robertson, Howard S. (trans.), *The Song of Roland* (London: Dent, 1972).

Robertson, Merle Greene, "The Quadripartite Badge: A Badge of Rulership," in Merle Greene Robertson (ed.), *Primera Mesa Redonda de Palenque, Part I* (Pebble Beach, CA: Pre-Columbian Art Research, Robert Louis Stevenson School, 1974), pp. 77–94.

Rodin, A., E.B. Havell, and A.K. Coomaraswamy, *Sculptures Çivaites* (Paris and Brussels: G. van Oest, 1921).

Roling, Bernd, *Drachen und Sirenen: die Rationalisierung und Abwicklung der Mythologie an den europäischen Universitäten* (Leiden and Boston: Brill, 2010).

Romm, James, "Dragons and Gold at the Ends of the Earth: A Folktale Motif Developed by Herodotus," *Marvels & Tales* 1/1 (1987), pp. 45–54.

——, "Belief and Other Worlds: Ktesias and the Founding of the 'Indian Wonders,'" in George E. Slusser and Eric S. Rabkin (eds), *Mindscapes: The Geography of Imagined Worlds* (Carbondale: Southern Illinois University Press, 1989), pp. 121–35.

——, "Alexander, Biologist: Oriental Monstrosities and the *Epistola Alexandri ad Aristotelem*," in Scott Westrem (ed.), *Discovering New Worlds: Essays on Medieval Exploration and Imagination* (New York: Garland, 1991), pp. 16–30, reprinted in Bill Readings and Bennet Schaber (eds), *Postmodernism Across the Ages: Essays for a Postmodernity that Wasn't Born Yesterday* (Syracuse, NY: Syracuse University Press, 1993), pp. 31–46.

——, *The Edges of the Earth in Ancient Thought: Geography, Exploration, and Fiction* (Princeton: Princeton University Press, 1992).

——, "New World and *novos orbes*: Seneca in the Renaissance Debate over Ancient Knowledge of the Americas," in W. Haase and M. Reinhold (eds), *The Classical Tradition and the Americas*, vol. 1, part I, *European Images of the Americas and the Classical Tradition* (Berlin and New York: De Gruyter, 1994), pp. 78–116.

——, *Herodotus* (New Haven and London: Yale University Press, 1998).

Ronca, Italo, "*Semper aliquid novi Africam adferre*: Philological Afterthoughts on the Plinian Reception of a Pre-Aristotelian Saying," *Akroterion* 37/3–4 (1992), pp. 146–58.

Rood, Tim, "Herodotus and Foreign Lands," in Carolyn Dewald and John Marincola (eds), *The Cambridge Companion to Herodotus* (Cambridge: Cambridge University Press, 2006), pp. 290–305.

Roscher, Wilhelm Heinrich, "Omphalos, eine philologisch-archäologisch-volkskundliche Abhandlung über die Vorstellungen der Griechen und anderer Völker vom 'Nabel der erde,'" in *Abhandlungen der philologisch-historischen Klasse der königlichen sächsischen Gesellschaft der Wissenschaften* 29/9 (1913).

Rose, Carol, *Giants, Monsters, and Dragons: An Encyclopedia of Folklore* (New York: W.W. Norton, 2001).

Ross, D.J.A., *Illustrated Medieval Alexander-Books in Germany and the Netherlands: A Study in Comparative Iconography* (Cambridge, UK: Modern Humanities Research Association, 1971).

Ross, Doran H., "Artists Advertising Themselves: Contemporary Studio Facades in Ghana," *African Arts* 37 (2004), pp. 72–9.

Rossi-Reder, Andrea, "Wonders of the Beast: India in Classical and Medieval Literature," in Timothy S. Jones and David A. Sprunger (eds), *Marvels, Monsters, and Miracles: Studies in the Medieval and Early Modern Imaginations* (Kalamazoo: Medieval Institute Publications, 2002), pp. 53–66.

Roussineau, Giles (ed.), *Le Roman de Perceforest*, 9 volumes (Geneva: Droz, 1987).

Roxburgh, David J., "Baysunghur's Library: Questions Related to its Chronology and Production," *Journal of Social Affairs* 18 (Winter 2001), pp. 11–41.

——, *The Persian Album, 1400–1600: From Dispersal to Collection* (New Haven and London: Yale University Press, 2005).

Ruberg, Uwe, "Die Tierwelt auf der Ebstorfer Weltkarte im Kontext mittelalterlicher Enzyklopädik," in Hartmut Kugler and Eckhard Michael (eds), *Ein Weltbild vor Columbus. Die Ebstorfer Weltkarte. Interdisziplinäres Colloquium 1988* (Weinheim: VCH, 1991), pp. 319–46.

Rubiés, Joan-Pau, "Hugo Grotius's Dissertation on the Origin of the American Peoples and the Use of Comparative Methods," *Journal of the History of Ideas* 52/2 (1991), pp. 221–44.

——, "New Worlds and Renaissance Ethnology," *History and Anthropology* 6 (1993), pp. 157–97.

Rudloff, Diether, *Zillis: die romanische Bilderdecke der Kirche St. Martin* (Basel: P. Heman, 1989); also published under the title *Kosmische Bildwelt der Romanik: die Kirchendecke von Zillis* (Stuttgart: Urachhaus Johannes M. Mayer, 1989).

Rudolph, Conrad, *The "Things of Greater Importance": Bernard of Clairvaux's Apologia and the Medieval Attitude toward Art* (Philadelphia: University of Pennsylvania Press, 1990).

Ruiz García, Elisa, and Soledad de Silva y Verástegui, *Beato de Navarra (ms. nouv. acq. Lat. 1366 de la Bibliothèque Nationale de France)* (Madrid: Millennium Liber, 2007).

Ruppert, Brian O., "Beyond Death and the Afterlife: Considering Relic Veneration in Medieval Japan," in Jacqueline I. Stone and Mariko Namba Walter (eds), *Death and the Afterlife in Japanese Buddhism* (Honolulu: University of Hawai'i Press, 2008), pp. 102–36.

Rush, Dana, "The 'Convulsive Beauty' of Mami Wata," MA thesis, University of Iowa, 1992.

——, "Eternal Potential: Chromolithographs in Vodunland," *African Arts* 32 (1999), pp. 60–75, 94–6.

Sáenz-López Pérez, Sandra, "La representación de Gog y Magog y la imagen del Anticristo en las cartas náuticas bajomedievales," *Archivo Español de Arte* 78 (2005), pp. 263–76.

——, "Imagen y conocimiento del mundo en la Edad Media a través de la cartografía hispana," PhD dissertation, Universidad Complutense de Madrid, 2007.

——, "El vuelo de oriente a occidente del mítico pájaro Rujj y las transformaciones de su leyenda," in María Victoria Chico and Laura Fernández (eds), *La creación de la imagen en la Edad Media: de la herencia a la renovación, Anales de Historia del Arte* (2010), volumen extraordinario, pp. 325–41.

Said, Edward, *Orientalism: Western Conceptions of the Orient* (New York and London: Pantheon Books, 1978).

Saint-Denis, Eugène de, *Le rôle de la mer dans la poésie latine* (Paris: C. Klincksieck, 1935).

Saitō Jun, "Yōkai to kaijū," in Tsunemitsu Tōru (ed.), *Yōkai-henge* (Tokyo: Chikuma shobō, 1999), pp. 66–101.

Saitō Shūhei, "Uwasa no fōkuroa: Kuchi-sake-onna no denshō oboegaki," *Kenkyū kiyō* 7 (March 30, 1992).

Salih, Sarah, Anke Bernau, and Ruth Evans, "Introduction: Virginities and Virginity Studies," in Sarah Salih, Anke Bernau, and Ruth Evans (eds), *Medieval Virginities* (Cardiff: University of Wales Press, 2003), pp. 1–13.

Sánchez, Jean-Pierre, *Le mythe des Amazones du Nouveau Monde* (Kassel: Edition Reichenberger, 1991).

——, "Myths and Legends in the Old World and European Expansionism on the American Continent," in W. Haase and M. Reinhold (eds), *The Classical Tradition and the Americas*, vol. 1, part I, *European Images of the Americas and the Classical Tradition* (Berlin and New York: Walter de Gruyter, 1994), pp. 189–240.

——, *Mythes et légendes de la conquête de l'Amérique* (Rennes: Presses Universitaires de Rennes, 1996).

Sandison, Alan, *Robert Louis Stevenson and the Appearance of Modernism: A Future Feeling* (Basingstoke and London: Macmillan, 1996).

Sandys, George, *Ovid's Metamorphoses, Englished, Mythologiz'd, and Represented in Figures*, ed. Karl Hulley and Stanley Vandersall (Lincoln, NE: University of Nebraska Press, 1970).

Santarem, Manuel Francisco de Barros y Sousa, *Essai sur l'histoire de la cosmographie et de la cartographie pendant le Moyen-Age* (Paris: Maulde et Renou, 1849–52).

Santi, Francesco, "Utrum Plantae et Bruta Animalia et Corpora Mineralia Remaneant post Finem Mundi: L'animale eterno," *Micrologus* 4 (1996), pp. 231–64.

Santner, Eric L., *On Creaturely Life: Rilke, Benjamin, Sebald* (Chicago: University of Chicago Press, 2006).

Sarmiento, Domingo Faustino, *Facundo: Civilization and Barbarism*, trans. Kathleen Ross (Berkeley, CA: University of California Press, 2003).

Sartre, Jean-Paul, *The Family Idiot: Gustave Flaubert 1821–1857* (Chicago: University of Chicago Press, 1989).

Sato, Masayuki, "Imagined Peripheries: The World and its Peoples in Japanese Cartographic Imagination," *Diogenes* 44/173 (1996), pp. 119–45, reprinted in Anthony Pagden (ed.), *Facing Each Other: The World's Perception of Europe and Europe's Perception of the World*, vol. 2 (Aldershot, UK and Burlington, VT: Ashgate, 2000), pp. 367–94.

Saunders, Rosalyn, "Becoming Undone: Monstrosity, Leaslicam Wordum, and the Strange Case of the Donestre," *Different Visions: A Journal of New Perspectives on Medieval Art*, vol. 2 (2009), <http://www.differentvisions.org/Issue2PDFs/Saunders.pdf>.

Sayfan, Liat, and Kristin Hansen Lagattuta, "Scaring the Monster Away: What Children Know about Managing Fears of Real and Imaginary Creatures," *Child Development* 80 (2009), pp. 1756–74.

Scafi, Alessandro, *Mapping Paradise: A History of Heaven on Earth* (Chicago: University of Chicago Press, 2006).

Schele, Linda, "Accession Iconography of Chan-Bahlum in the Group of the Cross at Palenque," in Merle Greene Robertson (ed.), *The Art, Iconography and Dynastic History of Palenque Part III* (Pebble Beach, CA: Pre-Columbian Art Research, Robert Louis Stevenson School, 1976), pp. 9–34.

Schele, Linda, and David Freidel, *A Forest of Kings: The Untold Story of the Ancient Maya* (New York: William Morrow, 1990).

Schele, Linda, and Mary Ellen Miller, *The Blood of Kings: Dynasty and Ritual in Maya Art* (Fort Worth: Kimbell Art Museum, 1986).

Schellhas, Paul, *Die Gottergestalten der Mayahandschriften* (Berlin: Verlag von A. Asher, 1904).

Schilder, Günter, *Monumenta cartographica Neerlandica* (Alphen aan den Rijn, Holland: Uitgevermaatschappij Canaletto, 1986–).

Schmidt, G.D., *The Iconography of the Mouth of Hell: Eighth-Century Britain to the Fifteenth Century* (Selinsgrove, PA: Susquehanna University Press, 1995).

Schröder, Stefan, "Die Klimazonenkarte des Petrus Alfonsi. Rezeption und Transformation islamisch-arabischen Wissens im mittelalterlichen Europa," in Ingrid Baumgärtner, Paul-Gerhard Klumbies, and Franziska Sick (eds), *Raumkonzepte: Disziplinäre Zugänge Unter Mitarbeit von Mareike Kohls* (Göttingen: V&R Unipress, 2009), pp. 257–77.

Schwanbeck, E.A., *De Megasthene Rerum Indicarum Scriptore* (Bonn, 1945).

Schwarz, Hillel, *The Culture of the Copy* (New York: Zone Books, 1998).

Schweder, E., "Die Angaben über die Völker von Innerafrika bei Plinius und Mela," *Philologus* 47 (1889), pp. 636–43.

Scobie, Alex, "The Origins of 'Centaurs,'" *Folklore* 89/2 (1978), pp. 142–7.

Sconduto, Leslie (trans.), *Guillaume de Palerne* (Jefferson, NC: McFarland, 2004).

——, *Metamorphoses of the Werewolf: A Literary Study from Antiquity through the Renaissance* (Jefferson, NC: McFarland & Co., 2008).

Scott-Dixon, Krista, "The Bodybuilding Grotesque: The Female Bodybuilder, Gender Transgressions, and Designations of Deviance," *Mesomorphosis* 2/10 (December 15, 1998).

Secomska, Krystyna, "The Miniature Cycle in the Sandomierz *Pantheon* and the Medieval Iconography of Alexander's Indian Campaign," *Journal of the Warburg and Courtauld Institutes* 38 (1975), pp. 53–71.

Sedat, David W., *Margarita Structure: New Data and Implications*, ECAP Paper No. 6 (Philadelphia: Instituto Hondureño de Antropología e Historia and the University of Pennsylvania Museum Early Copan Acropolis Program, 1997).

Sedgwick, Eve Kosofsky, *Epistemology of the Closet* (Berkeley: University of California Press, 1990).

Seed, Patricia, "'Are These Not Also Men?': The Indians' Humanity and Capacity for Spanish Civilisation," *Journal of Latin American Studies* 25/3 (1993), pp. 629–52.

Segal, Charles, "Divine Justice in the *Odyssey*: Poseidon, Cyclops, and Helios," *The American Journal of Philology* 113/4 (1992), pp. 489–518.

Seler, Eduard, *Gesammelte Abhandlungen zur Amerikanischen Sprach- und Alterthumskunde*, 5 volumes (Berlin: A. Asher, 1902–23).

——, *Observations and Studies in the Ruins of Palenque* (Pebble Beach, CA: Robert Louis Stevenson School, 1976).

Semonin, Paul, "Monsters in the Marketplace: The Exhibition of Human Oddities in Early Modern England," in Rosemarie Garland Thomson (ed.), *Freakery: Cultural Spectacles of the Extraordinary Body* (New York, NY and London: New York University Press, 1996), pp. 69–81.

Seneca, *Seneca's Tragedies*, with an English translation by Frank Justus Miller (London: William Heinemann, and Cambridge, MA: Harvard University Press, 1960).

Serres, Michel, *Angels: A Modern Myth*, trans. Francis Cowper (Paris: Flammarion, 1993).

——, *Genesis*, trans. Geneviève James and James Nielson (Ann Arbor: University of Michigan Press, 1995).

——, *The Natural Contract*, trans. Elizabeth MacArthur and William Paulson (Ann Arbor: University of Michigan Press, 2001).

——, *The Parasite*, trans. Lawrence Schehr (Minneapolis, MN: University of Minnesota Press, 2007).

Serres, Michel, with Bruno Latour, *Conversations on Science, Culture, and Time*, trans. Roxanne Lapidus (Ann Arbor: University of Michigan Press, 1995).

Seymour, M.C. (ed.), *The Defective Version of Mandeville's Travels*, EETS, ns 319 (London: Oxford University Press, 2002).

Shaw, Donald, "Gallegos' Revision of Doña Bárbara 1929–30," *Hispanic Review* 42/3 (1974), pp. 265–78.

Shaw, Rosalind, *Memories of the Slave Trade: Ritual and the Historical Imagination in Sierra Leone* (Chicago: University of Chicago Press, 2002).

Sheller, Mimi, *Consuming the Caribbean* (London: Routledge, 2006).

Shelley, Mary Wollstonecraft, *Frankenstein; or, The Modern Prometheus* (London: Lackington, Hughes, Harding, Mavor & Jones, 1918).

——, *Frankenstein or, The Modern Prometheus*, ed. Maurice Hindle, rev. edn (London: Penguin, 2003).

——, *Frankenstein, or The Modern Prometheus*, unpaginated electronic edition, Project Gutenberg, <http://www.gutenberg.org/ebooks/84>, accessed 2011.

Shen, Xu, *Shuowen jiezi* (Shanghai: Shanghai guji chuban she, 1981).

Shibayama, Saeko (trans.), "Japanese and Chinese Poems to Sing, *Wakan rōeishū*, ca. 1017–1021," in Haruo Shirane (ed.), *Traditional Japanese Literature: An Anthology, Beginnings to 1600* (New York: Columbia University Press, 2007), pp. 285–92.

Shirley, Rodney W., *The Mapping of the World: Early Printed World Maps 1472–1700* (London: Holland Press Cartographica, 1983, and Riverside, CT: Early World Press, 2001).

Silleras-Fernández, Núria, "*Nigra sum sed formosa*: Black Slaves and Exotica in the Court of a Fourteenth-Century Aragonese Queen," *Medieval Encounters* 13/3 (2007), pp. 546–65.

Simek, Rudolf, "The Journey to the Centre of the Earth: Jerusalem as the Hub of the World," in Rudolf Simek, *Heaven and Earth in the Middle Ages: The Physical World Before Columbus*, trans. Angela Hall (Woodbridge, UK: Boydell Press, 1996), pp. 73–81.

——, *Heaven and Earth in the Middle Ages: The Physical World Before Columbus*, trans. Angela Hall (Woodbridge, Suffolk, and Rochester, NY: Boydell Press, 1997).

Simpson, Marianna S., and Jerome Clinton, "How Rustam Killed the White Div," *Iranian Studies* 39/2 (2006), pp. 171–97.

——, "Word and Image in Illustrated Shahnama Manuscripts: A Project Report," in Charles Melville (ed.), *Shahnama Studies I* (Cambridge: University of Cambridge, Center for Middle Eastern and Islamic Studies, 2006).

Sims, Eleanor, *Peerless Images: Persian Painting and its Sources* (New Haven and London: Yale University Press, 2002).

Skurski, Julie, "The Ambiguities of Authenticity in Latin America: Dona Bárbara and the Construction of National Identity," *Poetics Today* 15/4 (1994), pp. 605–42.

Smith, Ian, *Race and Rhetoric in the Renaissance: Barbarian Errors* (New York: Palgrave Macmillan, 2009).

Smith, Moira, "The Flying Phallus and the Laughing Inquisitor: Penis Theft in the *Malleus Maleficarum*," *Journal of Folklore Research* 39/1 (January–April 2002), pp. 85–117.

Smith, Norman R., "Loathly Births Off Nature: A Study of the Lore of the Portentous Monster in the Sixteenth Century," PhD dissertation, University of Illinois at Urbana-Champaign, 1978.

——, "Portent Lore and Medieval Popular Culture," *The Journal of Popular Culture* 14/1 (1980), pp. 47–59.

——, "Portentous Births and the Monstrous Imagination in Renaissance Culture," in Timothy S. Jones and David A. Sprunger (eds), *Marvels, Monsters, and Miracles: Studies in the Medieval and Early Modern Imaginations* (Kalamazoo: Medieval Institute Publications, 2002), pp. 267–83.

Smith, Paul Julian, "Quevedo and the Sirens: Classical Allusion and Renaissance Topic in a Moral Sonnet," *Journal of Hispanic Philology* 9/1 (1984), pp. 31–41.

Solinus, *Collectanea Rerum Memorabilium*, 2nd edn (Berlin: Weidmann, 1895).

Solomon, Anne, "The Myth of Ritual Origins? Ethnography, Mythology, and Interpretation of San Rock Art," *South African Archaeological Bulletin* 52 (1997), pp. 3–13.

——, "Landscape, Form, and Process: Some Implications for San Rock Art Research," *Natal Museum Journal of the Humanities* 9 (1997), pp. 57–73.

——, "Ethnography and Method in Southern African Rock Art Research," in C. Chippindale and P.S.C. Taçon (eds), *The Archaeology of Rock Art* (Cambridge: Cambridge University Press, 1998).

——, "Meanings, Models, and Minds: A Reply to Lewis-Williams," *South African Archaeological Bulletin* (June 1999), pp. 51–60.

Sorabji, Richard, *Animal Minds and Human Morals: The Origins of the Western Debate* (Ithaca: Cornell University Press, 1995).

Soranus, *Soranus' Gynecology*, trans. Owsei Temkin (Baltimore: Johns Hopkins University Press, 1991).

Soudavar, Abolala, *Art of the Persian Courts: Selections from the Art and History Trust Collection* (New York: Rizzoli, 1992).

Spade, Dean, "Methodologies of Trans Resistance," in George E. Haggerty and Molly McGarry (eds), *A Companion to Lesbian, Gay, Bisexual, Transgender, and Queer Studies* (Oxford: Blackwell, 2007), pp. 237–61.

Speck, Gordon, *Myths and New World Explorations* (Fairfield, WA: Ye Galleon Press, 1979).

Spencer, John, *A Discourse Concerning Prodigies: Wherein the Vanity of Presages by them is Reprehended, and their True and Proper Ends are Indicated* (Cambridge, 1663).

Spinden, Herbert J., *A Study of Maya Art, Its Subject Matter and Historical Development*, Memoirs of the Peabody Museum of American Archaeology and Ethnology, Harvard University, vol. 6 (Cambridge, MA: Peabody Museum of American Archaeology and Ethnology, 1913).

Spinks, Jennifer, "Wondrous Monsters: Representing Conjoined Twins in Early Sixteenth-Century German Broadsheets," *Parergon* 22/2 (2005), pp. 77–112.

——, *Monstrous Births and Visual Culture in Sixteenth-Century Germany* (London: Pickering & Chatto, 2009).

Spinoza, Benedict, *Ethics*, trans. Edwin Curley (London: Penguin, 1994).

Spittler, Janet E., *Animals in the Apocryphal Acts of the Apostles: The Wild Kingdom of Early Christian Literature* (Tübingen: Mohr Siebeck, 2008).

Stallybrass, Peter, and Ann Rosalind Jones, *Renaissance Clothing and the Materials of Memory* (Cambridge: Cambridge University Press, 2000).

Stanley, Henry M., *Through the Dark Continent* (New York: Harper & Brothers, 1878).

Stannard, David E., *The Puritan Way of Death* (Oxford: Oxford University Press, 1977).

Stark, Rodney, *What Americans Really Believe: New Findings from the Baylor Surveys of Religion* (Waco, TX: Baylor University Press, 2008).

Stead, Evanghélia, *Le Monstre, le singe, et le fœtus: tératogonie et décadence dans l'Europe fin-de-siècle* (Geneva: Droz, 2004).

Steel, Karl, "How to Make a Human," *Exemplaria* 20 (2008), pp. 3–27.

Steeves, H. Peter, *The Things Themselves: Phenomenology and the Return to the Everyday* (Albany: State University of New York Press, 2006).

Stein, Aurel, *Innermost Asia*, vol. 2 (Oxford: Clarendon Press, 1928).

Steinicke, Marion, "Apokalyptische Heerscharen und Gottesknechte: Wundervölker des Ostens in abendländischer Tradition vom Untergang der Antike bis zur Entdeckung Amerikas," PhD dissertation, Freie Universität Berlin, Fachbereich Geschichts- und Kulturwissenschaften, 2002.

Steintrager, James A., "Perfectly Inhuman: Moral Monstrosity in Eighteenth-Century Discourse," in Andrew Curran, Robert P. Maccubbin, and David F. Morrill (eds), *Faces of Monstrosity in Eighteenth-Century Thought, Eighteenth-Century Life* 21, n.s., 2 (1997), pp. 114–32.

Stephens, Walter, "Witches Who Steal Penises: Impotence and Illusion in *Malleus Maleficarum*," *Journal of Medieval and Early Modern Studies* 28/3 (1998), pp. 495–529.

——, *Demon Lovers: Witchcraft, Sex, and the Crisis of Belief* (Chicago: University of Chicago Press, 2002).

Stevenson, Edward L., *Maps Illustrating Early Discovery and Exploration in America 1502–1530* (New Brunswick, NJ: n.p., 1903).

——, *Genoese World Map, 1457* (New York: American Geographical Society and Hispanic Society of America, 1912).

——, *Geography of Claudius Ptolemy* (New York: The New York Public Library, 1932); republished as *The Geography/Claudius Ptolemy* (Mineola, NY: Dover, 1991).

Stevenson, Robert Louis, *Strange Case of Dr Jekyll and Mr Hyde*, in Roger Luckhurst (ed.), *Strange Case of Dr Jekyll and Mr Hyde and Other Tales* (Oxford: Oxford University Press, 2006), pp. 1–66.

Stipriaan, Alex van, "The Ever-Changing Face of Watramama in Suriname: A Water Goddess in Creolization since the Seventeenth Century," in Henry John Drewal (ed.), *Sacred Waters: Arts for Mami Wata and Other Water Divinities in Africa and the African Atlantic World* (Bloomington: Indiana University Press, 2008), pp. 525–47.

Stone, Andrea, "The Zoomorphs of Quirigua," PhD dissertation, Department of Art History, University of Texas at Austin, 1983.

——, "Variety and Transformation in the Cosmic Monster Theme at Quirigua, Guatemala," in Virginia Fields (ed.), *Fifth Palenque Round Table, 1983*, Palenque Round Table Series 7 (San Francisco: Pre-Columbian Art Research Institute, 1985), pp. 39–48.

Stone, Andrea, and Marc Zender, *Reading Maya Art: A Hieroglyphic Guide to Ancient Maya Painting and Sculpture* (London: Thames and Hudson, 2011).

Stoneman, Richard (trans.), *The Greek Alexander Romance* (New York: Penguin, 1991).

——, "Romantic Ethnography: Central Asia and India in the Alexander Romance," *Ancient World* 25 (1994), pp. 93–107.

——, *Alexander the Great: A Life in Legend* (New Haven: Yale University Press, 2008).

Strange News out of Kent (London, 1609).

Strassberg, Richard E., *A Chinese Bestiary: Strange Creatures from the Guideways through Mountains and Seas* (Berkeley: University of California Press, 2002).

Strickland, Debra Higgs, "The Iconography of Rejection: Jews and Other Monstrous Races," in Colum Hourihane (ed.), *Image and Belief: Studies in Celebration of the Eightieth Anniversary of the Index of Christian Art* (Princeton: Princeton University Press, 1999), pp. 25–46. (As Debra Hassig.)

——, *Saracens, Demons, and Jews: Making Monsters in Medieval Art* (Princeton, NJ: Princeton University Press, 2003).

——, "Artists, Audience, and Ambivalence in Marco Polo's *Divisament dou monde*," *Viator* 36 (2005), pp. 493–529.

——, "Introduction: The Future is Necessarily Monstrous," *Different Visions* 2 (2010), pp. 1–13.

——, "The Sartorial Monsters of Herzog Ernst," *Different Visions: A Journal of New Perspectives on Medieval Art* 2 (2010), pp. 1–35, <http://differentvisions.org/two. html>.

——, "Antichrist and the Jews in Medieval Christian Art and Protestant Propaganda," *Studies in Iconography* 32 (2011).

——, "Meanings of Muhammad in Later Medieval Art," in Christiane J. Gruber and Avinoam Shalem (eds), *Picturing Prophetic Knowledge: The Prophet Muhammad in Cross-Cultural Literary and Artistic Traditions* (forthcoming).

——, "Saracens, Eschatological Prophecies, and Later Medieval Art," in Jerold C. Frakes (ed.), *Medieval Christian Discourses of the Muslim Other* (forthcoming).

Stryker, Susan, "My Words to Victor Frankenstein Above the Village of Chamounix: Performing Transgender Rage," in Renée R. Curry and Terry L. Allison (eds), *States of Rage: Emotional Eruption, Violence, and Social Change* (New York: New York University Press, 1996).

——, "Transgender Feminism: Queering the Woman Question," in Stacy Gillis, Gillian Howie, and Rebecca Munford (eds), *Third Wave Feminism: A Critical Exploration* (London: Palgrave Macmillan, 2007), pp. 59–70.

Stuart, David, "Royal Auto-Sacrifice among the Maya," *RES: Anthropology and Aesthetics* 7/8 (1984), pp. 6–20.

——, *Ten Phonetic Syllables*, Research Reports on Ancient Maya Writing 14 (Washington, DC: Center for Maya Research, 1987).

——, "Blood Symbolism in Maya Iconography," in Elizabeth P. Benson and Gillett G. Griffin (eds), *Maya Iconography* (Princeton, NJ: Princeton University Press, 1988), pp. 175–221.

——, *Corpus of Maya Hieroglyphic Inscriptions*, vol. 9, part 1 (Cambridge, MA: Peabody Museum of Archaeology and Ethnology, Harvard University, 2003).

——, "A Cosmological Throne at Palenque" (2003), <www.mesoweb.com/stuart/ notes/Throne.pdf>, accessed July 1, 2009.

——, *The Inscriptions from Temple XIX at Palenque* (San Francisco: Pre-Columbian Art Research Institute, 2005).

——, *Sourcebook for the 29th Maya Hieroglyph Forum, March 11–16, 2005* (Austin: Department of Art and Art History, University of Texas, 2005).

Stuart, David, Nikolai Grube, and Linda Schele, "A New Alternative Date of the Sepulturas Bench," *Copán Note* 61 (Copán: Copán Acropolis Project and the Instituto Hondureño de Antropología e Historia, 1989).

Stuart, David, and George Stuart, *Palenque: Eternal City of the Maya* (London: Thames and Hudson, 2008).

Stückelberger, Alfred, and Gerd Grasshoff (eds), *Klaudios Ptolemaios: Handbuch der Geographie* (Basel: Schwabe Basel, 2006).

Subtelny, Maria E., "The Sunni Revival under Shah Rukh and its Promoters: A Study of the Connection between Ideology and Higher Learning in Timurid Iran," in *Proceedings of the 27th Meeting of Haneda Memorial Hall Symposium on Central Asia and Iran, August 30, 1993* (Kyoto: Institute of Inner Asian Studies, Kyoto University, 1994), pp. 14–23.

Subtelny, Maria E., and Anas B. Khalidov, "The Curriculum of Islamic Higher Learning in Timurid Iran in the Light of the Sunni Revival under Shah Rukh," *Journal of the American Oriental Society* 115/ 2 (1995), pp. 210–36.

Sutherland, Gail Hinich, *The Disguises of the Demon: The Development of the Yakṣa in Hinduism and Buddhism*, SUNY Series in Hindu Studies (Albany: State University of New York Press, 1991).

Tachikawa Kiyoshi (ed.), *Hyaku-monogatari kaidan shūsei* (Tokyo: Kokusho kankōkai, 1995).

Tada Katsumi, *Edo yōkai karuta* (Tokyo: Kokusho kankōkai, 1998).

——, *Hyakki kaidoku* (Tokyo: Kōdansha, 1999).

Takahashi Toshio, *Gojira no nazo: Kaijū shinwa to Nihonjin* (Tokyo: Kōdansha, 1998).

Takeuchi, Melinda, "Kuniyoshi's Minamoto Raikō and the Earth Spider: Demons and Protest in Late Tokugawa Japan," *Ars Orientalis* 17 (1987), pp. 5–23.

Talbot, D.A., *Woman's Mysteries of a Primitive People: The Ibibio of Southern Nigeria* (London: Cassell, 1915; London: Frank Cass, 1968).

Tapia y Rivera, Alejandro, *La Antigua Sirena* (Mexico: Orión, 1959).

Tate, Carolyn, *Yaxchilan: The Design of a Maya Ceremonial City* (Austin: University of Texas Press, 1992).

Taube, Karl A., "A Study of Classic Maya Scaffold Sacrifice," in Elizabeth Benson and Gillett Griffin (eds), *Maya Iconography* (Princeton, NJ: Princeton University Press, 1988), pp. 331–51.

——, *Itzam Cab Ain: Caimans, Cosmology, and Calendrics in Postclassic Yucatán*, Research Reports on Ancient Maya Writing 26 (Washington, DC: Center for Maya Research, 1989).

——, *The Major Gods of Ancient Yucatan*, Studies in Pre-Columbian Art and Archaeology 32 (Washington, DC: Dumbarton Oaks, 1992).

——, *Aztec and Maya Myths* (Bath: British Museum Press, 1993).

——, "The Jade Hearth: Centrality, Rulership, and the Classic Maya Temple," in Stephen D. Houston (ed.), *Function and Meaning in Classic Maya Architecture* (Washington, DC: Dumbarton Oaks, 1998), pp. 427–78.

——, "Turquoise Hearth: Fire, Self-Sacrifice, and the Central Mexican Cult of War," in Davíd Carrasco, Lindsay Jones, and Scott Sessions (eds), *Mesoamerica's Classic Heritage: Teotihuacán to the Aztecs* (Niwot: University Press of Colorado, 1999), pp. 269–340.

——, "The Symbolism of Jade in Classic Maya Religion," *Ancient Mesoamerica* 16 (2005), pp. 23–50.

——, "Catalog Entry 1," in Daniel Finamore and Stephen D. Houston (eds), *Fiery Pool: The Maya and the Mythic Sea* (New Haven and London: Yale University Press, 2010).

——, "Where Earth and Sky Meet: The Sea in Ancient and Contemporary Maya Cosmology," in Daniel Finamore and Stephen D. Houston (eds), *Fiery Pool: The Maya and the Mythic Sea* (New Haven and London: Yale University Press, 2010), pp. 202–19.

Tavernier, J.B., *Collection of Travels through Turkey into Persia and the East Indies …
being the Travels of Monsieur Tavernier and other Great Men*, vol. 1 (London: Moses
Pitt, 1884).

Tawara Seiji (ed.), *Poketto monsutaa zukan* (Tokyo: Ascii, 1997).

Taylor, Dicey, "The Cauac Monster," in Merle Greene Robertson and Donnan C.
Jeffers (eds), *Tercera Mesa Redonda de Palenque, 1978* (Monterrey: Pre-Columbian
Art Research Center, 1978), pp. 79–90.

Taylor, E.G.R., "Idée fixe: The Mind of Christopher Columbus," *The Hispanic
American Historical Review* 11 (1931), pp. 289–301.

Tedlock, Dennis, *Popol Vuh* (New York: Simon and Schuster, 1985).

Teiser, Stephen F., *The Scripture on the Ten Kings and the Making of Purgatory in
Medieval Chinese Buddhism* (Honolulu: University of Hawaii Press, 1994).

Terajima Ryōan, *Wakan-Sansaizue 7* (Tokyo: Heibonsha, 1994).

Thackston, Wheeler M., *The Tales of the Prophets of al-Kisa'i* (Boston: Twayne
Publishers, 1978).

Thavis, John, *Catholic News Service*, March 2, 2011, <http://www.catholicnews.com/
data/stories/cns/1100846.htm>, accessed March 12, 2011.

*The ranters monster: Being a true relation of one Mary Adams, living at Tillingham in
Essex … with the manner how she was deliver'd of the ugliest ill-shapen monster that
ever eyes beheld …* (London: Printed for Geoge Horton, 1652).

Thomas of Cantimpré, *Liber de natura rerum: Editio princeps secundum codices
manuscriptos*, ed. Helmut Boese (Berlin: W. De Gruyter, 1973).

Thomas, Keith, *Man and the Natural World* (New York: Pantheon, 1983).

Thompson, C.J.S., *The Mystery and Lore of Monsters: With Accounts of Some Giants,
Dwarfs and Prodigies* (London: Williams & Norgate, 1930).

Thompson, J. Eric S., *The Moon Goddess in Middle America, With Notes on Related
Deities*, Carnegie Institution of Washington Publication 509, Contributions
to American Anthropology and History 5/29 (Washington, DC: Carnegie
Institution of Washington, 1939), pp. 121–74.

——, *Maya Hieroglyphic Writing: An Introduction* (Norman: University of Oklahoma
Press, 1960).

——, *Maya History and Religion* (Norman: University of Oklahoma Press, 1970).

Thompson, Lloyd A., *Romans and Blacks* (London and New York: Routledge;
Norman, OK: Oklahoma University Press, 1989).

Thompson, Stith, *Tales of the North American Indians* (Cambridge: Harvard University
Press, 1929).

Thomson, Rosemarie Garland, "Introduction: From Wonder to Error: A Genealogy
of Freak Discourse in Modernity," in Rosemarie Garland Thomson (ed.),
Freakery: Cultural Spectacles of the Extraordinary Body (New York, NY and London:
New York University Press, 1996), pp. 1–19.

Throop, Priscilla (trans.), *Isidore's Etymologies: Complete English Translation*, vol. 2
(Charlotte, VT: Lulu.com, 2005).

Titchkosky, Tanya, *Disability, Self, and Society* (Toronto: University of Toronto Press,
2003).

Tobin, Joseph (ed.), *Pikachu's Global Adventure: The Rise and Fall of Pokémon* (Durham, NC: Duke University Press, 2004).

Todorov, Tzvetan, *The Conquest of America: The Question of the Other* (New York: Harper and Row, 1984).

Tōji Hōbutsukan, *Tōji no mandara zu: mihotoke no gunzō* (Kyoto: Tōji Hōmotsukan, 1992).

Tolan, John V., *Saracens: Islam in the Medieval European Imagination* (New York: Columbia University Press, 2002).

Tolkien, J.R.R., "Beowulf: The Monsters and the Critics," *Proceedings of the British Academy* (1936), reprinted in John Ronald Reuel and Christopher Tolkien (eds), *The Monsters and the Critics, and Other Essays* (Boston: Houghton Mifflin, 1984).

Tombs, Pete, "The Beast from Bollywood: A History of the Indian Horror Film," in Steven Jay Schneider (ed.), *Fear Without Frontiers: Horror Cinema Across the Globe* (Godalming, England: FAB Press, 2003), pp. 243–53.

Tooley, Marian J., "Bodin and the Mediaeval Theory of Climate," *Speculum* 28/1 (1953), pp. 64–83.

Toorawa, Shawkat M., "Wâq al-wâq: Fabulous, Fabular, Indian Ocean (?) Island(s)," *Emergences* 10/2 (2000), pp. 387–402.

Tornesello, Natalia L., "From Reality to Legend: Historical Sources of Hellenistic and Islamic Teratology," *Studia Iranica* 31/2 (2002), pp. 163–92.

Toulouse, Sarah, "Marine Cartography and Navigation in Renaissance France," in David Woodward (ed.), *The History of Cartography*, vol. 3, *Cartography in the European Renaissance*, Part II (Chicago: University of Chicago Press, 2007), pp. 1550–68.

Troup, Calvin L., "Augustine the African: Critic of Roman Colonialist Discourse," *Rhetoric Society Quarterly* 25 (1995), pp. 91–106.

Tsutsui, William, *Godzilla on My Mind: Fifty Years of the King of Monsters* (New York: Palgrave Macmillan, 2004).

Tsutsui, William M., and Michiko Ito (eds), *In Godzilla's Footsteps: Japanese Pop Culture Icons on the Global Stage* (New York: Palgrave Macmillan, 2006).

Tupper, Frederick, "Chaucer and the Seven Deadly Sins," *PLMA* 29/1 (1914), pp. 93–128.

Turner, William, *A Compleat History of the Most Remarkable Providences* (London, 1697).

Tuve, Rosemond, "Notes on the Virtues and Vices," *Journal of the Warburg and Courtauld Institutes* 27 (1964), pp. 42–72.

Tuzin, Donald F., *The Cassowary's Revenge: The Life and Death of Masculinity in a New Guinea Society* (Chicago: University of Chicago Press, 1997).

Tyler, Royall (trans.), *Japanese Tales* (New York: Pantheon, 1987).

Tyler, Tom, "Deviants, Donestre, and Debauchees: Here be Monsters," *Culture, Theory and Critique* 49/2 (2008), pp. 113–31.

Tzanaki, Rosemary, *Mandeville's Medieval Audiences: A Study on the Reception of the Book of Sir John Mandeville (1371–1550)* (Aldershot: Ashgate, 2003).

Uebel, Michael, "Unthinking the Monster: Twelfth-Century Responses to Saracen Alterity," in Jeffrey Jerome Cohen (ed.), *Monster Theory: Reading Culture* (Minneapolis, MN: University of Minnesota Press, 1996), pp. 264–91.

——, *Ecstatic Transformation: On the Uses of Alterity in the Middle Ages* (New York: Palgrave Macmillan, 2005).

Uluç, Lâle, *Turkman Governors, Shiraz Artisans, and Ottoman Collectors: Sixteenth-century Shiraz Manuscripts* (Istanbul: İş Bankası Kültür Yayınları, 2006).

Ury, Marian (trans.), *Tales of Times Now Past: Sixty-two Stories from a Medieval Japanese Collection* (Berkeley: University of California Press, 1979; Ann Arbor: Center for Japanese Studies, University of Michigan, 1993).

Vachhani, Sheena J., "Vagina Dentata and the Demonological Body: Explorations of the Feminine Demon in Organisation," in Alison Pullen and Carl Rhodes (eds), *Bits of Organization* (Copenhagen: Copenhagen Business School Press, 2009), pp. 163–83.

Valtrová, Jana, "Beyond the Horizons of Legends: Traditional Imagery and Direct Experience in Medieval Accounts of Asia," *Numen* 57/2 (2010), pp. 154–85.

Van Duzer, Chet, "The Cartography, Geography, and Hydrography of the Southern Ring Continent, 1515–1763," *Orbis Terrarum* 8 (2002), pp. 115–58.

——, "Cartographic Invention: The Southern Continent on Vatican MS. Urb. Lat. 274, Folios 73v–74r (c.1530)," *Imago Mundi* 59/2 (2007), pp. 193–222.

——, "Floating Islands Seen at Sea: Myth and Reality," *Anuario do Centro de Estudos de História do Atlântico* 1 (2009), pp. 110–20.

——, "A Northern Refuge of the Monstrous Races: Asia on Waldseemüller's 1516 Carta Marina," *Imago Mundi* 62/2 (2010), pp. 221–31.

——, *Sea Monsters on Medieval and Renaissance Maps* (The British Library, forthcoming).

Vansina, Jan, *Art History in Africa* (New York: Longman, 1998).

Van Stekelenburg, A.V., "*Ex Africa semper aliquid novi*—A Proverb's Pedigree," *Akroteriòn* 33/4 (1988), pp. 114–20.

Varthema (Barthema), L., *Itinerario*, in J.W. Jones (trans.), *The Travels of Ludovico di Varthema* (London: Hakluyt Society, 1863).

Vega, Ana Lydia, *Pasión de historia* (San Juan, PR: Ediciones de la Flor, 1991).

Velásquez García, Erik, "The Maya Flood Myth and the Decapitation of the Cosmic Caiman," *The PARI Journal* 7/1 (2006), pp. 1–10, <www.mesoweb.com/pari/publications/journal/701/Flood_e.pdf>, accessed July 1, 2009.

Vergil, *The Aeneid*, trans. Robert Fitzgerald (New York: Vintage Classics, 1990).

Vermeule, Emily, *Aspects of Death in Early Greek Art and Poetry* (Berkeley, Los Angeles, London: University of California Press, 1979).

Verner, Lisa, *The Epistemology of the Monstrous in the Middle Ages* (New York: Routledge, 2005).

von Albrecht, Michael, *Roman Epic: An Interpretative Introduction* (Boston: Brill, 1998).

von den Brincken, Anna-Dorothee, "Weltbild der lateinischen Universalhistoriker und -kartographen," in *Popoli e paesi nella cultura altomedievale: 23–29 aprile 1981* (Spoleto: Presso la Sede del Centro, 1983).

——, *Kartographische Quellen, Welt-, See-, und Regionalkarten* (Turnhout: Brepols, 1988).

——, "Fines Terrae": Die Enden der Erde und der vierte Kontinent auf mittelalterlichen Weltkarten (Hannover: Hahnsche Buchhandlung, 1992).

Von Folsach, Kjeld, For a Privileged Few: Islamic Miniature Painting from the David Collection (Humlebæk: Louisiana Museum of Modern Art and The David Collection, 2007).

Von Glahn, Richard, The Sinister Way: The Divine and the Demonic in Chinese Religious Culture (Berkeley: University of California Press, 2004).

Wakabayashi, Haruko, "Tengu Images and the Buddhist Concepts of Evil in Medieval Japan," PhD dissertation, Princeton University, 1995.

——, "Hell Illustrated: A Visual Image of Ikai that Came From Ikoku," in Susanne Formanek and William R. LaFleur (eds), Practicing the Afterlife: Perspectives from Japan (Vienna: Verlag der Österreichischen Akademie der Wissenschaften, 2004), pp. 285–318.

Waldby, Catherine, Visible Human Project: Bodies and Posthuman Medicine (London: Routledge, 2000).

Walker, Henry J., Theseus and Athens (Oxford: Oxford University Press, 1995).

Wallis, Helen, "Java la Grande: The Enigma of the Dieppe Maps," in Glyndwr Williams and Alan Frost (eds), Terra Australis to Australia (Melbourne: Oxford University Press, 1988), pp. 39–81.

Walsham, Alexandra, Providence in Early Modern England (Oxford: Oxford University Press, 1999).

Wang, Chia Chi Jason, "The Iconography of Zhong Kui in Chinese Painting," MA thesis, University of California, Berkeley, 1991.

Warner, George (ed.), The Buke of John Maundeville (Westminster: Nichols and Sons, 1889).

Waterhouse, Edward, A Declaration of the State of the Colony in Virginia [1622] (Amsterdam and New York: Da Capo Press, 1970).

Watson, Burton (trans.), and Haruo Shirane (ed.), The Demon at Agi Bridge and Other Japanese Tales (New York: Columbia University Press, 2010).

Wattenbach, W. (ed.), Die Apologie des Guido von Bazoches (Berlin: Sitzungsberichte der Königlich Preussischen Akademie der Wissenschaften zu Berlin, 1893).

Weckmann, Luis, "The Middle Ages in the Conquest of America," Speculum 26/1 (1951), pp. 130–41.

Wenzel, Siegfried, "The Seven Deadly Sins: Some Problems of Research," Speculum 43/1 (1968), pp. 1–22.

West, M.L. (ed.), Hesiod: Theogony (Oxford: Clarendon Press, 1966).

——, (ed.), Hesiod: Works and Days (Oxford: Clarendon Press, 1978).

Weston, Lisa, "Queering Virginity," Medieval Feminist Forum 36 (2003), pp. 22–4.

Westrem, Scott D., "Against Gog and Magog," in Sylvia Tomasch and Sealy Gilles (eds), Text and Territory: Geographical Imagination in the European Middle Ages (Philadelphia: University of Pennsylvania Press, 1998), pp. 54–75.

——, The Hereford Map: A Transcription and Translation of the Legends with Commentary (Turnhout: Brepols, 2001).

Wey-Gómez, Nicolás, "Cannibalism as Defacement: Columbus's Account of the Fourth Voyage," Journal of Hispanic Philology 16/2 (1992), pp. 195–208.

——, *The Tropics of Empire: Why Columbus Sailed South to the Indies* (Cambridge, MA and London: MIT Press, 2008).

White, David Gordon, *Myths of the Dog-Man* (Chicago: University of Chicago Press, 1991).

Whitehead, Neil L., "South America/Amazonia: The Forest of Marvels," in Peter Hulme and Tim Youngs (eds), *The Cambridge Companion to Travel Writing* (Cambridge, UK: Cambridge University Press, 2002), pp. 122–38.

Whitfield, Roderick, and Anne Farrer, *Caves of the Thousand Buddhas: Chinese Art from the Silk Route* (London: British Museum Publications, 1990).

Wiesner-Hanks, Merry, *The Marvelous Hairy Girls: The Gonzales Sisters and Their Worlds* (New Haven, CT and London: Yale University Press, 2009).

Wilde, Oscar, *The Picture of Dorian Gray* (London: Simpkin, Marshall, Hamilton, Kent, 1913).

William Rockhill Nelson Gallery of Art and Mary Atkins Museum of Fine Arts, Wai-Kam Ho, and Cleveland Museum of Art. *Eight Dynasties of Chinese Painting: The Collections of the Nelson Gallery–Atkins Museum, Kansas City, and the Cleveland Museum of Art* (Cleveland and Bloomington: Indiana University Press, 1980)

Williams, David, *Deformed Discourse: The Function of the Monster in Mediaeval Thought and Literature* (Montreal: McGill-Queen's University Press, 1996).

Williams, John, *The Illustrated Beatus: A Corpus of the Illustrations of the Commentary on the Apocalypse* (London: Harvey Miller, 1994–2003).

Williams, Megan Hale, *The Monk and the Book: Jerome and the Making of Christian Scholarship* (Chicago: University of Chicago Press, 2006).

Williams, Paul, *Mahāyāna Buddhism: The Doctrinal Foundations*, 2nd edn (London: Routledge, 1989).

Winckelmann, Johann Joachim, *Winckelmann: Selected Writings on Art*, ed. David Irwin (London: Phaidon, 1972).

Winslow, Matthew Scott, review of John Gardner's *Grendel*, in *The Greenman Review*, <http://www.greenmanreview.com/book/book_gardner_grendel.html>, accessed June 27, 2010.

Wittkower, Rudolf, "Marvels of the East: A Study in the History of Monsters," *Journal of the Warburg and Courtauld Institutes* 5 (1942), pp. 159–97; reprinted in Rudolf Wittkower, *Allegory and the Migration of Symbols* (Boulder, CO: Westview Press, 1977), pp. 45–74.

——, "Marco Polo and the Pictorial Tradition of the Marvels of the East," in E. Balazs (ed.), *Oriente Poliano* (Rome: Istituto italiano per il Medio e Estremo Oriente, 1957), pp. 155–72; reprinted in Rudolf Wittkower, *Allegory and the Migration of Symbols* (Boulder, CO: Westview Press, 1977), pp. 76–92.

——, *Selected Lectures of Rudolf Wittkower: The Impact of Non-European Civilizations on the Art of the West*, ed. Donald Martin Reynolds (Cambridge: Cambridge University Press, 1989).

Wolf, Armin, "Mapping Homer's Odyssey," in George Tolias and Dimitris Loupis (eds), *Eastern Mediterranean Cartographies* (Athens: Institute for Neohellenic Research, 2004), pp. 309–34.

Wolfe, Cary, "Introduction," in Cary Wolfe (ed.), *Zoontologies* (Minneapolis, MN: University of Minnesota Press, 2003).

——, *What Is Posthumanism?* Posthumanities Series, no. 8 (Minneapolis, MN: University of Minnesota Press, 2010).

Wolff, Hans (ed.), *America: Early Maps of the New World* (Munich: Prestel-Verlag, 1992).

Wood, Ian, "Missionaries and the Christian Frontier," in W. Pohl, I. Wood, and H. Reimitz (eds), *The Transformation of Frontiers from Late Antiquity to the Carolingians* (Leiden: Brill, 2001), pp. 209–18.

Woodford, Susan, *Images of Myths in Classical Antiquity* (Cambridge: Cambridge University Press, 2003).

Woods, John, "The Rise of Timurid Historiography," *Journal of Near Eastern Studies* 46/2 (1987), pp. 81–108.

Woodward, David, "Medieval *Mappaemundi*," in J.B. Harley and David Woodward (eds), *The History of Cartography*, vol. 1 (Chicago: University of Chicago Press, 1987–), pp. 286–370.

Woolley, Jacqueline D., "Thinking About Fantasy: Are Children Fundamentally Different Thinkers and Believers from Adults?" in Margaret E. Hertzig and Ellen A. Farber (eds), *Annual Progress in Child Psychiatry and Child Development* (Philadelphia: Brunner/Mazel, 1999), pp. 57–88.

Wright, John K., *The Geographical Lore of the Time of the Crusades* (New York: American Geographical Society, 1925).

Wu Zimu 吳自牧. Mengliang Lu 夢梁錄, *Donjing Menghua Lu, Wai Sizhong* 東京夢梁錄外四種 (Shanghai: Gudian wenxue chuban she, 1957).

Wyman, Leah M., and George N. Dionisopoulos, "Primal Urges and Civilized Sensibilities: The Rhetoric of Gendered Archtypes, Seduction, and Resistance in Bram Stoker's *Dracula*," *Journal of Popular Film and Television* 27/2 (Summer 1999), pp. 32–9.

Wyngaert, Anastasius van den (ed.), *Itinera et relationes Fratrum Minorum saeculi XIII et XIV* (Florence: Colle S. Bonaventurae, 1929).

Xu Shen 許慎, *Shuowen Jiezi Zhu* 說文解字注. (Shanghai: Shanghai guji chubanshe, 1981).

Yanagita Kunio, *Yanagita Kunio, Teihon Yanagita Kunio shū* 5 (Tokyo: Chikuma Shobō, 1969).

——, "Yōkai meii," *Teihon Yanagita Kunio shū* 4 (Tokyo: Chikuma Shobō, 1970).

Yang Bojun 楊伯峻. *Chunqiu Zuozhuan Zhu* 春秋左傳注 (Beijing: Zhonghua shuju, 1990).

Yokoyama Shigeru, and Matsumoto Ryūshin (eds), "Ibukiyama Shuten dōji," in *Muromachi jidai monogatari taisei*, vol. 2 (Tokyo: Kadokawa shoten, 1973).

Young, Ellen, "The Slaying of the Minotaur: Evidence in Art and Literature for the Development of the Myth, 700–400 B.C.," PhD dissertation, Bryn Mawr University, 1972.

Yuan Ke 袁珂, (ed.) *Shanhai Jing Jiaozhu* 山海經校注 (Shanghai: Shanghai guji chubanshe, 1991).

Yule, Henry (ed. and trans.), *Cathay and the Way Thither: Being a Collection of Medieval Notices of China* (London: Hakluyt Society, 1866).

Yūyo Shōsō, *Taima mandara so*, in Jōdoshū Kaishū Happyakunen Kinen Keisan Jimukyoku (ed.), *Jōdoshū zensho* 13: *Shūgi kenshō* (Tokyo: Sankibō busshorin, 1971).

Zamora, Margarita, *Reading Columbus* (Berkeley: University of California Press, 1993).

Zarncke, F., "Der Brief des Presters Johannes an den byzantinischen Kaiser Emanuel," *Abhandlungen der königlich sächsischen Gesellschaft der Wissenschaften, phil.-hist. Klasse* 7 (1879), pp. 873–934; reprinted in Charles F. Beckingham and Bernard Hamilton (eds), *Prester John, the Mongols, and the Ten Lost Tribes* (Aldershot, Hampshire, and Brookfield, VT: Variorum, 1996), pp. 40–102.

Zeitlin, Judith, *The Phantom Heroine: Ghosts and Gender in Seventeenth Century China* (Honolulu: University of Hawai'i Press, 2007).

Zhu Junsheng 朱駿聲. Shuowen Tongxun Dingsheng 說文通訓定聲 (Wuhan: Wuhan shi guji shudian, 1983).

Žižek, Slavoj, and Mladen Dolar, *Opera's Second Death* (New York: Routledge, 2002).

Index